Democratic Innovations
in Nepal

BHUWAN LAL JOSHI

and LEO E. ROSE

Democratic Innovations
in Nepal

A Case Study of Political Acculturation

Berkeley and Los Angeles

University of California Press

1966

UNIVERSITY OF CALIFORNIA PRESS
Berkeley and Los Angeles, California
Cambridge University Press, London, England
© 1966 by The Regents of the University of California
Library of Congress Catalog Card Number 66–14092
Printed in the United States of America

To
His Majesty King Mahendra Vir Vikram Shah Deva,
King of Nepal,
and
Sri Bishweshwar Prasad Koirala, the first elected
Prime Minister of Nepal—

> *Two Nepali leaders who, although placed at*
> *opposite ends of the political spectrum by a*
> *not too uncommon irony of Nepali history,*
> *are in a real sense the two most important*
> *co-authors of Nepali political acculturation*
> *surveyed in this book.*

Preface

MODERN Nepali political history can be divided into two periods
—with the 1950 revolution as the dividing line—in which the
form and the dynamics of the political process demonstrated
certain distinctive characteristics, but in which there was also a
high degree of survival and persistence of traditional institutions
and modes of behavior. The revolution which overthrew the
oligarchic Rana family regime in 1951 unleashed complex and
multifaceted forces in this previously isolated, sternly regimented
society. A renaissance in the sphere of literature was one of the
first evidences of a new awakening. Leading figures in the minute
but influential Nepali intelligentsia began experimenting with
literary forms and subjects that had been frowned upon by the
tradition-oriented Ranas. Educational facilities also multiplied
rapidly, if often on a tenuous basis, under the leadership of a
newly emerging youthful elite that had been educated in the few
Western-style schools sponsored by the Ranas or in the colleges
and universities of neighboring India.

The aftermath of the revolution was indeed an exhilarating
and creative period for this new elite, gratefully released from the
deadening oppression of Rana-imposed conformity and authoritarianism. Inevitably, this almost frantic search for innovation
had a considerable impact on political and social attitudes.
Perhaps the most distinctive aspect of the immediate postrevolutionary period—setting it apart both from what had existed
before and what eventually emerged—was the broad political
freedom conceded to virtually all political elements, even those
frankly counterrevolutionary. From a society in which voluntary
political associations had been most conspicuous by their absence,
Nepal was suddenly transformed into a society in which virtually
all forms and idioms of contemporary world politics received at
least token expression.

Political and bureaucratic institutions, shaken from their
traditional moorings with insufficient time or opportunity to
adjust to the new situation, were necessarily subjected to a long

period of experimentation which has not yet come to an end. To both the active participants and the society as a whole, the politics of this transitional period has often seemed to be little more than an exercise in frustration as experiment has succeeded experiment after what seemed to be only a nominal trial. This obvious failure to achieve a meaningful consensus on many of Nepal's basic political questions has proved a serious handicap to all the political innovators—the Crown, the political parties, and the articulate Nepali elites.

In view of this substantial lack of agreement on fundamentals, it is hardly surprising that there has been a gradual renewal of interest in and appreciation of certain aspects of the traditional political structure and process. There is, indeed, a broad degree of continuity between pre-1951 and post-1960 politics in Nepal. Innovation is still a predominant characteristic of contemporary Nepali politics, but the limits within which these experiments are structured are now more rigidly defined than in the 1951–60 period.

The present study is thus an analysis of a political system in transition in its most critical and formative period. Doubtless, many of the problems and situations under discussion are those faced at present by most Asian states, as also those of Africa. Nepal offers certain advantages, however, for a study of politics in a neo-traditional, pseudo-modern society. The long and comparatively effective isolation of Nepal from the outside world up to 1947 facilitates a study in depth of the Nepali political process. The origin, role, and position of the elites, whether traditional or modernist, are probably more clearly defined in Nepal than elsewhere in Asia because of their shorter and less intensive exposure to external influences. Political behavior still tends to follow familiar traditional paths. The sources and impact of external influences are more easily identified and isolated by the social scientist, and the processes of political and social transition are more susceptible to analysis on the basis of well-defined categories in Nepal than in most other Asian countries, where contacts with the West and reactions to Western influences have a longer and more pervasive history. The impact of a Hindu social system on political institutions and behavior, for instance, is probably more easily studied in Nepal than in India, where extraneous and adventitious influences have intruded for several centuries.

Nepal's strategic, if uneasy, position between the largest Communist and democratic powers in Asia adds further interest to this study. Kathmandu has frequently expressed its determination to avoid the paths charted by either of its giant neighbors, but it is still to be proved that an alternative system is feasible under such stressful conditions. The natural reaction might well be for Nepal to retreat to the protective shell long provided by its isolation from the harsh realities and ambiguities of international politics. But withdrawal has been specifically and repeatedly rejected by the Nepali political leadership in favor of a policy aimed at carving out a separate and unique international personality, distinguishing Nepal from both Communist China and democratic India.

Much of this study consists of a detailed political history of a crucial transitional period in Nepal. The method of inquiry we have employed in delineating political events and in describing political personalities is the case-study approach, focusing intensively on continuous trends and patterns emerging over a period of time. While thus trying to disentangle the complex skein of political developments, we have also emphasized the discontinuities or the disjunctures that marked the emergent political process at its various crisis points. We hoped that our reliance on the case-study method of inquiry would enable us to underscore the multidimensional nature of political change and bring out as fully as possible the psychic dimension of change—in particular, the overriding influences of a few key individuals on the transitional politics. For in Nepal political change not only has brought correlated changes in the social, economic, and intellectual life of the country, but also has produced profound changes in the behavior, values, and ideals of the small group of persons composing the new "modernizing" oligarchy. These behavioral and ideological modifications in turn caused further alterations in the developing political process, and this active interaction between the change agents and the nature of the change process itself has continued unabated till now.

Indeed, this study of political change in Nepal can be compared to the study of behavioral and attitudinal modifications in a person undergoing a program of stimulated change. Nepal's hectic political experiences since 1951 are analogous with those of a person who has subjected himself to psychotherapeutic treatment. It was in that year that the long-sequestered Himalayan kingdom was catapulted out of its medieval coma into the bewildering stream of twentieth-century existence. The crisis in Nepal's national identity precipitated by such a revolutionary upheaval continues to affect deeply the individual and social lives of the small band of Nepali elites. The groping for directions, the search for anchor values, the intense desire to grow rapidly, the frantic impatience to catch up with the rest of the world, the demand for equality in the comity of nations—all these preoccupations have marked the years of Nepal's infantile and adolescent politics, if one could label the years of transitional politics until 1959 as the period of political infancy and the years after that as the period of political adolescence. The dominant mood in Nepali politics has been self-expression and self-aggrandizement rather than problem solving. The successive governments formed between 1951 and 1959 were so enmeshed in interpersonal, intraparty, and interparty conflicts that task orientation was all but lost from the public life of the country; the crisis in Nepal's national identity became truly a crisis in the personal lives of all Nepali elites. The attendant atmosphere of frustration and cynicism virtually ruled out the possibility of any rational, predictable, and stable party politics, and the rise of political influentials made the nature of transitional politics more personality-centered than ever before.

By bringing together the political facts and events of these "infantile" and "adolescent" periods in one place, and by collating them so that their underlying motivations and meanings become apparent, we may have brought to light some aspects of political life and behavior in contemporary Nepal which many Nepali politicians would perhaps wish were best left in undisturbed oblivion. We hold no brief for any political individual or system, and as social scientists our primary allegiance is to facts; whenever we have brought to surface some unpleasant political facts, this has been done only to provide an accurate and objective delineation of significant events.

We have purposely refrained from theorizing about the process of political change. We feel that the first concern in any scientific study of a problem should be to provide a full and objective description of the relevant facts pertaining to that problem, and that theoretical concerns should succeed rather than precede the empirical process. We also feel that we are too close to events in Nepal since 1960 to have the necessary emotional and temporal remoteness to engage in theoretical abstractions. It is our hope, however, that the present study of political change in Nepal will provide the factual substructure for qualified social scientists to undertake the next phase of scientific inquiry—that of analyzing and abstracting the interrelationships of significant political events and processes into formal propositions and hypotheses of social and political change in a traditional society. We would also like to see any theoretical model thus derived further cross-validated with political experiences of comparable countries and societies so that eventually a general theory of social-political change with predictive power can emerge.

Even though we have favored a descriptive case-study approach, some hidden biases may have entered into the study through the manner in which we have catalogued and collated specific political events or persons for discussions. Selection of any kind is unquestionably a subjective process, but we believe that awareness of possible biases can act as a useful restraint on any preëxisting proclivities in data collection. To make our possible biases explicit we can state that we have consciously guarded ourselves against omitting references to events or persons we have judged to be politically significant. Likewise, we have exercised our discretion in excluding all references to events or persons we deemed to be trivial or inconsequential with respect to the total political process. For each head and prominent member of the Cabinet we have included a brief sketch of his political career and socialization, and for each government we have provided a detailed and objective account of its record; where political controversies were involved, we have plunged headlong into the discussion of the political issues and the participants concerned as impartially as possible.

The basic objective of the study is to describe, understand, and explain, in all its many and varied forms, the course of modernization in an essentially backward society. Our main efforts, however, have been geared to describing and understanding the processes of political change in a traditional society; whatever explanations we have offered from time to time are more in the nature of descriptive hypotheses derived from the relevant domain of data (i.e., political facts and events) than of hypotheses derived from any subsumed theory or model. We believe that in

exploratory investigations like the present one, excessive preoccupation with general theories or comprehensive models may lead to
the one-sided collection of only those facts which are congruent
with the predilections and thus support the theory. Such exercises
in scholarship fail to provide an objective test of the subsumed
theory and only lead to its perpetuation and, eventually, institu-
tionalization under a misleading façade of scientific objectivity. In
social sciences, most theories at the present time are still descriptive, hindsight theories whose main criterion for survival is the
plausibility of their *post hoc* explanations rather than their
capacity to anticipate new events. Before social science theories
can claim the status of scientific theories surviving by the power
and generality of their predictive hypotheses, we must first
construct theories based on dependable facts, and then test such
theories constantly in the crucible of new facts and events to
refine their validity and generality. We hope that the present study
will prove a modest contribution toward this long-range goal of
constructing a theory of social change.

At a nontheoretical but practical level, we feel that this study
may have some value for the political elites in Nepal who are,
indeed, the ultimate authors of the processes and events we have
investigated. In the heat of political controversy, many political
distortions and misperceptions have arisen in Nepal, some acci-
dentally and some deliberately. Our hope is that this study, by
mirroring the facts and events of these crucial years faithfully, will
enable the Nepali political elites to analyze past events with
better perspective and greater objectivity, and to continue their
political "prospecting" with better successes and accomplishments
than heretofore. If in some measure it will contribute to a
clarification of national political goals in Nepal, improved political understanding and maturity, a sense of regard for facts and
honest dissent, we will feel that our efforts are amply rewarded.

A brief description of the source materials utilized in this
study would be appropriate in view of the virtual lack of
secondary sources available to the public outside Nepal. The
Rana regime maintained a strict control over all publications in
Nepal and even sometimes used their influence with the British
Government of India to muzzle or suppress Nepali-language
publications in India. Only one journal, the official *Gorkhapatra*,
was permitted to be published in Nepal, serving both as an
official gazette and as a newspaper. One or two privately published

monthlies were also licensed in the last stages of the Rana period, but these printed only noncontroversial articles and literary contributions.

Indian independence in 1947 ended most restrictions on Nepali publications in India, and the 1950 revolution had a similar result in Nepal. The Nepali press has undergone a substantial growth subsequently, particularly in Kathmandu, but also in an incipient form in some outlying areas. The quality of most of the dailies and weeklies leaves something to be desired, of course, as is to be expected in a country with only a brief journalistic history. The news reporting is usually scanty, biased, and unreliable, with editorial comments freely interspersed. But the press has one saving grace from the viewpoint of our study—it is a political press and, until 1961 at least, broadly representative of the political spectrum in Nepal. Most of the significant political factions in the capital published a daily or weekly which clearly and faithfully reflected their views on the political issues of the day. Not all of these went out of publication after the ban on parties in December, 1960, although their official connections with parties had to be terminated. Nevertheless, several of these journals seem to have retained an unofficial status as the voice of a political faction or leader.

Government publications have also had a rapid growth since 1951. The *Gorkhapatra* has been continued; it still serves as a semiofficial source for official views. The *Nepal Gazette,* which publishes the texts of legislation, ordinances, and official announcements, was established in 1951. In addition, many government reports on specific topics are now published by the department concerned or by the Department of Publicity and Broadcasting of the Central Secretariat.

Party manifestos, programs, reports on party meetings and conferences, and pamphlets on various subjects, including party histories, were published by most of the major political parties before December, 1960. In addition, a large number of books and pamphlets have been privately published in the last decade, illuminating certain aspects of the political history of Nepal. Some of these are in the form of memoirs; others are indifferently disguised and often vituperative attacks on political opponents; and some others have been published under the guise of political histories. All were invaluable—indeed, indispensable—to this study, not only for their contents, but also for their incisive depiction of the atmosphere and character of the Nepali political scene.

Finally, mention should be made of the substantial coverage given to Nepali political developments in the Indian press. These often suffer from the biases and political predilections of the newspapers or their correspondents, adding a new and sometimes tricky facet to the task of political analysis of Nepali affairs. Nevertheless, the Indian press serves a useful function as a necessary supplement to the Kathmandu press, particularly in the spheres of consistent chronology and news interpretation.

There were, obviously, serious deficiencies in the published source materials available to the authors. These were met as far as possible through personal contacts and interviews on an extended basis with political and governmental leaders.

It is with pleasure and gratitude that we make the following acknowledgments:

To His Majesty's Government in Nepal, and in particular to the many officials in the Central Secretariat who were generous both with their time and their assistance on innumerable occasions.

To the Institute of International Studies, University of California, Berkeley, under whose ultimate sponsorship this study was undertaken.

To the Center for South Asia Studies of the Institute of International Studies, and in particular to Dr. Joan V. Bondurant and Dr. Thomas Blaisdell, the chairmen of the Center at different stages of the study.

To the Ford Foundation and the American Institute of Indian Studies, which sponsored the field work of one of the authors in 1957–58 and 1963–64.

To Mahesh C. Regmi, the prominent Nepali economist, whose assistance in all aspects of the study, including the collection of elusive published materials, has been invaluable.

And finally to Dr. Margaret W. Fisher and Professor Robert A. Scalapino, whose advice, guidance, and support were essential to the inauguration of the project and to the completion of the study.

BHUWAN LAL JOSHI
LEO E. ROSE

Institute of International Studies
University of California, Berkeley
September 1, 1964

Contents

Introduction to Nepal

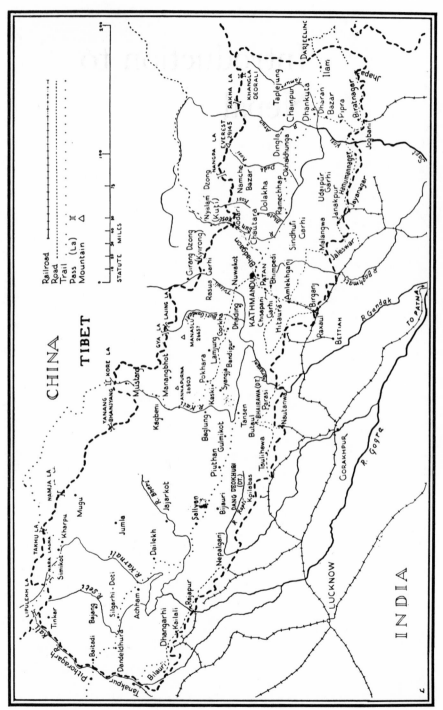

Map 1. Political map of Nepal.

1

The Setting

This throne of Nepal is a fort . . .
A fort built by God himself.

It was in these dramatic terms that King Prithvi Narayan Shah,[1] the founder of modern Nepal, described the kingdom centered in Kathmandu Valley that he conquered in the mid-eighteenth century. From the tiny principality of Gorkha, in the mid-montane area of Nepal approximately forty air-miles from Kathmandu, this remarkable scion of the Shah dynasty steadily expanded his authority until by 1775, the year of his death, much of present-day Nepal had been incorporated into his empire. In the next four decades his successors continued the process of unification and expansion until the whole of the sub-Himalayan hill area from Bhutan in the east to Kangra in the west was under Gorkha dominion. Nepal even challenged Chinese suzerainty in Tibet (1788–92) and British authority on the plains of northern India (1814–16), with predictably adverse consequences. Nevertheless, in the process a unified political entity emerged, which has subsequently retained its essential characteristics intact, though with somewhat more restricted boundaries than at the apex of Gorkha imperial expansion.

HISTORICAL POLITICAL DIVISIONS

Nepal's present international boundaries are of comparatively recent origin, extending back only to the mid-nineteenth century. A number of empires, usually based in Kathmandu Valley, had occasionally extended their sway over the surrounding hills, but large political units had been the exception rather than the rule. Politics in the hills before 1775 was characterized by a multiplicity of small principalities, often mutually antagonistic, whose rivalries sometimes dated back for centuries. When Prithvi

Narayan Shah commenced his campaign of conquest and unification, he had to contend with more than a hundred rajas, most of whom ruled territories that were at least as large as Gorkha and were roughly comparable to it in material and human resources.

There were, however, certain broader traditional political groupings to which most of the hill principalities belonged. In the western hill areas, two clusters of states seem to have had a long historical background—the twenty-two Baisi states of the Karnali region in far western Nepal and the twenty-four Chaubise states in the area directly to the west and south of Kathmandu. The wealthy and powerful kingdoms in Kathmandu Valley were separate political entities, and in the eastern hills numerous small local rulers were bound together in a very tenuous fashion within the loose confederation of Kirati tribal communities.

The significance of these traditional lines of affiliation varied from time to time and often may have been virtually meaningless. There is little evidence, for instance, to indicate that any of these groupings functioned as effective alliances or political associations; indeed, some of the most intense rivalries were found within rather than beyond their confines. Nevertheless, they did have a historical and, at times, cultural and ethnic base, some effects of which can still be detected in contemporary Nepali politics.

The Baisi states in far western Nepal had all formed part of the Malla kingdom of the eleventh to fourteenth centuries which, centered in the Jumla district, included also Kumaun and Garhwal to the west and western Tibet to the north of the Himalayas.[2] Once this empire disintegrated, some form of loose affiliation persisted among several of its component parts down to the time of the Gorkha conquest.

The Chaubise states in the Gandaki area may initially have represented a loose affiliation of Hindu rulers in a region that was still predominately non-Hindu in population.[3] In any case, by the eighteenth century these states could be divided into several categories, based on diverse dynastic lines. Of these, the most important were the Sen principalities of Palpa, Danahun, Rising, Gulmi, Makwanpur, and Morang, and the Shah (or Sahi Thakuri, as they were known earlier) kingdoms of Kaski, Lamjung, Tanahun, Khor, Bhirkot, Nuwakot, Garahun, and Satabun.* In the middle of the sixteenth century, a member of the Shah family, Dravya Shah, conquered Gorkha, replacing a non-Rajput, non-

---

* These subdivisions doubtlessly varied from time to time, and different sources cite different states within the Sen and Shah groupings. The affiliations noted here are based on the various listings in D. R. Regmi, *Modern Nepal* (Calcutta, 1961), p. 11.

Hindu dynasty. Gorkha, however, was never a Chaubise state, perhaps because the lines of affiliation had been formalized before this principality was brought under the rule of a Hindu dynasty.

According to Nepali historical traditions, a Hindu dynastic family bearing the prestigious Malla name established its rule over Kathmandu Valley in the thirteenth century, not long after the Malla rulers of Jumla had conquered a large empire in the hill area to the west. One of the more prominent of the Kathmandu Malla rulers, Yaksha Malla, divided the kingdom among his three sons on his death in 1480. Subsequently three separate kingdoms —Kathmandu, Patan, and Bhadgaon—flourished in the valley, deriving much of their wealth from their central position in the inter-Himalayan trade complex between India and Tibet. But chronic internecine warfare wore down the strength of all three kingdoms, and eventually they had to seek the assistance of adjacent hill rajas and martial communities against each other. The conquest of the valley by Prithvi Narayan Shah in 1768–69 was greatly facilitated by Patan, which first invited the Gorkha ruler to intervene in the valley's politics, and by Bhadgaon, which provided him with support at a crucial period in his campaign.

The term "Kirati" has been widely used to distinguish the tribal communities of the eastern Nepal hills, and that area is sometimes referred to, in historical contexts, as Kirat. A further subdivision is sometimes made between Majh ("middle") Kirat, the homeland of the Rais to the west of the Arun River, and Pallo ("further") Kirat, or Limbuwan, the homeland of the Limbus between the Arun River and the Sikkim border. Throughout this region there was only a very tenuous political authority before the Gorkha conquest in 1771–74; local rulers and elites enjoyed a fully autonomous status. The Sen ruler of Palpa, and later of Makwanpur, at times laid claim to suzerainty over the Majh Kirat areas, but it is questionable whether this ever had much political significance.* According to Sikkimese historical accounts, the Limbus in Pallo Kirat once had intimate political and cultural ties with Sikkim, but these gradually disintegrated in the century preceding the Gorkha conquest of eastern Nepal.

The various political divisions that antedated the unification of Nepal under the Shah dynasty never completely lost their

---

* In one source the army that resisted the Gorkha onslaught against Makwanpur in 1761 is described as a "Kirati force," and the general in command has the distinctly non-Aryan, non-Hindu name of Chong Wang Hang. But whether these Kirati warriors were stationed at Makwanpur as subjects or as mercenaries is not clear. Iman Singh Chemjong, *Kirat Itihas* [History of Kirat] (Gangtok, Sikkim, 1952), p. 1.

political significance. The regional administrative units into which Nepal was subsequently divided usually followed traditional political boundaries. The subdistricts (*thums*) in the western hills were largely coequivalent with the old Baisi and Chaubise principalities, and in the eastern hills the traditional subdivisions within the Kirati and Limbu communities were retained in drawing district and subdistrict boundaries.[4] Morever, there were until 1961 approximately twenty "Rajyas," with limited political and administrative autonomy, outside the regular district adminstrative system. These represented the last remnants of principalities whose ruling families merged their territories with the Gorkha kingdom through agreement, in the process retaining certain rights and privileges. In 1961 the Nepal government inaugurated a program under which existing regional administrative structure—consisting of thirty-two districts and the three magistracies in Kathmandu Valley—is being reorganized. Fourteen "zones" and seventy-five "development districts" have been established. The latter, however, usually coincide with the old subdistricts and thus retain the traditional political divisions.

DOMINANT TOPOGRAPHICAL FEATURES

The rapid extension of Shah dominion in the latter half of the eighteenth century was all the more remarkable in view of the excessively rugged terrain in which it occurred and the racial and cultural diversity of the many communities inhabiting the area. In the approximately seventy-five air-miles between the great Gangetic plain and the Tibetan plateau, three major mountain ranges, running east to west, intrude on the topography. On the northern border lie the fabled Himalayas, the Home of the Gods in both Hindu and Buddhist tradition, which include most of the highest mountains in the world—such as Everest, or Sagarmatha (29,028 ft.) Kanchenjunga (28,216 ft.), Makalu (27,824 ft.), and Dhaulagiri (26,975 ft.), all in or on the border of Nepal. Parallel and to the south are two lesser but still impressive ranges, the Mahabharat (5,000–15,000 ft.) and the Siwalik (1,000–3,000 ft.), the latter called the Churia in Nepal.

No less spectacular are the major river systems in Nepal. Originating on the Tibetan plateau, these rivers cut deep, narrow gorges and river valleys through the Himalayas and sub-Himalayan ranges before sweeping down to the plains of India, where they eventually join the most sacred of rivers in Hindu tradition —the Ganges. There are three principal river systems in Nepal—

the Karnali in the west, the Kosi in the east, and the Gandaki in the central part. In the area between the Himalaya and the Mahabharat ranges, innumerable other streams rise, eventually joining one of the main river systems at some point to the north of the Siwalik Range.

Topographically, Nepal can be conveniently divided into three distinct regions—the Terai, the Inner Terai, and the hills. The Terai constitutes the southernmost section of the country, commencing at about 200 feet above sea level at the Nepal-India border and rising to around 1,000 feet at the foot of the Siwalik hills. The name, derived from Persian, means "damp" and is appropriate in view of the hot, humid climate of this area. In the ancient and medieval period, the Terai was a rich agricultural region that provided the economic base for several important political and cultural centers. Ruins of many cities—among them Lumbini, the birthplace of Gautama Buddha, and Simrongadh, once the center of a flourishing kingdom that included the Tirhut area of present-day Bihar state in India—are found in the midst of the dense forests which now cover much of this area.

The circumstances under which large sections of the Terai were abandoned to the jungle are still unclear. Possibly the Muslim conquerors who crossed and recrossed northern India between the twelfth and the seventeenth centuries destroyed the existing political and agrarian system. Once depopulated, the area may have quickly reverted to jungle. By the time of the Gorkha conquest of the hill areas to the north, the Terai was mostly a heavily forested region inhabited by a few tribal communities which had developed some degree of immunity to the virulent forms of malaria prevalent there. Initially, the Gorkha rulers did little to develop their newly acquired lands at the foot of the hills, presumably because it was considered expedient to retain the Terai as a malarial jungle and thus as a barrier to British encroachment on the hill areas. The British discovered as early as 1767 that military operations were feasible across the Terai only in the "cold" season from October to April.

By the middle of the nineteenth century, the strategic considerations that had made the development of the Terai inadvisable earlier were no longer so persuasive. British power in India was overwhelming and firmly established. In Nepal any serious contemplation of military resistance disappeared; it was now considered expedient to seek an accommodation with the ruling power in India and to encourage the development of the Terai through the expansion of cultivation. Since the hill people were reluctant to move to this hot, fever-ridden area, the Terai was opened to settlement by plains dwellers from across the border. Thus even today most persons of the cultivator class and several of the large landowning and commercial families in the Terai are Indian in origin and still have extensive kinship and marriage ties across the border. Hindi, in the form of several regional dialects such as Maithili and Bhojpuri, is widely spoken and is often the medium of education and even, unofficially, of local administration.

The Inner Terai, lying between the Siwalik and the Mahabharat ranges, consists of several fairly broad valleys running from east to west. Until recently, this was a region of swamps and jungles whose tigers, elephants, and rhinoceroses attracted big-game hunting expeditions. Hunts are still feasible, but only in the cold season, as the climate is subtropical and virulently malarial. The first major efforts to transform these potentially productive areas into settled agrarian communities were undertaken in the mid-1950's, when the Nepal government, with the assistance of the United States aid program, commenced the development of the Rapti Valley at Chitaun. The immense and valuable forest resources of the Inner Terai are also now being exploited in a systematic fashion for the first time.

The hill region, as commonly understood in Nepal, comprises the Mahabharat and Himalayan ranges and the area lying between, and takes in nearly 75 per cent of the total land area of the country. The eastern hills—i.e., to the east of Kathmandu—are characterized by steep and narrow valleys, mostly running from north to south, and by poor, stony soils. The central hill area, in contrast, includes several broad and well-watered valleys, such as those of Kathmandu, where the capital is situated, and Pokhara, an important market center. Being the most productive agricultural region in Nepal, except for the eastern Terai, it supports a fairly dense population. The western hills, from the Karnali River to the Indian border, are thinly populated and largely undeveloped. Here "the soil is in general fertile, [but] steep slopes, inadequate rainfall, and excessive erosion have resulted in the lowest proportion of cultivated land to the total area" in Nepal.[5]

The hill region can also be divided into meaningful social and economic categories, on the basis of altitude, as *besi* ("valley"), mid-montane, and *lekh* or alpine pasture areas. The *besi* areas, formed by rivers and streams, contain fertile alluvial soil, but are often highly malarial. With the exception of the few large valleys in central Nepal, these river valleys have usually been avoided by the main hill communities and are inhabited by small aboriginal tribes such as the Danuwar, Kumkale, and Majhi.[6] The mid-montane areas (below 7,000 ft.) are the most productive agriculturally and hence the most heavily populated. The *lekh* areas (above 7,000 ft. and rising to between 16,000 and 18,000 ft. in the immediate vicinity of the Himalayas) are primarily pastoral and only secondarily agricultural; in addition, small-scale cottage industries such as wool spinning and weaving, paper-making, and basket-making are important, as is the position of some of the communities as trade intermediaries between Nepal and Tibet.[7] The social structure in the mid-montane area reflects Brahmanic Hindu social values and customs. In the *lekh* area, the influence of Lamaistic Buddhism or a synthesis of Buddhism and Hinduism is prevalent.

THE PEOPLE OF NEPAL

While there is only the vaguest and most unreliable documentation on the racial and regional origins of the numerous communities now inhabiting Nepal, it is generally agreed, even within communal myths, that most of them migrated to Nepal at some time during the past two or three thousand years. The reasons for migration are not difficult to comprehend, and, indeed, the process still continues. The mass flight of Tibetans to Nepal as a result of the ruthless suppression of Tibet's rebellion against Chinese Communist authority in 1959 is doubtless one of many comparable events in the history of these two countries. The opening of the Nepal Terai to cultivation in the nineteenth century attracted numerous settlers from India, some of whom later moved into the hill areas as merchants or to Kathmandu as politicians, government servants, and teachers. Indian Brahmans were frequently invited to Nepal by its Hindu kings, and were given extensive land grants in exchange for their indispensable ritualistic services and their advice on social and political questions. Nepal has thus served for centuries as a political and religious refuge, and as an area open for economic exploitation. The traffic, however, has not always been "one way." Banaras in India has long been a refuge for Nepali political exiles as well as a religious pilgrimage center. In recent decades unemployment in the hills has forced hundreds of thousands of Nepalese to seek employment in India or recruitment in the Indian and British armies.

REGIONAL DISTRIBUTION OF MAJOR ETHNIC GROUPS

Complexity and diversity are as much aspects of Nepal's population, an estimated ten million in 1964, as of its topography. At least three major racial strains have been discerned by ethnologists and anthropologists, though a consensus on the origins and subdivisions within each group is still to be achieved. The most important racial group numerically, socially, and politically in much of Nepal is composed of Indo-Aryans, migrants from the plains or from the hill areas of northern India. Almost as numerous, but less prominent except in some local areas, are communities of Mongolian origin which inhabit the higher hill areas in the west and east. A third and much smaller stratum comprises a number of tribal communities, such as the Tharus and the Dhimals of the Terai, which may be remnants of indigene communities whose habitation of Nepal predates the advent of Indo-Aryan and Mongolian elements. Most of these tribal groups have gradually been driven back into the more isolated sections— the Terai jungles and the hot, malarial river valleys in the hill areas—during the course of the Indo-Aryan and Mongolian incursions.

At least three distinct categories of Indo-Aryans are found in Nepal. The most numerous, possibly, are the inhabitants of the Terai. Many of them are relatively recent immigrants. The Pahari, or hill Indo-Aryan groups, are concentrated in the lower hill areas in far western Nepal. They resemble in many respects Indo-Aryan communities in the hill districts of northern India.[8] The third category, the most prominent socially and politically, is composed of descendants of high-caste Hindu families which migrated to Nepal several hundred years ago in the wake of the Muslim invasions of northern India. These families, mostly of Brahman or Kshatriya status, have spread through the whole of Nepal with the exception of the areas immediately adjacent to the northern border. They usually constitute a significant proportion of the local elites and are frequently the largest landowners in an area.

The Mongolian element in Nepal's population can be divided into two categories, based upon different areas of origin and cultural affiliations. One branch probably entered from the east or southeast, for they bear a distant physical and cultural resemblance to tribal communities inhabiting the intermediate hill areas between China and Southeast Asia.[9] Included within this category are the Kirati tribal communities—the Limbus and

Rais. Certain historical traditions of the important Newar community in Kathmandu Valley relate them to the Kiratis, though the connection must have been in the very distant past.

In the other Mongolian category are the several communities of Tibetan derivation. They inhabit chiefly the northern border area and are almost indistinguishable from their neighbors in Tibet physically, linguistically, and culturally, and usually are referred to as Bhotias (i.e., Tibetans) by other Nepalese. Some of the groups, resident south of the Himalayas for a longer period, have less obvious ties with Tibet and have some of the cultural attributes of the dominant Nepali hill groups.

The ethnic structure in Nepal is made more complex by the fact that there are a number of communities, such as the Newars of Kathmandu Valley and some of the Chettri castes, in which it is evident that there has been a profuse admixture of Indo-Aryan and Mongolian strains. Further, some communities, such as the Magars, are physically and linguistically Mongolian in origin but have gradually adopted Hindu (i.e., Indo-Aryan) social and ritual practices. This process of Sanskritization, as it is termed in popular anthropological parlance, is apparent over much of Nepal. There can be little doubt that it has been a dominant social phenomenon for several centuries at least. Nor is there much doubt that the process leading toward the adoption of Hindu social customs is even more widespread today, although it is now in conjunction with other and in some respects contradictory modernization processes.

Sanskritization has been aided and abetted in the past by the enforced imposition of Brahmanic social systems and codes of behavior by the Hindu dynasties that have dominated much of Nepal for the past thousand years. The most important of these social codes were introduced and formalized under the regimes of three of the greatest leaders in Nepal's history—Jayasthiti Malla of Kathmandu (1382–95), Rama Shah of Gorkha (1606–33), and the founder of the Rana political system, Jang Bahadur Kunwar (1846–77). All three were orthodox Hindus who attempted to codify the structure of Nepali society—both Hindu and non-Hindu—within a basically orthodox Hindu framework.

The social code introduced by Jayasthiti Malla was formulated, according to the chronicles, under the guidance of five Indian Brahmans. As far as was feasible, it adhered to the rules of conduct specified in the Manu dharmashastra of orthodox Hinduism. The Newari population of Kathmandu Valley was divided into sixty-four subgroups, essentially along occupational or craft lines, and these subgroups had the essential characteristics of jatis in the Hindu caste system. For the most part, Buddhist elements among the Newars were given a position equivalent with that of Hindus of a similar status. The Buddhist clergy, for instance, were placed on a footing of parity with Brahmans or Kshatriyas, depending upon their familial origin. This social code was retained virtually intact throughout the Malla period. Today, with only slight modifications, it still forms the basis for the Newari social system.

Rama Shah's role in the formalization and stabilization of the Gorkha social system was similar to that of Jayasthiti Malla in Kathmandu. An incipient caste structure was introduced, rigid for the orthodox Hindu Brahmans and Kshatriyas, but flexible for the still largely non-Hindu tribal communities in Gorkha.* A legal code based upon shastric (i.e., dharmashastra) principles, suitably modified to accommodate tribal customs and practices, was introduced, as were rules regulating weights and measures, irrigation facilities, land tenure, grazing land, and other important features of economic and social relations. The Rama Shah social code seems to have been the first codified system in the hills. It had a tremendous impact upon surrounding areas and, indeed, may have been an important factor in the expansion of Gorkha rule throughout the hill area.

Both the Jayasthiti Malla and Rama Shah social codes were formulated for comparatively small communities inhabiting a very limited area. After the unification of Nepal under the Shah dynasty, a social and legal code applicable to the entire country was required. The first steps in this direction were taken during the reign of Rana Bahadur Shah (1777–99), but it was Jang Bahadur Kunwar, the first Rana Prime Minister, who finally completed the task. As with the Rama Shah code, Jang Bahadur's Muluki Ain, or Legal Code, incorporated a few basic Brahmanic principles, primarily those applicable to intercaste relations and caste pollution. For the most part, however, the customs of each community or ethnic group in Nepal were retained insofar as they did not conflict with the dharmashastras. The Muluki Ain was modified on several occasions during the Rana period, always in the direction of enhanced Hindu orthodoxy. This process was reversed in the postrevolutionary period when, in 1963, a new edition of the legal code modified most of the caste, marriage, and social regulations.

---

* The social code specified four castes (i.e., varnas) and 36 subcastes (i.e., jatis). It is likely, however, that the latter figure was only symbolic, for the code did not distinguish anywhere near that number of subcastes. Buddhi Man Singh, "Bhasa Vansavali" [Nepali Genealogy] (MS in collection of Leo E. Rose), leaf 122a.

The national language, officially, is Nepali. Stemming from Sanskrit, it may have had a common origin with similar dialects spoken in the northern hill areas of India, but it has been subjected to diverse influences from various sources, including, possibly, Rajasthani dialects. It is closely related to Hindi, particularly in its written form, and utilizes the same script. There are numerous other languages spoken in Nepal, usually associated with particular communities or regions of the country. Some of these, such as the Kumauni dialects of the far western hills, and Bhojpuri and Maithili in the Terai, are also Sanskrit-derived and are closely related to Nepali. Others, including the Bhotia, Kirati, Newari, Magar, and Gurung languages, belong to the quite distinct Tibeto-Burman linguistic family. Thus, language has long been an important divisive factor in Nepal. At present, however, Nepali is widely spoken throughout the country, at least as a second language, except in the isolated northern and eastern border areas. The increasing use of Nepali as the medium of instruction in the rapidly expanding educational system should soon make it a national language in fact as well as by legal prescript.

Cultural influences from India—whether from traditional Hindu or Buddhist sources, or from modern political ideologies—have been extremely influential in defining the character of contemporary Nepali society. But it would be inaccurate to conclude that Nepal is merely India writ small. Many non-Hindu social attitudes and values are still prevalent in Nepal, even within communities that have adopted Brahmanic rituals and the Hindu caste system. Moreover, it is apparent that under the impact of nationalizing and centralizing influences, a distinctive Nepali political personality is gradually emerging, drawing inspiration from its own historical and cultural background as well as from India, from other Asian neighbors, and from the West. These trends in the development of a Nepali national identity provide, perforce, one of the central themes of this study.

THE ECONOMY

The predominance of agriculture in the Nepali economy is readily apparent from any set of statistical references available: rural-urban ratio, employment, production, or commerce. Probably 85 per cent of the people of Nepal depend directly upon agriculture for their livelihood, a phenomenally high figure even for the underdeveloped areas of Asia. Yet only in the past half-century has pressure on the land become a serious problem. Indeed, the land policy of the Rana government, as reflected in tenure and revenue regulations, was directed more toward encouraging the extension of cultivation in the hills and the Terai than to carrying out the systematic regulation of landlord-tenant or landowner-government relations.[10] By 1900, however, surplus lands suitable for cultivation were no longer available in some of the more heavily populated hill areas, as was indicated by the massive migrations to other parts of Nepal and to India, Burma, Sikkim, and Bhutan. Concerted efforts to revise government policies to meet new conditions had to await the overthrow of the *status quo*-minded Rana regime in 1951.

As should be expected from Nepal's historical and sociological background, the land tenure structure is a fantastic conglomeration of systems derived from numerous sources. Virtually all land-tenure forms extant in northern India at some point during the past two milleniums can be found in Nepal. In addition, the Bhotias of northern Nepal have retained certain features of the Tibetan land system, while the Kirati and Limbu communities in the eastern hill areas have their own distinctive system, which bears certain resemblances to communal ownership practices prevalent among tribal communities in the Assam hill areas and in Burma.

The first steps in the direction of a standardized land-tenure system followed the expansion of the Shah dynasty's dominions in the eighteenth century. Eventually, five broad categories of land tenure emerged: (1) *Raikar* land was that on which revenue was paid directly to the state and for which the government acted the role of the landowner. (2) *Birta* was a form of land tenure, often tax exempt, in which the state assigned land to an individual. In effect, the state divested itself of ownership rights, usually on conditional terms. (3) *Guthi* land was that donated by the state or individuals for religious or philanthropic purposes. It was usually tax exempt. (4) *Kipat,* a form of communal land tenure, was particularly prevalent in the eastern hill areas. (5) *Rakam* and *Jagir* were forms of tenure under which lands were assigned by the state to individuals for the performance of specific services (e.g., military or civil appointments). All of these tenure systems, with the possible exception of *Kipat,* were based ultimately on the theory that land belonged to the state, a legal fiction that has been maintained until the present day. Nevertheless, most aspects of private ownership of land exist in Nepal, and government efforts to exercise its nominal rights in the land inevitably meet with intense resistance from landowning groups.

Manufacturing, even on a traditional cottage-industry scale, seems never to have reached significant proportions in pre-1951 Nepal. Even so, it is likely that more Nepalese were engaged in what were essentially manufacturing or artisan activities in 1850 than in 1950, both in proportionate and absolute terms. Cotton and wool cloth production, for instance, was substantial enough to permit exportation to Tibet; copper and iron mining, primarily in the eastern hill area, was sufficient to meet local needs and provide a surplus for export to India; production of brass and paper was flourishing; and the output of armaments had reached proportions that caused concern among the British in India. By the early decades of the twentieth century, most such activities had ceased or were in decline. Cloth production was limited to the remote hill areas where cheap mill-made textiles from India, England, and Japan could not be easily obtained. The primitive techniques used in mining were no longer economic, and the lack of communications, capital, and technical competence deterred modernization of the mines. The armament industry virtually disappeared once the British decided it was expedient to provide Nepal with military equipment, thus eliminating the necessity for Kathmandu to produce its own.

Trade and commerce, on the other hand, have long been important in the Nepali economy. The affluence of Kathmandu has traditionally been associated with its position in a well-developed trans-Himalayan trade system. From the sixteenth to the twentieth century, a large share of the commerce between northern India and central Tibet was channeled through Kathmandu Valley. Lamaistic monastic insitutions in Tibet, Newari commercial families in Kathmandu Valley, and Hindu and Muslim trading communities in north-central India coöperated in the operation of a complex, highly profitable trade structure.

The Gorkha conquest of Kathmandu in 1768 temporarily disrupted the established trade pattern, much to the concern of everyone involved. The process of reconstruction proved to be long and involved, absorbing the interest of Nepal, Tibet, and the British in India for at least two decades. Part of the motivation for the rapid expansion of the Shah dominions after 1770 seems to have been connected with the Nepal government's determination to control all the access routes between India and Tibet in the sub-Himalayan hill areas and thus to force both the Tibetans and the British to recognize Kathmandu's monopoly as entrepôt for the Indo-Tibetan trade.

By the beginning of the nineteenth century an accommodation had been reached anew between Kathmandu and Lhasa;

once again most trans-Himalayan commerce was routed through Kathmandu. The easier road through Sikkim and the Chumbi Valley in Tibet was deliberately kept closed on Tibet's insistence until the last decade of the century, despite the objections of the British government of India. But the British were not to be permanently denied. Tibet was eventually "opened," though not until the Younghusband expedition (1903–05) had fought its way to Lhasa. With the opening of the Sikkim route, Kathmandu's importance rapidly declined. A number of Newari commercial families transferred their operations to Kalimpong and were able to make good use of the special privileges (e.g., exemption from custom duties) that they enjoyed in Tibet. Not until the fortunes of politics once again closed the Sikkim route, in 1959, could Kathmandu aspire to regaining its lost prestige and affluence as the major trading center in the Himalayas.

The communications network in Nepal has long been a crucial factor in the country's political, economic, and cultural life. Topographical features—east-west ranges and north-south river systems—have made east-west communications extremely difficult and north-south communications, at least to the south of the Himalayas, comparatively easier. Even today, the hill areas in the eastern and western extremities of the country have readier access to the plains to the south than to Kathmandu. Similarly, the Nepal Terai sends most of its surplus agricultural production to markets across the border in India, since markets in Nepal are both limited and difficult to reach. The Nepali authorities have usually found it worth while to encourage the continuation of this trading system, which brings in substantial quantities of Indian rupees, even though they sometimes find it necessary to purchase food at the nearest access points in India in order to relieve shortages in Kathmandu Valley and the hills.

The Nepali economy is, thus, closely intertwined with that of northern India. In 1964, approximately 95 per cent of Nepal's external trade was with India,[11] and most of the rest was channeled through India. Until recently, at least, the Indian rupee was the standard medium of exchange in the Terai and much of the hill area, and the efforts of the Kathmandu authorities to extend circulation of Nepali currency were usually unavailing. Further, many Nepalese from the hills are regularly recruited for the famous "Gurkha" regiments of the Indian and British armies, and others descend to the plains during the cold season in search of seasonal employment, providing important outside supplements to the nearly marginal economic structure in much of the hills.[12]

Somewhat similarly, but in a far more restricted fashion, the economy of the northern border area of Nepal is interconnected with that of Tibet. Whereas the southern border is open along its entire length, the Himalayas are a formidable though not impass-able barrier to the north. There are at least eighteen pass areas between Nepal and Tibet, of which only two are really feasible for extensive commercial purposes. All the passes are at elevations from 15,000 to 20,000 feet above sea level and are closed through-out the winter months to any but the most intrepid and resource-ful of travelers. The Bhotia communities in northern Nepal, in particular the Sherpas and the Thakalis, have long acted as intermediaries in a local border trade with Tibet. But trade with Tibet has amounted to no more than 2 or 3 per cent of Nepal's total external commerce in modern times. Its complete disruption would adversely affect a few small communities in the northern hills and several commercial houses in Kathmandu, but would be almost imperceptible in the country's economic structure as a whole. Indeed, Kathmandu's persistent efforts to maintain and expand economic ties with Chinese-controlled Tibet would seem to be attributable more to optimistic appraisals of commercial potential than to any great concern for preserving the existing system.

THE CENTRALITY OF KATHMANDU IN NEPAL'S POLITICAL DEVELOPMENTS

Kathmandu, in its manifold functions as the administrative capital, the locus of political decision-making, the vortex of Nepali nationalism, the home and sanctuary of Nepali elites, and the center of cultural and intellectual activities, occupies a unique position in the body politic of Nepal. It is at one and the same time the most modernized, most highly educated, and most sophisticated city in Nepal and the least representative. Politics as a Nepali phenomenon has been largely restricted to the urban areas of Kathmandu Valley and its population of less than three hundred thousand. In a real sense, Kathmandu serves as the prototype of progress for the rest of Nepal, and public leaders envisage the development of little Kathmandus over the length and breadth of the country.

Kathmandu has excited both jealousy and admiration among the Nepalese living beyond its periphery—jealousy of its atypical modernization, which is regarded as having been achieved in large part at the expense of outlying areas, and admiration for its role as a pacesetter. This ambivalence in the attitude of non-Kathmandu political leaders has contributed its share of irrationality and unpredictability to Nepal's political development.

Historically, the Kathmandu area was conterminous with that of Nepal, and even today residents of the hill areas will say they are going to Nepal when traveling to Kathmandu Valley. As the administrative capital of the ancient Lichhavi kings (first to eleventh centuries) and the later Malla dynasties (thirteenth to eighteenth centuries), it prospered as the meeting point of two great cultures, the Indian and the Sino-Tibetan, and developed as the focus of a unique cultural synthesis along the entire Himalayan range. The heritage of this cultural syncretism is extant today in Kathmandu in the form of numerous architectural, intellectual, and artistic treasures and has provided a historical basis for current definitions of Nepal's cultural and political individuality.

Kathmandu underwent a significant political transformation when the Shah kings of Gorkha made it the capital of their new, expanding nation-state. In the process, Kathmandu's political primacy over the rest of Nepal was established, in form as well as in fact. It became the residence of the Shah kings and their courtiers, and the seat of government. Even under the Rana regime (1846–1951), which deliberately segregated Kathmandu politically from both India and the rest of Nepal, its political primacy was preserved intact.

During the more than a hundred years of Rana rule, Kathmandu was naturally the site of the limited concessions to modernization that the ultraconservative Rana regime was prepared to introduce. It became the first modern city in Nepal—and for a long time was the only city with electricity, telephones, automobiles, radios, and other appurtenances, few though these might be, of the twentieth century. Even in Kathmandu, exposure to the modern world is a recent phenomenon. The first high school and hospital were established only in the last decade of the nineteenth century. The first college was opened in 1918, and the first university in 1960. Electricity was introduced in 1904. The first modern highway linking Kathmandu with the outside world was completed in 1956.

Under the impact of this gradual modernization, Kathmandu, the ancestral home of traditional Nepali political, military, and sacred elites, became also the sanctuary of elites of a new kind. These individualistically oriented, liberal cosmopolitan elites, educated in Western-style institutions, were mainly instrumental in the overthrow of the Rana regime in 1951 and the introduction of political experimentation based upon democratic principles of government. Their origin can be traced directly to the establishment of the first high school and college in Kathmandu and to exposure to modernizing, liberalizing influences from India. Since 1951 they have challenged the dominant position, in the political process, of the traditional oligarchy composed of the military and sacred (i.e., Kshatriya and Brahman) elites, and have established themselves as the core of a new "modernizing" oligarchy.

From 1951 to 1959, the political primacy of Kathmandu was maintained intact, and its newly emergent Western-educated elites dominated Nepali politics. Even leaders of political factions based in other sections of the country felt it necessary to come to Kathmandu to have their credentials approved and their political legitimacy established. In the process these regional political leaders were absorbed into the Kathmandu political system; they adopted both the political goals and the tactics of the Kathmandu politicians.

The 1959 general elections constituted the most serious threat to the political primacy of Kathmandu since the unification of Nepal under the Shah dynasty. For the first time, Kathmandu's political status was diminished, for the valley was allotted only five seats in the 109-member Lower House of Parliament. Nepali politics were on the way to becoming national politics rather than Kathmandu politics. The royal *coup* of December 15, 1960, which led to the abolition of parliamentary democracy and the institution of a "guided" and tradition-oriented form of democratic politics—called Panchayat Raj—restored the political preëminence of Kathmandu at the all-important decision-making level. The centrality of Kathmandu in the country's political development has been preserved and continued amid the political innovations introduced by King Mahendra. Thus, once again, Kathmandu's role in all aspects of Nepali politics is vital and usually determinant.

Historical
Background

2

The Shah and Rana
Political Systems

UPON THE EMERGENCE of Nepal as a nation-state in 1768 under the
dynamic leadership of the ruler of Gorkha, Prithvi Narayan Shah,
participation in the political process became the virtually exclusive prerogative of two high-caste Hindu groups, Brahmans and
Kshatriyas, which were further subdivided into several factions
and families. This pattern was in consonance with ancient Hindu
scriptural requirements that the rulers of a state should always be
recruited from the Kshatriya, or warrior, caste and that they
should exercise their political functions with the advice and
consent of the Brahmans, the intellectual elite and spiritual
preceptors.

The traditional role of the Brahman was that of an adviser
rather than a governor or administrator, and it was usually in that
capacity that the Brahman elite families operated under the Shah
political system. They fulfilled a variety of responsibilities for the
ruler as priests, lawgivers, astrologers, and diplomatic emissaries.
Seldom did they seek direct and open confrontations with other
political groups. Their involvement in the political process typically took the form of behind-the-scenes efforts to persuade the
rulers to adopt certain courses of action or, alternatively, of
participation in *sub rosa* intrigues and conspiracies aimed at the
ruling group. They constituted, nonetheless, a powerful body in
the Nepal Court under the Shahs.

Until the emergence of the Rana family in 1846, the elite
factions most directly involved in the political process were the
members of four prominent Kshatriya families—namely, the
Shahs, who were the ruling or royal family, and the Pandes,
Thapas, and Basnyats, who can be termed noble families. In

23

theory, the royal family occupied the pivotal position and the noble families contested with one another for positions of executive authority and military command under the general supervision of the Shahs. The hostility and sense of rivalry between the three principal noble families was so long-standing and deep-seated that no one family could enhance the scope of its own political power except at the expense of the others. Such coalitions or alliances as were formed among them were of the most expedient and temporary character; when one family rose to power, the others invariably suffered not only a political eclipse but also a diminution in the economic base, mainly landholdings, upon which their political position depended. It is not surprising that the political history of Nepal during the Shah period was largely confined to incessant familial intrigues and conspiracies conducted within the indulgent arena of the royal palace at Kathmandu.

While in theory the Shah ruler was the ultimate political authority in the country, his effectiveness as a ruler was badly hampered by internal conflicts and tensions within the royal family and by the defensive political tactics of the nobility. The King had the final voice (*Hukum*) in the selection of the executive head of his government, the Mukhtiyar, as well as in all matters pertaining to the government. But the vicissitudes of politics occasionally forced the King to delegate his *Hukum* to the Queen or the Crown Prince, and the Mukhtiyar was usually chosen on the basis of a consensus among the royal family and the nobles active in the Court—the Bharadars or "bearers of burdens."

Frequently there was as little cohesion among the Shahs as within the other leading Kshatriya families. The royal family was usually divided by the more or less conflicting interests of (1) the King, (2) the Senior Queen, (3) the Junior Queen, and (4) the King's brothers and cousins, each of the four having a coterie of supporters among the officials known as Bharadars. The Crown Prince and his brothers, when they had attained their majority, constituted a fifth and occasionally unruly faction. By tradition, the Shah kings always married two wives at the same time, presumably to ensure succession to the throne. An important side effect of this practice was a gradual corrosion of the royal powers. The Senior and Junior Queens were not merely competitors for the status of favorite wife; they were at times involved in bitter struggles with each other over the King's *Hukum* and over the succession rights of their respective children. The Junior Queen, in particular, was likely to resort to extreme tactics to counter the established convention under which the sons of the Senior Queen had prior rights of succession to the throne. Since succession was based on the principle of primogeniture—that is, the eldest son succeeding his father—the King's brothers, cousins, and uncles were cast in the role of dependent relations who were accorded regal status without its authority and power. The men of this group, known collectively as the Choutariyas, could gain political prominence only as regents for a minor king or as partisans of one of the noble families. This fragmentation of the Shah family provided the court nobility with the opportunity to play off its different members or factions against one another. Indeed, for purposes of self-aggrandizement it was best to keep the Shahs as badly divided as possible.

Thus, the matrix of politics permitted a great variety of moves and countermoves among political elite groups. Any durable political system had to be the outcome of a process of equilibration among all the contending forces. But alliances and coalitions among the contenders could not be maintained on a long-term basis, and equilibrium could be achieved only through the destruction of hostile groups on as broad a scale as possible. It is, therefore, small wonder that the political process was soaked in blood and violence. None of the Mukhtiyars or regents between 1769 and 1846 died a natural death; their lives were ended abruptly either by the assassin's bullet or sword or by their own hand. The rise to power of one family or faction was inevitably marked by the purging of the others from the administration and frequently by the execution of their leading members. Over the period from 1769 to 1846, the Choutariya group was in power from 1786 to 1794, the Pande group from 1801 to 1805, and the Thapa group from 1806 to 1837 and again from 1843 to 1845.[1] The Basnyat group, although prominent in the court and the army, never headed a government during these years. Any change of regime and accompanying elimination of the former dominant faction brought a complete reversal of political alignments. Any faction in power sought to perpetuate itself by continual and systematic persecution of all real or potential threats to the regime. Thus, Court conspiracies and intrigues were the only means available to induce changes in the government, and change came about usually as the climax of a successful treacherous scheme.

To add to the instability of the Shah system, a new political factor emerged in the early part of the nineteenth century: the presence of British power in India. The British had sought to penetrate Nepal for commercial and strategic reasons as early as 1767, when they dispatched Captain Kinloch with a small force to assist the beleaguered Newar King of Kathmandu against Prithvi

Narayan Shah.[2] In 1801, the British Government, by capitalizing on a split between the King and his Court, and by siding with the incumbent powers in Nepal, obtained a treaty of commerce and alliance which, among other things, provided for the permanent stationing of a British Resident in Kathmandu.[3] This marked the formal entry of British influence into the unstable political process of the Nepali Court, an influence which lasted in one form or another until the departure of the British from India in 1947. The British presence, besides dividing the Court into pro-British and anti-British factions, led to the emergence of pro-Chinese and anti-Chinese alignments and thus to additional disruptive influences.

In sum, the political process under the Shah rulers was a deadly game of political poker played by the few privileged elite groups of the Court, comprising primarily those families that had accompanied King Prithvi Narayan Shah when he transferred his capital from Gorkha to Kathmandu. The unification and territorial expansion of the country widened the scope of Court politics from its previous narrow base in the small mountainous principality of Gorkha, but the actors and the pattern remained essentially the same.

The Shah government, while retaining with minor modifications the political apparatus brought over from Gorkha, seemed to lose some of its responsiveness to local opinion in the new surroundings of Kathmandu. In Gorkha the governmental system had often associated the local populace with its composition and functions. For example, when the King had to choose a minister, he obtained a consensus of his Court and subjects.[4] In such cases, public opinion meant the consensus of six elite families prominent in Gorkha social and political life. These families, belonging to different caste and ethnic groups, were known collectively as the Thar Ghars.

The Shah king, although technically an absolute monarch responsible to no one but himself and ruling by divine right, had to reckon with the restraints imposed by religious and social traditions as well as with the active influence enjoyed by the Thar Ghar aristocracy at the Court and in the administration. It was on them that he had to depend for recruiting talent to carry on the administration of the state.

Under the early Shah kings administration was based on a simple delegation of royal powers to a small group of officials, the Bharadars, who constituted the Court of Nepal. Their designations, and the order of their importance, were (1) Choutariya, (2) Kazi, (3) Sardar, (4) Khardar, (5) Kapardar, (6) Khajanchi, (7) Takshali, (8) Dharmadhikar, (9) Vichari, (10) Dittha, (11)

Jetha-Boora, (12) Subba, and (13) Umrao. All these officials held office for a period of one year only, being screened annually by the king in a ceremony called the Pajani, after which they were either reappointed or dismissed. Generally speaking, the Choutariya acted as the *de facto* head of the day-to-day administration. As the senior member of the Shah family, he was entitled to precedence over other officials and functioned as the King's proxy in supervising the various branches of the government. Usually when the King was a minor, the Choutariya, functioned also as regent and exercised wide powers. It was during the minority (1777–94) of King Rana Bahadur Shah that Bahadur Shah, the Choutariya, functioned both as regent and as Mukhtiyar (i.e., Prime Minister) ; from that time on, the new office of Mukhtiyar was a regular part of the administrative system.

This innovation eventually weakened the traditional role of the Choutariya in day-to-day administration, for the office of Mukhtiyar fell into the hands of non-Shah noble families. Damodar Pande held it from 1799 to 1805, and Bhimsen Thapa from 1806 to 1837. A Brahman, Ranga Nath Gurujyu, served as Mukhtiyar for eight months in 1837–38. Ranajang Pande held the office from 1839 to 1841. It was filled again by a Choutariya, Fateh Jang Shah, from 1841 to 1843. The title was changed to that of Prime Minister when Mathabar Singh Thapa was appointed to the post in 1843. Later, under the Ranas, Mukhtiyar was the title held by the Commander in Chief, who was the next in line of succession to the Prime Ministry.

Among the other officials of the Shah administrative system, the Kazis, or Ministers, exercised supervisory functions over civil and military affairs. Usually there were four Kazis; the one who was entrusted with the Lal Mohur ("red seal") of the king followed the Choutariya and the Mukhtiyar in order of precedence. Kazis usually headed the army during military campaigns. Subordinate to the Kazis, but invested with the command of small army units, were the Sardars, of whom there were usually four in the government. More or less routine details of administration were handled by the Khardars, who acted as secretaries, writing dispatches to foreign states or to officers of the government. The Kapardar was in charge of the King's wardrobe, jewelry, and kitchen. The Khanjachi was the treasurer and bursar of the government. The Takshali was master of the mint.

On the judicial side, the Dharmadhikar acted as the chief criminal judge of the country and dipsensed justice in all cases of litigation on behalf of the Crown, although sentences pronounced by the Dharmadhikar had to be approved by the King before they could be carried out. The Vicharis recorded the proceedings and verdicts in the court over which the Dharmadhikar presided. The Dittha acted as a superintendent of the police system. The Jetha Booras ("elder statesmen") held intermittent positions as emissaries to district officials or to the courts of foreign states. The Subbas were district officials who collected taxes and revenues on behalf of the King; they also supervised the maintenance of law and order in their districts. Finally, the Umraos were commanders of the military posts scattered over the country.[5]

Before the reign of Prithvi Narayan Shah, the Gorkha military forces were bands of militia maintained by the Umraos, who were assigned lands called *Jagir* to support themselves and their followers. The service of the Umraos, however, was by annual tenure, and the grants of land were coterminous with the period of service. The large turnover of these military personnel each year was intended partly to ensure that a larger body of trained men would be available throughout the country than the state could afford to support at one time, and partly to discourage the formation of cliques among ambitious military officers. Any officer retired from the military roll was entitled to continue to use the title he had earned while on active duty; he was regarded as having an honorary position in the administration and was, moreover, eligible for immediate recall at the government's discretion. There was little or no stigma attached to the fact that a person was *Dhakre,* or off the payroll; by the same token, anyone on active duty could expect to be laid off at some time or other. During Prithvi Narayan's reign regular regiments were established for the first time, and the militia was then gradually relegated to a secondary position in Nepal's military system.

During the reign of Rana Bahadur Shah (1777–99), and especially during the prime ministry of Bhimsen Thapa (1807–37), there was a vigorous central administration in Nepal. The government sought to strengthen its own position vis-à-vis local political elites by preventing grants of land from becoming hereditary, by confiscating permanent assignments of land to the temples and monasteries and adding their revenues to the government treasury, and, most significantly, by organizing a state army holding allegiance to the Crown rather than to the Umraos or Sardars.

THE RISE OF THE RANA FAMILY

The Rana family rose to political power as the result of a massacre of the leaders of the other important political families in

1846. Although the massacre was precipitated by the assassination of the Junior Queen's favorite, Gagan Singh, it can be seen as the violent culmination of intrigues and counterintrigues that had beset the court since the downfall of Bhimsen Thapa in 1837. The Pande family, in power from 1837 to 1841, had taken the opportunity to persecute the Thapas. When the Thapa family came to power again late in 1843, General Mathabar Singh Thapa, Bhimsen's nephew and godson, was appointed Prime Minister and Commander in Chief. He in his turn wreaked bloody revenge on the Pandes. The royal household was at this time badly split between the King, the Junior Queen, and the Crown Prince. The King was anxious to fix the succession on the Crown Prince, but without his own abdication; the Junior Queen was conspiring to put her son on the throne in place of the son of the late Senior Queen; the Crown Prince was conspiring against both his father and his step-mother in his eagerness to be seated on the throne at the earliest opportunity.

In January, 1843, King Rajendra formally invested the Junior Queen, Lakshmi Devi, with the *Hukum,* promising that in all matters pertaining to the government he would seek her counsel and abide by her advice. In December, 1844, Crown Prince Surendra suddenly left Kathmandu for the Terai, vowing that he would not return until his father had abdicated. The King followed him and was finally able to persuade him to return home by making a political settlement under which he retained the throne but conceded some royal prerogatives to his son, who was given authority to issue orders and enforce their compliance. This three-way division of authority within the royal family, known popularly as the Tin Sirkars ("three governments") , paved the way for its political eclipse.

In 1845, Prime Minister Mathabar Singh was assassinated, and subsequently Fateh Jang Shah was restored to the office. The assassination of Mathabar Singh was carried out by his nephew, Jang Bahadur Kunwar, on the order of King Rajendra. For this service, Jang Bahadur, a member of a minor noble family of Kshatriya status, was raised to the rank of Kazi.[6] Taking advantage of the anarchic state of court politics, he established virtually dictatorial control over the government. His place in the history of Nepal is assured not merely as the protagonist of the Rana regime, but as a man of great personal courage and political astuteness.

The event which catapulted Jang Bahadur and his family into political prominence was, as we have noted, the massacre that followed upon the assassination of Gagan Singh, the favorite of the Junior Queen. Gagan Singh, the most influential member of the Council of State, had been assigned command of seven regiments and had been charged with the responsibility of supervising all the arsenals and magazines in the country. His rise into the limelight of Court politics from the lowly station of a Chobdar (a personal attendant in the palace) had evoked great jealousy and animosity among other members of the Court. It is believed that the King and his sons were determined that Gagan Singh should die, because of his rumored amorous affair with the Junior Queen, and that the Prime Minister, Fateh Jang Shah, helped select an assassin.[7]

In any case, the murder of Gagan Singh led to a violent tragedy in the Kot, or courtyard, of the royal palace, an event usually referred to as the Kot Massacre of 1846. Immediately after hearing of Gagan Singh's assassination, the Junior Queen visited his house and vowed vengeance on those responsible. Carrying the sword of state in her hand, she proceeded to the Kot and ordered the sounding of a general alarm for an assembly of all civil and military officials. By design or caution, Jang Bahadur hastened to the Kot at the head of the three regiments under his command, accompanied by all his brothers and relatives. He deployed his troops at all the entrances and exits of the Kot courtyard, giving instructions that no one was to enter or leave without express orders from himself. Jang was one of the first to reach the Kot; shortly afterwards all the important civil and military officials of the government assembled there. The Queen demanded that whoever was responsible for the death of Gagan Singh be made known. Her suspicion settled on a Kazi, Birkishor Pande, who pleaded innocence; nevertheless the Queen ordered General Abhiman Singh to behead him immediately. For confirmation of the execution order, Abhiman Singh looked to King Rajendra, who refused to give his sanction without a trial of the accused. Prime Minister Fateh Jang and other royal councilors were disinclined to press charges against anyone in the prevailing atmosphere and tried to temporize.

While the councilors were involved in argument, Jang Bahadur sparked the massacre by informing (or misinforming) the Queen that General Abhiman's troops were fast approaching the Kot to overpower the Queen's party, and by demanding his immediate arrest, to which the Queen acceded. Upon Abhiman Singh's refusing to submit himself to arrest, one of Jang's soldiers stabbed him to death with a bayonet. This was the first casualty of the Kot Massacre; a general melee ensued, in which Jang Bahadur, his brothers, and the soldiers under their command engaged in widespread slaughter of their real or potential political foes. The massacre began on the night of September 14 and continued into the early hours of the following morning. When the last blow had been struck, the courtyard presented a ghastly scene. It was as if the long internecine struggles and endemic intrigues of the Nepali Court had resolved themselves in a grand finale. The casualties at the Kot were staggering in both the number and the rank of the persons involved. The entire Council of State, with the exception of Jang Bahadur, was wiped out. Prominent members of the Choutariya, Pande, and Thapa families were killed, and many who managed to escape from the scene of the massacre fled the country immediately.

According to one source, twenty-nine prominent nobles were killed during the Kot Massacre, twenty-six fled the country, and twenty-five others were banished. Among those killed were eleven Choutariyas, six Pandes, three Thapas, and nine members of other Kshatriya families. In addition, seven Choutariyas, two Pandes, two Thapas, two members of the Rajguru family, and thirteen other persons fled to India. Shortly thereafter several whole branches of the Choutariya and Thapa families, as well as a number of Pandes and other Kshatriyas and Brahmans, were banished from Nepal.[8]

On the day following the Kot Massacre, the Queen bestowed on Jang Bahadur the office of the Mukhtiyar with the title of Prime Minister and Commander in Chief, and this appointment was soon confirmed by King Rajendra. Jang Bahadur's brothers also received high offices in the government. His elder brother, Bhakta Bir Kunwar, received the title of Kapardar and was entrusted with supervision of the King's wardrobe, jewelry, and kitchen. His second brother, Kazi Bam Bahadur Kunwar, was put in charge of the Bara Kausi (the treasury). His third brother, Kazi Badri Narsingh Kunwar, was put in charge of the Kumari Chowk (accounts and audits). His fourth brother, Krishna Bahadur Kunwar, became a commander-colonel and received the responsibility of administering the important district of Palpa. The remaining three brothers, Ranodip Singh Kunwar, Jagat Shamsher Jang Kunwar, and Dhir Shamsher Jang Kunwar, became colonels in the army. Thus Jang and his family acquired control over most of the key posts in the administration of the country.

The Kot Massacre assured the security and continuity of Jang's hold on the government. The Thapa family, which earlier had been weakened considerably by its political vendetta with the Pande family and the capricious intrigues of the royal family, was eliminated from the political scene; the Pande family, which had suffered under long years of Thapa rule and the uncertain patronage of the royal family, was decimated. The internecine feud between these two noble families had caused a gradual attrition of their political power, to which the massacre adminis-tered the *coup de grâce*. A further aspect of the Kot tragedy was the political annihilation of the Choutariya family, which had seemed to be emerging as the dominant faction at the Court with the waning of the Thapas and Pandes. With these three promi-nent families thus removed, Jang Bahadur had only to contrive the destruction of two more families before his political control over the goverment would be complete. The Basnyat family, though not in the forefront in the days of the Pandes and the Thapas, was still a potential political threat. Above all, the power of the royal family had to be curbed quickly before its members could plot his overthrow.

Opportunity presented itself almost immediately, much to Jang Bahadur's political advantage and convenience. Barely a month and a half after the Kot Massacre, the Junior Queen entered into a plot with the Basnyat family in order to secure her son's immediate succession to the throne. This plot, usually called the Bhandarkhal Parva, or Basnyat conspiracy, contemplated both the political elimination of Jang Bahadur and his family and the assassination of King Rajendra and Crown Prince Surendra. Also participating in the plot was Wazir Singh, the son of Gagan Singh, whose murder had led to the Kot tragedy a few weeks earlier. The scheme of the conspirators failed when one of them, Vijaya Raj Pandit, revealed the entire plan to Jang Bahadur, who turned the tables against the Queen and her associates. According to one account, thirteen Basnyats were killed on the night of October 31, the most prominent among them being Kazi Bir Dhoj Basnyat.[9] Thus the last potential Kshatriya family rival to the Kunwars was destroyed. At the same time, the political power of the Junior Queen was utterly shattered. Expelled from the royal palace, her royal prerogatives revoked on the advice of the Council of State and with the approval of the King and Crown Prince, the Queen made preparations to leave for Banaras. King Rajendra re-confirmed Jang as Prime Minister and conferred on him addi-tional honorary titles. Even the lands that had been confiscated from his granduncle, Bhimsen Thapa, in 1837 were restored to him.

Soon thereafter King Rajendra expressed a desire to accom-pany the Queen, probably because he feared assassination if he remained in Kathmandu. On November 21 he gave his *Hukum* to

Crown Prince Surendra.[10] Two days later, he left with the Queen and her two sons for Banaras. Thus the threat from the royal family to the security of Jang's regime was diminished, although the intractable and capricious nature of Crown Prince Surendra still provided an element of uncertainty. Jang was able to complete the political emasculation of the royal family on May 12, 1847, when he formally deposed King Rajendra, on charges of having conspired against the state from abroad, and proclaimed Surendra King of Nepal. This action received the endorsement of the military and civil officials of the Nepali Court, and its subsequent acceptance by the British Government lent it a degree of international validity. As a final measure, former King Rajendra was arrested on July 28 at Alau in the Terai, where he was involved in plans for a rebellion. He was escorted to Kathmandu as a prisoner, and spent the rest of his life at Bhaktapur under close surveillance.

In a matter of seven years since his appointment as a captain of artillery, Jang Bahadur had succeeded in outmaneuvering the Thapas, Pandes, Basnyats, Choutariyas, and the Shah rulers, and in establishing himself as the undisputed master of the country. He could probably have deposed the Shah dynasty and placed his own family on the throne if he had been prepared to risk a political upheaval. Indeed, in 1857 a deputation of Court nobles petitioned him to seize the throne of Nepal for himself. Jang Bahadur had, however, already settled for a less controversial political arrangement under which King Surendra invested him and his family with hereditary rights in perpetuity to absolute authority in Nepal. This was the famous Royal Sanad of August 6, 1856, which provided the legal basis for the Rana regime until 1951.

By the Sanad ("order") of 1856, King Surendra reduced himself and his descendants to the position of political nonentities and bestowed on Jang Bahadur's family effective political authority over Nepal. Additionally, Jang Bahadur was appointed Maharaja of Kaski and Lamjung—two small principalities in west-central Nepal and supposedly the home region of his ancestors—and the title of Maharaja was made inheritable within his family. Succession to the office of Prime Minister and to the Maharajadom, which was to be for life, was based on seniority, first among Jang's brothers and then later among his sons and nephews. Jang was also invested with special powers to impose or commute capital punishment; to appoint or dismiss government officials; to declare war against or make peace with Tibet, China, and the British Government or other foreign powers; to dispense justice and punishment to criminals; and to formulate new laws and repeal or modify old laws pertaining to the judicial and military departments of the government.[11] It is noteworthy that while Jang was being equipped with all these political prerogatives, he was technically out of office. He had resigned as Prime Minister on August 1, and his brother, Bam Bahadur, had been appointed in his place. The implication, therefore, was that Jang enjoyed these special powers in his capacity as Maharaja of Kaski and Lamjung rather than as Prime Minister.

The title "Rana" was conferred on Jang Bahadur Kunwar by King Surendra in 1858, in recognition of the Kunwar family's claim to descent from the famous Rajput Ranas of Rajasthan in India. Later, descendants of Jang Bahadur and his brother Dhir Shamsher adopted the practice of appending the name and title "Jang Bahadur Rana" to their own names and eventually came to be known as the house of the Ranas, or the Rana family.

The Rana regime lasted from 1847 to 1951. During this period there were ten Rana Prime Ministers, of whom at least one was assassinated, two resigned, and the last one, Mohan Shamsher, was overthrown by a popular revolution. The year 1885 is an important landmark in the history of the regime, as it signifies the violent end of the "rule of the seven brothers"—that is, Jang Bahadur's seven brothers. In that year the last living brother, Ranodip Singh, was murdered by his nephews and the political succession was taken over not by Jang's sons, as should have been the case under the succession proposed by Jang and approved by King Surendra, but by the group of seventeen brothers, all sons of Jang's youngest brother, Dhir Shamsher. Jang's nephew Bir Shamsher initiated the "rule of the seventeen brothers" and either killed Jang's direct descendants or banished them from the country. This year also marked the beginning of the rule of the second-generation Ranas, which lasted until 1945. The office of Prime Minister was held from 1945 to 1951 by two third-generation Ranas, one of whom, Padma Shamsher, was forced to resign by the other, Mohan Shamsher, who became his successor in 1948 and in turn was overthrown by the 1950 revolution.

Jang Bahadur sought to consolidate the future of the Rana regime by neutralizing all potential political foes among the noble families through a series of marriage alliances with them. He himself married the sister of his Choutariya opponents, Guru Prasad Shah and Fateh Jang Shah. He allied his branch of the Rana family with the throne by marriages of his sons into the royal family. His eldest son, Jagat Jang, married King Surendra's eldest daughter in 1854, and a year later his second son, Rana Jit Jang, married the King's second daughter.

Perhaps the most significant political marriage arranged by Jang Bahadur was that of his daughter to Crown Prince Trailokya Vikram in 1857. Out of this marriage was born Prithvi Vir Vikram Shah, who reigned as the seventh Shah king from 1881 to 1911. Similar attempts to infiltrate the royal family were continued by the different Rana factions that emerged at the top of the Rana hierarchy from time to time. After his successful *coup d'état* against Jang's brother and sons in 1885, Bir Shamsher had his two daughters married as third and fourth wives to King Prithvi Vir Vikram Shah (who was already a half Rana by blood) in the hope —unfulfilled, as it turned out—of having a grandson seated on the throne of Nepal. Later, Chandra Shamsher, who became Prime minister in 1901 after staging a *coup* against his half-brother, Deva Shamsher, had his turn in arranging marriage alliances with the already Rana-infused royal family. Chandra went even a step farther than Bir when he had his son married to King Prithvi Vir Vikram Shah's eldest daughter and, soon afterward, passed a new regulation on succession making it possible for the royal princess to accede to the throne. As fate would have it, King Prithvi Vir Vikram died only after the birth of a male heir, the future King Tribhuwan, and Chandra was foiled in his schemes. But he continued to cement kinship ties with the royal family by arranging marriages between his two other sons, Singha and Krishna, and King Tribhuwan's two other sisters. Again, the last strong Rana Prime Minister, Juddha Shamsher, established kinship links with the royal family by having his granddaughter marry Crown Prince Mahendra and his great-granddaughters marry the two younger sons of King Tribhuwan.

THE RANA POLITICAL SYSTEM

The Rana political system as it eventually evolved was largely the creation of three consolidators of Rana rule—the prime ministers Jang Bahadur (1847–77), Chandra Shamsher (1901 –29), and Juddha Shamsher (1932–45). Jang Bahadur, the innovator of the system, laid down the legal, militaristic, and administrative foundation; Chandra Shamsher brought the system to the apex of its consolidation; Juddha Shamsher sought to inject a note of modernity, feeble though it was, into the medieval Rana government.

The paramount goal of the Rana political system was to keep effective political control over the civil and military administration in the hands of the Rana family. The basic policy was to ensure perpetuation of the system as prescribed under King Surendra's Sanad of 1856, which had assigned all political power to the Rana Prime Minister. The Sanad had further, as we have seen, established the principle of dual sovereignty inasmuch as the Rana Prime Minister was named Maharaja of Kaski and Lamjung, and sovereignty over these two small states was inheritable by all succeeding Rana Prime Ministers. Since he was thus elevated to the level of kingship, his office was considered superior to that of the traditional Mukhtiyar or executive head of the government, and the latter office was therefore assigned to the nearest claimant to the prime ministership. The Rana Prime Minister was known as Sri Tin Maharaj and Supreme Commander in Chief; his nearest brother became Mukhtiyar and Commander in Chief.

Succession to the hereditary prime ministership departed from the rule of primogeniture that was followed in the royal family. Since Jang Bahadur had seven brothers who had all been extremely valuable assets in his rise to power, he had to devise a system under which their individual aspirations to the highest office could be recognized. Thus a line of succession was provided by King Surendra in the Sanad of 1856, according to which each of Jang's brothers should in turn become Prime Minister in the event of a vacancy in the office, the succession thereafter going, in order of seniority, to Jang's sons and to his brother's sons.

Control of the military was the key to the survival of the Rana political system. The rank and file were recruited from the hills, but most of the higher officers were members of the Rana family. Rana boys were appointed generals and colonels in the army soon after their birth, and sometimes even before. This practically exclusive control over the army was zealously safeguarded.

For uninterrupted continuation of the system, there were at least four requisites besides control of the military, and these the Ranas tried to maintain in one way or another until the very end of their regime. First and foremost, the political neutralization of the royal family was an absolute necessity. This was obtained by confining the Shah kings to the Royal Palace and keeping strict surveillance over their activities. The highest royal orders during the Shah period were issued under the Lal Mohur, the King's red seal, and all executive heads of government during the pre-Rana period had conducted the affairs of state on the authority of the

Lal Mohur. To accommodate various categories of governmental transactions, at least six kinds of Lal Mohur had been developed over the years. The seal was held by the Rana Prime Minister, but, as the political role of the King had become largely nominal, the use of the Lal Mohur for executive functions was both superfluous and inexpedient. Prime Minister Bir Shamsher therefore introduced a new seal of his own, called the Khadga Nishana, to legitimize the use of his wide discretionary powers over all branches of the government. The Khadga Nishana, became, in effect, a substitute for the King's Lal Mohur. In the course of time, the Rana Prime Minister's seal became the most frequently used imprimatur of governmental authority, and, like the Lal Mohur, it became differentiated into various categories for different levels of governmental transactions.

Second, the continuation of the Rana system required persistent political suppression to forestall the rise of any rival family or faction, or the beginning of any mass revolt. Systematic persecution of hostile elements in the Thapa, Basnyat, and Choutariya families continued, while the more friendly elements among them were made part of the system through a discreet distribution of subordinate posts in the civil and military administration. As far as the general public was concerned, the Rana rulers sought to perpetuate backwardness and ignorance by discouraging the spread of education or travel abroad, and by intensifying communal disputes and rivalries through social controls exercised by the royal priests, who in the name of religion or the dharmashastra code sternly punished any attempt on the part of the people to modify social, ethnic, and caste inequalities.

Third, the survival of the Rana oligarchy required continued support and friendship on the part of the British Government. The successive Rana rulers courted British support in various ways. Jang Bahadur helped the British during the critical days of the 1857 Indian revolt by personally leading a military campaign against the Indian rebels. For this act of friendship the British conferred honors and titles on him, and also returned part of the territories ceded by Nepal in the Anglo-Nepali war of 1814–16. Bir Shamsher, after his successful *coup de'état* of 1885, granted permission for the open recruitment of Gorkhas from Nepal for the British Indian Army. During the First World War, Chandra Shamsher provided thousands of Gorkha recruits. In return the British agreed to pay an annual subsidy to the Nepali government and in 1923 signed a treaty formally recognizing Nepal's independence. During the Second World War, Juddha Shamsher provided extensive support in men and materials again to the

British Government. It is much more than a historical coincidence that serious opposition to the Rana regime arose in the
country upon the exit of the British from India in 1947.

Fourth, Rana rule required a highly centralized administration. Thus, trusted relatives of the incumbent Rana Prime
Minister were installed at supervisory levels. All government
employees, both civil and military, were directly responsible to
the Prime Minister, who continued their appointments on a year-
to-year basis through the system of scrutiny known as the Pajani.
The administrative apparatus was divided into four main
branches, namely: the Khadga Nishana office, that is, the Prime
Minister's office; the Muluki-Bandobast, the routine administration of the country, entrusted to the Mukhtiyar; the Munshi-
khana, or foreign office; and the Jangi Adda, the military administration. Subordinate offices were created in each branch to
provide for a better division of labor, usually under the supervision of Ranas. The penetration of the Rana family into the higher
echelons in both civil and military administration was all-perva-
sive; only a few non-Rana elements rose to positions of authority
within the government during the period of Rana rule.

Related to the fourth requisite was the fact that the Rana
Prime Minister also functioned as the judicial head of the
country. Appeals of criminal and civil cases from all over Nepal
were presented to him for final disposition, and his judicial office,
later known as the Binti Patra Niksari during Chandra
Shamsher's prime ministry, served as the last court of appeal. Jang
Bahadur deserves credit for his significant contribution in compil-
ing and codifying the various laws and sanads of the land. Soon
after his return from a trip to England in 1850–51, he convened a
council of Gurus, Pandits, Bharadars, and military officers to
prepare uniform rules of justice applicable to all subjects and in
all districts. The result of these deliberations was the compilation
of books of law (the Muluki Ain) and the inauguration of a
penal system. These law books were sent to the various districts,
and district officials were given instructions to administer justice
according to their provisions. Thus, for the first time, an attempt
was made to enforce uniform laws all over the country. Later
Rana rulers made minor modifications in the judicial system
established by Jang Bahadur. Chandra Shamsher separated the
Diwani (civil) and Fouzdari (criminal) courts, and Juddha
Shamsher established appeal courts in the districts and a high
court in the capital.

The Rana political system was an undisguised military
despotism of the ruling faction within the Rana family over the

King and the people of the country. The government functioned as an instrument to carry out the personal wishes and interests of the ruling Rana Prime Minister; its main domestic preoccupation was the exploitation of the country's resources in order to enhance the personal wealth of the Rana ruler and his family. No distinction was made between the personal treasury of the Rana ruler and the treasury of the government; any government revenue in excess of administrative expenses was pocketed by the Rana ruler as private income. No budgets of the government's expenditures and revenues were ever made public. As a system accountable neither to the King nor to the people, the Rana regime functioned as an autochthonous system, divorced from the needs of the people and even from the historical traditions of the country, and served only the interests of a handful of Ranas and their ubiquitous non-Rana adherents. No peaceful dissent or protest was possible, and internal changes within the Rana system could take place only through *coups* and conspiracies. The system was continued fundamentally unchanged, so far as its reliance on force and coercion was concerned, until its overthrow in 1951. The few changes that occurred during its more than a hundred years were changes not in its aims and methods, but merely in leadership, the consequence of the endless struggle for power within the Rana family itself.

3

Oppositional Politics Under Rana Rule

FROM THE very first days of the Rana regime, Jang Bahadur had to utilize all his skill and determination to counter the intrigues and conspiracies of hostile political factions. The royal family and the remnants of the Thapa, Pande, and Basnyat families were not prepared to accept the ruthless treatment they received at the hands of this upstart leader from a minor noble family. Jang Bahadur's efforts to win the support of these families through marriage arrangements, tax-free land grants, and appointments at the middle level of the civil and military administrations were only partially successful. The Rana political system was as much against the traditions of the Shah dynasty as it was against the traditional political process, and most of the old nobility eagerly awaited the opportune moment to revenge themselves on the Rana leaders.

Nor was the Rana system immune to internal dissension and sabotage. The prolixity of Rana marriages and their high rate of fertility, when combined with a roll of succession based upon seniority by birth, produced an ideal set of circumstances for the festering of discontent within the family. Ranas low on the roll, or excluded therefrom because of the accident of birth, the caste of their mothers, or the whims of the Rana ruler, were usually prepared to conspire against those at the top of the family hierarchy. These "underprivileged" Ranas had only a feeble sense of identification with their family and were disposed toward collaboration with non-Rana elements whose objective was elimination of the Rana system.

The Rana Prime Minister was usually more apprehensive of danger from his immediate successors on the roll than from extrafamilial enemies. As the protagonist of the Rana system, he was in the position of having both to trust and to suspect those directly under him on the roll. He was also frequently under pressure from his own sons, who wanted to be advanced as many steps as possible on the roll of succession while their father was still in power. As this usually coincided with his own interests, it became common practice for the Prime Minister to revise the roll of succession to suit the interests of his particular branch of the family. The leadership at the top was, naturally, sworn to the continuation of the Rana system by any means, but those Ranas who had been victimized by manipulations of the roll of succession were not averse to the destruction of the system, if thereby their ambitions would be better served.

Thus, opposition to the Rana system in the latter part of the nineteenth century developed out of two kinds of politics: the politics of revenge, and the politics of self-aggrandizement. The principal actors in the politics of revenge were the external opponents of the system within the ruling family and the Thapa, Pande, and Basnyat families; their accessories were usually the dissident elements among the Ranas. The politics of self-aggrandizement was played at the top of the Rana hierarchy by the Prime Minister and his immediate successors. Although the goal in this case was not the uprooting of the system, the contending factions and individuals sought support from external political elements who were fundamentally opposed to it.

Oppositional politics during this period was the monopoly of the members of the traditional ruling order, the Bharadars. Except for two or three incidents, the commoners (*Duniyadars*) were largely uninvolved and, indeed, apolitical. The overriding concern of the non-Rana Bharadars was the restoration of the power structure as it was before 1846. The Brahmanic sacred elite in general supported the Ranas because of their espousal of conservative traditions. Occasionally, however, Brahmans were involved in opposition plots by such incidents as Jang Bahadur's caste defilement during his visit to England in 1850–51.

Oppositional tactics at this early stage took the traditional forms so familiar to the Nepali Court—intrigues, conspiracies, and assassinations. Similarly, the consequences of an unsuccessful conspiracy followed the traditional pattern of swift retribution: summary trial and execution, physical torture and mutilation, caste defilement, and banishment. Even the dead were not spared humiliation. Stories of how Bhimsen Thapa's body had been mutilated and denied a proper Hindu cremation, and of how Mathabar Singh Thapa's body was dragged through the streets of

Kathmandu before it was finally cremated were long remembered. The possibility of such dire consequences made it imperative that conspiracies and intrigues against the established political order be carred out not merely covertly, but with great deliberateness and caution.

One exception to this general pattern of clandestine opposition was the open challenge from the deposed King Rajendra in 1847. In that year Guru Prasad Choutariya and Jagat Bam Pande raised a small force in the Terai with the intention of overthrowing the Rana regime, and Raghu Nath Pandit persuaded the old king to join the rebels on assurances that the state troops would side with him as they had done with his grandfather, Rana Bahadur Shah, under similar cirumstances some forty years earlier. Bolstered by such hopes, he returned to Nepal from Banaras, but he and his followers were routed by Jang's troops. As we noted earlier, Rajendra was taken prisoner and kept in confinement for the remainder of his life.

OPPOSITION TO THE RANAS—CONSPIRATORIAL POLITICS

The conspiratorial politics that characterized the first six decades of the Rana regime can be divided into four categories—those in which the initiative was taken by (1) other Kshatriya families, (2) groups outside the usual political factions, (3) Shah-Rana coalitions, and (4) dissident elements within the Rana family itself.

The Kot Massacre in 1846 and subsequent events had decimated and disorganized the non-Rana noble families, which for many years were unable to marshal either the capacity or the will to challenge the regime, except for one halfhearted attempt by remnants of the Basnyat family in 1857. While Jang Bahadur was making preparations to proceed to India in the winter of 1857–58 to assist the British in suppressing the revolt that had broken out in the northern provinces, the Basnyats planned to assemble two thousand men, ostensibly for enlistment in the army, and use this force to assassinate Jang Bahadur and his brothers. The plot was revealed to the Prime Minister before his departure for India, and the persons most directly involved were arrested and executed.[1]

Far more serious was the conspiracy of 1881, which was perhaps the most broadly based of all the plots against the Ranas. It involved members of the Thapa, Basnyat, Pande, and Choutariya families as well as less influential Kshatriya and Brahman families such as the Adhikaris, Bistas, and Karkis. Prime Minister Ranodip Singh left Kathmandu for a hunting expedition in the Terai in December, 1881, providing the conspirators with an opportunity to lay their plans more openly. At the last moment, however, one of the conspirators—the grandson of Gagan Singh, whose death had sparked the Kot Massacre—revealed the entire plot to the Commander in Chief, Dhir Shamsher, who had remained in the capital. All the suspects in Kathmandu were arrested, and Prime Minister Ranodip Singh was apprised of the presence of conspirators in his entourage and advised to return to Kathmandu immediately. Twenty-three conspirators were executed, seven imprisoned, and four exiled. Among those executed were Thapas, Pandes, Shahs, Basnyats, and Adhikaris.[2] This was the last conspiracy in which members of these families played a prominent role.

Although Nepali politics was a virtual monopoly of a few Kshatriya and Brahman families, there were two anti-Rana incidents of some importance in which the initiative stemmed from outside these closed circles. The first was the disaffection within several Gurung regiments in 1857, shortly after Jang Bahadur had decided to side with the British in the revolt in northern India. It was alleged that a sergeant in one of the regiments had been inciting his comrades to assassinate Jang Bahadur and that many were ready to follow his leadership. Jang Bahadur ordered a review of all the troops at the Tundikhel, or parade ground, in Kathmandu, with the intention of decimating the Gurung regiments if they proved mutinous. The Gurung sergeant was summoned in front of the regiments, and the charges against him were read out. His comrades "consulted together for a short time and then suddenly fell on him and cut him to pieces." The troops were then dismissed without any further disturbance.[3]

Of a distinctly different character was the agitation which broke out in 1876 in Gorkha district, the home of the Shah dynasty, which may be considered the first popular movement against Rana rule. Since the movement was both anti-Brahmanical and anti-Rana, its true aims and methods were undoubtedly distorted in official accounts as well as in chronicles of the period. The government represented the movement as the work of a religious fanatic and charlatan, but in fact it was a local popular movement aimed at the overthrow of the regime.[4] It is apparent, however, that the leader was an intelligent, resourceful person, who made use of the symbols and legends of his district that would be effective in mobilizing the people of Gorkha. To justify his program, he claimed divine inspiration from a local goddess, Mankamana, who had commanded him to destroy the government of Jang Bahadur; to justify his leadership, he presented himself as the reincarnation of Lakhan Thapa, a widely known saint of an earlier period in Gorkha. One of the chronicles speaks of the leader of the movement in derogatory terms, but acknowledges his success in winning the sympathies of the people: "During the time of this Raja [Jang Bahadur], in the district of Gorkha, an impostor of the Magar caste proclaimed himself to be the reincarnation of Lakhan Thapa and persuaded people to worship Mankamana at his place without going to her shrine. He had built a five-storied house. He used to perform the Yajna [sacrifice] at his palace. People became convinced. The villagers went to him with all kinds of offerings, including the five animal sacrifices. In this way, they dropped the habit of going to Mankamana for worship." [5] The chronicle also attributes a communal character to this movement by describing its followers as "mostly Magars."

On receiving news of the popular agitation in Gorkha, Jang Bahadur was quick to act. A military force was sent to suppress the movement and arrest its leaders. Lakhan Thapa and twelve of his staunchest supporters were brought to Kathmandu in bamboo cages, the rest being herded in on foot. A trial was held at Thapathali, Jang's private residence, and Lakhan and six of his followers were sentenced to death. According to a semi-official account, the leaders of the agitation had planned to kill Jang Bahadur at Deorali on his return from a hunting expedition with the Prince of Wales in the Terai and "to march to the capital, where Lakhan was to be proclaimed king amidst the shouts of the whole population." [6]

But doubtless the most serious threats to the Rana regime in these decades came from coalitions between members of the royal family, who never accepted their relegation to a position of minor importance in Nepal's political structure, and dissident elements in the Rana family. These conspirators could also usually depend on support from various Brahman and Kshatriya families who either were directly attached to them on an interfamilial basis or were prepared to support any move to overthrow the detested Rana rule.

The first conspiracy of this type occurred in 1851, while the Rana regime was still in a primitive stage of development. In the view of many conservatives at the Nepali Court, Jang Bahadur had violated religious and social traditions by his trip to England in 1850–51. Partly to allay such suspicions, Jang Bahadur visited important Hindu pilgrimage centers at Dwarika, Rameshwaram, and Banaras and underwent rites of purification soon after his return to India. His enemies in Nepal, however, were determined to make a political issue of his alleged caste defilement during his overseas travel. One of the members of his entourage circulated eye-witness reports of how Jang Bahadur had lost caste by dining and socializing with Europeans. On the strength of these reports, a group of conspirators agreed that Jang Bahadur should be removed. The key persons involved were two of his brothers, Bam Bahadur and Badri Narsingh; a cousin, Jaya Bahadur; and Prince Upendra, one of the King's brothers. The plan, according to one report, was to assassinate both Jang Bahadur and King Surendra, and to replace them with Bam Bahadur and Prince Upendra.[7]

On February 16, 1851, the day before the plan was to be carried out, Bam Bahadur revealed the entire scheme to Jang Bahadur. Moving swiftly against the other conspirators, Jang had them apprehended and then tried and convicted at an emergency meeting of the court, which first recommended that all should be put to death and later that they should live but be deprived of their eyesight.[8] Jang eventually had their punishment reduced to internment at Allahabad under the supervision of the British authorities in India.

With Prince Upendra safely removed from the scene and King Surendra so intimidated that he meekly followed the instructions of the Prime Minister, the royal family was bereft of any real political leadership until Crown Prince Trailokya Vir Vikram Shah reached his majority in 1875. This vigorous young man immediately set about to regain the royal prerogatives lost by his father in 1856. In conjunction with Jagat Jang, the eldest son of Jang Bahadur, Prince Trailokya formed a plan whereby the order of succession prescribed in the Sanad of 1856 would be set aside on the death of Jang Bahadur. King Surendra would be forced to abdicate in favor of the Crown Prince, who would then appoint Jagat Jang as Prime Minister. The plan was, however, thwarted by Dhir Shamsher, Jang Bahadur's youngest brother. When Jang Bahadur died at Patharghatta, some distance from Kathmandu, in February, 1877, Dhir Shamsher suppressed the news and instead circulated reports that Jang was critically ill. When Prince Trailokya and Jang Bahadur's sons hastened to Patharghatta, Dhir Shamsher took advantage of their absence from the capital to force King Surendra to appoint Ranodip Singh, Jang's elder brother, as Prime Minister and himself as Commander in Chief.[9]

As might have been predicted, Crown Prince Trailokya soon died under suspicious circumstances, early in 1878. His younger brother, Prince Narendra, assumed the leadership in the royal family's plots against the Ranas, again with the coöperation of Jang Bahadur's sons. It is probable that Prince Narendra planned a reënactment of the Kot Massacre, except that this time all the leading members of the ruling branch of the Rana family would be eliminated. The plot was never carried out, reportedly because Jang Bahadur's sons insisted that nothing should be undertaken in the year of mourning following their father's death; what prevented a later attempt is not known. This conspiracy only came to the attention of the Rana ruler in 1881, when one of the persons arrested for implication in another plot revealed that Prince Narendra and two of Jang Bahadur's sons had conspired together to end the Rana system three years earlier. All three were sent to India and were kept under supervision by the British authorities for several years before being permitted to return to Nepal.

CONFLICT AND DISUNITY IN THE RANA FAMILY

The nature of opposition to the Rana rule underwent a transformation toward the end of the nineteenth century as the Rana family became more segmented and disunited. Because of their affluence, Ranas could afford several wives and mistresses, and usually sired numerous children. The inevitable result was that ambition and impatience overrode traditional family loyalties. Soon after Jang Bahadur's death in 1877, the Rana family became divided into two hostile factions: the Jang faction, consisting of the ten sons of Jang Bahadur, and the Shamsher faction, consisting of the seventeen sons of his youngest brother, Dhir Shamsher. The Shamshers were determined to advance their relative positions on the roll of succession, as otherwise their line would have succeeded to the hereditary prime ministership only after four of Jang Bahadur's sons had served their turns.[10]

In November, 1885, the Shamsher faction, led by Bir Shamsher, staged a *coup d'état*. Bir Shamsher had been deputed by his uncle, Prime Minister Ranodip Singh, to lead four regiments of the Nepali army to participate in an exercise of the British Army in India. This force was scheduled to leave on November 23 and was held in a state of readiness at Tundikhel, the parade ground in the center of Kathmandu. On the night of November 21 Bir Shamsher and his brothers went to the Prime Minister's palace and obtained a private audience on the pretext of presenting an urgent letter from the British

Residency. They then fired point blank at their uncle and murdered him in cold blood. Bir Shamsher used the four regiments under his personal command to round up all his political foes, alleging that the Prime Minister had been assassinated by the sons of Jang Bahadur. Most members and supporters of the Jang faction were killed; a few saved their lives by seeking asylum at the British Residency. Bir Shamsher proclaimed himself the new Rana Prime Minister and went through the motions of receiving confirmation from the five-year-old King Prithvi Vir Vikram. Thus the political power of Jang Bahadur's immediate family was ended and the Shamsher faction of the Rana family took control of the government.

Within sixteen months of Bir's seizure of power, Khadga Shamsher, the Commander in Chief and next in succession to the prime ministership, was discovered plotting against the life of his brother. He was banished to the hinterland of the country, and two years later was made governor of Palpa district. Early in 1888 Rana Bir Jang, one of the surviving sons of Jang Bahadur, tried to invade the Nepal Terai from India, but this feeble attempt was repulsed by troops dispatched by Bir Shamsher.

In 1901 Bir Shamsher died and was succeeded by Deva Shamsher, a Rana with unusually liberal views, who set about establishing elementary schools and charitable organizations. He even asked the *Duniyadars,* or commoners, to submit proposals for administrative and judicial reforms. These minor but progressive gestures struck terror in the hearts of the other Shamshers, who feared that the new Prime Minister was undermining the regime, and thereby their chances of succession, by awakening public consciousness. Deva's younger half-brothers forced him to abdicate at gun point after about four months of rule and banished him to Dhankuta, in eastern Nepal. The leader of the *coup,* Chandra Shamsher, then became the fifth Rana Prime Minister.

Thus the Rana roll of succession instituted by Jang Bahadur had been changed abruptly, once by assassination and once by deposition; also the order of the names in the roll of succession had been altered on several occasions. When the roll was drawn up in 1856, it was a fairly simple matter to specify the succesion of the brothers of Jang Bahadur, who were all born of the same parents; it was not foreseen that caste distinctions within the Rana family might become a seriously complicating factor.

In the course of time, Jang and his brothers produced Rana descendants of at least three caste groups. In the highest or "A" class were those born of Ranas and wives of equivalent caste status, with whose families the Ranas could interdine freely. Ranas of the middle or "B" class were born of wives from families of good but not equivalent Kshatriya caste status, with whom all social intercourse except the partaking of boiled rice was permissible. Ranas of the lowest or "C" class were born of mistresses whose caste status usually was such as not to permit marriage or interdining with Ranas, and therefore they were not entitled to social assimilation within the Rana family. Since such a three-way division of the Rana family was not anticipated, the Sanad of 1856 did not specify that any particular branch of the Rana family was entitled to succession to the hereditary prime ministership, but it was natural to assume that the custom in most inheritances of property would be followed and that only Ranas of unpolluted caste would be eligible to succeed to the office. Jang Bahadur himself violated this convention, however, when in 1868 he revised the roll of succession to include his infant sons and grandsons as well as two illegitimate sons.[11] Bir Shamsher followed suit by putting his three favorite sons on the roll despite their C class origin.* Although these significant developments were not openly opposed, the Ranas of the A or B class seem to have been considerably agitated by them. Since the Ranas had innumerable mistresses and concubines in their palaces, there was a real possibility that the C class Ranas might outnumber those of the A or B classes and subvert the roll of succession to favor themselves.

It was partly to forestall such a contingency that the consolidator of the Rana regime, Chandra Shamsher, institutionalized the three-way division in the Rana family by specifying the privileges and functions of each group. By differentiating the powers and prerogatives of the A Ranas from those of the other two groups, socially and politically, he sought to preserve the hegemony of the A class in the highest echelon while at the same time formally associating the B and C groups with lower echelons of authority in the army and the government. For example, Ranas of the A class automatically became major-generals at the age of twenty-one years and could rise to the highest rank; those of the B class became lieutenant-colonels and could rise to the rank of commanding colonel; and those of the C class became second lieutenants and could rise no higher than the rank of major. Thus Ranas of B and C status were in effect debarred from succession to the prime ministership, since they were not eligible to hold appointments as commanding generals.

---

* Of the seventeen Shamsher brothers who helped Bir in his *coup,* only nine were high-caste Ranas; the remaining eight were of the C class.

The official recognition of the caste system among the Ranas during Chandra Shamsher's rule provided the first systematization of the power structure in the family and secured the A Ranas' monopoly of the prime ministership. It also advanced Chandra's sons several steps in their position on the roll of succession. Yet Chandra could not apply the division retroactively to exclude B or C Ranas previously installed on the roll. To make matters worse, his successor, Bhim Shamsher, modified the system to advance the interests of his three favorite C sons, whom he elevated to the rank of general and included on the roll of succession.

Upon Bhim's death, in 1932, Juddha Shamsher succeeded to the prime ministership. By that time a C Rana, Rudra Shamsher, had become Commander in Chief and was next in the line of succession. A few other C Ranas had also advanced on the roll to qualify as Rudra's successors, thereby delaying the succession of Chandra Shamsher's numerous sons. In March, 1934, the A-class families of Juddha Shamsher and Chandra Shamsher joined forces and effected a bloodless purge of the Rana family—bloodless, reportedly, at the insistence of the British Government. All C Ranas who had been included on the roll of succession by Bir Shamsher and Bhim Shamsher were stripped of their rights of succession and banished from the capital. Among those affected by this purge were two brothers, Hiranya Shamsher and Prakash Shamsher; their sons, Suvarna Shamsher and Mahavir Shamsher, both played prominent roles in the 1950 revolution against the Rana regime.

Soon after the removal of the C Ranas, Juddha applied himself to loosening the grip of Chandra Shamsher's sons on the government. He placed his own sons in positions of authority and sought to relegate the Chandra Shamsher faction to the background. Eventually a serious split developed among the A Ranas; meanwhile the dispossessed and disgruntled C Ranas bided their time, awaiting opportunity to avenge their political humiliation. Juddha resigned voluntarily in November, 1945, and was succeeded by Padma Shamsher, who was in turn forced to resign by Chandra Shamsher's sons in April, 1948.

Thus the Rana regime was hastened toward its demise by its divisive caste composition and its system of succession to political office. There were widespread feelings of insecurity and suspicion among the Ranas. One measure of this sentiment was the stationing in the Prime Minister's palace of a well-armed regiment of bodyguards—called the Bijuli Garath ("Electric Guard") because of its state of constant alert—while the rest of the Nepali Army was kept in a state of partial disarmament. This special regiment became the basic defense for the power of the Rana Prime Minister.* Political threats from the numerous Ranas of the B and C classes mounted steadily, and when a new type of political opposition developed in Nepal after 1946, the Rana family could not maintain a unified or effective response.

OPPOSITION TO THE SHAMSHER FACTION OF THE RANA REGIME

Soon after 1900, new ideas about social and political change, taken over from reformist and independence movements in India, were adopted by some opponents of the Rana system. These innovators belonged to the miniscule middle-class groups in Kathmandu Valley who could afford to travel to India or send their children to school there.

Exposure to the Indian nationalist movement and Western education led the handful of educated commoners in Nepal to the view that the elimination of British rule in India was a prerequisite for the fall of the Rana regime, since British power in India had become a major bulwark of the Rana system. Eventually a large number of Nepalese participated in the Indian National Congress and *satyagraha* movements of the 1920's and 1930's, and received instruction and practical training in the new ideology and methods of mass movements initiated by Gandhi.

Another impact on Nepal in the early part of the present century came from an Indian movement for religious reform, the Arya Samaj, which was particularly strong in the Punjab. Swami Dayananda, the protagonist of this movement, reinterpreted Hinduism according to the ancient Vedas and urged the reformation of existing Hindu belief and practices on that basis. Arya Samaj reformers held public meetings to explain their point of view and challenged the tradition-minded Hindu priests to engage in open debates. Arguing that Hinduism had been reduced to a complex of rituals and mythologies by Brahman priests in the post-Vedic period, they were highly critical of what they regarded as the corrupting influence of the Hindu sacred elite. According to the Arya Samaj reinterpretation, such social practices as child marriage and restrictions on the marriage of widows were not consonant with the spirit of Vedic Hinduism and ought to be abandoned. Thus the Arya Samaj, although fundamentally religious in character, was also a social reform movement.

---

* The guard regiment was transferred to the royal palace in April, 1951, as a symbol of the restoration of the Shah kings' lost prerogatives.

Arya Samaj ideas were a clear threat to the interests of the Brahman priests and preceptors of the Rana regime, most of whom had long since put aside the intellectual and scholarly traditions of their caste and settled down to lives of luxury and comfort, emulating the manners and traditions of the Rana palaces. Moreover, they had built up a convenient source of income based on caste distinctions. For instance, it had been made mandatory for the tens of thousands of Nepalese who went to India as "Gurkha" recruits for the British Indian Army to reclaim their caste upon their return by the payment of a specified fee to the Rajguru, the head of the Brahman family that served as priests to the royal and the Rana families. The amount of monetary expiation was determined according to a graduated scale designed to cover all categories of caste pollution. Besides having final authority in questions of caste pollution, the Rajguru alone could make the final determination of anyone's caste status; he was empowered also to excommunicate violators of caste and other social practices. It was inevitable that the Brahman priests who profited from the Rana system would vigorously combat the egalitarian and anticlerical ideas of the Arya Samaj, not merely to preserve ancient traditions, but also to protect their considerable vested economic interests.

The first Nepali innovator in the new religious opposition to Rana rule was Madhava Raj Joshi of Kathmandu, who during a trip to Banaras in 1893 had been deeply influenced by the ideas and techniques of Swami Dayananda. He sent his sons to Arya Samaj schools in India and began to propagate unconventional vedic ideas in Nepal. When he proposed a scholarly debate on the interpretation of Hindu scriptures, the Brahman priests of the Rana regime refused to engage in an open meeting with the young challenger; instead, they had other Brahmans debate with him in the presence of Prime Minister Chandra Shamsher and had him beaten severely for his allegedly sacrilegious remarks about the deities of Nepal during the debate. Madhava Raj was socially disgraced and paraded through the streets of Kathmandu, and was later sentenced to two years in jail.[12] In 1920, Madhava Raj's sons returned to Nepal, after finishing their education at Arya Samaj schools, and began to resume the interrupted program of their father. Again the Rana government launched an onslaught on the Arya Samaj, and Madhava Raj's sons were banished to India.

The Arya Samaj movement, although suppressed by force in Nepal, had some far-reaching consequences. It created a social and political ferment among the previously inert middle-class families of the capital, and by exposing the social and religious hypocrisy institutionalized by the Rana government, it produced a new awakening among the people. To the younger generation, especially, it provided experience in a new kind of agitational technique in support of social change, and underlined for them the necessity and even the validity of the reforms it urgently advocated. The seminal influence of Madhava Raj's introduction of Arya Samaj ideas later sprouted into many social and political movements. One closely allied offshoot of this movement, which was suppressed by force in 1930, was an anti-Brahmanical agitation launched by a number of young men in Kathmandu.

Two other factors which aroused political consciousness among the Nepali people in the first quarter of the twentieth century were the First World War and the first Indian civil disobedience movement in 1920. Nepali soldiers fought gallantly in the theaters of war in Europe and elsewhere, and in the process were exposed to the world of the twentieth century. The Rana government, fearing that the veterans might bring modern ideas into their villages, specifically asked the British authorities not to promote Gorkha recruits beyond the rank of sergeant, and upon their return rigidly enforced on them the rules of Patiya, or caste purification.[13]

One reflection of the new social consciousness engendered by foreign travel and exposure among the Gorkha servicemen was Thakur Chandan Singh's establishment in 1921 of the Gorkha League and two weekly papers, the *Gorkha-Sansar* ("Gorkha World") and *Tarun Gorkha* ("Young Gorkha"), at Dehra Dun, an important Gorkha recruiting depot in India. The main object of this organization was to effect social reforms in Nepal. Since the Rana government interpreted any proposal for change as a potential threat to its political authority, the activities of the Gorkha League came under its disapprobation.

At about the same time, Devi Prasad Sapkota founded a weekly, the *Gorkhali,* in Banaras, to arouse Nepali nationalism and public consciousness against Rana rule. Historically, Banaras had been the home in exile for Nepali political expatriates for many centuries. By 1921 the Nepali community at Banaras had been deeply influenced by the Indian nationalist movement led by Gandhi, and their own nationalistic feelings had been aroused. Dharanidhar Koirala's poems and Surya Vikram Jnawali's historical writings in Nepali also helped promote nationalistic sentiments among literate Nepalese.

Although the Ranas were generally hostile to the Indian nationalist movement, not all aspects of Gandhi's constructive work-program were arbitrarily dismissed as inappropriate for

Nepal. Indeed, the Rana regime seems to have viewed certain features of the program as an effective check upon the modern ideas and attitudes that were being enthusiastically adopted by Nepali students at Western-style educational institutions at home and in India. The Charkha ("spinning wheel") movement for the production of hand-woven cloth was officially endorsed by Chandra Shamsher, who sent a young social reformer, Tulsi Mehar, to India on a government scholarship to receive training in cottage industry at Gandhi's ashram.* In 1947 the Rana government sought to encourage Gandhi's "basic education" system as the prototype educational system for Nepal. The consensus among the new educated elites in Kathmandu at the time was that the regime was attempting to exploit Gandhi's name and program in order to discourage a higher-education system based on the Western model, which the Ranas considered politically more dangerous.

In the 1920's a small group of middle-class Nepalese emerged in Kathmandu as the nucleus of a new educated elite. Most of them had received a college-level education, had traveled abroad, and had been exposed to the nationalistic political winds blowing in India. Being in Kathmandu and under the vigilant supervision of the Rana government, they had to conduct their political activities circumspectly, in contrast to the Nepali expatriates at Banaras. The Kathmandu group sought to awaken consciousness mainly through their writings. A tragic instance of Rana repression in this period was the prosecution of Krishna Lal, who published a book on the cultivation of maize. In the Preface to the book he remarked that "dogs of foreign breed were being pampered in Nepal while native dogs were the only useful animals as far as protection against thieves was concerned." This was interpreted by the authorities as an implied comment on the pro-British proclivities of the Ranas, and the author was sentenced to nine years in jail, where he eventually died.[14] In another incident, in 1930, some forty-five persons in Kathmandu petitioned the government for permission to establish a public library. Because it was illegal at that time to establish a public library or school, the sponsors of the petition were prosecuted by the government for contemplating an unlawful action, and each of them was fined a hundred rupees.[15]

Two significant political conspiracies against Rana rule occurred in the 1930's, one of which followed the pattern of

---

* In 1930, after Chandra Shamsher's death and during the second non-coöperation movement in India, Tulsi Mehar was imprisoned as a political agitator and the Charkha movement was allowed to continue only under strict government supervision.

traditional conspiratorial opposition, while the other was conceived along the more modern lines of a political party organization. The first is often referred to as the Prachanda Gorkha
("Resurgent Gorkha") conspiracy of 1931. A few young men,
influenced by terroristic tactics prevalent in India at that time,
laid plans to overthrow the Ranas by force and introduce a
parliamentary system of government. The members of this group
were rounded up before they could initiate any action. The other
opposition group was more broadly conceived and included
within its ranks much of the emerging educated elite in Kathmandu. It operated under several different covers, including an
elementary school (the Mahavir School) and a social service
organization, the Nagarik Adhikar Samiti ("Citizen's Rights
Committee"). The school provided a meeting place for liberal
elements and also initiated some new directions in public education. The social service organization sought to promote public
enlightenment by undertaking seemingly innocuous welfare activities such as the holding of prayer meetings and the organizing
of relief societies in support of religious programs. Sukra Raj
Shastri, one of the sons of Madhava Raj Joshi, served as president
of the organization. Eventually he was arrested and imprisoned
for having delivered an unauthorized lecture on the Bhagavad
Gita.

The political organization of the Kathmandu intellectuals
was a secret society, the Praja Parishad ("People's Council"). It
was a comprehensive political party which included in its fold
members from several castes and ethnic groups in Nepal. It aimed
at the overthrow of Rana rule and the inauguration of a democratic political system. Even King Tribhuwan was reported to be
among its supporters. The nucleus of the Praja Parishad party was
established as early as 1935. A general election of its officers was
held in 1940, and Tanka Prasad Acharya was chosen as president
of the party.[16]

The Praja Parishad party conducted its publicity abroad in
Indian newspapers, exposing the Ranas' tyranny over the King
and the people and their ruthless exploitation of the entire
population for the enrichment of one family. Articles critical of
the regime began to appear in a Bihar periodical, *Janata,* in 1938.
These alerted the Ranas, and later the Parishad's pamphleteering
in the streets of Kathmandu confirmed their suspicion that a
conspiracy was forming. In August, 1940, the government announced a reward of 5,000 rupees for any information leading to
the arrest of Parishad leaders. In October it was able to induce
one party member to disclose the secrets of the organization,

whereupon five hundred suspects were rounded up in Kathmandu alone.

A summary trial of the prisoners was held at the Prime Minister's palace, and the Rana tribunal pronounced its verdict on January 23, 1941. Four persons—Sukra Raj Shastri, Dharma Bhakta, Dasarath Chand, and Ganga Lal—were sentenced to death, and thirty-eight were given prison sentences ranging from six years to life.* King Tribhuwan was interrogated by the tribunal on his alleged involvement in the Praja Parishad movement, but the Prime Minister's plan to depose him was unsuccessful because the Crown Prince (the present King Mahendra) "stolidly refused to accept the Maharaja's offer of his father's throne," [17] and also because the British Minister to Kathmandu was opposed to any major political upheaval in Nepal which might disrupt the recruitment of Gorkhas for the British Indian Army during the Second World War.

Two centers of opposition to the Shamsher faction of the Rana rule emerged in the 1930's, one at Banaras and the other in Kathmandu. The Banaras group consisted mostly of expatriates and exiles connected with earlier political episodes in Kathmandu, together with the large community of Nepali students. Among the prominent expatriates were Hom Nath Upadhaya, who had been involved in the 1881 conspiracy, and Devi Prasad Sapkota and Krishna Prasad Koirala, both of whom had aroused the hostility of Prime Minister Chandra Shamsher. (Krishna Prasad Koirala's two sons, Matrika Prasad Koirala and Bishweshwar Prasad Koirala, were to play leading roles in the overthrow of the Rana government in 1950 and also in the politics of the subsequent decade.) The Banaras group, because it was operating on Indian territory, functioned openly and conducted its program through newspapers, magazines, public meetings, and public organizations. As early as 1935, Nepali students had established the Nepali Sangha ("Nepali Association") in Banaras and the Chhatra Sangha ("Students' Association") at Banaras Hindu University. Similarly, in 1945, expatriate Nepalese established the Dalit-Nibarak Sangh ("Amelioration League") in Calcutta, and the Nepali students at Calcutta University formed the Himanchal Vidyarthi Sangh ("Association of Students from the Himalayas").[18] Leaders of these Nepali groups used methods and

---

* Sukra Raj Shastri had no formal relationship with the Praja Parishad, but was implicated by the government and was executed along with the three Parishad leaders a few days later. The Rana government, and particularly several Brahman priests, had long since earmarked him as an enemy because of his open avowal of Arya Samaj views, Sanskritic scholarship, and personal contacts with Indian leaders like Gandhi and Malaviya.

programs borrowed from the Indian nationalist movement to strengthen their organizations, and adopted the political vocabulary and goals of the Indian political leaders. The Kathmandu group, which had to operate under the fear of Rana repression, could not function openly. The political roots and inspiration of this group, too, were linked with the Indian nationalist movement, but its location in Kathmandu and its affiliation with local families gave it an indigenous political character that was less evident in the émigré group at Banaras.

4

The 1950 Revolution

THE POLITICAL CONSEQUENCES of the Second World War in the Indian subcontinent were so cataclysmic that even the carefully insulated Rana regime in Nepal could not escape their impact. True to its traditional loyalty to the British Raj, the Rana government had pledged a loan of eight battalions of the Nepal Army for the maintenance of internal security in India as early as the days of the Munich crisis. On the outbreak of the war in Europe two Nepali brigades were speedily dispatched to India. A few months later, permission was given for twenty Nepali battalions to cross the "black waters" in order to participate in military campaigns in Africa and Europe.* Before long, hundreds of thousands of Nepalese were participating in the war in one capacity or another. The return of these widely traveled Nepali servicemen presented to the Rana government not only a considerable problem of economic rehabilitation, but also an important, if still only potential, political threat.

A more immediate threat stemmed from the political turmoil in India. The outbreak of the war intensified nationalist sentiments in India, and Indian leaders demanded the end of British rule as a precondition for mobilizing Indian men and materials for the war effort. In 1942 the British Government sought to meet this demand by proposing limited home rule at that time and independence later, but the Indian National Congress turned

---

* The strict Brahmanic social code which prohibited Nepalese from going overseas on pain of losing their caste applied equally to the Gorkha soldiers employed in the British Indian Army. The oceans were designated as the "black waters."

down the offer as inadequate and launched a movement demanding full independence for India without delay. The British suppressed this agitation by force. Thousands of Indians—and along with them some Nepalese domiciled at Darjeeling, Banaras, and Calcutta—were thrown into jail. The Rana government, apprehensive that the Indian independence movement might prove contagious, requested the British authorities to take into custody several other Nepalese living in India.

By early 1945 the end of the war was in sight, and the British adopted a more conciliatory approach. Before the year was out, most political prisoners, including the detained Nepalese, had been released, and open political activities had been resumed in India. In June, 1945, the British Government announced its willingness to let representatives of prominent Indian political parties form a popular government. The landslide victory of the Labour party in the British general elections strengthened the prevalent belief that the end of the British Raj in India was a matter of months rather than years.

The Rana ruler, who had so far shielded his archaic political system from the winds of change blowing in India, suddenly found his southern flank exposed to stronger currents generated by the rapid Indian advance toward independence. There was an increasingly uncomfortable realization among the Ranas that political events in India were taking a course historically and ideologically inimical to the Rana regime. With their long history of collaboration with the British in the suppression of the Indian independence movement, they had little reason to hope that they could effect a *rapprochement* with the new political forces emerging on the Indian scene. The most shattering blow must have been the Ranas' awareness that the British Raj, which they had so sedulously cultivated over the years, seemed eager to lay down its burdens in India with only nominal solicitude for its erstwhile Rana allies.

As if cognizant of his incompatibility with the emerging political order in India, Juddha Shamsher—the strong-willed Rana Prime Minister who believed the world to be divided permanently by divine design into two classes, the rulers and the ruled—made history by voluntarily relinquishing the prime ministership in November, 1945. Upon his exit from the Rana political hierarchy, power in Nepal passed into the hands of the third-generation Shamsher Ranas. In order to ensure a peaceful succession, Juddha personally crowned the new incumbent, Padma Shamsher, before retiring from the political scene.

PADMA SHAMSHER'S RULE—NOVEMBER, 1945, TO FEBRUARY, 1948

Padma Shamsher's elevation to the prime ministership coincided with ominous developments both inside and outside Nepal. India was on the verge of independence. The New Labour government in Britain dispatched a Cabinet Mission to India in March, 1946, to work out plans for the smooth transfer of power to Indian hands. At home, thousands of Nepali soldiers were returning from abroad in the course of the demobilization of the British Indian Army. Most of them faced uncertain futures, and almost all had been exposed to modernizing influences. The Ranas feared that the returnees' stories of army life abroad might cause disaffection in the state army, which had been maintained in a primitive condition. Most of the 45,000 soldiers were stationed in Kathmandu or its vicinity, but there were virtually no barracks, and the men had to find their own billets. In the best-paid unit, soldiers of the grade of private received a meager fifteen rupees a month; from this they had to buy food and keep up their uniforms, of which one free issue was given on enlistment. This underpaid, ill-clothed army, the Ranas feared, would prove susceptible to the admonitions of returning veterans or fall prey to the schemes of politicians.

Thus Padma Shamsher had to assume immediate responsibility for the formation of new and effective responses to the rapidly emerging challenges to the Rana regime. Had the determination and assertiveness of his predecessor been added to his own innate good sense, he might have become the catalytic agent of enduring political change in Nepal, and Rana rule might have undergone a liberal transformation rather than a violent overthrow.

As later events proved, Padma Shamsher was beset with too many doubts and fears to give practical expression to his often-stated reformist intentions. He took the whole country by surprise in his inaugural speech in 1946, when he described himself, in a style uncharacteristic of the Ranas, as the servant of the nation. This dramatic statement was taken at face value by many Nepalese who believed that his background as an "underprivileged" Rana—he had been disowned by his father and rejected by his son—had brought him closer to the sentiments of the people. What was not understood was that his penurious upbringing had also produced in him a strongly pessimistic and suspicious attitude. At the beginning of the war he was convinced that Britain would fall before the Axis onslaught, and he made no secret of his views.[1] When the British were preparing to transfer power in India, he was convinced that the subcontinent would be torn by political chaos. Above all, he feared that the sons of Chandra Shamsher, who were next in the line of succession, were determined to force him from office and that his life was in constant danger.

Despite all the momentous political changes in India in 1946, Padma Shamsher moved cautiously in his efforts to liberalize the Rana regime. Like most Ranas, he had persuaded himself that forces of disintegration would soon emerge in India as a result of the transfer of authority and that the British Government, foreseeing such a possibility, would not push the plans for Indian independence. Some substance was given to his beliefs by the widespread riots in India in August, 1946, following the Muslim League's call for direct action. But there was also the disturbing fact that in the same month Nehru, the Indian National Congress leader, was invited by the British Viceroy to form an interim government.

The Rana government under Padma Shamsher did make certain moves in 1946 to counter the new political situation fast developing in India. A landlords' conference was held at Kathmandu, in an effort to ensure stability in the areas of southern Nepal bordering on India by appealing for the support of the landlords, who had a vested interest in the continuation of the Rana political system. What the Rana government chose to ignore was the fact that the new political influences from India were as hostile to the landlords as to the Rana system. A second response came in the form of token improvements in the condition of the underpaid soldiers. A salary increase was announced, and rice was made available to army personnel at subsidized rates. Third, efforts were made to extend Nepal's diplomatic relations by seeking new allies and resuming old contacts abroad. Babar Shamsher visited the United States, and Krishna Shamsher, like Babar Shamsher a highly placed Rana general, led a political mission to China. One direct outcome of this diplomatic activity was the signing of a treaty of friendship and commerce with the United States in April, 1947, and the exchange of diplomatic representatives between the two countries in February, 1948. Nothing of consequence resulted from the mission to China, presumably because the Chiang Kai-shek government was deeply embroiled in internal problems.

A fourth response of the Rana government was an effort to gain support from Indian political groups other than the National Congress. One obvious choice was the All-India Hindu Mahasabha, a group whose leaders had often glorified the Ranas as the custodians of the only Hindu state in the world. The Mahasabha leaders opposed the secular political programs of the Indian National Congress and were committed to the establishment of a Hindu state in India. The Rana government used the Hindu Mahasabha press in India to present its point of view to the Indian public. In 1945–46 the Ranas played host to Dr. B. S. Moonjee, a prominent Hindu Mahasabha leader, in Kathmandu and allowed him to address the students and faculty at Tri-Chandra College. Moonjee praised the Ranas for upholding Hindu ideals of government in Nepal and criticized the leaders of the Indian National Congress, including Gandhi, for their ideas and policies. The next political visitor the Rana government recruited was Dambar Singh Gurung, a Nepali of Indian domicile and president of the Gorkha League in Darjeeling. Gurung's visit and his public speeches did little to improve the Kathmandu intellectuals' opinion of the Ranas and was indicative of the mistrust with which the regime viewed the Nepali communities in India, rightly apprehending that they would participate in future anti-Rana agitations launched from the south.

The year 1947 was ominous for the Ranas in several respects. A mass political party had been organized in October, 1946, by the Banaras group of Nepali political exiles. In January, 1947, it was expanded, under the name of the Nepali National Congress (Nepali Rashtriya Congress), to include Nepalese both inside and outside Nepal. The avowed object of the new party was the overthrow of the Rana regime by nonviolent *satyagraha* tactics and its replacement by a democratic government under the consitutional leadership of the King. On February 20 the British Government solemnly declared its intention of withdrawing from India not later than June, 1948. This announcement must have shattered any remaining illusions of the Ranas about the continuation of British rule in India.

The most immediate danger was posed by the activities of the Nepali National Congress. The organization of this mass political party had been enthusiastically welcomed by a number of prominent Indians as an earnest of a new awakening in Nepal, and their congratualatory messages could hardly have been a source of complacency for the Ranas. Shortly after its formation, the Nepali National Congress participated in a labor strike at the Biratnagar Jute Mills, in the Nepal Terai. The Rana government had considerable difficulty in meeting this overt and widely publicized challenge to their regime. No longer could the Indian railway system be used to transport state army units to the threatened area; troops had to be sent to Biratnagar over long and difficult mountain trails.

The strike commenced on March 4; B. P. Koirala, the Nepali National Congress leader, joined the strikers on March 9. State troops arrived only on March 24. Koirala and his associates were arrested, some being sent to Kathmandu and others to Dharan, and the strike was temporarily suppressed by force. The Congress held a delegates' conference at Jogbani, across the border from the mills, and resolved to initiate a country-wide *satyagraha* or civil disobedience movement on the Indian model.

This unprecedented anti-Rana movement began on April 13 as scheduled, with thousands of Nepalese courting voluntary arrest at Biratnagar, Birganj, Janakpur, and Kathmandu. The satyagrahis demanded the release of all political prisoners and the institution of civic rights. The turnout in Kathmandu probably had the most unnerving effect on the regime. The capital city, well policed by its huge state army concentrations, witnessed spectacular anti-Rana processions involving tens of thousands of men and women, students and peasants. Nothing like this had ever occurred before, and the Rana rulers were seized by indecision and uncertainty as to the best way of coping with the situation. Several satyagrahis were arrested and were detained in palace compounds. After weeks of deliberation with other Ranas, Padma Shamsher made a historic speech on May 16, announcing his desire to associate the people with the government to a greater degree than in the past. He outlined the following measures to further this objective: (*a*) establishment of a Reforms Committee to consider plans for political liberalization, (*b*) establishment of elected municipalities and district boards in various districts, (*c*) separation of the judiciary from the executive branch of the government, and the establishment of an independent judiciary, (*d*) authorization of seven new schools in Kathmandu Valley, and (*e*) publication of the annual budget of the country.

These announcements, although they did not presage any sweeping reforms, were viewed as major concessions, and the Nepali National Congress called off its agitation in consideration of the liberal professions of the Rana government. In June, at the request of the Rana government, the Indian government sent a three-man team of constitutional experts under the leadership of Sri Prakash Gupta to advise in the preparation of political reforms. In the same month the first popular elections of officials of the Kathmandu municipality were authorized.

In July students at the Sanskrit School in the capital launched an agitation, demanding that the curriculum in their school be modernized to include such subjects as geography, history, economics, and social science. This movement was directed as much against the Rana regime as against the Brahman priests who were directly responsible for the supervision of the school. The agitation was suspended on assurances from the Prime Minister that the students' demands would be fulfilled shortly. But reportedly, the Rajguru and the Commander in Chief opposed Padma Shamsher's liberal attitude and took advantage of the cessation of agitation to have the leaders arrested. The stipends of these students were discontinued, and they were expelled from the school and banished from Kathmandu Valley. Most of them later joined the ranks of the Nepali National Congress in India.

After the Prime Minister's historic speech promising reforms, most of the *détenus* connected with the *satyagraha* were released, but not B. P. Koirala and his associates, who had been arrested in Biratnagar in March. Several Indian political leaders requested that Koirala be released for reasons of health, and finally on Gandhi's intercession the Rana ruler freed him in August, 1947—the month that India became independent.

The timing of this release seems to have been decided in part by the hope of creating a split in the Nepali National Congress. After B. P. Koirala's arrest in March, the party workers elected M. P. Koirala interim president and entrusted him with authority to conduct the *satyagraha* campaign. In July a general conference of party workers was held in Banaras. On the assumption that B. P. Koirala would not be released in the near future, the conference elected D. R. Regmi as acting president. Koirala's unexpected release and subsequent statement that he had resumed leadership of the party brought him into conflict with Regmi, who insisted that he was entitled to serve as president for a full term. This split in the party could not be resolved, and until April, 1950, the Nepali National Congress functioned as two factions with identical names and flags. It has been alleged that the Rana government engineered the split with the help of Brahman supporters who had close kinship ties with Regmi.

The year 1948 opened on a hopeful note for the future political development of the country. On January 26 Padma Shamsher announced a new Constitution, which the Nepali National Congress, again meeting in Banaras, accepted in spite of its obvious shortcomings. The Constitution was a Rana version of the proposals prepared by the team of constitutional experts headed by Sri Prakash Gupta. As the most imaginative and potentially most pragmatic response of the Rana regime to the challenge of the times, the 1948 Constitution has a significant place in the political history of Nepal. It was eventually nullified, not by opposition from the Nepali people, but by the insincerity and duplicity of the dominant wing of the Rana family—the sons of Chandra Shamsher—who refused to allow its implementation in form or spirit.

Promulgation of the Constitution had been an act of supreme courage on the part of the usually timid Padma Shamsher. Then his nerve faltered. Three weeks later he left Kathmandu for India, ostensibly for medical reasons, but the care with which he disposed of his private property made it apparent that he was leaving the country for good. One of the sons of Mohan Shamsher accompained the Prime Minister, and it was through him that Padma sent a letter of resignation on April 26, 1948. Reportedly, Nepali political leaders and Indian authorities tried to persuade him to refuse to abdicate and to continue his rule from India, but without success. Padma was determined to pursue a life of retirement in India.

THE 1948 CONSTITUTION

The 1948 Constitution contemplated no substantive changes in the prerogatives of the Rana Prime Minister, and it accepted the right of succession of the Ranas to the prime ministership as "for all time inalienable and unalterable." [2] It provided for the establishment of a Council of Ministers, a bicameral Legislature or Parliament, and a High Court (Pradhan Nyayalaya). All executive authority was vested in the Rana Prime Minister, who functioned as head of the government and chairman of the Council of Ministers. There were to be five Ministers in the Council, all of whom were to be appointed by the Prime Minister and were to hold office for a term of four years at his pleasure. Two of the five Ministers were to be chosen from among the elected members of the Legislature. The Prime Minister could dismiss any or all Ministers if they ceased to command his confidence. Also there were reserved to him wide discretionary powers to suspend or modify the Constitution by promulgating special ordinances, which were to have the force of law for six months.

The Council of Ministers was to transact all executive business and to "define the policies of the government, scrutinize the budget of the various departments, give final consideration to the government bills to be placed before the Legislature, and bring about coordination and cooperation between various departments of the government."

At the village and district levels the Constitution envisaged the establishment of a *panchayat* ("council") system. The basic units of the governmental bodies at these levels were the *gram panchayat* ("village council"), having five to fifteen elected members and representing one or more villages, and the *nagar panchayat* ("town council"), having ten to fifty elected members and representing a town or city. The chairmen of the village and town panchayats were to elect a *zilla panchayat* ("district council"), of fifteen to twenty members. The panchayats of all categories were empowered to expend whatever revenue they could raise, presumably by taxation, and whatever grants were allocated to them by the government, for such local services as education, health, transport, public buildings, and water-supply systems.

The Legislature was to consist of two houses: an upper house, the Bharadari Sabha ("Council of Nobles"), consisting of twenty to thirty nominated members, and a lower, the Rashtra Sabha ("National Council"), consisting of forty-two elected and twenty-eight nominated members. Elections to the Rashtra Sabha and the panchayats were to be based on adult suffrage.

The jurisdiction of the Legislature was severely restricted. It could not discuss the list of expenditures charged upon the revenues of the state, nor could it consider a demand for a grant without the permission of the Prime Minister. Its defined activities consisted mainly of adopting necessary legislation for promoting public welfare and improving the administration of the country. The Prime Minister reserved to himself discretionary powers to stop or veto any legislation contemplated or approved by the Legislature if he deemed it harmful to the public welfare. All bills approved by the Legislature were to be enacted into law only after the Prime Minister's seal had been affixed.

The Prime Minister was empowered to appoint a Judicial Committee consisting of two outside members and ten members of the Legislature. The Judicial Committee was to act as the Supreme Court of Appeal in special cases and was authorized to frame rules and regulations for the administration of justice. As we have noted, the Constitution also provided for the establishment of a Pradhan Nyayalaya or High Court. This was to consist of one chief justice and twelve judges, and was to function as a court of records and have supervisory jurisdiction over lower courts. The Prime Minister was given discretionary authority to appoint or dismiss any judge of the Pradhan Nyayalaya.

Perhaps the most significant features of the Constitution, as far as the public was concerned, were the acceptance of the principle of representative local self-government at the village and district levels, the projected establishment of invigilatory administrative bodies such as the Auditor General's Office and Public Service Commission, and, above all, the recognition of civil rights and liberties for the citizens of Nepal. For the first time in the history of Nepal, a constitution laid down that the Nepalese could exercise freedom of speech, expression, religion, and assembly "in conformity with established practices of public policy and morality."

MOHAN SHAMSHER'S RULE (FEBRUARY 1948, TO FEBRUARY, 1951)

Mohan Shamsher took over the Prime Minister's power and duties in February, 1948, once Padma Shamsher had departed for India. One of his first acts was to ban the Nepali National Congress throughout the country. This action, coming soon after the announcement of the Constitution, was indicative of the new Prime Minister's conservative approach to political reforms. The Constitution was scheduled to go into effect in April and to be fully operative within twelve months. Mohan Shamsher's scarcely disguised disinclination to implement the Constitution eventually cost the Ranas whatever political support they might have gained from the measure.

In his inaugural speech, in April, Mohan Shamsher showed a belated awareness of the Rana government's diplomatic isolation on the world scene after the withdrawal of British authority from India. To improve this situation, he proposed extending Nepal's diplomatic relations with foreign countries, including the United States, France, the Netherlands, Brazil, and Belgium. Ambassadors from the United States and France presented their credentials to King Tribhuwan in 1948 and 1949, respectively; Nepal applied for membership in the United Nations in February, 1949 and the Brazilian Minister to India was decorated with a Nepali medal in August, 1949. It would seem that Mohan Shamsher was counting more on diplomatic support from abroad than on internal political reforms as a means of stabilizing the Rana political system.

The extension of relations overseas was only one aspect of this diplomacy of survival. Equally important was the regime's continued efforts to gain the support of the new nationalist government in India. Although the Ranas must have exulted over the serious internal difficulties in India after the partition of the country, Mohan Shamsher was willing to assist New Delhi through the loan of Nepal Army units as long as this served the interests of the Rana system in Nepal. When the Indian government became involved in military campaigns against the princely state of Hyderabad in 1949, for instance, Mohan Shamsher quickly supplied ten battalions under the personal command of his son, Sharada Shamsher, to assist in the maintenance of law and order in other parts of India. In February, 1950, the Prime Minister paid a state visit to India and expressed in his speeches the determination of his government to assist India in any hour of difficulty, as it has assisted the British Raj.[3] Reportedly, the Indian leaders, Nehru in particular, sought unsuccessfully to impress upon him the necessity of liberalizing his government. The only tangible result of Mohan Shamsher's visit was the signing of treaties of peace and friendship and of trade and commerce between the two governments in July, 1950. The treaties were subsequently the subject of intense controversy in Nepal, and Mohan Shamsher was accused of conceding Nepal's sovereignty in his anxiety to solicit Indian support for his regime.

Mohan Shamsher's political conservatism can be attributed in part to his religious orthodoxy and Rana heritage, but it was also stimulated by the constant pressures exerted by his ambitious younger brother, Babar Shamsher, against any concessions to internal or external demands for political reforms. Even the few educated Ranas were so hopelessly entrapped in the elaborately cultivated family protocol, based on obedience and seniority, that they could not offer serious opposition to the political orthodoxy of these two stalwarts.

One direct result of this coalition between the two Rana brothers had been the resignation of Padma Shamsher in April, 1948 (which had been involuntary, despite the grounds of ill health offered in explanation of it). Another and more serious result was the estrangement of two prominent C Ranas, Suvarna Shamsher and Mahavir Shamsher. These two cousins, along with their parents, had been among the victims of the bloodless Rana family purge in 1934 and had been exiled from Kathmandu Valley at that time. When Padma Shamsher came to power in 1945, they were allowed to return to the capital, and Suvarna was even appointed to the Constitutional Reforms Committee. But they soon found themselves at odds with the conservative bloc in the Rana family, led by Mohan and Babar Shamsher. After Padma's abdication their private property in Kathmandu which Padma had restored to them was reconfiscated and their political rehabilitation rescinded by order of Mohan Shamsher. This proved to be a serious political miscalculation. Mahavir and Suvarna, alienated by this action, established in 1948 a political party of their own, the Nepal Democratic Congress (Nepal Prajatantrik Congress).

The headquarters of this new political organization was in Calcutta, where both Suvarna and Mahavir had extensive business establishments. Better equipped financially than the strife-torn Nepali National Congress, the party even published a newspaper of its own, the *Nepal Pukar* ("Call of Nepal"), which advocated the overthrow of the Rana regime by any means, including violent insurrection. The Nepal Democratic Congress had only a limited popular appeal, however, because of its Rana leadership and financial backing. Opponents alleged that the two founders were motivated solely by personal grudges. And, indeed, in the initial stage of its organization, the party's supporters and followers were mostly persons sympathetic to Suvarna and Mahavir because of ties of kinship or traditions of familial service. Subsequently, the party was able to attract the support of persons who were dissatisfied with the factional politics of the Nepali National Congress, among them a number of Gorkha ex-service-men and some former members of the Indian National Army.* The Democratic Congress organized the nucleus of a private army which later evolved into the Mukti Sena ("Liberation Army") of the 1950 revolution.

The organization of the Nepal Democratic Congress was an ominous development for the future of Rana rule. It committed several influential and wealthy C Ranas, whether from motives of personal revenge or from dedication to democratic principles, to the destruction of the political system dominated by A Ranas. Thus the Rana family, at a time when its political existence was seriously challenged by a common front of non-Rana elements in the country, could no longer count on internal cohesion and solidarity. Furthermore, the Nepal Democratic Congress did not restrict itself to nonviolent (i.e., Gandhian) tactics in its plans to overthrow the regime; to the question of means it adopted a

---

* The Indian National Army was organized during World War II by Subash Chandra Bose, an Indian nationalist leader, to liberate India from British control. Its headquarters was in Singapore and its personnel were mostly Indian officers and soldiers captured by the Japanese, and Indian residents of Southeast Asian countries under Japanese control.

strictly pragmatic approach. Violent revolutionary tactics and traditional conspiratorial methods of effecting changes in the government were not ruled out. Reportedly, the Nepal Democratic Congress planned a military revolt in January, 1949, but was never able to carry it out.

In September, 1948, a third political party was organized, this time in Kathmandu, under the name of the Nepal Praja Panchayat ("Nepal People's Council"). In contrast to the other two Nepali political parties, the Praja Panchayat was not opposed to the continuation of the Rana regime and was willing to function as a political party within the framework of the 1948 Constitution. Prominent among its leaders were Gopal Prasad Rimal, Tripurawar Singh, and Vijaya Bahadur Malla. When the party held a series of public meetings to test the fundamental rights provisions of the Constitution, the Rana government suspected more serious designs and tried to suppress its activities. A more flexible ruler might have put the Praja Panchayat to profitable use as a counter to the far more radical political agitation emanating from Banaras and Calcutta.

After it had become clear that Mohan Shamsher was not willing to honor the reforms solemnly announced by Padma Shamsher, the Praja Panchayat launched a *satyagraha* movement in the three cities of Kathmandu Valley, demanding the implementation of the constitutional provisions relating to fundamental rights. In October, 1948, while this agitation was going on, B. P. Koirala and some of his associates secretly came to Kathmandu to establish contacts with the Praja Panchayat leaders. In December the visitors were discovered and arrested. The Rana government, alarmed by their presence, then began severe suppression of the Praja Panchayat. Hundreds of political suspects were rounded up from among students, businessmen, and intellectual groups. Many of the *détenus* were maltreated and even tortured in jail as Mohan Shamsher followed a policy of treating political critics and opponents far more harshly than Padma Shamsher had done in 1947. Consequently the public began to entertain serious doubts about the efficacy of nonviolent tactics of the Gandhian type.

This second arrest of B. P. Koirala brought the Rana government under heavy criticism by several Indian political leaders. In March, 1949, the annual conference of the Indian Socialist party adopted a resolution on Nepal that strongly condemned the repressive policy of the Rana government and urged the early release of all Nepali political prisoners and *détenus*. In May, when Koirala and his associates began a hunger strike in jail, the Indian Socialist party observed "Nepal Day" in demonstrations all over India, and party leaders organized processions in front of the Nepali Embassy in New Delhi to demand the immediate release of Koirala and other political prisoners.

The unfavorable publicity resulting fom Indian pressures and the threat of a nationwide *satyagraha* by the Nepali National Congress made the Rana government reconsider. Since Koirala was a Brahman, there was fear of the consequences if he sould die while in confinement, since responsibility for the death of a Brahman is one of the five grievous sins of orthodox Hinduism. Koirala had a long private audience with Mohan Shamsher, who reportedly expressed himself as eager to democratize the Rana administration in the near future. Koirala was released in June, and his talk with Mohan Shamsher probably led him to persuade the Nepali National Congress leadership in India to call off the further agitation which had been planned.

In 1949 mainland China fell to the Communists and the Kuomintang government was evacuated to the island of Formosa. This momentous political upheaval, the long-range effects of which were quickly anticipated in political circles in both India and Nepal, strengthened the Indian government's determination to establish in Nepal a stable political system capable of withstanding any political challenge that might eventually develop from across its northern border. Yet the Rana government seemed to view the rise of Communist power in China more as an excuse for retaining its political system intact than as a reason for liberalizing it. In speeches made during his state visit to India in February, 1950, Mohan Shamsher defended the Rana system as a bulwark against Communist subversion from the north. Thus again the Rana government compromised its long-range interests by seeking refuge in temporary expedients. Unwillingness to face up to the unpalatable fact that drastic reforms were needed if the system was to continue led the Rana rulers to cultivate comforting political fancies and myths, and their numerous parasitic followers did little to awaken them from their world of make-believe.

The self-assurance of the Ranas was shaken in September, 1949, when some Nepali National Congress leaders, pursued by police in the Terai, opened fire and wounded one of the policemen. This action demonstrated that the Nepali National Congress's avowed policy of nonviolence was more a matter of profession than observance. Confirmation of the shift in policy came in March, 1950, when the party president, M. P. Koirala, and the Nepal Democratic Congress president, Mahendra Vikram Shah, issued a public statement announcing the merger of the two parties—the one with an avowed policy of nonviolence and the other pledged to overthrow the Rana regime by any possible means. The formal merger took place in April at a general conference of workers of both parties in Calcutta, and a new organization, the Nepali Congress, was born. The flag of the Democratic Congress was adopted for the new party, and M. P. Koirala of the National Congress was elected its president. At the conference a decision was reached to conduct the campaign against the Rana regime on two levels. Publicly, the party president was authorized to organize nonviolent opposition; privately, B. P. Koirala and Suvarna Shamsher were entrusted with the responsibility of procuring arms and forming a "liberation army."

The Nepali Congress quickly began preparations for revolution. In its main outlines, their plan called for (1) the abduction of King Tribhuwan, who would be taken from Kathmandu to western Nepal, presumably to Palpa; (2) the establishment of a constitutional government under the King; and (3) a revolt against the Rana government by sections of the Nepal Army. The abduction of King Tribhuwan was to take place in September, during the week-long Indra Jatra festival (held at the old royal palace and traditionally attended in person by the kings of Nepal), and the revolt in the army was to be sparked by several C Rana and Shah family officers.

The seriousness of the situation was recognized by the Rana regime, which hastily introduced a number of countermeasures. On September 22, Prime Minister Mohan Shamsher finally inaugurated the two houses of the Nepal Parliament, as provided for in the 1948 Constitution, but did so in an extraconstitutional manner. The Upper and Lower Houses were both filled with Ranas and their followers, and even the so-called elected representatives in the Lower House were appointed without so much as the formality of a pretended election. Mohan Shamsher in his address to the Parliament announced that the Constitution was fully operative. He had, he said, formed a Council of Ministers, including two elected members in accordance with the provisions of the Constitution, but he neglected to mention the names of those selected.

On September 24, the Rana government arrested several Nepali Congress leaders who had been secretly organizing an armed insurrection in the capital. Those arrested included Colonels Toran Shamsher Rana and Noda Vikram Rana, along with some other C Rana military officers. In a subsequent press announcement the government reported that it had seized arms, ammunition, and wireless equipment at the residence of Captain

Pratap Vikram Shah, Suvarna Shamsher's brother-in-law.[4] The discovery of the plot aroused suspicions concerning King Tribhuwan's possible involvement, and it has been alleged that the depositions of those arrested did implicate him in the secret plans of the Nepali Congress. King Tribhuwan, presumably to avoid interrogation on this question, feigned illness and on that ground canceled his periodic interviews with the Prime Minister.

King Tribhuwan's strong anti-Rana sentiments had been an open secret in Kathmandu ever since his implication in the Praja Parishad conspiracy of 1940. He had been allowed to make unofficial visits to India in 1944 and 1946, and during the second trip he had established contacts with anti-Rana political elements in India through Suvarna Shamsher, who was at that time in Padma Shamsher's good graces. There is little doubt that the plans of the Nepali Congress had the blessing of the King and that he supported the party's efforts to organize a military *coup* in September, 1950.

Mohan Shamsher, reportedly, planned to force the abdication of King Tribhuwan after obtaining depositions as to his involvement with the Nepali Congress. Again, however, Crown Prince Mahendra refused to supplant his father, and the Prime Minister concocted a scheme by which the King's third grandson Jnanendra, was to be placed on the throne and the rest of the royal family banished to Gorkha.

While a major political crisis was brewing in the capital, Nepali Congress leaders gathered at Bairaganiya, a border town in India, and prepared for an armed struggle with the Ranas. The usual constitutional processes within the party were suspended temporarily, and M. P. Koirala, the party president, was given dictatorial powers to lead the fight.

Certain events now occurred which led directly to the outbreak of the revolution in November. By tradition the Rana ruler had to obtain the King's Lal Mohur on any order inflicting capital punishment on Nepali subjects. Reportedly, King Tribhuwan refused to permit the use of the seal when the Prime Minister demanded authority to execute ten persons for involvement in the September conspiracy. Mohan Shamsher, like his predecessor Juddha in 1940, then decided to go ahead with the executions anyway. He was, however, thwarted, for at this point King Tirbhuwan made a dramatic and public action of protest.

On November 4, the King asked permission to see the Prime Minister at the latter's residence. This being granted, he drove there alone in his car. On November 5 he informed the Prime Minister that he would go on a hunting trip the next day with his family. (Presumably, the earlier visit had been for the purpose of getting permission for this.) The Rana ruler agreed and provided the necessary military escort, unaware that among the escort were several whom King Tribhuwan had already won over to his side. On the morning of November 6 King Tribhuwan and his entire family, with the exception of his four-year-old grandson Jnanendra, departed by automobile from the Royal Palace on what was ostensibly a hunting trip. The Indian Embassy was on the road the royal party was supposed to follow. On reaching the gates of the Embassy, the King and his sons, who were all driving their own cars, suddenly swung through the gates and into the grounds, to the surprise and consternation of those Rana guards who had not been apprised of the King's plan. Thus the royal family took sanctuary and escaped from the Rana ruler's control. It seems probable that the Prince Jnanendra was left behind both to avoid suspicion about the hunting trip and to provide protection for him and the royal line in the event of mishap to the others if the plan should fail.

THE 1950 REVOLUTION

The royal flight into the Indian Embassy took both the Nepali Congress and the Ranas by surprise. The Nepal government was thrown into utter confusion. Mohan Shamsher, who had always relied on his spies for information on the King's activities and on army officials for restricting his movements, was stunned. The Prime Minister's first reaction, reportedly, was to order the forcible removal of the royal family from the Indian Embassy, but the idea of military action against a foreign embassy, if it was considered, was dropped, and it was decided that emissaries should be sent to persuade King Tribhuwan to return to the royal palace. Accordingly, Vijaya Shamsher and Ananda Shamsher were deputed to seek an audience with him, but he refused to see them.

Early in the morning of November 7, the Parliament was convened in an emergency session. This Rana-dominated body unanimously approved the Prime Minister's proposal that King Tribhuwan should be asked to recognize his eldest grandson as his successor and that if he refused the third grandson should be placed on the throne. The request, transmitted to the King through the Indian Ambassador, was refused. The Rana government then crowned the four-year-old Prince Jnanendra formally at 2:45 P.M. of the same day. With remarkable speed, coins bearing the name of the new King were brought out, and this, although in accord with the traditional practice during coronations, was interpreted as an indication of the Rana government's lack of interest in a political settlement with King Tribhuwan.

The next move was to seek diplomatic recognition of the new monarch from foreign powers. Representations were made to India, Great Britain, and the United States. The British Government, because of its traditional ties with the Ranas, initially seemed to be more solicitous of the welfare of the Rana family than was Washington. But after the visit of its representative, Sir Esler Dening, to Kathmandu on December 3, it, too, decided to follow India's leadership on the matter and to refuse recognition.

The Nepali Congress's plans for insurrection had to be put into action promptly because of the opportune situation provided by the royal family's sudden and unexpected flight to the Indian Embassy. The revolt can be said to have begun on November 10, the same day the royal family was flown to New Delhi in a special airplane of the Indian Air Force under an agreement between Indian and Nepali officials. Late that afternoon, an airplane dropped anti-Rana leaflets over Birganj and Kathmandu. On November 12, leaflets were dropped over Biratnagar, Dhankuta, and parts of the Nepal Terai. The aircraft belonged to Himalayan Airways, a line based in Calcutta and owned by Mahavir Shamsher, one of the C Rana leaders of the Nepali Congress.[5] On November 16, the Indian government announced that no further unauthorized flights over Nepal from Indian territory would be allowed.

Upon learning that King Tribhuwan was to be flown to New Delhi, the Nepali Congress leaders had mobilized their volunteers at nine different points on the Nepal-India border. In the early hours of November 11, two or three hundred armed men in about forty trucks—the vehicles, according to the Rana authorities, bearing the "marking and numbers of Bihar State in India" [6] —attacked Birganj, in south-central Nepal, and captured the government offices there. A revolutionary government was proclaimed under the Mukti Sena, or Liberation Army, of the Nepali Congress. The volunteers, reinforced and supplied with newly captured arms, continued to advance northward.

Other Nepali Congress volunteers, stirred by reports of the capture of Birganj, launched insurrectionary activities all along the border. In the first week of operations Parasi, Rangeli, and Udaipur Garhi fell to the rebels, and attacks were launched against Biratnagar and Jhapa in the eastern Terai and Bhairawa in the west.

The state army was handicapped in the struggle against the

Nepali Congress by inadequate communications with Kathmandu and by difficulties in obtaining supplies and reinforcements. Only in Biratnagar and Bhairawa did the rebels meet stiff resistance from local military units and the district government. On November 15, however, the government of the Indian state of Uttar Pradesh announced a formal restriction of anti-Rana activities on the Indian side of the border. This seriously hampered the movements of the Nepali Congress volunteers by preventing their use of Indian railways and roads to transport men and material. But the Rana government faced even greater difficulty in moving troops to the relief of rebel-infested areas in eastern and western Nepal, since the journey from Kathmandu to these areas over mountain trails took weeks rather than days.

On hearing of the rebels' capture of Birganj, only two days' march from Kathmandu, the government dispatched a force of battalion strength. These state army troops, led by Rana officers, reached a point within five miles of Birganj and then awaited reinforcements, although they heavily outnumbered the rebels. An additional battalion arrived a few days later, and Birganj was retaken in the third week of November.

The armed struggle between Rana and Nepali Congress forces continued through December with varying fortunes on both sides. Among the places captured by the Nepali Congress were Kailali Kanchanpur, Narayanpur, Bhagavanpur, Bhojpur, Dhangarhi, Biratnagar, Malangwa, Okhaldhunga, and Dhankuta. Probably more demoralizing for the government were the developments in Kathmandu and within the Rana family. Massive demonstrations in the capital, on November 26 and 28, demanded the restoration of King Tribhuwan and an end to Rana tyranny. The government had to resort to gunfire, and two demonstrators were killed. The mass protest exposed the falseness of the Rana claims that the Nepali Congress rebellion was manned and engineered solely by foreign elements.

A highly serious development was the disaffection within the ranks of the Rana family. By the end of December forty C Ranas had resigned from their positions in the army and administration in protest against the oppressive policies of the A branch of the family and in support of the restoration of King Tribhuwan to the throne. Several of them took part in the mass demonstrations. In the first week of 1951 the situation deteriorated further when Rudra Shamsher, a C Rana who had been the Bada Hakim of Palpa District, organized a *coup d'état* and seized control of the government there. The 1,500-strong garrison at Palpa, the largest military unit outside Kathmandu, sided with Rudra Shamsher. This action exposed most of the western hills to the Nepali Congress forces.

The Rana government suffered further from difficulties in communication with the troops it had dispatched by way of the mountain trails to points in the far east and far west of the country. The soldiers of the state army were clearly divided in their loyalties. The Nepali Congress had given wide publicity to the theme that the King had withdrawn his approval of the Rana government and that the rebellion had as its objective his restoration to the throne. Naturally, morale in the army ebbed very low. It was a shattering blow to the Ranas when, on January 3, a body of state troops on the banks of the Kosi River in eastern Nepal surrendered to Nepali Congress volunteers.[7]

The military contest probably would have continued for a protracted period had not the diplomatic contest between the Rana and the Indian governments come rather quickly to a settlement. In early November, the Indian government had announced that it would give asylum to the King as he requested, and would make arrangements to bring him to India. The Rana government had argued that the King had no right or reason to seek asylum without its permission and that he should therefore be returned from the Embassy. Nevertheless, as we have seen, King Tribhuwan and his family were flown to New Delhi on November 10, 1950. Then, when the insurrection broke out, the Ranas issued a series of publicity releases from the Nepali Embassy in New Delhi, purporting to establish that the Nepali Congress rebels had been encouraged, trained, and equipped by interested Indian elements who, by implication, included the Indian government. A second setback to the Rana government was the failure of the effort to secure recognition of the hastily crowned boy-king, Jnanendra, by foreign powers. It was clear that this failure resulted from the Indian government's refusal to accept the new monarch and the disposition of other foreign powers to follow Indian leadership in the matter.

Convinced that there was now no alternative to negotiation with the Indian government, the Rana government sent two representatives, Vijaya Shamsher and Keshar (Kaiser) Shamsher, to New Delhi. The initial discussions were held, it seems, only between these representatives and the officials of the Indian government, as if the latter were representing both King Tribhuwan and the Nepali Congress as well as their own government. The Rana representatives did not meet with King Tribhuwan until December 8, presumably after the Indian government had prepared its final proposals for a settlement.

In a memorandum submitted to the Government of Nepal on December 8 the Indian government stated:

The Government of India's primary objective is that Nepal should be independent, progressive and strong. For this purpose they regard immediate constitutional changes which will satisfy popular opinion and be acceptable to important nonofficial organizations of Nepalese nationals as urgent. They suggest the following measures: (1) that a Constituent Assembly composed entirely of properly elected members should be brought into being as soon as possible to draw up a Constitution for Nepal; (2) pending the meeting of the Constituent Assembly mentioned above an interim government, which will include persons representative of popular opinion and enjoying public confidence should be established. This body should also include members of the Rana family, one of whom should be Prime Minister. This body should act as a Cabinet on the principle of joint responsibility and should frame its own rules of business; and (3) King Tribhuvan should continue as King in the interests of the realm.[8]

The Rana government did not formally acknowledge receipt of the memorandum until December 19. As if to add force to the Indian memorandum, King Tribhuwan issued a public statement from New Delhi on December 22, expressing his hope that the future political order in Nepal would be based on public participation and representation. The reaction of the Rana government was embodied in the proposals that Mohan Shamsher presented to a special meeting of the Nepal Parliament on December 24. He suggested the immediate formation of a new Cabinet, consisting of nine persons, three of whom were to be popular representatives, and the holding of elections to a constituent assembly in about three years. There was no mention of king Tribhuwan's return to the throne; neither was there any reference to the role of democratic parties. Thus ended the first round of negotiations between the Rana government and the Indian government.

At this stage, it would seem that the Rana government was trying to accomplish two main objectives: to bar King Tribhuwan from returning to Nepal, and to underplay the role of the Nepali Congress both as an agent of political change and as a participant in any future government. The Indian government, however, remained firm in its refusal to accept Prince Jnanendra as king and insisted that King Tribhuwan should preside over the proposed political changes in his country.

In the second round of negotiations, which began on January 1, 1951, the Rana government accepted the Indian proposals *in toto.* On January 8, Prime Minister Mohan Shamsher announced the new political order in a public proclamation. He admitted the failure of his government to obtain foreign recognition of the new king and cited the advice of the Indian government that King Tribhuwan should continue as King of Nepal. Then he agreed that since "lawless elements" had exploited the situation arising out of the monarch's absence, King Tribhuwan should be restored to the throne and should be authorized to appoint a regent in his absence. The other significant political changes announced were that (1) elections, based on adult suffrage, would be held not later than 1952 in order to form a constituent assembly, which would draw up a constitution for the country; (2) pending the completion of the constitution and the formation of a government based on it, an interim Cabinet would be established for the transitional period and would consist of fourteen members, seven of whom would be representatives of the people; and (3) an amnesty for all political prisoners would be granted.[9]

On January 10, King Tribhuwan issued a public statement, signifying his approval of Mohan Shamsher's proclamation and appealing to the Nepali Congress's liberation army to lay down its arms.[10] The Nepali Congress, which had not been a participant in the negotiations, at first reacted negatively to the royal appeal. M. P. Koirala characterized the political compromise reached at New Delhi as a "disillusionment" and observed that no interim arrangement could be acceptable to the people unless there was "an effective transfer of power to the people of Nepal." He defined the aims of the Nepali Congress as the liquidation of the feudal regime rather than a compromise with it. On January 14, however, at the invitation of the Indian government, M. P. Koirala, B. P. Koirala, and Suvarna Shamsher flew to New Delhi for political consultations. Two days later, M. P. Koirala, in his capacity as party president, issued an order for a cease-fire in Nepal and appealed to "everyone to assist in the restoration of peace." [11]

The limited participation of the Nepali Congress leaders in the negotiations at New Delhi failed to produce within the rank and file of the party the consensus that would have helped in the implementation of the new political arrangments. The leadership of the party had acquiesced in the decisions reached between the two governments, but at the time when the party president issued the cease-fire order, on January 16, the Bairaganiya decisions of the General Conference of the party—namely, the overthrow of the Rana rule and the liquidation of the feudal order—were still far from realization. Only a "middle way" had been found under the auspices of the Indian government, and the Nepali Congress party was now committed to a policy of compromise with the Rana rule. The "Delhi compromise," as it came to be called in Nepali political circles, resulted in bitter dissension within the party. A serious situation soon developed in the western Terai, where the local commander of the party forces, K. I. Singh, refused to heed the cease-fire directive of the president and continued the armed rebellion.

Once the Nepali Congress had subscribed to the basic formula proposed by the Indian government, its leaders were directly involved in a third round of negotiations, on the composition of the interim government, which began in New Delhi on February 1. These tripartite talks between King Tribhuwan, the Nepali Congress, and the Rana government were successfully concluded on February 8, when the personnel of the Rana-Congress interim coalition government was agreed upon. A week later, King Tribhuwan and the Nepali Congress leaders returned triumphantly to Kathmandu. Prime Minister Mohan Shamsher was present at the airport to receive the King he had repudiated and had sought to dethrone. The political monopoly of the Rana family had come to an end.

The revolution of 1950 was, thus, a relatively brief episode, but its consequences were epoch-making for contemporary Nepal. The military struggle between the Ranas and the Nepali Congress had been marked by few serious encounters; nevertheless, the century-old Rana political edifice had crumbled as if built on a foundation of sand. The decisive battles of the revolution were fought in New Delhi between the Indian government and the Rana government, at the diplomatic level. The odds were all in favor of the Indian government, which had decided to pursue a policy of the "middle way" in Nepal based on a compromise between a chastened Rana ruling family, the reform-minded King Tribhuwan, and the enthusiastic, if somewhat immature, Nepali Congress leadership. The Indian government spoke both on behalf of King Tribhuwan and the Nepali Congress, while the Rana government had to face not merely a divided country, but also, and at the critical moment, a divided family. Thus, with his back to the wall, Prime Minister Mohan Shamsher made the historic proclamation on January 8 which virtually ended the monopoly rule of the Ranas.

The revolution was only a partial success as far as the avowed objectives of the Nepali Congress revolution were concerned. When the party decided to launch an armed struggle, it had presented programs for a comprehensive revolution to end not only the political monopoly of the Ranas but also the social and economic bases of their power. Since the Indian government reserved to itself all the crucial political decisions during the revolution, the Nepali Congress was forced to modify its programs and policies in accordance with terms defined in New Delhi.

Under this new political arrangement, any real consideration of the social and economic goals of the revolution had to be postponed, and first priority was given to the achievement of a viable political compromise between the custodians of the *status quo* and the proponents of change. The "Delhi compromise" was decried by critics of the Nepali Congress leadership as a sell-out to the Ranas and the Indian government, and that theme has been reiterated time after time in subsequent years, not infrequently by those who assumed a safely neutral position during the revolution itself. The leaders of the revolution had now to make an adjustment to a new kind of struggle against the Ranas—this time within the governmental structure. It was on this mixed note of hope, disappointment, and uncertainty that the first experiment under the new "democratic order" was launched in February, 1951.

The Search for
Constitutional
Democracy
(1951–55)

5
The "Revolutionary" Governments

A DRAMATIC CHANGE occurred in the Kathmandu political atmosphere while negotiations on the composition of the future Nepali government were under way in New Delhi. The Ranas released 247 political prisoners on January 17, 1951, and, without making a formal announcement, assumed an attitude of indifference toward political activity in the capital. Processions and demonstrations sprang up spontaneously in the streets of Kathmandu, Patan, and Bhadgaon, and continued intermittently for several days. The climax was reached on February 15, when King Tribhuwan and his family returned from India amid spectacular public jubilation. Prime Minister Mohan Shamsher was at the airport to receive the King whom he had tried to dethrone, and this occasion might be said to have marked the end of the old and the beginning of a new political era in Nepal.

THE RANA-CONGRESS COALITION CABINET

On February 18, King Tribhuwan issued a historic proclamation establishing an interim government and outlining the significant features of the new political system. The interim government, a coalition of Rana and Nepali Congress representatives, was charged with the responsibility of conducting a smooth transition to a new political order "based on a democratic constitution framed by elected representatives of the people."

King Tribhuwan stipulated explicitly that the new Ministers, including the Prime Minister, would hold office at his pleasure and would be collectively responsible to him for their actions. This constituted a drastic transformation in the status of the Prime Minister, which in the Rana period had become synonymous with *de facto* rule.[1]

King Tribhuwan's proclamation, in the absence of relevant conventions or traditions, provided the sole legal basis for the new government. Further, it restored royal prerogatives to the Shah monarch and delineated, however vaguely, the contours of the future political landscape in the country.

THE COMPOSITION OF THE COALITION GOVERNMENT

In accordance with the policy of the "middle way" proposed by the Indian government and set forth in Nehru's speech of December 6, 1950,[2] the interim Cabinet was based on equal representation of Ranas and the Nepali Congress. Each group was allotted five representatives in the Cabinet, and Mohan Shamsher

TABLE 1

The Coalition Cabinet of 1951

Name	Rank	Portfolio	Political affiliation
THE RANA BLOC			
Mohan Shamsher	Prime Minister	Foreign Affairs	Senior leader of the A Ranas; and the last ruler under the Rana regime
Babar Shamsher	Minister	Defence	The next in line of succession of the A Ranas; Minister and Commander in Chief under the Rana regime
Chudaraj Shamsher	Minister	Forests	Representative of B Ranas
Nripa Jang Rana	Minister	Education	Representative of C Ranas
Yajna Bahadur Basnyat	Minister	Health and Local Self-Government	Representative of the Rana Bharadars; a lieutenant colonel in the army under the Rana regime

TABLE 1—*Continued*

Name	Rank	Portfolio	Political affiliation
THE NEPALI CONGRESS BLOC			
Bishweshwar Prasad Koirala	Minister	Home	Former president of the Nepali National Congress; a working committee member of the Nepali Congress
Suvarna Shamsher	Minister	Finance	Leader of the Nepal Democratic Congress; treasurer of the Nepali Congress
Ganesh Man Singh	Minister	Industry and Commerce	Member of the Praja Parishad conspiracy in 1940; leader of the Nepali National Congress and the Nepali Congress
Bharat Mani Sharma	Minister	Food and Agriculture	Nepali Congress leader of the Dang Deokhuri area in the western Terai
Bhadrakali Mishra	Minister	Transport	Nepali Congress nominee; leader of a social organization in the eastern Terai

was retained as Prime Minister. Of the five Rana representatives, two were of the A, one of the B, and one of the C class, and the fifth, a non-Rana, was designated as the elected representative of the Rana-appointed Bharadars. Of the five Nepali Congress representatives, three represented the dominant leadership of the party and two were newcomers to the party ranks, presumably appointed to provide territorial balance. The members of the Cabinet, their portfolios, and their political affiliations are listed in table 1.

POLITICAL BACKGROUND OF THE MINISTRY

Mohan Shamsher's long indoctrination and training during the rule of his father, Chandra Shamsher, when Rana autocracy reached its peak, had made him a staunch conservative in both religious and political matters. His political background, therefore, was incompatible with his new role as the leader of a government committed to establishing political democracy. Indeed, his retention as Prime Minister must have been due to the Indian government's discouragement of sudden and radical political change in Nepal, since it is inconceivable that either King Tribhuwan or the Nepali Congress supported his continuation in office under the new setup.

Mohan Shamsher's position in the coalition Cabinet was further complicated by the lack of cohesion within the Rana bloc. At best, he could be sure of the support of only two loyal Rana followers—his brother Babar and the B Rana, Chudaraj Shamsher. The C Rana, Nripa Jang, was predisposed toward the Nepali Congress bloc. The fifth member of the Rana bloc, Yajna Bahadur Basnyat, also found it politically expedient to side with the Nepali Congress and to play down his Rana affiliations.

The Nepali Congress was comparatively better organized, sharing strong anti-Rana attitudes and a unanimity of view on the party's role as the agent of social and political change. Three members—B. P. Koirala, Suvarna Shamsher, and Ganesh Man Singh—were leaders of the party's secret Emergency Committee which had been set up in April, 1950, to organize the armed insurrection against Rana rule. They held the key portfolios of Home, Finance, and Industry and Commerce and wielded considerable influence on the entire government. Because of the importance of the Home portfolio and his position in the party hierarchy, B. P. Koirala was the official leader of the Nepali Congress bloc in the coalition Cabinet and was easily the most influential member of the government.

The Nepali Congress bloc was, however, not entirely homogeneous. The two other members, Bharat Mani Sharma and Bhadrakali Mishra, were not as closely associated with the party hierarchy as their three colleagues. Sharma, the youngest member of the Cabinet, held a lower position in the party hierarchy; he had participated in insurrectionary activities in western Nepal and had been nominated to the cabinet on that basis. Bhadrakali Mishra was a more serious dissident threat, since his nomination had been the result of intense "politicking" at New Delhi. Mishra, who was not a member of the Nepali Congress during the 1950 revolution, joined the party only after becoming a Minister in the Cabinet. His political experience was largely restricted to the organization of a social service organization along Gandhian lines in the Nepal Terai in 1950. He had spent some time at

Gandhi's ashram and in 1948 was in Gandhi's entourage when he visited villages affected by communal riots in Bihar. Mishra had been critical of the insurrection because of his support of Gandhian nonviolent tactics, although he sympathized with the Nepali Congress objectives. Several leaders of the Indian government, who had advised Nepali political leaders to eschew violence in their activities against the Rana government, are believed to have been displeased when the Nepali Congress launched its armed revolt, and in subsequent negotiations at New Delhi in January, 1951, the Indian government may have indicated the desire that an avowed Gandhian be included in the new Nepali Cabinet. Bhadrakali Mishra satisfied this criterion; moreover, he was an inhabtiant of the Terai, a region which had never before been represented in the government. His appointment reportedly was recommended by C. P. N. Singh, the Indian Ambassador in Kathmandu and one of the key figures in the 1950 revolution.

THE FUNCTIONING OF THE COALITION GOVERNMENT

Since the coalition Cabinet was formed on the basis of a peculiar dialectic logic of combining the incumbent Rana regime with an antithetical Nepali Congress in the hope of producing a democratic political synthesis, conflict was inherent in the scheme of things. It was clear from the very outset of the negotiations in New Delhi that the Nepali Congress had been assigned a secondary role in the Indian government's discussions with the Ranas. Indeed, the Nepali Congress leaders were only invited to New Delhi in time to ratify the Indian proposals after these had been accepted by the Rana regime. Thus, the Nepali Congress viewed the coalition as a temporary truce and accepted it with the intention of fighting the Ranas from within the government. Presumably the Ranas accepted it in order to gain time to evaluate the strength of the opposition or, alternatively, to prepare for the evacuation of their families and property from Nepal. The spirit of political reconciliation, which theoretically underlay the Rana-Congress coalition, was absent from the very beginning.

The first clash between the Rana and the Nepali Congress blocs occurred over the question of precedence in the seating arrangements at the swearing-in ceremony on February 18, when B. P. Koirala, as head of the Nepali Congress group, insisted that he be seated next to the Prime Minister. Significantly, each group used separate flags, the one flying the Nepali Congress flag and the other the traditional Rana flag.

The uneasy relationship between the two blocs deteriorated further when reports began to circulate that sons and grandsons of Babar Shamsher, the Defence Minister, were organizing an armed group, the Vir Gorkha Dal ("Brave Gorkha Organization"), to subvert the army and overthrow the government. Reportedly discussions in the Cabinet turned into angry exchanges over Babar Shamsher's alleged involvement in this organization, which the Nepali Congress leader characterized as a terrorist communal group. Since Babar refused to repudiate or obstruct the political activities of his family, Home Minister B. P. Koirala on April 11 ordered the arrest of several members of the Gorkha Dal, including the general secretary, Bharat Shamsher, who was Babar's grandson. The next day, Gorkha Dal members raided the Kathmandu prison, released Bharat Shamsher and his associates, and then proceeded to attack the Home Minister's residence. After his private secretary was wounded, B. P. Koirala dispersed the Gorkha Dal mob by shooting down his nearest assailant.

The Gorkha Dal counterrevolution had far-reaching consequences. King Tribhuwan issued a statement condemning Gorkha Dal fanaticism and praising B. P. Koirala's behavior during the attack. On April 14, as a precautionary measure, the King took over direct command of the army from the Prime Minister and assumed the title of Supreme Commander in Chief. The Gorkha Dal was declared illegal, and its leaders and their alleged supporters in the army were arrested. The attempted counterrevolution gave the Nepali Congress an excuse for retaining the party's "liberation army," which was maintained as an auxiliary police force under the name of the Rakshya Dal ("Protective Organization").

Within the government, a deadlock was reached on May 2 when the Nepali Congress group formally accused Babar Shamsher of connivance with the Gorkha Dal and demanded his removal from the Cabinet. A new *modus vivendi* had to be negotiated before the Cabinet could resume its operation on the basis of collective responsibility. The Nepali Congress demanded that the crisis should be resolved in Kathmandu under the direction of King Tribhuwan. Mohan Shamsher, presumably in search of more nearly nonpartisan auspices, insisted that the negotiations should be held where the original agreement had been concluded, in New Delhi. His view prevailed, and within a few days members of the Rana and the Nepali Congress factions met in New Delhi under the supervision of Prime Minister Nehru and the Indian Ministry of External Affairs.

A joint statement to the press on May 16 announced "complete agreement that the Nepali cabinet should work in a cooperative and progressive spirit for the political development and economic prosperity of Nepal." [3] It was agreed further that the coalition should continue in office with only minor changes in personnel and that a nominated Advisory Assembly should be established to function as a "little parliament," thus giving the government a more representative character.

In conformity with the terms of the agreement, Mohan Shamsher offered the resignation of the coalition government to King Tribhuwan, who in turn announced a reconstituted Cabinet on June 10. Babar Shamsher, the Nepali Congress bloc's *bête noire*, was replaced by Singha Shamsher, Nepal's Ambassador to India. On the Nepali Congress side, Bharat Mani Sharma was replaced by Surya Prasad Upadhyaya. Prime Minister Mohan Shamsher assumed the Defence portfolio in addition to Foreign Affairs, and there was a minor reshuffling of portfolios among the rest of the Ministers.

The reconstituted Cabinet seemed to function with greater harmony, at least until the beginning of October. By this time the Nepali Congress had decided to force the Rana bloc out of the government. That King Tribhuwan sided with the Nepali Congress bloc became evident on October 2, when he announced the composition of the Advisory Assembly, of whose thirty-five members the large majority belonged to the Nepali Congress, while the rest were independents. There was no representation of the official Rana bloc—and only one Nepali Congress Rana had been included. Evidently the Prime Minister was ignored in the nomination of members, for on October 8 Mohan Shamsher publicly expressed his regrets that the King had not consulted with the Cabinet before announcing the composition of the Advisory Assembly.[4] Nepali Congress leaders interpreted these remarks as a rejection of the King's constitutional authority and demanded Mohan Shamsher's resignation.

On November 6, police fired on a procession of students, killing one. This touched off the long-expected crisis in the government. Prime Minister Mohan Shamsher issued a public statement on November 9, expressing sympathy with the bereaved family and sorrow over the tragic event. He indicated also his determination to conduct an impartial official enquiry. Home Minister B. P. Koirala interpreted these remarks as proof of the Prime Minister's repudiation of the principle of collective responsibility—the basis of Rana-Congress coalition. On November 10 —the first anniversary of the 1950 revolution—the Home Minister spoke over Radio Nepal and expressed his party's disillusionment with its experience of collaborating with the Rana group in what he termed an "unnatural coalition." He demanded their elimination from the government and the formation of a politically homogeneous Cabinet. More significantly, he admitted that the goals of the revolution had been only partly achieved, and called for a new, more comprehensive revolution to complete the task. With this purpose in mind, he said, it was his intention to release all political *détenus* to enable them to participate in a maximum public consensus as the basis for such a revolution.[5]

The impact of B. P. Koirala's radio address was reinforced by the resignation of the Nepali Congress bloc from the Cabinet on the same day, and of the Rana bloc on November 12. A new political atmosphere typified by a mood of expectancy and frenetic activity was evident in Kathmandu. It was universally agreed that the final hour of Rana political power had arrived, but there was considerable division of opinion among the political parties—indeed, within the Nepali Congress itself—with regard to the nature and form of the next political arrangement.

The opposition political parties held public meetings to air their views on the crisis. The Praja Parishad voiced opposition to the formation of a Nepali Congress government, on the grounds that this would lead to the initiation of a new political tyranny, and demanded the formation of an all-party government as the most judicious arrangement. Similarly, leaders of the Nepali National Congress (D. R. Regmi faction) expressed their suspicion that a Nepali Congress government would not permit democratic institutions, such as an independent judiciary and Public Service Commission, to function freely, and also demanded the formation of an all-party government. The political independents of Kathmandu echoed similar sentiments and cited the use of gunfire by the police on November 6 as reason enough for not entrusting the reins of government to the Nepali Congress.

The firing on students by the police had aroused considerable local hostility toward B. P. Koirala, and King Tribhuwan had been so apprised both by the local politicians and by his private staff. B. P. Koirala assumed full responsibility for the firing (which seems to have been carried out without his knowledge) and the subsequent tragedy. He refused to meet with the student leaders, however, even after the King repeatedly commanded him to do so, on the grounds that the students' agitation was politically manipulated and that their demands lacked any substance. His refusal probably influenced King Tribhuwan's later decision not to entrust the prime ministership to him.

Serious dissension appeared in the ranks of the Nepali

Congress soon after its nominees resigned from the Cabinet. The majority of the party's Working Committee were reportedly supporters of B. P. Koirala, but King Tribhuwan insisted on nominating M. P. Koirala to head a new government.* The committee reluctantly accepted the King's decision. M. P. Koirala then submitted to the King the names of eight Nepali Congress members and six independents to comprise his Cabinet.

THE FIRST M. P. KOIRALA GOVERNMENT

A Royal Proclamation was issued on November 16, 1951, announcing the establishment of a new government under the leadership of M. P. Koirala. In his prefatory remarks the King admitted that the coalition government had not succeeded in its tasks, and that the people had not been "happy and contented" with it. The need for a representative, broadly based government during the interim period was emphasized. Once again the King expressed his determination to establish a "fully democratic political system functioning in accordance with a constitution prepared by a Constituent Assembly," although for the interim period, he argued, the leader of the largest party, favored by a majority of the people, was the most eligible to lead the government, subject to the proviso that the Cabinet should reflect the ethnic and territorial divisions in the country. M. P. Koirala was commanded to practice "enlightened statesmanship" in the discharge of his duties and was advised to supervise the functioning of the Cabinet in a manner that would ensure the "continued good will, impartiality, and respect of the people toward the government." [6]

Specifically, the new Prime Minister was instructed to clarify and precisely define the civic rights of the people without prejudicing public security and the existing legal system. The Cabinet, as a group, was instructed to implement as speedily as possible measures to (1) establish an independent judiciary

---

* According to the then general secretary of the Nepali Congress, K. P. Bhattarai: "When the Coalition Ministry resigned, the Congress Working Committee proposed that B. P. Koirala should head the new Government. But Mahavir Shamsher who was very intimate with King Tribhuwan, informed us that the Palace would like to have only M. P. Koirala as the Premier. We refused to believe this and sent a delegation of three members to meet the King. Tribhuwan definitely suggested M. P. Koirala's name and warned that, in case this was not accepted by the Party, he would impose direct rule with the help of General Keshar Shamsher. We had no option but to acquiesce." Quoted in A. Gupta, "Politics and Parties in Nepal, 1950–60: A Study of Post-Rana Political Developments and Party Politics" (Ph.D. Dissertation, Indian School of International Studies, 1963), p. 80.

entirely separate from the executive branch of the government, (2) ensure a better organization and functioning of the Public Service Commission, and (3) set up arrangements for elections—if possible, before the end of April, 1953—to the Constituent Assembly. Finally, King Tribhuwan called upon the people to extend their full coöperation to the new government and cautioned civil servants to discharge their obligations loyally and competently without concern for political changes at the top.

THE COMPOSITION OF THE NEPALI CONGRESS CABINET

In accordance with King Tribhuwan's instructions, the new Cabinet was more broadly based than the previous one; indeed, it established a model for future "democratic" governments. Representatives of the eastern and western hills and the Terai were included, and ethnic groups such as the Gurungs and the Limbus were represented for the first time. The Ranas, however, were still overrepresented, holding four posts; two were "liberal" Nepali Congress Ranas, descendants of disinherited C Ranas; the other two were A Ranas, members of the recently dissolved political oligarchy.

The two A Ranas and four independents were nominated to the Cabinet by M. P. Koirala, with King Tribhuwan's approval. They looked to the King for leadership, however, and to that degree acted as his pressure group within the Cabinet. The role of these independents in the Cabinet later assumed some importance in the conflict between M. P. Koirala and the Nepali Congress party.

The members of the new Cabinet are listed in table 2.

A significant feature of the Cabinet was the creation of several new portfolios. Separate ministries were established for General Administration, Planning and Development, Land Reform, Parliamentary Affairs, and Law and Justice. The jurisdiction of the Home Ministry, as established during B. P. Koirala's tenure, was curtailed severely; several of its functions were divided between General Administration, and Law and Justice. Prime Minister M. P. Koirala's assumption of the new portfolio of General Administration gave him strategic control over all other departments, since this new ministry dealt with all Cabinet affairs, government appointments, the Public Service Commission, the coördination of the work of different ministries, and the supervision of district administration. The new Home Minister, unlike his predecessor, was left with only the residual departments of police, jails, and broadcasting.

TABLE 2

THE NEPALI CONGRESS CABINET OF 1951

Name	Rank	Portfolio	Political affiliation
Matrika Prasad Koirala	Prime Minister	Foreign Affairs and General Administration	President, Nepali Congress
Surya Prasad Upadhyaya	Minister	Home and Food	Nepali Congress
Suvarna Shamsher Rana	"	Finance	"
Narada Muni Thulung	"	Local self-government	"
Mahendra Vikram Shah	"	Industry, Commerce, and Civil Supplies	"
Bhadrakali Mishra	"	Transport	"
Mahavir Shamsher Rana	"	Planning and Development, Mines, Forests, and Electricity	"
Ganesh Man Singh	"	Agriculture, Animal Husbandry, and Land Reforms	"
Khadga Man Singh	"	Parliamentary Affairs	Independent
Keshar Shamsher Rana	"	Defence	"
Bhagawati Prasad Singh	"	Law and Justice	"
Sharada Shamsher Rana	"	Education	"
Nara Bahadur Gurung	Deputy Minister	Health	"
Dharma Ratna "Yami"	"	Forests	"

The administrative setup at the Central Secretariat level required strengthening, and it was hoped that the new General Administration department would answer to this particular need. Preparations for convening an elected Constituent Assembly were to be the responsibility of the new Ministry of Parliamentary Affairs. Similarly, it was expected that the separate Ministry of Law and Justice would contribute toward the revision and codification of existing Nepali laws and the preparation of new "democratic" laws and, eventually, toward the functioning of an independent judiciary.

The new Cabinet was relatively free of Rana obstructionism of the type that had beset the coalition government. The multi-ethnic composition of the Cabinet was expected to produce a national outlook in the general orientation of its members. Bhadrakali Mishra and Bhagawati Prasad Singh represented the Hindi-speaking Terai areas; Ganesh Man Singh and Dharma Ratna "Yami," the Saivite and Buddhistic sections, respectively, of the Newar community of Kathmandu; Nara Bahadur Gurung, the Gurung community of the western hills and also the former servicemen of the "Gurkha" regiments in the British and Indian armies; and Narad Muni Thulung, the Limbu community of the eastern hill area. The new Cabinet was thus a test of the capacity of Nepali leaders to operate in a true coalition of national interests, setting aside their personal and ethnic interests and sharing a common political consensus.

POLITICAL BACKGROUND OF THE PRIME MINISTER AND OTHER MINISTERS

M. P. Koirala dominated the new Cabinet, perhaps the most crucial of all the interim governments. His elevation to the prime ministership was the result both of his influence within the Nepali Congress and of his personal accommodation with King Tribhuwan. His influence in the party, however, was the result not of leadership and initiative, but of his capacity for coördination and compromise. In contrast to his brother, B. P. Koirala, the new Prime Minister was known for his caution and practical wisdom, his conservatism and religious orthodoxy—in short, he was the more traditional type of Brahman. Since he had served the Ranas briefly in a subordinate capacity, he was familiar with the rules and protocol of the Rana palaces and could accommodate himself to traditional authority. Of all Nepali Congress leaders, he was the one most inclined to deal with the monarchy respectfully and without indulging in the newfangled practices of egalitarian speech and irreverent manners.

M. P. Koirala also lacked his brother's socialist convictions and intensity, and was not committed to any ideological reconstruction of society except on the most pragmatic terms. His political philosophy can perhaps be best characterized as adherence to moderation as a practical policy and to the desirability of a policy of slow evolutionary change rather than drastic reforms. This emphasis on evolutionary social and political changes made him a supporter of some traditional Nepali social institutions and later brought him into direct conflict with the radical elements in the party, represented by B. P. Koirala, who believed that Nepal's "feudal" society could not be transformed by means short of a social revolution or upheaval.

Thus, M. P. Koirala's appointment as Prime Minister represented the emergence of a new point of view in Nepali Congress circles, a view which contrasted with the prevailing revolutionary sentiment and B. P. Koirala's recent call for a comprehensive revolution. The party was divided on the question of the nature of transitional politics in Nepal. M. P. Koirala viewed the interim period as one in which no serious efforts would be made to implement the principle of constitutional monarchy and in which the scope of the government's activities would be restricted to routine administration. Major social or economic reforms were to be avoided. The alternative viewpoint, represented by B. P. Koirala, envisaged the interim period as necessarily a formative stage in the transition to a new democratic order under which the King had to grow accustomed to functioning as a constitutional head of state and the Cabinet had to initiate basic social and economic changes to prepare the groundwork for a new political system. The conflict between these two points of view later developed other ramifications leading to mutually exclusive interpretations of the proper relationship between the ruling party and the government.

M. P. Koirala's political biases were clearly reflected in the selection of the independent members of the Cabinet, none of whom was distinguished for any particular political ideology or commitment; the independents were, in fact, associated with the existing political order. The two avowed politicians in the group were Khadga Man Singh and Dharma Ratna "Yami," neither of whom had strong political ties or commitments. Among the eight Nepali Congress representatives in the Cabinet, three were members of the original dominant group in the party—namely, Suvarna Shamsher, Ganesh Man Singh, and Surya Prasad Upadhyaya. Their political preëminence was somewhat modified by the presence of the five other party nominees, who represented heterogeneous political elements more closely associated with M. P. Koirala's approach to transitional politics.

Although the Ranas were in a minority, they seemed to dominate the attitudes and the policies of the new government indirectly. Indeed, its efforts to decelerate the tempo of social, economic, and political reforms initiated during B. P. Koirala's tenure as Home Minister were interpreted by his followers in the Nepali Congress as Rana-inspired. The Prime Minister's inability and unwillingness to check this trend was seen as a sign of his growing alignment with the forces of political revivalism. The role of the independents in the Cabinet was also construed as encouraging those forces at the expense of democratic elements and as presaging a new kind of court politics centered in the royal palace. These views were shared by the party's hard-core triumvirate—B. P. Koirala, Suvarna Shamsher, and Ganesh Man Singh—and by their followers, who were chagrined at the exclusion of B. P. Koirala from the new government.

DISPUTE BETWEEN B. P. KOIRALA AND M. P. KOIRALA

The relationship between the Nepali Congress and M. P. Koirala was from the very beginning the most crucial variable in the functioning of the Cabinet. The success of the new government depended on the resolution of the ideological dispute between the two Koirala brothers over the nature of transitional politics. M. P. Koirala's appointment of several former supporters of the Rana regime to key administrative positions cost him much support and sympathy in the party.* The tight grip maintained by the Prime Minister over other departments through the General Administration ministry antagonized several of his Cabinet colleagues. His reputation in the party was further tarnished when, in February, 1952, he headed the Civil Offices Coördinating Committee, consisting entirely of adherents of the Rana regime, and when the new budget, announced that same month, doubled the size of the King's privy purse over that allocated by the Rana-Congress coalition government.

All these developments undoubtedly disturbed the B. P. Koirala faction in the party. On February 20, B. P. Koirala announced his intention of contending for the presidency of the party against M. P. Koirala on the grounds that the same person should not hold the offices of both party president and Prime Minister. He charged the Indian Ambassador, C. P. N. Singh, with trying to balance one leader against another, and called for Singh's replacement in the interests of Indo-Nepali friendship. He characterized the government's ban on the Communist party as "unwise" and appealed for a vital economic policy designed to "prevent the Chinese Communists from taking advantage of the situation in Nepal with the help of K. I. Singh." [7]

In response to B. P. Koirala's challenge, M. P. Koirala

---

* For instance, in the first administrative reorganization, announced on November 28, 1951, the former chief of the Rana police force, Chandra Bahadur Thapa, was appointed Home Secretary, and Gunja Man Singh, another Rana supporter of long standing, was appointed Cabinet Secretary.

indefinitely postponed the party's annual election meeting, giving the explanation that the expansion of membership had complicated the central organization's task in determining the number of delegates from each district. On March 1, the constitutionality of this decision was challenged by B. P. Koirala, who reiterated his views on the need to achieve progress through revolutionary means. The dispute between the two brothers, now brought into the open, divided both the party and the government into two factions.

The rift was fast approaching crisis proportions when the Indian Socialist leader Jaya Prakash Narayan intervened. At his invitation the Koirala brothers met with him in Calcutta. On March 8, they returned to Nepal together, after reaching an agreement under which the mutual recriminations indulged in by both factions were to be terminated. It was agreed that there should be an uncontested election of the party president, and that the same person should not hold that post and be Prime Minister as well. B. P. Koirala conceded that the party should not attempt to provide day-to-day guidance to the government in the execution of policy, while M. P. Koirala agreed that the government should be guided in general by the policies and programs adopted by the party's annual conference. Finally, it was agreed that the party's Working Committee should be constituted on the basis of joint consultations between the party president and the Prime Minister.[8]

The Calcutta agreement resulted in a temporary truce between the two brothers and a measure of harmony among the Nepali Congress representatives in the government. M. P. Koirala withdrew his candidacy for the party presidency and recommended the unanimous election of B. P. Koirala to that office. But B. P. Koirala's subsequent election did not halt the deteriorioration in his relations with M. P. Koirala, who showed less inclination than before to take his party colleagues in the Cabinet into confidence and sought to use King Tribhuwan as his main political support. His colleagues were not consulted in the selection of recipients of the honors and titles conferred by King Tribhuwan on his birthday, July 2, 1951, nor in the preparation of the Royal Address delivered at the inaugural session of the first Advisory Assembly on July 7.[9] This situation led to open disagreements between government factions on the Assembly floor. B. P. Koirala charged that the Royal Address failed to reflect the revolutionary spirit of the times, that its land reform programs were vague, and that its reference to the Constituent Assembly was casual.[10]

The political tug of war between the Koirala brothers began
in full earnest in the first week of July. The party Working
Committee (ten of whose fourteen members had been selected by
the Prime Minister) sided with the views of the party president.
The basic thesis of the Working Committee was that the government was too cautious in its approach to social and economic
reforms, and that it had encouraged the resurgence of conservative
and revivalist elements in Nepali society. In order to check this
dangerous trend, it was argued, the size and composition of the
Cabinet had to be revamped by dropping the independents. The
party president was, however, faced with a delicate political
situation, since M. P. Koirala was still the only Congress leader
acceptable to King Tribhuwan as Prime Minister.

Accordingly, the Working Committee decided on July 19 to
reduce the size of the Cabinet from eleven to seven members, and
a list of nominees—five Nepali Congress members and two
independents—was sent to the Prime Minister, who had stayed
away from the deliberations of the Committee. The Prime
Minister was reported to have objected to the inclusion of three
persons on this list—Suvarna Shamsher, Surya Prasad Upadhyaya,
and Ganesh Man Singh—whom he held "responsible for hetero-
geneity." [11]

On the following day, M. P. Koirala sent his reply to the
Working Committee, criticizing its directives on the reconstruction of the Cabinet. He alleged that (a) the Working
Committee had reached its decision without the participation of
other party Ministers,* (b) the reasons for the reconstitution of
the Cabinet had not been clarified, (c) the leader of the
government had not been given a free hand in the selection of the
Cabinet, (d) the principle of separation of the offices of the Prime
Minister and the party president had been violated by the latter's
dictation of the names for the new Cabinet, and (e) the clause in
the gentleman's agreement concluded between the two brothers
in March which stipulated that the party executive would not

---

* Apparently, at an earlier meeting the party Ministers had decided against
participating in the meetings of the Working Committee relating to the
reconstitution of the Cabinet, but had expressed their willingness to abide by the
decision of the party president, the Prime Minister, and other members not
associated with the Cabinet. Nepali Congress, *Nepali Congress ra Nepal ka Pradhan
Mantri* [The Nepali Congress and Nepal's Prime Minister] (Kathmandu, 1952), p. 7.

interfere in day-to-day administrative matters had been violated.

On receiving this reply, the Working Committee called upon M. P. Koirala and his colleagues to resign from the government by July 22. The Prime Minister challenged the authority of the nominated Working Committee to make this demand, and refused to follow its directives. He demanded instead an immediate meeting of the All-Nepal Nepali Congress Committee to settle the dispute. In reply the Working Committee called upon him and other Nepali Congress Ministers to submit their resignations to the King within forty-eight hours, and warned them that if they failed to do so, the Committee would be constrained to suspend them from active membership in the party for a period of three years.

Three Ministers—Suvarna Shamsher, Ganesh Man Singh, and Surya Prasad Upadhyaya—resigned from the Cabinet in compliance with the Working Committee's directives. But three other Ministers—Narada Muni Thulung, Mahendra Vikram Shah, and Mahavir Shamsher Rana—chose to follow the Prime Minister's lead and refused to resign, maintaining that the actions of the Working Committee were both unwarranted and unconstitutional.

With the exit of the three Nepali Congress Ministers from the Cabinet and the expulsion of the Prime Minister and other refractory Ministers from the party in the last week of July, 1952, the M. P. Koirala government ceased to function as a party government. The Prime Minister, at a meeting of his partisan followers on August 6, expressed his willingness to resign, but also accused the three former Ministers who had resigned of conspiring against him since February 21, the day he had announced the postponement of the annual session of the party. On August 10 the Prime Minister resigned from the government, together with the remaining members of the Cabinet. In a statement issued shortly thereafter he explained that he wished to attend the meeting of the All-Nepal Nepali Congress Committee, scheduled for early September, as a "common soldier of the Congress and not as the Prime Minister." [12]

Thus the career of the Nepali Congress government was marked from the very beginning by continual conflict between M. P. Koirala and B. P. Koirala and by serious collision between them as Prime Minister and party president. These, however, were not the only developments that jeopardized the functioning of the government. There had been two serious revolts against its authority—an armed uprising by a section of the government's special police force in January, 1952, and an unprecedented, paralyzing strike by low-grade employees in the Secretariat in June. Both of these events shed revealing, if somewhat disconcerting, light on the institutional weaknesses of the government.

THE RAKSHYA DAL REVOLT

The Rakshya Dal revolt, known more commonly if inappropriately as the K. I. Singh revolt, was a multifaceted conspiracy involving various factions. In the forefront were some unruly elements, including undisciplined and disaffected recruits from far eastern Nepal to the Rakshya Dal—the paramilitary police force that B. P. Koirala as Home Minister had created out of the military wing of the Nepali Congress. In the background, instigating the disaffected elements of the Rakshya Dal, were reactionary political elements ranging from revivalist Ranas to political malcontents.

On the night of January 21, 1952, a segment of the Rakshya Dal staged a revolt in Kathmandu and seized such key government offices and installations as the Secretariat, the prisons, the radio station, the wireless, and telephone offices, and the artillery and cartridge stores. Among those released from prison were K. I. Singh and his associates, who had been under detention in the capital since September, 1951, and A. P. Kharel and R. P. Rai, leaders of the secessionist Kirati organization, the Rashtriya Mahasabha ("National Council"). The rebels then acclaimed K. I. Singh as their leader, and A. P. Kharel and Tek Bahadur Malla as his assistants.

All these dramatic events took place at night, and the inhabitants of Kathmandu knew nothing about them until the following morning. All the Ministers had hurried to the royal palace that night, both for consultations and for protection. K. I. Singh summoned a Nepali Congress Minister, Ganesh Man Singh, and the Praja Parishad leader, Tanka Prasad Acharya, and appointed them as intermediaries between himself and King Tribhuwan. The two shuttled back and forth between the royal palace and the Secretariat (where Singh was stationed), carrying proposals and counterproposals. K. I. Singh presented a five-point program to King Tribhuwan.* But while these negotiations were

---

* Singh's demands were for establishment of an all-party representative government; convening a conference of all political parties to outline a program of action for the government; preparation of a five-year development plan with the coöperation of all political parties; establishment of friendly and equal relations with all neighboring countries; and performance of all actions peacefully. G. B. Devkota, *Nepal ko Rajnaitik Darpan* [Political Mirror of Nepal] (Kathmandu, 1959), p. 63.

underway, the state army, led by the King's personal bodyguards, was closing in on the Secretariat after recapturing most other government buildings in the city. By early afternoon of January 22 it was obvious that the negotiations with the King were leading nowhere. K. I. Singh and a band of his long-time followers fled through a back door of the Secretariat and succeeded in escaping to Tibet and eventually to Peking.

King Tribhuwan promptly declared a state of emergency and invested Prime Minister Koirala with full power to govern without the advice of the Cabinet, if deemed necessary. The Rashtriya Mahasabha, whose leaders had been involved in the uprising, was declared illegal on January 25, as was the Communist party for its alleged support of the revolt.

Although the K. I. Singh episode was easily suppressed, it dramatized the vulnerability of the government to an armed *coup,* highlighted the insensitivity of the government to developments within its own organs, and demonstrated the need for a reliable, well-disciplined army. The bulk of the Kirati section of the Rakshya Dal, which had played a prominent role in the K. I. Singh revolt, was disbanded, and the remaining units were incorporated into either the state army or the civil police.

An important aftermath of the K. I. Singh episode was the government's decision to invite an Indian military mission to Nepal to reorganize the state army along modern lines. Reorganization and modernization implied, in addition to improved military training, the end of Rana traditions in the army and the creation of a new military hierarchy based on merit rather than birth and capable of formulating basic military policies. The Indian Military Training Mission, which arrived on February 27, was originally expected to stay in Nepal for only one year; six years were to pass before it finally did leave, in 1958. With its arrival in Kathmandu, a new and explosive issue was inserted into Nepal's politics, as will be seen.

THE LOW-GRADE GOVERNMENT EMPLOYEES' STRIKE

Shortly after the revolution, a "Union of Low-Grade Government Employees" had been established in Kathmandu with the avowed purpose of securing improved salaries and working conditions. The main promoters of the union were associated with the "popular front" organizations of the Communist party. On March 2, 1951, Home Minister B. P. Koirala issued an order instructing government employees not to participate in any form of party politics or union activities. But the Union of Low-Grade Government Employees continued to function, and on May 25 presented a list of demands to the government, urging their early implementation. The government, however, paid no serious attention to the demands, probably under the impression that the union represented only a handful of professional agitators.

A year later, on May 16, 1952, the union presented its grievances to the M. P. Koirala government. This time it served notice that, unless appropriate measures were undertaken to meet its demands, a strike would commence from June 1. Once again the government ignored the union, minimizing its strength and appeal. As a result, a general strike of the low-grade government employees—mostly members of the clerical staff—began on June 1 in Kathmandu. Members of opposition political parties, together with students, provided the strikers with both moral and physical support, by serving as pickets and propagandists and by organizing a sympathy strike. On June 2 a government press communiqué notified all striking employees of their dismissal. The strike continued until King Tribhuwan intervened with a Royal Proclamation on June 6, under whose provisions Prime Minister M. P. Koirala announced revised pay scales for government employees, beginning with a minimum salary of thirty rupees per month.

The strike of the government employees, which was unprecedented in the history of public administration in Nepal, revealed the internal weakness of the administrative machinery as well as the penetration of party politics, especially of the pro-Communist variety, into its rank and file. The strike contributed to the deterioration in the position of the M. P. Koirala government that led finally to its resignation on August 10, 1952, and a sudden turnabout in the trend of postrevolutionary transitional politics in Nepal.

6

King Tribhuwan's Political Experiments

THE DEMOCRATIC experiment suffered a serious setback on August 14, 1952, when, contrary to expectations, King Tribhuwan did not invite the Nepali Congress to form a government to replace the M. P. Koirala Cabinet. Nor did he approach the leaders of the opposition parties. Instead, he decided to act as his own Prime Minister, assisted by a committee consisting of six Royal Councilors. In his proclamation, however, the King emphasized that the new political setup was a temporary arrangement which would be terminated as soon as an "influential, action-oriented, popular government" could be installed.[1]

THE ROYAL COUNCILORS' REGIME

The Royal Proclamation of August 14 defined the primary functions of the Councilors in the following terms: "eradication of bribery, corruption, and nepotism in the government, establishment of an independent judiciary, and an unambiguous definition of the people's fundamental rights." [2] In a notification published by the Royal Secretariat on August 26, the duties of the Councilors were set forth in more detail. They were charged with the responsibility of improving the administrative machinery in their respective departments, and were instructed to undertake a scientific reorganization of the departments by replacing dishonest and incompetent officials, and by drafting rules concerning

promotion, security of tenure, and grade levels of the administrative personnel.

There was no constitutional basis for the establishment of
the Royal Councilors' regime under the provisions of the 1951
Interim Government Act. To circumvent this legal difficulty,
King Tribhuwan promulgated a Special Circumstances Power
Act on September 9, 1952, effective retroactively, which suspended
all those clauses of the Interim Government Act referring to the
Cabinet.[3] According to this Act, all executive powers were vested
in the King, and the original concept of the King-in-Council was
at least temporarily nullified. Thus, the Special Circumstances
Power Act not only provided the legal foundation for the Royal
Councilors' regime, but also marked the introduction of the
King's absolute authority in political affairs.

The suspension of important clauses in the Interim Government Act made the continuation of the Advisory Assembly
politically incongruous. The second session of the Assembly was
scheduled to commence on August 16, but one of the King's first
actions after the establishment of the Councilors' regime was to
prorogue the Assembly. Three weeks later, the Assembly was
formally dissolved on the recommendation of the Councilors, and
the Nepal Interim Government (Second Amendment) Act, which
provided the legal basis for the Assembly, was suspended.[4]

The composition of the Royal Councilors' government is
given in table 3.*

POLITICAL BACKGROUND OF THE ROYAL COUNCIL

None of the Councilors had any significant political affiliations or influence to recommend their inclusion in the new
regime. Only two, Khadga Man Singh and Mahavir Shamsher
Rana, had some kind of political record. Singh, who was still
trying to find his political bearings after nearly twenty years in a
Rana prison for complicity in the "Prachanda Gorkha" plot, had
been an independent politician without party affiliations since
July, 1951. Mahavir, a C Rana member of the Nepali Congress,
resigned from the party a few hours before joining the Councilors' regime. In a public statement shortly thereafter he described

---

* The Royal Proclamation of August 14 named only five Councilors. In the
notification of the royal palace Secretariat dated August 26 a sixth participant,
Sharada Shamsher Rana, was added as an adviser and assigned the education
portfolio (*Nepal Gazette*, Vol. II, No. 3, Bhadra 10, 2009 [August 26, 1952]). The
Adviser was not officially part of the Royal Council and was not obligated to attend
Council meetings at the palace, but his powers over the Education Department
approximated those of the Councilors.

TABLE 3

THE ROYAL COUNCILORS' GOVERNMENT OF 1952–53

Name	Rank	Portfolios
Keshar Shamsher Rana	Chief councilor	General Administration; Finance; Defence
Mahavir Shamsher Rana	Councilor	Home; Planning and Development
Surendra Bahadur Basnyat	Councilor	Industry, Commerce, Food and Civil Supplies
Manik Lal Rajbhandari	Councilor	Public Works and Communication; Law and Parliamentary Affairs; Health and Local Self-Government
Khadga Man Singh	Councilor	Foreign Affairs; Revenue and Forest
Sharada Shamsher Rana	Adviser	Education

the Nepali Congress as a party which had become "inordinately weak as a result of intra-party jealousy, hostility and avarice" and his severance of relationship with it as "an attempt to rise above the recent events precipitated by low-level, stupid party politics." [5]

The other members were either old-line Ranas or non-Rana nobles under the former Rana regime. Keshar Shamsher and Sharada Shamsher were A Ranas. The former was related to King Tribhuwan by marriage and the latter was Mohan Shamsher's eldest son. The two non-Rana nobles were political newcomers. Surendra Bahadur Basnyat came from a non-Rana Kshatriya aristocratic family which had long been identified with the Rana military oligarchy. Manik Lal Rajbhandari belonged to a prominent Newar family long associated with the Rana civil administration. The career experiences and personal attitudes of both could be termed outdated.

THE FUNCTIONING OF THE ROYAL COUNCILORS' REGIME

Being little more than instruments of the King's will, the Royal Councilors had no personal axes, political or ideological, to grind. Consequently there were no internal conflicts to push them in diverse directions. But the functioning of the regime was severely hampered by King Tribhuwan's determination to reestablish a party government as soon as possible in view of his failing health. The King initiated a first round of negotiations with leaders of various politcial parties at Calcutta in January,

1953. The Calcutta negotiations produced no tangible result, probably because of B. P. Koirala's opposition to what he called the King's "individual approach," whereby the importance of individuals was exaggerated without reference to their position or influence in their respective party organizations. Probably, also, King Tribhuwan wished to delay making a final decision on the new government until the dispute between M. P. Koirala and the Nepali Congress could be settled, one way or the other. It was a foregone conclusion that M. P. Koirala was the King's first choice as Prime Minister. By February, however, relations between the M. P. Koirala group and the Nepali Congress had deteriorated 'further. On February 13 supporters of M. P. Koirala met in 'Kathmandu and decided to make a final break from the parent 'organization and form a new party of their own.

The Nepali Congress Working Committee, meeting in Kathmandu March 10–13, passed a resolution which welcomed the coöperation of other parties in its political programs, but ruled out any compromise with former members of the party "at the cost of democratic principles, and traditions of the party and its prestige and honor." [6] Clearly, this resolution destroyed any prospect of a *rapprochement* with M. P. Koirala at the party or the governmental level. Further, the Working Committee decided to press for an early termination of the Councilors' regime and appointed a special committee to draw up an action program. As a part of this studied hostility toward the Councilors' regime, B. P. Koirala refused to comply with a request from the palace for a list of party representatives to the proposed Advisory Assembly on the grounds that he had no information on the Assembly's composition, structure, and powers.

It was in this context that King Tribhuwan initiated a second round of political negotiations. Prominently involved in these discussions were leaders of other political parties, such as D. R. Regmi, of the Nepali National Congress, and Tanka Prasad Acharya, of the Praja Parishad. Various political formulas were under consideration, such as a Cabinet of popular persons (favored by King Tribhuwan), a coalition Cabinet of two or three major parties (favored by M. P. Koirala), and an Executive Council consisting of representatives of several parties.[7] Once again the negotiations were inconclusive and the life of the Councilors' regime was extended.

King Tribhuwan continued his search for a representative government. In a New Year (Nepali calendar) message to the nation on April 12 he reiterated his desire to usher in a popular ministry the moment it was feasible. The Royal Councilors' regime was at this time badly shaken by the discovery of an anti-government plot in the police force, believed to have been instigated by revivalist political elements seeking to organize political cells among the police with the ultimate objective of effecting a revolt. Eighty arrests had been made in connection with this conspiracy.

Meanwhile the Councilors' regime had to deal with unrest among peasants in Taulihawa and Pokhara subdistricts, and, more seriously, a "no rent" campaign launched by the Nepali Congress in eastern Nepal. The final date for the annual payment of land revenue to the government was May 15. The Nepali Congress leaders exhorted the peasants to participate in a civil disobedience movement against the government by refusing to pay the revenue until their demands for agrarian reforms were met.

The most serious opposition to the Councilors' regime came from M. P. Koirala, who had earlier been one of its few supporters. His faction of the Nepali Congress met at Birganj on April 30 and formed the National Democratic Party, electing him as its president and Mahendra Vikram Shah as general secretary. In an inaugural address M. P. Koirala charged that corruption and inefficiency were rampant among government officials both in the capital and in the districts. He asserted that the King was helpless to "stop the rot" without a popular Cabinet and urged him to institute such a Cabinet immediately.

Thus the stage was set for a third round of negotiations in Kathmandu during the middle of May. King Tribhuwan seems to have continued to insist upon a Cabinet consisting of political leaders nominated on a personal rather than a party basis. In any case, Suvarna Shamsher and Surya Prasad Upadhyaya, two Nepali Congress leaders who were reported to have been selected for inclusion in the proposed Cabinet, issued a joint statement on May 22, announcing their refusal to join a government composed on a personal basis. A few days later B. P. Koirala criticized such a basis for the proposed government as impossible and unrealistic, and demanded instead that the majority party—by implication, the Nepali Congress—be allowed to form a popular government in coöperation with other parties sharing its views.

On June 15, however, King Tribhuwan ended the Councilors' regime and again entrusted the reins of administration to M. P. Koirala, and thus brought the newly organized National Democratic party to power.

THE SECOND M. P. KOIRALA GOVERNMENT

The sudden assumption of office by M. P. Koirala's new party, barely six weeks after its inception, led to a rapid expansion of its ranks. Political fortune seekers and opportunists of all kinds were able to attain easy access to the party's inner sanctum. This stream of new members led M. P. Koirala to claim a primary position for the National Democratic party in Nepal's politics, followed, according to his scale, by the Nepali Congress, the Gorkha Parishad ("Gorkha Council"), and the Communist party, in that order. Although King Tribhuwan did not publicly accept M. P. Koirala's assessment of his party's influence, the haste and speed with which he installed the party in power exceeded the wildest expectations of the membership.

The Royal Proclamation of June 15, 1953, which established the new government, reflected the King's dilemma and also conveyed his sense of despair at the lack of political unity in the country:

It is difficult to decide which party is great and which small until general elections are held. And, as all parties claim to be the largest of all, our difficulty is aggravated rather than simplified. If the politicians had only given up their individual and partisan outlooks and taken a national outlook, this problem would have been solved and our burden, too, which we have been compelled to carry on contrary to our taste and health, would have been lightened. The Prime Minister shall, with our consent, be entitled . . . to make any additions or subtractions in the Cabinet or make any alteration in the portfolios of the Ministers as and when necessary . . .[8]

The King's pronouncements highlighted four important points: (1) The present Cabinet was a temporary arrangement until it could be further expanded. (2) Party leaders and influential independents were to continue negotiations with M. P. Koirala. (3) M. P. Koirala had *carte blanche* to make changes in the Cabinet. (4) Independents were to be accorded representation in the Cabinet. M. P. Koirala, thus, in his dual role as leader of the government and dispensor of ministerial posts, emerged as the strongest authority after the King.

These developments resulted in a highly unstable political equilibrium, in which all parties were involved in a scramble for office. Political alliances were formed and dissolved as and when they maximized the bargaining power of the participant groups, and the party newspapers alternately cooed political amity and spewed political blackmail. The Gorkha Parishad, stung by M. P. Koirala's refusal to negotiate with it, asserted its right to form a one-party government. The independents—a mixed crowd of businessmen, landlords, educators, and eccentrics—began to organize themselves, rather paradoxically, into a pressure group, thus compounding the political instability. These independents, playing the role of political mediators, helped undermine the prestige and reputation of the political parties by their self-righteous, "holier than thou" attitude in which they rationalized their own existence by condemning the party system and questioning the appropriateness of a democratic system in the context of existing social, educational, and economic conditions in Nepal. The democratic experiment should be scrapped, they argued, and Nepal should revert to the absolute but benevolent rule of the King.

THE COMPOSITION OF THE NATIONAL DEMOCRATIC PARTY CABINET

The unusual haste and secrecy with which the new Cabinet was selected suggested that M. P. Koirala conceived of it not merely as a tentative political arrangement, but also as a *fait accompli,* with which his political opponents would be forced to reckon.* Predictably, potential challengers to the Prime Minister's leadership were excluded from the Cabinet, which was composed of party colleagues of limited political stature. The Ministers and their respective portfolios are listed in table 4.

There were only two newcomers in the Cabinet. Tripurawar Singh, a Kathmandu political leader and one of the organizers of the Praja Panchayat in 1948, had been associated with the Kathmandu Valley branch of the Nepali Congress since 1951, and had supported M. P. Koirala during the latter's dispute with the party executive in 1952. Suryanath Das Yadav, a landlord from Saptari in eastern Nepal, was a friend of the Koirala family and

---

* An editorial in *Nepal Pukar,* the Nepali Congress organ, stated on June 25, 1953: "Nobody had any inkling of a new cabinet in the making until a few hours before it was actually formed. In fact, even the Royal Councilors came to know about it only an hour before it was sworn in. Tanka Prasad and Dilli Raman Regmi had also been invited to the Royal Palace, and they learned only there that they were to take part in the swearing-in ceremony as members of the new Cabinet. But these two gentlemen did not want to join the government in haste, and returned without taking part in the ceremony. On July 20, D. R. Regmi and Tanka Prasad issued a joint statement, saying that they returned from the Royal Palace without taking part in the swearing-in ceremony because M. P. Koirala had violated the previously agreed-upon basis of the new government." Quoted in Devkota, *Rajnaitik Darpan,* p. 218.

TABLE 4

THE NATIONAL DEMOCRATIC PARTY CABINET, 1953

Name	Rank	Portfolio
M. P. Koirala	Prime Minister	Foreign Affairs; General Administration; Finance
Narada Muni Thulung	Minister	Defence; Revenue; Forests
Tripurawar Singh	Minister	Health and Local Self-Government; Education; Public Works; Communications
Suryanath Das Yadav	Minister	Law and Parliamentary Affairs
Mahavir Shamsher Rana	Minister	Home; Planning and Development; Industry and Commerce; Civil Supplies and Food

had no significant political background. He had joined the Nepali Congress after the 1950 revolution, and had supported M. P. Koirala in his dispute with the Working Committee. None of the Ministers in the Cabinet, with the possible exception of Mahavir Shamsher, who was a special favorite of King Tribhuwan, would have had the audacity to assert themselves against the Prime Minister, to whom they owed their elevation to high office.

THE FUNCTIONING OF THE NATIONAL DEMOCRATIC PARTY GOVERNMENT

Soon after its inauguration in June, 1953, the new government was faced with problems of financial instability in the capital and lawlessness in certain districts in western Nepal. The exchange rate between Nepali and Indian currency had reached the record high of 162 Nepali rupees for 100 Indian rupees. The price of imported goods had gone up, and the business community was hard hit by the adverse exchange rate. The government called a hurried conference of officials, political leaders, economists, and businessmen on July 4 to consider ways and means of handling the currency crisis, but nothing consequential resulted from these deliberations.[9]

Even more embarrassing to the government was the incident in western Nepal in which a well-known local figure, Bhim Datta Pant, and a large number of followers attacked the police station at Brahmadev Mandi and captured the government treasury.[10] Official sources depicted Pant's activities as pure, unmitigated brigandage, but in some political circles he was considered to be a

Communist-oriented social leveler following the example K. I. Singh had set earlier in the same region. Pant's armed defiance of the government spread to other towns, including Billary and Kanchanpur, and the central authorities found it difficult to handle the situation because of the problems in transporting troops to this area over rugged mountainous terrain from Kathmandu.

Beset with these problems, M. P. Koirala visited Prime Minister Nehru in Delhi on July 19. At the request of the Nepali Prime Minister, the Uttar Pradesh Provincial Armed Constabulary crossed into Nepali territory and joined with Nepali troops in mopping-up operations against Bhim Datta Pant. In the first encounter with the insurgents, two rebels were reported killed, 50 injured, and 276 taken prisoner.[11] Pant himself was killed on August 23 in an accidental shooting.

In his conversations with Nehru, M. P. Koirala also mentioned that a blueprint for Nepal's first Five-Year Plan had been prepared and that one of the objects of his visit to Delhi was to seek India's guidance and assistance in the implementation of this plan. The news of the existence of a draft plan was heartening to the Nepalese, but nothing further was heard of it after the Prime Minister's return to Kathmandu. Nor was M. P. Koirala's record on his own order of priorities in meeting Nepal's most pressing problems any more impressive. His program had listed: administrative reorganization, including the army and police; land reforms; and development of communications, industrialization, and education. He proposed to tackle the land problem by converting *Birta* (tax-free) lands to *Raikar* (government) lands, and then granting permanent tenancy rights to the tillers. He also stated his intention to introduce income taxes and death duties as one means of diminishing differences in economic levels. But none of these programs was implemented, in part because of the Prime Minister's preoccupation with complex political negotiations.

Early in its existence, the new government also had to face a public agitation launched by the Nepali Congress in Biratnagar in support of a no-rent campaign. The day before the inauguration of the new government, fourteen Nepali Congress *satyagrahis* were arrested in Biratnagar. More troop reinforcements were flown out to Biratnagar from Kathmandu, and the Commander in Chief himself was present. The formation of the new government, however, slowed the tempo of the Nepali Congress agitation, which had been mainly directed against the continuation of the Councilors' regime. On August 1 all the *détenus* were released and the government claimed that "the no-rent campaign had failed, as it had been able to realise the revenue." [12]

From 1953 until his death in March, 1955, King Tribhuwan's health was an important factor in Nepali politics. The King was physically unable to exercise direct authority over the government, and was forced to delegate sweeping powers to the Prime Minister. The removal of the King as an active mediator between the various political factions left the other political parties at a disadvantage in negotiations with M. P. Koirala, whose background and career often did not inspire a sense of mutual trust.

King Tribhuwan flew to Calcutta for a medical check-up on August 12, 1953, and remained there for more than a month. He then returned to Kathmandu, but only for three days before leaving for Europe, where he stayed until January 4, 1954. During this time, most political alignments and schisms were directly related to the King's itinerary. On the eve of his departure for Europe and on his return, political activities reached feverish heights, in contrast to more routine forms during his absence.

On September 1, 1953, municipal elections were held in Kathmandu, the first since 1951. Seventy-three candidates contested the elections, nearly all of them as independents. The active politicking of the independents in the capital had diminished the prestige of political parties, and intraparty squabbles had made matters even worse. Most candidates, therefore, chose to play down their party affiliations. All parties, however, including the banned Communist party, actively campaigned for their favorites or protégés. The attention of the entire country was focused on the election, and there was a predisposition in many quarters to read the election results as a political barometer for all of Nepal. Kathmandu was the nerve center of political activity both for and against the government, and local agitation there had caused, either directly or indirectly, the dissolution of several governments. In this context the municipal elections assumed national importance, and the parties conducted vigorous campaigns. Nearly 53 per cent of the estimated 56,000 voters went to the polls. Six of the seven Communist-supported candidates won; the Nepali Congress and the Nepal Praja Parishad each supported four victorious candidates, and the Gorkha Parishad one; the remaining four winners were nonaffiliated independents.[13]

The results of the municipal elections clearly indicated the National Democratic party's lack of support in Kathmadnu. M. P. Koirala correctly interpreted this as demonstrating the necessity to strengthen his Cabinet by including representatives of other parties. On September 12, he flew to Calcutta to consult with

King Tribhuwan, who had already decided to go to Switzerland for further medical treatment. The Nepali Congress and other political parties, alarmed by the victory of the Communist-supported candidates, exerted pressure on the King and M. P. Koirala to recompose the existing Cabinet before the King's departure for Europe.

On September 17, King Tribhuwan returned to Kathmandu to make the necessary political arrangements before proceeding to Europe. But to the dismay and annoyance of the other parties, he left for Europe on September 21 without effecting changes in the Cabinet. A Regency Council, consisting of the two Queens and Crown Prince Mahendra, was established to act on the King's behalf in his absence. The Council was granted only strictly limited powers, however, and M. P. Koirala was entrusted with full responsibility for making changes in the Cabinet at his discretion.[14]

THE NATIONAL COALITION CABINET

When King Tribhuwan returned to Nepal in January, 1954, the scene had been set for yet another change of governments. On February 18, Nepal's "National Day," a Royal Proclamation terminated the one-party National Democratic party government and introduced a novel experiment—a four-party coalition government. The new government was termed a "national coalition." The King demonstrated sensitivity to the prevailing political mood in Nepal when he said:

The atmosphere of political instability and uncertainty that has arisen in the country today can benefit neither the country nor the people. If this uncertainty continues for long, it will prove fatal . . . We understand that the existing situation in the country has filled the people with a sense of frustration and apathy.[15]

Nevertheless, it was obvious that the "national" character of the government was in some respects more hypothetical than real. The Nepali Congress was not included, although three portfolios were left unfilled in the hope that the Congress would elect to participate at a later date. Moreover, the illegal but active Communist party and the Gorkha Parishad—the parties that had been most vociferous in their demand for an all-party government —had been debarred even from the preliminary negotiations leading to the formation of the new government.

Indeed, it was apparent that M. P. Koirala, the agent chosen by King Tribhuwan to achieve his objective, viewed political developments in a somewhat different light. For him the concept of a national government was useful as a means of maneuvering different parties into positions of subservience to himself and the National Democratic party. In his negotiations with the Nepali Congress, for instance, he acted with a great deal of ambivalence, as if both desiring and fearing Nepali Congress participation. When the Nepali Congress Working Committee nominated representatives to participate in the proposed new government, M. P. Koirala's sense of insecurity was enhanced. He suddenly dropped his plans for a coalition with the Nepali Congress and proposed instead the establishment of a Cabinet on an "individual basis," although the new Ministers were to be "drawn from different parties." [16]

Following this policy reversal, M. P. Koirala started serious negotiations with the parties which, more pliable than the Nepali Congress, could be satisfied with one representative in the Cabinet. The three parties which agreed to participate on this basis were the Nepali National Congress (D. R. Regmi faction), All-Nepal Jana ("Peoples'") Congress, and the Praja Parishad. The first two, it may be recalled, were splinter organizations that had broken off from the Nepali Congress because of personal disagreements with the party leadership. The Praja Parishad, the oldest political party in Nepal, had the largest number of "jail-returned patriots" in its ranks, but having never really developed as a mass party, it lacked a popular base and a coherent ideology.

M. P. Koirala seems to have assumed that the inclusion of representatives of these parties in his Cabinet was not a threat to his own leadership. But to reinforce his position even further, he included two Rana independents—although, in fact, both were more his partisans than independents—in addition to one more nominee of his own party. Thus, in a seven-man Cabinet, he was usually assured of the support of at least four members. The assignment of portfolios was also contrived to secure a maximum number of key departments for the Prime Minister and his supporters, as can be seen in table 5.

THE FUNCTIONING OF THE NATIONAL GOVERNMENT

The new government was bedeviled from the very outset by King Tribuwan's continued illness, and by intra-Cabinet disputes, which later manifested themselves on a magnified scale in the meetings of the Advisory Assembly. Early in June, 1954, the

TABLE 5

THE NATIONAL COALITION CABINET, 1954

Name	Rank	Portfolio	Political affiliation
M. P. Koirala	Prime Minister	General Administration; Finance	National Democratic
Mahavir Shamsher Rana	Minister	Planning and Development; Agriculture and Food; Industry and Commerce	Independent
Narada Muni Thulung	Minister	Revenue; Forests	National Democratic
Keshar Shamsher Rana	Minister	Defence	Independent
Dilli Raman Regmi	Minister	Foreign Affairs; Education; Health; Local Self-Government	Nepali National Congress
Tanka Prasad Acharya	Minister	Home	Praja Parishad
Bhadrakali Mishra	Minister	Public Works; Communications; Law and Parliamentary Affairs	All-Nepal Jana Congress

King's condition took a turn for the worse. The people of Kathmandu, perturbed over his failing health, offered mass prayers and performed propitiatory rites. More than a hundred priests offered prayers at the Hindu temples of Guheshwari and Pashupatinath, and the Buddhist monks performed special ceremonies at Swayambhunath. This demonstration of anxiety was partly political in motivation. The public felt that the King was the only one who could save the country from the malaise created by the political parties, while the party leaders, including members of the coalition Cabinet, apprehended that the Prime Minister would be invested with special powers as a result of the King's increasing ill health. King Tribhuwan's bestowal of the military title of General of the Army on M. P. Koirala on July 9, 1954, had, in particular, aroused speculations and rumors concerning this possibility.

The representatives of the other parties in the Cabinet showed resentment of M. P. Koirala's dominant position from the very beginning. Unable to unseat him through direct action, they strove to undermine his position from within. Tanka Prasad

Acharya, the Praja Parishad member of the Cabinet, took the initiative in challenging the Prime Minister's authority, demanding an immediate reorganization of the Secretariat, the preparation of the budget and a proper audit of accounts, an end to overcentralized control by the Prime Minister's department of General Administration, a better definition and distribution of powers, the establishment of an effective and independent anti-corruption department, and proper coördination among the various Ministers and political parties in the Advisory Assembly.[17]

Controversy within the Cabinet came to public attention in a rather abrupt manner in August, when Home Minister Tanka Prasad Acharya issued an order to his departmental staff requiring them to obtain his permission if they wished to see the Prime Minister on official business. He contended that such an order was necessary because the Prime Minister had been tampering with his department. This crisis arose as a result of the Home Secretary's issuing instructions to the staff that verbal orders of the Home Minister should not be implemented since they occasionally happened to be contradictory. Tanka Prasad Acharya charged that the Prime Minister had instigated the Home Secretary to issue this unprecedented order. In retaliation he prohibited his staff from meeting the Prime Minister without permission. King Tribhuwan had to intervene in order to reconcile his Ministers. The unfortunate Home Secretary, caught in the ministerial tangle, was shunted off to another department.

THE SECOND ADVISORY ASSEMBLY

Animosities within the Cabinet were further heightened over the composition of the Advisory Assembly. On April 13, 1954, King Tribhuwan issued a Royal Proclamation announcing the formation of an expanded Advisory Assembly to "associate a greater measure of public coöperation with the government" and to "promote the growth of democratic institutions in the country." [18] This second Advisory Assembly was conceived on a much wider scale than its predecessor of 1952. Members were nominated from every administrative district and, for the first time, special representation was provided for women, peasants, merchants, labor, the depressed classes (i.e., untouchables), and intellectuals. The size of the Assembly was increased from 61 members (14 Ministers and 47 nominees) in 1952 to 113 members (7 Ministers and 106 nominees) in 1954. All political parties except the Communists were granted representation, based on an arbitrary assessment of their comparative strength in the country. Among the government parties, the National Democratic party was allotted 45 seats, the Praja Parishad 12, the Nepali National Congress 8, and the Jana Congress one; among the opposition parties, the Nepali Congress received 11 seats and the Gorkha Parishad one.[19] The remainder, presumably, were independents nominated on the recommendation of the district Bada Hakim or at the discretion of the King. Later, on May 11, eight more names were added to the list of 113 members, and the representation of the Praja Parishad and the Jana Congress was increased.

The Nepali Congress refused to participate in the Assembly, on the grounds that it was underrepresented, while the National Democratic party was overrepresented. And even one of the four ruling parties—the Nepali National Congress—refused to join the Assembly, while the Praja Parishad and the Jana Congress accepted their nominations only after objecting to the preponderant representation allotted to the Prime Minister's party. The Assembly began with such lukewarm public enthusiasm that only 61 out of 121 members were present at its inauguration on May 28.

Balchandra Sharma, the general secretary of the National Democratic party, was elected chairman of the Assembly on June 1, and M. P. Koirala, in his capacity as Prime Minister, became the leader of the house. The Assembly proceedings were marked by vigorous debates and, frequently, sharp criticisms of the government. Widely rumored rifts in the Cabinet encouraged party representatives in the Assembly to engage freely in attacks on some Ministers. Indeed, the party whips exerted only nominal control over party members, most of whom tended to act in their individual capacities rather than under party discipline, and the government suffered repeated defeats in the Assembly. On July 23, for instance, the Prime Minister presented the statement of expenditures for the financial year 1953–54 (which, according to the Nepali calendar, ended on July 16) and the statement of estimated expenditures for the first four months of the current year. One member, Krishna Gopal Tandon, demanded twenty-four hours to study the Accounts Bill, to which the government bench did not agree. Another member then put a resolution to postpone consideration of the bill for twenty-four hours, which was passed. The Prime Minister stormed out of the Assembly hall angrily, and relations between him and other Assembly members became increasingly strained as weeks passed by. Again, on August 5, Home Minister Tanka Prasad Acharya's bill giving extensive powers to magistrates and public officers was rejected by a majority in the Assembly.*

The generally tense relations between the government and the Assembly was also brought into the open when Balchandra Sharma, the Speaker of the Assembly and chairman of the fifteen-member Flood Relief Committee constituted by the house, resigned from the chairmanship of the committee as a protest against the lack of coöperation from the Cabinet. The first session of the Assembly was recessed on August 17 to enable members to perform relief work in various flood-devastated areas of the country.

This session of the Assembly had demonstrated widespread disaffection in the ranks of the government parties. Overtly critical and often hostile, the members reflected the temper of the people whom they were supposed to represent and with whom they were certainly in more direct contact than the Ministers. The pattern of the debates assumed the form of a struggle between the government benches and various members who often treated the government as if it were on trial charged with incompetence and antinational intentions. If King Tribhuwan and his Ministers had ever hoped that the Assembly would serve as a ballast to the shaky coalition, these hopes had disappeared by the end of the first session. But the Ministers themselves were far from blameless. Frequently, in order to counteract the Prime Minister's majority in the Cabinet, they encouraged their own party members in the Assembly to take an antigovernment position in this larger arena, where they could be certain of support from rebels in the Prime Minister's party as well as from their own ranks.

Intra-Cabinet disputes continued after the adjournment of the Assembly and were, in fact, intensified in the fall of 1954. On September 25, King Tribhuwan announced the appointment of a three-member Regency Council while he was undergoing prolonged medical treatment in Switzerland; its powers were broadly similar to those of its predecessor in 1953. Crown Prince Mahendra was the chairman of the Council, assisted by his brothers, Prince Himalaya and Prince Vasundhara.

King Tribhuwan's departure for Europe was delayed at the last moment by a new ministerial crisis. Prime Minister M. P.

---

* Prime Minister M. P. Koirala told journalists on August 8 that the government's defeats in the Assembly were largely owing to the members' lack of familiarity with parliamentary procedures. The members of the Assembly took strong exception to these remarks. Forty-three of them, including fourteen members of the Prime Minister's own party and eighteen from other government parties, issued a statement demanding that M. P. Koirala retract his "undignified and unparliamentary remarks." *The Statesman* (Calcutta), August 13, 1954.

Koirala told journalists on September 28 that he would quit office
if proper homogeneity and understanding were not forthcoming
from his colleagues in the Cabinet, and that he had informed the
King of his intention. The King asked all the Ministers to place
their differences before him at a special meeting, and a tentative
reconciliation was achieved. Later, the Ministers, under the
leadership of the Prime Minister, issued a joint statement:

Minor differences of opinion are unavoidable, but press reports in this
connection have been unduly exaggerated. To remove any misunderstanding in the public mind, we feel it our duty to announce that we
have renewed our pledges before His Majesty the King, prior to his
departure, to work in absolute harmony and cooperation for the
proper functioning of the government and for the peace and prosperity of the country.[20]

King Tribhuwan then bade farewell to his subjects in a broadcast on October 2, in which he said that members of the Cabinet
had pledged themselves to work in harmony. He left for Switzerland the next day, on a trip from which he was never to return.

The months of October and November were particularly
difficult for the coalition government. There was widespread
unrest in various parts of the country. A *satyagraha* movement was
carried on for twenty-four days in Palhi, in western Nepal—and
this under the leadership of the local branch of the National
Democratic party! A platoon of the Sher battalion had to be
dispatched to Dang, also in the west, to assist troops already
engaged in suppressing troublemakers in the area. The situation
in Bardia in the western Terai was also reported to be explosive.
Followers of K. I. Singh were rumored to be active in north-
eastern Nepal, and a strong police force had to be sent to
Dhankuta to suppress the activities of A. P. Kharel.

Tanka Prasad Acharya, the Home Minister, suggested an
immediate political conference of all democratic parties to decide
how to combat these subversive elements, thus indicating a lack
of confidence in the government's ability and competence to
handle the situation. On October 10, the Working Committee of
the National Democratic party met in Kathmandu under the
chairmanship of M. P. Koirala. A resolution was adopted which
viewed the situation in Nepal with great concern "particularly
because of the present political atmosphere in which a general
feeling of hostility and indifference towards the government
predominates." [21] The party admitted that no progress had been
made in implementing the party program, but the blame was
placed on "political elements which had recently joined the
Cabinet." This ran counter to the spirit of the pledge of harmony

and coöperation signed by all the Ministers on October 2, and engendered further suspicion and hostility among the other constituent parties in the Cabinet.

It was under such unfavorable auspices that the second session of the Advisory Assembly was opened by Crown Prince Mahendra on November 17. Discussion of his inaugural speech continued until November 23. Although the session was sparsely attended, some 134 amendments were moved, relating to criticisms of government policy toward land reforms, exchange control, and flood-relief measures. One of the significant actions of the Assembly at this time was the approval of a resolution recommending that any social discrimination among various castes at public places be made punishable, but this suggestion was ignored by the government.

In the meantime, the Cabinet seemed to be heading for another crisis. On December 11, Prime Minister M. P. Koirala made a strong plea for a merger of all major parties, on the grounds that the necessary coöperation and homogeneity was lacking in the Cabinet. Accusing the supporters of some Cabinet members of being more hostile than helpful, he said that he was no longer capable of leading such a Cabinet and that he would decide the future of the government in another fortnight. On December 23, the Cabinet suffered yet another crushing defeat in the Assembly on a nonofficial resolution demanding the cancellation of the government's power to enact laws without consulting the Assembly when it was not in session. This defeat was the first in this session and the sixth suffered by the government. Although, technically, the government was not responsible to the Assembly, this particular setback was a severe blow to the prestige of the Cabinet. The fact that a nominated Assembly with a majority of government party members could question the *bona fides* of the government to enact legislation only reflected the deeper dissensions in the Cabinet itself.

This became even more apparent on December 17, when Tanka Prasad Acharya, the Home Minister, secured the Regency Council's dismissal of the Cabinet Secretary, an M. P. Koirala appointee, on charges of nepotism and favoritism. Countering the Prime Minister's call for a merger of the major parties, Tanka Prasad Acharya called for a national democratic convention, from which Communists and reactionaries would be excluded, to achieve unity among the parties. He was instrumental in planning a meeting of Praja Parishad, Jana Congress, Nepali National Congress, and Nepali Congress leaders to explore ways and means for forging unity among their parties—obviously in an attempt to isolate the National Democratic party. In retaliation, the General Council of the National Democratic party passed a resolution on December 30 charging that "it was impossible to work in the government in the present form." [22] By all indications, the stage seemed to be set for the final showdown between the Prime Minister and his colleagues in the Cabinet.

THE NEPALI CONGRESS SATYAGRAHA

While the government was thus beset by conflicts in the Cabinet and in the Assembly, the Nepali Congress was preparing a test of strength by launching a *satyagraha* campaign for "safeguarding the interests of democracy." On October 18, the party executive announced a six-point program as the basis of its agitational campaign: preservation of peace and security, protection of life and property; protection of civic rights and establishment of an independent judiciary; abolition of the "farcical" Advisory Assembly, and the holding of early general elections; reduction in the price of rice and the generally high price level; currency control and reduction in the exchange rate; and protection of national independence and preservation of the "prestige" of the nation.[23]

These demands drew strong criticisms from M. P. Koirala and his party, and from the Gorkha Parishad and the Communist-controlled Janadhikar Surakshya Samiti ("People's Rights Protection Committee"). The Prime Minister suggested that the Nepali Congress could implement its demands by joining the ranks of the government and shouldering responsibility for them. The Gorkha Parishad leader, Ranadhir Subba, characterized the demands as "all vague except the one for an independent judiciary." [24] He suggested that the different political parties should set January, 1956, as the goal for holding general elections and, in the meanwhile, form a caretaker government for the next twelve months. The Janadhikar Surakshya Samiti accused the Nepali Congress of trying to improve its bargaining position in future negotiations with M. P. Koirala.

Although support from other political parties was lacking, the Nepali Congress announced a nationwide *satyagraha* movement, to commence on January 10, 1955. Inaugurating the campaign, B. P. Koirala appealed to the people to refuse to pay taxes, to boycott government offices, and to observe general strikes. The Communist-dominated Janadhikar Surakshya Samiti joined the movement on its own volition, despite its earlier criticisms. After two days, B. P. Koirala called off the movement, having received a letter from Crown Prince Mahendra stating that the Nepali Congress' demands for an independent judiciary, general elections, and peaceful conditions in the country would be implemented shortly. The party leaders hailed their victory, but on the same day angry Communist-led mobs raided the Nepali Congress office in Kathmandu, charging the party with "betraying the people's movement." The pro-Communist group continued its campaign independently and violence soon broke out. Twenty-six persons were arrested on January 17, including the sons of Prime Minister M. P. Koirala and Foreign Minister D. R. Regmi.[25]

The Nepali Congress *satyagraha* heightened the intra-Cabinet disputes further. On the eve of the *satyagraha,* the Prime Minister secured an order from the Regency Council relieving Tanka Prasad Acharya and Bhadrakali Mishra of their portfolios and took personal charge of the Home Ministry. Both Acharya and Mishra continued as members of the Cabinet. On January 17, however, Tanka Prasad Acharya staged a walkout from the Assembly with five members of his party when the Speaker disallowed an adjournment motion, introduced by R. P. Kharel of the Praja Parishad, which maintained that the Regency Council's assurances to the Nepali Congress on the implementation of the party's demands amounted to a censure of the government.

On January 23, M. P. Koirala, in his additional capacity as Finance Minister, presented the government budget for 1954–55 to the Assembly. The budget was strongly cirticized in the Assembly as thirty-six members, representing all political parties, expressed their discontent. Even a member of the Prime Minister's party joined the chorus, denouncing the budget as "an insult to the party manifesto and resolutions." [26] The provisions calling for a 10 per cent surcharge on land revenue and the exemption of *Birta* land from taxation were bitterly criticized. Violent scenes accompanied the debate.

Finally, the Prime Minister dropped the proposed land revenue surcharge and introduced provisions for income tax and for taxation of *Birta* lands. On January 30, Foreign Minister D. R. Regmi moved demands for grants for the Foreign Affairs Ministry. Seven cut motions were tabled, five of which were withdrawn; but two introduced by R. P. Kharel of the Praja Parishad were passed by a vote of 43 to 39, with members of the Praja Parishad and the Jana Congress and even some of the National Democratic party voting with the opposition. That evening, M. P. Koirala submitted the resignation of the coalition Cabinet to the Regency Council. As the Council was not empowered to accept the resignation, it was referred to King Tribhuwan in Europe. Meanwhile, the Council rejected a petition by the National Democratic party calling for the dissolution of the Assembly, but agreed to its adjournment for one month.

The government was in a state of chaos. The adjournment of the Assembly forced the deferment of the payment of government bills, since the sanction of the Regency Council for the budget of the current year had not been received and, indeed, could not be until the Assembly had been prorogued rather than adjourned. At the request of the Prime Minister, Crown Prince Mahendra finally prorogued the Assembly on February 9 and ordered the dismissal of Tanka Prasad Acharya and Bhadrakali Mishra from the Cabinet. On the same day he left Kathmandu for Europe to seek further instructions from King Tribhuwan.

Crown Prince Mahendra returned from Europe on February 16. Two days later—on the fourth anniversary of the introduction of democracy—King Tribhuwan's message, in which he delegated full royal powers to the Crown Prince, was broadcast over Radio Nepal. On the same day, Crown Prince Mahendra dissolved the Regency Council. In a message to the nation he first enumerated all the steps he had taken as chairman of the Regency Council and then announced that he would take personal control of the Anti-Corruption Department, Public Service Commission, Central Intelligence Bureau, and Civil Servants' Registration Office. He further pledged to remove, within fifteen days, any misunderstanding over the independence of the Supreme Court. In his assessment of the past four years, he indicated a skeptical attitude toward democratic experimentation in Nepal. On March 2, he accepted the long pending resignation of the Prime Minister and his Cabinet, thus bringing to a dismal conclusion both the "national coalition" political experiment and the postrevolutionary Tribhuwan era.

7

Party Politics in Postrevolutionary Nepal

PRIME MINISTER MOHAN SHAMSHER'S announcement on January 8, 1951, accepting New Delhi's proposal for the gradual liberalization of Nepal's political system, and the subsequent release of all political prisoners on January 17, unleashed a wave of frenetic activity in Kathmandu. Freed along with the rest were such prominent anti-Rana leaders as Tanka Prasad Acharya, Chuda Prasad Sharma and Ram Hari Sharma of the Nepal Praja Parishad, Khadga Man Singh of the Prachanda Gorkha, Ganesh Man Singh of the Nepali Congress, and Tripurawar Singh of the Nepal Praja Panchayat.

The interval between the release of the prisoners and King Tribhuwan's triumphant return to Kathmandu provided local political elites with a month in which to organize before the Nepali exiles, now free to return and mostly affiliated with the Nepali Congress, could gather again on the scene. Since the Nepali Congress did not have an official unit in the capital, the Kathmandu political leaders had no reliable source of information on the negotiations under way in New Delhi between the King, the Ranas, and the Nepali Congress.* Most of the old-time leaders, including Tanka Prasad, were undecided as to whether they should revive their own political organizations or join with the Nepali Congress. Two questions were uppermost in their

---

* The only Nepali Congress leader of any significance in Kathmandu at this time was Ganesh Man Singh. He had been arrested by the Rana government in September, 1950. When released in January, 1951, he was as much in the dark about what was transpiring in New Delhi as the other Kathmandu leaders.

124

calculations: would the Nepali Congress include leaders of other Kathmandu factions in the interim government, and was the Nepali Congress prepared to accommodate these leaders in the party's higher hierarchy?

Both questions had been answered in the negative by the end of February. The only Kathmandu leader included in the new government was Ganesh Man Singh, already a member of the Nepali Congress. The organization of the party's Kathmandu unit was also entrusted to Ganesh Man Singh, assisted by another Kathmandu resident, Surya Prasad Upadhyaya, who had been in exile in India and had played a prominent role in the formation of the Nepali Congress. These two men ignored most of the Kathmandu factions, and chose instead the newest and weakest of the local organizations—the remnant of the Praja Panchayat, but with the important exclusion of Gopal Prasad Rimal—as their local core organization. This alienated the other, more influential Kathmandu leaders, who turned to either anti-Nepali Congress or independent politics, to the serious detriment of Congress strength and influence in the capital.

The speeches by Nepali Congress leaders at the first public meeting of the party in Kathmandu after the establishment of the new government did not help to bridge the growing gulf between the local elites and the party. The party president, M. P. Koirala, for instance, spoke in disparaging terms about the contribution of the Kathmandu populace to the 1950 revolution. This haughty attitude was regarded as evidence that the Nepali Congress had become indifferent to popular sentiment at its moment of success.

Several social and political organizations sprang up in Kathmandu after February, 1951, underscoring the failure of the Nepali Congress to incorporate local political elements within the ranks of the party. The Praja Parishad was revived under the leadership of Tanka Prasad Acharya and Khadga Man Singh, and many members of the Nagarik Adhikar Samiti ("Civil Liberties Union") and the Sewa Samiti ("Social Service League") founded around 1937, resumed their allegiance to this party. Some factional elements of the old 1937 groups associated with the Praja Parishad, however, reorganized themselves independently. One prominent example was a short-lived new party, the Janavadi Prajatantra Sangha ("People's Democratic Union"), under the leadership of Prem Bahadur Kansakar (who had organized a public library in 1946 and later joined the Nepali National Congress in India) and Purna Bahadur Manav, a former teacher at the Mahavir school.

There were also several social and political organizations

which emphasized their nonparty character and thus provided another type of platform and outlet for those persons who did not want to identify themselves with the Nepali Congress. Some examples were the Shanti Rakshya Swayam Sevak Sangh ("Union of Volunteers for the Protection of Peace"), an *ad hoc* organization established in the three main cities of Kathmandu Valley in January, 1951, to provide protection against anticipated Rana counterrevolutionary activities; Paropakar ("Assistance Society"), a social service organization; and a new Nagarik Adhikar Samiti, organized by Kathmandu "neutrals," mostly educators and writers, to protect the most tangible if momentary achievement of the 1950 revolution, the exercise of civic rights.

The Nepali Congress leaders were successful in winning the support of some unaffiliated Western-educated members of the Kathmandu elites by offering them important positions in the new administrative setup. But those in this group who felt that they were either ignored or undervalued by the party later became bitter critics of the new coalition government and the Nepali Congress. Such persons, most of whom belonged to the staff of Tri-Chandra College or the government-sponsored high schools, voiced their political opinions in public until Home Minister B. P. Koirala's order of March 2, requiring all government employees to refrain from party politics, finally silenced them—at least, in public.

By March, 1951, therefore, large sections of the avowedly political elements in Kathmandu were openly opposed to the coalition government and the Nepali Congress. Most of them had suffered long periods of incarceration in Rana prisons and considered themselves more deserving of recognition as popular representatives in the coalition government than the Nepali Congress nominees. As they had been denied such recognition by the Nepali Congress leadership, their oppositional politics tended to take the form of vehement and unrestrained denunciation of the *bona fides* of the Nepali Congress leaders.

REVIVALIST POLITICS

By the end of January, 1951, the Rana family had been fragmented into a number of factions signifying various degrees of adjustment and accommodation to the new political order. Most B Ranas and C Ranas had aligned themselves closely with King Tribhuwan and expected to play an important role in the stabilization of the new political system. These Ranas were consciously striving to abandon their feudal verbal habits and behavior, and were avidly learning the use of democratic manners and egalitarian speech. They were, moreover, opposed to any kind of revivalist politics that would endanger the new political system and restore the former A Rana political monopoly, even if under a modified form. The C Ranas, in particular, identified themselves closely with the ideology and the leadership of the Nepali Congress and especially with the restoration of King Tribhuwan's royal prerogatives.

The A Ranas, which by 1950 meant the families of Chandra Shamsher and Juddha Shamsher, were divided into several groups with conflicting loyalties. The crucial factor among those A Ranas who supported the new system seemed to be their kinship relations with the royal family. Obviously, these elements were not so much supporters of the new system or the Nepali Congress as they were of the revitalized role of the royal family in the politics of the country. Two A Ranas in this category were Keshar (Kaiser) Shamsher, Chandra Shamsher's son, who was married to King Tribhuwan's sister, and Hari Shamsher, Juddha Shamsher's son and Crown Prince Mahendra's father-in-law. Among those A Ranas who were not reconciled to the new political order were the sons of Mohan Shamsher and his brother, Babar Shamsher, both members of the newly formed coalition government.

Vijaya Shamsher, Mohan Shamsher's son, had played a leading role as the Rana representative in the crucial New Delhi negotiations in 1950–51. As one of the few Ranas with a higher education, he had built up a small coterie of educated non-Ranas, mostly instructors at the local college, as personal followers even before the outbreak of the 1950 revolution. By January, 1951, when it was clear that the days of Rana rule were numbered, he sent one of his coterie to India as an emissary to invite D. R. Regmi, the dissident leader of the Nepali National Congress, to organize an opposition party in Nepal. Regmi had publicly opposed the 1950 revolution, on the grounds that it was contrary to the Gandhian principles of nonviolence to which his party was committed. With the promise of financial support from Vijaya Shamsher, D. R. Regmi and a few other political workers returned to Kathmandu in January, 1951. There were angry demonstrations in Kathmandu at the time, protesting the circumstances under which he had returned, but D. R. Regmi continued his efforts to expand his party, reportedly with Rana financial support. In any case, the Nepali National Congress publicity bulletins became the most acrimonious mouthpiece for revivalist politics, condemning the coalition government and the Nepali

Congress for both their policies and their motives. It is noteworthy, however, that Vijaya Shamsher, unlike his cousins in Babar Shamsher's family, never engaged directly in party politics at this time. His appointment as ambassdaor to India in June, 1951, associated him formally with the coalition government and brought him closer to King Tribhuwan in subsequent years.

Babar Shamsher's son, Mrigendra Shamsher, and grandson, Bharat Shamsher, played more direct roles in organizing revivalist politics. Their activities began shortly after the establishment of the coalition government, and their anti-Nepali Congress attitude was probably strengthened by reports of Babar Shamsher's repeated humiliations at Cabinet meetings. They organized the Vir Gorkha Dal as early as March, 1951, with the help of their loyal palace guards and other personal attendants. As it was still inexpedient to have avowed Rana leadership at the top, they imported Ranadhir Subba, a leader of the Gorkha League in Darjeeling (India), as a front man. The leaders of the Vir Gorkha Dal sought to discredit the Nepali Congress and its leaders as creations and puppets of the Indian Government, exaggerated reports of Indian interference in the affairs of the government, and invoked the spirit of militant Gorkha nationalism as the basis of their policies.

OPPOSITIONAL POLITICS

Oppositional politics in 1951 were thus primarily the preoccupation of three political groups of diverse motivations, namely, (*a*) the discontented, indigenous Kathmandu political elites, (*b*) the revivalist political groups sponsored or supported by sections of A Rana families, and (*c*) the embryonic Communist party, which had been established in Calcutta in September, 1949.[1] All three groups were constantly searching for—and, indeed, often fabricating—issues to oppose the new coalition government and, in particular, the Nepali Congress.

The newly revived Nepal Praja Parishad, whose leaders had long prison records and whose followers had known political backgrounds, probably best reflected the attitudes and sentiments of the Kathmandu political elite. But the party lacked a coherent ideology and, moreover, was confined to the city of Kathmandu as a base of operation. In its attempt to demarcate its position vis-à-vis the Nepali Congress, the Praja Parishad leadership found a distinctive ideological slogan in what it called "New Democracy." The ideology of New Democracy was never elaborated beyond vague generalities that included the destruction of feudalism and the institution of a people's socialist government, reminiscent of "people's democracy" in Communist China. But, perhaps, for the kind of politics practiced by the Praja Parishad leaders and followers, a well-developed ideology was not only unnecessary but would have proved a hindrance to their political maneuvers.

The revivalist political groups, as represented by the Vir Gorkha Dal and Regmi's Nepali National Congress, lacked both firm ideologies and a substantial following. Each group was limited to a few personal adherents of the leaders, whose party loyalties were mostly defined in terms of familial ties or service. Each operated on *ad hoc* demands and issues rather than long-term policies. Regmi's group did pick up a few avowed anti-Rana political malcontents, but these elements, unable to penetrate the hard-core monopoly of the leader and his familial followers, soon departed for greener political pastures.

The Vir Gorkha Dal was inspired by no political ideology other than the contempt and the anger of some prominent Ranas toward the Nepali Congress members in the coalition Cabinet. The very name, Vir Gorkha, signified an attempt to arouse the militant parochialism of the inhabitants of the hills against the people of Kathmandu and the Nepal Terai, who were presumed to be Nepali Congress supporters.

The Communist party had a ready-made ideology, but lacked followers and sympathizers. It characterized the 1950 revolution as "bourgeois" and the Nepali Congress leadership as a "clique of the nationalist-capitalist bourgeoisie composed of the Suvarna Shamsher and B. P. Koirala group," and called for preparations for a real democratic revolution. Tactically, it attempted to organize numerous front organizations and to unite all "progressive forces" into a broad "People's Front" to fight the Rana-Congress coalition government. It concentrated its attention on three groups in the capital—students, intellectuals (mainly writers and poets), and peasants. A pro-Communist student organization, the "Vidyarthi Federation," was set up, and the Nepal Peace Council, with international Communist affiliations, was established to solicit the support of the intellectuals. A peasants' organization (Nepal Kisan Sangh) was organized, as well as a women's organization (Nepal Mahila Sangha) and a labor organization (the All-Nepal Trade-Union Congress). As in most cases these various fronts were merely products of the interlocking leadership of the same individuals, their influence and effectiveness was questionable. But they helped the Communists to present to their political opponents an impressive appearance, however inflated, of broad-based public appeal.

When the Vir Gorkha Dal was banned in April, 1951, after its attack on B. P. Koirala, only three political groups—the Nepali National Congress, the Praja Parishad and the Communist party —remained in the field to provide opposition to the coalition government and the Nepali Congress. The Nepali National Congress fought the government through its publicity bulletins, attacking especially Home Minister B. P. Koirala, against whom all sorts of personal accusations were hurled, ranging from "fascist dictator" to "plunderer." * Because of its limited following, it did not participate in direct agitation and demonstrations as did the other two parties, although it held many more public meetings to propagate its point of view.

The Praja Parishad and the Communist party worked closely together in their agitational programs. In contrast to the Nepali National Congress, these two parties resorted to direct action by organizing public demonstrations against the government and the Nepali Congress. They were able to muster the support of a wide variety of groups, but perhaps their most distinctive asset was their success in courting the student community in Kathmandu at an earlier stage than other political groups.

The issues involved in the oppositional politics of 1951 were mostly nonideological in character and personal in spirit. One common feature of all opposition groups was that their hostility was aimed solely at the Nepali Congress leaders in the government, and Home Minister B. P. Koirala in particular, and not at all at the Rana Ministers. The main burden of their allegations was that the Nepali Congress, as a signatory to the Delhi compromise, had helped to introduce Indian influence in Nepal to the point where it constituted interference in the affairs of government. The activities of the Indian Ambassador, C. P. N. Singh, were called into question and the Nepali Congress leadership was accused of collaborating with him on plans to compromise Nepal's independence and sovereignty.

The intervention of Indian Army units in the capture of K. I. Singh and his followers in February and again in July, 1951, was

---

* The intemperateness of personal attacks and accusations, which filled the pages of the publicity bulletins, landed the party leaders in serious difficulties in September, 1951. Because of the comments in a publicity bulletin on a *sub judice* case, Chief Justice Hari Prasad Pradhan cited D. R. Regmi for contempt of court and sentenced him to imprisonment for six months and a penalty of 500 rupees. Regmi was released on December 19, 1951, after he had paid the fine.

quickly seized upon by all opposition groups as verification of their allegations against the Nepali Congress. The country's sovereignty and independence had been impaired, they charged, and the coalition government was functioning as a subservient instrument of the Indian government. It was reported that C. P. N. Singh regularly attended the meetings of the Nepali Cabinet. In March, when he attended a conference of Bada Hakims in Birganj, his presence was interpreted as a proof of the extension of Indian interference in district affairs. The visit of Nepali Cabinet Ministers to New Delhi in May for mediation of their disputes, the involvement of the Indian government in the arbitration of these disputes, and the consequent reorganization of the Cabinet in June—all these events were cited by opposition groups as irrefutable evidence of the subservient status of the coalition government.

In June, Nehru made his first official visit to Nepal, and this event separated the opposition groups into those which were anti-Indian for opportunistic reasons and those which were anti-Indian for ideological reasons. Among the first category was D. R. Regmi and the Nepali National Congress. Regmi's anti-Indian speeches and activities were directed mainly against the activities of C. P. N. Singh and the Ambassador's private secretary, S. K. Sinha, whom he considered to be biased toward the Nepali Congress leaders and hostile to himself. There was also an element of personal frustration in his anti-Indian nationalism arising from the fact that, despite his status as one of the few members of the educated elite, he had been excluded by both the Nepali Congress and the Indian government from the coalition Cabinet. Regmi's political slogan in 1951, therefore, called for immediate dissolution of the coalition government and its replacement by a government composed of representatives of all political parties.

Regmi and his party, however, did not participate in the anti-Nehru demonstrations, which were prepared by the Praja Parishad and the Communist party. These groups and their sympathizers depicted Nehru as a tool of Anglo-American imperialism, and his policies vis-à-vis Nepal were construed to be aimed at reducing Nepal to the status of an Indian colony for the benefit of capitalists and monopolists. The demonstrations against Nehru's visit received scant public support, but the sponsoring groups held a public meeting after he left, to explain their opposition to his policies.

The most obvious political target of all opposition groups was B. P. Koirala, the Nepali Congress Home Minister. As the

Minister responsible for the restoration and maintenance of law and order, he had to exert his authority, and rather forcefully at times, over many scattered areas of Nepal. As a result of the political climate engendered by the 1950 revolution, respect for authority had diminished all over the country, and many political elements, including counterrevolutionary groups, were attempting to take advantage of a confused situation. There were rebellious activities in Bhairawa and Nepalganj, peasant agitation in Bardiya, labor unrest in Birganj, and students' agitation in Kathmandu. At some of these places the government had restored law and order by force, resorting to gunfire. Several people were killed, and many more were wounded. The responsibility for all these repressive measures was laid on the shoulders of the Home Minister by all opposition groups, who charged that his promulgation of the Public Security Act was proof of dictatorial intentions. The Rakshya Dal was described as his private army, and the Nepali Congress as a party of foreign origin and loyalty. Public sentiment against members of the Rakshya Dal was aroused to such a point that the opposition groups organized a general strike and procession in Kathmandu on September 23, protesting against alleged abuses during a football match.

Perhaps the most significant alignment of opposition groups was the "United Front," formed by the Praja Parishad, the Communist party, and various Communist front organizations in July, 1951. Tanka Prasad Acharya of the Praja Parishad was elected chairman, but the United Front was in reality heavily dominated by a few Communist individuals and their phantom-like organizations. In November, the Front issued a manifesto outlining its objectives and policies. The coalition government was characterized as a stooge of the Indian government, which "held the final authority to dismiss Ministers, including the Prime Minister." The goals of Anglo-American imperialism were alleged to be the conversion of Nepal into a military base against Communist China. Taking this interpretation of the context of Nepali politics, the United Front announced the following as its main objectives: (a) establishment of a people's government representative of labor, peasants, the middle class, and national capitalists under the leadership of truly democratic elements, (b) establishment of a joint advisory committee representing all progressive political parties and social class organizations, and (c) appointment of a Cabinet under the auspices of the Advisory Committee. The Cabinet was to be held responsible to the Advisory Committee, and its main responsibility was defined as that of convening a constituent assembly.[2]

PARTY POLITICS UNDER THE FIRST M. P. KOIRALA GOVERNMENT

The appointment of the first Nepali Congress Cabinet, headed by M. P. Koirala, in November, 1951, did not basically alter the trends of political party development. Oppositional tactics continued to be essentially negative and highly personal in character, although now M. P. Koirala replaced the former Home Minister, B. P. Koirala, as the primary target of criticism. The attacks on the Prime Minister were extended to include also those leaders who were considered to be the main supporters (and manipulators) of the Cabinet—primarily Ambassador C. P. N. Singh and Prime Minister Nehru of India, and King Tribhuwan. The issues which generated the most heat were M. P. Koirala's alleged alignment with reactionary Rana-Shah groups, and New Delhi's supposed designs upon the sovereignty and independence of Nepal.

The curious circumstances under which M. P. Koirala had been foisted upon the Nepali Congress as Prime Minister by King Tribhuwan led the party to function as a quasi-oppositional group almost immediately after the formation of the Cabinet. On December 5, for instance, B. P. Koirala accused C. P. N. Singh of exceeding his authority by meddling in the internal politics of Nepal. The Indian Ambassador was charged with fomenting rivalries among Nepali political leaders and, by implication, was held responsible for the exclusion of B. P. Koirala from the prime ministership.[3]

Other political parties, such as the Nepali National Congress and the United Front, were understandably delighted to receive this support for their allegations that Ambassador Singh was the creator and the preserver of the M. P. Koirala government. But they, unlike the Nepali Congress, attributed expansionsist motives to the Indian government and interpreted Singh's activities as part of a conspiracy for the gradual annexation of Nepal. They found ready ammunition for their anti-India compaigns in the arrival of the Indian Military Mission and Indian civil service study teams in Kathmandu, and in the visits of the Nepali Prime Minister and Cabinet members to New Delhi.

The question of alleged Indian interference in Nepal's internal affairs was easily the most complex and the most emotionally charged political controversy of the time. So much passion was aroused in both India and Nepal over this issue that it became very difficult, if not impossible, to view the problem with any degree of objectivity. On the Indian side, the advent of independence from British rule had given birth to an ideological renaissance, whose protagonists emphasized India's historical and cultural influence in neighboring South Asian countries. The concept of a Greater India (*Maha Bharat*) was broached as a cultural entity, transcending the political boundaries of India. Moreover, the Indian government, under Sirdar Patel's vigorous leadership, had embarked on a vast program of integrating some six hundred Princely States—which had enjoyed limited internal automony under British rule—into the new Indian Union.

These developments caused considerable alarm in Nepal, where the highly sensitive political elites regarded Indian policies toward the three Himalayan kingdoms of Nepal, Bhutan, and Sikkim as being inspired by the same exuberance for integration evident within India itself. When the Indian government entered into new treaty relationships with Sikkim in 1950, and assumed control over its foreign relations, defense, and strategic communications, politically conscious elites in Nepal were alarmed as to the possible future intentions of India toward their own country.*

This situation was somewhat alleviated in 1950, when Nepal and India entered into new treaty relationships recognizing, *inter alia,* one another's independence and sovereignty. But this formal recognition became suspect when the Nepali Congress came into power in 1951, owing to the Indian government's intimate involvement in the negotiation of the Delhi compromise that ended Rana rule.

The year 1951 also marked the end of Nepal's long political isolation from the rest of the world and the rediscovery of nationalism by Nepali elites. During the long period of political quarantine imposed by the Rana rulers, the Nepalese had been indoctrinated with profound fears and suspicions of outsiders— and particularly of reformist and revolutionary ideas from India. The sudden influx of Indian influence in 1951 and 1952—in the form of Ambassador Singh's activities, the arrival of Indian advisers and experts, and the visits of Nepali Ministers to New Delhi—was too overwhelming and unsettling for the Nepali elites. The rapidity of change within Nepal itself made it even more difficult for them to obtain a sense of perspective.

In such an atmosphere, the arrival of the Indian Military

---

* It was quickly noted in Kathmandu that these were the same terms upon which the Princely States had first been integrated into the Indian Union, and conclusions as to their significance were hastily and, as it turned out, incorrectly drawn by the intensely nationalistic Nepali political leaders.

Mission in March, 1952, proved to be the last straw. Even some of the non-Rana Kshatriyas, who had previously been only peripherally involved in party politics, came to accept the allegations of Indian interference which opposition parties had been exploiting assiduously for the past year in their desperate search for substantive political issues. Even King Tribhuwan came in for indirect— and, from the Communists, direct—criticism for the alleged surrender of his prerogatives to Indian will and direction. His commissioning of M. P. Koirala to form a new government was criticized by anti-Nepali Congress parties as indicative of inability to withstand Indian pressure, while the retention of him as Prime Minister, after the party had disavowed him, was interpreted by Nepali Congress leaders as evidence of the King's being involved in a reactionary political game aimed at excluding the progressive elements of the Nepali Congress leadership from the government.

THE RISE OF SPLINTER GROUP POLITICS

The establishment of a one-party government and the formal end of Rana rule brought about an undeclared race for power within the ranks of the political parties, most of which were ideologically unaligned and organizationally weak. But, predictably, all internal splits were invariably justified by their partisans either on ideological grounds or on constitutional niceties.

Ironically, the Nepali Congress, the first ruling party, was also one of the precursors of this kind of centrifugal party politics. The ideological background for the split between the two Koirala factions in the party was carefully spelled out by B. P. Koirala in early 1952 in an article on "The Nepali Congress and the Government." [4] His main thesis was that the Nepali Congress party was not merely distinctively different from the government, but was also the guide and the pace setter for the government. He made it clear that the party was more than a publicity department of the government; it was to function as a watchdog commission, ready to criticize and oppose the policies of the government when these went astray. In the absence of an elected parliament or assembly, the party itself would function in this capacity. Finally, he proposed that the party president should remain outside the government and that the majority of the Working Committee members of the party should be selected from among party leaders not included in the government.

B. P. Koirala's views on the relationship between the party and the government, which were accepted by the party executive after his election as president at the annual party conference in

May, 1952, precipitated the Cabinet crisis of July and the formal separation of the M. P. Koirala group from the party fold. The same conference was marked by the secession of two other factional groups. One of these, led by Balchandra Sharma and Kedar Man "Vyathit," briefly maintained an independent existence as the Leftist Nepali Congress; the other, led by Bhadrakali Mishra, later functioned as a separate political party under the name of the Nepali Jana Congress.

Subsequent to the ban imposed on the Communist party in January, 1952, the United Front had become a truncated organization, and the Praja Parishad had to bear most of its organizational and agitational responsibilities. In these circumstances, the Front functioned on anything but a united basis, and the Praja Parishad leaders gradually lost interest in their association with the Communist party and even with Marxist ideology. Finally, the Parishad formally withdrew from the Front in September, 1952, terminating all connections with the Communist party and the allied front organizations, and launching itself on an independent political career.

The diminutive Nepali National Congress was also split in May, 1952. The party president, D. R. Regmi, expelled four members of his Working Committee, including the party's general secretary, Rishikesh Shah, and deprived them even of ordinary membership. On June 3, these persons then established a dissident Nepali National Congress and announced the expulsion of D. R. Regmi, charging him with violations of the party constitution and misuse of party funds.

Thus by August, 1952, when the M. P. Koirala government was dissolved, the political scene in Kathmandu was cluttered with a number of splinter groups. The original Nepali Congress had been divided into four distinct factions; the Nepali National Congress had been segmented into two groups with identical names and party flags; and even social groups such as the Women's Association and the Students' Union had been divided into parallel organizations.

The rise of splinter group politics had far-reaching adverse effects on the development of the democratic process in Nepal. The most salient effects were (*a*) the dissociation of most such groups from any base of popular support and (*b*) the rise of a new breed of professional politicians whose primary goal was the achievement of high office in the government by currying favor with the royal palace. Party loyalties and ideologies assumed secondary importance in such a context; personalities and influence at the royal palace became the paramount considerations.

PARTY POLITICS UNDER THE ROYAL COUNCILORS' REGIME

The establishment of the Councilors' regime produced an unprecedented if short-lived consensus among most political parties. The party leaders feared that this supposedly tentative political arrangement might prove durable because of the strong Rana and pro-Rana associations of its leading members. These apprehensions were accentuated by the knowledge that there were many revivalists outside the ranks of the government and strongly entrenched in feudal religious and economic institutions, who were eagerly awaiting the opportunity to reverse the political process introduced in 1951. These fears loomed larger and larger in the minds of the political public with the passage of time and produced a new politics of consensus, which manifested itself in several alliances and coalitions among splinter groups.

On October 25, 1952, the Nepali Congress (Bhadrakali Mishra faction) and the Nepali National Congress (Shankar Prasad–Rishikesh Shah faction) merged and set up a coördinating committee of eleven members, with Jiva Raj Sharma of the Nepali National Congress faction as chairman and Bhadrakali Mishra as general secretary. Similarly, the M. P. Koirala faction of the Nepali Congress (called the Nepali Congress Ad Hoc Committee), the Praja Parishad, and the Nepali Congress Leftist Bloc faction (led by Balchandra Sharma) announced their decision to coördinate their activities on February 24, 1953, and subsequently set up a committee to explore the possibilities of bringing about a merger of the constituent groups. This was followed, in May, by a decision to form a united front of the constituent groups.

Since the primary objective of all these maneuvers was access to ministerial posts, the alliances and coalitions were, *ipso facto,* little more than tentative moves and countermoves toward that goal. Ideologies and principles were of secondary importance, and the overriding concern was to "prove" by means of publicity campaigns the popular and representative status of the leading political figures.

In conjunction with the tenuous politics of consensus, however, the trend toward factionalism in party politics continued unabated. The breach between the two factions of the Nepali Congress remained unbridged despite the efforts of King Tribhuwan and some Indian leaders. In August, 1952, the All-Nepal

Nepali Congress Committee ratified by a vote of 118 to 7, with nine abstentions, the Working Committee's decision to suspend M. P. Koirala and two former party Cabinet members— Mahendra Vikram Shah and Narada Muni Thulung—from active membership for three years.[5] Followers of M. P. Koirala called the decision "farcical and manipulated ratification" and formed a separate "Ad Hoc Central Committee" to launch a country-wide campaign against the current leadership of the parental organization.[6]

In September and October the Koirala brothers made separate trips to Poona, where the Indian socialist leader, Jaya Prakash Narayan, attempted to mediate their disputes. But his efforts were of no avail, and the rift continued and, in fact, widened in the succeeding months under the plethora of charges and counter-charges from both sides. In March, 1953, M. P. Koirala estimated that about sixty of the 150 members of the All-Nepal Congress Committee had joined his group.[7] He further disclosed that B. P. Koirala had rejected his proposal to bring back the three Nepali Congress splinter groups (i.e., the M. P. Koirala, the Bhadrakali Mishra, and the Balchandra Sharma factions) into the parental organization by reconstituting the party executive to represent all dissident factions. He claimed that negotiations with B. P. Koirala broke down because of the latter's insistence on the dissolution of the Ad Hoc Committee as a precondition for unification. B. P. Koirala, on the other hand, maintained that the total strength of the three factions which had seceded from the Nepali Congress did not exceed 20 per cent of its total strength.[8] A few days later, the party executive officially announced a policy of no further negotiations with leaders of dissident groups.

While the so-called national parties were engaged in tactical coalitions or factional conflicts, two parties with avowed parochial leanings—the Terai Congress and the Gorkha Parishad—were trying to reap political advantage from the generally confused situation. The Terai Congress had been organized in 1951 with three principal objectives: (a) establishment of an autonomous Terai state, (b) recognition of Hindi as a state language, and (c) adequate employment of the Terai people in the Nepal civil service. Its leader, Vedananda Jha, claimed in May, 1953, a membership of 60,000 for his organization and demanded adequate representation of the Terai in the proposed Advisory Assembly.[9]

The Gorkha Parishad, which had been organized in February, 1952, in the place of the Vir Gorkha Dal, canvassed for support among the people of the hill areas by playing on their fear of non-Gorkha elements in Kathmandu and the Terai, and by invoking the militaristic traditions of the hill people. Most of the local Gorkha Parishad leaders in the hills had been associated with the old Rana military establishment and soon ran into conflict with local Nepali Congress leaders. The result was widespread political tension in the hill districts, which led to disturbances in Pokhara in January, 1953, between supporters and opponents of the Gorkha Parishad. The government finally resorted to force of arms to restore law and order, and arrested Bharat Shamsher, the general secretary of the party.

PARTY POLITICS UNDER THE NATIONAL DEMOCRATIC PARTY GOVERNMENT

A carefully fostered ambivalence characterized party policies toward the National Democratic party government appointed in June, 1953. Publicly, most parties attacked the Cabinet for alleged sins of omission and commission; privately, the party leaders engaged in tortuous negotiations with Prime Minister M. P. Koirala to settle the terms under which a coalition government could be established. Political mergers and alliances occurred when these were considered expedient in the process of bargaining. In brief, the political arena was no different from the Kathmandu bazaar, where the prices of goods and wares are determined only after protracted haggling between the seller and the customer. This comparison, however, is not completely accurate, as there was only one customer (M. P. Koirala acting as King Tribhuwan's proxy), surrounded by many sellers (various political parties); but it conveys the spirit of the negotiations. The various contending parties were clearly at a disadvantage in their bargaining with M. P. Koirala.

POLITICS OF MINISTRY-MAKING

During the first week of the new government, the various political parties were preoccupied with preparations for welcoming the Everest heroes, Tensing Norkay (Norbu Tenzing) and Edmund Hillary, to the capital. The Nepali Congress Working Committee, therefore, did not meet until June 21, when it adopted a resolution which stated:

This government [i.e., the new M. P. Koirala Cabinet] is a product of palace intrigue and is as unrepresentative and undemocratic as the Councilors' regime. It is wholly incapable of solving any problem facing the country, particularly in the transitional stage through which the country is passing. This meeting condemns the undemocratic and conspiratorial manner in which the so-called Cabinet has been created, and is of the view that it has no sanction whatsoever behind it. A splinter group of the Nepali Congress, baptized as a party only a few weeks ago, has been in a most objectionable manner installed in the government to the amazement of the people of Nepal.[10]

The Nepali Congress had suffered both insult and injury. Previously, it had negotiated with the King and M. P. Koirala with a sense of confidence in its status as the largest party in Nepal. A few weeks earlier, it had even rejected the idea of a coalition Cabinet in which it would have had equal status (three Ministers) with the National Democratic party. After the formation of the new government, the Nepali Congress was confronted with the choice of either negotiating with M. P. Koirala on his terms or continuing as an opposition party.

B. P. Koirala issued a statement on July 4 indicating the terms under which his party would be willing to join the government. These were : (a) that his party be allowed the same number of seats in the Cabinet as the National Democratic party; (b) that his party's program be accepted by the government; and (c) that the government be dissolved upon the resignation of any one group.[11] M. P. Koirala in a presidential address to his party's conference in Biratnagar on July 11, rejected the Nepali Congress demands and reiterated his former offer to include three Nepali Congress nominees in an expanded Cabinet consisting, in addition, of three independents and three National Democratic party nominees. All would be recruited on an "individual basis" outside the control of their affiliated parties, according to the Prime Minister. Once again, the Nepali Congress rejected the proposal.

M. P. Koirala's visit to New Delhi that same month aroused expectations in Kathmandu that Prime Minister Nehru would intervene and mediate the dispute between the two Koirala brothers. These reports led D. R. Regmi and Tanka Prasad Acharya to issue a joint statement criticizing any agreement between the Nepali Congress and the National Democratic party based on equal representation in the Cabinet. They accused M. P. Koirala of reneging on the settlement negotiated in King Tribhuwan's presence in April under which, they claimed, a Cabinet of seven was to be formed, including one representative from each of the four main parties—Nepali Congress, Nepali National Congress, Nepal Praja Parishad, and National Democratic—and three independents.[12]

POLITICS OF MERGERS AND ALLIANCES

The politics of ministry-making continued at a somewhat abated pace from July to October, but in the meanwhile the parties regrouped and realigned on a substantial scale. On June 23, B. P. Koirala, president of the Nepali Congress, and Jiva Raj Sharma, president of Nepali National Congress (dissident group), announced that their respective parties had dissolved and merged to form the Nepali Congress (National Congress–associated). After the merger, B. P. Koirala dissolved and reconstituted the Working Committee, parliamentary board, and all subcommittees of the Nepali Congress to accommodate the new elements in these bodies. At the same time, delegates of the Nepali Jana Congress met at Birganj on June 28 with delegates of a dissident Nepali Congress group and formed the All-Nepal Jana Congress, under the presidency of Bhadrakali Mishra.

The Leftist Nepali Congress, which had separated from the parent organization in May 1952, was also actively engaged in political acrobatics. Its leader, Balchandra Sharma, signed a pact with the Nepali Congress president on July 28, pledging to remerge his group with the parent organization.[13] But this pledge was never honored. Subsequently, Sharma obtained better terms from M. P. Koirala, who promised the Leftist Nepali Congress one-third representation in the National Democratic party's Working Committee, twenty to twenty-five seats in the party's general conference, and a speakership for Sharma in the prospective Advisory Assembly.[14] Attracted by these terms, Sharma announced the merger of his group with the National Democratic party on August 28. Two days before, his co-leader, Kedar Man "Vyathit," resigned from even ordinary membership in the Leftist Nepali Congress, accusing Sharma of opportunism and self-aggrandizement.

Perhaps the most significant political coalition during the tenure of the National Democratic party Cabinet was brought about by King Tribhuwan's Royal Proclamation of September 20. Among other things, the proclamation empowered M. P. Koirala to modify the Cabinet during the King's absence in Europe. This delegation of the royal authority was strongly criticized by the Nepali Congress, the Praja Parishad, and the Nepali National Congress.[15] Party leaders B. P. Koirala, D. R. Regmi, and Tanka Prasad Acharya pledged publicly to work together on the basis of a common program, and formed a "Council of Action" consisting of themselves and Chuda Prasad.

Suvarna Shamsher, and K. P. Rimal. On September 23, two days after the King's departure, the three parties announced the formation of a "League of Democrats," in which each party was to function as an equal partner with equal rights, and the leaders claimed that they had agreed upon a minimum program based on the principles of nationalism, democracy, and social justice. The program, as put forth by the League, consisted of nine points: no foreign association with the internal administration of the country (no explicit statement was made about the Indian Military Mission) ; acceptance of foreign economic and technical aid only if these did not encroach upon the independence of the country; revision of treaties with foreign governments with a view to removing such articles as were derogatory to the prestige and interests of Nepal; no ownership of agricultural lands by foreigners; acceptance of Nepali currency as legal tender throughout the country; membership for Nepal in the United Nations; opposition to all imperialist forces, and sympathy for all democratic and anti-imperialist elements; early holding of elections; and formation of a coalition Cabinet of democratic parties.[16]

These points, mostly vague and unspecific, indicated only a superficial agreement among the constituent parties, and had more the character of party shibboleths and slogans than of commitment to any program. All three parties sought to capitalize on the prevailing nationalistic sentiment without naming any particular source of threat, real or imaginary, to national sovereignty. The implication, however, was clear. Interested political parties had lately fed the public with copious reports of alleged Indian armed intervention, and people were becoming uneasy at the sight of Indian military officers roaming around Kathmandu.

The failure to specify concrete measures to be taken to constitute a coalition Cabinet of democratic parties led to the undoing of the League as a political alignment. M. P. Koirala, with his well-developed political acumen, was quick to seize on this fatal flaw in the organization, and effectively undermined the League within a month of its inception. On October 16, he publicly offered four seats in the Cabinet to the Nepali Congress negotiator, Suvarna Shamsher, with the option of filling them either with Nepali Congress representatives or with nominees of the League.[17] Members of the other parties rejected the offer outright, with strong criticisms of M. P. Koirala's high-handedness in not dealing directly with the League. The Nepali Congress Working Committee, however, voted to allow its members to join the Cabinet.[18] B. P. Koirala, Suvarna Shamsher, Surya Prasad

Upadhyaya, and Rameshwar Prasad Singh were approved as the party's nominees. The League's Council of Action met on November 2 and adjourned *sine die* after an inconclusive and recriminatory two-hour meeting. From that time on the League was defunct for all practical purposes. No sooner was the League dissolved and bad blood created between the three parties than M. P. Koirala changed his tune and began to talk in terms of a five-party Cabinet, which would include the Praja Parishad, Nepali National Congress, and independents in addition to the National Democratic party and the Nepali Congress. He stressed the point that King Tribhuwan preferred a national government and that a five-party Cabinet would be the closest approximation of the King's desire.

On January 10, 1954, M. P. Koirala told newspaper reporters in Calcutta that negotiations concerning the Cabinet expansion had reached a final stage and that new Ministers, although drawn from different parties, would be appointed on an individual basis.[19] A few days later he revealed that the new Cabinet would have ten to fifteen Ministers and that he was going to set a deadline for talks with other political parties. When he formed a new Cabinet on February 18, he chose two representatives from his party, one representative each from the Nepali National Congress, the Praja Parishad, and the All-Nepal Jana Congress, and one independent.

PARTY POLITICS UNDER THE NATIONAL GOVERNMENT

On February 20, two days after the formation of the "National" government, M. P. Koirala announced that two Nepali Congress members and an independent would be added to the Cabinet. The Nepali Congress, however, decided to reject this somewhat casual invitation. On March 2, the party Working Committee adopted a resolution expressing opposition to the new government, which it charged had been formed "as a private affair." [20] Chagrined by M. P. Koirala's allegedly devious tactics, the committee decided to launch an agitation against the curtailment of the powers of the High Court and to hold an "Anti–Black Act Day" on March 28, in protest against the Royal Proclamation of January 10 and subsequent legislative enactments which had deprived the High Court of much of its power.

The demand for the restoration of an independent judiciary

drew varied degrees of support from such parties as the Nepali Congress, the Communist party, and the Gorkha Parishad. The Communist party—through a front organization, the Janadhikar Surakshya Samiti ("People's Rights Protection Committee") —demanded the removal of the ban on its legal existence. The Gorkha Parishad was motivated by the fear that the new coalition government might clamp down on its activities. It did not, however, fully share the negativistic attitude of the Nepali Congress. Indeed, the Gorkha Parishad was relieved that the King had not installed "another unmitigated Nepali Congress tyranny." Its general attitude amounted to an acceptance of the new regime as a lesser political evil. Even the Communists were encouraged by the prospect of a weak government, which would not be in a position to repress their activities to the same extent as a Nepali Congress government would have been.

The Nepali Congress observed the "Anti–Black Act Day" by calling a general strike, holding mass meetings, and leading processions throughout the country. A new feature of the agitation was a signature collection campaign, demanding an independent judiciary. In Kathmandu, B. P. Koirala and eighteen other Nepali Congress leaders were arrested at a public meeting, but were released on the same day after being in police custody for some six hours.[21]

Another issue which unified most of the opposition parties was the alleged intensification of Indian interference in the internal affairs of Nepal. This theme was developed more vigorously following Prime Minister Nehru's statement to the Indian Parliament, on May 18, that Nepal's foreign policy would be coördinated with that of India, which was interpreted in Nepal as evidence of India's intention to manage Nepal's foreign policy. An outburst of anti-Indian sentiment occurred on May 28 at the Kathmandu airport on the occasion of a visit by an Indian Parliament good-will mission, which had come to attend the inaugural session of the second Advisory Assembly. A hostile demonstration, shouting slogans against Indian interference, was staged by a crowd of about two thousand. The government blamed the Gorkha Parishad and the Nepali Congress for the demonstration and arrested some of their leaders on charges of inciting the demonstrators against the visiting Indian parliamentarians.

Opposition leaders, however, interpreted the demonstrations as indication of popular reaction against the policies of the Nepal government toward India and vice versa. B. P. Koirala, disavowing his party's responsibility for the mob at the airport, analyzed the situation in these words:

The Kosi agreement, the presence of an Indian Military Mission, a large contingent of Indian advisers and technicians, and the India-Nepal trade agreement have been irritating the national sentiments of the Nepalese people. . . . The incident at the airport was not an organized event but an outburst of pent-up feeling." [22]

A similar position was taken by Ranadhir Subba, the Gorkha Parishad leader, who expressed his sympathy for the airport demonstrators and outlined some of the reasons why anti-Indian feeling was running so high. It was to be desired that "the foreign policies of India and Nepal should be coördinated, not that Nepal's foreign policy should be coördinated with that of India," the Gorkha Parishad leader asserted. [23]

King Tribhuwan, in his inaugural address to the Advisory Assembly, felt compelled to reply to these political allegations by insisting that "India's assistance constituted no interference in Nepal." [24] Prime Minister M. P. Koirala was vehement in his denials of Indian interference. Answering Nepali Congress critics, he said:

The Indian Military Mission came to train and reorganize the Nepalese Army at our request during the Rana-Congress coalition government in 1951. There was not a single adviser for the government. Certain Indian officers were here for public relations. I definitely know that those who shout at the top of their voice about Indian interference had sought the help of Indian advisers themselves to the extent of taking them into cabinet confidence and associating them in every administrative execution. During recent times these practices have stopped completely. [25]

Nevertheless, questions were raised persistently in the Advisory Assembly on the date of the withdrawal of the Indian Military Mission and the number of Indian Army checkposts on Nepal's northern border. One member of the Advisory Assembly even attributed the fluctuations in the rate of exchange between Nepali and Indian currency to an Indian government "plot" to undermine Nepal's economic stability. The growth of anti-Indian sentiments culimated on September 21 in a public demonstration organized by the pro-Communist Janadhikar Surakshya Samiti as "Anti–Indian Interference Day."

Fairly indicative of the strength of the Communist hold on public sentiments in Kathmandu at this time was the fact that the United States, also, was frequently the object of malignment in political circles. The government of Nepal, unwittingly perhaps, played into the hands of the Communists when Mrigendra Shamsher, a Gorkha Parishad leader, was arrested on charges of illegally importing four American-made wireless transmitters. The government claimed that the instruments bore the inscription, "Signal Corps, U.S. Army."

According to the Gorkha Parishad, this wireless equipment had been purchased from army surplus stores, but the Communists seized this opportunity to attack the United States by alleging that the transmitters were to be used for revolutionary purposes to establish a pro-Western government. George Allen, the American Ambassador to India and Nepal, paid a hurried visit to Kathmandu on June 12 and characterized reports of American involvement in the internal politics of Nepal as utter nonsense. Unsuccessful in his efforts to persuade the government to allow him to examine the wireless equipment allegedly supplied from the United States, he vented his frustrations at a press conference in Kathmandu:

I have begged, implored, and beseeched the Nepalese officials to give me details of the equipment to help us find out how and from where it came. No details have been given to me yet, and I have been told that they would be supplied if the necessity arose.[26]

On August 8, the Janadhikar Surakshya Samiti put on an anti-American rally with the support of the banned Communist party and the Kisan Sangh, a pro-Communist peasant organization, protesting against American "imperialist" activities in Nepal. Effigies of Eisenhower and Dulles were burnt. Even the Prime Minister's party sent a letter to the Janadhikar Surakshya Samiti, expressing sympathy for the demonstration while mentioning its inability to send volunteers.

THE DISSOLUTION OF THE NATIONAL GOVERNMENT

After the proffered resignation of the coalition Cabinet on January 30, 1955, swift realignments occurred among the constituent parties. M. P. Koirala dissolved his party's twenty-one-member Working Committee, which had been formed only a month earlier, charging that five of the members had violated party discipline by voting against the government. Balchandra Sharma, the general secretary of the party, then announced that he and two thirds of the members of the party's General Council had now rejected M. P. Koirala's leadership and would merge with the Praja Parishad.

The formal merger of the Praja Parishad, Balchandra Sharma's faction of the National Democratic party, and Bhadrakali Mishra's All-Nepal Jana Congress took place on February 3. Sharma was elected president of the new party, which retained the name of the Praja Parishad and adopted the flag of the Jana Congress. The president asserted that forty-seven members of the Advisory Assembly had joined the new party, and, in a representation to the Regency Council, claimed the right to form a one-party Cabinet. M. P. Koirala, on the other hand, set up a coördination committee and commenced merger negotiations with the Nepali Congress.

The epitaph of the entire Tribhuwan period was written by two members of the National Cabinet, Tanka Prasad Acharya and Bhadrakali Mishra, in an angry, intemperate letter to M. P. Koirala upon their dismissal from the Cabinet. They charged:

The independence of the judiciary is lost. All over the country anarchy, famine, corruption, bribery, unemployment, and inflation are rampant. The currency situation has reached a dangerous state. The peasants are exploited more than ever. Facilities for communication, irrigation, education, and public health are almost nonexistent. The lawful rights of students, labor, women, and merchants have been ruthlessly suppressed. Reactionary elements are receiving full encouragement from you. Big landlords and capitalists are having a field day in exploiting the people and the resources of production.[27]

This was intended as an indictment of the Prime Minister, but in a far more real sense it was a popular indictment of political parties and the irresponsible role they had played in the governance of the country. Thus, the sentiment expressed was more than an epitaph for an era: it was also the epitaph for the political party system in Nepal, which henceforth had to accommodate itself to a new ruler with an attitude toward the transitional political process in Nepal fundamentally different from that of his predecessor.

8
Policies and
Programs: 1951–55

THE ANTI-RANA LEADERS returned victoriously to Kathmandu in February, 1951, fully determined to remold Nepal's political, social, and economic structure along egalitarian, democratic lines as quickly as possible. The gradualist spirit which underlay the Delhi compromise represented the viewpoint of the Indian government, but not of the Nepali Congress. How frustrating it was, then, to discover that reforms could not be introduced suddenly and effectively within a democratic context, and that many of their favorite programs did not evoke an enthusiastic response from broad segments of Nepali society. The Tribhuwan era proved to be, therefore, a period of maturation for the political leaders not only in the tactics of politics, but in the politics of government.

CONSTITUTIONAL DEVELOPMENTS

The primary task of the first post-Rana government was the creation of a new political order to replace Rana autocracy. Undoubtedly the most substantial progress in this direction was represented by the Interim Government of Nepal Act, which went into effect on March 30, 1951. The new organic law, or Interim Constitution, abolished the personal absolutism of the Rana Prime Minister, as defined in the 1856 Sanad and the 1948 Constitution, and provided for a collective sharing of power between the King and the Council of Ministers. It stipulated that "the executive power of the State shall be vested in the King and his Council of Ministers," and thus established a King-in-Council system as an important aspect of the new political process.

The powers of the Prime Minister were drastically reduced

from what they had been under the Rana system, as he was henceforth merely the appointed head of the Council of Ministers, which was collectively responsible only to the King. Specifically, the duties of the Prime Minister were (*a*) to communicate to the King all decisions of the Cabinet relating to administrative affairs, (*b*) to furnish information relating to such administrative affairs as the King might request, and (*c*) if the King so required, to submit for consideration by the Cabinet any matter on which a decision had been taken by a Minister but which had not been discussed by the Cabinet as a whole. In the sphere of legislation, the King-in-Council was vested with the power to promulgate ordinances which had "the force and effect of the law of the country," subject to the proviso that such ordinances would cease to operate three months after the assembly of a validly constituted legislative body.

The most significant aspect of the Interim Constitution, as far as a democratic process was concerned, was the separation of the judicial and the executive branches of government. The Pradhan Nyayalaya, or High Court, was unequivocally declared to be the highest court of justice in the country, and no provision was included for an appeal to the Prime Minister or the King for a reversal of the court's decision. The Pradhan Nyayalaya was also designated as the Court of Record and was authorized to mete out punishment on contempt charges.

The Interim Constitution provided for several administrative innovations such as a Public Service Commission, a Comptroller and an Auditor General. The Public Service Commission was entrusted with the responsibility of conducting examinations for appointments to all the civil services of the government, and was also assigned a consultative role on all administrative matters relating to methods of recruitment to the services and to decisions concerning promotions, transfers, and disciplinary matters affecting a person's employment. The Comptroller and Auditor General were empowered to examine the accounts of all branches of the government. Both of these offices marked revolutionary departures from the traditional administrative practices of the Shah and Rana administration, under which appointments to government service were made on a familial basis with no consideration for skills or merit and the financial records of the government were maintained and scrutinized unsystematically.

The Act of 1951 defined expressly the aims of the interim government as those of "creating conditions as early as possible for holding elections to a Constituent Assembly, which will frame a Constitution for Nepal." For this purpose, the establishment of an Election Commission with authority to "superintend, direct, and control preparation of electoral rolls and the conduct of elections" was envisaged. The elections were to be conducted on the basis of universal adult suffrage.

One significant feature of the Interim Constitution was the lengthy first section, entitled "Directive Principles of State Policy," borrowed for the most part from the Indian Constitution, which set guidelines for the policies and programs of the government. The duty of the state was declared to be "the promotion of the welfare of the people by securing a social order in which social, economic, and political justice will infuse all the institutions of national life." On the international plane, the state should promote peace and security, just and honorable relations between nations, and settlement of disputes by arbitration. Like the Indian Constitution, the Interim Government Act of 1951 guaranteed, within the limits of national peace and security, the rights of the citizens to freedom of speech and expression; freedom of assembly, association, and movement throughout the country; and the right to private property and practice of any profession or business. These directive principles were undoubtedly ambitious and unrealistic in the context of Nepali social life, but they served to underline the visions and aspirations of the new political elites that had emerged as the leaders of the democratic political order.

THE FIRST ADVISORY ASSEMBLY

The establishment of an Advisory Assembly was first approved by King Tribhuwan in October, 1951, as one means of strengthening the position of the Nepali Congress bloc in the Mohan Shamsher Cabinet. A thirty-five-member Assembly was appointed, but events intruded before it could meet. The Rana-Congress coalition resigned in mid-November, and the new Prime Minister, M. P. Koirala, preferred to govern without the assistance of an advisory body whose members had been chosen by his principal rival in the Nepali Congress. Once the Prime Minister's relations with the party had deteriorated to the breaking point, however, M. P. Koirala decided that an Assembly, suitably recomposed, might prove advantageous. The first Advisory Assembly, expanded from thirty-five to forty-seven members, was eventually convened in July, 1952.

To provide a legal basis for the Assembly, it was necessary to amend the Interim Government Act. The amendment, approved in April, 1952, defined the purpose of the Assembly as that of securing a greater participation of the representatives of the people in the administration of the country and of providing assistance and advice to the King and the Cabinet. The members were selected by the King from among the prominent citizens of the country, and the Cabinet Ministers were *ex officio* members.

The Assembly, which was to hold at least two sessions every year, was empowered to consider any question connected with the legislative and executive programs of the government, subject to the following exceptions: (*a*) relations with foreign countries, (*b*) the conduct of the King and members of the royal family, (*c*) matters described as contrary to public welfare by the government, and (*d*) a vote of no confidence against the Cabinet or any Minister. The Cabinet was forbidden to submit to the King any bill that had not been considered and approved by the Assembly while it was in session, but could still enact legislation if the Assembly was not in session. The King could veto any bill or resolution passed by the Assembly or could return the bill to the Assembly with suggested changes or amendments.

LEGISLATIVE MEASURES

Two important pieces of legislation, enacted during the Royal Councilors' regime, reflected the changed political atmosphere in Nepal after the resignation of the M. P. Koirala government. These were the Press and Publications Act of 1952 and the Nepal High Court Act (Amendment) promulgated in December, 1952. The former gave sweeping powers to local and district officials to punish publishers of newspapers on the following counts: leading government officials astray from their duty and loyalty; causing hatred and disrespect toward the King and his family; causing hatred and disrespect toward the government established according to law and toward its actions, or toward any race or caste of any of the subjects of His Majesty; pressuring any government official to act in a manner not required by his work, or to make him abstain from or delay any work already undertaken by him, or to induce him to resign from his work; and causing mutual enmity and hatred among the different classes of the subjects of His Majesty.[1] A system of graduated financial penalties for various degrees of offense was imposed. All newspaper publishers and press owners were required to deposit a security with the government, and this security could be confiscated by the local and district officials for violations of the Press Act. The officials were also given wide discretionary powers to confiscate unauthorized newspapers, pamphlets, or books, and to seize any such material sent by post.

The Nepal High Court Act of 1951,[2] which received royal assent on May 8, 1952, was also amended by the Royal Councilors. In its original form, the High Court consisted of a chief justice and four puisne judges who could not be removed except through resignation or by a two-thirds' majority vote of the Cabinet on charges of misconduct or incompetence. The High Court was declared to be the highest court of the land, and its orders and decisions were deemed final. In many respects the Court's functions, powers, and structure corresponded generally to those of the Supreme Court of India, including full authority over all subordinate courts and tribunals under its jurisdiction.

The first amendment of the High Court Act,[3] approved by King Tribhuwan on the recommendation of the Royal Councilors, raised doubts as to whether the Interim Constitution was, in fact, the supreme law of the land. The High Court Act included an oath in which the judges swore allegiance to the 1951 organic law; as amended, however, the judges merely swore—through an oath to "Pashupatinath, Guheshwari, and the family deity, by touching copper, tulsi [sacred plant], Ganga jal [holy water from the Ganges], and the holy book of Hari Vansha"—that they would carry out their duties, and no mention was made of the Interim Government Act.

The process of delimiting the constitutional role of the judiciary was continued under the National Democratic party government appointed in June, 1953. The new government faced an unprecedented constitutional crisis in November, which it met through a further attrition of the status and powers of the High Court. The crisis was largely the result of High Court decisions in two suits filed against the government for infringement of civil and political rights. The first was filed by B. P. Koirala, who had been restricted to Kathmandu Valley on September 20 by the Deputy Secretary of the Home Ministry on orders from the Prime Minister, on charges of having fomented disaffection among government civil servants.[4] The second suit was filed by Bharat Bahadur Pande and Min Bahadur Shahi against the Bada Hakim of West No. 1 District for repeal of an order of internment that had been issued against them.[5]

The High Court ruled that in both cases the internment of the plaintiffs violated Article 18 of the Interim Government Act of 1951:

No person shall be deprived of life or personal liberty except according to procedures established by law or rules made by the government for the public good, or for the maintenance of public order or the security of that state.

The Court also ruled that the restriction or internment powers of the Kathmandu Valley magistrates violated Article 16 of the Act, which guaranteed to Nepali citizens the right to reside and settle in any part of Nepal. Accordingly, on November 19, the High Court ruled in favor of the plaintiffs in both suits. The implications of these court rulings were: (1) The Interim Government Act of 1951 and the Vyaktigata Swatantrata ("Individual Freedom") Act were held to comprise the Constitution of Nepal, conferring certain fundamental rights on the Nepali people. (2) Any laws which were repugnant to these fundamental rights, whether made before or after 1951, were invalid, and the Public Safety Act and the Kathmandu Commissioner and Magistrates' Act were *ultra vires*. (3) The King had no power to enact legislation, and could only promulgate ordinances. (4) The Prime Minister had no power to issue executive orders; only the King-in-Council could do so.[6] As a result, the process of government was thrown in utter confusion since these decisions rendered illegal most of its practices and procedures. Both the King and the Prime Minister were denied powers that they had exercised frequently since 1951.

To end the constitutional crisis, King Tribhuwan issued a Royal Proclamation on January 10, 1954, in which he declared that: (*a*) supreme rights in the legislative field should be vested in the King as long as a Constitution had not been framed by an elected Constituent Assembly; (*b*) as long as the Constituent Assembly had not framed a constitution, all those judicial powers which had not been given to the Supreme Court should be vested in the King; and (*c*) all powers exercised by the Ministers and their subordinates, according to the rules and laws enforced by the King or by royal authority, should always be regarded as proper and valid, and as such should not be questioned in any court.[7] The Royal Proclamation stated also that the supreme executive, judicial, and legislative powers of the Shah sovereign, which had been "delegated" to the Rana Prime Minister in 1856, had been "revoked" in 1951, and that supreme authority in all these spheres was once again vested in the monarch. This was, thus, the first unequivocal affirmation of the King's inherent powers as the supreme executive, legislative, and judicial authority in Nepal since the end of Rana rule.

The Royal Proclamation was followed by three legislative enactments, promulgated on February 13, which clipped the powers of the High Court even more drastically and formally reaffirmed the King's inherent powers and prerogatives in the legislative, executive, and judicial fields.[8] Two of the enactments amended existing laws—the Interim Government Act and the High Court Act—while the third promulgated the Nepal Laws (Interpretation) Act, which clarified the procedures and technicalities involved in the enforcement, repeal, connotation, and interpretation of both old and new Nepali laws.

The third amendment of the Interim Government Act of 1951 included several important provisions that seriously impaired the powers of the judiciary. The Directive Principles of State Policy were defined as guidelines for the government rather than constitutional directives. Since they were held to be nonjusticiable in any court, no Nepali law could be deemed invalid because it was incompatible with the Directive Principles. Under this ruling, the Public Security Act and the Kathmandu Commissioner and Magistrates Act were reinvalidated. Furthermore, the government was vested with the power to grant pardons, reprieves, and respites or remissions of punishment and to suspend, remit, or commute the sentence of any convicted persons—powers that the High Court had declared could be exercised only by the King. Finally, three articles of the Interim Act relating to the composition of the judiciary were deleted and a new article inserted which merely stated that this should be "as determined by law." [9]

This last provision set the stage for the second amendment of the High Court Act, in which important changes were made in the powers and jurisdiction of the High Court. The Court was no longer the "highest court of justice in the country," in view of the King's declaration that he was the supreme judicial authority in Nepal. The High Court was no longer a "court of record," and thus it lost all powers of such courts, including the authority to punish for contempt. Section 30 of the High Court Act was omitted, depriving the Court of the power to issue directions and orders, including writs of *habeas corpus*.

The government, despite Prime Minister M. P. Koirala's preoccupation with political haggling, was also curtailing individual rights in the country by other means. In September, 1953, the government published a notice in the official gazette prohibiting employees of government-recognized educational institutions, whether aided financially by the government or not, from taking part in politics or making speeches. In October, the government published an order requiring all military and civil employees to report the receipt of political materials, such as leaflets and circulars, within three days of delivery.

Thus, by the end of the Tribhuwan era, the democratic political system introduced in 1951 had been severely eroded. The ultimate sovereignty of the King had been established as the basic premise of the Nepali constitutional system, and all the institutional barriers to the exercise of this authority, hastily erected in the first year after the overthrow of the Ranas, had been abolished one by one. As long as King Tribhuwan sat on the throne, to be sure, absolute monarchy was a constitutional theory rather than a political fact in Nepal. During most of this period, real political authority and power was exercised by political leaders in the Council of Ministers. But there were few obstacles to making the theory fact by the time King Tribhuwan's successor had ascended the throne in 1955, as the history of the succeeding period testifies.

MODERNIZATION OF THE ADMINISTRATIVE SYSTEM

The administrative reorganization tasks facing the Rana-Nepali Congress coalition government in 1951 were both complex and urgent. The traditional machinery for the maintenance of law and order had been seriously impaired in several parts of the country in the course of the 1950 revolution. Equally serious, if not quite as urgent, was the need to create a modern, viable administrative system as an institutional bulwark to a democratic political order.

The traditional administrative machinery had constituted, in essence, an extension of the Rana-controlled military hierarchy into civil administration. The task of the new government was to revamp the entire system to suit the conditions of a democratic polity. Trained administrative personnel were scarce, and the few civil servants associated with the Rana regime were both temperamentally and technically unsuited for most branches of the new administration, with the important exception of the police. Thus, the small community of Western-educated elites, mostly college professors and schoolteachers, was called upon to staff the key positions in the new administrative system. A Central Secretariat was hastily organized at Singha Darbar, the residence of Rana Prime Ministers since 1903, and ten ministries were established in accordance with the portfolios announced by King Tribhuwan on

February 18. A Secretary functioned as the permanent head of each ministry under a politically appointed Minister, and was assisted by deputy secretaries, assistant secretaries, nongazetted officers, and senior and junior clerical staff—all members of the civil service. Offices formerly scattered around the city were brought together and assigned to the jurisdiction of the appropriate ministry.

The coalition government found it necessary to apply to the Indian government for technical assistance in drawing up rules of procedure for the new administrative setup. Accordingly, three senior members of the Indian civil service worked in Nepal for about a year and prepared administrative rules and instructions for office procedures on the basis of the Indian Secretariat manual. They also assisted in the preparation of the Interim Government Act of 1951, which provided the constitutional basis for the new political order.

One significant administrative innovation was the publication of the *Nepal Gazette,* commencing on August 6, 1951. Any notice published in the *Gazette* had the same status as orders of the government, and was to be implemented without delay even if separate executive orders had not been received from the ministry concerned. The publication of the *Gazette* brought some degree of uniformity and universality to the decisions of the government, which in the past had often been exercised with varying latitudes of interpretation by district and local officials. This standardization of government orders and regulations, as typified by publication of the *Nepal Gazette,* helped to create a new role for officials in the administrative structure—the role of the bureaucrat.

RESTORATION AND PRESERVATION OF LAW AND ORDER

One paramount responsibility of the Rana-Congress coalition government was the restoration of law and order in parts of the country which had been badly affected by the 1950 revolution, a task which fell upon the not unwilling shoulders of the Nepali Congress Home Minister, B. P. Koirala. In the period immediately after the revolution there was some doubt about the effectiveness and loyalty of the Rana-officered state army in an emergency. One of the first objectives of the government, therefore, was the reorganization of the army under the direct command of the King. Most A Rana officers were gradually eliminated, either voluntarily or involuntarily, from positions of command, and B and C Ranas were promoted in their place. Kiran Shamsher, a C Rana, was appointed Commander in Chief, but final command responsibility was assumed by the King, who took the title of Supreme Commander in Chief.

Nevertheless, the only trusted instrument for the maintenance of law and order in the capital for some months after the revolution was the Rakshya Dal, the old "liberation army" of the Nepali Congress. This tended to create bad feelings between some sections of the regular army and the Rakshya Dal, whose lack of tradition and discipline also brought it into conflict with the local populace.

The coalition government armed itself with legislative authority to tackle problems of lawlessness by enacting two important pieces of legislation—the Public Security Act and the Emergency Powers of the Bada Hakim Act. The Public Security Act invested the government with wide discretionary powers to arrest a person and hold him in custody for a period of six months without trial, "in the interests of the security of the nation and public stability." [10] The government was empowered to extend the period of internment from time to time, subject to the proviso that no one should be ordered interned for more than six months or, in case of extension, be kept interned for more than one year continuously. The Emergency Powers of the Bada Hakim Act, which was valid for only six months, conferred more or less similar powers on the district administration to handle local problems of lawlessness and public disorder. The Bada Hakims, or magistrates at the head of the district administrations, were invested with authority to imprison any suspected offender for three months without trial and to disperse any armed assembly in their areas, by force if necessary.

ADMINISTRATIVE REORGANIZATION

The first comprehensive reorganization of the Secretariat at the Departmental Secretary level was announced on November 28, 1951, about two weeks after the installation of the M. P. Koirala government. This did not result in a major change in the composition and character of the Secretariat, however, as a majority of the new Secretaries had been prominent members of the Rana bureaucracy. There were only three new Secretaries, recruited from the Western-educated elite, and these were assigned to such minor departments as Health, Local Self-Government, and Parliamentary Affairs. Indeed, the so-called reorganization of the higher administrative staff marked, in fact, a revival of Rana-associated attitudes and procedures in the civil service.

This revivalist tendency was further buttressed in February, 1952, when a Civil Service Coördination Committee, composed entirely of former Rana administrators, was appointed by M. P. Koirala. The committee produced no significant changes in administrative procedures and machinery, but its composition did underscore the conservative orientation of the Prime Minister.

While M. P. Koirala was thus encouraging the revival of traditional administrative practices in the government, Indian advisers, brought in by the previous government, were preparing and recommending "modernizing" rules and procedures. The model followed was the Indian civil service system, suitably modified to conform to Nepal's needs and experiences. The first team of Indian experts left in February, 1952, and a new team, popularly known as the Buch Committee, after its leader, N. B. Buch, arrived in July to conduct a thorough investigation of the administrative machinery.

The report of the Buch Committee, which included a long list of recommendations, was submitted to the government at approximately the same time that the Royal Councilors' regime was appointed to office. In his instructions to the Councilors, King Tribhuwan stated that their foremost duty was "to establish immediately a system of administration consisting of honest, loyal, unprejudiced, impartial, and public welfare–minded officials, and to draft laws and rules for every part and branch of administration." [11] One of the first actions of the Councilors' regime, therefore, was the reorganization of the Secretariat into eleven departments, as recommended by the Buch Committee.* This was followed by an overhaul of the administrative staff at the district level, in which several officials appointed by B. P. Koirala during his stint as Home Minister in 1951 were dismissed. Unfortunately, this action made little contribution to the "depoliticization" of the bureaucracy, as the dismissed officials were replaced in most instances by members of the royal family or relatives of the Councilors.

In September, new pay scales for government service were announced. A few months later a Civil Service Screening Committee, formed to scrutinize the competence of civil servants, published the curriculum for examinations in different categories of the Nepal Civil Service. For the first time, all government employees were divided into two classes: the Nepal Civil Service and the Nepal Technical Service.

The process of administrative reorganization was continued

---

* These were: General Administration; Foreign Affairs; Defence; Finance; Home; Revenue and Forests; Commerce, Industries, and Civil Supplies; Public Works and Communications; Education, Health, and Local Self-Government; Planning and Development; and Law and Parliamentary Affairs.

and expanded under the National government headed by M. P. Koirala. The Home Minister, Tanka Prasad Acharya, initiated a major reorganization of the Police Department in May, 1954. At that time there were five different forces with police duties: the civil police (2,000 men), the Ram Dal (500), the Rakshya Dal (4,500), the militia (15,000), and military detachments assigned to police duties (1,000).[12] The reorganization plan provided for the reduction of the police force from 23,000 to an integrated unit of 6,500 officers and men. The militia stationed in mountainous regions was to be reorganized for use as a "road army."

Another reorganization scheme of the National government pertained to the improvement of the administrative system in the districts. In a policy statement, the Cabinet announced that Bada Hakims were to be appointed on a nonpolitical basis and be drawn from the staff of the Civil Secretariat.[13] In November, 1954, the Bada Hakims were incorporated in the regular civil service, but this lasted only until the ascension of King Mahendra to the throne, when once again they were appointed on an *ad hoc,* political basis.

By the beginning of 1955, substantial changes had been effected in the form and structure of the administration in Nepal. On paper, Nepal had a modern civil service engaged in a wide variety of public welfare activities, in addition to the revenue-collecting and security functions that had been the sole concern of the Rana bureaucracy. But the changes were more in form than in substance, as the Rana psychology of administration was still virtually unchallenged. This was reflected most pervasively in the operating procedures within the Secretariat, which proved to be much less susceptible to reform and reorganization than the administrative superstructure. The general trend of political developments towards the end of the Tribhuwan era, moreover, tended to encourage and support resistance to effective modernization of the administrative machinery.

SOCIAL AND ECONOMIC REFORMS

One of the more surprising aspects of the first post-revolution government was the adoption as government policy of certain measures for economic and social reforms proposed by the Nepali Congress bloc in the coalition. It had been expected that the Rana bloc would strongly oppose these measures, most of which were aimed at undermining the prestige and interests of the Rana family, but this did not prove to be the case. For example, on the initiative of the Nepali Congress, but with the support of the Rana Ministers as well, the Cabinet abolished many feudal practices which had been an integral part of the Rana political system. These comprised a wide variety of administrative practices, such as monetary exactions in the form of mandatory gifts and presents, forced labor to maintain public works or facilitate the tours of government officials, free allowances from the Treasury to members of the Rana family and their favorites, and supplementary land grants to favorite officials. The monopoly of the Rana family over all high positions in the army was also ended, and command posts were now made accessible to officers from any ethnic or caste community.

The sharpest point in the Nepali Congress's attack on the feudal privileges of the Rana family was its proposal to abolish the holding of *Birta* (rent-free) lands—the traditional base of Rana economic power. Yet on September 26, 1951, the Cabinet accepted unanimously the principle of the abolition of *Birta* and decided to establish the necessary administrative machinery for the implementation of this policy. As a first step in the process of recording *Birta* holdings, the transfer of *Birta* land by sale or mortgage was prohibited for all holdings larger than 25 *Ropanis* (about 3.25 acres) in the hill districts and Kathmandu Valley and 25 *Bighas* (about 40 acres) in the Terai.[14]

The coalition government also undertook several significant social measures to dramatize the end of the Rana political order and the inauguration of a democratic system. In September, the Cabinet decided to discontinue the traditional military parade in Kathmandu during the Indra Jatra festival, which the Rana rulers had used to overawe the local populace. Some of the traditional festivities involving the ceremonial sacrifice of animals, associated with the Durga Puja festival, were discontinued, and gambling during the festivals of Kojagrat and Panchak was banned. In October, the Ministry of Education published an order requiring both government-sponsored and government-aided schools to admit students of untouchable castes.

The first M. P. Koirala Cabinet, although ostensibly dominated by the Nepali Congress, proved to be much more conservative and cautious than its predecessor.* On the question of land

---

* Prime Minister M. P. Koirala's conservatism was best reflected in his attitude toward social reform. In December, 1951, a group of untouchables attempted to force entry into the sacred Hindu temple of Pashupatinath in Kathmandu, a right which had theoretically been assured to them by the provision of the Interim Constitution abolishing untouchability. The Brahman Prime Minister, however, had them arrested on charges of breach of peace, thus helping sustain archaic social and religious principles.

reform and *Birta* abolition, for instance, M. P. Koirala adopted a go-slow approach. A new Ministry of Land Reform was created, but the focus of governmental activity in this regard shifted from such drastic measures as abolition and reallocation of inequitable landholdings to organizing studies and surveys of land problems. Within a month of its formation, the new government withdrew the restrictions imposed by the previous Rana-Congress coalition on sales, transfers, mortgages, gifts, and subdivisions of *Birta* land. Later, in a notification dated March 18, 1952, the government assured landowners that the abolition of the *Birta* system would not be done on a rough-and-ready basis, and indicated that the government would confine itself to collecting records or figures on various classifications of *Birta* lands, the extent of their cultivation, and the amount of rent payable on different categories. To avoid entanglement in a complicated program of land redistribution, the government also announced a policy under which new land would be brought under cultivation. To that end, applications were invited from the interested public, with first priority going to landless laborers and political sufferers.

Almost the only important measures of the M. P. Koirala government in the field of land reform were the institution of *ad hoc* land enquiry commissions to study peasant-landlord conflicts in western Nepal, and the publication of the draft of a Tenancy Rights Acquisition Act.[15] According to the draft, tenants cultivating land belonging to landlords would be entitled to legal protection against capricious eviction. The guidelines motivating this legislation and subsequent land policy were stated as follows: (*a*) tenants should be allowed to settle permanently on the land they cultivate; (*b*) the number of landless laborers should be decreased; (*c*) improved feelings of security on the part of tenants would improve agricultural productivity, and (*d*) general improvement in the relationship between the landlord and the peasants would result from a clear definition of the rights and privileges of both groups.

THE FIRST GOVERNMENT BUDGET

Perhaps the most notable single administrative measure of the M. P. Koirala government was the publication of the first government budget in the history of Nepal. In his historic broadcast over Radio Nepal on February 2, 1952, Finance Minister Suvarna Shamsher presented the budget for the year 1951/52 and compared it with that of the previous year, which had never been published. The financial assets left by the last

Rana government in the form of gold, silver, old coins, Indian coins, Nepali and foreign currency notes, and shares in the Nepal Bank were estimated at approximately 80 million Nepali rupees. Out of these reserves, the Finance Minister established a Currency Reserve Fund, an Exchange Stabilization Fund, and a Budget Equalization Fund, with capitals respectively of fifty, twenty, and ten million rupees.

The budget for the preceding year (1950/51) was estimated as follows: total income during 1950/51, Rs. 29,081,000; total expenditure during 1950/51, Rs. 24,687,000; surplus, Rs. 4,394,000. The budget for the year 1951/52 was estimated as follows: total income during 1951/52, Rs. 30,516,000; total expenditure during 1951/52, Rs. 52,521,000; deficit, Rs. 22,005,000. Expenditures for the current year were expected to rise by nearly 30 million rupees, more than double the amount for the preceding year. Increased expenditures were earmarked for the new administrative organization and the new role of the government as the promoter of social services, such as education and public health. The army, the police, and the Secretariat consumed nearly 40 per cent of the additional expenditures.[16]

The budget also outlined, in broad prospectus, the government's intentions and policies in the area of economic development. Improved accounting methods had been introduced; the establishment of a State Bank was proposed; and a National Savings Scheme was suggested for the mobilization of indigenous resources. The aim of the government was defined as that of raising the standard of living of the people, not by leveling down and distributing existing wealth, but by developing the resources of the country and by increasing national wealth and production. The government announced its adherence to a "mixed economy" policy, under which private enterprise would be guaranteed full scope, but the government would prevent the exploitation of any class or individual.

As might be expected, the ultraconservative Royal Councilors' regime was even more cautious in its approach to economic and social reform than the first M. P. Koirala government. The only measure of any significance in these spheres was the appointment of a Land Reform Commission on August 27, 1952, to investigate the land tenure system in Nepal and to recommend appropriate measures for the improvement of the agricultural system. The reports of the Commission formed the basis for most subsequent land legislation. Two other commissions, a Pay Commission and an Education Commission, were established in April,

1953. The former was charged with the responsibility of systematizing the pay scale of government employees and the latter with the formulation of a national scheme of education.[17] The Councilors' regime, however, was dismissed long before the reports of these commissions were completed.

The four-party National government entered office in 1954 on the basis of a forty-point "minimum" program of action which supposedly incorporated the programs of the constituent parties. It quickly became obvious that the minimum program had been motivated by political considerations and that neither the parties nor the government had serious concern with its implementation. Indeed, the only significant achievement of the National government, and certainly the most controversial, was the agreement with India on the multipurpose Kosi River project. The Kosi River, often described as the "River of Sorrows," annually devastated thousands of square miles of agricultural land in Nepal and the Indian state of Bihar. The Kosi project envisioned construction of a barrage, headworks, flood banks, and canals on Nepali territory. The costs of the project were to be borne by India, while Nepal was assured of irrigational and power facilities. On April 23, 1954, the Indian Minister for Planning, Gulzari Lal Nanda, arrived in Kathmandu and, three days later, negotiated an eighteen-point agreement with the Nepali government on the Kosi project.

This agreement was assailed immediately by various political parties and newspapers. The criticisms usually centered around the fact that Nepal had surrendered extraterritorial rights to India at the project sites for an indefinite period of time without obtaining adequate compensation and without securing adequate benefits from the project. Prime Minister M. P. Koirala defended the agreement on the grounds that it would save annually about 2,000 acres of fertile land from erosion by the Kosi River, and also dwelt at length on the irrigational facilities and hydroelectric power that would accrue to Nepal from the project. But his arguments that, in the past, Nepal had purchased land at Jayanagar and Raxaul in India for its railways and had sold land to the British Residency at Kathmandu without losing its sovereignty failed to convince the opposition. From this time on, the Kosi agreement was a hot political issue in Nepal. Even the gift of nearly 100,000 rupees' worth of ammonium sulphate, presented to the government of Nepal at the conclusion of the Kosi agreement, was interpreted in some political quarters as a bribe to compensate Nepal for what it had lost through the Kosi agreement.

FOREIGN POLICY

In the aftermath of the 1950 revolution, the first interim government was so much involved in domestic affairs that it could spare little time for attention to foreign policy questions. Nor was there any great urgency about this, as the circumstances under which Nepal had emerged from a century of Rana-imposed isolation and autocracy served to define the general features of Nepali foreign policy. New Delhi had set the terms of the tripartite compromise that ended the revolution; India's leadership in the determination of Nepal's newly acquired role in the world community of nations was generally accepted in Kathmandu. India's "special relationship" with Nepal was recognized at this stage of developments by virtually all the political leaders of the country except the Communists. Indeed, in 1951, the opposition party leaders often sought New Delhi's intervention in Nepal's internal politics, and only later, when it became evident that the Indian government would not intervene on their behalf, did elements of the opposition begin to assume an openly critical attitude toward India's Nepal policy.

By the time of the establishment of the first Nepali Congress government, in November, 1951, developments both within Nepal and abroad—in particular, the Chinese Communist conquest of Tibet—had made it imperative for the new government to define its foreign policy in more precise terms. On January 6, 1952, Prime Minister M. P. Koirala and several other ministers visited New Delhi for consultations with the Indian government, and on their return the Prime Minister addressed the nation on his government's foreign policy. He emphasized the necessity of close relations with India and disclosed that the Nepal government was negotiating a loan of 150 million rupees, "with no political strings attached," from New Delhi. On the international level, he characterized his policy as one of steering clear of "power blocs" and of obtaining membership in the United Nations.[18]

Perhaps the most concrete development in Nepal's foreign relations during the first M. P. Koirala government was the initiation of several foreign aid projects, some of which had been negotiated earlier by the Rana government or the Rana-Congress coalition. Construction on the Indian-supported highway, the Tribhuwan Rajpath, linking Kathmandu with India, was inaugurated on February 19, 1952. In addition, the Indian government also undertook the tasks of modernizing Kathmandu's airport, reorganizing the Nepali Army, and improving the civil administration. Chester Bowles, the American Ambassador to India and Nepal, who visited Kathmandu in February, held preliminary discussions with the government on the question of a Point Four aid program in Nepal.

One other controversial development in this period was the conclusion of an agreement with the United Kingdom, in July, permitting British recruitment of Gorkhas for battalions stationed in Malaya. A tripartite agreement between England, India, and Nepal in July, 1947, had allowed the British to recruit Gorkhas up to twelve battalions' strength at recruitment depots located in India. In 1952, however, the Indian government announced its intention to close the British recruiting facilities on Indian soil, and this necessitated a new agreement providing for British recruitment facilities within Nepal itself. Nepali political parties, including the Nepali Congress, had long agitated against the recruitment of Nepalese by foreign powers, and had demanded the abrogation of the agreement with England. Nevertheless, the M. P. Koirala government negotiated a new agreement which permitted the British to establish two recruitment depots in Nepal—one at Taulihawa in the western hills and the other at Dharan in eastern Nepal—at which a limited number of Gorkha soldiers could be recruited over a five-year period.

Foreign policy issues continued to play a comparatively minor role in the government's proceedings until the spring of 1954, when several events at home and abroad forced the question of Nepal's relations with China to the fore. Since 1951, opposition party leaders had been clamoring for diplomatic relations with the People's Republic of China. The government's reply had been that Peking had demonstrated little interest in the establishment of diplomatic relations and that, in these circumstances, Nepal was also disinclined to attach much urgency to the question.

This situation changed drastically in the view of the Nepal government with the signing of the Sino-Indian treaty on Tibet on April 29, 1954, in which New Delhi surrendered the special privileges it had enjoyed in Tibet and also recognized Chinese sovereignty over that state. It was in this agreement that the "five principles" (*Panch Shila*) of peaceful coexistence were first enunciated as the basis of relationship between the two countries.

The modification of India's relationship with Tibet inevitably had serious repercussions upon Nepal's policy toward both Tibet and China. One of the first came when, in 1954, there was no payment of the annual tribute of Rs. 10,000 which Lhasa had sent to Kathmandu since 1856. Prime Minister M. P. Koirala's announcement in October, 1954, that Nepal had no interest in the continuation of the tribute system, but wished to revise its century-old treaty relationship with Tibet, was a somewhat belated recognition of the drastic change in circumstances to the north of the Himalayas. Chou En-lai's statement in Peking proposing the establishment of normal diplomatic relations with Nepal received an immediately favorable response from the Nepali Foreign Minister, D. R. Regmi.

The question of Sino-Nepali relations was one of the subjects raised by Nehru during his visit to China in October, 1954. M. P. Koirala met Nehru in Calcutta both before his departure for Peking and on his return to India. After these consultations the Nepal government decided to establish diplomatic relations with Peking. The Nepali and Chinese ambassadors in New Delhi commenced exploratory talks, and by December D. R. Regmi could report that satisfactory progress had been made. Domestic political developments and King Tribhuwan's death intervened to delay a final agreement, and it was only in July, 1955, that diplomatic relations with China were formally resumed. Nevertheless, by the end of the Tribhuwan era Nepal was in the process of introducing important innovations in its foreign policy that have since substantially altered Nepal's role in inter-Himalayan political developments.

9

The Tribhuwan
Period in Retrospect

ALMOST EXACTLY four years elapsed between the restoration of
King Tribhuwan to the throne in 1951 and his death in 1955.
These were remarkable years in many respects, and the accomplishments of the various governments that held office in Nepal
during this period were not as insignificant and ephemeral as
some later political leaders have implied. The record is, at least,
mixed, and this should not be obscured by the sense of frustration, cynicism, and disenchantment that was rampant at the end of
the Tribhuwan era.

Despite its brief tenure in office, the first post-revolutionary
government—the Rana-Congress coalition—left a durable impression on the politics of contemporary Nepal. It gave the
country an interim Constitution in which the ideals of a constitutional monarch and a cabinet form of government were im-
bedded, and it laid the basis for a new political process in Nepal.
Familial politics was replaced by party politics, and Rana autocracy gave way to a liberal Shah polity. The country was given its
first independent judiciary. A modern, national administrative
system, no longer the monopoly of privileged families, but open
to all qualified candidates irrespective of caste, religion, sex, and
family connections, was introduced. The Nepali Army was "nationalized" by opening the ranks to recruits from any ethnic
group or geographical area of the country, the exclusive control of
the Rana family over command posts was abolished, and all
officers became eligible for promotion to the highest ranks. The
principle of the abolition of *Birta* land was accepted as a
government policy aimed at the eradication of the feudal order,
the forests were brought under the control of the government,

and many degrading feudal administrative practices were abolished.

Yet, the coalition government also left a political legacy which in the long run prejudiced the interests of a democratic political system. The Nepali Congress leaders made only a feeble attempt to obtain the support of Kathmandu political elites, and these elites, in turn, abetted by the Communists and goaded by their sense of injured pride, initiated a highly unstable, personalized type of party politics based primarily on nonsubstantive, emotional issues which had as its objective the humiliation of the Nepali Congress. The Rana family, in contrast, escaped serious public or political criticism.

In its eagerness to dislodge the politically effete Rana minority from the Cabinet, the Nepali Congress leaders also ignored the Rana Prime Minister's thoughtful suggestion that the importance of his office should not be downgraded even under a democratic system. Because of their personal dislike and disrespect for the Rana incumbent, the party agreed to a diminution of the Prime Minister's power and an expansion in the powers of the King. The Delhi compromise had envisaged a three-way division of power during the interim period between three more or less equal political entities—the King, the Ranas, and the Nepali Congress. But the Nepali Congress, stung by memories of its exclusion from crucial negotiations in Delhi and by public criticisms of its alleged betrayal of the goals of the revolution, sought to undermine the interim political compromise from the very beginning, little realizing that the expulsion of the Ranas would probably prove advantageous to the Palace, but could also result in a proportionate reduction in the capability of the party to serve as an instrument of political change.

Moreover, the emergence of party politics in Kathmandu produced a political situation which was, on balance, favorable to reactionary elements and unfavorable to the Nepali Congress. Indeed, the Nepali Congress had only one thing in its favor during the tenure of the coalition government, and that was the continued solidarity of its leadership at the top. Few Nepalese seemed to realize that the weakening of the Nepali Congress during the interim period also meant a general debilitation of the embryonic democratic political structure.

The Nepali Congress government, the second political experiment of the interim period, began as democracy's finest hour in Nepal and ended as its swan song. The failure of the one-party government to accomplish any substantial reforms or improvements and its ignominious dissolution in the clash of personal ambitions and party strife were a great blow to the cause of democracy and the prestige of the Nepali Congress. The only benefactors were revivalist political elements, who hoped for either a resurgence of Rana power or the absolute rule of the Shah monarch. Political opportunists and elements opposed to change and reform won the upper hand in the political arena, and from this time on the cult of personality became the theme of party politics.

Perhaps the most harmful effect of the failure of the Nepali Congress was the general frustration which ensued among the public, which had been misled by a constant barrage of political speeches and propaganda into assuming that the end of Rana rule had brought the millennium. With the fall of the Nepali Congress government, the momentum for change was abruptly halted, and the spiral of rising popular expectations was stopped. In such circumstances, the politically articulate public became increasingly cynical and hypercritical, seeking security and hope in the mushrooming of new political parties and associations which only abetted the further deterioration of an already critical situation.

The Councilors' regime halted, and temporarily reversed, the evolution of the transitional political process initiated in 1951. Party politics were further sidetracked from the goals of political democracy as the parties themselves turned into the pawns of individuals concerned with power rather than principles or programs. Even the consensus among the parties on the undesirability of the Councilors' regime was not especially significant, since the parties, enmeshed in the personal ambitions of their leaders, could not agree on any common course of action to oppose or replace the regime.

The Councilors' regime also marked the beginning of the Crown's direct participation in the political process during the period of democratic experimentation. The King had now veered away from his original intention to assume a constitutional role and allow popular representatives to run the government, and took an increasingly active part in decision and policy making. Similarly, Ministers began to be selected not for their popularity, influence, or party strength, but on a strictly personal basis, which basically altered the nature of political activity in Nepal.

The eight-month-long government of the National Democratic party, although conceived as a strictly interim arrangement, had a strong, but essentially negative impact on the evolution of a democratic system in Nepal. The Royal Proclamation of January 10, 1954, and the subsequent legislative enactments formally marked the recognition of royal autocracy and the denigration of the independent judicial process. Since King Tribhuwan was temperamentally and physically incapable of acting the role of an autocrat, much of the newly revived royal authority passed on to M. P. Koirala, not as a leader of his party or even as Prime Minister, but in his personal capacity as the King's favorite. His nondescript colleagues in the Cabinet were mostly his political creations and as such were incapable of countering his authority in any way.

More importantly, M. P. Koirala had in his hands the power to dispense Cabinet seats to various political parties. With this as a base, he negotiated with other parties from a position of advantage and strength, merged one political faction with his own party, and disrupted attempts by other parties to form coalitions and alliances. Under such circumstances, the political process degenerated into unstable political alignments and factions motivated by rank opportunism and exaggerated personal ambitions. The main beneficiaries of this situation were the independents, the Gorkha Parishad leaders, and the Communists, all of whom, despite their vastly dissimilar political orientation, stood to gain from the general loss of reputation of the democratic political parties. In general, during the tenure of the National Democratic party the democratic process reached its lowest point, and political opportunism, its zenith. Political dissidents obtained a fresh lease on life, but the people of Nepal began to exhibit even greater distress with the results of the so-called democratic political experiments.

The functioning of the National coalition Cabinet was another illustration of the overwhelming importance of personalities in the new political process in Nepal. The basis of the government itself had been the promised coöperation of political leaders acting in their individual capacities rather than as representatives of their parties. The so-called coalition had really been a simple combination of several prominent party leaders rather than a fusion of party objectives or ideologies. Thus the forty-point "minimum" program adopted by the coalition was little more than a symbol of a token consensus among the members of the government, and as such was never translated into practice.

There can be little doubt that it was M. P. Koirala who insisted on forming the National government with "individuals" rather than "representatives of political parties," presumably because he wanted to avoid a repetition of the events that had unseated him from power in August, 1952. This novel basis for a government may have been a cleverly conceived device for protecting the Prime Minister's favored position with King Tribhuwan, but it was hardly a valid basis for forming a government, let alone a "national" government. In principle, a coalition of individuals rather than parties implied a denigration of the party system as an effective instrument for the social, economic, and political transformation of Nepal. It was contrary to the spirit of parliamentary democracy, one of the avowed goals of the 1950 revolution. More insidiously, it helped create conditions which encouraged the further disintegration of political parties, thereby bringing them into greater public disrepute. The organizational structure of all the parties was weakened, as rank-and-file members saw in this situation an opportunity to reap greater political rewards as individuals than as party members; thus the authority of the party leaders was undermined.

This diminution of the Prime Minister's authority over party followers as well as Cabinet colleagues was the fatal flaw in the functioning of the coalition government. M. P. Koirala had little control over the activities of the other-party members in the Cabinet, and the latter in their turn—Tanka Prasad Acharya, in particular—sought at every opportunity to undermine the Prime Minister's leadership in the government. The motivations for their course of action, oriented neither to party nor ideology, were essentially personal. While the Cabinet was caught in the cross-currents of personal ambitions, the government could do little else besides carry on routine administration, and even this was not performed in a very creditable manner.

The coalition government virtually signed its death warrant when it decided to establish an Advisory Assembly, since the Assembly only helped project intra-Cabinet disputes into a wide-open public forum. In the process, the disputes among the Cabinet party members, who liked to think of themselves as equals among equals, were intensified by the differential allocation of seats in the Assembly. The party members in the Assembly generally acquitted themselves in the same political style as the party members in the Cabinet—that is, regarded themselves as individuals rather than party members and held themselves bound by only nominal ties of party discipline and loyalty.

The establishment of the Assembly created a curious spectacle in which a government-nominated body set itself up as the critic and judge of that government's activities. To some extent, individual party members of the Cabinet encouraged this essentially negativistic tendency of the Assembly by instigating their party followers against selected Cabinet colleagues. The net result of such imprudent, if perhaps personally satisfying tactics was that party Ministers or party whips were unable to marshal the votes of their followers even on nonpartisan issues. The successive defeats suffered by the government in the Assembly were reminders of the general loss of control all around, and the confusion became worse when the government finally collapsed.

An incongruous feature of the coalition Cabinet was its pretense at being the first "national" government since the end of Rana rule. King Tribhuwan had conceived of a national government in which all the major political parties would participate. With the exclusion of the Nepali Congress, the Gorkha Parishad, and the Communists from the coalition, however, the new government was hardly "national" in the King's terms.

The end of the coalition government signified the end of an epoch of political experimentation under King Tribhuwan's aegis and the rise of a new political era under that of Crown Prince Mahendra—shortly afterwards King Mahendra. During the four years between King Tribhuwan's historic proclamation of February 18, 1951, and his delegation of full royal authority to Prince Mahendra on February 18, 1955, the democratic experimentation in Nepal had undergone several vicissitudes.

On the positive side, the end of the century-old Rana rule had released the creative impulses of the people in many directions—in the field of arts, literature, and language—and the Nepalese began to rediscover their national identity after years of nondescript existence. The Nepali intellectuals—the Western-educated, the literati, the pamphleteers, the newspaper editors, the public orators, and the politicians—were all engaged in feverish political activities. And Kathmandu, the traditional home of these elites, became both the political and the cultural Mecca of Nepal.

The release of the creative energies of the people saw its varied manifestations in the phenomenal expansion of educational facilities in the form of new schools and colleges, adult schools, professional schools, and libraries all over the country, mostly on private initiative. The people also exhibited an enormous desire for education for themselves and for their children; and girls in unprecedented numbers enrolled in schools and colleges, in most cases defying existing social traditions and restrictions.

Another manifestation of the release of creative energies was the mushrooming of new political and social organizations. These corporate activities affected almost every sphere of national and social life. Trade-unions were started for such working people as taxicab drivers and tailors; "depressed" classes established their own organizations to fight for social equality; women and young people organized groups to enhance their future and protect their rights. By 1955 there were more than 130 social and political organizations in Nepal.

Thus these first four years of democratic experimentation were a period of excitement, euphoria, and emotional lability on the one hand, but were also the period during which political leaders demonstrated their inability to assist in the establishment of a constitutional democracy. Perhaps the most serious deficiency was the absence of national leaders who could clearly and intelligibly articulate the potentialities of the new political age and thus help the nation make the giant step from feudal medievalism toward the twentieth-century horizon. The person best situated to serve this function was King Tribhuwan, but unfortunately his health began to fail at the very time when, owing to the weaknesses of the political party system, his leadership had become most imperative. The practical politics of ministry-making superseded the more fundamental politics of transition.

The one political party that had the opportunity to provide transitional guidance and leadership was the Nepali Congress, which could have played a role similar to that of the Congress Party in India after independence. The Nepali Congress leaders, however, lacked the maturity and experience of Nehru and his colleagues, and tended to be somewhat arrogant in their relations with other political factions. They neglected to recognize the aspirations and sentiments of the Kathmandu elites, thus alienating themselves from influential groups of students, intellectuals, and political workers. In their moment of success and triumph, moreover, they seemed to ignore the fact that constitutional democracy, as prepared and packaged in New Delhi, had to somehow strike roots in Nepal. A hopeful beginning was made under the Rana-Congress coalition government in 1951 when the Nepali Congress introduced several fundamental reforms such as the interim constitution, an independent high court, and the abolition of a number of feudal socioeconomic practices. But the party lost its golden opportunity in 1952 when the first M. P. Koirala government disintegrated in a clash of personal ambitions and conflicting ideologies.

Politics after August, 1952, when the Nepali Congress government laid down its burden as well as its responsibility, became less party politics and more personal politics. Alliances and coalitions of competing individual politicians were often misleadingly dignified with such high-sounding appellations as a United Front or a League of Democrats. Political parties, including the

Nepali Congress, became enmeshed in the new politics of expediency—the only politics that led to seats in the Cabinet. During King Tribhuwan's declining health, M. P. Koirala became the high priest of this brand of politics, and other political leaders engaged in zigzag bargaining negotiations, using the traditional principles of *Sama, Dana, Danda,* and *Bheda.** As a result, the political process became arbitrary, irrational, and unpredictable, animated by the same traditional spirit of Court politics which, ironically enough, had been the mode of politics under both the Shah and the Rana regimes.

In accordance with the irrational nature of the political process, political issues tended to be equated either with the momentary irritations of the party leaders or with the deep-seated suspicions and fears of the people. And the issues became so highly charged with emotion that it was well nigh impossible to settle them on the basis of any rational, external criteria; the motives of the protagonists and the antagonists were dominant. Further, the abrupt termination of the century-old geographical, cultural, and political isolation of the country led to the influx of foreign ideas and influence, and the suddenly aroused public of Nepal was too confused and overwhelmed to form a correct perspective of the nature of events in the country and abroad. Opposition leaders, in their search for political issues, found a convenient handle on the question of foreign interference. India, with its close involvement in the initiation of the political change and in the stabilization of the new system thereafter, became an easy target for political criticism. The alleged interference of the Indian government, in such forms as the use of Indian troops in the capture of Nepali rebels and the presence of an Indian Military Mission, was not considered half as important as suspicion concerning India's motives and future intentions with regard to the sovereign status of Nepal.

While the political process deteriorated with the gyrations and counter-gyrations of contending political factions, the embryonic democratic system introduced by the Rana-Congress coalition government in 1951 underwent serious attrition. The Interim Government Act of 1951 and the High Court Act of 1951 were amended several times until by February, 1954, the independence of the judiciary was all but lost and the concept of a

---

* These four principles were recommended by ancient Hindu texts on statecraft as the most effective ways of dealing with a political opponent. The principle of *Sama* meant making peace with the enemy; the principle of *Dana,* making concessions to the enemy; the principle of *Danda,* inflicting punishment on the enemy; and the principle of *Bheda,* fomenting divisions within the ranks of the enemy camp.

constitutional King-in-Council system in which the King acted in conjunction with a Cabinet had become invalid. It was solemnly proclaimed that the King was the supreme legislative, executive, and judicial head of the country and that the High Court and the government operated only with the limited powers delegated by the King. The "Directive Principles of State Policy" embodied in the Interim Government Act of 1951, which envisaged the establishment of a society based on equality and social justice, were declared to be nonjusticiable in any court. The elections to a Constituent Assembly, which King Tribhuwan had hoped would meet not later than April, 1953, seemed as remote as ever in 1955. Thus, the epoch of democratic political experimentation under King Tribhuwan's aegis came to an end on an unhappy note of increasing political frustration and economic stagnation.

King Tribhuwan reigned for slightly over four years after the introduction of political democracy in 1951, the culmination of his lifelong mission to oust the Rana government. During this crucial transitional period, he was frequently in indifferent health and spent a total of twelve months abroad seeking medical treatment. He was, thus, unable to make a full contribution to the consolidation of the new political order, and had to rely on the judgment of the few politicians he trusted.

By temperament, also, King Tribhuwan was content to function as a constitutional monarch. Perhaps the best demonstration of his dedication to democratic principles was his historic proclamation of February 18, 1951, in which he expressly promised that the new political system would be based upon a Constitution framed by the elected representatives of the people. To concede that true sovereignty resided in the people was, indeed, an enormous personal concession, and one which King Tribhuwan was willing to make in behalf of what he conceived to be the interests of true democracy. Critics and cynics have sometimes deplored the lack of royal direction in the governments formed during the Tribhuwan era, but the sincerity of the King has seldom been questioned. It was only right and proper, therefore, that King Tribhuwan should be acclaimed as "the father of the nation" and "the chief architect of Nepali democracy."

Innovations in
the "Interim"
Political System
(1955-59)

10

King Mahendra's Political Innovations

By the time King Mahendra had formally ascended the throne, it was unmistakably apparent to the Nepali political leaders that they had to accommodate themselves to an entirely different kind of ruler from his predecessor. Only thirty-five years old at the time of his accession, the new King had spent a greater part of his life in the involuntary seclusion of the royal palace under the Ranas. But even as Crown Prince he had demonstrated a self-assertive character and a proclivity for experimentation on occasion. At the time of his first marriage, to a Rana princess in 1940, for instance, he ignored the royal tradition of wedding two wives at the same time. Again, after the death of his first wife, the Crown Prince married his late wife's sister in spite of strong vocal opposition to the match from various sources. King Tribhuwan implied his displeasure by departing for Calcutta a few days before the ceremony. Political party leaders objected that a marriage alliance with an A Rana family was inappropriate for the monarchy in democratic Nepal. But Mahendra proved to be unbending and unresponsive to criticism, even though at one point his insistence upon the marriage seemed to threaten his succession to the throne.

The circumstances surrounding the second marriage gave the Nepali public its first real opportunity to appraise their next ruler. Mahendra's earlier incursions into politics in the postrevolutionary period had merely left the impression that he was close to one section of the Rana family and was vaguely hostile to the democratic political experiment. In July, 1951, for example, he had issued a public statement in which he declared:

Administration of a democratic nature has been established in Nepal, but real democracy can be realized only when the people shed their narrow outlook and do not contribute to rumor-mongering and unrest, but try to arouse feelings of nationalism and national progress. I have seen that some people interpret democracy as the spread of unrest and useless rumors. . . . Such rumors cause me not just sadness, but great pain and hatred.[1]

This statement was the initial expression of the Crown Prince's personal concept of democracy and his impatience with the principles of a democratic administration. It also evidenced a predilection toward ethical judgments of a democratic system in isolation from its political manifestations.

There can be little doubt that Crown Prince Mahendra was strongly critical of the democratic experiment in Nepal from the very beginning. On the first anniversary of the Royal Proclamation of February 18, 1951, to cite another of his views, he declared:

Today instead of our golden dreams we have in our country innumerable organizations, in none of which can we see a selfless leader. Every government department was organized along new lines. But why does bribery alone succeed in it? As prices rise higher, why do foreign fashions entrench themselves stronger? Why are the simple and the honest people dying? And why are the reckless prospering? Similarly, new schools and colleges were established, but they are conducted without books. Freedom of speech was established, but there is no place where we can hear the expression of a pure heart. Rather it has turned into an instrument of name-calling among brothers. Freedom of the press was granted, and, even under a king like ours, anarchic materials inimical to the good and the gentle were published, abetting the activities of the unscrupulous. The so-called complete democracy violated every rule and regulation, and all around we heard only desperate, muddled, and panicky voices. And when the opportunists forgot the interests of their country, the so-called progressives fell victim to a selfish devilishness, and humanity began to spew poison and illusions. . . . Therefore, it is my hope that this one-year-old infant "democracy" which, by mistake or design, is on its death-bed, can be salvaged by our united efforts.[2]

The clearest expression of his views was made three years later, on the fourth anniversary of the introduction of democracy and after his assuming full royal powers:

Today marks the completion of four years of democracy in the country, but it is a matter of great shame that we cannot point to even four important achievements that we have made during this period. If we say that democracy is still in its infancy, we have seen such qualities as selfishness, greed and jealousy which are not found in an infant. If we say that it has matured, unfortunately we do not see it flourishing anywhere, and, I presume, this is not hidden from anyone in the country.[3]

It was, however, the concluding section of the message—in which the Crown Prince announced his decision to supervise several departments himself and to settle the "misunderstanding concerning an independent judiciary in fifteen days"—that was unprecedented both for content and style in royal proclamations. Here for the first time was a ruler with enough confidence in himself to promise specific accomplishments by a self-imposed deadline, and enough determination to back up his words by assuming personal control over the relevant governmental departments. To advocates of constitutional monarchy, this was indeed ominous; but to those who were concerned primarily with practical results rather than with political systems, the Crown Prince's new political role was a heartening development. Subsequently, political controversy in Nepal has mainly centered around the debate between these two groups.

THE COUNCIL OF ROYAL ADVISERS

No political activity was possible in the last half of March, 1955, as the entire nation was plunged into mourning by the news of King Tribhuwan's death in Zurich on March 14. In a Royal Proclamation of that same date, King Mahendra pledged himself to the promotion and preservation of democracy in Nepal in continuation of his father's sacred intentions, and at a large public condolence meeting eight days later he reiterated this pledge.

The period of mourning for King Tribhuwan ended officially on March 25, and the business of political negotiations was resumed. Former Prime Minister M. P. Koirala submitted a memorandum to King Mahendra in which, citing his own experiences, he argued that a coalition government would fail and would be unable to solve pressing social and economic problems. Advising against the formation of an "independent nonparty Cabinet," he recommended that the King select a party of his choice to form a government.[4] The Nepali Congress leaders, apprehensive that King Mahendra's direct rule would be continued indefinitely, demanded that their party, as the largest and the best organized, be asked to form a government. On April 4, King Mahendra announced that he would call a political conference shortly to determine a course of action for himself and the country.

On the Nepali New Year's Day, April 14, King Mahendar took the entire country by surprise by announcing a Council of Royal Advisers, consisting of five members (see table 6).

TABLE 6

The Council of Royal Advisers, 1955

Name	Title	Portfolio
Gunja Man Singh	Principal Royal Adviser	Foreign Affairs; Finance; Industry and Commerce; Food
Lt. Gen. Ananda Shamsher	Deputy Principal Royal Adviser	Home; Law and Parliamentary Affairs
Guruju Bhogendra Raj	Royal Adviser	Health; Local Self-Government; Communications and Works
Purendra Vikram Shah	Royal Adviser	Defence
Aniruddha Prasad Singh	Royal Adviser	Irrigation; Forests and Revenue

This use of royal advisers was a throwback to the days of Rana autocracy, under which all of them had been schooled, trained, and rewarded. It was, clearly, a group that would never be inclined to question authority, since by training and inclination, its members represented the mentality of an earlier generation. It included a Rana, a hereditary royal priest, a protégé and beneficiary of the Rana system, an obscure relation of the royal family, and a former official in the district administration. The group was not only reactionary, but it lacked any apparent talent or special skills to commend itself to the public. The only conceivable reason for the selection of these persons was the King's confidence in them as instruments through whom he could implement his own program.

A comparison of this advisory team with that established by King Tribhuwan in 1952 reveals significant differences in the approach of the two men toward administration. King Tribhuwan's advisory team had contained at least two political workers, while King Mahendra's group lacked any members with experience in party politics. The first advisory regime was headed by a liberal Rana, the second by a former career man in the Rana administration who had the reputation of being a useful flunky. Much of the initiative in the new regime came directly from the King, and there was little possibility of effective influence by the advisers upon the King, as there had been under King Tribhuwan.

All the political parties, with the exception of the Gorkha

Parishad, strongly criticized the new setup. The Nepali Congress leader, Suvarna Shamsher, attacked the new regime as a painful challenge to democratic elements all over the country, and emphasized the danger of the throne's being exposed to direct public criticism as a consequence of this undemocratic step. M. P. Koirala described the new regime as a revival of the Rana regime and warned that Nepali politics had reached a crossroads.[5] The Praja Parishad leader, Tanka Prasad, charged that the new setup was contrary to the wishes of the late King as well as the publicly stated aims of King Mahendra, and implied that the new ruler was opposed to the establishment of a democratic government.[6] The strongest criticism, however, came from B. P. Koirala, the Nepali Congress president, who said:

. . . The direct rule by the Crown was not only undemocratic, reactionary and a shame-faced acknowledgment of defeat in the endeavor of building democratic institutions in the country, but also definitely fraught with grave consequences for the country. The King's reliance on the advice of unprogressive and reactionary elements is causing anxiety among those interested in the democratic development of the country. . . . The theory that the King can do no wrong, on which the entire concept of a constitutional monarchy hinges, would certainly lose its luster if he were to be mixed up in the day-to-day governance of the country.[7]

KING MAHENDRA'S POLITICAL PROGRAM

In line with his announced intention to proceed carefully in establishing a new political system, King Mahendra called a conference of all political, social, and cultural organizations at the royal palace on May 8. Four major political parties—Nepali Congress, Praja Parishad, Nepali National Congress, and National Democratic—boycotted the meeting, which was, however, attended by 129 organizations of a widely varied character. The leaders of the four parties, after a two-day conference of their own, issued a joint statement declaring that the conference could serve no useful purpose and calling upon the King to set up a "popular Cabinet" as soon as possible.

Instead, in his opening address to the conference, King Mahendra reviewed the political history of the past four years in these words:

It was more than four years ago that democracy came to the country with the help of everyone. During this period Cabinets of various political parties and involving twenty-five or thirty individuals were formed on several occasions, and one-party governments, coalition governments, and advisory governments were established. On various occasions advisory assemblies were formed, but how much the country and the people have benefited from these events is known to all and needless for me to repeat. But whenever a new ministry was formed, following proper consultations so far as I know, that Cabinet considered itself new for two or three months, then in the following two or three months somehow produced conflicts within itself, and in the next two or three months discussed ways and means of dissolving itself, by which time that Cabinet would have been dismissed, only to start the same cycle all over with another Cabinet, thus resulting in no accomplishment of any kind, and only succeeding in making a laughingstock of the country.[8]

King Mahendra did not fail to comment on the nonparticipation of the major political parties. With a characteristic use of innuendo, he deplored their superior attitude and accused the parties of unwillingness to participate on an equal footing with other social and cultural organizations. He concluded his opening remarks by stressing three main points: (1) He would not let democracy lapse in the country, though he would in no case lay the country waste by repeating the so-called democratic experiments of the past four years. (2) The conference should tell him whether the Advisory Assembly should be continued. (3) He attached the utmost importance to the holding of general elections as soon as possible, and hoped to announce the election date within three months.

The conference met in four sessions and lasted until May 17. The dominant group in these proceedings was comprised of so-called "independents," whose only common platform was their detestation of political parties and their leaders. On the last day of the conference, its major recommendations were summed up by King Mahendra as calling for termination of direct rule, the holding of elections, continuation of the democratic system, and dissolving of the present Advisory Assembly. He accepted these recommendations, but commented that caution and patience were required to promote the growth of true democracy and that it was necessary for him to ponder over these "serious matters" for some time, searching for the best ways to implement them.

Another policy of King Mahendra, which was cleverly conceived to put the political parties on the defensive, was his program of establishing direct contacts with the people. This was a further illustration of his basically empiricistic approach to the study of popular opinion in different parts of the country. Nine *Daudahas* (Tour Commissions), composed of pro-royalist independents, were formed on April 18, and were dispatched to the districts to survey public opinion and to submit appropriate proposals for the reform and development of those districts. In practice, the commissions turned out to be fact-finding committees for assessing the influence of the various political parties outside Kathmandu. Naturally, this aroused vigorous opposition from the political parties, some of which went to the exent of staging demonstrations against the commissions. King Mahendra then abandoned the Tour Commissions device for the time being, but presumably only after it had served his purpose.

After the political conference in May, King Mahendra initiated a series of consultations with party leaders. Prospects for an early restoration of the democratic system seemed good and, at the insistence of the King, the leaders held a number of meetings among themselves to discuss party coalitions or mergers. Nothing came out of these discussions, however, and King Mahendra forged ahead with his own political and administrative reforms, most of which seemed to be designed to steal the thunder of the political parties by implementing those specific demands for which they had long been agitating. On August 1, for instance, his government signed a treaty which normalized diplomatic relations with China. On August 8, King Mahendra announced that general elections, demanded by virtually all political factions, would be held on the full moon day of October, 1957.

In the last week of August, King Mahendra renewed negotiations with the leaders of the Gorkha Parishad, the Nepali National Congress, the Nepali Congress, and the Praja Parishad. This time he circulated a seven-point questionnaire which sought the parties' views on the composition of the Cabinet and the policies and programs to be adopted, questions upon which the parties had been badly divided in the past.[9] In this instance, however, the Nepali Congress, Nepali National Congress, and Praja Parishad together recommended the exclusion of the Gorkha Parishad from the Cabinet and proposed that any one of them be invited to form a government on the guarantee of coöperation from the other two. The Gorkha Parishad, which had earlier suggested that a new government should be entrusted to a political party which had not been tried before (i.e., the Gorkha Parishad), now offered to withdraw from the negotiations and to function as an opposition party. It was reported that King Mahendra insisted upon some form of coalition Cabinet, arguing that no single party should be entrusted with the administration because of the pending general elections. But the leaders of the three other parties failed to evolve a common formula which could serve as the basis of a coalition government. The negotiations proved abortive, and direct rule continued.

Toward the end of October, King Mahendra called for a third round of negotiations with political parties. The announcement that the King would tour India in the following month added an air of expectancy to these proceedings, for it was widely speculated that a new Cabinet would be sworn in before his departure. It was reported that an agreement had been reached between the King and the leaders of the Nepali Congress, Nepali National Congress, and Praja Parishad under which each party would have two representatives in a Cabinet which would also include two to four independents and over which the King himself would preside. The three parties were asked to draw up a joint minimum program by October 27. After some initial difficulties, the three parties submitted a draft program to the King. At this stage, however, a new controversy arose over the King's novel method of selecting the party members for the Cabinet. Each of the three parties was sent a panel of three names which excluded all former Ministers (i.e., virtually all of the top leadership in the parties), and was instructed to select two names from the list. The party leadership were surprised and distressed by this development, and rejected the procedure as an indefensible intrusion into party affairs. By October 30, a deadlock had been reached, and the negotiations were adjourned until the King's return from India.

A fourth round of political negotiations began in January, 1956, after the King's return to Kathmandu. It was reported that the King repeated his offer of a Cabinet in which he would select six party representatives and over which he would preside, and that the parties again rejected these terms. The King then announced that he would undertake a three-week tour of western Nepal. Kathmandu political circles concluded that for the time being the King had abandoned his efforts to form a Cabinet, and that the present Advisory Council would be retained. It was, therefore, wholly unexpected when on January 27—the day of his departure for western Nepal—the King announced the formation of a Cabinet consisting of four Praja Parishad members and three independents, with the Praja Parishad leader, Tanka Prasad Acharya, as Prime Minister.

THE PRAJA PARISHAD GOVERNMENT

The appointment of the new Cabinet was greeted with astonishment. Through months of unsuccessful parleys, the King had repeatedly insisted upon a multi-party coalition which excluded former Ministers and over which he himself would preside. Indeed, as recently as five days before, the royal palace communiqué announcing the failure of negotiations with the parties had specified that the King's plan for a Cabinet without a Prime Minister had been rejected by the party leaders.

The new government was, thus, a complete reversal of the King's earlier positions. Presumably, if he had offered similar terms a week earlier, a broadly based coalition government could have been formed. Furthermore, the new government, which from the viewpoint of popular support was probably the weakest formed thus far, seemed incompatible with the King's numerous public statements stressing the need for a strong, durable government. The three Praja Parishad Ministers, exclusive of Tanka Prasad Acharya, represented different factions of a party not distinguished for its ideology, for the intellectual integrity of its leaders, or for its influence with the public. These so-called "popular Ministers," nominees of a weak and segmented party, could hardly be expected to exert much influence in a government dominated by the three royalist independents—the former Chief Royal Adviser, a cousin of the King, and one of the King's favorites. Moreover, King Mahendra chose as Prime Minister a man who was not the president of the ruling party, and thus, intentionally or fortuitously, sowed seeds of discord which tore the party apart once it was forced out of power.

COMPOSITION OF THE PRAJA PARISHAD CABINET

The members of the Praja Parishad Cabinet and their respective portfolios are listed in table 7.

TABLE 7

THE PRAJA PARISHAD CABINET, 1956

Name	Portfolio	Party affiliation
Tanka Prasad Acharya	Home; General Administration	Nepal Praja Parishad
Chuda Prasad Sharma	Foreign Affairs; Food and Agriculture	Old-line Praja Parishad faction
Gunja Man Singh	Finance; Planning	Independent; former Chief Royal Adviser; King's nominee
Pashupati Ghosh	Public Works; Transport and Communications	Jana Congress faction of Nepal Praja Parishad

TABLE 7—*Continued*

Name	Portfolio	Party affiliation
Purendra Vikram Shah	Defence	Independent; King's cousin
Balchandra Sharma	Education and Health	National Democratic Party faction of Nepal Praja Parishad
Anirudha Prasad Singh	Law and Parliamentary Affairs	Independent; King's nominee

The only person in the Cabinet on whom Tanka Prasad Acharya could rely for support was Chuda Prasad Sharma, who had been a fellow political prisoner for nearly a decade. The other Ministers were divided in their loyalties and had their own axes to grind. Balchandra Sharma had floated in and out of parties and party alignments with amazing frequency since 1951, and it was only natural that Tanka Prasad should handle him with considerable circumspection. The other Praja Parishad Minister, Pashupati Ghosh, was something of an accident. He was a political nonentity from Birganj who had close personal relations with Bhadrakali Mishra and the Jana Congress faction of the Praja Parishad. Bhadrakali Mishra's election as party president had disqualified him from inclusion in the Cabinet. But it was necessary that there be a Minister from the Jana Congress faction, and Pashupati Ghosh was the choice. Ghosh's primary allegiance, then, was to Bhadrakali Mishra rather than to the party or the Prime Minister, and he functioned later as Mishra's man in the bitter intra-party disputes that ensued. Thus, Tanka Prasad Acharya was uncertain of his personal influence even with the Praja Parishad Ministers, not to mention the independents. In assessing this government, it is to be borne in mind that King Mahendra exerted a dominant influence behind the scenes and that the Praja Parishad was scarcely more than a façade behind which the King continued the direct rule system in a somewhat modified form.

POLITICAL DEVELOPMENTS

It was perhaps symptomatic of the trend of political developments that the first organized opposition to the new government came not from the political parties, but in the form of a quasi-military plot in the first half of 1956. It is difficult to ascertain the objectives of the conspirators, because the government, reportedly embarrassed by the royal connections of some members of the group, never made the facts public.* According to newspaper accounts, eleven persons were arrested, most of them former army officers.[10] Reportedly, papers seized from the arrested persons showed that the plot called for the simultaneous storming, at midnight, of the royal palace, the Secretariat buildings, and the houses of Ministers in a bid to capture the government. The conspirators were reported also to have made overtures to the army in seeking support for their plans. Although the political affiliations of this group did not come to light, their possible connections with the royal palace and the army were widely speculated upon in Kathmandu.

Perhaps the weakness of the Praja Parishad government explains its comparative longevity—nearly eighteen months. This Cabinet may have seemed to King Mahendra to be the best of the conceivable alternatives, as it was incapable of challenging his leadership and yet had some viability and, at least for the first year of its existence, favor with the public. Indeed, during much of this period the government had the tacit support of most political parties, which welcomed the termination of the direct rule system. The attitude of the Nepali Congress and the Nepali National Congress toward the government was also conditioned in part by the hope and expectancy of eventual inclusion in the Cabinet. Bhadrakali Mishra, the Praja Parishad president, had left this prospect open in one of his pronouncements. Later, however, it became evident that this goal could be attained only if the other parties recognized the preëminence of the Praja Parishad and accepted its leadership. Once this was clear, the unofficial moratorium on political opposition to the government ended. The Nepali Congress formally withdrew its support in August, 1956, and the Nepali National Congress shortly thereafter. The United Democratic party and the Gorkha Parishad continued to support the government, though indirectly, until 1957, and then became increasingly critical. Only the Communists, indebted to Tanka Prasad for their newly won legal status, supported the government throughout its tenure in office.

Without doubt, the most controversial issue raised during the tenure of the Acharya Cabinet was the Prime Minister's attempt to change the purposes for which the general elections were to be held. Since February 18, 1951, when King Tribhuwan announced that the country would in the future be governed by elected representatives under a Constitution framed by a Constituent Assembly, it had been a foregone conclusion that the

---

* Bazaar gossip had it that King Mahendra's second brother, Prince Vasundhara, was implicated in this plot. There has never been a verification from any reliable source.

general elections would be held to elect representatives to such a body, and it was believed highly unlikely that King Mahendra would even consider compromising the wishes of his late father in this respect, for he had in numerous public declarations asserted an unswerving commitment to King Tribhuwan's ideals, including presumably the election of the Constituent Assembly. There was a sense of shock in Kathmandu, therefore, when Tanka Prasad Acharya and his party began to agitate for a Parliament with limited powers operating under a Constitution granted by the King—a strange reversal indeed for a party used to parading Marxist ideology, defending people's rights, and castigating the feudal-minded.

Tanka Prasad first broached his proposal in June, 1956, in an address to the Praja Parishad party congress in Birganj. He argued that there could not be two sovereigns in the country at the same time, and that the people of Nepal were not quite prepared for a full-fledged democracy. By emphasizing the absolute rather than the Constitutional sovereignty of the King he may have endeared himself to the palace and other elements associated with it, but he alienated himself and his party from the democratic movement in Nepal that alone could have given the party any real strength. There was, moreover, democratic sentiment within his party against this proposal; it was a full year before the party finally voted formally in favor of elections for a Parliament, and then only after Tanka Prasad had promised as a *quid pro quo* a homogeneous party Cabinet.

Tanka Prasad and his party found a ready following on this issue among so-called independents, landed-interest groups, orthodox religious groups such as the Karmavir Mahamandal ("Brave-in-Action Society"), and some regional and ethnic organizations such as the Kirat League. These assorted organizations of questionable popular influence not only supported Tanka Prasad, but outdid him. They wanted no elections whatsoever, and called for the revival of an absolute monarchy.

The only political party that supported the Praja Parishad on this question was the United Democratic party of K. I. Singh. The other parties, led by the Nepali Congress and including such diverse groups as the Communists and the Gorkha Parishad, demanded that elections be held for a Constituent Assembly. The Nepali National Congress leader, D. R. Regmi, insisted that the people alone were sovereign and the repository of all authority. The Nepali Congress party executive demanded the dissolution of the government and accused the Praja Parishad leaders of "fouling the political atmosphere of the country and dragging in an unnecessary controversy, and seeking to make the King a subject of political wrangle." They called upon King Mahendra to fulfill the solemn vow of his predecessor by permitting the elected representatives of the people to frame a Constitution. Further, the party decided to arouse public consciousness on the election controversy through extensive tours of the country by members of the party executive.

One dramatic aspect of the debate on this issue was the suit filed by B. P. Koirala in the Supreme Court against the Prime Minister, accusing him of violating Royal Proclamations and the existing law by his statements supporting general elections for a Parliament. The Nepali Congress leader contended that King Tribhuwan's proclamation of February 18, 1951, and the People's Representation Act of 1952 had legally defined the aims of elections. He requested a writ of mandamus against the Prime Minister requiring him to abide by these laws. In reply, Tanka Prasad contended that a Royal Proclamation did not constitute law by itself and that the Act in question had not received authentication, since no royal seal had been affixed to it. Further, he argued that his statement at Birganj had been made in his capacity as a private citizen and that he was within his rights to express his views on the subject. On August 6, 1956, the Court dismissed the petition, upholding the Prime Minister's rights under the Civil Rights Act.

The Praja Parishad Cabinet reached its lowest ebb in July, 1957, when even its own members were openly denouncing the party high command and the government. Although the immediate internal differences were covered over momentarily, the embers of discord were glowing underneath and it was only a matter of time before the party would be rocked by another violent explosion. Tanka Prasad Acharya, evidently disturbed by the mounting criticism from without and within, became at times almost desperate and incoherent in his speeches and statements. Addressing a sparsely attended public meeting at Kathmandu on May 25, 1957, for instance, he attacked the supporters of a Constituent Assembly as agents of feudalism—too ludicrous a charge even for his own followers.

Right-wing and communal organizations and individuals were also opening fire on the government. The Terai Congress, at its third party meeting, on May 29, demanded that the southern districts of the Terai should be granted regional autonomy. A new orthodox Hindu organization, the Karmavir Mahamandal, demanded a revival of the ancient Hindu monarchical system on the grounds that Western democracy was alien to the culture and traditions of the country and that political parties had proved utterly incapable of running the government. Under its dynamic ethnocentrist leader, Narahari Nath Yogi, a man of broad classical learning, the new organization had the potential to serve as a strong rallying point for conservative elements in the country. The Kirat League, a regionally oriented group from eastern Nepal, demanded that elections should be postponed indefinitely until the people were competent to govern themselves. But far more important was the fact that the Acharya government was caught in a deadly conflict with the Shanti Rakshya Swaya Sevak Sangh Kendra ("Central Committee of Volunteers for the Preservation of Peace"), a nonpolitical social organization in Kathmandu, over a vital although nonpolitical issue—food scarcity in the valley.

The Kendra had been formed as a vigilante body in Kathmandu in January, 1951, at a time when the country was in a state of near chaos owing to the impending collapse of the Rana regime and the delay in King Tribhuwan's return to Kathmandu. It was a valley-wide organization, having separate branches in the three principal cities in the valley. The Kendra provided an effective outlet for political activists who were either opposed or indifferent to parties, and it also functioned as a valuable public service agency, helping the government to distribute rice and other essential commodities equitably through its local branches. In the course of time, the Kendra amassed considerable public support in recognition of its services and its influence within the government.

In June, 1957, a shortage of rice caused much distress in the valley. Prices rose steadily, and the public clamored for action by the Kendra to bring pressure on the government to alleviate the situation. When verbal representations to the government produced no effect, the Kendra decided to dramatize the food situation by organizing a hunger march on June 15. A procession, of about twelve thousand persons, shouting "Give us food or quit office," paraded through the streets of Kathmandu.

The struggle for food turned into a symbolic struggle for the overthrow of the Praja Parishad government. On June 24 and 27, the Kendra called general strikes in Kathmandu. These were completely successful, and the Kendra branches elsewhere resolved to launch their own struggles against the government. The Cabinet finally yielded and promised to take immediate measures for relief. Food Minister Chuda Prasad Sharma talked in grandiose terms of a plan to utilize airplanes and helicopters to import 200,000 maunds of rice from India and an equal amount from Burma, at a cost of 10 million rupees.[11] But it was apparent that the government was incapable of effective action, and the Cabinet was totally discredited as far as Kathmandu Valley was concerned.

Out of sheer desperation, Tanka Prasad Acharya during a speech on June 30 denounced the Kathmandu populace, accusing them of standing by as spectators when "a few goondas" paralyzed the whole city, and even implying that the people were not as yet fit for democracy.[12]

Partly as an expression of his frustration and partly to highlight the supposedly obstructionist role of the independents in the Cabinet, Tanka Prasad Acharya submitted a letter of conditional resignation to the King on July 5, stating:

It is now seventeen months and a few days since the government was formed under my leadership as the Prime Minister appointed by your Majesty. . . . I have made it clear to your Majesty that the Mahasa-miti [Grand Council] of my party has resolved on the formation of a homogeneous government. This resolution stemmed from a conviction that the demands of the people could be fulfilled only through a more homogeneous and efficient government and administration. Therefore, I beg your Majesty either to allow me to form a homogeneous cabinet or to consider this letter as my resignation from the government.[13]

The motivations behind Tanka Prasad Acharya's sudden decision to press for a homogenous government at this stage of developments are difficult to comprehend unless it is assumed that he desired to lay down the burden of an unpopular government. Clearly, King Mahendra would never accede to a proposal which would exclude his representatives from the Cabinet or would minimize the close supervision he had maintained over the government. Moreover, the widely publicized rifts in the Praja Parishad would certainly discourage the King from seriously considering the delegation of broader powers to a government based on this party. Tanka Prasad Acharya blamed the independents in the Cabinet for all its defects. This argument might have carried weight with his disgruntled party men and some sections of the political opposition, in particular the Communists, but not with the King.

King Mahendra waited a full week before acting on Tanka Prasad Acharya's request. Meanwhile, he consulted with leaders representing a wide variety of viewpoints before reaching a decision about the next government. B. P. Koirala, Surya Prasad Upadhyaya and Suvarna Shamsher were called to the palace separately on several occasions, giving rise to speculations that the Nepali Congress would be asked to form the next government, much to the alarm of the other political parties. The Nepali National Congress demanded a national Cabinet, comprising representatives of the major political parties. The Communists, in an effort to minimize the central role of the King, proposed that a conference be convened by all political parties to discuss the government crisis. The so-called independents met in a conference at Kathmandu and appointed a twenty-five-member *ad hoc* committee which was authorized to present to King Mahendra their demand that they be allowed to form the new government.

Contrary to prevailing expectations, however, King Mahendra once more frustrated the Nepali Congress. He dissolved the Acharya government on July 14 and the next day called upon K. I. Singh, the sworn enemy of the Nepali Congress and "the Koirala brothers," to form the next government. What is more, he charged that the Praja Parishad government had admitted its inability to hold the elections and run the government—allegations which came, in the words of Bhadrakali Mishra, as "a great surprise and a rude shock to all lovers of democracy." [14]

The Royal Proclamation, strangely enough, did not refer to the demand of the Praja Parishad leader for a homogeneous government, which was the stated reason for the resignation of the government. The Praja Parishad leaders reacted quickly to King Mahendra's implicit accusations of incompetence. The party president, Bhadrakali Mishra, stated on July 16 that his party's government had only desired to remove obstructive elements from the Cabinet and had at no time expressed its inability to conduct the elections on the announced date.[15] On the same day the outgoing Prime Minister denied King Mahendra's allegations and issued a copy of his letter of resignation to the press to corroborate his statement. Tanka Prasad contended that he had informed the King about the possibility of holding elections on the fixed date, despite several difficulties mentioned in the Election Commissioner's report, if timely action should be taken by allowing him to form a homogeneous government. The independent members of the outgoing Cabinet, however, supported the Royal Proclamation. One of them told a press correspondent that the Cabinet had officially informed the King of its inability to hold elections on the scheduled date.[16]

THE UNITED DEMOCRATIC PARTY GOVERNMENT

The Royal Proclamation of July 15, 1957, commissioned K. I. Singh, president of the United Democratic party, to explore the possibility of forming a Cabinet within two weeks. The proclamation appealed to all political parties to rise above "mutual differences of opinion, jealousy, and malice" and to dedicate themselves to "the supreme duty of service to the Motherland." [17] King Mahendra also stipulated his preference for a Cabinet that would have the "coöperation and good will of the majority of the political parties as far as possible." If this was really what the King hoped for, however, the commissioning of K. I. Singh to hold discussions with the other political parties was self-defeating. The Prime Minister–designate, whose reputation was more that of a rebel against constituted authority than a mediator between conflicting viewpoints, was hardly the type of person to negotiate the formation of a coalition Cabinet with other parties. Moreover, his public pronouncements since his return from China in 1955 had generated so much public controversy and animosity toward him that his choice as a candidate for the leadership of a new, "national" government cannot be understood on any rational basis other than his and King Mahendra's common dislike for the Nepali Congress.

The selection of K. I. Singh as the leader of the new government, therefore, indicated that King Mahendra had once again embarked on a course of unusual political experimentation. Characteristically, he had first listened to all points of view, and had then decided on an independent course of action which no one had recommended. It was an act of courage on his part, for he knew full well that K. I. Singh's appointment was certain to antagonize most of the political parties. It was even more of a calculated risk if he actually had in mind using the unpredictable Singh as a means of destroying the political potential of the Nepali Congress.

Criticism from political parties and other organizations was instantaneous and vehement. B. P. Koirala characterized the decision as a "danger signal for democrats and the forerunner of dictatorship." [18] The Working Committees of the Nepali Congress, Praja Parishad, and Nepali National Congress adopted resolutions decrying the appointment of K. I. Singh and questioning his competence to hold the general elections successfully. The Gorkha Parishad, on the other hand, did not publicly condemn the King's decision, but adopted a cautious wait-and-see approach. To this party, a government headed by K. I. Singh was preferable to a coalition of democratic parties in which the Nepali Congress undoubtedly would play the leading role.

The consensus of reaction toward the Royal Proclamation from social and cultural organizations was, on the whole, negative. The Kendra deplored the omission of any reference to the elections and also expressed regret that "the destiny of 8.4 million Nepalese" had been entrusted to a person who was "noted mainly for his aggressiveness and physical qualities." [19] The president of the All-Nepal Women's Conference described the announcement as a challenge to democracy. The secretary of the Nepal Students' Union stated that it "ignored political realities by asking K. I. Singh, who was well known for his irresponsible utterances, to conduct talks with political parties." [20] The Buddhist Sabha Sangha (association) stated that K. I. Singh was objectionable because "his party wanted the elections to be held for a parliament." It appealed to the people to take appropriate action to defend the rights conferred on them by the late King Tribhuwan.[21] A meeting of various social and professional organizations such as the Nepal Yuvak Sangh ("Youth League"), Nepal Tarun Dal ("Youth Corps"), and the Nepal Drivers' Union requested the King to reconsider his decision and to entrust the reins of government to democratic elements.

Support for King Mahendra's new experiment came from such minor organizations as the Karmavir Mahamandal, Rashtriya Jana Rajya Parishad ("National People's Government Council"), Nepal Socialist Peasant's party, and All-Nepal Peasant's Association, all modest in size and influence. Significant support, however, was received from several newly formed splinter political organizations such as the Parallel Nepali Congress, Parallel Praja Parishad, and Jiva Raj Sharma faction of the Nepali National Congress. With the exception of the last named, these political bodies came into existence in the wake of the Royal Proclamation of July 15, and their leaders seem to have assumed that K. I. Singh—who had himself been treated as a political untouchable by other parties—would welcome renegades from the opposition ranks into his government. In this they were sorely mistaken, however, for K. I. Singh ignored both the parallel and the parental organizations. Only one dissident leader, Jiva Raj Sharma, who had left the Nepali National Congress in 1954, was eventually included in the Singh Cabinet.

K. I. Singh did not discharge the responsibility of seeking support from other political parties with any visible enthusiasm. For the most part, he did not involve himself directly in this task, choosing instead to delegate his party functionaries to negotiate with other political leaders. On a few occasions he wrote "chits" to other leaders, but these had more the characteristic of a summons to his presence than an invitation to discussions. Of all the leaders whom he summoned in this fashion, only Bhadrakali Mishra and Bharat Shamsher actually appeared, and the exchanges with them were hardly cordial, conciliatory, or productive of results.

The party secretaries, perhaps more cognizant than Singh of the United Democratic party's real strength, seemed to have taken more interest and initiative than their leader in meeting with the other parties. A seven-man Emergency Committee was formed within the party to conduct political negotiations. K. P. Srivastav, the general secretary of the party, held discussions with leaders of the Praja Parishad and the Nepali National Congress. G. B. Sen, a joint secretary in the party, met with leaders of the Gorkha Parishad and the Jiva Raj Sharma faction of the Nepali National Congress. Shamsher Chand, another general secretary, had a one-hour talk with B. P. Koirala. This talk seems to have been a failure, for on July 18 Singh wrote a personal letter requesting Koirala to come to his house by 4:00 P.M. of that day and intimating that if the Nepali Congress leader did not come, this would be interpreted as proof of his party's lack of interest in a coalition government. In his reply, declining the invitation, B. P. Koirala pointed out that he had received Singh's letter only an hour before the time specified for the interview, and went on to describe the basic differences between the Nepali Congress and the United Democratic party.

On the evening of that same day, Singh met with King Mahendra and, presumably, told him of such progress as had been made. By July 21, reportedly, all the major parties had declined to coöperate with the Singh government. On July 24, Singh again met with the King and may then have asked for permission to form a one-party government with the support of a few "independents." On the next day the Emergency Committee of the United Democratic party decided to terminate negotiations with other parties and resolved to form its own government with the help of some independents. A list of the party members to serve in the government was agreed upon and submitted to the King. On July 26, King Mahendra issued a Royal Proclamation announcing the formation of an eleven-member Cabinet under the Prime Ministership of K. I. Singh. Hoping to forestall the establishment of this Cabinet, the Nepali Congress, Praja Parishad, and Nepali National Congress approached the King with a joint memorandum, offering to form a government on the basis of a minimum program and promising to hold elections on the scheduled date, but this was ignored.

In the July 26 proclamation, King Mahendra charged that a coalition Cabinet had proved impossible, "either owing to the lack of mutual good-will in the political field or owing to the paucity of a sense of sacrifice among political elements." Emphasizing the necessity of national unity for the greater good of the country, the King indicated that he did not wish to undertake direct rule and that he was "firmly desirous of laying strong foundations of a democratic system in the country." [22] In addition to the Cabinet, he announced the prospective early formation of a seven-member National Council, a five-member Work-Expediting Committee, and a National Planning Council. The powers and functions of these special bodies were not defined at the time and, indeed, only one of them, the National Council, was formed during the K. I. Singh regime. Opposition political parties interpreted the King's announced intention to form these bodies as being indicative of distrust in the democratic system and also as measures to restrict the authority of the K. I. Singh Cabinet.

COMPOSITION OF THE UNITED DEMOCRATIC PARTY CABINET

The eleven-member Cabinet consisted of seven members of the United Democratic party, three "independents," and one member of the dissident Nepali National Congress (table 8).

TABLE 8

THE UNITED DEMOCRATIC PARTY CABINET, 1957

Name	*Portfolio*	*Political affiliation*
K. I. Singh	Home; Foreign Affairs	United Democratic party
Purendra Vikram Shah	Defence	Royal cousin; King's nominee
Parushuram Bhakta Mathema	Industry and Commerce	United Democratic party
C. B. Singh	Finance	United Democratic party
Damar Bahadur Singh	Law and Parliamentary Affairs	United Democratic party
Ramdin Mahato	Forests	United Democratic party
Kula Bahadur Limbu	Health	United Democratic party
Padma Narsingh Rana	Public Works; Communications	United Democratic party
Bhupal Man Singh	Food and Agriculture	King's nominee
Lakshmi Prasad Devkota	Education; Local Self-Government	Independent; King's nominee
Jiva Raj Sharma	Development and Planning	Nepali National Congress

The United Democratic party members in the Cabinet were without question the most incongruous collection of Ministers ever inflicted upon Nepal. Without exception, they were political nonentities who owed their rise to high office entirely to K. I.

Singh's favor. None of them had any substantial influence in the country, even in the areas from which they had come, nor were they important even in the ruling party's hierarchy. Most of them had only recently become political activists, having been drawn into politics as followers of Singh after his return from China rather than as dedicated party workers. K. I. Singh could expect—and he obtained—their unquestioning support within the Cabinet; he was thus assured of an automatic majority in Cabinet decisions. The K. I. Singh government was in this respect quite different from its predecessor, more difficult for the King to handle and potentially more dangerous to the throne. And, indeed, dissension between the Prime Minister and King Mahendra's main spokesman in the Cabinet, Purendra Vikram Shah, developed very quickly.

The new Prime Minister did not waste much time before commencing a campaign aimed at discrediting most of his political rivals. On September 2, he issued an incredible press note in which he accused the Ministers in the other post-revolution governments of having wasted more than 38 million Nepali rupees and 57 million Indian rupees. Wild rumors that he intended to arrest most of his political opponents began to circulate in the capital. The Prime Minister's public expression of his determination to retrieve the "lost national wealth" at the "cost of my life, if necessary," added to the tension in Kathmandu.[23] Apart from its sensational impact on the public, however, this announcement did not seem to disturb the opposition leaders, and perhaps only increased the sense of urgency in their projected program of direct action aimed at the dismissal of the K. I. Singh government.

POSTPONEMENT OF GENERAL ELECTIONS

In a broadcast to the nation on October 4, K. I. Singh announced, as was expected, that the general elections promised two years before in the 1955 Royal Proclamation would not be held. King Mahendra confirmed the Prime Minister's statement on October 6. The reasons for the indefinite postponement of the elections were not elaborated, but it was noted that both the Election Commission and the Cabinet had reported to the palace that the elections could not be held on schedule.

The reaction to the announcement was sharply negative throughout the country. Political parties and social-cultural organizations of all varieties issued strongly worded statements critical of the King's action. Kathmandu witnessed strikes, processions, and demonstrations in protest. October 8 was observed as a "black day," and all parties coöperated with student organizations in conducting black-flag demonstrations and in observing a two-hour blackout in the evening. Most criticism centered around the failure of the King to announce a new date for the elections. The practical difficulties mentioned in the Election Commission's report, it was argued, should not deter the King from setting a new date, if he really was in favor of general elections.

The only dissident voice in this chorus of public protest was *Karmavir,* the organ of the staunchly royalist Karmavir Mahamandal, which cautioned the King against holding elections in the present circumstances because, in its opinion, "the political party leaders would even sell their morality to become Ministers." The paper asked the King to "concentrate power in his hands and use it for introducing an organized democracy in the future under improved conditions of employment opportunities and educational level." [24]

The General Conference of the Democratic Front, organized by the Nepali Congress, Nepali National Congress, and Praja Parishad, met at Birganj on October 8. Some four hundred delegates, representing various parts of the country, were present at the meeting. The Front, which had apprehended the postponement of the elections since the establishment of the K. I. Singh government, resolved to launch a country-wide civil disobedience movement on December 12, and claimed that any "honest" government could hold the elections within six months. An Action Committee consisting of B. P. Koirala, Bhadrakali Mishra, and D. R. Regmi was formed to lead the movement, which began immediately in the form of public meetings, processions, signature collections, and the recruitment of volunteers in every district in support of the Front's program.

The postponement of the elections made it politically awkward for those parties outside the Front that had tacitly supported the Singh government. With the exception of the United Democratic party and the Gorkha Parishad, the other minor parties came out with strong statements protesting the postponement. The general secretary of the United Democratic party, K. P. Srivastava, replied to the Front's demands by declaring that the holding of elections could be expedited only "with the power of the khukri" (i.e., by naked force).[25] His party paper, *Samyukta Prayas,* sought to belittle the decision of the Birganj conference of the Front by representing the Front as "nothing more than a temporary compromise of leaders who had neither the strength, nor the desire, nor the public support for conducting the movement." [26] The Gorkha Parishad accused the Front leaders of "trying to disrupt the elections under an appearance of trying to expedite them." [27] The Communist party, while pledging support for the Front's limited objectives, expressed regret that the Front leaders had decided to exclude the Communists from their organizations.

THE LANGUAGE ISSUE

The Singh government aroused another loud political controversy by its policy with regard to the Nepali-Hindi language problem. The issue had become an acute political problem in the Terai in 1956 when some Terai politicians, including M. P. Koirala, demanded that Hindi be granted the status of a national language. The precipitating factor in this controversy was the attempt by teachers in the newly established "national" elementary schools in the Terai to introduce Nepali as the medium of instruction in the classrooms. The education system in the Terai had been developed largely on the initiative of prominent local leaders, mostly Nepali landlords and Indian merchants. Before 1955 the Education Department of the government of Nepal had intervened at the local level more as an auxiliary to local efforts than as a policy maker, primarily because the government lacked an articulated and coördinated educational policy. Another factor, which had accentuated the effects of the government's indifference to the Terai schools, was the dearth of Nepali teachers, owing partly to their limited availability and partly to their unwillingness to work in the humid, malarial Terai. Consequently the schools had imported a large number of Indian teachers from across the border, and these teachers naturally preferred to teach in Hindi or English rather than Nepali. Furthermore, there was considerable support for Hindi as the primary medium of instruction among the Indian business and landowning communities in the Terai.

The new Nepali teachers, many of whom were products of the Teacher Training Center in Kathmandu, had a very different orientation from that of the older staff members. In their training in Kathmandu, the need for viewing education from a national perspective was emphasized. Education was not only an instrument of social change, they were told, but also a powerful means for developing the sense of national identification. The use of Nepali—the national language—in the classrooms was of fundamental importance in the achievement of this latter goal. But when the new teachers attempted to make Nepali the sole medium of instruction, they aroused the hostility and anxiety of other teachers and of important sections of local society, and a widespread controversy ensued.

The language issue divided the politicians not along ideological or party lines, but on the basis of regional loyalties. The Terai Congress and the Terai members of the Nepali Congress both demanded that Hindi be accorded the status of a national language. Most Nepali politicians from the hill areas took somewhat equivocal positions on the controversy, usually to conform with the attitude of the audience they happened to be addressing.

By 1957 the language question was arousing strong passions on both sides in parts of the Terai. At Jaleshwar, Hindi partisans had established an organization for the propagation of Hindi. At Biratnagar, a pro-Nepali organization, the Nepali Pracharini Sabha ("Publicity Committee"), had inaugurated a vehement public campaign against the pro-Hindi demands of the Terai Congress. Public feelings ran high. Bhadrakali Mishra, the Praja Parishad leader from the Terai, was shouted down by an audience because of his inability to speak in Nepali. It was in this context of public agitation that the Singh government announced its language policy on October 12, 1957. To qualify for government aid and recognition under this policy, Terai schools were required to use Nepali as the language of instruction in the middle and high schools, and to use textbooks approved by the government. Furthermore, all teachers had to be Nepali citizens and were required to attain a specified degree of proficiency in Nepali by 1959.

This formulation of language policy by the government found the United Democratic party divided in its ranks. K. P. Shrivastav, the general secretary of the party and a Terai leader, held a protest meeting at Raj Biraj and declared publicly his "opposition to the government's forcible imposition of Nepali on the Terai people." [28] The Education Minister, Lakshmi Prasad Devkota, King Mahendra's nominee and a distinguished Kathmandu poet, and the United Democratic party's publicity secretary, G. B. Devkota, strongly endorsed the priority of Nepali as the national language.

Partisans of Hindi interpreted the action of the government as a threat to their language and issued an ultimatum to the government to withdraw the order of the Education Ministry. At their instigation, a general strike was called at Birganj on November 11 to protest the anti-Hindi policy of the government. The strike was held even though the government had issued a clarification of its policy on October 31 in which it reaffirmed the designation of Nepali as the principal medium of instruction in Nepali schools but disclaimed any intention of suppressing regional or local dialects.

THE GANDAK PROJECT

Another policy of the Singh government which aroused a loud controversy was its readiness to negotiate with India on projects for the Gandak River. This project was to consist of a barrage and headworks near Bhainsalotan in southwestern Nepal, half of which was to be located on Nepali territory. On October 17, an Indian administrator announced that a draft proposal of the Gandak project agreement was ready for the consideration of the Nepali government. The government set up an investigation committee under the chairmanship of Purendra Vikram Shah, the Defence Minister, to collect information about the project. Kathmandu politicians reacted in their usual vehement fashion, accusing the Cabinet of an excessively generous attitude toward India. Although the Singh government was dismissed before the negotiations between the two governments made any headway, the Prime Minister earned additional public odium by banning newspapers critical of the negotiations.

Relations of the Singh government with the local press had been strained from the very outset, for within a fortnight of Singh's assumption of office the "repressive hand of the government" had fallen upon five dailies and two weeklies.[29] With mounting criticisms from the Democratic Front and with increasing attacks by the local press on the Indo-Nepali negotiations on the river project, the Singh government imposed further restrictions on the freedom of the press. After printing editorials critical of the negotiations with India, the daily *Samaj* was banned and its editor was arrested. A week later, another daily, *Desh Sewa,* was banned. One mitigating factor in this period of government encroachments on the freedom of the press was a decision of the Supreme Court which permitted most of the banned newspapers to resume publication pending the final disposition of their appeals. A hopeful, although somewhat ironical, development was the final acceptance by the government of the long-standing demand of the Nepali journalists for a Press Commission to study the problems and difficulties of the press in Nepal. Formation of the Press Commission was announced on November 7; it was instructed to submit its report by April 12, 1958. But long before the Press Commission had completed its assignment, the K. I. Singh government was out of office. On November 14, King Mahendra dismissed the United Democratic party Cabinet as suddenly and unexpectedly as he had appointed it, and as usual with the minimum of explanation.

11

The Prelude to the 1959 General Elections

THE ABRUPT termination of the K. I. Singh regime caught the entire country by surprise, and possibly the Prime Minister himself was the most surprised of all. According to one report, Singh had to telephone to the Kathmandu radio station for the text of the Royal Proclamation, which had just been broadcast, announcing the acceptance of his resignation.[1]

The news of the dissolution of the United Democratic party government was enthusiastically welcomed by the Kathmandu press and the other political parties. The press generally commended King Mahendra for his timely action in curbing the dictatorial ambitions of K. I. Singh. Among the politicians, the reaction, although varying in interpretations, was one of relief and expectancy. B. P. Koirala commented that the unpredictable nature of Nepali politics no longer held many surprises for him, but that both the appointment and the dismissal of Singh had caught him completely unaware. Suvarna Shamsher hailed the event as the end of a reign of terror and attributed Singh's sudden fall to his mistake in overestimating his strength and to his harassment of the civil servants. Tanka Prasad Acharya commented that Singh's dismissal had become inevitable in the interests of national welfare because he lacked administrative abilities and was incapable of meeting the current needs of the country. D. R. Regmi dismissed Singh's resignation as a matter of no consequence and preferred to emphasize instead the importance of early elections. In a somewhat noncommittal manner, Bharat Shamsher, the Gorkha Parishad leader, explained that the latest political event in no way affected his party's programs and policies with respect to the general elections. The Communist party, disavowing any surprise at the end of Singh's tenure, characterized the royal palace as the source of political instability in the country and appealed for vigilant unity by all democratic forces so that any future government could compel the royal palace to conduct general elections for a Constituent Assembly. The business community in Kathmandu Valley reportedly celebrated the event by distributing sweets and cigarettes.

The dramatic fall of Singh's government gave rise to wild rumors and speculations in the capital. It was even whispered in some circles that Singh's sudden exit was caused by his involvement in a high-level armed conspiracy to seize power, and that Singh and his colleagues were restricted to the confines of Kathmandu Valley pending a full inquiry into the alleged conspiracy. Although the consensus of public opinion had never credited Singh's government with a long life expectancy, no one had anticipated that it would collapse so soon. Singh himself added to the mystery by his persistent refusal to explain his sudden resignation. In interviews with the press he restricted himself to the observation that no honest person could live and work "in the cobweb of dishonest conspiracy that prevailed in the government." When queried further by the press correspondents about his future plans, Singh gave only vague replies, and was specific only in his pledge of unstinted loyalty to the King and the country.

The political situation following Singh's loss of office was, to say the least, extremely fluid and uncertain. From one point of view, it seemed that King Mahendra had exhausted all possible political experiments based on unstable, royalist-oriented parties. He was now left with only antithetical choices, such as the Gorkha Parishad or the Nepali Congress, both of which he had carefully excluded from office since ascending the throne in 1955. The Communist party, of course, did not count in his political calculations. He had consistently refused to recognize their existence (though he permitted their legalization) by debarring them from participation in the political conferences at the royal palace. From the point of view of the general public, the political arena was a chaotic hodgepodge of parties and parallel splinter organizations, and their unprincipled alliances. Also in the forefront was a group of businessmen and landlords under the label of the Independent League, which burst into activity every time there was the prospect of a new government. Most significant of all was the birth of a new party, called the Nepal Prajatantrik Mahasabha ("Nepal Democratic Convention"), under the leadership of Ranga Nath Sharma, who had been one of the King's nominated members in Tanka Prasad's expanded Cabinet. The new political organization was formed at a conference in Nepalganj in the last week of November, 1957. Quite unequivocally, it declared its support of a limited democracy under the aegis of King Mahendra and advocated elections for a Parliament rather than a Constituent Assembly. It was also rumored at the time that the new party was blessed with unlimited financial resources, presumably supplied by the royal palace. In any case, Ranga Nath Sharma astounded the country by demanding the right to form the next government barely a week after his party was founded. This was a clear example of the inflated political pretensions of some leaders in Nepal, and was symptomatic of the level of opportunism to which the political party system had degenerated.

THE SECOND DIRECT-RULE PERIOD

Once the general relief at the end of Singh's government had diminished, the public and the press undertook various post-mortem analyses of that government, all ending in a search for another political arrangement, which, it was hoped, would not repeat the mistakes of the past. In his Royal Proclamation, King Mahendra had merely mentioned, without suggesting any alternative courses of action, that he had been "compelled, in spite of his reluctance, to conduct the administration of the affairs of the country for a few days." It was apparent that he wanted to study the reaction of the political parties and the public before embarking on another major political venture.

The parties, for their part, were sharply divided among themselves with respect to future plans for the government. Although each of them, regardless of size and ideology, aspired to inclusion in the next government, none was confident that King Mahendra shared its political perspective. The most feasible arrangement, therefore, was a coalition government in which the parties would be represented according to King Mahendra's wishes and terms. Since the parties were hardly in a position to lay down terms, all they could do at the time was to make glib promises of accomplishment if they should be allowed to form the government.

There was, however, an immediate problem that the King had to reckon with—the projected countrywide *Satyagraha* organized by the United Democratic Front (Nepali Congress, Nepali

National Congress, and Praja Parishad), which was scheduled to commence on December 8. In the first week of December, B. P. Koirala and Tanka Prasad Acharya issued public statements urging the King to announce a date for the general election so that the proposed movement could be canceled. True to his characteristic approach to such situations, King Mahendra's response was as ambiguous as possible. He invited a wide variety of political organizations to a political conference at the palace, set for December 6. The composition of the conference was such as to place the Democratic Front parties in a conspicuous minority.

The response of the Front leaders was scarcely enthusiastic. While they did not specifically reject the invitation, they did announce that the conference would not affect preparations for the proposed agitation. On the evening of December 5, the three leaders of the Front—B. P. Koirala, D. R. Regmi, and Bhadrakali Mishra—met with the King and expressed their uneasiness at participating in the conference scheduled for the next day. According to newspaper reports, the King disavowed any intention on his part to undermine the Front parties by inviting all political organizations to the conference, and urged the Front leaders to participate. Further, it was reported that the King assented to their launching the proposed agitation regardless of the outcome of the conference. On the strength of this, the Front leaders decided to participate.

The conference of political party representatives and leaders was held at the royal palace on the afternoon of December 6. King Mahendra took the chair, and eighteen representatives of various political parties were present. In an opening speech King Mahendra described himself as more impatient than they that elections be held as soon as possible. Then, interrupting his speech, he asked the Election Commissioner to report on the current status of preparations for the elections. On resuming his speech, King Mahendra asked the participants to express their opinions on the timing and the purpose of the elections and the type of arrangement that would be suitable during the interim period. He appealed to them to rise above petty selfish or party interests and to address themselves to the problems at hand, keeping in mind the interests of the country and the unity and the sovereignty of the nation. In an obvious reference to the Front leaders, he advised that thought be given to the probable consequences of the proposed movement "at a time when the country was faced with serious problems of drought, food scarcity, and natural calamity in various areas." [2]

The discussions at the conference, as the King had expected, showed a sharp division of opinion between the three United Democratic Front parties and the other political parties. The Front leaders reiterated their conviction that the elections could be held within six months, and justified their proposed civil disobedience movement as a means of emphasizing this point both to the government and the people. They acknowledged that there was a diversity of opinion among them with regard to the purposes of the election, but they felt that this question could be resolved easily, once the date of elections was announced. The other participants were generally opposed to the Front's insistence upon holding elections within six months. Some of them wanted the government to direct its attention to solving food problems before holding the elections; and it was suggested that the elections should be held only when the Election Commissioner deemed it appropriate. The Terai Congress representative demanded elections for a Constituent Assembly, but in general the non-Front political organizations expressed a preference for elections for a Parliament.

After all the representatives had expressed their opinions, King Mahendra made a concluding speech before adjourning the conference. The consensus of opinion at the conference had been strongly critical of the Democratic Front's approach to the problem of elections. Perhaps emboldened by the critical attitude of the majority, King Mahendra expressed his emphatic disapproval of the proposed civil disobedience movement and urged the Front leaders to redirect their energy, money, and effort to educating the people about "what the situation in the country is, what democracy means, and how elections should be conducted." [3] He also advised B. P. Koirala and other interested parties to confer with the Election Commissioner as to the date and procedure of the elections and to report their conclusions back to him. This was the only tangible outcome of the conference at the royal palace.

As far as the Front leaders were concerned, the conference had only succeeded in upsetting the timetable of their agitation, which was scheduled to begin in about thirty-six hours. They had also been charged by the King to investigate the current status of preparations for the elections in consultation with the Election Commissioner. Since the time factor was so crucially important, and since they did not want to disobey the royal command, they proceeded to the Election Commissioner's office immediately after the conference, where they were joined by leaders of other political parties. For about two hours they studied the necessary files and records and held discussions with the commissioner. The next day, December 7, the Front leaders addressed a joint petition to the King in which they reiterated their view that elections could be held within six months and requested the King to issue a proclamation to this effect.[4]

The non-Front parties continued the discussions at the office of the Election Commissioner on December 7. Present at these discussions were the United Democratic party, Gorkha Parishad, Terai Congress, Parallel Nepali Congress, Nepali National Congress (Jiva Raj Sharma faction), Prajatantrik Mahasabha, Parallel Nepal Praja Parishad, and Rashtriya Praja party representatives. They also prepared a joint report, which advised the King to commence the elections on February 12, 1959.

THE UNITED DEMOCRATIC FRONT'S SATYAGRAHA

Since no Royal Proclamation was forthcoming, the United Democratic Front launched its civil disobedience movement on December 8. Satyagrahis picketed the gates of government offices and tried to dissuade government employees from entering. B. P. Koirala and others were arrested while picketing at the main gates of the Secretariat, but were released after a few hours. The movement continued and there were reports of passive resistance at Bhaktapur, Kalaiya, Bhojpur, Lalitpur, Nuwakot, Sindhuli, Upardang Garhi, Hetaunda, and Biratnagar. The Communists joined in on their own initiative.

While the movement was under way, the publicity departments of the government and the royal palace were busy issuing communiqués alleging that the Front had launched its *Satyagraha* with unbecoming haste, disregarding the advice of other political parties and the wishes of King Mahendra for a careful study of the election problem. The King continued to confer with two former Prime Ministers, Tanka Prasad Acharya and M. P. Koirala, and the leaders of non-Front political parties.

On December 15, King Mahendra broadcast a Royal Proclamation over Radio Nepal, naming February 18, 1959, as the day of general elections. Almost all political parties immediately welcomed the announcement. The Action Committee of the Front called off its agitation, and adopted a resolution stating: ". . . although the Front's entire demands have not been fulfilled, the declaration of a date for conducting the elections shows that the people have been victorious." [5]

The announcement of the election date marked a change of phase in the evolution of the political process in Nepal. The Royal Proclamation, although significantly silent on the goals of the election, was a recognition of the popular demand for a government composed of elected leaders rather than nominees of the royal palace. The uncertain conditions under which various governments had risen and fallen since 1951 had created widespread yearning for a stable administration which would be accountable to the people rather than the royal palace. The announcement also had a healthy effect on the political parties, most of which lacked any bases of public support and, hence, had turned into small in-groups constantly bickering among themselves and with other similar groups. The fractionalization of the parties had frequently been motivated by ambitious politicians who used such tactics to curry favor with the King. For the first time in seven years of political experimentation, the parties now had to reckon with the need to cultivate the support of the people rather than the royal palace. The announcement virtually wiped out the splinter groups—in order to survive, they were forced to negotiate mergers among themselves or return to their parental organizations.

There remained the problem of forming a suitable government to conduct the administration in the interim period and to make necessary preparations for the elections. By all indications King Mahendra was not eager to terminate the direct-rule system quickly, as he continued to form advisory bodies to assist him in the administration. On January 5, 1958, a Planning Council was established under the chairmanship of his younger brother, Prince Himalaya, and in the same month a high-powered Food Management Board was formed to meet the difficult food situation in various parts of the country. On February 22, King Mahendra dissolved the Election Commission and replaced it by a new three-member body. On February 25, he set up a Work Expediting Committee and charged it with the responsibility of ensuring the smooth functioning of the various branches of the government.

While making all these changes in the government, the King was holding negotiations with leaders of political parties, presumably over the composition of the next government. The Front parties were once again divided over the issue of the purpose of the elections. On December 24, 1957, the Praja Parishad executive reiterated its previous demand for elections to a Parliament, while the Nepali Congress and the Nepali National Congress continued to espouse elections for a Constituent Assembly. Since the Royal Proclamation had fulfilled the main objective of the Front, the constituent parties—particularly, the Nepali Congress —began to drift away from their alliance.

In January, 1958, therefore, the alliance of the Front parties was sustained only because of the necessity of making a good showing at the municipal elections in Kathmandu and Patan. All political observers, including King Mahendra, had their attention focused on these elections as a gauge of the popular appeal of the Front. The elections took place in the middle of January. The Front failed to capture a majority of seats in either city, and independents carried the polls. Only one avowed Front candidate won in Kathmandu, and none of the five Front candidates was victorious in the Patan elections. A pro-Nepali Congress paper claimed that the Front had won nine seats in Kathmandu, on the ground that most of the victorious independent candidates had affiliations with the Front. This assumption was challenged by the Communists, who sought to prove that they had supported or put up most of the winning independents. Whatever the interpretation of these results, it was clear that the Front had failed to demonstrate any overwhelming influence in Kathmandu Valley. It was against this disappointing background that the Front's general conference began in February at Birganj.

Before heading for the conference, the Front leaders held a joint interview with King Mahendra on January 24. It was reported that the King proposed the formation of an Executive Council consisting of the Front and other political parties, and that the Front leaders accepted the proposal. This development touched off a series of impassioned appeals to the King by the leaders of parallel splinter organizations and the new formed Prajatantrik Mahasabha, asking for "a chance to win the new leadership." [6] These groups sought to strengthen their case by exposing the "dishonest, corrupt, and opportunistic" background of the Front leaders and by arguing for a Cabinet with a Prime Minister rather than an Executive Council.

THE ROYAL PROCLAMATION OF FEBRUARY 1, 1958

On February 1, 1958, when some five hundred political party leaders and workers were converging on Birganj for the conference of the Democratic Front, King Mahendra made a momentous Royal Proclamation from Kathmandu which ranks in importance with King Tribhuwan's Proclamation of February 18, 1951. The King singled out continuing political instability as the principal reason for a lack of progress in the country during the past seven years. In order to remedy this situation he proposed the early establishment of (a) a Constitution Drafting Commission in order to prepare a Constitution incorporating the idea of a bicameral Legislature, (b) a nominated Advisory Assembly in the interim period before the elections, and (c) a government without a Prime Minister, consisting of independents as well as representatives of political parties. The functions and duties of the proposed government would be to implement development programs, assist in the preparation and promulgation of the Constitution, conduct the day-to-day administration, and conduct the first general elections.

The first tangible result of the Proclamation was the Third Advisory Assembly, which was announced on March 5. Why King Mahendra considered it necessary to establish another Assembly, when elections were scheduled for the early part of the next year, was never explained. The Assembly did not meet until October and, to add to the mystery behind King Mahendra's motives, it was dissolved after being in session for just twenty-two days. Perhaps the Advisory Assembly was nothing more than a tactical maneuver on the King's part. This impression is further strengthened when one examines the novel technique used in forming the Assembly. The King instructed "the Nepalese of every district . . . to gather together at a place on a date fixed by the Bada Hakim of the District and to elect five representatives from each district." He also ordered six persons from each district, including the Bada Hakim, the head of the Revenue Office, the head of the Apellate Court, the head of the Amini Court, and two prominent local persons selected unanimously by these officers to forward the names of persons elected by the majority of the people by April 12, 1958. The King himself made the final nominations from the lists obtained from different districts.

Having received universal support from all social organizations and political parties for his proposals of February 1, King Mahendra went about the business of forming the next government in a relaxed and unhurried manner. As usual, he continued his exploratory talks with leaders of various parties and factions, at the same time giving no indication of when he would set up a new government. The first clue, vague as it was, came in the form of an announcement, on February 11, that he had accepted an invitation to visit the Soviet Union later in the year. It was expected that the new government would be sworn in before his departure for the Soviet Union, but nobody knew at the time when his trip would begin.

On the evening of April 30, King Mahendra called a conference of five political parties to discuss the composition of the next government. Those invited were B. P. Koirala of the Nepali Congress, D. R. Regmi of the Nepali National Congress, B. Mishra of the Nepal Praja Parishad, Ranadhir Subba of the Gorkha Parishad, and K. I. Singh of the United Democratic party. K. I. Singh did not attend; reportedly he submitted a written message to the King explaining that the recent meeting of his party's Working Committee had decided against participation in the proposed Cabinet, or, as it should be called owing to the omission of a Prime Minister, Council of Ministers. At the conference in the royal palace, according to newspaper reports, King Mahendra asked the participants to submit the name of one representative from each party for the Council. B. P. Koirala submitted the name of Suvarna Shamsher, and the representatives of other parties offered to name their representatives within two or three days.

The inauguration of the Council of Ministers was delayed, however, by the continuing friction between Tanka Prasad Acharya and B. Mishra within the Praja Parishad. Their differences of opinion, perhaps accentuated by the necessity of choosing a party representative for the Council of Ministers, came to public notice in the form of an exchange of letters between them. In an interview with King Mahendra on May 6 they aired their grievances against each other, and the King "assured them of his willingness to hear their mutual complaints against each other in the interests of preserving political unity in the country."[7] Finally, on May 15, King Mahendra issued a Royal Proclamation establishing a Council of Ministers under the interim chairmanship of Suvarna Shamsher. Representatives of four parties—the Nepali Congress, Gorkha Parishad, Nepali National Congress, and Nepal Praja Parishad—and two independents were included.

A few days before the installation of the Council of Ministers, King Mahendra announced two politically significant measures. First, he let it be known that the Indian Military Mission, having completed its assignment, would depart in three or four months. This announcement was hailed by the local press as a token of King Mahendra's recognition of public sentiments. He also announced—just two days before the new Council of Ministers was set up—a sweeping reorganization of the district administration involving the dismissal of thirteen Bada Hakims and the appointment of twelve new ones. Some others were promoted or transferred. Thus, the King presented a *fait accompli* to the new Council of Ministers as far as the district administration was concerned.

THE COALITION COUNCIL OF MINISTERS

In a Royal Proclamation on May 15, King Mahendra charged the new coalition Council of Ministers with the fourfold responsibility of implementing development projects, assisting in the preparation of the Constitution, conducting the daily administration of the government, and holding general elections. In establishing a Council of Ministers rather than a Cabinet led by a Prime Minister, the King was expressing his conviction that only a government with limited power functioning under his supervision could prove to be enduring and effective. Previous governments, as he stated on February 1, "had usually disintegrated under conditions of endemic internal conflicts." [8] There was, however, one significant shift from his earlier position that he himself should assume the chairmanship of the new government. To the surprise of the political parties and the public, he also announced on May 15 the appointment of Suvarna Shamsher, the Nepali Congress representative, as the interim chairman of the Council, giving no indication as to when this interim arrangement would end.

Whatever the King's motivation was in this instance, his decision helped to generate some degree of tension within the Council of Ministers from its inception. Suvarna Shamsher's sudden and unexpected elevation to the chairmanship of the Council was construed by the representatives of other parties as a recognition of a special position for the Nepali Congress, implying thereby a denigration of their own status and a nullification of the mutually agreed basis of interparty equality in the Council. The feeling of injured pride was immediately perceptible in the statements of D. R. Regmi, the representative of the Nepali National Congress. Just three days after the Council had been sworn in, Regmi was quoted as saying that Suvarna Shamsher commanded no special privileges in his capacity as the temporary chairman and that all Ministers of the Council were equal in terms of authority and discretionary power.[9] And, indeed, the subsequent activities and policies of other Ministers did not often reflect favorably on the authority of the chairman of the Council. At times, in fact, they seemed to be motivated by a desire to flout his authority from a sense of spite more than from any genuine ideological difference.

The initial reaction of the public, press, and political parties to the Royal Proclamation was one of joy and relief at the termination of the direct-rule system. Although skeptical comments were heard from some quarters with regard to the heterogeneous composition of the Council, there was not a single note of dissent in the chorus of appreciation which greeted the King's decision to end direct rule. Public enthusiasm for the new government arose largely from the fact that the political party representatives in the Council were all pledged to the holding of general elections at an early date. The Royal Proclamation of February 1 had reassured the public about King Mahendra's determination to hold elections as soon as possible, and it was widely assumed that his two representatives in the Council would assist in the preparations for the elections with at least as much zeal as the party representatives. Thus, the composition of the Council and the prevailing nationwide yearning for governmental stability produced a political climate in which the very term "election" came to acquire properties of word-magic and the purposes of the elections were often considered secondary to the overwhelming importance of the preparations under way.

This excessive preoccupation with the process of elections was partly responsible for the suddenness with which most political parties abandoned their previous demands for a full-fledged constitutional monarchy and settled for limited democracy under a benevolent monarchy. This same concern seemed to underlie the seemingly uncritical acceptance, by the press and the public alike, of the new political experiment. Only one newspaper, reflecting Nepali Congress views, refused to accept the democratic façade of the Council of Ministers and described the new arrangement as an indirect form of direct rule. Explaining the circumstances under which the Nepali Congress was participating in such a political arrangement, the paper commented:

Any political party sincerely desirous of holding the elections will wish to coöperate with the government under any conditions. All the four parties are committed to holding the elections. The Nepali Congress is the most eager of all. It wants the elections in any circumstance. It will, therefore, participate in any setup in any capacity because it hopes to gain a victory in the elections. If direct rule can hold the elections, it will coöperate with direct rule. It will work even as a departmental secretary if thereby the elections can be held.[10]

THE COMPOSITION OF THE COUNCIL OF MINISTERS

Despite a seemingly broad-based composition, the Council of Ministers was in many respects a political anomaly. For the first time since the end of Rana rule in 1951, the Nepali Congress and other "democratic" parties were in coalition with a representative of resurgent Rana power in the government. The nomination of Ranadhir Subba, the president of the Gorkha Parishad, as one of the members of the Council made it appear as if the evolution of democracy in Nepal had turned full circle. In November, 1951, the Nepali Congress had abandoned the coalition with the Ranas on the grounds of incompatible and irreconcilable differences. In the intervening eight years the Ranas had gone through innumerable vicissitudes, but now they had emerged as the leaders of an ostensibly democratic party, strong enough to claim a seat in a coalition Council of Ministers. During the same period the Nepali Congress had undergone phases of organizational splintering and political meandering and had finally agreed to join a government dominated by a Rana representative, King Mahendra's nominees, and representatives of two weak "democratic" parties. Its minority of one in 1958, in contrast to its parity with the Ranas in 1951, was an indication of resurgent Rana influence in the government and of the devious nature of Nepali politics. Furthermore, the Democratic Front of the three non-Rana political parties had virtually ceased to function since their unsuccessful joint conference in February. The alignment of democratic political forces was, thus, in its weakest phase both within and outside the new government. The Rana–royal palace coalition, on the other hand, was by far the most potent force in the country.

There was, therefore, little public surprise when Kathmandu newspapers began to speculate on conflicts that had arisen within the Council at its very first meeting. It was assumed that the delay in the allocation of portfolios was owing to a tussle for key departments among the representatives of the political parties. According to these reports, the Gorkha Parishad member demanded the Home, Finance, and Foreign departments, while D. R. Regmi had earmarked the Home and Foreign departments for himself.[11] One party which lost badly in the grab for key departments was the Praja Parishad, whose representative, C. B. Pandey, was away from Kathmandu and was not sworn in until May 19. By then, rumors had it, King Mahendra had solved the crisis confronting the Council by distributing the portfolios according to his own preference.

A glance at the membership of the Council (see table 9) reveals its heterogeneous character, whence came the complex interplay of diverse motivations and attitudes which often characterized its performances. Suvarna Shamsher's appointment as chairman did not invest him with additional powers or prerogatives. For the most part, his duties seem to have been confined to the routine of conducting Council meetings and to have involved only minimal coördination of the various departments, as each member of the Council displayed a remarkable degree of autonomy in departmental affairs. The principle of collective responsibility was more a matter for verbal profession than for observance, and even the political parties represented in the Council

TABLE 9

THE COUNCIL OF MINISTERS, 1958

Name	Portfolio	Party affiliation
Suvarna Shamsher (*chairman*)	Planning and Finance	Nepali Congress
Dilli Raman Regmi	Home	Nepali National Congress
Chandra Bhusan Pande	Transport and Communications	Praja Parishad
Purendra Vikram Shah	Defence; Foreign Affairs	King Mahendra's relative and representative
Bhupal Man Singh	Food, Agriculture, Irrigation, and Forests	King Mahendra's representative
Ranadhir Subba	Law and Parliamentary Affairs; Commerce and Industry; Education and Local Self-Government	Gorkha Parishad

usually dissociated the departments of their representatives from any criticism of the government. It should be noted, however, that the preparations for elections were treated as a joint responsibility, for the obvious reasons of public commitment on the part of the political party representatives and royal command on the part of the King's nominees.

ATTITUDE OF POLITICAL PARTIES TOWARD THE COUNCIL

Although the non-participating parties generally welcomed the end of direct rule, they were critical of the extremely heterogeneous character of the Council. Tanka Prasad Acharya, who was now openly critical of his party's president, B. Mishra, publicly expressed his misgivings about the efficacy of the Council, which he dubbed King Mahendra's unique attempt at a conciliation of two mutually contradictory political forces.[12] N. M. Thulung, president of the Parallel Nepali Congress, issued a public statement expressing his belief that the Council would not be able to discharge its responsibilities impartially and that his party would provide an active democratic opposition.[13] Dayanidhi Sharma, president of the truncated National Democratic party, welcomed the termination of direct rule, but was disinclined to welcome the Council of Ministers.[14] The Communist party adopted a resolution on the Council at its second plenum, held June 3–6 at Rautahat, in which it declared:

The Communist party is of the opinion that the constitution of the Council of Ministers without a Prime Minister is contrary to all democratic conventions. The party is opposed to such arrangements. The party feels that the Council of Ministers will prove unsuccessful in solving the problems of the country quite in the same way as all other Ministers and ministries of the past. The question of coöperating with the Council of Ministers, therefore, does not arise at all. But the party is ready to extend its full coöperation to them in any work concerning the holding of general elections and in any other sincere step taken to solve problems concerning the general welfare of our people.[15]

Even the Nepali Congress, one of the four ruling parties, deemed it necessary to comment upon the heterogeneous character of the Council—presumably to dissuade the public from entertaining unrealistic expectations of accomplishment from the new government. On May 29, the Working Committee and the Parliamentary Committee of the party issued a joint statement:

The Nepali Congress does not . . . want to make the people believe that its representative will be able to implement big schemes for the development of the country. It is not reasonable for the people to expect great things from this Council of Ministers which has been formed to conduct the general elections and run the day-to-day administration. The Nepali Congress has ordered its representative to coöperate with his colleagues and to give top priority to the elections.[16]

In general, however, the Council of Ministers entered office with a fund of political good will unprecedented in the past seven years of democratic experimentation. All the party organs of the four constituent parties supported the new experiment, and for once the political air of Kathmandu was free of the vituperative press campaigns which had usually greeted the birth of new governments in the past. In particular, the mild tone of discussion in the pages of the *Rashtravani,* the Gorkha Parishad paper, and the *Samyukta Prayas,* the United Democratic party paper, was a significant departure from their usually rancorous style.

THE PROSECUTION OF K. I. SINGH

One serious decision facing the new Council was the course of action to be followed by the government with regard to the long list of accusations leveled at high-ranking government officials by K. I. Singh in a public speech on April 26. The local press, while critical of the intemperate tone of his speech, had demanded a thorough investigation of the charges. King Mahendra ignored the former Prime Minister's bitter comments, but it was commonly assumed that the Council, which was more sensitive to public opinion, would initiate appropriate measures. According to newspaper reports, the Council was divided on the matter. On May 23, however, a special court was instructed to issue a summons ordering K. I. Singh to appear before it within two weeks.

The case against K. I. Singh was of considerable import for a number of reasons. He was, after all, the first Prime Minister to be called into court to explain his behavior. Moreover, by accusing highly placed civil and army officials of deliberate intrigues he had sought to emphasize the conspiratorial nature of vested interests entrenched in the government and the army. And, finally, the public attached a special significance to the fact that the government had decided to investigate his allegations through a special court rather than through the usual channel of the Magistrate's office. The report filed by the Police Superintendent on May 2 had requested that legal action be taken against Singh on the grounds that he had (1) incited the army "to disloyalty," (2) embittered Nepal's relations with friendly countries, and (3) fomented parochial feelings.[17] The summons repeated these charges and asked him to appear before the Court for clarification of his speech.

K. I. Singh appeared before the special court on May 29 and skillfully exploited the occasion. In refuting the charges leveled against him, he read out a seven-page document in which he first denied vehemently whatever was attributed to him in the police report and then went on to repeat his accusations against most of the persons whom he had attacked in his April 26 speech. He also questioned the legality of the Court's procedure in interrogating him without specifying the government as a plaintiff, and then sought to implicate the police inspector in a conspiracy aimed at defaming him for personal motives and accused him of forging evidence, for which irregular and corrupt practice, he demanded, the police official ought to be duly punished.

Going into detail, Singh submitted a list of persons who, he charged, were for personal reasons interested in bringing about the current action of the government against him. They were: Chief Secretary Chandra Bahadur Thapa, whom Singh alleged he had found corrupt and tyrannical during his Prime Ministership and had accordingly reported to the King; Secretary Bhim Bahadur Pande, who was charged with amassing a personal fortune out of foreign aid programs in his capacity as Secretary for the Planning and Development Departments and co-director of foreign aid programs; Education Secretary Keshar Bahadur Khatri Chhetri, who had allegedly violated government regulations by carrying an unlicensed firearm for three years; Finance Secretary Nir Raj Rajbhandari, who was accused of enriching himself by manipulation of the exchange rate of Indian currency in collusion with Nepali merchants and the former Finance Minister, Gunja Man Singh; Commander in Chief Toran Shamsher, who early in 1951 had violated army discipline by working with politicians such as Suvarna Shamsher and Mahavir Shamsher, and who now allegedly wanted to avenge himself on K. I. Singh because the latter had dismissed his son, Harihar Shamsher, from his position as Police Superintendent on grounds of corruption and collusion with black marketeers; B. P. Koirala and Suvarna Shamsher, who were charged with placing an order of 400,000 rupees for wireless sets in 1951, when they were Ministers, none of which had yet arrived; and Mahavir Shamsher, who had acknowledged the receipt of 990,000 rupees from the Kailali Kanchanpur treasury but had never provided any information on the disposition of this sum.

K. I. Singh denied that he had accused the royal palace of fomenting communalism, but he pointed out that Secretary Hansa Man Singh of the palace secretariat had violated traditional administrative practice by employing his brother in his office. K. I. Singh also denied that he had sought to create bad feelings between Nepal and foreign powers, but almost in the same breath went on to elaborate his allegation that American aid was being spent lavishly mainly to benefit a few Nepali landlords and the American personnel.[18]

The Special Court dismissed this intriguing case without any further action and before any further enlightenment could be shed on Singh's allegations. After some correspondence with the Secretariat, the Court decided that the government, which had been embarrassed by Singh's performance, was not prepared to pursue the case any further inasmuch as Singh had denied all the charges leveled against him. The case was handed back to the Home Department, which also dropped all proceedings against the wily, obdurate former Prime Minister. This ended the legal proceedings, but the repercussions of K. I. Singh's startling accusations were felt in Kathmandu for months to come.

THE THIRD ADVISORY ASSEMBLY

On June 2, King Mahendra announced the appointment of sixty-two persons, whose names had been selected from a panel consisting of approximately two hundred names submitted by the district Bada Hakims in accordance with the royal proclamation of March 5, to a third Advisory Assembly. Under this procedure, the Bada Hakims of each district had called a public meeting which had nominated at least five persons for inclusion in the panel list submitted to the King. In forming the Advisory Assembly, King Mahendra stated that he had also intended originally to include representatives from every political party, including parallel organizations, but that the Council of Ministers had dissuaded him from this course. He had decided, therefore, to include representatives from only six parties—the Nepali Congress, Gorkha Parishad, Praja Parishad, Nepali National Congress, United Democratic party, and Communist party.* All the parallel organizations and the newly organized Nepal Prajatantrik Mahasabha were excluded. The United Democratic party refused to send representatives to the Assembly, and even advised members who had been appointed by King Mahendra from the nominated list to resign.

The sudden announcement of the membership of the Advisory Assembly over Radio Nepal caused a sensation in Kathmandu political circles. The reaction was universally critical. It was contended in some quarters that the list of members had not been confined to the winners of direct elections in the districts, but contained the names of many defeated candidates as well. A more fundamental criticism was the charge that the Assembly could scarcely prove of benefit to the country when its first meeting could not be held until two or three months before the elections.[19]

PREPARATIONS FOR THE ELECTIONS

Despite its heterogeneous composition, the Council of Ministers was unusually vigorous in making preparations for the elections. Chairman Suvarna Shamsher allocated sizable funds for election expenses as early as August, 1958. Ranadhir Subba, who held the Law and Parliamentary Affairs portfolio, moved swiftly in appointing election officers for all the constituencies. Official and unofficial organizations held mock elections in various parts

---

* Home Minister D. R. Regmi contradicted the reference in the Royal Proclamation to the Council's advice on the formation of the Advisory Assembly. He told journalists that the King had sought the Council's advice only at the last minute. The Council, therefore, refused to offer advice on the nomination of the sixty-two members selected from the district panels, but did advise the King on the nomination of an additional eleven members to the Assembly and on the inclusion of representatives from six political parties. (*Halkhabar*, June 6, 1958; *Nepal Times*, June 3, 1958).

of the country for demonstration purposes, and the Election Commission solicited the services of poets, song writers, and literati in planning and executing their publicity campaigns. As the election date moved closer and the preparations intensified, the opposition parties, with the exception of the Communists, grew increasingly concerned that the elections might actually be held this time, a development that was unlikely to prove advantageous to them. They became increasingly cool toward the whole electoral process, and some even suggested that the elections should be postponed. Indeed, it was obviously for this reason that several minor parties suddenly raised the citizenship issue. They organized the Nepalitwa Rakshya Sangha ("Union for the Protection of Nepali Citizenship"), and demanded that the proper criteria for citizenship be determined before elections were held. Nothing came of this.

A serious threat to the elections was posed by the third Advisory Assembly, which began its session on November 19, with a total membership of ninety-one, including the six members of the Council of Ministers.* A large majority in the Assembly were "independents," most of whom were also unfavorably disposed toward the elections. The imbalance between these elements and the political party representatives was clearly demonstrated in the contest for the chairmanship of the Assembly on November 23–24. There were, in all, four contestants—representing the independents, Nepali Congress, Praja Parishad, and Nepali National Congress. On the third ballot, the independent candidate, Surya Bahadur Thapa, won over his nearest opponent, Hora Prasad Joshi of the Nepali Congress, by a thirteen-vote margin. The government party representatives were not only outnumbered by the independents, but also badly divided among themselves. The election of the independent candidate was, for example, supported by Praja Parishad and Gorkha Parishad members.

As soon as the Assembly had finished some of its procedural arrangements, several political resolutions were brought to the floor, first in the form of amendments to the Royal Address of November 26 and later in the form of specific proposals to the government. On December 10, D. S. Pariyar, one-time president of the Parallel Nepali Congress, moved the following resolution:

---

* The Advisory Assembly was composed of the following: sixty-two members nominated by the King from the district panels; ten from political parties (Nepali Congress, Gorkha Parishad, Nepali National Congress, Praja Parishad, and Communist—the United Democratic party refusing to depute two representatives) ; and thirteen, including seven women, nominated by the government.

Whereas the royal proclamation of February 1, 1958, stipulated that elections should be held on the basis of a Constitution to form a Parliament of two houses, and since the aforesaid Constitution has not been brought before the public as yet, and since the People's Representation Act does not distinguish one house of the Parliament from the other, the Advisory Assembly requests the postponement of the elections until the Constitution is published.[20]

The resolution was approved by a voice vote. A similar resolution was moved on December 16 and was carried by a vote of 29 to 15. King Mahendra, however, prorogued the Assembly on December 20 "in order to facilitate the participation of the members in the general elections, scheduled to begin on February 18, 1959." [21]

In support of the Advisory Assembly resolution recommending postponement of elections, some thirty-odd social, cultural, and political organizations presented a joint petition to the King on December 16.[22] Most of these organizations were nothing more than a handful of persons who, through the clever use of mass media and agitational techniques, had increased their nuisance value in a manner out of all proportion to their actual strength.*

On December 19, the representatives of forty-two social organizations held a public meeting in Kathmandu to explain their demand for postponement of the elections. About 3,000 supporters of the major political parties demonstrated against the meeting, and, according to newspaper reports, about a hundred persons were manhandled by the hostile audience. The police intervened and arrested twelve supporters of the Nepali Congress and the Communist party. The demands of the forty-two organizations were not taken seriously by any political party, but their representatives continued to press their position before King Mahendra, even when he left the capital on December 25 for a five weeks' tour of central and western Nepal. It was reported that some of them followed the King's entourage and were able to present their petitions to the King in person.[23] There was, of course, no significant outcome to their meeting with the King, and the preparations for the election went ahead on schedule. Nepal's first general elections were, thus, able to commence on February 18, 1959, the date specified by King Mahendra in his Royal Proclamation of December 15, 1957.

---

* The most extreme case was the couple that established at least three different social organizations, whose membership was confined to themselves and their children. Most of the others were also limited to a family circle or a friendship group.

12

King Mahendra's First Four Years: The Record

CONSTITUTIONAL DEVELOPMENTS

IN THE latter stage of the Tribhuwan era, political controversy in Nepal had largely centered around two constitutional issues—the independence of the judiciary, and the proper definition of political and civil rights. Popular agitation against the Royal Proclamation of February 13, 1954, which had formally established the King's ultimate authority in the judicial as well as the legislative and executive spheres of government, had not diminished by the time of King Tribhuwan's death. Indeed, Crown Prince Mahendra had moved quickly and impressively on this question even before ascending the throne. On March 4, 1955, exercizing the royal prerogatives granted to him by his incapacitated father, the Crown Prince restored Sections 2, 4, and 30 of the 1951 High Court Act, which had been abrogated by the February 13 Proclamation. Once again, the High Court became the supreme judicial authority in Nepal, as well as a court of record and a court of final appeal, with full power to institute contempt of court proceedings at its own discretion and to issue writs to the executive branch of government.

The independence of the High Court was seemingly even further strengthened fourteen months later with the enactment of the Supreme Court Act of 1956 by the Tanka Prasad Acharya government. Under the provisions of the new law, the High Court was transformed into the Supreme Court of Nepal. Its status as a court of record was retained, as was its power to initiate contempt of court proceedings and to issue writs of *habeas corpus* and *mandamus,* to issue prohibitory orders, and to initiate *quo warranto* proceedings. It was also authorized to frame rules and regulations concerning the efficient discharge of justice by the lower courts and was given limited consultative powers in the selection of District Court judges.

Although King Mahendra described the Supreme Court as more powerful and prestigious than the former High Court, in certain respects the powers of the new judiciary were more limited, perhaps most significantly and ominously by the provisions of Section 24 of the new Act, which reserved the royal prerogatives in judicial matters with the explicit statement that the King could reduce or enlarge the scope of the judicial processes and the provisions of the courts at his own discretion. The 1956 Act also relaxed the criteria for the appointment of Supreme Court judges, who, under the 1951 Act, were required to have had at least ten years' judicial experience. Under the new regulations, no previous experience in law was needed. Shortly thereafter, the Law Minister in the Praja Parishad government, who had virtually no legal training or experience, was appointed Chief Justice of the Supreme Court. Such appointments tended to weaken the prestige of the court and to add political factors to its consideration of cases.

From the viewpoint of over-all constitutional development, however, the most significant clause of the Supreme Court Act of 1956 was the oath required of judges. Under the High Court Act of 1951, the judges had sworn allegiance to the Interim Constitution; in the Supreme Court Act all references to the 1951 organic law were eliminated and the judges were required to apply only existing laws and conventions. The new Act thus constituted an indirect repeal of the 1951 Interim Constitution, which had included a provision obligating the government to hold elections for a Constituent Assembly. This helped set the framework within which the "Constituent Assembly versus Parliament" controversy that dominated Nepali politics from 1956 to 1958 was conducted.

The Praja Parishad government, though headed by a Prime Minister who had often bitterly criticized the efforts of other governments to limit the political and civil rights of the people, attempted to introduce the most coercive measure in this field since the Rana period. The draft of the Penal Code, published September 18, 1956, was given a universally hostile reception by parties, press, and public. Particular exception was taken to the provision that "anyone causing, inspiring, or aspiring to any efforts at creating contempt toward the King and his government by means of speech, expression, or signal" would be liable to a sentence of "life imprisonment or fourteen years' imprisonment or a heavy fine." [1]

The opposition did not object, at least publicly, to the sections of the draft requiring allegiance to the throne, but was aroused by what they considered an insidious attempt by the government to entrench itself in power. The intensity of the public reaction forced the government to proceed cautiously on this legislation. The two-month period stipulated for eliciting public opinion on the draft was extended by a month. Finally, chastened by the public outcry, the Praja Parishad Cabinet quietly dropped the proposed legislation.

POLITICAL INSTITUTIONS

King Mahendra's propensity for experimentation with political institutions and processes was clearly evident in the period between his accession to the throne and the 1959 general elections. Some of these experiments took the form of actions aimed at bypassing the Council of Ministers and the Secretariat in a bid to establish direct relations with the people. The dispatch of Royal Commissions to the districts in 1955 and his own intensive walking tours of areas of Nepal that had never been visited by a reigning monarch are obvious examples. In other cases, the King seemed to aim at the creation of alternative institutions which could be used as balances to the Cabinet in those periods in which he ruled through a government composed in part of political party representatives and headed by a party leader. On appointing K. I. Singh as Prime Minister, for instance, the King also announced that three high-powered bodies—a National Council, a Work-Expediting Committee, and a Five-Year Planning Board—would also be established to "assist" the United Democratic party Cabinet in its onerous duties. A National Council Act was promulgated on December 3, 1957. The terms of the Act did little to clarify the functions and role of the Council; it merely specified that the Council would act as an advisory body on questions of national welfare and improvement. But the general conclusion in Kathmandu political circles was that the Council was intended as another institutional support for the Crown in case of conflict with a Cabinet or political parties.

Another indication of the trend of developments was the Royal Decree issued on April 17, 1958, which changed the name of the Government of Nepal and its foreign embassies to "His

Majesty's Government" and the "Royal Nepalese Embassies." The term "Government of Nepal" had been used both in the Rana period and since 1951. Although the change in nomenclature did not mean much in an objective sense, it did symbolize King Mahendra's increasingly close identification with the administration.

ADMINISTRATIVE REORGANIZATION

It was inevitable that the new political look introduced by King Mahendra in 1955 would be accompanied by major changes in the administration, and, indeed, the new monarch undertook a major reorganization of the Secretariat personnel with characteristic zeal and thoroughness. The first objective was the district administration. On August 23, 1955, sixteen district magistrates were dismissed. Their replacements were mostly Ranas and Shahs —seven Ranas and four Shahs—drawn from the same old-line groups as were the persons whom the King had selected for his Council of Advisers.* Changes in the district administration had barely been completed when a major reorganization of the Central Secretariat was announced on October 14. An entirely new set of departmental secretaries was appointed, and their number was reduced from twelve to nine. A new position, that of the Chief Secretary to the Government, was created; this official also served as head of the Anti-Corruption Department.

All of these new appointments, which were made without consultation with the Public Service Commission, were strongly criticized by the parties and the press. Nevertheless, the King pressed on with the administrative reorganization. On October 7, he announced new pay scales for government employees. For the first time, cadres of five classes were established, namely: gazetted officers, nongazetted officers, senior clerks, junior clerks, sepoys, and orderlies. The system of double payment of salaries was abolished.† Limits on government salaries were fixed at a maximum of 975 rupees and minimum of 30 rupees per month. The last of this series of administrative changes was announced on October 21, when King Mahendra made changes in the personnel of such statutory bodies as the Public Service Commission, the

---

* It was claimed that these changes in the district administration were made in response to local demands transmitted to the King through the Royal Commissions.
† Under the Rana regime, Ranas had automatic appointments as officers in the army. Whenever they obtained a civil appointment as well, they were entitled to receive the salaries attached to both their appointments. This practice had been continued after the overthrow of Rana rule.

Election Commission, the Census Commission, and the Law Commission.[2] In addition, he also established seven temporary judicial benches to dispose of accumulated cases pending in the Supreme Court.

The appointment of the Praja Parishad government in January, 1956, led to another frantic spate of administrative reorganization. In this instance, however, it was the Secretariat's structure rather than personnel that was the object of the new Cabinet's reorganization zeal. An Administrative Reorganization Commission was established under the chairmanship of Prime Minister Tanka Prasad Archarya to draw up rules under which the procedure for the transaction of government business was to be modernized. The first codified Civil Service Act was approved on September 9, providing for a civil service organization that encompassed all the different branches of the administration. The government service was divided into nine categories: the Education Service, Judicial Service, Health Service, Administrative Service, Engineering Service, Forest Service, Agricultural Service, Foreign Service, and Royal Palace Service.

The Prime Minister also announced that all of the 600 gazetted officers and some 21,000 nongazetted employees of the government would be incorporated into the new service on a tenure basis only after having been carefully examined and approved by a screening committee. Two such committees were established. The first, headed by the Prime Minister, handled the screening of "selection grade" officials—i.e., ambassadors and Departmental Secretaries; the other, headed by Foreign Minister Chuda Prasad Sharma (the Prime Minister's only completely dependable colleague), screened high-level officials below the Secretariat level. A standard grading procedure was established, allowing up to 100 points for qualifications (primarily academic), 100 for previous experience, 50 for service records (i.e., efficiency ratings), and 50 based upon personal interviews. A total of 100 out of the 300 possible points was set as the passing grade. The screening process of the upper-level civil servants was completed by mid-1957, but the Acharya government was dismissed before the results could be published. Nothing was done subsequently to apply the results of the screening, and officials who had failed were often retained and even promoted, while some who had passed were dismissed from service for essentially political reasons. Thus, this effort to introduce a degree of formal structuralization in the civil service system proved abortive, and the consternation it had caused within the Secretariat turned out to be wholly unnecessary.

The dismissal of Tanka Prasad Acharya and the appointment of K. I. Singh as his successor in mid-1957 caused yet another uproar in the Secretariat. On August 6, the new Prime Minister addressed a gathering of civil servants at Singha Darbar and announced that junior government employees would be screened shortly just as the senior officials had been under Tanka Prasad Acharya. This announcement, combined with Singh's warning of dire consequences that would fall on corrupt officials, led to the expectation of major changes in the administrative staff. The announcement on August 12 that a special police organization and a special intelligence section, staffed by former servicemen of the "Gurkha" battalions in the British and Indian armies, would soon be organized under the direct supervision of the Prime Minister, added substantially to the sense of foreboding that prevailed in the Secretariat, as well as to the serious deterioration in morale that ensued.

But the senior officials within the administration were by this time all royal appointees, who could count on some degree of support from the palace. Within a week of the inauguration of the new government, rumors of friction between the Prime Minister and the Departmental Secretaries began to circulate in Kathmandu. The situation worsened steadily as the strong-minded, obdurate Prime Minister pressed on with his plans for an administrative reorganization even if this should bring him into conflict with the palace. K. I. Singh was reported to have prepared a list of senior officials whose dismissal from office by October 17 had been requested of the King. The request was, of course, ignored by the palace; on October 23, however, the Prime Minister on his own initiative suspended the Acting Home Secretary and an Assistant Education Secretary. Two days later, the Chief Secretary went on special leave and returned to his office only on November 14—the day King Mahendra suddenly announced his acceptance of the resignation of the Singh government. Later, K. I. Singh acknowledged that one of the chief reasons for tendering the resignation of his Cabinet was the lack of coöperation he had encountered among the senior officials in the Secretariat, who continued to look to King Mahendra as the *de facto* as well as the *de jure* head of the administration.

ECONOMIC POLICY

King Mahendra inherited a severe economic crisis as well as political chaos from the last M. P. Koirala government. Immediate action was necessary, particularly with respect to the currency exchange rate, if the steady deterioration in the value of Nepali currency was to be stemmed and a potentially dangerous threat to the stability of the regime avoided. Three days after being sworn in, the Royal Advisers announced a fifteen-point program which was aimed specifically at the stabilization of the exchange rate between the Indian and Nepali rupee, and in the process also checking the rapid rise in the prices of essential commodities imported into Nepal. Shortly thereafter, the government published a report on the reserves and securities held by the government as backing to the currency notes in circulation. This was intended to strengthen public confidence in the paper money, which at that time was so low that most metal coins had disappeared from circulation and currency notes were being discounted at 10 per cent below their face value.

Currency reform was also a major preoccupation of the Praja Parishad government, which, priding itself on its strongly nationalistic character, initiated a program under which Nepali currency would gradually come into use throughout the country.* On April 16, 1956, the government announced that Nepali rupees must be accepted by all government treasuries in the Terai for the payment of land taxes, custom duties, and telephone-wireless rates. This bold measure, which was justified on nationalistic rather than economic grounds, had an immediately adverse effect both on government revenues and the price structure in Nepal. The exchange rate of Nepali and Indian currency in the Terai was set arbitrarily at the unrealistic figure of 128 to 100. Landlords were quick to seize the opportunity to make a handsome profit by paying land taxes in Nepali currency (which they could easily obtain at a devalued rate on the open market), while demanding rent from tenants in Indian rupees, as had traditionally been the practice.

Another policy of the Praja Parishad government had a somewhat better, but only slightly more durable, effect on the currency. This was the policy introduced in 1957 under which part of the 20 million Indian rupees received under the Chinese economic aid program was used to stabilize the exchange rate between Indian and Nepali currencies. The exchange rate was set at 135 to 100 and was maintained at this level until the Chinese-donated rupees were finally expended.† In 1958, this arbitrary rate had to be

---

* In 1957, Nepali currency was in general use only in Kathmandu Valley and the adjacent hill areas. Indian currency was the normal medium of exchange in the Terai and outer hill areas.

† The government's decision to utilize the Indian rupees obtained from China for stabilization of the currency meant, of course, that these funds could not be used for their stated purpose—capital support for factories to be constructed under the Chinese aid program.

abandoned on the grounds that it operated against the interests of the government and the public alike. By that time, however, the State Bank which had been established in 1956 was functioning effectively and was able to utilize the wide powers it had been given in the regulation of Nepali currency and in the setting of flexible exchange rates with Indian and other currencies.

LAND REFORM

Several tentative gestures in the direction of a basic land-reform program were made during King Mahendra's first direct-rule period. The most important of these was a thirteen-point program, the first authoritative definition of the government's policy on such questions as tenancy rights and land rents, which was announced on September 3, 1955.[3] Under the terms of this policy statement, landlords could not demand more than 50 per cent of the produce as rent—a traditional rate in much of Nepal—or charge more than 10 per cent interest on loans in cash or kind. Tenants who cultivated a plot of land for two consecutive years and paid the rent regularly were granted tenancy rights automatically. A 10 per cent land tax was also imposed on previously tax-free *Birta* lands.

The thirteen-point program was merely a statement of policy, however, and did not have the force of law. The Land Tenancy Act—an ordinance incorporating the principles defined in the royal announcement—was drafted by the Acharya government, but was not finally promulgated until August, 1957, when the K. I. Singh government was in office. A number of additional features—e.g., a ban on forced labor (*begar* or *beth*)—were included in the Act as finally adopted, but the provisions were essentially those stipulated by King Mahendra two years earlier. In any case, the 1957 Land Tenancy Act was never implemented to any degree, and made little improvement in tenancy conditions in Nepal.

PLANNED ECONOMIC DEVELOPMENT

Most of the leaders of the 1950 revolution were ardent and vocal advocates of planned economic development, but the governments established after the fall of the Rana regime were in no position to devote much attention to this subject. The first step in the direction of a planned economy was not taken until October 8, 1955, when King Mahendra announced that a National Planning Commission would be formed and would be entrusted with the responsibility of formulating a Five-Year Plan to raise the standard of living of 8.4 million Nepalese.[4]

It does not seem that this first Planning Commission ever functioned. Indeed, the procedure under which the first Five-Year Plan was prepared and even the precise date it came into effect, is something of a mystery. The plan, as it eventually evolved, was less a coördinated program for economic development than a description of the various village-development, teacher-training, malaria-control, and irrigation projects which had been undertaken at one time or another in the early 1950's on the personal initiative of various Ministers with either American or Indian aid.

The first reference to a functioning Five-Year Plan came from King Mahendra during his tour of India in December, 1955. Speaking to a group of Nepali residents in Calcutta, he said:

With a view to ensuring the economic progress of the country and in order to solve the problem of unemployment, a Five-Year Plan for our country has already been prepared. We are convinced that the implementation of that plan will solve the problem of emigrant Nepalese.[5]

Details, however, were not divulged for almost ten months, when the plan—which was first drafted by a foreign adviser to the government and then later discussed within the Secretariat by a series of committees that lacked the technical training to scrutinize it with the necessary competence—was finally imposed from above on an unsuspecting public. In August, 1956, before any further announcement had been made, the Development Minister, Gunja Man Singh, confided to a press representative that the plan had been revised and that the original cost estimate of Rs. 210 million had been expanded to Rs. 350 million. The plan had already been started, he revealed, and was based on an estimated foreign aid of Rs. 100 million from India and Rs. 60 million from the United States during the five-year period.[6] More details were brought to light on September 21, when Tanka Prasad Acharya, on the eve of his departure for China, called upon the people to help the government in fulfilling the goals of the plan. According to his outline of the plan, about 33 per cent of the total expenditure was earmarked for developing transportation and communication, 25 per cent for agriculture, 17 per cent for hydroelectric projects, 16 per cent for health education, and 6 per cent for cottage industries.[7] It was estimated that the government revenues in the next four years could be raised by a maximum of Rs. 170 million, out of which Rs. 75 million would be earmarked for stabilizing the national budget and the remaining Rs. 95

million for the plan. The latter figure, added to the estimated Rs. 100 million from India as well as Rs. 60 million from the United States, would bring the resources available for the plan to a total value of Rs. 220 million. The conclusion of an economic treaty with China would provide an additional Rs. 20 million in Chinese aid for the first three years of the plan period. All this led Tanka Prasad Acharya to claim at a press conference in January, 1957, that he had succeeded in procuring Rs. 240 million in foreign aid for the implementation of the Five-Year Plan.

It was only *after* the first Five-Year Plan had been announced and public coöperation had been solicited that a twenty-eight-member Planning Commission, consisting of officials, non-officials, and political party representatives, was established. Inaugurating the Commission, the Prime Minister suggested the formation of four panels, namely: (1) agricultural and village development, (2) industry, transport, communications, and public works, (3) social services and manpower, and (4) fiscal and financial policies. The Nepali Congress withdrew its representatives from the Commission on March 31, and the Nepali National Congress followed suit on April 3, both charging that the Commission, as composed, lacked competence to formulate or implement plans and that it had been established somewhat on the lines of a "political circus" to delude the public into thinking that planned economic progress was in the offing.

K. I. Singh evidently accepted this view of the Commission and of the first Five-Year Plan. On his appointment as Prime Minister in mid-1957, he discarded the plan and used his Cabinet as the agency for formulating a modified Two-Year Plan. The government moved swiftly and on September 1 published a 16-item outline of the plan, in which the main emphasis was on the development of transport and communications. The Two-Year Plan envisaged the construction of 100 suspension bridges and several all-weather roads in various parts of the country, and the establishment of eight hydroelectric power stations. Each district would have a minimum of two irrigation dams, and paper mills would be erected at various places in the Terai and a cement factory at Bhainse. The plan also provided for the construction of barracks and family quarters for army units stationed at Kathmandu and Pokhara.

No mention was made of the resources available to the government to support these various undertakings, some of which were expensive. But perhaps this was unnecessary, for the plan was obviously motivated by political rather than economic considerations. The vagueness surrounding the various projects and the two-year time limit doubtless reflected K. I. Singh's calculation of the date of the general election. In any case, the Two-Year Plan was in turn discarded after the dismissal of the Singh Cabinet, and the first Five-Year Plan was revived. Finally, on December 3, King Mahendra promulgated a Planning Commission Act which provided for the formation of a Planning Commission with a tenure of five years to "prepare and implement development schemes, prepare the budget for development works, and advise the government on matters of national interest." [8] The Commission was formally established on January 5, 1958, under the chairmanship of Prince Himalaya, King Mahendra's first brother, presumably to prepare the revived Five-Year Plan, though this was not made clear in the Commission's terms of reference.

OTHER ECONOMIC DEVELOPMENTS

The coalition Council of Ministers appointed by King Mahendra in May, 1958, had been expected to devote its full attention to preparations for the elections and day-to-day administration. It was something of a surprise, therefore, that several important economic measures were introduced during the Council's tenure in office. Some of these had obvious, if complex, political explanations involving either the Council's relations with the palace or the political maneuverings of the component parties which were busily jockeying for an advantageous position in the coming general election.

One of the best examples of how the palace used party governments as fronts for the introduction of unpopular but necessary legislation occurred just five days after the coalition Council took office. On May 24, 1958, the government suddenly and without warning promulgated a Taxation Imposition Act to be enforced immediately throughout the country. The ordinance levied new taxes on houses, land, water, and vehicles in both urban and rural areas. This announcement fell like a bombshell upon the public in Nepal, which had no previous experience with taxes on income, property, houses, or "God-given" water. And this Act, announced so suddenly, caused widespread indignation. From later reports, it became evident that the new Act had been framed during the direct rule and had been put into effect by the palace without the approval or, indeed, the knowledge of the Council.[9] But it was the Council, of course, that had to bear the brunt of the criticism of the measure from the public and the opposition parties, and it was Suvarna Shamsher, as Finance Minister, who had to announce the suspension of the Act in the course of his budget speech on August 19, thus by implication also assuming responsibility for its having been enforced.

Another political controversy, this time within the Council of Ministers, was caused by the unilateral announcement of a new industrial policy by the Gorkha Parishad Minister of Commerce and Industry, Ranadhir Subba, on June 7.[10] According to the Home Minister, D. R. Regmi, Ranadhir had made his announcement without prior consultation with the Council, and certainly without its approval.[11] The policy statement, which followed by three days the government's approval of the establishment of an Industrial Development Center with a capital of Rs. 2 million to assist and coördinate the development of small- and medium-scale industries, reflected the private-enterprise bias of the Gorkha Parishad. Probably it would have been opposed by the Nepali Congress representative if the Council had considered the matter. In any case, the Nepali Congress government formed after the 1959 general elections formulated its own industrial policy that differed in some respects from that announced by Ranadhir Subba.

The Gorkha Parishad Minister's policy was predicated on the conviction that private investment, both national and foreign, should play a major role in the industrial development of the country, and that the role of the government should be limited to providing attractive facilities and concessions to national and foreign entrepreneurs so as to stimulate investment in industrial and commercial enterprises. The formulation of this industrial policy had no perceptible impact on foreign investors, but it did arouse some apprehensions among Nepali entrepreneurs. A spokesman of the Nepal Chamber of Commerce, while generally welcoming the government proposals, pointed out that the government would be treating national and foreign investors alike, despite the fact that the latter usually had huge capital reserves and superior technical knowledge. While conceding that foreign investment was badly needed for the economic development of the country, he pleaded for special considerations for national capital so that it could eventually forge ahead and compete on an equal basis with foreign capital.[12] It must be pointed out that these discussions were highly theoretical at the time, in the absence of any known overtures by foreign entrepreneurs to undertake any industrial enterprise in Nepal. The prevailing political instability and uncertainty alone would have been an effective deterrent, no matter how attractive the government's industrial policy might appear at first sight. Nevertheless, the establishment of the Industrial Development Corporation was a significant accomplishment, inasmuch as it provided a basis for coördinating and implementing plans for industrial development in the future, and the Gorkha Parishad may have benefitted to some extent from Ranadhir Subba's catalytic role in the formulation of this policy.

IMPORT LICENSE DISTRIBUTION ISSUE

Ranadhir Subba was also the central figure in another intra-Cabinet controversy, this time over the distribution of import licenses. On August 17, a number of Kathmandu newspapers reported that businessmen were "attending" the Commerce and Industry Minister at his residence in order to obtain import licenses. It was alleged that Ranadhir had issued a license for the importation from India of 600 tons of iron of which only twenty tons had actually been brought into Nepal, while the rest had been disposed of in the Indian black market.[13] It was further charged that the Gorkha Parishad leaders were using the distribution of import licenses to collect money for the party's election funds.

Subba denied that any license had been issued for importing iron from India. It turned out, however, that of thirty-two import licenses available, eleven had been granted to one person.[14] Local businessmen were seriously agitated by what they termed monopolistic contracts granted by the Minister. On this, the Nepal Chamber of Commerce issued a statement on September 7:

The way His Majesty's government has granted import quotas for such essential materials as iron, cement, salt, corrugated iron sheets, and coal cannot be considered moral or justifiable. Till now the government had been consulting with the Chamber of Commerce and also businessmen in general while making such arrangements. But it is surprising that no regard was paid to this healthy tradition this time. Special favor has been shown toward some five or ten businessmen by granting them such quotas in a very arbitrary manner. Such an act on the part of the government strikes at the very root of the interests of the business community.[15]

The Gorkha Parishad, grimly aware of the political import of such allegations on the eve of elections, denied all the charges and even sued one paper for defamation of the party secretary. But the press note issued by the Industry and Commerce Department, partly to explain its policies and partly as a rejoinder to the press campaigns, was rather unconvincing:

The local press published certain misleading and confusing reports about the distribution of quotas to certain businessmen for importing salt, iron, cement, and coal into the country for the year 1958. It was evident from observation of the practices of past years that the work could not be carried out satisfactorily when quotas were granted to several persons. Also, as it was difficult for the authorities of both India and Nepal to maintain contact with so many persons for one item, it was found expedient to grant quotas to the fewest possible persons this year. Therefore the Department has appointed handling agents, keeping in view the capabilities of the businessmen. In order to provide encouragement to new traders, some twenty new importers, too, have been appointed this year.[16]

It was after the publication of this press note that the local papers began to demand the resignation of the Gorkha Parishad Minister. According to reports, near pandemonium had erupted in the Council when the question was brought up for consideration by Suvarna Shamsher. Ranadhir Subba reportedly threatened to resign from the government if his departmental decisions were brought under scrutiny at the Council meeting, and there the matter ended. Nevertheless, the unfavorable publicity given the Gorkha Parishad came at a most inopportune time, with general elections only a few months away.

Another complaint leveled against Ranadhir was his appointment of 109 election officers, of whom 77 were alleged to be Gorkha Parishad members or sympathizers.[17] As these appointments were of a nongazetted rank, they did not fall directly within the jurisdiction of the Public Service Commission, and the Minister concerned had full discretion in making the appointments. But the local press raised a hue and cry against Subba's appointments and demanded that they be scrutinized by the Council of Ministers so as to ensure impartiality in the elections.

CONTROVERSY OVER THE BUDGET

Suvarna Shamsher, the Finance Minister, presented the budget for the year 1958–59 on August 19, just three months after the formation of the Council. This budget of the last interim government was of historical significance. In scope and character the budgets usually provided the most eloquent commentary on the economic implications of the democratic experiments in the country. All budgets since 1951 had been more or less deficit budgets, and the vexatious problems posed by a dual currency system had made the task of balancing the budget very arduous. Planning and development expenditures had risen steadily, owing partly to political pressures and partly to the availability of foreign aid. By and large, the government had become increasingly dependent upon foreign aid rather than internal resources as the key factor in balancing the budget.

The 1958–59 budget presented by Suvarna Shamsher reflected all these features, yet by an ingenious manipulation of the exchange rate it provided for a nominal surplus of Rs. 162,000. In a speech over Radio Nepal, Suvarna Shamsher explained that he had incorporated the principle of a minimum level of taxes in the budget since he felt that only the elected representatives of the people were qualified to impose new taxes. About Rs. 110 million was earmarked for development projects; since the national income did not exceed Rs. 70 million, most of the balance was to be covered by foreign aid. One politically significant measure was the curtailment of the King's privy purse by nearly Rs. 300,000.

The critics of the budget focused their attention on the way in which a small surplus had been obtained by raising the official exchange rate between Nepali and Indian currencies from 128–100 to 150–100. This was characterized as a political stunt and as an example of fiscal immorality since it involved an artificial raising of the national income by devaluating the national currency. Some newspapers and political parties, charging that the Finance Minister had let his proposals become known before the official presentation of the budget, demanded his resignation. It was claimed that local merchants had put the unofficial exchange rate at 164–100 and fixed the price of imported commodities proportionately even before the Finance Minister announced his budget. The steep rise in the price level and the criticisms of the political press led to stories of collusion between the Finance Minister and the black marketeers.[18] Leaders of opposition parties sought to inflame the discontent of the hard-hit middle class by pointing out that the new budget, with its significant omission of any mention of taxes on *Birta* lands, was framed to advance the interests of the rich at their expense.

ROYAL NEPAL AIRLINES CORPORATION ACT OF 1958

Nepal was first opened to air traffic in 1951, and since that time the Indian Airlines Corporation had been responsible for developing both internal and external services. By 1958, regular flights were in service, connecting Kathmandu with the eastern, southern, western, and central sections of the country and also with airports in India. Both as an expression of national sentiment and as a means of saving Indian currency, public opinion had long been demanding the establishment of a national airways. During K. I. Singh's brief tenure in office in 1957, preliminary plans had been formulated. On May 22, 1958, a week after the installation of the Council of Ministers, the government announced the enactment of the Royal Nepal Airlines Corporation Act, providing for the establishment of a national airways. The government held a controlling 51 per cent of the shares; the managing agents were required to subscribe for 25 per cent, and the remaining 24 per cent of the shares was made available to the public.

FOREIGN POLICY

The first year of King Mahendra's reign was almost entirely devoted to domestic political and economic developments. The only significant events in the realm of foreign policy—admission to the United Nations and the establishment of diplomatic relations with the People's Republic of China—represented the culmination of policy decisions that had been made under previous governments, the former in 1951 and the latter in 1954. They did not constitute, therefore, a major reorientation in Kathmandu's foreign policy at that time, although both events were to have important repercussions on Nepal's approach to foreign policy subsequently.

More obviously innovational in character were several of the foreign policy decisions of the Tanka Prasad Acharya Cabinet. On January 30, 1956, three days after assuming office, the new Prime Minister held a press conference to explain the programs and policies of his government. Striking a new note on foreign policy, Tanka Prasad expressed his determination to modify Nepal's "special relations" with India in favor of a policy of "equal friendship" with all countries.[19] His government was willing, he said, to accept "aid without strings" from all friendly countries such as India, China, Great Britain, the United States, France, and even Russia. Most significant was his comment that Nepal wanted to have direct trade relations with other countries, instead of conducting foreign trade through India as was the practice under the 1950 Indo-Nepali Trade Treaty. Here he struck a popular note with virtually all politically articulate elements in Nepal. The 1950 treaty had long irritated the Nepalese. It was, indeed, one of the few issues that cut across party lines and, as such, was an important facet of nascent Nepali nationalism. Previous governments, weak and divided as they were, had failed to initiate positive steps to amend the treaty, in part because they often had to solicit Nehru's tutelage in bolstering up their own shaky political structures. Although the Acharya government was not in office long enough to complete the negotiations for the revision of the treaty, it did initiate the process that led to the conclusion of a new trade treaty, more acceptable to Nepal, in 1960.

The attempts of the new government to pursue a foreign policy independent of Indian supervision culminated in a number of other measures, including a treaty with China on Tibet and the establishment of diplomatic relations with Japan, the Soviet Union, Egypt, and Ceylon. The decision to establish diplomatic relations with the Soviet Union was of far-reaching consequence as far as its implications for an independent policy were concerned. All parties, with the exception of the Gorkha Parishad and the United Democratic party of K. I. Singh, strongly endorsed the government's decision and described it as a just fulfillment of a long-standing public demand. The general secretary of the ruling Praja Parishad party showed unusual enthusiasm for the new relationship by forming a Nepal–Soviet Union Friendship Association on the day after the official announcement. Only K. I. Singh, who had consistently campaigned for a basically pro-India alignment on matters of foreign policy since his return from China, voiced his opposition to the new step.

Basic to the enthusiasm of the political parties over relations with the Soviet Union was the assumption that such world powers as the United States and the Soviet Union would guarantee Nepal's territorial integrity in the event that external (i.e., Indian or Chinese) interference should take more positive forms. There were also the usual expectations of additional aid from the Soviet Union for development and other purposes.

Relations with China were of more strategic importance to Nepal, in both the military and the political sense. In consideration of the inescapable geopolitical factors, opposition politicians and political parties, including the Nepal Praja Parishad, had agitated since 1951 for a renewal of relations with China as the best means of offsetting India's special position in Nepal. They argued that Nepal's survival as an independent nation depended on an adroit balancing of these giant neighbors against each other, and that in the event of strained relations between them, the only viable policy for Nepal would be one of equal and correct friendship with both. With this orientation as a framework, Tanka Prasad Acharya's government concluded a treaty on Tibet with Communist China on September 20, 1956.

Nepal's relations with Tibet, which had previously been regulated by the treaty of 1856, had come to an abrupt end in 1953, two years after the Communist Chinese seizure of Tibet. As a result of the Nepal-Tibet war of 1855–56, Nepal had obtained special privileges in Tibet. Lhasa agreed to pay a sum of 10,000 rupees annually to Nepal, and Nepalese domiciled in Tibet were exempt from taxes, duties, and, even, the processes of Tibetan law. The Nepalese, as privileged foreigners, had built up rather extensive commercial interests in Tibet. On the eve of the negotiations between Kathmandu and Peking over a revision of the treaty with Tibet, the Nepali Business Men's Association of Tibet presented a list of guidelines to the government of Nepal.[20] Most of these pertained to the retention of traditional privileges, in a somewhat modified form if necessary. They demanded that the rights of the Nepali businessmen to trade and the acquisition of property should be left as defined in the treaty of 1856, though they were willing to abandon extraterritorial privileges. Much to their surprise and disappointment, the government ignored their demands and concluded a treaty with China which bestowed no special protection or privileges on the Nepali merchants resident in Tibet. Tanka Prasad Acharya's government seemed to be motivated more by a desire to create a spirit of good will with the Chinese than to protect the interests of Nepali businessmen. In the larger scheme of things, perhaps, the commercial interests of a small group of Nepali traders must have been considered secondary to the more important objective of cultivating Chinese friendship as a counterpoise to possible Indian expansionist designs, which seem to have been highly exaggerated in the fertile imagination of the Prime Minister.

Tanka Prasad Acharya attempted to cement friendly relations even further through personal diplomacy. He visited China in 1956 to participate in the anniversary celebrations of the Chinese Communist revolution. There he concluded an economic aid agreement on October 7, and in a joint statement with the Chinese Premier, pledged to work in coöperation with China. For its part, Peking volunteered to make available to Nepal over the next three years Rs. 40 million in materials and Rs. 20 million in cash. The Chinese government, reportedly, even gave assurances that no Chinese technicians would be sent to Nepal except at the request of the Nepali government. The Chinese aid program caught the imagination of the Kathmandu populace more by its method of operation than by its size. It stood in direct contrast to the American and Indian aid programs, which were elaborately administered, often under the close supervision of the donor country. This procedure annoyed some Nepali officials, who complained of the high overhead costs of the programs and resented the dictations of the foreign technicians. To the Kathmandu public, the outright grant of foreign aid by China amounted to a recognition of the capacity of Nepalese to govern their own country without outside supervision.

Nepal's relations with India, however, continued to be cordial and friendly at the official level. The two governments exchanged frequent declarations of mutual coöperation and unity of purpose. The most notable example of this official amity was the visit of the Indian President, Dr. Rajendra Prasad, to Nepal in October, 1956, on his first trip to a foreign country since assuming office in 1950. A huge crowd, estimated at 50,000 persons, greeted him at the airport, along with the King and Queen. The two heads of state reaffirmed their countries' long-existing historical and cultural common bonds and interest in each other's security. At a public reception by the Kathmandu municipality, Dr. Prasad assured his audience that his government would aid Nepal to the utmost extent possible. But a statement he was reported to have made during the royal banquet set off a political controversy which to some extent diminished the good will engendered by his visit. The statement was the seemingly innocuous remark that India would consider Nepal's friends as her friends and Nepal's enemies as her enemies. The Nepali Congress, the Gorkha Parishad, and the Communists soon set to work analyzing the political ramifications of this remark and came up with sensational conclusions ranging from "India wants Nepal to be her obedient satellite" to "India is trying to foist her own enemies on Nepal."

One notable event during the tenure of the Praja Parishad government was the holding of the first international conference ever to use Nepal as its venue. The 2,500th anniversary of Lord Buddha's birthday came in 1956, and Buddhist organizations had scheduled the fourth Congress of World Buddhist Fellowship for Nepal—the birthplace of Buddha—to coincide with the occasion. Preparations were commenced during the reign of King Tribhuwan, with his active support, and King Mahendra also energetically assisted in them. Buddhist monks and scholars from thirty-two countries attended the Conference, which was inaugurated by King Mahendra, the only Hindu king in the world, on November 17, 1956. In his opening speech, the King emphasized the Nepali nationality of Buddha, and deplored the "lack of nonviolence, good conduct, tolerance, and fraternity in contemporary affairs at the social, national, and international levels." [21] The Conference lasted four days, and King Mahendra personally announced its adjournment. He ended by thanking all the delegates for accepting King Tribhuwan's invitation, issued two years earlier, to meet in Nepal. The Conference itself was a great success, and many Nepalese took pride in the fact that their country for the first time had succeeded in establishing direct relations with other countries without being under the cultural umbrella of India.

Viewed as a domestic event, the World Buddhist Conference was a great personal triumph for King Mahendra. As a Hindu monarch, advised by tradition-bound Hindu priests and preceptors, it was an act of personal courage and liberalism on his part to sponsor the Conference and, furthermore, to inaugurate and adjourn it. The Buddhists of the valley, who had suffered under the aggressive Brahmanic religious policies of the Ranas, felt that the King had restored the traditional Nepali spirit of religious tolerance. During the rule of the Rana Prime Minister Juddha Shamsher, the Buddhist monks of Kathmandu had been expelled from the country at the instigation of the Brahman priests. Most of them had scattered to India, Burma, and Ceylon. In India, some of the monks formed a Buddhist Association, the Dharmodaya Sabha, and under the same name published a monthly magazine in Newari. After the overthrow of the Ranas in 1951, and the release of the political *détenus,* the Buddhist organization shifted its headquarters to Kathmandu, and Buddhist monks, reëstablished in their viharas, worked toward a revival of Buddhism in the valley. The revival of the Newari language, long suppressed under the official educational policies of the Ranas, also closely followed the Buddhist resurgence, whose crowning success was the World Buddhist Congress in Kathmandu.

The dismissal of the Acharya government and appointment of K. I. Singh as Prime Minister resulted in a temporary reinstatement of certain features of Nepal's pre-1956 foreign policy. The Singh government's foreign policy was guided by the Prime Minister's oft-repeated statement, since his return from China in 1955, that closer relations should be developed with India and that no further extension of Nepal's diplomatic relations with other powers should be sought. His vocal adherence to a pro-India policy was apparent at his first press conference after assuming office, when he strongly endorsed India's claims in Kashmir.

There were factors other than political expediency, however, that may explain K. I. Singh's emphasis on Nepal's close ties with India. The new government, facing an acute food shortage in the capital and in several hill districts, approached New Delhi for help, and received some 3,500 tons of rice in August, 1957, to help tide over the immediate crisis. A few weeks later, the Indian government and the United States aid mission in Nepal were asked to assist in the implementation of the Two-Year Plan formulated by the Singh government. On September 4, the Deputy Finance Minister of India disclosed that India had promised aid to Nepal amounting to one hundred million rupees.

One facet of Tanka Prasad Acharya's policy that K. I. Singh did not modify was the attempt to diversify Nepal's trade relations. In a message to the nation on October 4, the Prime Minister stated that Nepal would soon develop its own foreign trade, free of the restrictions imposed by the 1950 Indo-Nepali treaty. The Singh government's tenure in office was too brief to permit much progress in this direction, but the fact that even this government, with its avowedly pro-India orientation, adopted revision of the treaty as a foreign policy objective was indicative of the widespread consensus within Nepal upon this issue.

Perhaps the only enduring legacy of the Singh government in foreign relations, however, was the creation of a Liaison Office in the Foreign Ministry to look after the condition of the millions of Nepalese domiciled abroad in India, Sikkim, Bhutan, and Burma. Mindful of his own forty years' residence in India and Burma, K. I. Singh placed considerable emphasis on this project from the outset of his term in office.

As had been the case during 1955, King Mahendra avoided raising potentially embarrassing foreign policy questions during the second direct-rule period, which began in November, 1957. One important exception was the Anglo-Nepali agreement on the recruitment of Gorkhas, which was renewed for an additional ten year period on April 17, 1958. Since 1951, one of the favorite slogans of the political parties had been the demand for the cancellation of this agreement and the recall of Gorkhas serving in the British Army, on the grounds that they were used to further the imperialistic designs of a foreign power. But the absence of any visible means of reëmployment within Nepal for these expatriates deterred the government from taking action, which would have been a sure way of arousing the opposition of the ethnic communities in the eastern and western hills whose economic prosperity was largely dependent upon the recruitment system.* King Mahendra, by extending the agreement for ten

---

* For an excellent analysis of the importance of the recruitment system for a western Nepal hill community see John Hitchcock, "A Nepalese Hill Village and Indian Employment," *Asian Survey*, I, No. 9 (November, 1961), 15–20.

years rather than the customary five years, acknowledged the problems involved in dealing with this situation and exposed the unrealistic and somewhat sanctimonious character of the political parties' demands.

THE AIDE-MÉMOIRE CONTROVERSY

Preparations for the elections absorbed the full attention of the coalition Council of Ministers appointed in May, 1958, and foreign policy issues were virtually ignored. One controversy, however, did arise and have an effect upon current Indo-Nepali relations, although it had to do with events of some years before. On July 7, a Kathmandu weekly, *Jhyali,* created a political sensation in the capital by publishing an allegedly authentic copy of a government *aide-mémoire* that had been submitted to the government of India in New Delhi by an unnamed Nepali minister on May 8, 1954.* The text of the document, published under the caption, "Aide-mémoire submitted by the Nepali Mirzaffar in Delhi," was as follows:

AIDE-MÉMOIRE—SECRET

It has already been accepted that the governments of India and Nepal should coördinate their policies in foreign and international affairs of mutual interest. In order to further the coördination in the policies of the two governments, discussions were held in the month of May between the Prime Minister of India and the Foreign Minister and other Ministers of the Government of Nepal, and the following agreements were reached:

1. The two countries will hold special discussions on matters of mutual interest in the area of foreign policy and relations.
2. The Government of India will consult with the Government of Nepal on any matter under consideration that is related to Nepal.
3. The Government of Nepal will consult with the Government of India on such matters and will seek advice and opinion from the latter on matters of establishing relations with any foreign country with a view to promoting better coördination in the policy of the two countries.
4. Especially on matters of Nepal's relationship with Tibet and China, special advice will be sought from the Government of India.
5. The Government of India is willing to represent Nepal and to take care of Nepali interests through its foreign missions in countries desired by the Government of Nepal.

---

* The *Jhyali,* it should be noted, was the mouthpiece of the dissident Nepali National Congress led by Jiva Raj Sharma, who had broken away from the parental organization on grounds of political and personal incompatibility with D. R. Regmi.

6. All Indian missions abroad will be instructed to accord all possible assistance to Nepali citizens abroad.
7. The two governments will hold consultations and exchange information on matters concerning foreign affairs and relations with foreign affairs.

The political impact of the publication of the document was immediate and far-reaching. Several local papers utilized the occasion to warn their readers against what they termed the activities of Mirzaffars, Jay Chands, and quislings.* They also demanded that the government conduct an investigation and bring to book persons responsible for drafting the *aide-mémoire*. One newspaper, accepting the document as bonafide, stated that it demonstrated India's intention to deprive Nepal of its independence and to treat the country like a constituent part of India.[22]

After a week of public controversy, a communiqué was issued by the Foreign Ministry:

The attention of His Majesty's Government has been drawn to a report published in a weekly paper on July 7, in connection with the foreign policy between the Government of India and the Government of Nepal.

The government would like to make it clear that the report published in that newspaper is entirely misleading and malicious.

No Cabinet Minister of Nepal visited New Delhi in 1954 and submitted an *aide-mémoire* to the Government of India.[23]

The government's comminiqué was neither an explanation nor a contradiction of the newspaper report. By making a statement that seemed to say that no Cabinet Minister had visited the Indian capital in 1954, when in fact three—D. R. Regmi, Mahavir Shamsher, and B. Mishra—had been there, the government added to the mystery surrounding the document and to the growing public confusion. D. R. Regmi's visit on May 5, 1954, had been made as Foreign Minister and in the company of King Tribhuwan; Regmi had met with Prime Minister Nehru at that time. Several local papers gave a different twist to the interpretation of the *aide-mémoire* by citing the government's communiqué as proof that the proposal had originated with New Delhi rather than Kathmandu, whereupon the ire of the press was turned against India rather than the so-called Nepali Mirzaffars. No voice was raised to point out that the terms of this *aide-mémoire,* if authentic, had not been accepted by either govenrment. In the

---

* Mirzaffar and Jaya Chand are two figures in Indian history, notorious for their unpatriotic acts. Mirzaffar collaborated with the British invaders against Muslim rulers in the eighteenth century, and Jaya Chand with the Muslim invaders against Hindu rulers in the eleventh century.

narrow, egocentric world of Kathmandu politics, where allegations were presumed to be true unless proven false, this controversy made a substantial contribution to the hypersensitivity of
the Nepali intellectual elites with regard to Indo-Nepali relations.

More significant from the long-range viewpoint, however, was
the economic aid agreement with the Soviet Union, signed on
April 24, 1959, the basis of which had been laid by King
Mahendra in his joint communiqué with the Chairman of the
Soviet Presidium of June 23, 1958.[24] Under the terms of the
agreement, the Soviet Union undertook to provide technical and
financial assistance to Nepal to the extent of 30 million roubles
for the establishment of a hydroelectric plant, sugar and cigarette
factories, a survey for an east-west highway, and a hospital. In this
way, the Nepal government deliberately invited the expansion of
power bloc rivalries within its own border, contributing further
to the conversion of Kathmandu into what Nepalese call "a
cockpit of international politics." What is usually forgotten in
Nepal is that this status was achieved on the invitation of its own
government rather than on the insistence of the various governments involved.

THE 1955–59 PERIOD IN PERSPECTIVE

The nine-month-long first period of direct rule was indeed
remarkable for the number of important decisions taken and new
policies initiated. Regardless of the political motivations and
implications, this was the most productive period of governmental
activity since the first interim government of 1951. The administration was reorganized at the center and also at the district level.
A positive step toward the regulation of currency fluctuations was
taken by the enactment of the State Bank Act. The long-awaited
date for the general elections was announced. The Planning
Commission was formed, and a comprehensive land reform program was proclaimed. The powers of the High Court were
reinstated. Diplomatic relations with the People's Republic of
China were established, and Nepal became a member of the
United Nations. Indirectly, the King helped to promote a new
political party, the United Democratic party headed by K. I.
Singh. The first census report was completed. One week before
the new Cabinet was sworn in, King Mahendra issued a royal
decree specifying that 5 per cent of the revenue of each district
should be spent in the district itself for development schemes,

whereby, for the first time, the central government accepted the principle of decentralized expenditure. These were—on paper, at least—an impressive series of achievements; but they did not bring political stability or an end to the demand for the implementation of a truly democratic structure through general elections.

Increasing attacks on the Royal Advisers' regime by the press and the parties had set the stage for yet another new political experiment. By January, 1956, the advisory regime, publicly described as a temporary government, had completed nine months of existence and seemed to be going strong. In the meantime, seemingly endless political negotiations had taken place between the new King and various political parties, while numerous Royal Commissions had toured the country for one purpose or another. Yet the shape of the country's political future was far from clear. General restlessness and despair had gripped most of the political parties. King Mahendra's open criticism of the previous regimes and his flat assertion that he would in no case repeat the mistakes of the past four years had cast grave doubts on their future. The royal scrutiny of the parties' programs, policies, and personnel had eventually taken the form of a rather unfavorable interrogation of their public record.

The first wave of public enthusiasm among the people, following upon some of the initial bold steps of the young King, dissipated into a mood of political fatalism. Public curiosity turned into rumor mongering, and the capital was rife with speculations of the most far-fetched nature, ranging from a restoration of Rana autocracy to the inauguration of K. I. Singh as the new Prime Minister. While the political parties were becoming dismayed and chagrined by the King's delaying tactics, conservative elements were taking comfort from the continuation of the authoritarian order. Some conservatives even banded together into a common front of "independents" opposed to the assumption of power by political parties, whom they condemned vociferously for lack of experience, ability, and, above all, integrity. The political parties, for their part, criticized these "independents" for their pro-Rana background and their vested interest in a feudal government—a charge which, in several instances, was not without substance.

King Mahendra was active on at least three fronts in the first year of his reign. First, he was conducting often-interrupted and long-drawn-out negotiations with the political parties. Frequently counseling extreme deliberation and patience to his people and emphasizing the delicate nature of his self-imposed assignment to establish "pure" democracy, he saw the various party leaders several times both separately and in joint conferences. He would seem to have been engaged in a long-range program of assessing very carefully the relative strengths, weaknesses, and potentialities of the parties. Meanwhile the parties, often working at cross-purposes in their negotiations with the King, made one concession after another to satisfy him, presumably on the theory that minor political concessions should not be grudged if the greater political evil of direct rule could be abolished thereby. Ironically enough, the public tended to place the blame for the lack of progress in these negotiations on the intransigence, party loyalties, and self-seeking interests of the party leaders.

A second objective of the King was to establish direct contact with his subjects. Some of the motivation for this may be traced to his determination to measure up to his late father's greatness and popularity. He sent personal representatives to all parts of the country in the guise of Royal Commissions, ostensibly to study public opinions and problems, but really, as Tanka Prasad Acharya charged publicly, "to elicit support for direct rule." He presided over a conference of social and cultural organizations in which he sought to present himself as the spokesman of the nonpolitically oriented public. In fact, he denounced in no uncertain terms the narrow-mindedness of the political parties which had refused to participate in the conference.

Finally, he undertook a series of drastic reforms in the government while emphasizing the supposedly temporary character of the advisory regime. In the minds of many the inevitable question was: Why should all these reforms be necessary in this interim period if he really intends to entrust the reins of government to party representatives? A plausible explanation can be found in his interest in surpassing the accomplishments of the previous four years during the first year of his reign and in his desire to place loyal elements in the key offices of the government while this could be easily done. The administrative machinery, it will be recalled, was thoroughly over-hauled both at the center and in the districts; appointments were thus provided for a number of Ranas, Shahs, and relatives of the Royal Advisers.

The Nepali Congress was the first political party to weary of unproductive political haggling at the royal palace. A strong group had emerged within the party which demended nonparticipation in negotiations with the King unless a clear mandate was received to form a government. It may have been partly because of the stiffening of this sentiment in the party that Birganj was chosen for the meeting of the general council rather than Kathmandu. By design or by coincidence, King Mahendra began his fourth round of negotiations with the Nepal Praja Parishad and the Nepali National Congress leaders in Kathmandu in the middle of January, 1956, when all Nepali Congress leaders were converging on Birganj. In fact, the King seems to have decided on the formation of a new government at a time when the attentions of the Nepali Congress were directed toward its party conference.

The Tanka Prasad Acharya Cabinet was formed after the collapse of almost year-long political negotiations at the palace, and against the consensus of opinion developed during these negotiations—indeed, even against the King's own publicly stated aims of creating a government based on the maximum possible coöperation between the political parties. The formation of the government under such paradoxical circumstances was an indication of the unpredictable logic of events that had overtaken the political process, which had now become a matter of seeking a *modus vivendi* between conflicting wills and motives.

The Praja Parishad seems to have been the sort of political party the royal palace had been seeking as a suitable façade for the continued leadership of the King. A weak, strife-ridden party was called to power when the demand of the time was for a strong coalition government. The Cabinet was dominated by royalist nominees, and the Prime Minister could not entirely count on the support of the other party members. The strains of running a government for seventeen months took a heavy toll of both the party organization and its leadership. But such a party government, by surviving as long as it did, underscored the circumstances under which a one-party government could come into being.

Yet the political legacy of the Praja Parishad government was considerable. A new look in Nepal's foreign policy was introduced by the adoption of a policy of equal and correct friendship with both India and China. Historical contacts between Nepal and China were renewed, and an economic aid treaty with China was signed. Extension of diplomatic relations and the meeting of the first international conference ever to be held in Kathmandu helped to project a new image of Nepal on the international scene.

On the domestic political side, the Praja Parishad government legalized the Communist party and divided the so-called democratic parties by proposing elections to a Parliament rather than the Constituent Assembly promised by King Tribhuwan in 1951, thus paving the way for King Mahendra's subsequent decision in favor of a Parliament and a King-given Constitution.

King Mahendra's activities during the tenure of the Acharya government underlined his emergence as a truly national political force. During the first year of his reign he had defined a new dynamic role for the Crown by direct participation in the affairs of government, and he continued these efforts during the Praja Parishad period. For nearly four months he toured different parts of Nepal as if he were a candidate for election, acquainting himself with the local inhabitants and redressing their grievances on the spot, and distributing sizable amounts of money for public welfare purposes. The King's supporters made much of the fact that he was the first monarch to go on foot to listen to his people's grievances and complaints. Undoubtedly, the emotional impact of this gesture on the people in the hills and the Terai redounded greatly to the advantage of the King; by contrasting his generosity with the widely alleged corruptibility of the political leaders, the people must have drawn conclusions unfavorable to the political parties. That this did not escape notice was indicated by the comment in a pro-Praja Parishad daily that the royal tours had "made a laughingstock" of the government.[25]

The King actually commenced the first of his tours on the day the Praja Parishad government was sworn in, visiting places in the western Terai, including the Rapti Valley, Nepalganj, Bhairawa, Butaul, Lumbini, and Pokhara. At most of these places the King addressed well-attended public meetings and explained his concern for "pure" democracy and the welfare of the people. His pronouncements were mostly patriotic and moralistic homilies, cast in appropriate democratic phraseology. His donations to various institutions such as schools, libraries, and hospitals provided substantiation of his concern with public welfare, since the local people assumed that these were his private donations although, in fact, most of them came out of the government treasury.

The results of this tour were so satisfactory that the King decided to traverse the rest of the country as quickly as possible. He toured the eastern Terai in December, 1956, and January, 1957, visiting Biratnagar, Dharan, and Rajbiraj and distributing 417,000 rupees as personal contributions. From January to March, he toured the eastern hills, visiting all the centers of government in those areas and returning by way of Biratnagar. The Finance Minister, an "independent," accompanied the King and distributed about 350,000 rupees from the government treasury in the King's name. The touring was interrupted while King Mahendra made a state visit to Ceylon, but was resumed in April and continued into May, this time to the far western hill area. By the middle of 1957, the King had covered most of the country.

By the time of the dissolution of the Praja Parishad government, King Mahendra had emerged as a powerful national political force. His popularization program had the characteristics of an organized movement backed by the entire resources of the Nepal government. The Praja Parishad Cabinet, grappling with the mundane problems of day-to-day administration, acted as a buffer between the King and the people, and absorbed public hostility and aggression, to its own utter ruin in the process. It was now clearly evident that King Mahendra was disinclined to accept a passive constitutional role and that, indeed, he seemed to entertain ambitions of becoming a charismatic national leader, surpassing even his father in popular esteem.

Without doubt the most questionable and potentially risky experiment yet attempted by the King was the appointment of K. I. Singh to replace Tanka Prasad Acharya in mid-1957. The proud Rajput from the hills of western Nepal was a basically different political personality from the cantankerous but easily managed Kathmandu Brahman, as the King soon discovered.

Yet, though the Singh government came in with a bang, it ended with a whimper. The Cabinet, during its brief tenure, functioned as the Prime Minister's personal creation, and after its dissolution the other Ministers quietly faded into the political obscurity from whence Singh had originally rescued them. K. I. Singh himself turned into a bitter, frustrated politician, venting his spleen not only against the Nepali Congress and other political opponents, but against intellectuals and students as well. He regressed to his viewpoint of 1950–51, from which he blamed India, the Nepali Congress and a multitude of foreign agents—including Americans—for his undoing, which he tended to equate with the downfall of the country.

The dismissal of the K. I. Singh government showed the limit to which King Mahendra was willing to tolerate the power-seeking activities of his own political creations. In putting Singh at the helm of the administration, the King may have hoped that his unconventional strong-arm approach to politics would help to subdue the growing political opposition, in particular that of the

Nepali Congress, against which Singh had been nursing a bitter personal grievance since 1951. What was accomplished, however, was probably the opposite of what the King intended. The Singh government's crude repressive measures had merely strengthened the opposition, improved the position of the Nepali Congress as the leading party, and antagonized the Nepali press and educated elite. Thus, in King Mahendra's scheme of things, the Singh government had quickly become a greater menace to his own position than the opposition which it had been designed to suppress, and consequently it had to be removed from office after only a short period of experimentation.

The six-month second period of direct rule that followed the Singh government was, like King Mahendra's nine months of direct rule in 1955–56, a period of tangible accomplishments as far as policies were concerned, despite the fact that on this latter occasion it was necessary to operate under a more difficult set of circumstances. In 1955–56 his role as the new King was still unclear in the public mind, but in 1957–58 the people had formed some evaluations and judgments about his increasingly dominant role in the government, based on their acquaintance with his two experiments in the intervening period. He weathered the first nationwide agitation launched by a combination of parties since 1951. Although initially he had to recognize the public demand for general elections by naming a date, he successfully overrode the political parties by forcing them to accept his proposals for elections to a Parliament under a Constitution he would finally approve. He established several advisory bodies such as the National Council, the Planning Commission, and the Work Expediting Committee to supervise the administration, and associated his two brothers openly with the government. He approved formally the first Five-Year Plan on March 15, 1958, and for the first time the public came to know officially that the plans had been in force since October, 1957. As an enduring symbol of his close identification with the administration, the government of Nepal and its embassies abroad came to be known officially as His Majesty's Government and the Royal Nepalese Embassies.

One notable feature of King Mahendra's second period of direct rule was the further concentration of administrative decision-making power in his personal secretariat. Since 1955 the Royal Palace Secretariat had become a superordinate governmental structure, invigilating and often overriding the decisions of the government Secretariat. Members of the Royal Palace Secretariat became involved during the second direct rule in large-scale malpractices, particularly in connection with forest lands, which local newspapers and the political parties brought to public attention. It was widely assumed that these elements were constantly at work to prolong the period of the direct rule as long as possible.

By accepting the Royal Proclamation of February 1, 1958, all political parties in effect accepted King Mahendra's personalized version of democracy rather than King Tribhuwan's vision of a government functioning within the framework of a Constitution framed by the people. King Tribhuwan's historic proclamation of February 18, 1951, was now a dead letter, and a new phase of political development had begun. The seven-year-old quest for democracy ended in a question mark: What kind of democracy did King Mahendra have in mind? All other definitions of democracy became suddenly irrelevant, and the parties, regardless of their political orientations, had lost the battle for constitutional democracy. The choice before them was, clearly, to attempt to build a tenuous democratic superstructure in which authority radiated from the King down rather than from the people up. Since the people of Nepal were to participate in the political process only to a degree predetermined by the King, the setting was laid for a clash of wills which was bound to come in the future when the people or their elected representatives would cross the political boundaries demarcated by the King.

Despite its heterogeneous character and unpromising inauguration, the coalition Council of Ministers was probably the most productive government in Nepal since the overthrow of the Ranas. This was the case even though the coalition of mutually antagonistic political elements encouraged a wide variety of centrifugal activities within the Council. But this characteristic operated to the government's advantage in certain respects, particularly as the general elections drew nearer. The customary bogey of foreign interference and domination was largely absent, and the dialogue between the parties did not attain the usual level of acrimony, even during the election campaign.

That a government such as the coalition Council of Ministers was the only one to achieve a comparatively broad measure of success in seven years of experimentation was, indeed, a revealing commentary on the political process in Nepal. Throughout this period, the people themselves had been only peripherally involved in the complex games played by the parties, the independents, and the palace. The 1959 Constitution represented the culmination of the process of change set in motion in 1951. The 1959 elections were to prove to be a remarkable demonstration of the nonpolitical public's overwhelming preference for a stable and forward-looking political order. The election results confounded the skeptics and cynics who had often gloomily prophesied that the illiterate and unsophisticated Nepali people were incapable of exercising their rights in an orderly and progressive fashion. The principal question that remained unanswered after the elections was the extent to which the Constitution granted to the country by King Mahendra was congruent with the kind of mandate the electorate had given to the winning party, the Nepali Congress.

13

The Parties Prepare for the Elections

THE POLITICAL chaos that surrounded the fall of the first National government, and the death of King Tribhuwan shortly thereafter, had a tremendous impact upon the situation of the parties. Undoubtedly the most dramatic immediate development was the virtually total eclipse of the once-powerful M. P. Koirala. His party disintegrated rapidly and passed quietly into limbo. Dissidents and opportunists, who had affiliated with the party in order to reap the spoils of office, quickly abandoned it when the rewards of membership were no longer forthcoming. A small, hard core, which continued to carry the standard of the National Democratic party, later followed M. P. Koirala back within the fold of the Nepali Congress in 1956.

The week following the dissolution of the M. P. Koirala government witnessed the emergence of an expanded Praja Parishad, as the tempo of party splintering and realignment reached a feverish level. In a political marriage of convenience, three pretenders to the Prime Minister's mantle—Balchandra Sharma, Tanka Prasad Acharya, and Bhadrakali Mishra—combined their factions under the Praja Parishad label. The first brought along several former members of the National Democratic party; the second provided the name for the organization, as well as the largest single block of members; the third contributed his party's flag to the new organization.

It must have been the context of these devious political alliances and schisms that encouraged Crown Prince Mahendra to devise an empiricistic approach to the assessment of each party's verbal insistence on its status as the largest and most representative in Nepal. A questionnaire was sent from the palace to every social and political organization in the country, requesting detailed information as to its structure, membership, and program. This investigation had a double advantage for the Crown Prince. Not only did it strengthen the Crown's position as a "neutral" in inter-party disputes, but it also provided valuable information on the ideologies and personnel of the various parties. On receiving the questionnaire, the parties were left with the unenviable choice of either revealing their party secrets or being considered uncoöperative and obstructive. However grudgingly, all the major parties complied with the royal instructions and sent the requested information to the royal palace by April 4, 1955.

THE FORMATION OF THE UNITED DEMOCRATIC PARTY

One of King Mahendra's more popular measures in the early period following his accession to the throne was his decision to grant an amnesty to K. I. Singh, who had been declared a traitor and criminal as a result of the violent episode at Singha Darbar on January 21, 1952. Singh and some thirty followers had fled to China and sought asylum there. After three and a half years, Singh left Peking, on June 7, 1951, bound for home. It was reported in Kathmandu that he had threatened a hunger strike if he were prevented from returning to Nepal. His supporters in Kathmandu, who had organized a "Friends of K. I. Singh Society," were able to get the backing of most political leaders and the educated elites for their demand that he be allowed to return. Public sentiment in favor of Singh rose perceptibly, and the people, disillusioned with the other leaders, began to impute all kinds of charismatic qualities to this colorful political personality.

On September 1, K. I. Singh reached the Nepal-Tibet border and from there wrote to King Mahendra, requesting pardon for his past activities and giving assurances of his lifelong loyalty to the Crown and his willingness to coöperate with the King in all nation-building activities. King Mahendra granted him an amnesty, and on September 13 he arrived in the capital amid great rejoicings and an impressive popular reception. He pleaded for termination of direct rule, although he supported the King's action in concentrating political power in his own hands. Addressing the largest public meeting that had yet been held in Nepal, Singh advised the people to take to Gandhian ideals and appealed to the government to seek closer economic ties with India. On October 9, he elaborated his ideas further by arguing that Nepal should prefer Indian aid and assistance to that from other sources, and stated that none of Nepal's problems would be solved by raising anti-Indian slogans.[1] Two weeks later, on October 22, he announced at a public meeting the birth of a new political party, the United Democratic party (Samyukta Prajatantra Sangha). He described his party as being democratic in character and pledged to work toward the establishment of a constitutional monarchy.

During the next several months, Singh made tours all over the country, trying to organize public support for his new party. The objectives of the party were set forth as (1) establishment of a genuine monarchical democracy by developing all sections of the society and the country; (2) facilitation of the return of foreign-domiciled Nepalese; (3) abolition of the *Birta* principle and landlord system, and distribution of land among the landless; (4) nationalization of the forests; (5) development of the natural resources of the country; (6) eradication of parochial feelings, and development of a spirit of harmony and coöperation between all classes and communities of Nepal; (7) maintenance of Nepal's nonalignment with power blocs, and establishment of friendly relations with all countries on the basis of mutual benefit and equality.[2] In spite of this ostensibly radical program, most of the party's supporters came from ethnic and interest groups that were frankly conservative and tradition-oriented—an indication of how inconsequential ideology was in the party system of Nepal.

Although the new party was singularly unsuccessful in attracting the support of the Kathmandu intellectuals, certain attributes made it appealing to the general public. Singh, the leading figure, was a first-rate demagogue. He had the uncouth, rugged manners of an uneducated Kshatriya and always spoke in blunt, direct language intelligible to the masses. He was incapable of indulging in ideological abstractions, and could visualize problems only in black and white categories. His view of the political process was uninhibited by any theoretical or ideological predilection. He had simple-minded solutions for complex problems and, while unable to convince the educated elites, could popularize his views among the people by relating them in the form of anecdotes, parables, and popular jokes. His reputation as a village homeopath and the legends of his self-abnegating qualities and political bravado cast on him the aura of a leader of the people who was at the same time a child of the soil.

Moreover, finances did not seem to be a problem with the United Democratic party. Although its sources were never made public, the energetic Singh seemed to have plenty of money on hand for party purposes. At several places he bestowed monetary grants on villagers in regal Rajput fashion for such purposes as building bridges or schools. The party conferences were held with considerable pomp and show. Funds were even available to fly in planeloads of guests and visitors for the conferences.

The United Democratic party was also significantly different from most other parties in that its leadership was mostly non-Brahmanic in origin and that the top-ranking persons in the party echelon came from areas other than Kathmandu. Out of a total Working Committee membership of thirty-two, only four were Brahmans. This was in contrast with the other parties, with the exception of the Gorkha Parishad, in which leadership was largely confined to Brahmans. Effective leadership in the United Democratic party was concentrated in the hands of K. I. Singh, a Kshatriya by birth, and it would not be inappropriate to characterize the dominant tone of the party as that of militant Kshatriya politics.* The U.D.P. shared this attribute with the Gorkha Parishad to some extent, but the latter party, in order to conceal its Rana support and background, veiled its militant qualities with the cloak of Gorkha nationalism and a commitment to parliamentary democracy.

THE NEPALI CONGRESS ADOPTS DEMOCRATIC SOCIALISM

The course of developments during the first year of the Mahendra era encouraged the Nepali Congress to devise new tactics and assume a new, revitalized public image. Most significant was the decision of the party's Working Committee, meeting at Birganj on November 27, 1955, to contest the pending general elections on a democratic-socialist platform. A subcommittee consisting of Suvarna Shamsher, Surya Prasad Upadhyaya and Rishikesh Shah was appointed to prepare an appropriate party manifesto for submission to the meeting of the general council, scheduled for the following January.

While broad agreement was achieved on the question of long-range goals, the party was badly divided over immediate programs and tactics. A strong faction led by Ganesh Man Singh and Tek Bahadur Panthi opposed the Working Committee's resolution pledging support to King Mahendra's efforts to set up a "democratic" government. The dissidents demanded an end to political negotiations with the palace until the King was prepared to commission the party to form a government. Ganesh Man Singh announced his intention to contest the party presidency

---

* K. I. Singh is from one of the former ruling families, claiming Rajput antecedents, in the hill area of far western Nepal.

elections on this issue at the general council meeting, the first instance in which these elections had been contested since 1952.

In the general council meeting, however, Suvarna Shamsher —with B. P. Koirala's support—was elected president of the party, defeating Ganesh Man Singh by a large majority. The delegates also adoped overwhelmingly the democratic-socialist platform presented by the subcommittee. At the same time, the attitude of the top leadership groups toward King Mahendra hardened perceptibly. B. P. Koirala rejected the King's offer of a seat in a six-member Council of Ministers—terms which the party had accepted a few months before in the hope of terminating the direct rule system.

With the appointment of the Praja Parishad government on January 22, 1956, the Nepali Congress's hopes for eventual participation in a coalition government rose once again. For several reasons, participation was deemed essential by the party leadership. First, in their judgment the political process in Nepal had steadily and increasingly fallen into the hands of reactionary elements, and the Congress might halt this dangerous trend by assuming power, even at the cost of some concessions on its part. Further, party morale had been sagging badly for some time. Party workers, with no constructive program to absorb their energies, had assumed a negativistic opposition to whatever government happened to be in office. Also, the prospect of joining a government headed by a weak ruling party with its attendant prospects for self-aggrandizement was attractive to some party workers, and tended to loosen party ties and loyalties. Most important, however, were apprehensions that a continuation of the present trends would mean an eventual victory for the Communists.

The dispute between the extremist group in the Nepali Congress that was opposed to all negotiations, either with the King or with other political parties, and the more moderate section of the High Command, which favored a policy that combined vocal criticisms of the government with cautious negotiations whenever possible, continued throughout the tenure of the Praja Parishad Cabinet. It was in part a reflection of this inner struggle when the Nepali Congress president, Suvarna Shamsher, dissolved the Working Committee and other committees in November, 1956, and on December 17 announced a new ten-member Working Committee, designed to "give new vigor to the party," which had decided to contest the forthcoming elections.[3] Most of the veteran leaders were conspicuously absent from the roster. The new executive adopted a different tactical approach under which it decided to pressure the government to hold elections for a Constituent Assembly by arousing public consciousness on this issue. Accordingly, the entire party personnel and organization was mobilized in January, 1957, to help prepare the people for the elections in October. Leaders of the Nepali Congress toured all sections of the country and in innumerable public meetings stressed the historical factors underlying King Tribhuwan's proclamation on elections for a Constituent Assembly, and exposed the Praja Parishad party's designs for vitiating the political atmosphere with an unnecessary controversy on the issue.

In order that the party might adopt a more aggressive policy toward the elections, the mild-mannered president, Suvarna Shamsher, indicated his willingness to retire from office in favor of B. P. Koirala. A special party conference at Biratnagar on May 25 elected B. P. Koirala to the presidency. The Executive Committee then adopted a more strongly socialistic election manifesto drafted by the new president, who offered to hold the elections within four months if his party should be entrusted with the reins of administration.

LEGALIZATION OF THE COMMUNIST PARTY

One of the more significant measures of the Tanka Prasad Acharya government was the lifting of the four-year ban on the Communist Party of Nepal in April, 1956, less than three months after assuming office. This came as no surprise, since Tanka Prasad's former alliance with the Communists in the 1951 United Front was well known. Even the Communists seemed confident. On the day before the ban was formally lifted, the general secretary of the party announced at an "underground" press conference that he would appear in public the next day, whether or not the ban was lifted.[4] Reportedly, the Communists had submitted proposals and counterproposals to Tanka Prasad—who seems to have been anxious to gain their support for his new directions in foreign policy—but had refused to give him the unconditional acceptance of the monarchy that he demanded as the price for lifting the ban, agreeing only to abide by the decision of the Constituent Assembly on this question. Nevertheless, the ban was lifted, and the Communists emerged from their curiously public "underground" existence.

The Communists paid a heavy price for legalization, in the form of greatly increased internal dissension. The exit from the "underground" quickly brought to the surface several unresolved internal disputes that divided the party into moderate and extremist wings. The moderates, led by Keshar Jang Rayamajhi, argued that the party should for the time being accept constitutional monarchy and seek a broad-based united front with all other "progressive" parties to insure that the monarchy remained constitutional and to forestall domination of the government by "reactionary" elements. The extremists, led by Pushpa Lal Shrestha, maintained that the party should struggle against all "feudal" institutions, including the monarchy, in alliance with other parties if possible, but single-handed if necessary. A party congress was convened at Kathmandu in June, 1957, to resolve these differences; it was ineffective, and the dissension within the Communist ranks continued unabated even in the period immediately preceding the first general elections, when party unity was essential.

OTHER PARTY DEVELOPMENTS

The political leader who had probably been most frustrated by the circumstances under which the Praja Parishad government was formed was D. R. Regmi, the president of the Nepali National Congress. His close association with Tanka Prasad Acharya in the past had led him to expect inclusion in any government headed by the Praja Parishad leader. After these expectations were shattered by the Praja Parishad resolution that made participation in the Acharya government conditional on a merger or alliance with the ruling party, Regmi came out with a strong denunciation of the government.

The Nepali National Congress was unable to initiate any action other than the expression of trenchant criticisms of the government through its party bulletins. The party enjoyed a brief renaissance in March, 1957, when several controversial "independents" (including Khadga Man Singh and Dharma Ratna "Yami") and a few party dissidents (such as Kedar Man "Vyathit" and Purna Bahadur "Manav") joined its ranks. Presumably these politicians were attracted by the prospect, which later turned out to be illusionary, of dominating the leadership of a weak party at a time when national elections were scheduled within a few months. The Nepali National Congress soon held a public meeting to present its recently acquired adherents. Khadga Man Singh attacked the government in scathing terms, and the government responded by arresting him for an alleged attempt to incite mutiny in the army and subversion among government employees. Although he was released shortly thereafter, the event dramatized the widening gap between the Nepali National Congress and the Praja Parishad, and helped to isolate the Praja Parishad even further from other parties.

The other major parties—the Nepal Communist party, the Nepal Gorkha Parishad, and the United Democratic party—were more or less equivocal in their criticisms of the Praja Parishad government. The Communists and the Gorkha Parishad dreaded the restoration of the Nepali Congress more than anything else. As they were both working with fairly long-range plans and goals, the government that would serve their interests best was undoubtedly a weak government, lacking in resources and engaged in frantic acts of self-preservation. Bharat Shamsher, the Gorkha Parishad leader, did not demand the dissolution of the Acharya government until June 16, by which time most other parties had raised a chorus of protest against its continuing; the Communists never officially pressed for a resignation. Thus, two parties as ideologically unlike as the Communists and the Gorkha Parishad functioned with remarkably similar attitudes toward the Praja Parishad government. Both made the demand that elections be held on the stipulated day their most important political slogan.

It was January, 1957, before the United Democratic party began to agitate for the dissolution of the Acharya government. This party, an unknown political force in 1956, had chalked out a distinctively personalized ideology which was unlike that of any other party in Nepal. The leader, K. I. Singh, stood for full-fledged monarchy, a Parliament rather than a Constituent Assembly, and close association with India in political, economic, and foreign policy matters—the last a complete *volte-face* from his anti-India attitude in 1951. The question was, how genuine was this sudden shift in K. I. Singh's political philosophy? Was it merely a tactical maneuver to expiate the political "sin" of exile in China and to rehabilitate himself with the Indian public and press, or was it something more than political opportunism? In any case, he opposed the establishment of diplomatic relations with China, criticized Nepal's aid pact with China, played down the necessity of seeking economic assistance from countries other than India, and accused the government of incurring a ten-million-rupee deficit in four months.

FACTIONAL CONFLICTS WITHIN THE PRAJA PARISHAD AND OTHER POLITICAL PARTIES

Since 1951, the intensification of intraparty squabbles and conflicts had usually coincided with the period when the particular party was in power. The Nepal Congress suffered from this nemesis in 1952 and the National Democratic party in 1955; the Praja Parishad was no exception in 1957. A weak party is perhaps more subject to unrealistic ambitions on the part of its leaders than is a broadly based one. The situation is likely to be exaggerated when the party is a conglomeration of opportunistic factions, as was the Praja Parishad. The key figures in the internal tussles of the party were the notoriously restless leaders of the three main factions, Tanka Prasad Acharya, Bhadrakali Mishra, and Balchandra Sharma. Mishra had changed political sides four times since 1951, and Sharma at least three times. Both had demonstrated little disinclination to use party labels to advance their own ambitions.

It is rather amazing that the internal conflicts in the Praja Parishad did not come to the surface until the end of 1956; but possibly the leaders of the various factions were reaping sufficient benefits from the new government to make a façade of unity desirable in view of the growing opposition from other parties. The first rumblings of discord were heard early in December, 1956, when Tanka Prasad Acharya appointed an independent member of the Cabinet, Gunja Man Singh, to serve as acting Prime Minister during his absence in India. Two Praja Parishad Ministers, Balchandra Sharma and Pashupati Ghosh, took strong exception to this decision and, reportedly, threatened to resign in protest against the Prime Minister's apparent lack of confidence in them. The crisis that finally wrecked the party did not arise until February 5, 1957, when the Prime Minister, empowered by the party executive to expand the Cabinet, appointed one Cabinet Minister, two Ministers of State and eight Deputy Ministers without consulting the party bureaucracy about the changes. The new Cabinet Minister was King Mahendra's brother-in-law and aide-de-camp; the two Ministers of State were former Commander in Chief Kiran Shamsher and a royal supporter; only the eight Deputy Ministers were drawn, mostly, from the party ranks.

If the expansion was intended to mollify critics within the party by elevating them to ministerial positions, subsequent events proved this to be a serious miscalculation, for, indeed, it merely increased the dissension. On the day following the Cabinet expansion, several party workers who had been ignored held a stormy meeting at the residence of the party president, Bhadrakali Mishra. Tanka Prasad Acharya was accused of hastening the disintegration of the party by encouraging factionalism. An emergency meeting of the party executive had to be called, and a compromise was effected only after the party leadership had assuaged the hurt feelings among the rank and file through more bountiful promises of rewards in the future.

The most severe, and nearly fatal, crisis within the Praja Parishad came to a head on May 31, 1957, during the deliberations of the party's general council. The meeting was attended by about a hundred delegates from various parts of the country, almost all of whom were bitterly critical of the high command. Bhadrakali Mishra bore the brunt of this attack, and was accused of having violated the party's principles and constitution. On the second day of the conference, charges and countercharges were hurled back and forth between the leadership and the rank and file, and the tense situation eventually erupted into violent scenes. The party president and secretary were forcibly driven out of the meeting, and the rebellious members then established a Parallel Praja Parishad.[5] Only on the intervention of Prime Minister Tanka Prasad Acharya was an open split finally averted. A number of compromise resolutions were adopted, to conciliate the belligerent factions. The radical wing forced the party to endorse a resolution demanding the confiscation of property and the abrogation of civil rights of capitalists who invested money abroad (i.e., the Ranas who had invested heavily in Indian industry). Tanka Prasad Acharya obtained support for two resolutions, one demanding elections for a Parliament rather than a Constituent Assembly and the other authorizing him to negotiate with the King for a homogeneous party government. The Prime Minister replied to criticism of inefficiency within his government by placing the blame on the "independents" in the Cabinet.

The appointment of the controversial K. I. Singh as Prime Minister, on July 15, caused yet another eruption in political party ranks. The immediate and unrestrained criticism with which almost all the leaders greeted King Mahendra's announcement of his choice was not, however, duplicated at all levels within their parties. In the Nepali Congress, a group of second-line leaders, including two former Ministers, formed a Parallel Nepali Congress on July 20 in protest against what they characterized the dictatorial tendency of the party leaders. The parallel organization submitted a memorandum to the King criticizing the parent body for compromising the dignity of the Crown and for casting aspersions on friendly neighboring countries. The implication was that the dissident group was committed to supporting King Mahendra's political action at home and seeking friendly relations with India in foreign affairs. In the process the dissident group brought itself in line with K. I. Singh's policies and may have hoped thereby to enhance its prospects of inclusion in the new government.

It is significant that the Parallel Nepali Congress chose to retain the original party name and flag, on the ground that their revolt was not directed at the party as such, but merely against "the upper stage leadership, the political monopoly of B. P. Koirala, Suvarna Shamsher, S. P. Upadhyaya and Ganesh Man Singh." [6] They claimed that their disagreement was entirely theoretical and constitutional, and they disowned any private motives. Enumerating their charges against the "non-nationalist, dictatorial, narrow, and vested interests of the leadership" in the Nepali Congress, they issued a pamphlet purporting to expose the unconstitutional, anti-party activities of these elements since 1951. The pamphlet, which was particularly vehement in its attack on B. P. Koirala, must have provided no small measure of comfort to anti-Nepali Congress forces. The political prospects of the parallel group, however, were severely damaged by the decision of the United Democratic party, on July 25, against negotiations with the parallel groups in the formation of a new Cabinet. Thwarted in the attempt to get into the government, the Parallel Nepali Congress faded into oblivion. Later some of its leading members came back into political prominence after King Mahendra's dismissal of the elected Nepali Congress government in December, 1960.

A Parallel Nepali Praja Parishad was also organized on July 22, after Jagat Bahadur Singh, the publicity secretary of the parental organization, and a few other members had publicly accused the party leadership "of incompetence, of fostering stagnation inside the party and of a conspiracy against the rank and file of the party to keep them at the bottom of the ladder." [7] They proclaimed themselves the true Praja Parishad and declared that more than forty-five General Council members and twenty-five district organizations had sided with them. Although the origins of these internal dissensions can be traced to the period when the Praja Parishad formed and later expanded the government, the precipitating cause for the open split undoubtedly was the July 15 Royal Proclamation, which aroused party workers and intermediate-grade leaders to entertain ministerial ambitions. This parallel group also failed to achieve recognition from K. I. Singh and, like its Nepali Congress counterpart, quickly faded from public view.

On August 31, the thirty-two-member executive committee of the United Democratic party had met in Kathmandu under the chairmanship of K. I. Singh to survey the state of public opinion throughout the country, evaluate the party's over-all political position, initiate preparations for the general elections, and draw up final lists of party candidates for the elections. After meeting for four days, the Executive Committee adopted a number of resolutions, expressing (1) deep gratitude to King Mahendra for allowing the U.D.P. to form its own government, (2) satisfaction at K. I. Singh's appointment as Prime Minister, (3) appreciation of the Prime Minister's efforts to ease the food problem in the country, (4) gratitude to the government of India for its speedy and valuable gifts of rice, (5) full support for the party government's modified Two-Year Plan; (6) appreciation of the Prime Minister's firm and determined steps to end corruption and nepotism in the administration and of his promise to recover the huge losses inflicted on the state treasury by previous governments and their members, (7) determination to put up candidates for all seats in the coming general elections, and (8) approval of K. I. Singh's policy of continuing and strengthening close relations with India.

This strong endorsement of the party leader did not survive the fall of the United Democratic party Cabinet in November, 1957. A revolt broke out immediately within the party against Singh's decision to submit his government's resignation without first consulting his colleagues in the Cabinet or the party. The dissidents were headed by one of the party's general secretaries, Shamsher Chand. Reports were received from Pokhara, Chand's political base, that a general meeting of the party members of the district branch had strongly condemned Singh's dictatorial attitudes and undemocratic policies. Singh retaliated by expelling Chand from the party, accusing him of violating party discipline and of participating in a conspiracy against the larger interests of the party. This was the first indication that Singh saw himself as an unwitting victim of a conspiracy in which Chand had had a major hand. He waited a full six months, however, before making a sensational disclosure at a public meeting in Kathmandu in which he accused Chand of collusion with top-ranking military and palace officials in a conspiracy to discredit him on trumped-up charges of armed subversion. He charged that Chand had met King Mahendra secretly at midnight and warned him that Singh planned to place a time bomb under the King's chair.

Chand retaliated by engineering Singh's expulsion from the midwestern branch of the party and, on November 23, called an emergency meeting of his faction "to consider the unpleasant atmosphere created by the fascist and undemocratic actions of K. I. Singh, who treated the party as his individual property." The meeting changed the name of the group to the People's United Democratic party so as to wipe out the "black stigma" of K. I. Singh's association with the original party name. The flag, the constitution, and the manifesto of the original party were retained. A new executive was formed, and Hobir Ale, a long-time colleague of K. I. Singh, was elected president of the new splinter group. On November 27, these dissidents held a public meeting and voiced strong criticisms of Singh's "individualist and fascist policies."

FORMATION OF THE UNITED DEMOCRATIC FRONT

After the United Democratic party government was installed, the Nepali Congress, Praja Parishad, and Nepali National Congress, which had petitioned the King unsuccessfully for authority to form a government, continued to hold talks for a common political action program. The three principal figures involved in these negotiations were B. P. Koirala of the Nepali Congress, D. R. Regmi of the Nepali National Congress, and B. Mishra of the Praja Parishad. On August 9, 1957, the three leaders issued a public statement, announcing the formation of a United Democratic Front. Asserting their belief in the principle that sovereignty resides in the people, they defined the objectives of the Front as the strengthening of democratic forces and the safeguarding of the fundamental civic rights of the people. While acknowledging that the three constituent parties had different opinions on the objectives of the elections, the leaders emphasized the necessity of forgetting minor differences in face of the impending grave threat to democracy. On August 15 a nine-man Executive Committee was formed, consisting of the presidents, the secretaries, and one Working Committee member of each of the constituent parties. On the following day they issued a further statement, criticizing (1) the theory that sovereignty resided in the Crown and (2) the appointment of K. I. Singh as Prime Minister.

At a meeting of the Front on August 20 it was decided that the branches of the three constituent parties should be instructed to work together to defend the democratic rights of citizens. The leaders of the three parties also decided to conduct country-wide tours to take their program to the people. At a public meeting in Kathmandu, they emphasized the theme of "democracy in danger," pointed out the contradictions in the royal announcement, and demanded an all-party government. B. P. Koirala observed: ". . . it is not the government of Sri K. I. Singh which has to be taken into account, but it is that systematic conspiracy to defeat democracy unfolding itself with the passage of time which we have to take note of today." [8] This was obviously a reference to King Mahendra's continued and direct interference in the political process.

The United Democratic Front was subjected to harsh criticism by other political groups for a variety of reasons. The Communist party and the Nepal Scheduled Castes Association criticised the narrow and selfish motives of the Front leaders in not including more social and political parties. The United Democratic party attributed the formation of the Front to personal feelings of jealousy on the part of its leaders. The Parallel Praja Parishad characterized it as a political game to win power. The Gorkha Parishad condemned it in strong terms and characterized it as "the height of ideological instability, a public deception, a bankruptcy of statesmanship and a begging-bowl for obtaining the reins of the government." [9] Even Tanka Prasad Acharya expressed his doubts about the success of the Front, emphasizing his feeling that it was based more on political expediency than on an ideological alliance.

The Singh government directly challenged the Front by ignoring it completely in the formation of the new Election Commission, to which representatives of the parallel parties were appointed on August 28. The Singh government even went so far as to characterize the parallel parties as the leading political organizations in the country. The Front called this "an act of dishonesty on the part of government against even the common canons of courtesy in not inviting major parties of the country to join the Election Commission and for including representatives of parallel organizations." [10]

More than on K. I. Singh, however, the Democratic Front concentrated its attack on King Mahendra's concealed political activities. The Front leaders charged that the King had clearly shown his opposition to democracy and a constitutional system and, thus, could no longer be above public criticism. They expressed their willingness to support the theory that the King could do no wrong, but only if he was willing to entrust the government to a Cabinet responsible to an elected Legislature. Indeed, the Front leaders argued that criticism of the Crown had become necessary in order to save it from its own indiscretions, such as the political gamble that had led to the appointment of the K. I. Singh government.

In the middle of September the Democratic Front leaders went on tour to popularize their proposed program of action. All regional branches of the three parties were instructed to organize public meetings and put emphasis on the growing danger to democracy from the King and K. I. Singh. On September 17, B. P. Koirala, B. Mishra, and D. R. Regmi were arrested at Janakpur, reportedly for having strongly criticized the King at a public meeting. All three were released after a few hours, presumably at the intervention of the King. The Front's organizational activities continued at a somewhat frantic pace until finally, on October 8, the general conference of the Front parties at Birganj decided to launch a civil disobedience movement two months later, on December 8, if the situation had not improved considerably.

The dismissal of the K. I. Singh government did not deter the United Democratic Front from its proposed course of action. On November 15, both B. P. Koirala and D. R. Regmi warned the King that the civil disobedience movement would be launched on schedule if a date for the holding of elections were not announced.[11] Preparations were intensified throughout the country. Action Committees were established in Kathmandu and in the districts, funds were solicited, and volunteer satyagrahis were given training at several camps. Support for the movement came from the Communist party's Central Committee and a substantial number of student and social organizations.

The failure of a last-minute conference at the royal palace on December 7 left the Democratic Front no choice but to launch the movement on the following day. The response tended to be one of indifference in most areas, but some degree of popular support was evident in Kathmandu Valley, a few centers in the Terai, and several places in the hills. It was, however, a relief to the Front parties when on December 15 the King issued a Royal Proclamation setting the date of the general elections for February, 1959. While this did not meet their demand that the elections be held within six months, the Front parties nonetheless accepted the King's date and called off the civil disobedience movement.

The Royal Proclamation of February 1, 1958, which stipulated that the elections would be held for a Parliament rather than a Constituent Assembly, posed a much more difficult problem for the Front parties. At this time, the general councils of each of the Front parties were holding separate meetings concurrently with a joint meeting of the Front at Birganj. The Praja Parishad extended a ready endorsement to the proclamation, which conformed with the party's platform on this issue. The response of the Nepali Congress and Nepali National Congress was ambiguous, as the proclamation ran counter to their basic policy objective—a constitutional monarchy operating within the framework of an organic law prepared by an elected Constituent Assembly. Indeed, these two parties were so preoccupied with the constitutional issue that they virtually ignored the resolution of the Praja Parishad's general council calling—"in view of the fact that democracy is in danger in the country"—for the merger of the Front parties.

Practical considerations dominated the deliberations of the Nepali Congress general council. Although one faction in the party was bitterly opposed to the Royal Proclamation, the majority opinion favored accepting the royal proposals on grounds of political expediency. The party leadership also seemed to have been chastened by their recent experiences in the civil disobedience movement and the municipal elections in Kathmandu and Patan, in which, as B. P. Koirala said in his opening address to the conference, "the Congress did not prove as strong organizationally as was generally considered." [13] On February 6, the general council accepted the Royal Proclamation of February 1 *in toto*. Explaining the reasons for the reversal of the position of the party on the subject of the Constituent Assembly, the official resolution stated:

It is self-evident from the Royal Proclamation that we are not moving forward. In fact, we are going backward. In such a context, the General Council of the Nepali Congress has considered seriously the situation arising out of an obstruction of the natural flow of the revolutionary process. Unfortunately, the revolutionary elements clashed with one another, and the general aim was deflected. It is a painful realization that a gulf seemed to separate the King and the subjects, who had jointly shared the oppression of the Rana regime and the dreams of a happier future . . .

In the opinion of the General Council of the Nepali Congress, reactionary elements have entrenched themselves strongly between the Crown, which had to date accepted the goal of democracy, and the democratic forces. If these retrogressive reactionary elements are allowed to remain effective, even the remaining few democratic rights will come to an end. It is said that the Constitution to be framed in accordance with the proclamation will secure the rights of the people. This conference believes that a delicate moment has arrived for all democrats who sincerely desire to make that Constitution democratic and to keep the evolutionary path of democracy unobstructed, and resolves to coöperate and collaborate with all democratic measures and elements which are determined to accomplish the task of holding elections and also to work toward the further development of all those democratic rights present in the proclamation in accordance with the demand and consciousness of the society.[14]

Acceptance of the proclamation was, indeed, a momentous decision for the Nepali Congress. It meant not merely a reversal of most of its policies, but also signified an acceptance of the concept of limited democracy. In effect, the party conceded King Mahendra's thesis that the people of the country were not yet sufficiently mature and competent to prepare a Constitution, and, thus, accepted a significantly reduced role for itself as an instrument of social and political change. After the Birganj conference, doubts about the wisdom of the party decision seem to have troubled most of the Nepali Congress leaders as well as the rank and file. Partly to reassure them, B. P. Koirala published in the Nepali Congress organ an article entitled "Yesterday, Today, and Tomorrow" which was intended, in part, as a defense of the pragmatic nature of the party decision. Explaining why the Nepali Congress had to abandon its demand for a Constituent Assembly as based on the Royal Proclamation of 1951, he wrote:

When we make a comparative study of the Royal Proclamation of 1951 and that of February 1, 1958, we can say with certainty that the latter is reactionary. But we must remember that the very spirit of the Royal Proclamation of the year 1951 was already dead. The reasons underlying this development will make up a separate article. I do not even intend to disclose the identities of those responsible for such a change. I only want to mention that the Royal Proclamation of February, 1951, could not get its roots firmly established among the people and that it had been nipped in the bud. Therefore, it will not be proper to compare it with the present Royal Proclamation. What we have to consider is whether it will be proper to conduct elections for a Parliament in the present circumstances. Is it not a step forward to conduct elections for a Parliament in the present intolerable situation? The comparison of the year 1951 with the year 1958 is not scientific. We must compare the year 1958 with the year 1959.[15]

The Nepali National Congress followed the example set by the Nepali Congress and endorsed the royal proposals on February 7, though it also expressed the hope that the proposed Parliament would serve as a Constituent Assembly as well. The reversal in the position of the Nepali Congress and Nepali National Congress was a significant victory for King Mahendra's policies. By accepting his proposals unreservedly, the two parties conceded more than had been demanded during the unsuccessful negotiations with them in the winter of 1955, when the King had tried to persuade the leaders of the three Front parties to participate in a Cabinet without a Prime Minister. Now, three years later, these parties not only endorsed his plan for an Executive Council, but also approved his program for holding elections to a Parliament rather than a Constituent Assembly.

Other political parties, such as the newly formed Prajatantrik

Mahasabha, the United Democratic party, and Rashtriya Jana Rajya Parishad ("National Council for People's Rule"), hailed the Royal Proclamation and considered it a vindication of their party objectives. From their very inception these parties had consistently upheld King Mahendra's right to grant a Constitution and to hold elections for a Parliament.

The Gorkha Parishad's reaction to the proclamation also indicated a significant political reversal. From its birth, in 1951, this party had strongly upheld such causes as civil liberties and the independence of the judiciary, in part because it feared the hostility of successive political party Cabinets toward its association with some members of the Rana family. Since it operated with a fairly broad time perspective with regard to inclusion in a government, it had in the past supported elections for a Constituent Assembly. After the Royal Proclamation of February 1, 1958, however, the Gorkha Parishad not only endorsed elections for a Parliament, but even maintained that it had espoused such elections in the past.

The Terai Congress, which was initially committed to elections for a Constituent Assembly, also reversed its position and on February 11 unanimously accepted the Royal Proclamation. The party's Working Committee demanded that enough powers should be vested in the Parliament to give adequate protection to the fundamental rights of the people. Indeed, only a few student organizations and the Communist party demonstrated some degree of resistance in accepting the proclamation. Sambhu Ram, secretary of the North Gandak Provincial Committee of the Communist party, called on "all democratic parties and elements" to "combine together so as to make King Mahendra withdraw his announcement about conducting elections for a parliament." [16] It was reported that the North Gandak committee endorsed Sambhu Ram's proposals at its meeting on February 4. The Central Committee of the party, however, meeting at Janakpur on March 2, voted to accept the proclamation with some reservations.

The so-called independents, consisting mostly of businessmen, landlords, and former officials of the Rana administration, banded together at a general conference in Birganj on February 13 and gave their unstinted support to the proclamation. It was reported that some four hundred delegates from one hundred and nine regions of the country participated in this conference, the first meeting of "independents" on a nationwide scale. Welcoming the delegates, Toya Raj Joshi observed that the numerous political parties were the main cause of the unstable conditions in the country, and stated that the people had begun to realize that "the inexperienced and selfish leaders of the political parties were leading the country to disaster." [17] According to newspaper accounts, the conference unanimously decided to establish a new party called the "All Nepal Independents Society" and formed a twenty-one-member Working Committee. A three-member presidium, consisting of Lok Nath Joshi, Gauri Narayan, and Sirdar Som Prasad, was formed to conduct the day-to-day affairs of the organization and Surendra Bahadur Basnyat was elected general secretary of the new party.

THE COALITION COUNCIL OF MINISTERS

The appointment of a four-party coalition Council of Ministers in May, 1958, had its first disintegrative impact, ironically enough, on one of the constituent parties, the Praja Parishad. The rift between Bhadrakali Mishra and Tanka Prasad Acharya over the party's representative in the Council delayed the formation of the Cabinet by nearly one week. The deadlock was finally resolved only after King Mahendra had intervened personally by nominating Chandra Bhusan Pande as the Praja Parishad Minister, but this only widened the gulf between the two senior party leaders.*

The two men had differed over the formation of the United Democratic Front in August, 1957. Tanka Prasad had been skeptical of the Front's utility from the beginning, while Mishra had been one of its most enthusiastic supporters. These disagreements came into focus at the joint session of the Praja Parishad's Working Committee at Gaur on July 17, 1958, in which the party divided into two mutually exclusive factions. Reportedly, Tanka Prasad was working toward a merger of the parallel organizations with the Praja Parishad, which would then leave the Front, but Mishra strongly opposed this. Tanka Prasad finally walked out of the Gaur meeting in protest against what he called the arbitrary policy of the party president, Mishra. On the following day, when the second session began, Tanka Prasad staged another walkout when the committee failed to approve his proposal for a prompt severance of the party's political ties with the Democratic Front. Having failed to convince his party colleagues on this matter, Tanka Prasad withdrew from further meetings and was reported to have said that he had ended all political relations with Mishra. The Working Committee, however, continued its deliberations.

---

* Balchandra Sharma had retired from any direct participation in politics after his appointment as Vice-Chancellor of the Royal Academy of Arts and Literature by King Mahendra in June, 1956.

It decided to send two party representatives to the Advisory Assembly, to open a training center for party leaders in preparation for the election campaign, and to set up a committee to draft an election manifesto. When Mishra formed a new Working Committee, Tanka Prasad Acharya, Chandra Bhusan Pande (the Praja Parishad Minister) and Ram Hari Sharma were excluded.

On August 11, 1958, Tanka Prasad organized a meeting of party workers from different districts to discuss the reorganization of the Praja Parishad on its original lines and to effect a complete dissociation from the Jana Congress. About a week later, Mishra wrote to Tanka Prasad demanding clarification of his political intentions. Tanka Prasad replied that he and his followers had decided to separate from Mishra and his group and to organize themselves "under the old red flag of the Praja Parishad with the spade and the hammer." [18] On September 8, Jiva Raj Sharma, president of the splinter Nepali National Congress, announced the unconditional merger of his organization with the new Praja Parishad. His action, however, was quickly repudiated by the general secretary of his own party and several members of the Working Committee as unconstitutional and unwarranted. From this time on, there were two splinter Praja Parishad groups, with identical names but separate flags, functioning in Nepal.

THE PARALLEL POLITICAL PARTIES AND SPLINTER GROUPS

Political splinter groups, which had proliferated in the time of the K. I. Singh Cabinet and the second period of direct rule, received what amounted to a kiss of death from King Mahendra when he set up the Council of Ministers. During the King's absence in the Soviet Union the leaders of these factions were involved in their own little private squabbles and political maneuvers. There was, however, a dawning realization by some of them that their only hope for political survival lay in some form of coalescence. As a result, a National Front was established on June 20, 1958, with Dayanidhi Sharma, the leader of the Rashtriya Praja party ("National Democrats"), as president. Sharma announced the formation of a Working Committee of the Front on July 20, consisting of representatives of the Rashtriya Praja party, Rashtriya Jana Rajya Parishad, the Parallel Nepali Congress and the Parallel Praja Parishad.

Political conflicts and intrigues, which had become practically a way of life with the dissidents, soon overcame the National Front. Shamsher Chand, the general secretary of the Peoples'

United Democratic party (the K. I. Singh splinter group), announced that his party had decided to join the Front with a view to strengthening democratic unity. This immediately led to dissension within the Front. The president of the Front issued a statement pointing out that it had not been possible to include Chand's party in the Front at the time of its formation as was intended, because Chand was not then in Kathmandu. Leaders of other Front parties took strong exception to this statement and criticized Sharma's action as unconstitutional. The presidents of the Rashtriya Jana Rajya Parishad, the Parallel Nepali Congress, the Parallel Praja Parishad, and the three secretaries of the National Front—Narad Muni Thulung, Purna Prasad "Brahman" and Jagat Bahadur—claimed that the inclusion of the Peoples' United Democratic party had not been discussed by the Working Committee.[19] Rivalry and tension within the Front continued unabated, leading a local paper to comment: "The parallel parties have no influence among the people. They have been working solely to fulfill their own selfish interests. They will be pacified only after the dissolution of the National Front." [20]

While the National Front tottered, the constituent splinter groups were caught in their own internal struggles. It was reported on July 21 that Jagat Bahadur, president of the Parallel Praja Parishad, had dissolved the old Working Committee and organized a new one. On the following day some workers of the party held a meeting, decided to expel Jagat Bahadur from the presidency on the ground that he had violated party discipline and attempted to weaken the National Front, and elected Keshav Raj Karki as the new president. A similar fate befell Dayanidhi Sharma, the president of the Rashtriya Praja Party, on September 13, when the presidium of the party expelled him from the party, elected Yajna Bahadur to his office, and then requested the secretary of the National Front to expel him from the Front.

CONCLUDING REMARKS

For the political party system, the period between King Mahendra's accession to the throne and the 1959 general elections was remarkable for one thing—the substantial revitalization and reorganization of the Nepali Congress. From August, 1952, to January, 1956, the Nepali Congress had functioned with two broadly opportunistic goals—to apply pressure on the party in power and to negotiate with the ruling party and the King to gain for itself a voice in the government. The sixth national conference of the party, at Birganj in January, 1956, marked a turning point in the party's history. A firm ideological stance was adopted, with the projection of a democratic socialist society as the party's ultimate political objective. The expedient tactics pursued during the preceding period were not abandoned entirely, but were downgraded in favor of a campaign aimed at forcing general elections as early as possible. But of most significance was the fact that the party deliberations had not been marked by intransigent factional struggles—a unique record for any Nepali political party and particularly one as broadly based as the Nepali Congress.

It was, in fact, the broadly representative character of the Nepali Congress that distinguished it from the rest of the parties in Nepal. The Nepali Congress was a pluralist party. Included within its folds were such diverse elements as Ranas, landowners, merchants, intellectuals, students, labor leaders, and former servicemen. It provided representation on a national scale to all the principal ethnic communities and regions of Nepal. Brahmans, Kshatriyas, Newars, Muslims, Limbus, Rais, and Gurungs all held important positions in the party hierarchy. The Terai, the eastern and western hill areas, and the urban centers were well represented at both the leadership and the membership level.

Organizationally the Nepali Congress was also virtually unique—the Communists were the only other example—in that it operated according to codified rules and procedures. This prevented the party from becoming a mere pawn in the maneuvers of ambitious politicians, in contrast to the personality-centered parties so characteristic of the political process in Nepal. The headquarters of the Nepali Congress functioned effectively, again unlike those of most other parties, and maintained close liaison with and supervision over party branches and units in the districts.

The only other parties that had some basis to claim a "national" status were the Gorkha Parishad and the Communist party, which were expected to pose the greatest challenge to the Nepali Congress in the 1959 elections. Both were well organized. The Communists, in particular, exercised rigid screening procedures before admitting prospective candidates to party membership. The rank and file of the Communist party was recruited primarily from students, lower-middle-class merchants, and urbanized peasants. The leadership of the party reflected a "national" pattern characterized by comparatively stable coalitions of persons belonging to different ethnic communities—Newars, Brahmans, Kshatriyas, and even one Muslim—all of whom belonged to the emergent Western-educated urban middle-class intelligentsia. The Gorkha Parishad drew its membership from the Kshatriya caste and from hill ethnic communities such as the Magars, Gurungs, Limbus, and Rais. Brahmans and the Terai communities were virtually unrepresented—at least, on the higher leadership level.

But both the Gorkha Parishad and the Communists were severely handicapped in their rivalry with the Nepali Congress by a number of factors. The Gorkha Parishad's influence was largely confined to the hill areas, and particularly to the area immediately around Kathmandu Valley. The Communists were similarly restricted territorially, having active centers of party strength only in Kathmandu Valley, two or three districts in the Terai, and a few places in the hills. The Communists were further weakened by serious internal disputes that aborted all efforts to form electoral alliances with other parties or political leaders.

The position of the other parties, most of which functioned in the context of the traditional Nepali political idiom in which the organization was invariably centered around an authoritarian personality supported by a small clique of adherents, was discouraging in the extreme. Most of them existed, in all but name, only in Kathmandu. None had made serious and persistent efforts to organize nationally except in those instances in which, owing to the quixotic character of Nepali politics in the pre-election period, one of these minor political factions had the mantle of the ruling party tossed lightly around its shoulders by royal whim. All of them approached the elections with well-justified forebodings of doom and with a basic disinclination to accept the passing of the palace-oriented political process under which they had prospered since 1952.

14

The 1959 Constitution and the General Elections

WHEN KING TRIBHUWAN announced the end of Rana rule in February, 1951, he had stated explicitly that the future governments of the country would function under a democratic Constitution prepared by elected representatives of the people. This statement served as the primary goal of the transitional politics until his death in March, 1955. There were differences of opinion among the political parties and their leaders on interpretations of the government's role during the interim period, but all were united in their insistence on the need for early nationwide elections to establish a Constituent Assembly, i.e., a legislative body that would prepare a Constitution for the country.

Despite this almost unique verbal agreement among the political parties, the successive governments formed under King Tribhuwan's aegis could only undertake a few preliminary steps toward the holding of general elections. In June, 1951, an Election Commission was established, followed by a Public Representation Act in December. But the absence of a national census, the lack of trained personnel, the delays and inefficiency of the fledgling administrative machinery, and, above all, the unwillingness of some political leaders in the government to have their credentials examined at the polls—all obstructed the activities of the Election Commission. The elections, once promised for no later than April, 1953, remained as remote as ever by the beginning of 1955.

Upon King Mahendra's accession to the throne in March,

1955, the situation changed drastically and quickly. The political parties and public, distressed by the unstable politics of the previous four years, intensified their demand for early elections. King Mahendra, no less eager than the party leaders for a new brand of politics, injected a bold note of certainty and determination when he announced in August, 1955, that the elections would commence on the full moon day in October, 1957. But soon thereafter a bitter controversy erupted among the parties because of a suggestion by the then Prime Minister, Tanka Prasad Acharya, that the elections be held for a Parliament under a Constitution granted by the King, rather than for a Constituent Assembly. This dispute further delayed the enactment of the amended Public Representation Act, which had been submitted to the government by the Election Commission in March, 1954. Meanwhile, the partly completed electoral rolls prepared by the Electoral Commission in the interim period had become obsolete, and an expanded staff, exercizing greater authority, had become necessary to bring them up to date.

Moreover, the new controversy concerning the purposes of the elections led to bitter divisions among the parties, with the result that the previous consensus on a Constituent Assembly was all but lost. Indeed, a new school of politics arose, supported by conservative social and political elements, which challenged not merely the concepts of a Constituent Assembly and elections, but also the validity of a democratic political system in the social and historical contexts of Nepal. The more sophisticated among these elements argued that in a country with a low literacy rate (6 per cent), and in which regional and communal loyalties were still potent, a political innovation such as national elections was potentially dangerous and disruptive; the less sophisticated argued that the concept of parliamentary democracy was wholly alien to the culture and traditions of the country and that a benevolent autocracy of the King should be instituted. These arguments were, of course, bitterly repudiated by most of the political parties.

In these circumstances the original date for holding elections fixed by King Mahendra in 1955 became infeasible. Consequently, in December, 1957, the King proclaimed a new date— February 18, 1959—as the day for commencing the nationwide elections. Further, he resolved the debate on a Constituent Assembly versus a Parliament by issuing a Royal Proclamation in February, 1958, stating that the elections would be held for a bicameral Parliament and that he would grant a Constitution to the people. The Election Commission was reconstituted in May,

1958, and the Public Representation Act was promulgated the following month.

THE ELECTION COMMISSION AND THE PUBLIC REPRESENTATION ACT OF 1958

The Election Commission had had a rather checkered history since its establishment in 1951. Its first action had been the preparation of voter's lists in different parts of the country under the authority of the Public Representation Act of 1951.* In 1953, the Commission prepared an amended version of the Act after consultations with Sukumar Sen, the Chief Election Commissioner of India, but four successive governments between March, 1954, and July, 1957, failed to complete its enactment. Under the K. I. Singh Cabinet, the Commission was reconstituted on September 5, 1957, to include five representatives of political parties and six government officials, among whom was the incumbent Chief Election Commissioner. Under a procedural innovation introduced by the Singh government, the expanded Commission published fortnightly reports of its activities and deliberations, and also made its records available to the interested public, who were invited to the Commission's office any working day after 2:00 P.M.

In its first meeting, on September 17, 1957, the expanded Commission decided that the general elections could not take place on the date previously announced, and reported accordingly to King Mahendra, who later postponed the elections until February 18, 1959. King Mahendra dissolved the expanded Election Commission in February, 1958, and announced its replacement by a new body consisting of only government officials, and it was under the auspices of the new Election Commission that the general elections of 1959 were held.

The Public Representation Act of 1958, promulgated by the King in June, 1958, provided for elections to a Parliament and insured the right to vote through a secret ballot to all Nepali citizens aged twenty-one years or more, irrespective of caste,

---

* It later developed that the Election Commission had been operating illegally under the provisions of the 1951 Public Representation Act. Although this law had been approved by the Cabinet, and published in the *Nepal Gazette* (Vol. I, No. 27, Magha 28, 2008 V.S. [February 10, 1952]), it had never received final authentication by the affixing of the royal seal. This legal anomaly, however, did not become known to the public until 1956, when a case filed against Prime Minister Tanka Prasad Acharya by B. P. Koirala on the basis of the 1951 Act was dismissed by the Supreme Court on the grounds that the Act had never attained the status of law, owing to the failure to affix the royal seal.

religion, and sex. With the exception of government employees, any Nepali national who had reached the age of twenty-five years was granted the right to stand as a candidate in the elections. The Act gave the Commission the necessary authority for preparing voters' lists, delimiting constituencies, judging the eligibility of candidates, and settling disputes and claims concerning the elections.

The Election Commission overcame many serious handicaps in holding the elections on the announced date. The physical terrain, the undeveloped state of communication and transportation facilities, the low rate of literacy, and, above all, the lack of historical and administrative precedents—these were only some of the major obstacles with which it had to cope. But, with exemplary vigor and resourcefulness, the Commission mobilized whatever indigenous help it could muster and also whatever technical assistance it could procure from abroad. Both the Indian and the British governments provided the Commission with wireless equipment and operators to facilitate communications. The Commission also enlisted the support of poets and song writers in its publicity campaigns to educate the people about the methods and purposes of the elections. Several mock elections were held in different parts of the country to acquaint the voters with election procedures; extensive use was made of Radio Nepal facilities; and the Commission even published a fortnightly periodical, *Nirvachan Sandesh* ("Election News"), to publicize reports about its activities and programs. The services of several thousand government employees at the Secretariat, district, and local levels were requisitioned to aid the Commission in its multifaceted responsibilities.

The Commission completed the delimitation of the country into 109 constituencies in May, 1958. A month later, the Chief Election Commissioner made an appeal over Radio Nepal for the coöperation of the people and, particularly, the press. He wrote letters to political parties inviting their suggestions and advice concerning the most expeditious method of holding elections. He announced over Radio Nepal some of the features of the impending event: (a) the country was to be divided into 109 constituencies; (b) each constituency was estimated to include an average of 78,000 voters, and separate polling booths were to be provided for population groups of about 2,000; (c) voters would not have to walk more than six miles to reach the nearest polling station; (d) Bada Hakims were to serve as Returning Officers and were to be assisted by Zonal Election Officers—each zone comprising four election constituencies—and Election Officers.[1]

In July, the Election Commission announced the deputation of 27 Zonal Election Officers, 6 Assistant Zonal Election Officers, and 109 Election Officers to various parts of the country.[2] The voters' lists were published in the various constituencies in August; any person who attained the age of twenty-one years after the lists had been prepared was advised to enter his name on the list at the nearest station. Final voters' lists were published on November 7 and were exhibited in each constituency for general information as well as last-minute scrutiny. Even after the expiry of the November 9 deadline, eligible voters were allowed to enter their names on the final voters' list until December 1 on payment of a late-enrollment fine of 25 rupees.[3] The candidates were given a month's time, from November 9 to December 8, to file their nomination papers, and the Returning Officer in each constituency was required to complete the scrutiny of nominations and publish the final list of candidates by December 15.

In October, the Election Commissioner announced that simultaneous elections in all constituencies, which had been requested by some political parties, would not be feasible, owing to the shortage of personnel. Instead, he proposed carrying out the elections in batches throughout the country. According to his plan, there would be balloting for only eighteen days, and elections in any constituency would be finished in one day. For example, on February 18, 1959, elections were to begin in eighteen constituencies spread over sixteen districts, on February 26 in the northern regions of Jumla district, and on March 2 in the western district of Dailekh. The Commissioner estimated that the elections would be completed in forty-five days, that is, by April 3.[4]

King Mahendra helped set the political mood for the first general elections by issuing a Royal Proclamation on November 9, 1958, calling upon the people to elect their representatives to the national Legislature. By December 15, a total of 942 nomination papers had been filed, from 107 constituencies, of which 98 were rejected.[5] This total did not include the nomination papers for the northern district of Jumla, where the deadline had not expired.

While the preparations for the elections were being pushed feverishly, both by the Election Commission and by the political parties, a major factor of uncertainty still existed and, in fact, continued until a week before the commencement of the elections. There had been no publication of the Constitution under which any elected government of the future would have to function. Finally, when King Mahendra proclaimed the new

Constitution at a special Durbar on February 12, 1959, the last hitch in the preparations was removed, and the first general elections in the history of Nepal began as scheduled on February 18.

THE 1959 CONSTITUTION

The 1959 Constitution was prepared by a special Constitution Drafting Commission established by King Mahendra in March, 1958. The Commission—headed by the chairman of the Public Service Commission, Bhagawati Prasad Singh—included Hora Prasad Joshi and the general secretary, Surya Prasad Upadhyaya, of the Nepali Congress; Ranadhir Subba, president of the Gorkha Parishad; and Ram Raj Pant, the principal of the Law College. Sir Ivor Jennings, the British expert on constitutional law, served as a consultant to the Commission at one stage in its deliberations. The Constitution, as drafted by the Commission, was first approved by the coalition Council of Ministers before it was submitted to King Mahendra for his approval.

The 1959 Constitution was ostensibly the product of a broad political consensus among four political parties—the Nepali Congress, the Praja Parishad, the Gorkha Parishad, and the Nepali National Congress—but in essence it represented the best possible political accomodation that could be achieved among these parties and with the King. While the Constitution generally followed the format and, in some cases, even the language of the 1950 Indian Constitution, in spirit it was much closer to the principles incorporated in King Tribhuwan's Royal Proclamation of January 10, 1954. The establishment of the Crown as the source of all legislative, executive, and judicial authority, an essential feature of the 1954 proclamation, was retained in the new Constitution. In the Preamble, it was clearly stated that the Constitution was granted as an "exercise of the sovereign powers and prerogatives vesting in Us,* in accordance with the tradition and custom of our country and which devolved on Us from Our august and respected forefathers." [6] This was explicitly affirmed in the "Executive Government" section:

. . . the executive power of Nepal is vested in His Majesty, extends to the execution and maintenance of this constitution and the laws of Nepal, and shall be exercised by him either directly or through

* The term "Us" refers to the King and his immediate family, consisting of his Queen and the Crown Prince. Traditionally, the Shah kings have used this plural form to identify themselves in their proclamations.

ministers or other officers, subordinate to him in accordance with the provisions of this constitution and of any other law for the time being in force.[7]

The objectives of the Constitution were stated in the following terms:

To help our subjects to attain all-round progress and achieve the fullest development of their personality; to insure to them political, social, and economic justice; and to cement the unity of the nation by bringing about political stability through the establishment of an efficient monarchical form of government responsive to the wishes of the people.[8]

One conspicuous omission in the statement of objectives was the lack of any reference to the establishment of a democratic system, which had figured prominently as the avowed goal of all successive governments since King Tribhuwan's historic proclamation of February 18, 1951. In contrast, the 1959 Constitution emphasized the primary responsibility of establishing a responsible monarchical system of government which would bring about the social, economic, and political well-being of the people.

The new Constitution was a fairly lengthy document, comprising seventy-seven articles in addition to the Preamble, and was classified into ten major parts covering sixty-six pages of text. It defined fundamental rights, the powers and functions of the executive government, the Parliament, the judiciary, and the Public Service Commission, the powers of the King, and fiscal procedures and organization.

FUNDAMENTAL RIGHTS

The section on fundamental rights paralleled closely the relevant portions of the Interim Constitution of 1951 and was based on extensive borrowings from the Indian Constitution. Like the Interim Constitution, the new Constitution guaranteed the equal protection of the laws to all citizens irrespective of religion, sex, race, caste, or tribe. Political liberties such as freedom of speech and expression, freedom of assembly without arms, freedom to form associations, and freedom to move to or reside in any part of the country were enumerated as part of the people's fundamental rights. Religious freedom was guaranteed subject to the proviso that "no person shall be entitled to convert another person to his religion." The right to private property was recognized and protected by the provision that "no person shall be deprived of his property save in accordance with the law."

A curious feature of the section on fundamental rights was the incorporation of provisions referring to preventive detention. Under these provisions, the government could place any person in custody under preventive detention for a maximum period of three months unless a specially constituted Advisory Board decided otherwise or any other specific law provided to the contrary. The government, moreover, reserved to itself the option of disclosing the grounds for his detention to the *détenu*.

Another feature of this section was the definition of the public good, which limited the conditions under which the fundamental rights could be exercised. Any law deemed necessary for the public good was beyond the scope of the constitutional provisions referring to fundamental rights. The following connotations of public good were defined: maintenance of law and order; maintenance of security; good relations among different classes or sections of the people or between the people of different areas; the health, comfort, convenience or public welfare of the public; economic prosperity of Nepal; observance of morality and decency; prevention of internal disturbance or any attempt to subvert the Constitution or any law in force; and prevention of contempt of court or of the Houses of the Parliament (Art. 3.2).

The Supreme Court was specified as the the judicial authority responsible for the enforcement of fundamental rights. It, or any other subordinate court authorized by it, was guaranteed the power to issue directions or orders or writs including writs in the nature of *habeas corpus,* mandamus, prohibition, *quo warranto* and *certiorari* for the enforcement of any of the fundamental rights enunciated in the Constitution.

THE PARLIAMENT

The Constitution provided for a Parliament of Nepal, which should consist of "His Majesty and two Houses, to be known respectively as the Senate *(Maha Sabha)* and the House of Representatives *(Pratinidhi Sabha)* ." The House of Representatives, or Lower House, consisted of 109 members elected for a period of five years on the basis of universal adult suffrage. The Senate, or Upper House consisted of thirty-six members, half of whom were to be elected by the Lower House on the basis of proportional representation and half to be nominated by the King. The term of the Senators was six years, with one third of them retiring at the end of every two years. The Speaker of the Lower House lost his membership in the house by virtue of his office if he was already a member. This novel provision, which was justified as a measure for insuring an impartial Speaker, made it possible for a non-member to serve as Speaker of the Lower House.

The Constitution granted differential powers to the two houses in the field of financial legislation. It was stated explicitly that all money bills must originate in the Lower House, but that the Upper House could delay their passage by at least one month and that of any other legislation by six months. The legislative powers of the Parliament were stated in the following terms: "Subject to the provisions of the Constitution, Parliament shall have powers to make laws for the peace, order, and good government of Nepal" (Art. 51) But the King reserved to himself the right to promulgate ordinances while the Parliament was not in session if he deemed them necessary, and these would have the status and validity of the law. These ordinances were to become inoperative if they were disapproved by a majority in both houses or after the lapse of forty-five days, once the Parliament commenced its next session.

The Parliament was granted authority to amend or repeal any of the provisions of the Constitution if two thirds of the total members of each house agreed to an amendment separately.

Several limitations on the authority of the Parliament were incorporated in the Constitution. It could not introduce any money bill without the consent of the King, and could pass no law without the formal assent of the King, who could withhold, refuse, or postpone his assent at his discretion and without any explanation (Art. 42). The King also reserved to himself wide discretionary powers to suspend either or both of the houses of the Parliament at any time he deemed necessary (Art. 56.1). The Constitution also insured the personal inviolability of the King by specifically debarring the Parliament from discussing his "private revenues" (Art. 44.4) and "the conduct of His Majesty and his successors" (Art. 34.1).

THE GOVERNMENT

The new Constitution provided for a Cabinet form of government roughly patterned after the British model. A Cabinet led by the Prime Minister and consisting of not more than fourteen ministers was envisioned. It was charged with the "general direction and control of the government" and was collectively responsible to the Lower House. The latter provision was at least technically an improvement over the 1951 Interim

Government Act, under which Ministers were individually or collectively responsible to the King for their actions and held their office at his pleasure. The Prime Minister was to be the leader of the majority party in the Lower House, but was, however, required to select at least two Ministers from the Upper House. He was also authorized to appoint a maximum of ten Assistant Ministers (of whom at least two had to be members of the Upper House) to assist the Ministers in the exercise of their functions.

The Prime Minister was required to communicate to the King the agenda, agenda papers, and conclusions of the Cabinet and any legislative or executive action either contemplated or implemented without reference to the Cabinet, and to furnish any information concerning the government whenever desired by the King. The King, however, again reserved to himself wide discretionary powers to formulate rules and regulations for government business by specifying relations between him, the Cabinet, and other government employees. The Constitution laid down explicitly that if ever a question arose over whether any matter was one in which the King could act on his own discretion, his decision was to be regarded as final and the validity of any of his actions was not to be questioned (Art. 10.5). These provisions created an anamolous position for any elected government, which was to be held responsible for both the constitutional and the discretionary actions of the King and also for their own actions as members of the government. In essence, these constitutional provisions brought into being a dyarchical form of government with two loci of power, one in the royal palace, staffed by the Palace Secretariat and based on the King's personal discretionary, emergency, and inherent sovereign powers, and the other in the Civil Secretariat, led by elected representatives of the people but based on only limited authority formally delegated and tolerated by the royal palace under the provisions of the 1959 Constitution.

Severe limitations were also placed on the Prime Minister in the exercise of his authority. The King was empowered to reject, on his own discretion, the Prime Minister's recommendation that the Parliament either be summoned or dissolved (Art. 26.2). This provision negated the basic principle of the Cabinet type of government and reduced the position of the Prime Minister to that of an ordinary civil servant. For example, if at any time the King rejected his recommendation, the Prime Minister had no choice but to resign if he adhered to the customs and spirit of parliamentary democracy; if, however, he continued in office, he would have to withdraw his rejected recommendation, and perhaps even apologize for it. Furthermore, the Constitution was unclear about a situation in which the King refused royal assent to a government bill passed by both houses. Should the Prime Minister then submit the resignation of his Cabinet or should he merely submit to the royal decision under duress? Thus, the basis of potential conflict was clearly woven into the future relationships between the King and the Prime Minister under the provisions of the 1959 Constitution. Indeed, the only way in which these potential conflicts could be avoided was through the manipulation of the Parliamentary process in such a way as to lead to the election of a King's man as Prime Minister. Any independent-minded Prime Minister who rejected a subordinate role was destined to fall into a headlong clash with the Sovereign's legislative, executive, and judicial powers sooner or later.

The Council of State (*Rashtriya Parishad*) was also used as a counterbalance to the Prime Minister. The King could dismiss a Prime Minister if, after consulting the Council of State, he was satisfied that the Prime Minister had lost the confidence of the Parliament or "persisted in acting contrary to the provisions of this constitution" (Art. 13.5,*d*). The Council was composed of all the Ministers, former Ministers, Speakers, and Deputy Speakers of the Parliament, and other royal apointees, and was conceived along the lines of the Privy Council in England to serve as a consultative body to advise the King. It was also assigned the functions of a Regency Council during the minority or mental or physical infirmity of the King (Art. 11.5,*b*). But some of the other functions of the Council overlapped with those of the Prime Minister. It was required, for example, to advise the King as to whether the constitutional machinery had broken down (Art. 17.42,2), or whether he should approve a bill passed by the Parliament (Art. 15.55,5).

THE JUDICIARY AND OTHER STATUTORY BODIES

The Constitution provided for the establishment of a Supreme Court and enumerated the procedures relating to the appointment of the Chief Justice and other judges. The Supreme Court was entrusted with the responsibility of deciding the final and definitive interpretations of the Constitution and was empowered to withdraw any cases involving interpretations of the Constitution from the subordinate courts to its own jurisdiction (Art. 58,*a*,*b*). The King reserved the right to appoint the Chief Justice and other judges at his discretion and, similarly, reserved the right to dismiss them for "misbehavior or incapacity" on the recommendation of a specially constituted Royal Tribunal (Art. 57.1, 57.4,*b*).

The Constitution also provided for the establishment of such statutory bodies and offices as the Public Service Commission, the Constituency Delimitation Commission, the Election Commission, and the Auditor-General. Members of these bodies were direct appointees of the King and, as such, were responsible to him alone for their actions.

THE POWERS OF THE KING

The King's exclusive control over the military was assured by the Constitution. The supreme command of the army was vested in him as part of his discretionary powers, and he alone was empowered "to raise and maintain armed forces; to grant commissions in such forces; to appoint Commanders in Chief and to determine their powers, duties and remunerations" (Art. 64.1, 64.2). It was laid down explicitly that "no bill or amendment relating to the armed forces shall be introduced in either House of Parliament without the recommendations of His Majesty" (Art. 64.3).

The King was also assured the power to grant pardons, reprieves, and respites, and to remit, suspend, or commute any sentence passed by any court, tribunal, or authority established by law. And, finally, all powers relating to matters not provided in the Constitution or covered by existing laws were stipulated to be the residuary powers of the King (Art. 68).

In addition to discretionary and residuary powers, the King was also vested under the 1959 Constitution with a wide variety of emergency powers. Under these latter powers the King could suspend or abrogate, in times of both war and peace, a part or all of the Constitution (Art. 55–56). The only restraint placed on him was that he could not suspend the constitutional provisions relating to the Supreme Court (Art. 55.1,*b*).

Furthermore, the King alone was assured the exclusive rights to enact a law relating to the succession to the throne (Art. 63). This was stated explicitly in Article 1: ". . . nothing in this constitution shall affect the law, custom, and usage relating to the succession to the throne by the descendants of His Majesty Shri 5 Maharajdhiraj [i.e., the King]."

The 1959 Constitution emphasized the inherent powers of the King, labeled variously as discretionary, residuary, and emergency, to such an extent that it raised questions as to whether it was a genuinely democratic document. What it represented was a political concession on the part of the King to experiment with limited delegation of powers to an elected Legislature in the conduct of the routine administration of the country. At best, it amounted to the adoption of a token democratic exterior for the future governments; at worst, it amounted to a calculated measure to create the illusion of political democracy under an essentially authoritarian system. Even the limited delegation of powers granted by the Constitution was hemmed in by so many safeguards and emergency provisions that the framers seemed to be preoccupied more with the tentative nature of the "democratic" experiment and the possibility of a political emergency than with the preparation of a democratic document.

POLITICAL PARTIES AND THE GENERAL ELECTIONS

The 1959 Constitution was not announced until February 12, 1959, when the general elections were only one week away. In contesting the elections, therefore, the political parties were operating in the dark for most of the campaign since they had no knowledge of the powers and functions of the government they were hoping to form. As a result, there was an aura of unreality in their election promises and manifestoes because of their assumption that the new Constitution would provide for the establishment of a strong, democratic government. It is unclear whether this was an example of their political naïveté, or whether the provisions of the Constitution, as drafted by the Commission, were revised in the royal palace without the knowledge of the parties that had been represented on the Commission. In any case, by the time the Constitution was promulgated, it was too late for the parties to do anything about it. Several parties, and notably the Communist party, criticized the new Constitution for its feudal character, but, like the others, they continued to contest the election in a spirit of political resignation.

The Election Commission had ruled that a party would have to nominate at least twenty-two candidates—that is, approximately 20 per cent of the total number of constituencies—to qualify for recognition as a national party. Under this ruling, only seven parties were so classified: the Nepali Congress, the United Democratic party, the Gorkha Parishad, the Communist party, the Praja Parishad (Tanka Prasad faction), the Praja Parishad (B. Mishra faction), and the Nepal Prajatantrik Mahasabha. Two other parties, the Nepali National Congress (D. R. Regmi faction) and the Terai Congress, set up only twenty and twenty-one candidates respectively, and did not qualify. None of the nine parties in the field entered into electoral alliances, and each continued to wage its campaign on its own resources. The only exception was the Communist party which supported Tanka Prasad Acharya and a few independents against the candidates of the Nepali Congress and the Gorkha Parishad, labeled as "enemies of the people" by its Politburo.[9] There were, in all, 786 candidates contesting the elections, of whom 268 ran as independents and the remainder under the auspices of political parties.[10]

Because of the low rate of literacy in the country, the Election Commission had to assign identifying pictorial symbols to the political parties and the independents so that the illiterate among the voters could cast their ballots according to the appropriate symbols. The symbols were divided among the parties as follows:

Party	*Symbol*
Nepali Congress	Tree
Gorkha Parishad	Hut
United Democratic party	Three ears of paddy
Paraja Parishad (B. Mishra faction)	Plough
Praja Parishad (Tanka Prasad faction)	Hammer and spade
Communist party	Three maize pods and a sickle
Prajatantrik Mahasabha	Hand
Nepali National Congress	Umbrella
Terai Congress	Man wearing a loincloth, carrying a sickle in his right hand and a load of wheat on his head

The independents were allotted the following symbols: lamp, horse, elephant, water-tap, scale, fish, flower, clock, bird, pitcher, bell, flute, pen, and inkpot.

Each candidate had to deposit a security of 250 rupees (about $35) for the constituency he was contesting. The security deposit was returned to all candidates who polled at least one sixth of the total votes cast in their constituency; those who polled less forfeited their security. The candidates were allowed to spend a maximum of 5,000 rupees (about $700) for their publicity campaigns after filing their nomination papers.[11] They were required to file an account of their election expenses to the Returning Officers of their constituencies within a month of publication of the election results.

The election campaigns of the various parties differed little in the promises and choices offered to the people. Their manifestoes and programs were broadly similar, barring minor differences in emphasis and a few trivial, idiosyncratic ideas of a party leader. The United Democratic party, for example, stressed the banning of religious proselytization and cow slaughter. The two factions of the Praja Parishad carried identical names and more or less similar programs and policies; the Tanka Prasad group, however, emphasized the responsibility of the state to protect the middle class as the potential reservoir of leadership in the country, while the B. Mishra group emphasized the necessity of a constitutional monarchy in which sovereignty was vested in the people. The Terai Congress demanded the formation of a federal union with autonomous political divisions. The Prajatantrik Mahasabha stood for the restoration and preservation of traditional religion. D. R. Regmi's Nepali National Congress gave top priority to the problem of developing the national and regional languages.

There were some significant differences in the emphasis and orientation of the Nepali Congress, the Gorkha Parishad, and the Communist party, as they represented roughly three different and distinct points on the political spectrum. They all, however, supported the establishment of a representative, popular government under the constitutional aegis of the King, abolition of *Birta* land, institution of land reforms, and a foreign policy based on nonalignment with power blocs and friendship with all countries.

The Nepali Congress advocated the establishment of democratic socialism in Nepal through the progressive elimination of the existing feudal land system and a program of rapid industrialization. It stood for abolition of big *Birta* landholdings and landlord intermediaries, and for administrative integration, a ceiling on landholdings, distribution of land to the landless peasants, guarantee of tenancy rights to the cultivators, and nationalization of forests. It pledged to carry out a scientific reorganization of the administrative machinery and the eradication of corruption in the government. Nepali was accepted as the national language, but the necessity of developing other regional languages was also recognized.

The Gorkha Parishad, laying particular emphasis on its patriotic and nationalistic character, promised urgent administrative reforms, development of the Terai areas, and the establishment of an efficient judicial system. It also pledged to carry out agrarian reforms without the socialistic tone of the Nepali Congress and promised to establish a mixed economic system allowing for both private initiative and government enterprises in the industrialization of the country.

The Communist party, while repeating its usual programs for agrarian reforms and the liquidation of the feudal system, had a specific three-point foreign policy based on abrogation of the treaty with Britain authorizing the establishment of Gorkha recruitment centers in Nepal, amendment of the 1950 trade treaty with India, and withdrawal of American "infiltration" in Nepal.

THE RESULTS OF THE GENERAL ELECTIONS

The first nationwide elections in the history of Nepal commenced as scheduled on February 18, 1959, when voters in eighteen constituencies went to the polls. For the most part, the elections were completed by April 3, the original deadline proposed by the Election Commission, although the last result was not declared until May 10.[12] Approximately 42 per cent of the eligible voters in the country exercised their franchise right, with the highest turnout (53 per cent) in Kathmandu city and the lowest in Dailekh in western Nepal.

The election results were disastrous to most of the prominent party leaders. The presidents (general secretary in the case of the Communist party) of all the contending parties, with the single exception of B. P. Koirala of the Nepali Congress, were defeated. Included in this list were most of the politicians who had dominated the poitical scene in Nepal since 1951—K. I. Singh, Tanka Prasad Acharya, Bhadrakali Mishra, Dilli Raman Regmi, Ranadhir Subba, Keshar Jang Rayamajhi, Pushpa Lal Shrestha, Ranga Nath Sharma, and Vedananda Jha. Both D. R. Regmi and Tanka Prasad Acharya forfeited their deposits, as they did not poll even one sixth of the total vote in their constituencies.

By April 3, the pattern of the election results was evident, and the Nepali Congress emerged as the winner of an absolute majority of seats in the House of Representatives. King Mahendra congratulated the Nepali Congress through Suvarna Shamsher, chairman of the Council of Ministers, for its victory in the general elections.[13] The results for the House of Representatives elections are shown in table 10.

THE AFTERMATH OF THE GENERAL ELECTIONS

The results of the 1959 general elections highlighted the emergence of three more or less national parties in the country—the Nepali Congress, the Gorkha Parishad, and the Communist party. The other parties were very nearly decimated. The few

TABLE 10

FINAL RESULTS OF THE 1959 GENERAL ELECTIONS

Party	Seats contested	Seats won	Per cent of total votes cast
Nepali Congress 108		74	38.0
Gorkha Parishad 86		19	17.0
United Democratic party .. 86		5	10.0
Communist party 47		4	7.0
Praja Parishad (Tanka Prasad faction) 46		2	3.0
Praja Parishad (B. Mishra faction) 36		1	3.0
Terai Congress 21		0	2.0
Nepali National Congress .. 20		0	0.7
Prajatantrik Mahasabha 68		0	3.0
Independents 268		4	16.0
Total 786		109	99.7

SOURCE: G. B. Devkota, *Nepal ko Rajnaitik Darpan* [Political Mirror of Nepal] (Kathmandu, 1960), p. 698.

which survived total destruction were reduced to the status of insignificant but cantankerous factions with no distinctive ideologies and programs of their own. But the independents probably suffered the worst defeat of all in proportion to their political ambitions, for only four of the 268 independent candidates managed to win election. This was probably the most surprising aspect of the elections, for it had been expected that a large number of independents would win seats.

It is significant that the three political parties which did comparatively well in the elections had one thing in common—a distinctive and fairly well-articulated ideology, presenting three distinct choices to the voters. The Gorkha Parishad represented the rightist end of the political spectrum; the Nepali Congress, a middle band leaning toward the left; and the Communists, the leftist end of the spectrum. In terms of party organization, the Communist party was the best disciplined, choosing its members in a highly selective fashion only after proper indoctrination and apprenticeship. The Gorkha Parishad was well financed and well organized, but applied only moderate restrictions in selecting members. The Nepali Congress was the most "open" of all parties and included within its rank and file people of diverse backgrounds and interests.

That the public was no longer prepared to accept politics based on personalities was clearly demonstrated by their clear rejection of most leading party politicians. These factional leaders were the by-products of the interim period, and their success in factional politics had resulted in the prolongation of the interim period to some nine years—seven years longer than had been expected. Their parties, with the exception of K. I. Singh's United Democratic party, had meandered through a multitude of tactical alliances and maneuvers; their policies had been guided in the main by expedient *ad hoc* ideologies, a common dislike and fear of the Nepali Congress and a keen desire to capture seats of power in the government.

These factional parties had always been organized around a leading figure and his small coterie of personal followers. When these parties did seek to extend their scope of operations to a national level, the main attractions for the new members were the political ascendancy of the party concerned or the financial munificence of the party leader. But this sudden inflation of the party ranks never seemed very lasting, probably because the leaders often changed policies to suit their own caprices, while the rank and file was seldom consulted about such changes.

Even more disturbing to organizational unity was the curious tendency of the party leaders to engage in bitter personal feuding once their party was dislodged from the government. Their followers, too, were equally uncommitted to the stated policies and programs of their party and often established their own autonomous party units or merged with other parties on the basis of immediate and expedient political advantage. The Praja Parishad, for example, was in power for about seventeen months, during which it managed to establish a skeletal nationwide party organization. Once it had resigned from the government, the party split into two factions and fought the elections as two political groups, with an identical name but separate flags. The results, of course, were disastrous.

A similar process undermined the strength of the United Democratic party, which held office for three months in 1957. While it did not have as long an association with the government as the Praja Parishad, it did have a forceful and resourceful leader in K. I. Singh. However, the dictatorial control of the party apparatus by Singh led to an atrophy of individual initiative and the abandonment of internal democratic processes. The United Democratic party's publicity organ issued enthusiastic reports of party units' being established in remote corners of the country, but the caliber of the personnel manning these units added very little real strength to the party. Even the party father-figure, K. I. Singh, failed to win election to the House of Representatives, being easily defeated by a relatively obscure Nepali Congress candidate.

The most interesting episode of the 1959 general elections was, perhaps, the dismal showing of the fourteen-month-old Prajatantrik Mahasabha, led by Ranga Nath Sharma. Reportedly, it was favored by politically nonalighed conservative elites and was well-financed by Ranas, the sacred elites, and landowners. This new party set up sixty-eight candidates in constituencies all over the country. While this may have been a deceptive token of the party's true strength, it certainly was a clear indication of its enormous financial backing. As it turned out, however, not a single party candidate was able to win at the polls.

The successful conclusion of the 1959 general elections was a remarkable accomplishment on the part of the Election Commission as well as the Nepali government. The fairness and impartiality of the elections was widely acclaimed by the parties and the press. All complaints concerning elections were referred to special election tribunals and were settled on an impartial basis. It is noteworthy, however, that K. I. Singh, Tanka Prasad Acharya, and Ranga Nath Sharma maintained a critical attitude toward the *bona fides* of the Election Commission before, during, and after the elections. K. I. Singh and Ranga Nath Sharma had submitted a memorandum to King Mahendra on February 20, accusing the election officials of partiality toward the Nepali Congress and demanding the dissolution of the coalition Council of Ministers. During the course of elections they alleged that foreign agents and foreign money were being used to manipulate the elections to their disadvantage and to the advantage of the Nepali Congress. On May 14, Tanka Prasad Acharya, K. I. Singh, and Ranga Nath Sharma submitted another memorandum to the King, alleging widespread irregularities and malpractices during the elections and demanding the formation of a special high-powered Royal Commission to investigate these charges.

In reply King Mahendra advised the three complainants to use the available legal facilities for redress of their grievances. Accordingly, K. I. Singh filed a suit in the Supreme Court against the Election Commission, Ministers, and high officials of the government in August, demanding a writ of mandamus from the court declaring the elections illegal and unconstitutional.[14] The court dismissed the case in November, ending K. I. Singh's efforts to denigrate the results of the elections.

The completion of the general elections in the spring of 1959 settled only the composition of the House of Representatives. The composition of the Upper House, or Senate, was determined in July, after the House of Representatives had convened in session. The house elected eighteen Senators on the basis of proportional representation on July 11. Of these, fourteen belonged to the Nepali Congress, two to the Gorkha Parishad, and one each to the Communist party and the United Democratic party. King Mahendra announced the names of eighteen nominated senators on July 13.[15] Thus, both houses of the Parliament as provided for under the 1959 Constitution were functioning by the middle of July, 1959.

Experiment with Parliamentary Democracy
(1959-60)

15

The Elected Nepali Congress Government

MAY 27, 1959, will long be remembered in the history of modern Nepal as the day on which King Mahendra established the last interim government before ushering in a new age of constitutional rule under the Constitution of 1959, thus in a sense marking the culmination of the political process that had begun with the installation of the first Rana–Nepali Congress coalition government on February 18, 1951. The interim period, which was initially expected to last two years at the most, had dragged on for eight years, and had been marked by the rise and fall of ten different regimes. This excessive fluidity in the political process was at once the cause and effect of endemic conflicts among and within the political parties, the exaggerated importance of personalities in determining party policies and programs, a singular lack of accomplishments on the part of the successive interim governments, and, above all, a nationwide sense of political frustration and fatalism.

One hope which helped sustain the fading aspirations of the politically articulate public during the long interim period was the prospect of national elections and the formation of a truly responsible, representative government. There was a broad agreement that only a national election could clear the political scene of unrepresentative political parties, opportunistic interest groups, vociferous patriots, and self-styled saviors. Eight years of political experimentation had given birth to a bewildering variety of political parties, each claiming to be the largest and the most representative, and a new breed of professional politicians

303

whose sole driving ambition was the capture of a ministerial post at any sacrifice of ideology and by any means of expediency. It was mainly owing to these unprincipled political elements that one goal of the 1950 revolution—a democratic Constitution framed by a Constituent Assembly in accordance with the wishes of the people—had become untenable by 1958. The Royal Proclamation of February 1, 1958, in effect laid down the contours of a new pattern of political democracy in Nepal, which, although at variance with the main objective of the 1950 revolution as far as Constitution making was concerned, envisaged a representative government elected by the people and responsible to a bicameral Parliament within the framework of a Constitution approved by the King.

It was in a way fitting that the Nepali Congress, which had spearheaded the 1950 revolution and was part of the first interim government, should have been called upon to terminate the interim period formally. The Nepali Congress had occupied a pivotal position in the political process in Nepal since 1951. Opposition political parties and alliances had grown out of disagreements—mostly personal, but sometimes procedural and ideological—within the ranks of that party. In its nine years of operation within Nepal, the Nepali Congress had survived four major splits and three tactical alliances with other political parties. Its rivals included such diverse elements as the Communists, Rana revivalists, religious conservatives, landowners, monarchists, and its own dissidents.

The relegation of the Nepali Congress to the status of an opposition party in the 1952–58 period had not been entirely its own choice. Ever since July, 1952, when its three representatives had resigned from the Cabinet in compliance with the instructions of the party executive, the Congress had sought to return to office on terms which at times seemed to compromise its stated policies and commitments. In the end, however, it invariably lost out to other political parties on the crucial matter of ministry making.

Thus for seven years the Nepali Congress had been deprived of the opportunity to enlarge its membership and influence by the distribution of political favors and patronage. The party's response to this difficult political situation took the form of an increasing ideological firmness and a gradual attrition of opportunistic followers. At a time when the political process in the country was veering away from the goals of the 1950 revolution, the Nepali Congress consolidated its ideological stance by adopting a strongly future-oriented program of "democratic socialism" and by a reiteration of the demand for a Constituent Assembly.

Despite the vagaries of political fortunes, the Nepali Congress was one of the few parties which succeeded in maintaining a hard-core party leadership and an organizational structure intact throughout the interim period.

The atmosphere in Kathmandu at the time of the inauguration of the elected Nepali Congress government was marked by a sense of relief at the clarification of the previously beclouded political scene, and also by a buoyant feeling of optimism on the future of the government. The success of democracy even in an illiterate and poor country seemed to be assured. Political observers and commentators throughout the world applauded the peaceful behavior of the voters and commended their electoral verdict as a mature political judgment in favor of strong, stable government. Above all, there was the expectation that Nepali politics for the next five years—that is, until the next general elections—would not be a repetition of the zigzag course of the interim period.

It was assumed that the Nepali Congress had learned the qualities of political wisdom and sobriety during its seven years in the political wilderness, and that the party would not abuse or misinterpret the clear-cut mandate it had received in the form of an absolute majority in the House of Representatives. The future of the country as well as that of representative government had been entrusted to the leadership of the Nepali Congress. After eight years of frustration and disillusionment, the leaders of the 1950 revolution were once again restored to power, in order to attain the still largely unfinished goals of that revolution.

B. P. Koirala, in his dual capacity as the president of the Nepali Congress and the first elected Prime Minister, emerged as a leader of national stature. Previously the Crown had been the only symbol—and, since 1951, a powerful instrument—of national unity. Now, B. P. Koirala and the Nepali Congress party provided a new focus of national identification. Although the prestige of the Crown continued undiminished, the new party government was expected to function as a custodian of the people's democratic rights and also as a catalyst for the achievement of prosperity.

B. P. KOIRALA'S POLITICAL BACKGROUND AND IDEOLOGY

From November, 1951, to May, 1959, B. P. Koirala's political career had been confined largely to the task of reorganizing and revitalizing the Nepali Congress. His political role, however, continued to be a crucial one and had considerable impact on the party as well as on the governments that were formed from time to time. He served as the chief spokesman of his party during protracted political negotiations with King Tribhuwan and, later, with King Mahendra. In these negotiations, however, he was consistently unsuccessful in his efforts to win a prominent role in the government for the Nepali Congress. Indeed, it was only when Suvarna Shamsher played the role of the leading party negotiator that the Nepali Congress was finally rewarded with a seat in the coalition Council of Ministers formed in May, 1958.

B. P. Koirala's ineffectiveness in political negotiations with the royal palace did not adversely affect his dominant leadership of the Nepali Congress or his powerful impact on the articulation of the party's socialistic ideology. He continued as president of the party from May, 1952, to January, 1956, and was again elected president at a special conference in May, 1957, when the outgoing president, Suvarna Shamsher, submitted his resignation in order to make room for a "dynamic, powerful and active President, who would handle the Congress election campaign in such a way as to bring [the party] a thumping victory." [1] B. P. Koirala was also responsible for the party's official adoption of democratic socialism as its main ideology at the party conference in January, 1956. He was the main author of the election manifesto on which the party fought and won the general elections of 1959.

B. P. Koirala's political career is really a case history of Nepali politics in the 1950's. More than any other leader, he seemed to typify the spirit of the 1950 revolution through his constant efforts to base the political decision-making process outside the royal palace and on the will of the people. He envisioned the goals of the 1950 revolution far beyond the political exigencies of the time and was constantly reminding his colleagues about the vital necessity of translating these into economic and social realities. To this end he chose the ideology of democratic socialism as his main political faith, although by any practical standards the possible attainment of even an attenuated form of socialism in Nepal was at best hypothetical. B. P. Koirala seemed to emphasize the need for developing an outlook which transcended the frustrations and achievements of the immediate present. Nepali politics, owing to the spectacular success of practical politicians, had become so preoccupied with expedient and immediate goals that the concept of a specific and bright future had ceased to be a motive force. Even the government of Nepal seemed to operate more on a day-to-day basis than on any long-range time perspective. Temporizing had become the most distinctive feature of administrative decision-making, and the maximization of immediate political gains had become the unverbalized but effective ideology of the political elites. In such a context of unenlightened practicality and unethical expediency, B. P. Koirala's future-oriented vision of a socialistic utopia was a sorely needed corrective. Even more creditable is the fact that eight years out of political office seemed not to tarnish his idealistic zeal, and in fact had probably intensified his dedication to a socialist ideology.

In addition to his well-articulated political ideology, B. P. Koirala had personal qualities which separated him from the rest of Nepali politicians. He was, for instance, an internationalist in outlook, and had maintained close contacts with developments in other countries of the world through active membership in the Socialist International. His brand of Nepali nationalism, also, did not conform with that adopted by a vocal ultranationalist school which claimed a special place for Nepal in the world on grounds of artistic, architectural, and intellectual accomplishments in some remote past. He could share but little of such backward-looking nationalistic sentiments. To him Nepal's glory was placed in the realm of the future, rather than in the ruins and remnants of the past. He saw the destiny of Nepal in the larger context of political events happening in the Indian subcontinent and from the perspective of Afro-Asian nationalism on the world stage. Since he was usually alienated from the group of rabid Nepali nationalists, he was at times suspected of being "soft" toward India, and was accused of compromising with Nepali independence and sovereignty. His relationship with India and Indian leaders was certainly deep and varied and often of a personal nature. He had spent the greater part of his childhood and youth in India, and had received his early political training in the Indian independence movement. He had strong personal friendships with Indian socialist leaders—Jaya Prakash Narayan in particular, with whom he had worked together in the 1942 "Quit India" movement. His early political activities in India not only served him as a period of valuable apprenticeship for his later political career in Nepal, but also provided him with models and plans for organizing the Nepali Congress. His socialistic ideals were undoubtedly the products of long years of association with Indian socialist leaders.

B. P. Koirala—unlike his brother, M. P. Koirala—had never served under the Rana civil service or been exposed to the artificial respectability of Nepali Court life. During the century of Rana rule, life at the Court had become encrusted with an elaborate structure of obedient decorum and politeness to the point that even the Nepali language spoken there had become differentiated into several layers of honorific usage. By his upbringing and rebellious youth, B. P. Koirala was a misfit in the complicated and often conspiratorial context of Court life. Although with the end of Rana rule the emphasis on Court etiquette had largely diminished, it was still maintained and cultivated at the palace with all the zeal befitting a restoration of royal prerogatives. In 1951, when B. P. Koirala became the Home Minister in the Rana-Congress interim government, several stories of his violation of Court protocol became current. When he was not selected as a member of the Nepali Congress Cabinet in November, 1951, it was seriously suggested in many quarters that his omission was occasioned by King Tribhuwan's distaste for his impertinent and irreverent personal conduct.

B. P. Koirala's image of himself as a rebel seems to have been shaped quite early in his life. In one of his early writings he pictured himself as a rebel asserting nonconformist behavior even at the moment of his birth—a reference to the fact that his birth had taken place only after a long and painful delivery. Two attributes which helped him sustain his self-image as a rebel were his youthfulness and daring. He was the only Nepali Congress leader operating in India who twice deliberately risked Rana imprisonment. And when the Gorkha Dal fanatics attacked him at his residence in 1951, he is reported to have handled the situation with great composure. Also, during his brief tenure as Home Minister, he had not shirked responsibility for police firings upon public processions if he felt such an action was justified. As a result he earned a good deal of opprobrium from the opposition parties and press as a "fascist" or "dictator," but these public criticisms did not seem to deter him from an intended course of action.

B. P. Koirala was only thirty-one years old when he became a member of the Cabinet in 1951. His youth had a great deal of appeal to young Nepali intellectuals not only in terms of his age, but also in terms of his youthful attitudes. He was reported to have antagonized orthodox Hindus and the conservatives in 1951 by remarking that the Nepali temple deities—according to one estimate there are some three thousand of them in Kathmandu alone—would be better protected if they were removed and housed in a museum. His impatience with the continuing social evils of caste restrictions, parochial feelings, and untouchability and his defiance of them in his personal living made him an appealing protagonist of change to anti-tradition-minded Nepali youth.

Another personal quality which distinguished B. P. Koirala from other political leaders was his remarkable sensitivity to universal human problems. He started on a literary career early in his adolescence, and, indeed, he has an established reputation in Nepali literary circles as an accomplished author of short stories which usually deal with the theme of social deviates who find themselves in conflict with the mores and conventions of society. In these stories he evoked sympathy for his characters by dwelling upon their human foibles and by exposing the relentless and often one-sided nature of social verdicts. His fascination with the dilemma of human existence led him to flirt with a wide range of Western writers, ranging from Freud to Camus.

VIEWS ON SOCIALISM

B. P. Koirala's views on socialism were expressed most frequently in speeches to student groups or party workers. On October 31, 1959, for instance, he spoke to a meeting convened by the Socialist Youth League of Bhaktapur and explained the government's attitudes toward the problem of land reform. He characterized the concentration of ownership of land in the hands of a few as rank injustice and feudal exploitation. As long as land was not in the hands of the tiller, he argued, industrial development was infeasible. He estimated that it would take at least twenty-five years to achieve socialism in Nepal.[2]

On November 7, Koirala addressed a meeting of the Kathmandu District Committee of the Nepali Congress. Discussing the role of the individual in a democratic and socialist society, he argued that individualism could not be tolerated at the expense of democratic and socialistic traditions.[3]

He expressed somewhat different views in a speech to students at the College of Education on December 7, wherein he elaborated his views on socialism in Nepal. On this occasion he declared that Nepal would not accept the principles of socialism at the cost of personal liberty. Socialism was a living doctrine, he argued, which should be suitably adjusted according to the time and the circumstances:

We can view the socialist principles from the standpoint of the countries of the east. The Vedas and the Upanishads speak of equality, fraternity, and service. Buddha propounded the principle of the golden mean. Even today [in India] Acharya Vinoba Bhave and Nehru regard socialism as their basic doctrine and are trying to reconstruct the country on that basis. In Nepal the Nepali Congress is trying to achieve economic equality and freedom on the basis of socialism. The revolution of 1950 put an end to the feudal regime, but the revolution will be successful only after Nepal attains economic freedom . . .[4]

On Semptember 12, 1960, Prime Minister Koirala, addressing a meeting convened by the Nepal Students Union, spoke on Marxism and the twentieth century. He remarked that the ideological rift between the U.S.S.R. and Communist China was an apt reply to those who still held that the Soviet socialism was the only true one. He warned the Communists of Nepal not to seek ideological support from abroad, and to help build socialism in Nepal according to the conditions of the country.[5]

On November 15, 1960, Prime Minister Koirala delivered an address on the role of intellectuals in Nepal to a gathering of students at Darbar College in Kathmandu. He described the contemporary period in the history of Nepal as the crossroads of transition, and an intellectual as one who could correctly and independently grasp the problems of the country. The two most significant problems of the day, he stated, were the abolition of the feudal order and the construction of a new industrial society. Referring to the disturbances in some parts of Nepal, he described them as phenomena not unnatural at a time when the country had reached a crisis on the road to progress. He pleaded for a new outlook in the task of constructing a new society and advised the college students not to be afraid of problems, but to face them bravely.[6]

Prime Minister Koirala's speeches, in his capacity as the unquestioned leader of his party and his government, highlight the ideologies and aspirations motivating the policies and programs of the Nepali Congress government. Even a cursory glance at them reveals that his speeches were imbued with a strong spirit of realism. His frankly political speeches seemed to be heavily weighted in favor of a cautious and deliberate approach to problems, and his references to the so-called socialistic policies of the government seemed to be animated more by a pragmatic awareness of the problems of the country than by any doctrinaire commitent to a partisan ideology.

Another notable characteristic of Koirala's speeches was the strong nationalistic tone of his utterances on the subject of Nepal's relations with the outside world. Clearly, in his mind the continued existence of Nepal's sovereignty and independence depended ultimately on the economic development of the country. But for the immediate present and the near future the only viable course for Nepal's foreign relations was to steer clear of military blocs on the larger world stage and of the Sino-Indian dispute nearer home. There were almost self-conscious attempts on his part on several occasions, particularly in the presence of Chinese or Indian leaders, to reaffirm the fact of Nepal's historical status as an independent and sovereign state.

A third characteristic of Koirala's speeches is their nonpolemical character. For a man who had spent his political career fighting political opponents of one kind or another, B. P. Koirala displayed a remarkable tolerance after assuming the reins of the government. At times he even went out of his way to persuade the opposition to lend coöperation to the government when a "national issue," such as economic development, was involved; evidently he considered the game of opposition politics too costly a political luxury in a country whose major national problem was the elimination of poverty and hunger.

If one were to criticize his speeches from any perspective, it would not be from the viewpoint of content, but by such criteria as political appropriateness or expediency. In the few months before the dismissal of his government, there were numerous indications that his real political opponents—not the political parties, but the landlords and other vested interests—were mortally frightened of the "socialistic" character of the government. Their apprehensions had led to disturbances in West No. 1, demonstrations in Kathmandu, appeals to the King, and accusations against the government. This situation was allowed to continue much longer than the circumstances warranted. The disturbances in West No. 1, for example, were permitted to simmer for some ten months, and meanwhile Ministers of the government, including the Prime Minister, were not spared public insults by demonstrators in the streets of Kathmandu and at the gates of the royal palace. During this critical period the Prime Minister's speeches, far from laying out a strong policy for restoring law and order in the disturbed areas, almost created an expectancy of inevitable disorder based on reasons of historical and dialectical necessity. His intellectual dissections of real problems in terms of Marxian history and economics before student audiences created an illusion that reports of lawlessness here and there were symbolic labor pangs of a new social order that was beginning to emerge on the horizon. Such an approach did not help to allay the prevailing fear and panic in the minds of the public. Moreover, the Prime Minister's ideological discourses during this period gave an unreal sense of strength and stability to the government, discouraged his colleagues from taking precautionary measures, and perhaps helped to engender a feeling of imminent threat in the minds of political opponents, who were biding their time to overthrow the Nepali Congress-dominated parliamentary democracy.

THE NEPALI CONGRESS GOVERNMENT

On May 27, 1959, when King Mahendra announced the establishment of the last interim government and the first elected government, B. P. Koirala was cast in the fateful role of the leader of that government. Although his elevation to the office of Prime Minister had been effected by an impressive victory at the polls, he was confronted in 1959 by a political situation much different from that he had faced in February, 1951. On the whole he was placed in a far less strategic role. In 1951, he was the victorious leader of an armed revolution, and there was the expectation that future governments would be based on the sovereignty of the popular will. By 1959 all that had changed. According to the 1959 Constitution the Crown was the sovereign entity from whence all executive, judicial, and legislative authority emanated. The Constitution had been ordained and granted by the King, the underlying assumption being that the popular will should assert itself only to the extent approved and authorized by the Crown, which remained the final authority to sanction or veto the actions of the government and the Parliament. The goals of 1950 had been aborted without even an attempt at their implementation. By 1959 those goals had been transformed into running an administration which for its survival would have to please two masters at the same time—namely, the electorate and the Crown. These two masters represented different, and under the peculiar circumstances of Nepali politics, contradictory forces; of the two, the Crown held final authority. After nine years of fruitless political experimentation, the electorate had expressed its approval of major changes in the *status quo* by electing a majority of Nepali Congress candidates. On the other hand, the Crown as a symbol of continuity and stability was cast in the role of a protagonist of the *status quo*. Moreover, the international situation had changed vastly since 1951. Nepal had now acquired a new role in world affairs as a member of the United Nations and a host of other international agencies and by an increasing diversification of her diplomatic relations. More directly, Nepal's location between increasingly antagonistic and powerful neighbors had exposed it to the possibility of armed conflict in a part of the world which had been traditionally hailed by poets and seers as a land of peace and tranquility. Relations between India and China were fast deteriorating, and the Chinese had cruelly suppressed the Tibetan demand for regional autonomy. The head of the Tibetan government, the Dalai Lama, had escaped from Lhasa in the wake of the Chinese repression and had sought political asylum in India. The critical problem for B. P. Koirala's new government was to evolve a balanced foreign policy which would alarm neither of her aroused neighbors.

The new Cabinet announced by King Mahendra on May 27 —by far the largest Cabinet established in nine years of political experimentation—included eight Ministers and eleven Deputy Ministers. It provided representation to most of the well-known Nepali Congress leaders and also broad regional representation to most ethnic groups in Nepal. For the first time, as a Deputy Minister, a woman, Dwarika Devi Thakurani, was appointed to the Cabinet. The personnel of the Cabinet and the division of portfolios as of May 28 are listed in table 11.

Five of the nineteen ministers had been members of previous Cabinets; the rest were recruited from the Nepali Congress rank and file. A common characteristic was their youth and enthusiasm. Soon after being sworn in, one Minister appeared on the street in Kathmandu without the military escort usually assigned to members of the Cabinet. To reinforce further this impression of difference and newness, and in part to justify the size of the Cabinet, the new Ministers voluntarily accepted a substantial cut in salary.

There was a reshuffle of portfolios when the new Constitution went into effect on June 30 and the Cabinet was transformed into a constitutional government. Three of the Deputy Ministers —Tulsi Giri, Suryanath Das Yadav, and Prem Raj Angdambe— were promoted to the rank of Cabinet Ministers. B. P. Koirala surrendered the Foreign Affairs portfolio to Tulsi Giri, and Surya Prasad Upadhaya gave Parliamentary Affairs to Suryanath Das Yadav. In the middle of July, B. P. Koirala repossessed the Foreign Affairs portfolio, and a new portfolio of Village Development was created for Tulsi Giri. On July 30, Prime Minister Koirala swore in Hora Prasad Joshi and Dr. Triveni Prasad Pradhan, both members of the Senate, as Assistant Ministers. There were no further Cabinet changes until September 15, 1960, when Assistant Minister Triveni Prasad was promoted to Minister to fill the vacancy caused by Tulsi Giri's resignation. At the same time, a new Assistant Minister, D. K. Sahi, joined the Cabinet.

While the Koirala Cabinet was the first truly homogeneous

TABLE 11

THE NEPALI CONGRESS GOVERNMENT, 1959

Name	Rank	Portfolio
B. P. Koirala	Prime Minister	Defence; Foreign Affairs
Suvarna Shamsher	Deputy Prime Minister	Finance; Planning and Development
Ganesh Man Singh	Minister	Transport and Communications; Land Reforms, Irrigation; Power and Public Works
S. P. Upadhyaya	Minister	Home; Law and Parliamentary Affairs
Ram Narayan Mishra	Minister	Industries and Commerce, Civil Supplies
Kashi Nath Gautam	Minister	Health and Local Self-Government
Parashu Narayan Chaudhari	Minister	Education
Shiva Raj Pant	Minister	Forests, Agriculture and Food
Dr. Tulsi Giri	Deputy Minister	Foreign Affairs
Mina Bahadur Gurung	Deputy Minister	Defence
Prem Raj Angdambe	Deputy Minister	Home
Suryanath Das Yadav	Deputy Minister	Law and Parliamentary Affairs
Shiva Pratap Shah	Deputy Minister	Finance; Planning and Development
Dwarika Devi Thakurani	Deputy Minister	Health and Local Self-Government
Yogendra Man Sherchan	Deputy Minister	Communications
Lalit Chand	Deputy Minister	Power and Public Works; Irrigation
Dewan Singh Rai	Deputy Minister	Forests, Agriculture and Food
Jaman Singh Gurung	Deputy Minister	Land Reforms
Neb Bahadur Malla	Deputy Minister	Education

government Nepal had had since 1951, it was not, of course, entirely free of internal dissension. In the working of any Cabinet, as a top decision-making body, some amount of tension and strain is perhaps functional and inevitable. In the case of the

Koirala Cabinet there were two situations which were often cited as reflecting lack of accord among the members. For one, there were persistent press rumors, circulated before or during any major administrative reorganization, hinting at a split into B. P. Koirala and S. P. Upadhyaya factions over the matter of appointments and promotions. The latter was often alleged to have personal ambitions, while B. P. Koirala was described as an idealistic hero trying to curb the rising passions of nepotism and favoritism among his colleagues. These rumors were probably wildly exaggerated in many cases, but were sustained by the common assumption that anyone in the government must necessarily be corrupt. Such was the legacy left behind by a century of Rana rule, and not much had happened in the past nine years to alter this impression.

The other instance of lack of accord was far more patent. It had to do with the role of Tulsi Giri as a member of the Cabinet. Giri was a problem child, alternately pampered and snubbed by his colleagues. The press was full of reports of his apathy and at times even hostility toward the programs of the government, but it was not until August 1960 that Giri finally resigned. How much of this indulgence was owing to B. P. Koirala's personal feelings toward him is a matter for conjecture. Koirala had first brought Giri to public attention by appointing him as one of the general secretaries of the Nepali Congress in 1957, and he may have been loath to see him leave the Cabinet. With all his partiality for youthfulness and new talent, B. P. Koirala must have seen in Giri a political leader of some promise.

Once Giri had dissociated himself from the Cabinet, he expressed increasingly vocal opposition to the Koirala government. On November 24 and 27, 1960, he accused the government of failing to fulfill its election pledges and thereby of forfeiting the people's trust. Specifically, he took issue with the statements of Prime Minister B. P. Koirala. Wherever the latter noted hope and progress, Giri was quick to perceive failure and stagnation. This recriminatory practice continued until the very week the Koirala government was overthrown by the King. On December 5, Prime Minister Koirala had addressed a press conference in Kathmandu, outlining the progressive steps undertaken by his government. Three days later Tulsi Giri issued a point-by-point refutation of the Prime Minister's statement.[7] On December 15, B. P. Koirala and his other Cabinet colleagues found themselves behind bars; on December 26, Tulsi Giri joined King Mahendra's Council of Ministers as one of its leading members.

On the whole, however, the Koirala Cabinet functioned

smoothly during its term in office. Between most members of the Cabinet, no serious acrimony was reported—a startling departure from the tradition of inter-Cabinet wrangles. Two factors probably explain this unprecedented stability. First and foremost was the element of personal leadership exercised by B. P. Koirala both within and outside the Cabinet. His control of the party, along with the accountability of individual members of the Cabinet to the party executive, helped to preserve balance and harmony in the highest executive organ of the government. Second, with the inauguration of an elected government, individual Cabinet members, unlike their predecessors, were no longer required to play the game of endearing themselves to the royal palace as their top-priority activity. Now they could focus their energy and talents exclusively on their work at the government Secretariat. For the first time in ten years of democratic experimentation, Cabinet Ministers had to concern themselves with their duties as administrators and formulators of government policies rather than with the process of political stabilization and survival. A new administrative practice followed by B. P. Koirala also helped discourage his colleagues from seeking favors at the royal palace. According to the new procedure, only the Prime Minister saw the King regularly on behalf of his Cabinet, and individual Cabinet members were not required to see the King regularly unless the latter expressly asked to meet any or all of them. As a result, the Koirala Cabinet functioned with considerable efficiency and harmony, without the open challenges to the leadership of the Prime Minister that had been endemic in most post-1951 governments.

16

Party Politics Under the Nepali Congress Government

THE ESTABLISHMENT of an elected government and the inauguration of a representative legislature did not result in a significant
change in the tactics of oppositional politics in Nepal. Responsible criticism of the government on the floor of the Parliament
was the exception rather than the rule, and outside its halls the
main challenge to the government came in the form of direct
public agitation under the auspices of opposition parties and
groups, the customary role of the political opposition in post-Rana
Nepal.

There were several reasons for the failure of the opposition to
devise new techniques. The novelty of the parliamentary democratic experiment did not elicit the necessary emotional and
attitudinal responses from the participants. Members of the
government benches as well as the opposition needed a period of
reëducation before adjustment to the new scheme of things could
be expected. Moreover, the widespread demand for rapid economic development did not presage the best psychological climate
for the smooth functioning of parliamentary democracy. Deliberation and caution, inherent facets of a parliamentary system, were
bound to irk both the government and the opposition. Furthermore, the absolute majority held in the Parliament by the Nepali
Congress instilled a sense of fatalistic desperation in the ranks of
its opponents, which assumed that the ruling party could and
would pursue its policies with dictatorial ruthlessness no matter
how responsible and constructive a role they played. The opposition members seemed to operate on the principle that since they

could not present a political alternative to the Nepali Congress through parliamentary techniques, their best strategy was to resort to direct public agitation against the government. By doing so, however, they were prejudicing the interests of parliamentary democracy and indirectly appealing to the King to exercise his wide discretionary powers under the Constitution.

Thus the elected Nepali Congress government faced its stiffest opposition from outside the Parliament. Tanka Prasad Acharya's faction of the Praja Parishad, the United Democratic party, and the Prajatantrik Mahasabha formed a direct action group called the National Democratic Front as early as June 1, 1959, with the avowed aim of arousing public opposition to the Nepali Congress government through extraparliamentary methods. In addition, there were *ad hoc* opposition groups formed from time to time to challenge the government on specific policies and programs. Most notable were the groups of landlords and merchants who were aroused by the new taxation and land reform measures, and who appealed to the King directly to redress their grievances. Their method of opposition was not only extraparliamentary, but was very strongly opposed to the concept of a parliamentary system.

It is interesting to compare the state of the opposition in 1959 with its status in 1951. There are some obvious similarities between the two periods, since the Nepali Congress occupied a dominant position in the political scene on both occasions. In 1951, the Congress had literally shot its way to office, while in 1959 it had won power through a spectacular victory at the polls. There was the same fervor and enthusiasm within the Nepali Congress for the new political order, although in 1959 the degree of enthusiasm may have been somewhat diluted by the experience of nine years of political frustration. Even more familar in 1959 was the disorganized state of the opposition. In 1959, as in 1951, some of the most active political leaders were once again out in the streets trying to muster whatever forces they could to oppose the new regime. The only significant differences were the emergence of a parliamentary opposition and a change in the political role of the students and youth.

Students, particularly in Kathmandu Valley, had played a key role in opposition politics throughout the period. In 1951 they presented the most active, articulate, and organized opposition to the government in power, and their support was solicited by almost all opposition political parties. Eight years later, the role of the students had changed considerably. Although students continued to be the most committed proponents of change, their organizations had been fragmented into various subgroups with conflicting ideologies and had been transformed into appendages of political parties. Moreover, their political effectiveness had been diminished by the new process of political change via the ballot box. Thus, in 1959, when the Nepali Congress formed its first elected government, it did not have to reckon with the opposition of students as a factor of consequence.

On the issue of nationalism, however, the students, irrespective of their party affiliations, continued to occupy a leading role, furnishing much of the noise and heat in the Kathmandu agitations against the Gandak agreement with India and the Chinese claims to Mount Everest. Otherwise, by and large, the students functioned as students, demanding the right to receive an education, seeking impartial selection of trainees for foreign scholarships, and sending delegates to youth festivals and forums abroad. By 1959 most of the students had determined their political loyalties, and there was a fairly clear-cut polarization of their sympathies. Some aligned themselves with the Communist party, others with the Nepali Congress, while others maintained an "independent" status. The Nepali Congress, profiting from its experience in 1951 and thereafter when it had neglected the students, organized its own auxiliary youth organization, the Nepal Tarun Dal ("Nepal Youth Corps"), on a country-wide basis and even helped it establish affiliations with socialist youth groups abroad. The Tarun Dal functioned less as a political organization and more as a rallying point for Nepali youths in support of the goal of a socialistic society. It is noteworthy that on December 15, 1960, when B. P. Koirala and his colleagues were arrested, they were attending the opening session of an all-Nepal youth rally under the auspices of the Tarun Dal. One remarkable aspect of this gathering of Nepali youths was their failure to seek King Mahendra's participation in any form, since it was the traditional practice that the King should patronize or inaugurate any significant social event of a comparable size in Kathmandu.

The political issues that animated the opposition in 1959–60 were both numerous and diverse, though obviously not of equal importance and intensity. While some of these were genuine instances of public protest, most of them were contrived and dramatized by interested political parties. Perhaps, the most emotionally charged issues were those involving any threat, real or imaginary, to the territorial integrity, independence, and sovereignty of Nepal. These were the Gandak River agreement with India, attributions of Indian influence on Nepal's foreign policy, and Chinese incursions into and designs on Nepali territory. Less important were the reported attempts by Indian or Chinese agents to promote pro-India or pro-China propaganda in the southern or northern border areas.

The economic issues raised by the opposition centered around the government's budget proposals and taxation policies, perhaps the area of most substantive disagreement between the government and its critics. Responsible opposition on these questions was provided by the opposition in the Parliament, but agitation in the streets and villages, sponsored by injured vested interests, and sometimes provoking retaliatory agitation from other political parties, was also widespread. Disturbances in West No. 1, Gorkha, and Dang were mainly inspired by the economic aspects of the questions at issue, although when the situation disintegrated in West No. 1 and later in Gorkha, the economic implications were quickly forgotten or suppressed, and the conflict turned into a straight fight against governmental "tyranny."

On administrative issues, the opposition concentrated its fire on the alleged "Congressization" of the administrative machinery both at the center and in the districts. It was charged that favoritism and party bossism were practiced in the appointment of officials in the Secretariat and of Bada Hakims in the districts, and that the Public Service Commission was not allowed to function effectively on questions of administrative recruitment. Perhaps the most sinister move of the government from the opposition parties' viewpoint was the appointment of local Nepali Congress leaders and workers as District Development Officers. The officials in this new cadre were entitled to special treatment since they were not subject to the usual administrative rules. They could function in a more or less semiofficial capacity, with authority to spend government funds on local development projects without close government supervision and without completely losing their party identification. The opposition also charged that the Nepali Congress had recruited new panchayat officers from the party rank and file, and it was insinuated that this was part of the Nepali Congress' plan to establish a permanent dominance in the local councils of the villages.

The principal issues raised by the opposition parties were: imbalance in the government's foreign policy; the need for an effective opposition party; demand for the use of royal discretionary powers to curb the alleged excesses of the government; the alleged criticisms of the Constitution by B. P. Koirala; the tension between nominated Senators' displeasure and the government; and interpretation of King Mahendra's only partly disguised warnings to the government as a formal censure of the government. There were also some strictly local and parochial issues indicative of little or no political import other than the momentary irritation of the local populace under constant prodding from interested political parties. And there was the spurious issue, contrived skillfully by the Communist party, of the government's decision to import vegetable oil. This policy was opposed on the grounds that imported Indian vegetable oil would injure the health of the people and destroy the domestic ghee (clarified butter) industry.

Finally, there was the all-encompassing, highly emotional issue of corruption, suspected or real, at all levels of the government. Whenever opposition politicians ran out of substantive issues, they would fall back on allegations of "corrupt conduct" by Ministers or their subordinates. This had become more or less standard practice in oppositional politics since 1951. Undoubtedly, some corruption existed under the Nepali Congress government as it had under all previous governments. Even the Prime Minister seemed to be seriously concerned with reports of corruption at the level of district administration. Opposition political leaders under the leadership of K. I. Singh sought to make capital out of the prevailing political mood by establishing an unofficial "anti-corruption committee" to "expose the extent of corruption practiced by the government."

Corruption as an issue in Nepali politics is of such a complex sociopsychological nature that it will be misleading to equate it with its literal meaning. If corruption denotes distribution of favors by persons in power, then it was the political way of life in Nepal long before democratic experimentation was introduced in 1951. The Rana administration was then nothing more than a colossal network of corruption practiced for the benefit of a particular family and at the expense of the people. The Nepali Court system—*Bharadari,* as it was called—had long been sustained and perpetuated by hopes of enlarging the share of individual courtiers in the revenues of the government. And the concomitant social order, based on *Birta* landholdings, private armies, and forced labor, was merely a ramification of the "corrupt" political system which had been in existence for centuries. Even the social life and the family structure of the Nepalese were not immune from the effects of institutionalized "corruption." Seeking favors from persons of position and influence, for example, was accepted as necessary for social and occupational advancement; persons of position and influence were required by the ethics of familial or caste obligations to help their kinsmen and dependents in obtaining employment or influence in the government. The results of this system of recruitment and promotion were readily visible in the composition of some of the branches of civil service which the Ranas had opened to non-Rana elements. Members of the Munshi family (Pradhan Newars of Kathmandu), for instance, had staffed the Foreign Office of the government so long that it was commonly known as a monopoly of the Munshi family. Similarly, the influential families of the Manis and the Raj Gurujus had held an absolute monopoly of certain other government offices under the Ranas.

With the collapse of the Rana regime, the administrative framework nurtured and promoted by the Ranas continued, but the criteria for evaluating "corruption" underwent a radical change, almost beyond recognition. A new ideology of public administration came into being. Its two fundamental propositions were: (1) the government must conduct itself as a servant of the people rather than as their master, and (2) members of the government, at all levels, must not practice favoritism in any form. The situation would have been improved somewhat if institutions for exercising control or supervision had existed. A Public Service Commission was established in 1951, but it never attained a strong influence over the government apparatus. The first year of democratic experimentation was a period of crisis and emergency, and a stable administrative structure could hardly have emerged in such circumstances. There was, thus, a general weakening of the "corrupt" administrative machinery inherited from the Ranas and at the same time the emergence of extremely puritanical criteria for evaluating the government on the part of the people. The upshot of such a paradoxical situation was that "corruption" became the most readily available weapon of the opposition against any government in power.

In the years following the revolution, reforms of the administrative machinery were introduced occasionally, mostly on an *ad hoc* basis. In 1956, the Tanka Prasad regime initiated the first systematic program to reorganize the administrative apparatus through the codification of civil service rules. The Nepali Congress renewed these efforts on assuming office in 1959 by formulating civil service regulations specifying conditions of tenure and promotion. Corruption was also curbed under the Nepali Congress by the presence of a vigilant opposition in the Parliament eager to bring examples of governmental corruption to public attention, and by the government's own realization that it would have to face the electorate again in 1964 for a renewal of its political mandate. The net result was a progressive narrowing of the scope and volume of corruption within the government, though certainly not its elimination.

THE NATIONAL DEMOCRATIC FRONT

On June 1, 1959, the presidents of the Nepal Praja Parishad, the United Democratic party, and the Prajatantrik Mahasabha announced the formation of a National Democratic Front to "fill in the gap of opposition both inside and outside the Parliament." [1] These leaders—all of whom had been defeated in the elections—contended that the Gorkha Parishad, the largest opposition party in Parliament, could not serve as a genuine opposition because of its reactionary leadership. It was asserted that the Front would not merely provide opposition through constitutional processes, but would also take steps to arouse sentiments of nationalism and democracy in the country.

The National United Front did not seek an alignment with other opposition groups, such as the Communists or the Gorkha Parishad, either within the Parliament, where it had five members, or outside, with the single exception of the addition of the miniscule Rashtriya Janata party of Purna Prasad "Brahman." The presidency of the Front was to rotate among the three presidents of the constituent parties every four months. Tanka Prasad Acharya was elected as the first president on June 6. In his presidential speech he suggested that a merger of the three parties would have been better than the formation of a Front. Confiding to his audience that this could not have been achieved under existing circumstances, he expressed the hope that the Front would function like a homogeneous party and lead eventually to a merger. Tanka Prasad then described the Nepali Congress government as the work of those elements who "by hook or by crook" wanted to "maintain their autocracy with the help of foreign elements." [2]

Thus, it was clear from the very beginning that the leaders of the Front would take a fiercely nationalistic stand in criticizing the Nepali Congress government. Their recourse to nationalism as a political issue was both a recognition of the lack of more substantive issues and an attempt to rationalize their own ignominious defeats in the elections. Earlier, in May, K. I. Singh, one of the three principal leaders of the Front, charged the Nepali Congress with receiving ten million rupees from a foreign power to insure its victory at the polls, committing itself to acceptance of a foreign military base, and being opposed to the continuation of the monarchy.[3] On May 10, when he was summoned by the Kathmandu magistrate to elaborate on his accusations, he refused to disclose the identity of the foreign power.

On June 6, the National Democratic Front issued a statement which listed the following objectives:

Preservation and furtherance of nationalism, and opposition to any internal or external attacks upon it

Popularization of democratic and social-justice principles

Neutrality

Popularization of the ideals of friendly relations with other countries on the basis of equality and mutual benefit

Struggle against bribery, mismanagement, and exploitation practiced by the government

Independence of the judiciary [4]

The first political campaign of the Front was connected with Nehru's visit to Nepal in the middle of June. The Front strongly criticized the joint communiqué issued by the two Prime Ministers which stated that their governments had an "identity of views" on national and international matters. This was interpreted as an abandonment of Nepal's neutral foreign policy and as proof that Nepal had become a satellite of India. The Front also criticized Nehru's skeptical comments on Panch Shila (or five principles of peaceful co-existence, which were first enunciated in the preamble to the Sino-Indian Treaty of April 29, 1954. The principles are: noninterference in each other's internal affairs; mutual respect for each other's territorial integrity and sovereignty; practice of non-aggression toward each other; mutual relations based on equality; pursuit of mutual benefits) which it claimed threatened the prospects of equal and honorable friendship between the two countries.[5] The Front vehemently attacked the Indian proposals for an agreement on the Gandak project, and demanded that the Nepal government reject treaties of this type with any foreign government as being detrimental to the sovereignty of Nepal. India was advised to implement the project on her own territory if she did not want to embitter relations with Nepal. The Front also seized the opportunity to attack the 1950 Indo-Nepali trade treaty, which it claimed had turned Nepal into a monopoly market for India. The early revision of the treaty in conformity with Nepal's sovereign rights to conduct foreign trade in her own best interests was demanded. Further, the Front demanded the removal of Indian commercial attachés from several towns in Nepal and the withdrawal of Indian personnel from the checkposts on the northern borders of the country. Finally, the Front called upon the government to take immediate steps to demarcate the Sino-Nepali borders.[6]

On July 12, at a public meeting in Kathmandu, the leaders of the National Democratic Front denied that they had organized merely to oppose Indian influence in Nepal. Speaker after speaker, however, castigated the Nepali Congress and its leaders as tools of Indian imperialism. The policy of the Nehru government toward Nepal was questioned, and demands were voiced opposing the Gandak project and calling for amendments in the Indo-Nepali trade treaty. The people were warned against meddling by Indian embassy officials in the politics of the country, and the Nepali government was again asked to remove Indian commercial attachés from interior towns and Indian military personnel from checkposts along the northern border.[7]

The general council of the Front met in the last week of September to consider the question of merger of the constituent parties, but no positive steps were taken in this direction. The meeting took note of the current public agitation launched by the Communists against the government's policy on the import of vegetable-oil ghee from India, and supported the Communist position.

The Nepali Congress government signed the Gandak agreement with India on December 4, over the opposition of the National Democratic Front. Tanka Prasad Acharya accused the Nepali Congress of subservience to India, and predicted that the Nepali Congress government, if allowed to continue in office, would hand over "all our streams and rivers and the areas around them to others."[8] The Front organized a protest demonstration against the agreement on December 20 and later the same day held a public meeting to present its points of view. All the speakers criticized the government for signing the agreement and suggested as an alternative that the Nepal government should seek funds from other, richer countries and build the project itself. K. I. Singh went a step further than all other speakers and threatened to file suit against the Nehru government in the International Court of Justice for seizing territories of a foreign country.[9]

Tanka Prasad Acharya made a statement to the press on February 9, 1960, criticizing the joint communiqué issued by Nehru and B. P. Koirala during the latter's visit to India, and charging that the Nepali Prime Minister had completely merged Nepali interests with those of India on matters relating to foreign, defense, and financial policies. He accused the government of India of deliberate designs against Nepal's independence and sovereignty, and referred to his experiences in trying to revise the

Indo-Nepali trade treaty when he was in office as Prime Minister to substantiate the charge. The Indian draft of the revised treaty, he alleged, had removed Indian custom restrictions over Nepali imports to and exports from other foreign coutries, but on "the condition that permission from India was required for the import of goods into Nepal." Indian aid programs also came in for their share of criticisms. Tanka Prasad characterized his experiences with such programs as consisting of, "mainly, lengthy accounts of expenditure without regard for the amount of actual work, and blaming Nepali officials for all kinds of failures." He demanded that the Nepali Congress government establish friendship with India strictly on the basis of Panch Shila to protect Nepal's rights of self-determination. Finally, he warned against the infiltration of Indian antinational elements in the Terai areas as "doctors, vaidyas [native phyiscians who practice Ayurvedic medicine] and teachers." Their main objective, he claimed, was merely to earn money, distort the nationalistic feelings of the Nepali people, and propagate the views of the Nepali Congress.[10]

By April, Ranga Nath Sharma had become president of the Front. In one of his first statements, the new president condemned B. P. Koirala and his government for alleged acts of omission and commission. The most serious allegation was leveled at the government's foreign policy, which he said was unable to act independently of India with regard to Nepal's relations with China. Hinting at Koirala's submission to Indian dictation, Ranga Nath asked why the Prime Minister had not signed a treaty with China in Peking during his recent trips as, he claimed, was proposed by the Chinese Premier.[11]

But the Front's anti-India stance was based more on the requirements of political expediency within Nepal than on the ideological considerations implicit in the Sino-Indian dispute, as became evident during the spring when the Chinese claim to Mount Everest and the border firing incident in Mustang aroused public sentiment against China. Characterizing these development as affronts to Nepal's sovereignty, the Front demanded the immediate resignation of the Nepali Congress government on the grounds that it was "compromising with the territorial integrity of Nepal by handing over Gandak to India and a large slice of Mustang to China." [12]

Growing dissension among the leaders and constituent units of the Front became increasingly apparent in the fall of 1960, reflecting in part new political alignments among opposition groups not included in the Front. The Gorkha firing incident in October served to rally the fast-disintegrating Front momentarily as each of its component units strove to gain an advantage from this situation. But the Front was steadily being pulled in different directions by its leaders and in particular by K. I. Singh, who reportedly was demanding the formation of a new party under his personal leadership. Singh was also reported to favor the launching of a nationwide movement against the government in December.[13] Although the other opposition leaders may have supported the proposal for a new party, they were not ready to accept Singh as its head, and presumably it was over this difference that Singh severed relations with the Front. Negotiations between the other constituent parties then rapidly diminished.

The National Democratic Front never amounted to much as an opposition group. The lack of unity among the constituent parties and the constant maneuvering for preëminence by Tanka Prasad and K. I. Singh—both of whom had been Prime Ministers —constantly obstructed coöperation between the leaders. The Front never grew into an independent popular movement, and served more as a tactical alliance of three profoundly discontented leaders who relied on personal qualifications rather than popular support in their attempts to oust the Nepali Congress government.

THE GORKHA PARISHAD

As the largest non-government party in the Parliament, the Gorkha Parishad dominated the parliamentary opposition. Bharat Shamsher was officially recognized as the leader of the opposition in June, 1960, and was accorded ministerial privileges and rank.* This was one of the factors, presumably, that led the Gorkha Parishad to abandon its previous direct-action tactics and confine itself to opposition to the government within Parliament. Even when disturbances broke out in West No. 1, a center of Gorkha Parishad strength, the party did not seem to participate in the local agitation with its customary zeal. Indeed, the local Gorkha Parishad leaders seem to have acted in response to the initiative of local Nepali Congress leaders.

There was, furthermore, a remarkable and totally unexpected reversal in the party's foreign policy position. The Gorkha Parishad, organized and nurtured as the party of militant Gorkha nationalism, had viewed the Nepali Congress as the stooges of Indian imperialism and India as a threat to the sovereignty and

---

* Up to this time, Bharat had only been the deputy leader of his party in Parliament, serving under his father, Mrigendra Shamsher.

independence of Nepal. It was, therefore, a shock to both his opponents and his followers when, on January 17, 1960, Bharat Shamsher suddenly proposed that Nepal and India initiate talks on a defense pact. He charged that Chinese incursions into Nepali territory in the Lipu area in Baitadi District, the territory north of Olanchok Gola in eastern Nepal, and the Limi area of Jumla District constituted aggression against Nepal. Although government spokesmen were quick to deny the accuracy of his charges, this statement did dramatize the potential threat of the Chinese build-up in Tibet to Nepal's largely unprotected northern border. On January 22, he demanded the formation of an all-party fact-finding commission, "parliamentary or otherwise," to investigate Chinese incursions into Nepal.[14]

On February 28, Bharat Shamsher submitted a memorandum to Prime Minister Koirala giving further details of Chinese incursions into Nepali territory in West No. 1 and at Namche Bazar in East No. 3.[15] In Parliament a few weeks later, he demanded that Nepal's absolute authority over Mount Everest be made emphatically clear to the Chinese, and also pleaded for a closer alignment of Nepal's foreign policy with that of India. In support of this stand, the Gorkha Parishad strongly endorsed the public demonstration held in Kathmandu on April 21, opposing the Chinese claim to Mount Everest. The Mustang border firing incident in June, according to Bharat Shamsher, was a "calculated move" by China against Nepal's sovereignty.[16] In some respects this incident added to the Gorkha Parishad leader's political stature. His January statements, which had been strongly criticized as alarmist by his political opponents, now seemed to be vindicated, and his plan for a stronger coördination of Indian and Nepali defense policies to be more reasonable. On August 3, the Gorkha Parishad demanded a "national" government because of what it termed the "failure of the Nepali Congress government in its foreign policy." [17] Presumably this was the opening maneuver in a campaign to win a Cabinet seat for its parliamentary leader.

It would seem, indeed, that by the latter half of 1960 the Gorkha Parishad, under the leadership of Bharat Shamsher, was following a policy of only nominal opposition to the government. Having been ostracized by the National Democratic Front and the Communist party, it may even have been considering an alignment with the Nepali Congress, with which it had at least a tacit agreement on foreign policy. In September, the Gorkha Parishad formed an alliance with D. R. Regmi's Nepali National Congress and Bhadrakali Mishra's wing of the Praja Parishad—probably in a tactical move to improve the party's bargaining position with the Congress or with other opposition parties and to prevent its total isolation in the political spectrum.

Bharat Shamsher's policy of moderate opposition to the Nepali Congress government was not acceptable to his party's militant wing, led by Bhuwan Bahadur Karki. Reports of a split in the Gorkha Parishad were current in October. Bharat Shamsher's refusal to join in the chorus of condemnation of the government on the Gorkha firing incident led B. B. Karki to berate him for his "pro-government" position.[18]

It is probable that the Gorkha incident was deeply disturbing to Bharat Shamsher and that he realized the dangers involved in violent opposition to the government at a time when developments in the Himalayas menaced the very existence of Nepal. In the month preceding the dismissal of the Nepali Congress government, when all opposition parties were taking advantage of the local agitation sponsored by anti-taxation groups, the Gorkha Parishad adopted a more or less neutral attitude. This led to a rift between Bharat Shamsher and his father, who was strongly critical of the Nepali Congress, and to the further reports of a split in the party that were circulating in the capital just two days before the Nepali Congress government was dismissed by King Mahendra.[19]

By the role it played, the Gorkha Parishad contributed to the development of parliamentary traditions and the functioning of the Parliament. Because of the party's preoccupation with parliamentary affairs, however, it was singularly ineffective in influencing the political situation in Kathmandu. As a party, the Gorkha Parishad left the entire field of public agitation and opposition to the Communists and the National Democratic Front, both of which in different ways were basically opposed to democratic traditions. However impressive the performance of the party spokesmen may have been within Parliament—where Mrigendra Shamsher demonstrated forensic skills in criticizing the government and Bharat Shamsher sounded the alarm on the threat from the north—they failed to inculcate a spirit of democratic opposition outside and were unable to enlist the support of the Nepali public for themselves or their party, which was still viewed by much of the articulate Nepali public as the tool of resurgent Rana forces.

THE COMMUNIST PARTY

The opposition role assumed by the Communist party was better conceived and more consistent ideologically than that of any other political group in Nepal. Taking advantage of the

Koirala government's determination to provide the fullest possible civil liberties, the Communists launched a relentless struggle
against the Nepali Congress both from within the Parliament and
with the public. Its four members in the lower house kept up a
continuous barrage of criticism of the government, and other
party members campaigned vigorously on the public front to
enlist the support of the people. While the Gorkha Parishad was
raising the specter of a Chinese invasion as its main political
gambit, the Communists stressed the threat to Nepal's independence and sovereignty from India.

On May 21, 1959, a week before the formation of the Nepali
Congress government, the Communist party Politburo met in
Kathmandu to review the current political situation. Resolutions
were adopted expressing satisfaction at the peaceful conclusion of
the first general elections and the advent of parliamentary democracy. In another resolution the Tibetan revolt was described as "a
rebellion engineered by a handful of Tibetan reactionaries with
the aid of imperialist and some undesirable anti-Communist
elements." [20]

About a month later, the plenum of the Communist party
met at Janakpur in western Nepal to define policies toward the
Nepali Congress government. The party expressed its concern
with the emergence of the Gorkha Parishad as the largest opposition group in the Parliament, and warned that the government
might join in a coalition with the Gorkha Parishad against the
interests of the people. For these reasons the party announced that
it would support all the "progressive" steps of the government,
but would also be ready to launch struggles for the solution of
immediate problems.[21] Further, the party warned the government
not to deviate from its neutral policy toward Tibet and not to
submit to Indian policies of interference in the internal affairs of
that country.

In August, Communist representatives in the lower house
criticized the government's budget as a disguised betrayal of its
announced intention to establish a socialistic society. Their main
objections were directed to relatively minor points, however, and
consisted of the charge that the government had allowed disparities in the pay scales of government employees, had proposed no
concrete plans to promote cottage industries, had shown no real
interest in solving the problem of unemployment, had not
advanced a nationalistic trade and commerce policy, and had
imposed inequitable import and export duties.[22]

The cancellation of the ban on the import of vegetable oil
into Nepal presented an opportunity which was seized avidly by

the Communists, who organized the first large-scale demonstration against the elected government on September 11, in opposition to the import of Indian vegetable-oil ghee (*Dalda*). The manifold implications of this seemingly nonpolitical issue were exploited to the full. It was hinted that the Prime Minister's brothers were in collusion with Indian vegetable ghee merchants; claims were made that the import of vegetable ghee, by reducing the use of clarified-butter ghee, would affect animal husbandry, thereby ruining agriculture and lowering the standard of living of the people; the statement of an Indian Health Minister was quoted out of context as proof that vegetable ghee was injurious to health; the government was accused of being utterly callous about the welfare of the people; and, finally, it was argued that the Nepali Congress was promoting the interest of foreign capitalists at the expense of Nepali ghee merchants. The anti-*Dalda* agitation continued unabated for nearly a year, with the National Democratic Front leaders teamed with the Communists on this issue. Finally, in June, 1960, the government capitulated to public pressure and reimposed the ban on the import of *Dalda*.

By December, 1959, the Communists had found an even better issue in the Gandak agreement signed with India. On this issue they could malign India and the Nepali Congress at the same time—India as the hypocritical, insidious threat and the Nepali Congress government as the submissive tool of Indian interests. On January 21, 1960, Tulsi Lal Amatya, leader of the Communist party in the Parliament, held a press conference in Kathmandu and detailed his party's criticisms of the Gandak agreement. He demanded the cancellation of the treaty and its replacement by a new treaty. He suggested a change in the project site so that it would be mutually beneficial to both countries, and maintained that the government had compromised Nepal's territorial integrity by handing over the project area to India. While emphasizing the desirability of the project, he maintained that it should have been constructed either by Nepal on the basis of a loan from India or jointly by the two countries.[23]

In order to rally public support for their stand on the Gandak agreement, the Communists held a public rally in Kathmandu on February 13. Communist speakers at the rally contended that: (*a*) instead of constructing the project with its own resources, the government had handed over responsibility for the project to a foreign government, thus depriving future generations of Nepalese of water and electricity—two main factors in increasing industrialization; (*b*) the project should have been truly a joint project under joint control and management if the

Nepal government considered itself incapable of constructing it alone; and (c) in its present form, the project agreement did not provide Nepal with equal benefits, either immediately or potentially. Most speakers demanded that the agreement be presented to Parliament for final ratification. Some even compared India's attempts to foist its terms on Nepal with the practices of the British East India Company two centuries earlier when it had conquered India by force or duplicity.[24]

As could be predicted, the Communists' attitude toward China was predicated on the necessity of representing the Peking regime in the best possible light to the Nepalese. Chinese achievements and successes were often painted in rosy terms, and comparable Indian accomplishments were denigrated. While the Communists maintained an ultranationalistic line in their attitude toward India, they became remarkably cosmopolitan on the subject of China. In 1959, the party demanded that the government pursue a neutral policy on developments in Tibet and on deteriorating Sino-Indian relations. When the Gorkha Parishad leader, Bharat Shamsher, publicly announced Chinese incursions into Nepali territory, the Communist party replied that it was inconceivable that there could be any threat from China. Tulsi Lal Amatya, the Communist spokesman in Parliament, charged that Bharat Shamsher was trying to foment anti-Chinese propaganda in Nepal under Indian influence and that he was paving the way for the entry of Indian troops into Nepal.[25]

Following B. P. Koirala's disclosure in April, 1960, that Chinese leaders had laid claim to Mount Everest, several anti-Chinese demonstrations were organized in Kathmandu with the support of the Nepali Congress and the Gorkha Parishad. The National Democratic Front adopted an equivocal position on this issue, while the Communists were placed in a dilemma. The party attempted to maintain a nationalistic façade by asserting that no Nepali territory should be surrendered to any foreign country, including China, but also compromised their patriotic purity somewhat by arguing that the dispute should be settled on the basis of sound historical research and not on emotional nationalism. Communist members of Parliament found themselves in an awkward position during the debates on this issue, and the Nepali Congress and Gorkha Parishad leaders had a field day in questioning their patriotic credentials.

The Communist party, however, was not to be trapped by what it called B. P. Koirala's "anti-Chinese" machinations. One party spokesman charged that the Prime Minister had created the Mount Everest issue to divert the attention of the people from the

Gandak agreement and the antidemocratic measures of his government.[26] The party then undertook its own diversionary tactics by
organizing a public agitation against the Gandak agreement. On
April 21, some eighteen social organizations organized a mammoth
pro-Mount Everest rally with strong anti-Chinese overtones in
Kathmandu; two days later the Communists organized an anti-
Gandak demonstration in front of the Parliament hall.

The Communist party's embarrassment on the Mount Ever-
est issue was somewhat mitigated by Premier Chou En-lai's visit to
Nepal toward the end of April. Speaking at a press conference in
Kathmandu on April 29, Chou was reported to have said:

[China] accepted the map given to us by Nepal. According to the
Nepali map, the southern slope belongs to Nepal, and the northern
slope to China. We never claimed Mount Everest. During our present
talks we accepted the idea that this peak belonged to Nepal. The
Nepal and Chinese governments will give their permission if any one
wants to scale the summit from the southern and northern sides
respectively.[27]

The Mustang incident of June 28 was another shattering
blow to the Communist insistence that China was not a military
threat to Nepal. On that day Chinese troops opened fire on Nepali
border guards near the Kore Pass in Mustang. One Nepali soldier
was killed, and ten others were taken prisoners. This incident
caused a strong nationalistic furor in which the Communists
found themselves out of step with the rest of the country. They
had to salvage what little they could from the difficult political
situation by concentrating on Chou En-lai's readiness to apologize
for the mistakes committed by the Chinese troops and to pay
compensation. At a news conference on July 4, Keshar Jang
Rayamajhi, the general secretary of the Communist party, declared that the Chinese had no aggressive designs against Nepal
and that Chou En-lai's friendly letters sufficed to prove China's
peaceful intentions.[28] The conciliatory attitude displayed by the
Nepali Congress government may have helped extract the Communists from their political dilemma, but the party was not able
to recover fully from the loss of prestige it suffered as a pro-China
party.

In September the Communist party issued a statement
clarifying its position on a much safer subject, the revision of the
Indo-Nepali trade treaty. The party laid down the following
proposed guidelines: (1) there should be no restriction on Nepal's
foreign trade with other countries, (2) Nepal should be allowed
to use any one of the Indian seaports in accordance with interna-

tional convention, (3) Nepal should control its own foreign exchange, and (4) Nepal should be allowed to pursue an independent tariff policy. The party warned that the Nepali Congress government was contemplating signing a trade treaty that would promote Indian interests rather than Nepal's.[29]

That same month the Central Committee of the party held a ten-day session in Kathmandu. The meeting adopted several resolutions, defining its policies and programs, and declaring that the responsibility of the party was to complete the "bourgeois democratic revolution" of 1950 by preparing for a truly proletarian revolution of the peasants. The Central Committee decided to launch a nationwide peoples' struggle in order to fight "right-wing reactionaries and the pro-feudal, pro-imperialist, and other weaknesses" of the government. The purposes of the struggle, which was to be launched in collaboration with "democratic and national forces," were (1) to oppose foreign capital, land evictions, Gorkha recruitment for the British Army, the presence of Indian personnel at northern border checkposts, and the Gandak agreement and (2) to strengthen the peasants' "no rent without receipt" movement.[30]

The Central Committee noted with satisfaction that party membership and influence had grown steadily in the preceding year. It claimed that the party had emerged as a truly national party representing progressive forces. To better adapt the party organization to continuing growth, it announced that it was contemplating important changes in the organizational structure. A National Council was proposed to replace the Central Committee; provincial committees were to be abolished, and a direct link was to be established between the National Council and the districts; cells were to be replaced by branches; and the National Council was to elect the Working Committee and the Politburo.[31]

While the Communist party was not directly involved in the disturbances in West No. 1 and Gorkha, it is an interesting commentary on the motives of the party that it sided with what it would have classified as "feudal elements" against the Nepali Congress government. The party denounced the government for alleged excesses and laid on the government the entire blame for the police firing, denying that local provocateurs had precipitated the action of the police.

The Communist party, thus, acted as both an ideological and opportunistic critic of the Nepali Congress government. In theory, it placed the highest priority on the struggle against reactionary revivalists—i.e., landlords, Rana supporters, and other vested interests; in fact, it spent more time and energy fighting the "socialistic" Nepali Congress. It often provided an effective opposition to the government both in Parliament and through direct public agitation. On balance, it is probable that the Communists fared better than any other opposition group during the tenure of the Nepali Congress government.

THE ROLE OF THE NOMINATED MEMBERS OF THE SENATE

Under the 1959 Constitution, King Mahendra appointed half of the membership of the Senate. On July 13, 1959, he nominated to this body eighteen senators of various political persuasions and ethnic backgrounds. It would seem probable that the King intended from the very beginning that the nominated members should serve as a restraining influence on the government by delaying measures proposed by the Cabinet and approved by the Lower House. In practice, in any case, the nominated members proved to be the most relentless and successful critics of the government, several times defeating the government on the floor of the Senate. They were instrumental in causing some of the most acrimonious debates and, in their attacks on the Treasury benches, often surpassed the performance of the elected opposition in the Lower House in fury and irresponsibility.

The Senators had been selected by the King in their personal capacities as prominent citizens. Included among them were two Nepali Congress leaders who were often in conflict with the party leaders in the Cabinet, and three ex-Nepali Congress leaders who had turned into sharp critics of their former party. Thus the Nepali Congress could hardly look for support from the ranks of the nominated Senators. The other eighteen members of the Senate were elected by the Lower House on July 11. Of these, only ten were loyal Nepali Congress members, and the others were either independents or representatives of opposition parties in the Lower House.* Thus, the Nepali Congress was distinctly a minority group in the Senate.

The virulent form of opposition in the Senate may in part have been due to the fact that, under the 1959 Constitution, this body had no real power to reject legislation introduced by the ruling party. At best, it could only delay the passage of govern-

---

* Several independents, including the brother of the Gorkha Parishad leader Mrigendra Shamsher, were included on the Nepali Congress list. This explains why the Congress elected only ten of its own members to the Senate despite its overwhelming majority in the Lower House.

ment bills for one to five months. On crucial matters such as the passage of money bills, the assent of the Senate was not even mandatory, the only stipulation being that the Senate had to be informed about the bill at least one month before the end of the session.

The Nepali Congress government's first defeat occurred in the Senate on July 21, when the ruling party set up a candidate for the post of deputy chairman of the Senate against an independent. Votes between the two candidates were evenly divided, and the chairman, who was not a Nepali Congress member, then resolved the tie by casting his vote in favor of the independent.

The government benches suffered another defeat in the Senate on September 1, over the reading of the Judicial Administration Reforms Bill. The nominated group was successful in adopting two amendments, which were intended to safeguard the judiciary against interference by the executive, over the objections of the government. In the face of this setback, the Home Minister observed that the amendments hit at "the very soul of the bill" and requested permission from the House to withdraw it.[32]

For the most part, however, the Senate was only an irritant, and the government tended to react in the same spirit. During May, 1960, when the Communists were once again reviving the anti-Gandak agitation, their representatives tabled an anti-Gandak treaty resolution in the Senate and the nominated Senators took turns in denouncing the government. On May 16, the opposition in the Senate voted down three sections of the government-sponsored Entertainment Tax Bill from what seemed to be sheer obstreperousness. On the following day, the Communist Senator submitted a resolution alleging that corruption was rampant throughout the country and demanding a "record of assets owned by the officials, from section officers to the Prime Minister."[33] The resolution—an indirect slur on the administration—was accepted unanimously.

Aroused by these obstructionist tactics, Prime Minister Koirala was reported to have stated at a press conference on May 28 that the nominated members of the Senate were failing to live up to their responsibilities as guardians of democracy and that they opposed every measure of the government for the sake of mere opposition.[34] On May 31, the nominated Senators raised a great clamor over the Prime Minister's remarks. Finally, to pacify them, B. P. Koirala had to deny that he had made the uncomplimentary remarks attributed to him. Later the nominated Senators were agitated by the publication of an article by Vishwabandhu

Thapa in the Nepali Congress party organ, the *Nepal Pukar*. Thapa, who was the chief whip of the party in the Lower House, was reported to have described the nominated Senators as unfit and unqualified. The majority of the nominated members staged a walkout from the Senate on August 4 as a token protest, and demanded that Vishwabandhu retract the unflattering remarks made about them.

There is no doubt that the Senate provided the Nepali Congress government with more uncomfortable and irritating opposition than did the Lower House, but it is doubtful that their opposition resulted in any change in the policies of the government or even in making the democratic system more viable. Often the opposition in the Senate was unrestrained, irresponsible, and of a personal nature, rather than judicious and constructive. Debates in the Senate were no less impulsive or more deliberate than those in the House. Indeed, it can be argued that most nominated Senators, who were not accountable to any party or group for their actions, exercized an excess of personal license in their speeches and actions in the Senate which often bordered on irresponsible amateurism.

THE JANA HITA SANGH

The economic measures of the Nepali Congress government faced strong opposition from several vested interest groups from the very beginning. The abolition of *Birta* tenure and the adoption of a tax structure aroused widespread apprehensions among wealthy landowners and some merchants. In many cases these persons were members of prestigious Kathmandu families whose wealth had been accumulated during the Rana period. They and their families owed their position and prosperity to the Rana regime, and they had been consistently skeptical and at times derogatory in their attitude toward the new political era. Their distaste for political parties, particularly those with an egalitarian bias, had caused them to band together as independents in the past. On several occasions they had demanded the right to form a government of their own, on the grounds that the parties were corrupt and incapable of running the administration. Less publicly, they had financed and organized several newspapers and conservative organizations, such as the Karma Vir Sangh. They had also helped foment political disunity within political parties by encouraging splinter groups and dissidents.

One such organization was the Jana Hita Sangh ("Union for

Public Welfare"), formed in April, 1960, with the avowed purpose of fighting the government's taxation policies and land reform measures. It was entirely a Kathmandu Valley phenomenon, and its public leadership was confined to a few middle-class merchants and small landowners. It never amounted to much as an organization, but it was able to capitalize on popular discontent over such issues as the Gorkha incident and property taxes by misrepresenting the government policies in an alarmist manner. One of its leaders, for example, charged publicly on April 22 that the government intended to undermine religion and culture by abolishing the Guthi system (the tradition of providing land endowments for temples and religious organizations to ensure their proper maintenance as well as the observance of prescribed rituals and ceremonies), in spite of firm government reassurances to the contrary.[35]

The "independent" political leaders of the Jana Hita Sangh sought King Mahendra's intervention more than once for repeal of the government's economic policies, and they were always alert to any opportunity to discredit the Nepali Congress government. Late in November, the Jana Hita Sangh set the stage for the dismissal of the government by organizing general strikes in all three cities of the valley. Coming just two weeks before the dismissal of the Nepali Congress government, these strikes have raised questions as to whether their timing was merely coincidental. Certainly there is reason for suspecting that the inspiration behind the strikes came from more authoritative sources than the few middle-class merchants and landowners who were the nominal leaders of the Sangh.

THE NEPALI CONGRESS AND INTRAPARTY OPPOSITION

The ruling party managed to maintain its organizational unity and strength intact throughout the incumbency of its government. There were no major splits or dissensions in party ranks, and the leadership of the party was retained by the same group that had led the party to victory in the 1959 elections. B. P. Koirala was in full control of the party organization, and there was no major challenge to his authority. Internal cat-fighting within a ruling party had become almost a political tradition during the previous nine years, but the Nepali Congress was a unique exception to this general rule.

The Nepali Congress continued to grow in strength and

membership during 1959–60. It was natural for any ruling party to acquire some additional political influence during its period in office, but the growth of the Nepali Congress seemed to be guided by careful planning and deliberation. Soon after the formation of the government, the party leaders drew up plans to strengthen the party at the district levels. Accordingly, beginning in September, 1959, a series of political conferences were held in districts all over Nepal. High-ranking party leaders and government Ministers addressed these meetings, trying to infuse a new spirit of responsibility in the party cadres. The role of the Nepali Congress as a bridge between the people and the government was emphasized, and the local party leaders were advised to enlist public support in carrying out the development programs of the government. These political conferences seem to have been used to combat any smugness that may have pervaded the district-level leadership as a result of the party's overwhelming victory at the polls, and to discourage opportunism and jobbery among them.

The appointment of District Development Officers on February 18, 1960, with authority to implement local development projects, was a further step in the government's plan to utilize the party as an instrument for the implementation of government programs. The recruitment of these officers, largely from the rank and file of the Nepali Congress, provided a new source of strength for the party at the district and local level. It was obvious that the Nepali Congress leadership was trying to consolidate the gains made in the election by implementing district development projects and by instituting panchayats at the village level. Priority was given to the implementation of development projects in districts dominated by opposition parties, and panchayat officers were recruited from the rank and file of the Nepali Congress. In these ways, the government hoped to strengthen the political base of the ruling party.

There is no question that the Nepali Congress party was well on its way to becoming an institutionalized nationwide political force by 1960. With the exception of the Communists, most of the other opposition parties either had disintegrated or were moving closer to the policies of the Nepali Congress. Against its own precedents and traditions, the Working Committee of the Nepali Congress nominated B. P. Koirala as president for two more years in January, 1960, thus continuing the system under which the roles of Prime Minister and party president were combined. On April 4, B. P. Koirala won the party presidency by an overwhelming majority, polling 5,973 votes against the token opposition of his opponent, Bhudeo Rai, who obtained only 865 votes.

The seventh general conference of the party met for one week in Kathmandu on May 8. Some 700 Nepali delegates were present, and delegates and observers from the socialist parties of Burma, Japan, Norway, Yugoslavia, Israel, and India were also in attendance. In his presidential address B. P. Koirala laid heavy emphasis on three main points: (1) the necessity of increased production and planning in the country, (2) the 1959 Constitution, which he said was not completely democratic, but was the best possible under the circumstances, and (3) the need for vigilance against antinational leftist elements in the country. The two general secretaries of the party were also reported to have made critical remarks about the Constitution.

Some opposition was voiced at the conference against the domestic policies of the government, particularly the industrial policy, but the foreign policy based on positive neutrality and nonalignment was endorsed and a number of policy resolutions defining the party's political, economic, and social objectives were adopted. The political resolution emphasized the party's immediate commitment to "safeguarding the rights of the Parliament, strengthening and stabilizing its comprehensiveness, building up a panchayat society with the help of local government bodies and other democratic institutions, and the ultimate establishment of a socialist Nepal through the medium of parliamentary democracy." The economic resolution called for the abolition of a feudal economy and the establishment of an industrial society. In separate resolutions the conference decided to make widespread use of the enthusiasm and revolutionary spirit of youth in the task of construction, and called upon the people to rise above petty personal and group interests and "participate in the establishment of a happy society free of exploitation." [36] The conference also adopted a seven-point program on industrialization: (1) the government should have full control over basic industries, (2) technical advice and loans should be provided to private investors, (3) steps should be taken to attract foreign capital where indigenous capital was not available, (4) full employment should be provided to replace workers in industries, (5) training centers should be opened for technicians, (6) centers for training in cottage industries should be opened where communications and electrical facilities were lacking, and (7) small-scale industries should be set up on a nationwide basis.[37]

On May 13, the conference held a secret session to consider the complaints of the rank and file against the party leadership and the Cabinet. This session restored the presidential prerogatives on the appointment of the party's Working Committee and empowered the president to accept or reject any resolution, and to amend the party constitution as he deemed fit "in order to make it more scientific and practicable." [38] This was a reversal of the earlier decision of the conference to reject the constitutional amendments proposed by the Working Committee.

The seventh general conference of the Nepali Congress, although initially marked by some vocal dissidence, ended in an affirmation of solidarity within the party and, more significantly, in a personal triumph for B. P. Koirala. He weathered all criticisms of the way he had handled the government and the party, and emerged as the undisputed leader of both organizations.

There were two other significant developments within the Nepali Congress in the months just before the dismissal of the government, the acceptance of the report submitted by the party's Work Expediting Committee, and the decision to launch a rent-receipt movement in East No. 1 and No. 2. The Work Expediting Committee outlined the measures which the government should adopt in order to liquidate feudalism, including the stricter enforcement of *Birta* abolition, protection of tenancy rights, institution of mobile courts, and control of nepotism. In tune with the theme of the report, the Working Committee published a resolution outlining its policies toward the peasants. The party noted that the government was sending out mobile courts to enforce the laws recently passed by the Parliament to protect tenancy rights, and called upon the landlords and landholders to adjust themselves to the new situation.[39] The All-Nepal Peasants' Association decided to launch a country-wide receipt movement on September 26, and welcomed the Nepali Congress statement of September 13 in favor of the peasants' movement in Dang and elsewhere, but the Nepali Congress commenced separate preparations for launching a receipt movement in East No. 1. The latter movement was just ready to get under way when the Nepali Congress administration was dismissed by King Mahendra.

The B. P. Koirala government was, of course, not entirely free from criticism and opposition within the party ranks. It was, however, readily apparent that the critics were in no position to influence party policies or challenge the party leadership. Occasional rumors of a rift between the Prime Minister and Home Minister Surya Prasad Upadhyaya were heard, but there were no public controversies between the two Ministers or their followers similar to those that had disrupted most previous governments. The opposition to the government within the party came mainly from M. P. Koirala and, to a lesser degree, from Dr. Tulsi Giri and Vishwabandhu Thapa. The latter was reported to have demanded the dismissal of two senior Ministers at the meeting of the party Working Committee in September.[40]

Tulsi Giri resigned from the government toward the end of August. The reasons for his resignation were never fully made public. Dr. Giri initially made only the cryptic comment that he had resigned to facilitate a Cabinet reshuffle by the Prime Minister.[41] On November 27 and December 9, however, he expressed his dissatisfaction with the government in interviews with the press.[42]

Perhaps the most outspoken critic of the Nepali Congress government was M. P. Koirala, former Prime Minister and former president of the party. He had many personal reasons to be aggrieved with the leadership hierarchy, the very men who were mainly responsible for his expulsion from the party in 1952. M. P. Koirala did not stand as a candidate in the 1959 elections, and therefore lacked the political credentials of the elected party leaders. His prestige and influence in the party must have been quite low as he was not among the party nominees to the Senate and only later obtained a seat there as one of King Mahendra's nominees.

M. P. Koirala was one of the first in the Nepali Congress to support the National Democratic Front. As early as June 7, 1959, he publicly welcomed the formation of the Front, emphasizing the need for a strong and healthy opposition.[43] Two weeks later he voiced his dissatisfaction with the composition of the Nepali Congress Cabinet, pointing out that all but "five or six members of the Working Committee of the party" had become Ministers and that the same person led both the government and the party.[44] The last comment was, doubtless, an implied reference to the situation in 1952 when he had been denied the right to hold both offices at the same time.

Most Nepali Congress members were inclined to view M. P. Koirala's criticisms as merely another device in his efforts to regain his former political status. It was not considered worth the effort at the time to punish or penalize him for his dissident role within the party. Indeed, his political prestige was considerably enhanced in 1959 when B. P. Koirala appointed him to both the party's Working Committee and Parliamentary Board, the first instances in which he was given positions of major responsibility since his readmission to the party in 1956.

But M. P. Koirala's most significant contribution in his self-imposed role as an intraparty critic was his attack on the government's foreign policy in April, 1960, and an article, entitled "King

Mahendra and Nepal" published in July. In an address to the Senate on April 12 he charged that the joint communiqué signed on different occasions by the Prime Minister with his counterparts in India and China had shown a lack of balance in the government's foreign policy. The joint communiqué signed with India, he noted, had stated that the two countries were separate only on domestic matters. He concluded, therefore, that the Nepal government feared India and was thus unable to exercize full sovereign powers. He also charged that the government had failed to assert itself in its relations with China by not refuting the Chinese claim to Mount Everest and by accepting a twenty-kilometer demilitarizated zone on either side of the border. The latter concession, he claimed, bestowed a strategic advantage on the Chinese, who had developed a comprehensive transportation network along much of the border.[45]

M. P. Koirala's article in a local paper, *Naya Samaj*, appeared immediately after King Mahendra had returned from an extended tour abroad. Presumably, M. P. Koirala wanted to inform the King about developments in Nepal during his absence. Focusing primary attention upon the alleged shortcomings of the Nepali Congress party and government, he concluded that both the foreign and domestic policies of the elected government had failed, and emphasized (1) the responsibility of the King for preventing party government from degenerating into a single party monopoly, and (2) the urgent need for a viable opposition. This article undoubtedly helped to lower the prestige of the Nepali Congress government in the eyes of the King as well as the public. In no small measure it contributed to a spate of rumors, in August, alleging that the King had virtually decided to terminate the Nepali Congress government. One newspaper went so far as to allege that M. P. Koirala had submitted a petition to the King, advising him either to take the reins of administration in his own hands or to call upon him (M. P. Koirala) to form a government.[46]

The Nepali Congress leadership was now clearly annoyed by M. P. Koirala's oppositional tactics. The Disciplinary Committee of the party declared on September 13 that M. P. Koirala's article was improper and objectionable, but recommended no disciplinary action against him. M. P. Koirala then resigned from the Working Committee of the party and began to play an even more conspicuous role in the attempts to form a united opposition. In a press interview on November 26 he remarked that if the constitution of the party were not changed fundamentally he would not be able to continue even as an ordinary member of the Nepali

Congress, and charged that the policies of the ruling party were antagonizing the people and helping the Communists to strengthen their influence. He interpreted the recent defeats of the Nepali Congress in the municipal elections of Dharan and Janakpur as the results of the jobbery practiced by the party leaders and also of their increasing alienation from the people.[47]

But the most that can be said is that by-election and municipal election results in 1959 and 1960 were inconclusive. Two of the three Parliamentary by-elections in 1960 were won by the Nepali Congress and the other by the Gorkha Parishad— results that conformed essentially with the pattern established in the general elections. The ten municipal elections held in 1959–60 were more confusing. The Nepali Congress's success in these elections were not as impressive as its record in the general election, although invariably it did emerge as the largest single party. It won a majority in Rajbiraj (January, 1960), five out of thirteen seats in Pokhara (June), seven out of thirteen in Butaul (February), and six out of fifteen in Nepalganj (June). The police firing in Gorkha in the latter part of 1960 would seem to have adversely affected the Nepali Congress's popularity, for it won only one seat in Dharan (October) and four in Janakpur (November).

It should be noted, however, that the municipal election results provided only a sampling of urban political trends. By and large, urban areas were prone to record a leftist predilection in elections because of the heavy concentration of a student population. In the eyes of the urban elite, the Nepali Congress had become identified with the established regime, and one that was introducing unpopular new taxation measures. The evidence from the rural areas, on the other hand, would seem to indicate that the Nepali Congress was strengthening its position. In contrast to the urban areas, where opposition found it easier to organize politically, in much of rural Nepal the Nepali Congress faced virtually no organized political opposition.

CONCLUDING REMARKS

It might be instructive to conclude this survey by listing some of the dominant political trends beginning to emerge at the time of the dismissal of the Nepali Congress government. Most notable, perhaps, was the ease with which the Nepali Congress and the two main opposition parties, the Gorkha Parishad and the Communists, adapted their tactics to parliamentary democracy.

This contrasted with the behavior of the parties humbled in the 1959 general elections, such as the constituent parties of the National Democratic Front, which consistently opposed the government on emotionally charged but essentially ephemeral issues. These parties, which had often proclaimed their adherence to democratic principles before the elections, now demanded repeatedly that the King exercize his extra-parliamentary powers and dismiss the government. Wedded as they were to the type of politics that had dominated the scene before the elections, these parties became increasingly aware of their status as political misfits in the Nepal of 1960. But their personalized brand of politics was so self-centered that they found it virtually impossible to strengthen their organizational structure or coöperate together on anything other than a strictly *ad hoc* basis.

In direct contrast to the failure of most opposition parties to adjust to the new situation was the success achieved by vested-interest groups in Kathmandu in capitalizing on popular reaction to the police firing in Gorkha. In the vanguard of these groups were a number of local merchants, assisted by a small band of political malcontents. Their primary objective was nothing less than the discrediting of parliamentary democracy through a concerted program of propagandization against and misrepresentation of government policies. The success of the strike and demonstrations they sponsored toward the end of November, 1960, symbolized the alienation of the Nepali Congress government from most articulate elements in Kathmandu and helped set the stage for the royal *coup* in December.

Nevertheless, developments in the months preceding the dismissal of the B. P. Koirala government were not particularly unusual or threatening. The Gorkha incident aroused widespread anxiety, but it did not confront the government with a major political crisis that was likely to bring about its downfall. The Nepali Congress was still exuding confidence in its preparations for the 1964 elections, and was entertaining foreign guests, including the Indian Commander in Chief, when the King suddenly ended the parliamentary system. A decade of experimentation directed toward the introduction of democratic parliamentary institutions and a constitutional monarchy was abruptly and effectively terminated, and a new era of political experimentation commenced.

17

Policies and Programs of the Nepali Congress Government

As THE FIRST elected government in Nepal, the B. P. Koirala Cabinet was accountable not only to the King, but also to the voters who had put it in office. In contrast to previous governments, it was morally and politically obligated to implement the party's comparatively detailed election manifesto which envisaged the progressive establishment of a socialistic pattern of society. The Cabinet was, thus, committed to ending the exploitation of the many—mainly peasants—by a privileged and wealthy minority. In concrete terms, this involved a gradual but radical change in the system of land tenure and ownership through the wholesale redistribution of land to tenants and landless laborers.

Equally significant were other land reform and economic measures cited in the party's election manifesto which struck at the very roots of the traditional social and economic order— abolition of the landlord system, abolition of Rajyas (the semi-autonomous small principalities in the western hills) , a ceiling on landholdings and redistribution of excess landholdings, nationalization of forests, and promotion of coöperative farming.[1] The party manifesto had accepted, in principle, the payment of compensation to the landlords and *Birta* owners for the appropriation of excess landholdings, but it was unlikely that the badly frightened landowners found this very reassuring.

346

The Nepali Congress had also pledged a "scientific" reform of the currency system and a planned and rapid industrialization. First priority had been assigned to the development of small-scale industries. While offering the Nepali entrepreneurs a full guarantee of freedom of choice and action in their industrial undertakings, the party also welcomed investment of foreign capital if the owners were prepared to abide by the restraints and regulations of the government.

In its election manifesto the Nepali Congress had paid particular attention to the problem of administrative reform. Recognizing that the present administrative system was "loose and unscientific," it had pledged itself to an elimination of corruption and bribery in government offices at all levels and had promised a scientific reform of the administrative machinery. The principle of administrative decentralization had been accepted as a guideline for future reforms, and the party had pledged itself to the recruitment of officials strictly on the basis of merit and qualifications.

In the realm of foreign affairs, the Nepali Congress had stated that friendly relations would be established with all countries on a basis of equality, and had pledged itself to a policy of noninvolvement with power blocs. Other highlights of the Nepali Congress election manifesto included: respect for religion and a guarantee of the right of any citizen to practice the religion of his choice without interfering with the religious rights of others; pursuit of a vigorous program for the development of health and education facilities and for the provision of drinking-water facilities; development of transportation; establishment of a judicial system in which justice was simple, impartial, cheap, and easily available to all; and recognition of Nepali as the national language while at the same time encouraging the development of regional and local languages.

Despite its short nineteen months' tenure in office, the B. P. Koirala government must be credited with a record of accomplishments unparalleled by that of any previous government in Nepal. As an elected government, commanding an absolute majority in Parliament, the Cabinet functioned with an unpredented sense of confidence. While its policies were directed to the vision of a Nepal twenty years hence, it did not ignore short-term projects intended to relieve urgent immediate problems. Some of these short-term "impact" programs were drawn up with the help and suggestions of Nepali Congress leaders at the district level who were familiar with economic and social conditions in their areas.

ECONOMIC DEVELOPMENT

In the field of economic planning and development, the Nepali Congress government initiated a series of pioneering attempts to mobilize Nepal's indigenous resources and to reduce existing economic inequalities. The Finance Minister, Suvarna Shamsher, in his budget speech to the Parliament on August 9, 1959, laid down the framework for the economic policies of the party government for the next five years. He listed five goals as the primary motivating forces behind the government's avowed policy of creating a socialistic system: (1) to increase the national income of the country, (2) to bring about fundamental changes in agriculture, (3) to provide adequate social welfare programs for the people, (4) to solve the problem of unemployment, and (5) to reduce inequalities in income levels and the distribution of wealth.[2] He emphasized the government's preference for labor-intensive projects on a short-term basis while at the same time carrying out some capital-intensive long-term projects. The budget included a sizable outlay of over 140 million rupees for development for the year 1959–60.* The list of priorities specified in the first Five-Year Plan was followed without any change, with the exception that the allotment for health and education was tripled in comparison with that of the previous year.

The most significant innovation in the development budget was the program aimed at the mobilization of internal resources through the inauguration of the first income and property taxation program in the history of Nepal. Cautioning against excessive dependence on foreign aid for development projects (which contributed 78 per cent of the development budget in 1958–1959), the Finance Minister pointed out the necessity of developing a sense of self-reliance in national planning. He quoted examples of other foreign countries, such as India and the United States, where the governments appropriated a considerable part of the national income as revenue. In Nepal, on the other hand, the government's share was only 2–3 per cent of the national income. This situation, he argued, could never justify allegations of excessive taxation by the government. He then announced taxes on *Birta* land, urban property, foreign investments, trade profits, watertaps, and radio receivers. How moderate the taxes were,

---

* The fiscal year, 1959/60, was the fourth year of the 330-million-rupee first Five-Year Plan, but less than one fifth of the total outlay had been expended in the first three years. According to a progress report of the Planning Ministry, 79 million rupees were spent under the Plan in 1959/60, while only 60 million rupees had been spent from 1956 to 1959. *Naya Samaj*, September 27, 1960.

however, could be ascertained from the fact that they were estimated to bring in only 2.5 million rupees in additional revenue.

The Finance Minister presented his government's second (1960/61) budget to Parliament on July 6, 1960. In general, he presented an encouraging report on the past year and had an optimistic outlook for the future. Referring to the past fiscal year, he noted that 53 per cent of the allocations of the Development budget would be spent and that about 81 per cent of the allocations for education and 56 per cent for health were likely to be expended. Regarding the short-term projects assigned to the District Development Boards, he noted two reasons—loss of time in making adequate arrangements and lack of technical staff—which had held up their quick implementation.

For the first time, the Finance Minister observed, the circulation of Nepali currency was on the increase in the Terai districts. Agricultural production continued to flourish, and more than 200 new private firms were granted licenses to establish small industries. The number of public servants continued to rise, and the price structure in general remained stable.

In his estimates for the year 1960/61, the Finance Minister proposed an expenditure of some 250 million rupees on the Development budget, a substantial increase over the past year. Explaining the increase, he observed:

The first Five-Year Plan was to cost 330,000,000 rupees. Till last year about 125,000,000 rupees had been spent on this score. If during the current year we can spend 205,000,000 rupees, the outlay target will be realized. But, moved by a desire to overfulfill the target, the budget has provided for expenditures to the tune of 250,000,000 rupees. This year we have to strive for the utmost fulfillment of the first Five-Year Plan. This year we will also prepare the second Five-Year Plan, which will go into operation next year. The budget was prepared with this also in view.[3]

Rather than rely on taxation as a means for mobilizing internal resources—assuming that such resources did exist in a subsistence economy—the Finance Minister proposed an interesting and less painful measure in the form of a National Debt scheme. He conceded that the scheme might not produce receipts adequate for Plan purposes, but he felt that it would serve a useful purpose by making the people "Plan-minded and perhaps encourage them to acquire the habit of saving." The government, he disclosed, intended to float government bonds to the value of Rs. 20 million at 5½ per cent interest, which would mature after five years.

The Finance Minister hinted about the preparation of the second Five-Year Plan, but merely noted that it would be submitted in about six months. Prime Minister Koirala had also given a few hints about the Second Five-Year Plan at a press conference on June 26. The total outlay was reported to be 1,960 million rupees, out of which nearly 450 million rupees were earmarked for investment in the agricultural sector, and 1,500 million in the nonagricultural sector.[4] Priorities were enumerated in the following order: industrial projects, road building, and agricultural production. It was hoped that the second Five-Year Plan would create 500,000 new jobs and lead to a 30 per cent increase in national income.

The confidence displayed by the Nepali Congress government in formulating policies could partly be gauged by the overtures it made to foreign entrepreneurs to encourage investment in Nepal. The eagerness of the government for investments from abroad—whether in the form of aid or private capital—was reflected in the Finance Minister's speech during the presentation of the second budget, in which he reversed his earlier position with regard to dependence on foreign aid for development projects.* A year earlier he had warned against dependence on foreign aid and called for the mobilization of internal resources. In his second budget speech, he estimated that 88 per cent of the development budget for 1960/61 would be financed by foreign aid, a 17 per cent increase over the previous year. Although the need for mobilizing internal resources had not diminished, the government had come to realize that it was unrealistic to place much emphasis on the mobilization of internal resources, and had concluded that any program of economic development could not be implemented without substantial foreign assistance.

On February 18, 1960, the Nepali Congress government announced the appointment of District Development Officers all over the country. These officers were given direct control over the administration of short-term development projects in their districts. A large majority were Nepali Congress party workers who were expected to be able to implement schemes speedily by enlisting coöperation from local people. These new officers held a quasi-official position in the government and were not encumbered by the usual red tape and rules of bureaucracy. In many

---

* Suvarna Shamsher signed an agreement with the United States on May 18, 1960, which aimed to encourage private American investment in Nepal by providing safeguards for such investment. On October 27, Prime Minister Koirala appealed to Indian businessmen and industrialists in Bombay to invest in Nepal, and assured them full guarantees and "industrial peace for the next ten years." (*Hindustan Times,* October 28, 1960) .

cases they could bypass circuitous official channels and obtain quick access to Ministers for early consideration of their schemes. Although this new system might have infused a new sense of urgency and zeal in the District Development Boards, it led to serious political repercussions both within and outside the administration.

On November 11, the tenth anniversary of the 1950 revolution was celebrated throughout the country. To mark the occasion the Koirala government decided to inaugurate projects all over the country at a cost estimated to total more than 100 million rupees. The Prime Minister himself made a flying tour of central and western Nepal to initiate development projects under the Indian and American aid programs. Two days earlier, while addressing a Revolution Day celebration at Biratnagar, he had told the public gathering that the Nepali Congress government was committed to making the country progressive while safeguarding individual liberty and justice. Specifically, he observed that he did not want to force social and economic changes through violent methods such as were used in Communist China. He estimated that in five years most of the objectives of his government would be accomplished, but he also pointed out that the establishment of a democratic society was only a means to the all-important goal of attaining comprehensive development throughout the country.

One notable economic achievement of the Nepali Congress government was its show of strength and self-confidence in concluding an agreement with the government of India over the controversial Gandak project, which had been the *bête noire* of Nepali politics since 1957. Negotiations between the two governments had led to acceptance of the project in principle. The project itself—a multipurpose hydroelectric dam on the Gandak River—was designed to benefit both countries. But since the site of the project was in Nepal, Nepali politicians had warned against a sellout of national sovereignty and rights to the Indian government. The opposition parties and press had grown so vociferous that previous governments had preferred to shelve the issue rather than take the political risk of concluding the agreement with India. But this risk the Nepali Congress government took on December 4, 1959.

The Gandak project envisaged the construction of a barrage at Bhainsalotan and two powerhouses—one on the Nepali side and the other on the Indian side. The total cost of the project, to be borne wholly by India, was estimated at more than 500 million Indian rupees. It was expected to be completed in ten years. On completion, the project would irrigate about 37,000,000 acres and generate 20,000 kilowatts of power. Nepal would obtain, free of cost, water for the irrigation of about 150,000 acres and electricity at the actual cost of production and transmission. The sovereignty and territorial jurisdiction of the government of Nepal over the project site was not affected.

Perhaps the most controversial economic measure of the government was the enactment of a law for the abolition of *Birta* land tenure. The bill was approved by the House of Representatives on September 17, 1959, and became law on October 7. For the Nepali Congress party, this law was the key frontal attack on Nepal's "feudal" economy. As far back as 1951 the party's representatives in the government had demanded the abolition of *Birta,* but none of the weak, unstable governments that were formed after 1952 had mustered the courage and will power to enact such a law.

Another achievement of the Nepali Congress, which had far-reaching political and economic repercussions, was the revision of the ten-year-old trade treaty with India which the last Rana Prime Minister, Mohan Shamsher, had concluded in 1950. Under that treaty, Nepal's foreign trade was intermixed with that of India. Nepali merchants could not export to or import from countries other than India without the latter's consent, and the Nepali government could not establish a separate foreign exchange account of its own. This treaty had long been a thorn in the Nepali economy, and politicians had often alleged that it constituted proof of India's desire to dominate Nepal economically, besides being an affront to Nepal's independent and sovereign status. Several previous governments had sought to amend the unequal trade treaty, but with no success. In 1960 the treaty was up for renewal and the Nepali Congress government soon gave clear indication that it intended to amend it in a way that would be consonant with Nepal's national honor.

On September 11, a new "treaty of trade and transit" was signed between Nepal and India. In general, it sought the expansion of trade between the two countries and the encouragement of their collaboration in economic development. In particular, while Nepal was to continue to levy import and export duties on goods imported from or exported to India, she could now permit imports from a third country by using her own foreign exchange resources. Another provision specifically recognized Nepal's right to pursue a trade policy divergent from that of India. The new trade treaty was widely acclaimed as one of the most significant accomplishments of the Nepali Congress government, even though some unpopular features of the 1950 treaty were not fully amended to the satisfaction of Nepali commercial interests.

On December 11, the Kathmandu branch of the Nepali Congress organized a public meeting in the capital, partly in response to a series of meetings and demonstrations organized by the Jana Hit Sangha (People's Welfare League) against the government's taxation and *Birta*-abolition measures. On this occasion Prime Minister Koirala made what was perhaps the most comprehensive statement on his political and economic beliefs and policy:

. . . People who had been suppressed for centuries are now awake. History has taken a new turn and the country is passing through a revolution. Election manifestoes, bills, blood, and fire alone do not make a revolution. The country is proceeding ahead toward a new situation, and a new wave of consciousness has pervaded it. From all quarters of the country, people who previously had been exploited and oppressed are demanding facilities such as roads, tunnels, schools, hospitals, bridges, and industries. Outdated systems are being replaced by new ones. In such a decisive hour of change some disturbances and excitement are inevitable. But it is surprising that some reactionaries are still making foolish attempts to stop these earth-shaking changes. The economy of the nation has so far depended on land alone. Now we have to discover alternative sources of employment for the establishment of a new industrial and socialistic order. The yield from the land alone is insufficient to bring economic development. The abolition of the *Birta* system and the levying of taxes are very ordinary aspects of our program. We are planning to take the country to the level of the advanced countries of the world.

Those who wear clean clothes, reside in palatial buildings, and live on the earnings of others are opposing the taxes because the system in which they were living idly is going to be eradicated. Air, water, sunshine, and land belong to those who consume them. It is the tillers alone that must own the land . . .

The country is not the same as it was before. A new order has come in. You have elected this government and it is up to you now to share the responsibility. If in the process of this change some persons suffer, this is natural. Without sacrificing personal interests we cannot build the country from resources obtained from land alone. How can we expect friendly countries to help us financially with funds raised as taxes from their people if we ourselves remain idle? How can we build the country in this way?

Fifteen months before the downfall of Mohan Shamsher's regime, when I was under detention by him, he told me at the Singha Durbar: "You aspire after the Prime Minister's throne. Take care—this must be written on one's forehead." I want to remind the feudal elements today that they should not be confused by writings on the forehead so far as landownership is concerned.[5]

This courageous speech turned out to be the last by the Prime Minister, for on December 15 B. P. Koirala and his colleagues were arrested by the army on orders from King Mahendra. The *coup* came as a surprise to Nepalese at home and abroad; from the tone of the Prime Minister's December 11 speech, it would seem that the victims of the *coup* also had not the slightest inkling as to what the monarch was planning.

ADMINISTRATIVE REORGANIZATION

The administrative machinery, which had been reorganized on an *ad hoc* basis after the 1950 revolution, had become one of the most unstable components in the governing of the country. Successive governments had invariably had their turn in changing the administrative system and personnel, both at the center and in the districts. Often these changes were justified as measures to bring about greater efficiency in the administration, but the opposition usually characterized them as nepotism or political favoritism. Since 1956, the overhauling of administrative personnel had been dignified with the pretentious label of "screening," and it was even announced that tests and interviews were to form the basis for determining the tenure of government employees. As the first elected government, it was essential that the Nepali Congress government tackle the problem of administrative reorganization with speed and confidence.

The urgency of improving the efficiency of the administrative system was undisputed. All the developmental programs of the government had been woefully hamstrung by the scarcity of efficient administrative personnel and by the incompetence of those already on the government payroll. Indeed, the success of the first Five-Year Plan depended far more on the availability of competent administrative personnel than on financial resources, which were already available in excess of what could be utilized.

The Nepali Congress government moved immediately on administrative reorganization. By July 25, 1959, the government announced the names of eleven top secretaries and other key officials as temporary appointments with a probationary period of one year. Although this procedure had an unpleasant association with the old Rana *Pajani* system, it also indicated the government's desire to give a period of trial to all officials before a final judgment was made with regard to their future. By August 22 the government announced a reorganization of gazetted officers in the Central Secretariat, who were also placed on a year's probation.

After completing the changes in the Central Secretariat, the government moved to improve administration in the districts. Bada Hakims were screened in September and November. On February 18, 1960, the government announced the appointment of District Development Officers to supervise the implementation of short-term development projects throughout the country. They were appointed for a period of one year and were outside the scope of the civil service regulations. On the same day, the government announced an increased pay scale for government employees and also the formation of several branches of government service under which all the technical staff of the government would be allocated. For example, doctors, engineers, and educators were assigned to different technical services, each with its own three-tiered hierarchy based on qualifications and length of service. On August 23, the government announced the permanent appointment of fifty-three high officials. The confirmation of other officials was expected to follow shortly. It seemed for the first time that Nepali officialdom would be able to function with a sense of self-assurance, with few worries about tenure, and with a stable administrative pattern. At long last an average official's career and future would not depend solely upon the caprices of the higher authorities and promotions would be earned by meritorious perfomance on the job rather than by skill in ingratiating oneself with momentary political masters. Imperfections and faulty judgments in the appointment of this or that person were, of course, to be expected. What was more significant was the prospect that, given time and patience, a civil service based on merit rather than tutelage would provide the administrative permanence and continuity so important for economic development.

One notable administrative achievement was the smooth functioning of the new elected legislature. Both houses of the Parliament discharged their duties creditably, with full observance of democratic procedures and niceties. Despite the overwhelming strength of the Nepali Congress in the Lower House, free and frank discussion was allowed; the opposition members had full opportunity to criticize the government without undue interference by the Speaker. In the Senate, half of whose members were appointed by the King and the remaining half elected by the Lower House, the Nepali Congress was in a minority; the independent members provided an active, and often aggressive, opposition to the government. The government was mindful not only of the rights and privileges of the members of the Parliament, but also of their needs for living quarters and maintenance. Plans were being drawn up early in 1960 to construct residential housing for the legislators. For a country with a low rate of literacy and education, the new institution of parliamentary democracy worked remarkably well.

MAINTENANCE OF LAW AND ORDER

One of the most serious charges leveled against the Nepali Congress government after its dismissal by King Mahendra was that it had failed to maintain law and order in certain parts of the country. Before discussing specific examples of public challenges to governmental authority and the latter's methods of coping with them, however, an important caution must be sounded to clarify how the Nepali Congress government conceived situations of so-called lawlessness and public disorder. Time and again the Nepali Congress leaders, particularly Prime Minister B. P. Koirala, warned that the transition of the country from a "feudal autocracy" to a socialistic pattern of society would inevitably be accompanied by open and bitter conflicts between the forces of change and those of reaction. The government would seem to have anticipated some amount of public unrest and agitation as not only inevitable, but also functional in implementing its economic measures, especially those concerning the abolition of *Birta* and the imposition of taxes on the propertied class. Consequently, when the press and the public circulated sensational and at times wildly exaggerated reports of tensions between the authorities and some sections of the population, the government on the whole was inclined to take a less than alarmist view.

To some extent, the Prime Minister accentuated this impression by his speeches and actions. For example, in August, 1960, at a time when disturbances in West No. 1 had assumed a critical state, he left for an official visit to Israel and ignored the request made by some members of the Parliament that he defer his trip until conditions in the disturbed areas of the country were normal. A somewhat similar incident took place in October, 1959, at the time of the police firing in Gorkha. Prime Minister Koirala flew to Bombay to inaugurate a conference of Nepali students in India; when questioned about the seriousness of the situation in Gorkha, he replied that his absence from Nepal alone was a proof of the minor nature of the incident. In this respect Prime Minister Koirala was wide of the mark in his assessment of the situation, but it was typical of him not to be swayed by public opinion, however strong.

The spring and summer of 1960 were especially trying periods for the Nepali Congress government from the standpoint of law and order. In April, Hindu-Muslim riots erupted in Mahottari District in the Terai. Three persons were reported killed in the clash, and 153 houses burned.[6] The parliamentary inquiry delegation which later visited the scene of the riots exonerated the government from any responsibility and attributed the riots to an exacerbation of religious sentiments, provoked by such causes as controversy over the building of a mosque or the alleged importation of beef into the area.

On July 21, use of gunfire by police in the district of Dang in western Nepal resulted in the death of one person and injury to two others. The district had been the scene of struggles between peasants and landlords in the past, and the latest incident seemed to fall into the same pattern. In a press note, the Home Ministry justified the police action on the grounds of self-defense and alleged that 500 people armed with sticks, spears, and other weapons had attacked the police.

But the most serious law and order incidents which confronted the Nepali Congress government were the disturbances in West No. 1 and 2, districts immediately beyond the periphery of Kathmandu Valley. Most political observers have maintained that these incidents were primary considerations in King Mahendra's sudden decision to scuttle parliamentary democracy in Nepal. Even if such were not the case, the disturbances in Nuwakot and Gorkha had great political significance in themselves, insofar as they represented the most tangled skein of current Nepali politics, in which all the important actors and agents of Nepali politics ultimately became involved.

Before discussing these incidents, it would be helpful to sketch briefly the historical and ethnic peculiarities of these areas. West No. 1 district, with its headquarters at Nuwakot, lies directly to the west of Kathmandu on the main trade routes to western Nepal and Tibet. West No. 2 district, with its headquarters in Gorkha, is contiguous with West No. 1. Both these districts had been the home base of the Shah kings before the conquest of Kathmandu Valley in the eighteenth century. Traditionally, these areas had long been the center of the most militant Gorkha nationalism in the country. The populace in these districts comprised a wide variety of ethnic groups, whose primary political identification was loyalty to the Shah dynasty and, perhaps somewhat inconsistently, to the Ranas.

In the 1959 general elections, the five constituencies in these two districts elected Gorkha Parishad candidates to Parliament. In West No. 1, the Kshatriyas were the politically active community, while in No. 2 politics were dominated by the Brahmans and Gurungs. The Gorkha Parishad and the Nepali Congress were the only two parties of any significance in those areas, but in the election the Nepali Congress candidates, although second on the ballot, trailed their Gorkha Parishad opponents by a wide margin. Only in Nuwakot constituency was the Nepali Congress able to run a close contest against the victorious Gorkha Parishad candidate. Thus the political complexion of these two districts was not favorable to the ruling party. More significantly, local Nepali Congress workers, smarting from their defeats in the elections, were eager to launch an agitation against the Gorkha Parishad leaders and supporters, most of whom had been supporters of the Rana regime. It is also possible that the high command of the Nepali Congress encouraged the local party functionaries in their political agitation in order to oust the Gorkha Parishad from its dominant position in the districts.

Since there were wide economic disparities and inequities in the districts, the political agitation of Nepali Congress soon assumed the form of an economic struggle. The Nepali Congress set itself up as the champion of the poor and indebted peasantry, and represented the Gorkha Parishad leaders as feudal exploiters, cruel moneylenders, and profiteers.* Thus, when the political animosity of the two parties was fanned into a much more serious and thoroughgoing economic agitation, conflict with the authorities became merely a matter of time.

What precisely happened in West No. 1 is hard to determine in the face of a plethora of politically motivated charges and countercharges. But there are several points which do emerge after sifting evidence from different sources. It seems that the local disturbances started as a result of quarrels between moneylenders and their debtors as early as the first week of November, 1959, barely six months after the installation of the elected Nepali Congress government. Subsequently, some amount of lawlessness spread in the district; robberies and thefts were reported here and

---

* For instance, as late as August 2, 1960, Bharat Prasad Upreti, vice-president of the Nepali Congress in the district of West No. 1, had issued a statement presenting five demands for immediate implementation as a prerequisite for the restoration of peace in his district. These were: distribution of wasteland registered in the name of wealthy people to landless peasants; enforcement of a maximum 10 per cent rate of interest; withdrawal of fictitious cases filed by the moneylenders; scrutiny of bonds executed since 1956 and determination of their exact value; and implementation of the 1957 Land Reform Act. *See Kalpana,* August 2, 1960.

there. After about six weeks of panic and fear the Bada Hakim invited both parties to meet with him and brought about a temporary reconciliation. He was even reported to have succeeded in restoring part of the looted property.

Gradually, the political parties, and particularly the local leaders of the Nepali Congress, became involved in the quarrels between the moneylenders and their debtors. Naturally, the Nepali Congress leaders had an advantage over their opponents in that they could invoke the aid of authority by appealing to their party government in Kathmandu. Reportedly, a local Nepali Congress leader was able to secure the release of two persons who had been arrested by the district authorities for alleged lawless activities. This frightened the followers of the opposition party, and, to add to their panic, the Assistant Home Minister visited the district for some time. His presence, however helpful for the maintenance of a temporary truce, was interpreted as an encouragement to Nepali Congress partisans. The apprehensions of the opposition groups reached a climax when a local Nepali Congress leader, whom they had held responsible for the instigation of local lawless elements, was deputed to the district as a Development Officer, blessed with the authority of the Nepali Congress government and holding considerable funds and power in his hands.

This touched off another series of disturbances in the district. More people, including a Gorkha Parishad member of Parliament, were arrested by the local officials. There was a generally heightened sense of insecurity throughout the district, and reports of rampant lawlessness began to circulate. Robbery and thefts took place, and the victims of the disturbances sent a delegation to Kathmandu on March 12, 1960, seeking what they termed royal protection against the wanton excesses of the government. Most of these people were men of means who had important connections —kinship or otherwise—with members of the traditional aristocracy in the capital. They paraded through the streets of Kathmandu, dramatizing their grievances against the government. To further advertise their plight they took quarters in the *Dharamshalas* (free quarters maintained by religious or philanthropic organizations) along the Bagmati river.

By this time the political parties seemed to have lost control of the political situation, and antisocial elements on both sides gained control. The local authorities had resorted to gunfire to suppress the disturbances, and several houses had been plundered and burned. On March 29 the Home Ministry imposed a ban on processions and meetings in West No. 1 and appealed to the refugees to return to their homes.

The disturbances in West No. 1 continued to simmer with occasional outbursts of violence and lawlessness until the very end of the Koirala regime. The government dispatched special courts and an Inquiry Committee to investigate the situation, but the findings of the investigations were never made public. The local press, often inspired by interested political elements, continued to publish so-called factual reports on the situation. The consensus of public opinion, as conveyed by the press reports, placed the blame on the ruling party for its acts of commission and on the Koirala government for its act of omission in failing to punish local miscreants, who were often reported to be Nepali Congress workers. By August the disturbances in West No. 1 had spread to the neighboring district of Gorkha, where the polarization of political forces assumed a much more violent form. As late as December 12—only three days before the overthrow of the Nepali Congress government—some seventy persons were reported to have arrived in the capital from West No. 1, seeking justice from the King and demanding the formation of a royal commission.

THE GORKHA DISTURBANCES

There is no question that unrest in Gorkha, the ancestral home of the Shah dynasty, was far more complex and foreboding than the disturbances in West No. 1. The principal party implicated in these disturbances by the government was the Karmavir Mahamandal. Originally a socioreligious organization, this organization had been transformed into a political party on the eve of the 1959 general elections. The Karmavir Mahamandal, whose political program aimed at the reinstatement of Nepal's ancient religious and cultural traditions, could not have chosen a better place than Gorkha to launch an agitation against the Nepali Congress government. Leaders of the Karmavir Mahamandal had often decried the institutions of parliamentary democracy and elections as alien to the history and culture of Nepal, and had upheld the appropriateness of a benevolent absolute monarchy, extolling the superior virtues of the traditions and policies of the Shah dynasty over those of contemporary political parties. The party's financial and political support came from the traditional aristocracy throughout the country. In their emphasis on religious and economic conservatism they were akin to some of the Gorkha Parishad leadership, though the latter party had expressly committed itself to democracy. It is thus probable that the Karmavir Mahamandal was able to enlist the support of the Gorkha

Parishad, at least unofficially, in its agitation in Gorkha against the Nepali Congress government.

The course of events in the Gorkha disturbances, like those in West No. 1, is difficult to follow because contradictory reports have been published by interested parties. It seems that opposition to the Nepali Congress had been strong in the district long before that party formed a government, partly for historical and traditional reasons and partly because of the unfavorable propaganda and publicity waged by the Gorkha Parishad and the Karmavir Mahamandal. After the formation of the Nepali Congress government, the political struggle between the parties had intensified in the district in consonance with developments in West No. 1. Critics of the ruling party were able to exploit a number of local grievances. The Nepali Congress government, for example, had introduced stricter regulations for the conservation of forest; as a result, the local inhabitants were unable to procure fuel wood and bamboo from nearby woods as had long been the custom.

The Nepali Congress, meanwhile, attempted to expand its following in the district by encouraging an economic struggle. The Gorkha Parishad was represented as a party of landlords and exploiters, and the Nepali Congress as a party espousing the causes and interests of the poor peasants. In Gorkha, as in West No. 1, the first disturbances erupted in the form of quarrels between creditors and debtors over rates of interest. But the difference was that the initiative in Gorkha was taken by the Karmavir Mahamandal, while the initiative in West No. 1 lay with the Nepali Congress. Indeed, in many ways, the developments in Gorkha would seem to have been a direct reaction to Nepali Congress initiative in West No. 1.

There are conflicting reports as to who was exercising active leadership in the Gorkha demonstrations. The government communiqué placed responsibility on Narahari Nath Yogi, president of the Karmavir Mahamandal, and described him, on the authority of the local Bada Hakim, as the person who was responsible for "inciting the people not to pay taxes, not to let the forests be nationalized by the government, and to overthrow the government by violent and terrorist methods."[7] It even quoted the Karmavir leader as claiming that he was the King's man and that he had photos and relevant papers to substantiate it. After a serious incident occurred on October 25, the Inquiry Committee sent by the Nepali Congress reported that Narahari Nath Yogi had entered Gorkha District on October 2.[8] The National Democratic Front report maintained that he had left the district on

September 28, almost a month before the incident. In any case, the central government ordered the local Bada Hakim to arrest him under the Security Act. But the Yogi had absconded by then, and he was not apprehended until November 1, in Jumla.

There are at least three versions of the Gorkha incident—those published by the government, the Nepali Congress organ (*Nepal Pukar*), and the opposition National Democratic Front. According to the government communiqué of October 28, the leaders of the Karmavir Mahamandal had been abetting destructive activities in the district in collusion with local landlords and other feudal elements. The Bada Hakim of West No. 2 was instructed to search the Karmavir Mahamandal office and to seize all papers and documents. The Bada Hakim, however, suspected that Mahamandal workers were conspiring to seize the government offices. Consequently, some prominent workers of that party were arrested and sent to Kathmandu. On October 23, the district government imposed a curfew in Gorkha under the Security Act. Two days later a crowd of 3,000 persons armed with sticks, *khukris,* and swords surrounded the government offices. The efforts of the Bada Hakim and other officials to pacify the mob failed, and gunfire was resorted to when the demonstrators began hurling stones at the police, injuring eleven of them. The government communiqué made it clear that it had no alternative other than to take strict action against those who opposed the constituted authority and sought to overthrow the legal government by force. Seven persons were reported to have been killed and six injured.

The report of the opposition National Democratic Front, on the other hand, accused the district government of firing on a peaceful procession, and alleged that the police had continued to fire upon the demonstrators when they were fleeing from the scene. It claimed that seven persons died instantaneously as a result of the firing and that scores of others were injured. The investigators reported their inability to find any corroboration of Narahari Nath Yogi's alleged claims to be acting on behalf of the royal palace. They also disputed the government's claims that twelve civil officials had been injured as a result of the mob violence. In conclusion, their report contended that the firing was unjustified and that the whole incident exemplified the callousness of the government and its intoxication with power.

On November 7, the government formally announced the formation of a Judicial Commission headed by a Supreme Court judge to investigate the Gorkha incident. It would seem that the seriousness of the violence in Gorkha had slowly begun to dawn even on the archcritics of the government, and a more cautious mood seemed to have pervaded discussions of the unfortunate episode. Prime Minister B. P. Koirala began a two-week inspection tour of the troubled district on November 21, and his tour was reported to have been a success. The last reference to the Gorkha incident before the overthrow of the Nepali Congress government appeared in the form of a newspaper report on December 3 stating that Narahari Nath Yogi was being sent to Gorkha to stand trial for his alleged role in instigating the disturbances.[9]

THE BAJHANG EPISODE

The Nepali Congress government undertook the task of integrating the regional administrative system by abolishing the semiautonomous Rajya courts in the few principalities that still existed in western Nepal. These small "native states" were a relic of the country's feudal past. Although their rulers were pledged to respect the central government's over-all suzerainty, they enjoyed nonetheless a degree of local autonomy within their territories in such matters as dispensation of justice and maintenance of law and order. By 1959 these tiny enclaves of feudal aristocracy had clearly become political anachronisms and, in some instances, centers of political reaction. It was reported, for instance, that the Raja of Bajhang, one of the states affected by the new policy of administrative integration, had become the president of the Karmavir Mahamandal, and even Narahari Nath Yogi was quoted as having advocated the secession of Bajhang state from Nepal.[10]

In May, 1960, the Nepali Congress government announced the abolition of Rajya courts and assigned their functions to existing regional courts. In the state of Bajhang the ruling family put up stiff opposition to the government's plan. According to the government communiqué, Om Jang Shah, the son of the Bajhang chief, on August 18, arrested the district judge and destroyed goods and papers belonging to the central government. A few days later his followers seized several Forest Department employees. To meet this challenge to the central government's authority, the Bada Hakim of Doti proceeded to the scene of disturbances with a contingent of state troops. Meanwhile, it was reported that Om Jang had set up a parallel government, declaring himself governor and appointing one of his lieutenants as Home Minister. There was an exchange of fire between the Bada Hakim's troops and Om Jang's followers, and two of the latter were reported to have been killed. In the face of the government's superior force, Om Jang and his father, Ram Jang, absconded; about one month later they turned up in India, where they held a press conference to publicize their grievances. They charged that the local Bada Hakim had committed atrocities in their state, and reaffirmed their right to rule Bajhang, which they claimed dated back to A.D. 1226, without interference from the center.[11] On November 23, Ram Jang was reported to be in Kathmandu, seeking redress of his grievances from King Mahendra. A week later, when he was preparing to hold another press conference, the government intervened and placed him under house arrest. His son, against whom a warrant for arrest was already pending, remained in India.

FOREIGN POLICY

The B. P. Koirala Cabinet was the only government in the decade of democratic experimentation which did not feel the need to use foreign policy as one means of strengthening its political position. Thus, it had a unique opportunity to redress whatever imbalances may have developed in Nepal's external relations since 1951.

During its seven years as an opposition party, the Nepali Congress had gradually reformulated its position on foreign policy. In the period from 1952 to 1959 the party had sometimes assumed a moderately critical position on Indo-Nepali relations, usually directed at the Indian Military Mission, the hydroelectric project agreements, and the 1950 trade treaty. On the other hand, relations with China during this period had never raised political issues in Nepal, with the exception of the Tibetan revolt in the spring of 1959. But even on this question the Nepali Congress's rather pungent criticism of Chinese behavior in Tibet was based on its distaste for totalitarian methods and not on any questioning of Peking's authority and suzerainty in Tibet.

On the whole, the foreign policy orientation of the Nepali Congress—like that of the other political parties, with the possible exception of the Communists—had been based on pragmatic rather than moral or ideological considerations. World peace was necessary if Nepal was to have any hope for economic development. The United Nations had to be supported as the best guardian and custodian of the independence, territorial integrity, and sovereignty of all small countries, since the tacit division of the world into power blocs had robbed the traditional concepts of independence and sovereignty of any real meaning. Nonalignment was viewed as the only policy for a country that wished to avoid being grouped with either major bloc and yet wanted to maintain a sense of identity with other countries in a similar situation.

Nepal's immediate neighbors, India and China, tend to dominate the Nepali world view. Nonalignment, hence, is coterminous with strict neutrality in the Nepali interpretation, at least as far as relations with China or India are concerned. The usual assertion that nonalignment involves judging issues on their merit rather than on their relation to established political ties thus has little meaning in the Nepali foreign policy context. At best, Kathmandu can hope to contribute to the easing of tension whenever disputes arise between its two giant neighbors, but only if it remains completely uninvolved.

The only unpragmatic ingredient in the Nepali concept of nonalignment between India and China has been the feeling of nationalism which developed during the anti-Rana movement, intensified by a peculiar combination of circumstances after the overthrow of the Rana regime. Indian influences in Nepal, mostly in the form of benign supervision of the fledgling democratic order, was skillfully exploited by opposition parties on the watch for political issues to be used against the government of the day. Most of the Cabinets formed between 1951 and 1955 were dubbed by the opposition as puppets dancing to the tune of the Indian government in New Delhi.

Thus, when the Nepali Congress formed a government in May, 1959, most of the constants in Nepali foreign orientations had become crystallized and to some extent even institutionalized. For example, anything that seemed to compromise even remotely or cast an unsavory reflection on national independence and sovereignty was a political anathema. In view of this attitude, the Nepali Congress government took an early initiative in revising the Indo-Nepali trade treaty of 1950, thus establishing its *bona fides* as a "nationalist" government. It concluded the long-delayed Gandak River agreement with India, but only after insisting on several revisions in Nepal's favor. When Nehru made a statement in the Indian Parliament hinting at unilateral Indian military action in Nepal in case of aggression on the latter by any third country, B. P. Koirala quickly retorted that the concurrence of the Nepali government must be first obtained. But similarly, when the Chinese created an incident on the Mustang border area in June, 1960, the Nepali Congress government took a strongly nationalist position, denouncing the Chinese as intruders on Nepali territories.

Even on the question of economic aid, the Nepali Congress

maintained an impartial position. The Indian aid program, which had always been the most substantial in Nepal, was maintained and even increased. But B. P. Koirala also signed a second economic aid agreement with China during his official visit to Peking in March, 1960. Under the terms of the new agreement, the Chinese government would give the Nepal government a free grant of aid to a total value of 10 million Indian rupees within a period of three years and without any political conditions attached. This aid did not include the remaining 40 million Indian rupees provided under the 1956 economic aid agreement between China and Nepal, which so far had not been used by the Nepal government.

The increasing of diplomatic contacts and relations with the rest of the world had become an even more important theme of the government's external policies since King Mahendra's accession to the throne in 1955. Except for the brief K. I. Singh regime in 1956, every government since the 1950 revolution had considered it a matter of prestige to establish diplomatic relations with a few additional countries. By April, 1960, Nepal had diplomatic relations with twenty-four countries. In part, this aspect of foreign policy was indicative of Nepal's vigorous search for a distinct national identity.

FOREIGN RELATIONS, 1959–60

The Nepali Congress government assumed office at a crucial stage in trans-Himalayan political developments. A major revolt against Peking's authority had erupted in central Tibet barely two months earlier and it would be nearly a year before Chinese control was firmly reëstablished over most of the Nepal-Tibet border. In the wake of the Tibetan revolt, Sino-Indian relations began to deteriorate rapidly, and the possibility of armed conflict between Nepal's two giant neighbors became a distinct, if incredible, possibility. Nepali foreign policy had to make adjustments—and quickly—to the new situation, and it was the Nepali Congress government that had to bear full responsibility for them.

Nepal's relations with China and India assumed even greater importance than previously in these circumstances, and the first moves in this intricate game were not long delayed. On June 11, 1959, just two weeks after the installation of the Nepali Congress Cabinet, Prime Minister Nehru of India paid a three-day official visit to Kathmandu. The occasion was marked by the issuance of a joint communiqué by him and Prime Minister B. P.

Koirala which affirmed an "identity of views" of the two countries, whose policies, both in the international and in the domestic sphere, were "animated by similar ideals and objectives." The two Prime Ministers were "further convinced that in the interests of peace as well as national and human progress no country should be dominated by another and colonial control in whatever form should end." There was "no conflict of interests between the two countries," which faced similar problems and had common approaches.[12]

B. P. Koirala elaborated on the "identity of views" at a press conference on June 20. He emphasized that there was no difference between the views of the two governments on international and allied problems, including the fate of Tibet. The following statement was attributed to him at the press conference:

It is true that India and Nepal have had many differences, but we are one in some things—and are so on the Tibetan issue. Nepal is not so different from India, and, in fact, Nepal has followed India's policy on Tibet by entering into an agreement with China to the extent of renouncing several claims, just as India has done. From the beginning, Nepal has been recognizing Tibet as part of China, and it has no concern over whether Tibet should enjoy provincial autonomy or not.[13]

On August 11, the Prime Minister disclosed at a press conference in Kathmandu that Nepal would have to finance the defense of its five-hundred-mile-long northern border. Although he was quick to point out that the northern border did not pose any problem at present, he felt it necessary to emphasize that henceforth the country would have to look after both its frontiers, northern as well as southern. This was in part an explanation of the more than 100 per cent increase in the defense budget over the previous year's revised total estimate of 14.3 million rupees.

The Prime Minister returned to the subject of Nepal's relationship with India and China on September 4 in a speech before the House of Representatives. He stated categorically that Nepal should not take sides or become involved in the current border dispute between India and China. He also pointed out that, considering the size of the country, the defense budget was inadequate, and went on to explain that the security measures adopted by his government on the northern border were limited mainly to guard duties and were not of an aggressive nature. Twelve days later, he informed the House of Representatives that Chinese troops had been sighted at some points across the northern border. He also reaffirmed his earlier statements that

Nepal would give asylum to refugees from Tibet, but would not permit them to indulge in political activites.

On October 1, B. P. Koirala stated in the House of Representatives that the Nepal-Tibet boundary was "already" determined, but admitted that there were differences with regard to certain regions. He disclaimed knowledge of reported incursions into Nepali territory by Chinese troops. Returning to the same theme on October 4 at a press conference, he reiterated Nepal's policy of neutrality, which he felt was viable both in the context of the "cold war" between the United States and the Soviet Union and in the context of Sino-Indian differences. He expressed the hope that the Chinese would not violate the Nepali border and thought that there was no need to seek fresh assurances from China in this regard.

On November 29, at a press conference, B. P. Koirala issued a statement reaffirming Nepal's position as a sovereign and independent country able to decide its external and internal policies according to its own judgment and preferences. This statement followed in the wake of Nehru's reference to Nepal during a debate in the Indian Parliament on November 27, in which the Indian Prime Minister had stated that aggression against Nepal and Bhutan would be treated as aggression against India. The remark touched off considerable public controversy in Nepal, leading B. P. Koirala to comment:

I take Mr. Nehru's statement as an expression of friendship that in case of aggression against Nepal, India would send help if such help is ever sought. It could never be taken as suggesting that India could take unilateral action.[14]

In January, 1960, B. P. Koirala paid an official visit to India. This trip was significant for a number of reasons besides the formal reciprocation of Nehru's visit to Nepal. Deteriorating relations between India and China had begun to cast an ominous shadow on the peace and tranquility of the Himalayas, and mutual misrepresentations between India and Nepal had preoccupied the respective presses of the two countries for some time. The Nepali press had reacted sharply to Nehru's statement that the defense of Nepal was India's military responsibility, while some sections of the Indian press had been demanding a closer integration of Nepal with Indian defense policies in the light of increased Chinese activities in the Himalayas. Finally, the Koirala government after eight months in office had acquired a sobering realization of the country's stupendous problems and felt it necessary to make a realistic appraisal of the resources available internally and externally for development purposes.

B. P. Koirala arrived in Patna on January 17 and then proceeded to Bhainsalotan—the site of the still controversial Gandak Project—Jamshedpur, Bareilly, Khatima, Phoolbagh, Agra, Poona, Khadakvasla, Bangalore, and Mysore before arriving in New Delhi on January 24. In the many speeches he delivered at various official functions, the Prime Minister, while constantly emphasizing the historical, cultural, and social contiguity of the two countries, was always careful to reaffirm the sovereignty and independence of Nepal. At a banquet he gave in honor of Nehru, he said:

For the cause of sovereignty and independence in the past, the Nepali and the Indian people have always advanced together . . . Your Excellency [Nehru] has always been a great friend and well-wisher of Nepal. We greatly appreciate your highest regard and respect for our sovereignty and independence, and we are convinced that your best wishes will always be there for the promotion of the dignity and respect of Nepal . . .[15]

On the evening of January 28 the two Prime Ministers issued a joint communiqué, affirming India and Nepal's "vital interest in each other's freedom, integrity, security, and progress." The communiqué revealed that India had promised financial assistance to the extent of 180 million rupees for Nepal's development programs, and had agreed to the revision of the Indo-Nepali treaty of trade and commerce.[16] Addressing a news conference at Chandigarh on January 31 before returning to Kathmandu, B. P. Koirala ruled out the necessity of a joint defense between India and Nepal. He termed any military alliance between such close friends as India and Nepal "worse than useless." [17] It is also significant to note in the light of future events that Koirala at that time categorically ruled out the possibility of war between India and China.

On February 18, speaking at a meeting convened by the United Nations Association of Nepal, B. P. Koirala declared that those who criticized the Indian aid promised in the January 28 joint communiqué were the same elements that had been frustrated by their defeat in the elections and that wanted to entangle Nepal in a military pact, presumably with China. Referring to the coördination of the foreign policies of Nepal and India, he said that the views of the two countries were identical with regard to world peace and nonalignment.[18]

Soon afterward, Prime Minister Koirala paid official visits to Burma and China. While in Rangoon, March 7–9, he signed a joint communiqué with the Burmese Premier, General Ne Win, in which it was agreed that relations between the two countries should be strengthened by establishing diplomatic relations at the embassy level. Both leaders affirmed their determination to strengthen the democratic process in their respective countries.

In China, March 11–23, Koirala held discussions on Nepal-China relations with Mao Tse-tung, Liu Shao-chi, Chou En-lai, and other Chinese leaders. Both sides reiterated their desire for mutual friendship and adherence to Panch Shila—the five principles of peaceful coexistence. At a formal ceremony in Peking on March 21 the two Prime Ministers signed a joint communiqué, an agreement on the boundary question, and an agreement on Chinese economic aid to Nepal.

In his speeches at public meetings in China, B. P. Koirala repeatedly stressed the need for peace and friendship among Asian countries and the consolidation of an Asian consciousness. On one occasion, in Peking on March 15, he hinted at apprehensions of Chinese expansionism and alluded, very guardedly, to China's ruthless suppression of the Tibetan rebellion:

I believe that efforts intended to suppress freedom-loving people or to rule over them by means of force are not only doomed to failure, but are also impossible. . . . Notwithstanding its size or might, if any power attempts to occupy or control even an inch of the territory of any Asian country, such attempts will definitely disrupt the peace of the world . . . If peace is again disrupted in the Asian countries, the Dark Age will once more cast a shadow over this continent. It will, therefore, be wise for Asia today firmly to adhere to the five principles of coexistence among all countries, big or small.[19]

On April 4, after returning from China, B. P. Koirala caused a sensation in Kathmandu when he informed newsmen that China had claimed Mount Everest and that he had refused to entertain such a claim.[20] For some reason he was not very specific about the Chinese claim. The most that newsmen could obtain from him was that China had claimed the peak on the ground that they had a name for it—Jhomolungma—and that the Nepalese had no name for it other than the British-bestowed "Everest." This unexpected disclosure touched off a frenzy of nationalistic protests throughout the country. Processions and meetings were held, and all political parties, with the exception of the Communists, demanded a categorical statement from the government on Nepal's rights to Mount Everest.

The Chinese Premier, Chou En-lai, who arrived in New Delhi on April 19 for discussions with the Indian government on Sino-Indian border disputes, was questioned about the alleged claim to Mount Everest. He parried the question by saying:

The situation with regard to this question is not like what you have learnt from the newspapers. This is a topic between the Prime Ministers of China and Nepal. I have no intention to disclose the discussions between the two of us on this. I will wait till I get to Kathmandu to disclose anything on this question.[21]

Chou En-lai paid an official visit to Nepal from April 26 to April 29, during which a treaty of peace and friendship, reaffirming the faith of the two countries in the five principles of peaceful coexistence, was signed. At a press conference on April 28 the Chinese Premier was questioned closely by Indian and Nepali correspondents about the claim to Mount Everest. He told the journalists that China was willing to accept the Nepali map which showed the boundary drawn along the peak. Asked how much territory was in dispute, he said that the area of divergence between the Chinese and the Nepali maps was so small that if Nepal wanted all of it, China would have no objection.

It was shortly thereafter, and probably not strictly coincidentally, that certain sections of the Kathmandu press alleged that India planned to seize Nepalganj and adjoining areas in southwest Nepal. B. P. Koirala dismissed these charges categorically at a press conference on May 26 and disclosed that India was prepared to settle the Narashai jungle issue, where six acres of Nepali land had been transferred to India as a result of a change in the course of the Gandak River.

But Kathmandu's attention quickly shifted back to the northern border on June 28, when Chinese troops fired on Nepali border guards near Kore Pass in Mustang. One Nepali soldier was killed and ten others were taken prisoner. B. P. Koirala called the Chinese action an "attack" and an "undermining of Nepal's sovereignty," as well as a violation of the border delimitation agreement concluded only three months earlier, under which China and Nepal pledged not to deploy armed forces or military patrols within twenty kilometers of the frontier. A brisk exchange of letters between Chou En-lai and B. P. Koirala ensued. The latter told the House of Representatives on July 4 that the Chinese had tendered an unqualified apology for the border incident and that there was no need to exaggerate the affair. He emphasized, however, that the Mustang incident had occurred on Nepali territory, three hundred yards from the border, thus contradicting Chou En-lai's contention that "the place of the incident was clearly Chinese territory" and that Chinese troops had not entered Nepal. On July 12, during a discussion in the Senate, he returned to the topic of the Chinese incursion and expressed his belief that the incident was "not indicative of any

Chinese designs against Nepal." [22] But again, speaking in the House of Representatives on July 25, Koirala charged China with violating its agreement with Nepal on the demilitarization of the border by sending her troops into the area without prior consultation with Nepal. In his reply to Chou En-lai, dated July 24, he reaffirmed his position that the unfortunate border incident took place in Nepali territory and not in Tibetan territory as claimed by the Chinese government; however, in the same letter he agreed to consider the question of the location of the incident closed, as "it would not serve any gainful purpose to continue arguing over the incident." [23] On August 27, B. P. Koirala told the House of Representatives that:

The position now therefore is that China has apologized for the incident and paid cash compensation but maintained that the event took place within Tibet—one furlong north of which she claimed to be Chinese territory—and denied the Nepali charge that Chinese troops violated Nepali territory.[24]

In the middle of September, the Prime Minister went to New York with the Nepali delegation to the United Nations General Assembly. He addressed the fifteenth General Assembly meeting on September 29, laying the strongest emphasis on Nepal's historical independence and its full faith in the United Nations as the custodian of its integrity and sovereignty. He exhorted the major powers to face up to the economic challenge of the underdeveloped countries, which he considered a more important issue than the political differences between the two power blocs. He pleaded strongly for an acceptance by the major powers of a plan for graduated disarmament concurrent with the establishment of a peace force under the auspices of the United Nations. He strongly endorsed the Secretary General's constructive role in the Congo and rejected the "troika" plan suggested by the Soviet Union for manning the United Nations Secretariat. This was B. P. Koirala's last important statement on foreign policy before his dismissal from office and imprisonment in December of that year.

CONCLUDING REMARKS

The preceding sections summarize briefly the notable activities of the Nepali Congress government in the realm of economic, administrative, and foreign policies. Certainly, no bold departures of policies were initiated, although the sheer volume and scope of the measures undertaken easily surpassed the record of all previous governments. In the matter of foreign policy, the dominant trends of the previous years were continued, although there was probably more realism in the planning and execution of policies than at any time in the past. By 1959, the political situation was less susceptible to the raising of foreign policy issues than previously. Political parties were directing as much attention to domestic developments as to the emotional, nationalistic appeals. The old slogans of Indian or Chinese interference in Nepali affairs, for example, no longer enjoyed political vogue; the focus of political concern seemed rather to center on the question of Nepali sovereignty and territorial integrity in the light of deteriorating Sino-Indian dispute in the Himalayas.

Similarly, the economic and administrative measures of the Nepali Congress government were in no significant way different from those pursued by the previous governments. During the second year of Nepali Congress rule there seemed to be an increasing awareness among party leaders that questions of economic development and administrative efficiency were basically pragmatic rather than ideological. There was more than a hint in the Prime Minister's speeches that he desired to enlist the support and collaboration of opposition political parties in national planning and development.

The situation with regard to law and order in the country was neither outstanding nor critical. Oppositional elements exercising the fundamental rights and privileges guaranteed by the 1959 Constitution had sprung up here and there, and were trying their best to discredit the party government, but they seldom constituted a serious threat to the authority of the government. In the districts of West No. 1 and Gorkha, however, the Nepali Congress government was outmaneuvered by local political elements who helped to continue the confused law-and-order situation much longer than was warranted by the points at issue. The culmination of the local "politicking" in the tragic police firing of October, 1960, shocked both the government and some of the opposition parties into a long overdue realization of their political responsibilities. Leaders of both the Nepali Congress and the Gorkha Parishad, for instance, initiated efforts to pacify their followers in the disturbed areas, and in the process were approaching an unofficial but working coalition between the two parties that was of great portent for the political future of the government.

18

King Mahendra and Parliamentary Democracy

FROM 1955 to 1959 King Mahendra had been an unusually active ruler, holding protracted negotiations with political leaders, exercising a close supervision over Cabinet and Secretariat, and undertaking extensive tours within Nepal and abroad. His direct participation in the processes of government imparted a new political dimension to the Crown, in contrast with the essentially constitutional role assumed by his predecessor. But the political system envisaged under the 1959 Constitution could function only if the crown relegated itself to a less central role. The results of the general elections reinforced this situation in certain respects. The absence of a strong opposition party, for instance, deprived the Crown of the leverage with which to counterbalance the ruling party within the constitutional system itself without recourse to more drastic steps such as the full use of the Crown's executive and emergency powers or, under extreme provocation, suspension of the Constitution. Thus the future of parliamentary democracy was contingent upon the degree of mutual trust and toleration that could be engendered between the Nepali Congress leadership and the Crown.

KING MAHENDRA AND THE NEPALI CONGRESS CABINET

King Mahendra experienced little apparent difficulty in making the transition to a constitutional role in 1959. His actions

374

and public statements during this period would seem to have been motivated by a genuine desire to give the institution of parliamentary democracy an honest trial. Once it was clear that the Nepali Congress had won an absolute majority in the general elections, the King unhesitatingly initiated negotiations with B. P. Koirala on the organization of a government. At the same time he admonished several of the opposition leaders who had petitioned him to invalidate the elections, suggesting that they make use of available legal channels for the redress of their grievances.

B. P. Koirala seems to have been given a completely free hand in selecting his Cabinet and in creating the post of Deputy Prime Minister, for which there was no provision in the Constitution. This was a complete break with the role played by the Crown since 1955, when the usual pattern had been for the King to select the party candidates for the Cabinet after protracted negotiations and then combine those selected with a few royal nominees. None of these procedures was followed in 1959. There were no royal nominees, and the list of Cabinet members was drawn up by B. P. Koirala in consultation with the party. Indeed, the list was made public on May 20, one week before King Mahendra announced it officially. Further, the King dissolved the three high-powered administrative bodies he had formed in 1957 to assist him in the supervision of the government. This was widely interpreted as an indication of the King's intention to give a clean slate to the new Cabinet and to allow it to function without direct guidance from the royal palace. King Mahendra also coöperated with the new Cabinet by issuing two executive orders that enabled the government to function until all provisions of the 1959 Constitution had become operative. One of these orders permitted the administration to expend funds on its own authority until a budget had been approved by the Parliament; the other provided for the formation of a Cabinet before the selection of the Upper House of Parliament.

There was only one incident in this initial period in which the King's actions were potentially embarrassing to the Nepali Congress government. In announcing his list of nominees to the Senate on July 13, the King excluded all Nepali Congressmen except for three dissident party leaders. This was interpreted in some quarters as indicative of the King's desire to create an institutional counterbalance to the otherwise overwhelming predominance of the Cabinet within the Parliamentary system. But it can also be interpreted as a token of the King's concern for the broadest representation within the Parliament, only imperfectly achieved in the elections to the Lower House. All major ethnic and minority groups, including a Muslim and a woman, received representation on the Senate's nominated list.

The assumption of broad administrative functions by the Crown in 1955 had led to what was in essence a dyarchical system of administration with two centers of decision making—one at the royal palace and the other at the Central Secretariat (Singha Darbar). The palace secretariat consisted of a complex hierarchy of civil and military officials, some inherited from King Tribhuwan's private staff and some newly recruited, and represented generally a diverse variety of interest groups. There were several important clusters within the palace staff, mostly centered around such factors as kinship relationships and ancestral service at the palace. But all these factions had a common interest in protecting their privileged and crucial decision-making position against the encroachment of the government functioning at the Central Secretariat.

Upon the installation of the Nepali Congress government in 1959, it was clear that the dyarchical pattern of administration was no longer viable. The palace secretariat had to be trimmed of its later accretions of administrative powers if it was to function primarily as a relay station between the King and the Cabinet, as originally intended by King Tribhuwan when he established a private secretariat in 1951. King Mahendra evidently sensed the potential conflict of interests and functions between the two secretariats under the new political system, for he moved to avert such a situation. He ordered the palace secretariat staff to pay their respects to Prime Minister Koirala at his residence shortly after the appointment of the new Cabinet. This formality was symptomatic of the new focus of political authority, and of the King's political perceptiveness.

This trend was reinforced by the care with which the Prime Minister established his personal authority over his colleagues in the Cabinet and thus, in effect, over the Central Secretariat. B. P. Koirala reserved for himself the right to report to the King on governmental affairs, and other members of the Cabinet could seek an audience with the King only with the permission of the Prime Minister. This was a clear break with past practices under which Ministers, and sometimes even Departmental Secretaries, had often sought private audiences with the King and had used these occasions to ventilate grievances against the Prime Minister or other colleagues with the inevitable consequence of endemic disharmony in the government. Presumably, the Prime Minister's ruling was resented in the palace secretariat, since it further restricted its scope of action, but King Mahendra seems to have accepted it as in conformity with his new constitutional status.

In October, 1959, an unprecedented episode took place in Kathmandu when King Mahendra participated in a football game at the invitation of Prime Minister Koirala. The sports event was held at the National Stadium and was open to the public. The proceeds from the game were donated to the Prime Minister's relief fund. King Mahendra and his brothers played on one side and the Prime Minister and his colleagues on the other. The political implications of the game were quickly noted by those sections of the press that were less than satisfied with the constitutional role of the King. To them King Mahendra's participation in the game was the result of a clever psychological assault, contrived by the Prime Minister, on the traditional prestige of the Crown. Other papers, which upheld the constitutional role of the King, hailed the event as one of historical importance not only "for the evolution of constitutional monarchy in Nepal, but also for the whole of the world."[1] The debate raged with such intensity that King Mahendra felt it necessary to justify his participation. In a statement issued on the occasion he claimed that he had as much right as any other citizen to take part in public welfare activities, and added that inasmuch as games developed a spirit of unity they had an important role in promoting national progress.

In many respects King Mahendra's participation in a public sports event was the most dramatic confirmation of his role as a constitutional monarch. By temperament and habit he was easily the most serious-minded monarch Nepal had known for a long time. It was considered somewhat unusual, if not astounding, for him to condescend to play against his Ministers, who held their offices at his pleasure, in a football game. By tradition the King of Nepal is revered as the reincarnation of Vishnu—the Hindu god of preservation. King Mahendra had never publicly debunked this tradition; and for countless numbers of his subjects, the restoration of royal prerogatives in 1951 had meant a revivified faith in the divinity of the King. Mahendra's numerous trips throughout the country since his accession to the throne had brought this concept nearer to reality for his subjects, especially those who received quick dispensations of justice or royal favors of one kind or another. That King Mahendra took part in a football game and, more significantly, justified his role, was hailed by many observers as a prelude to a redefinition of the Crown's role in Nepali politics. It is possible that the Prime Minister and his colleagues subscribed to this view and drew up their future plans on the assumption that the constitutional role of the Crown was an accomplished and irrevocable fact.

THE KING AND THE OPPOSITION

Opposition political parties organized a number of anti-government demonstrations in the fall and winter of 1959, but on what were obviously trivial or artificial issues. As such, they had little influence on King Mahendra's assessment of the political situation or his attitude toward the Nepali Congress government. Of a quite different nature was the demonstration in Kathmandu on December 3 in which a large crowd, consisting mostly of non-Ranas who had attained prestige and wealth under the Rana regime, gathered at the gates of the royal palace to protest against the imposition of taxes on urban land, water taps, and houses.[2] This demonstration, which was not the work of opposition parties, set the pattern for subsequent non-party political agitation which sought King Mahendra's direct intervention in the affairs of government.

These demonstrations may have aroused the first serious doubts in King Mahendra's mind as to the appropriateness of his strictly constitutional role. In any case, from this time on the King was more inclined to pass judgments, in public, on the activities and policies of the government. The first indication of this change in attitude came at the conclusion of his tour of western Nepal in January, 1960. On previous occasions the King had used his tours to redress local grievances by settling lawsuits, bestowing favors, and making liberal donations to local institutions. Upon the inauguration of an elected government, some aspects of the royal tours had become redundant, if not irrelevant. Nevertheless, the King's tour of western Nepal in the winter of 1959/60 was carried out along the same lines as his earlier tours and, as such, constituted a minor breach of his status as a constitutional monarch.[3]

Even more significant was the speech the King gave at a public reception at Nepalganj on January 30 upon the conclusion of the tour. He remarked:

. . . the people should direct the elected government on the right path. If the people fail to do so and corruption continues to increase in the country, we shall have to take another step to fulfill our duty. . . . Democracy was ushered into our country and the last elections were held with the coöperation of all the people for the achievement of these objectives. If democracy fails to achieve these things, it is meaningless. It is of no use if it brings harm to the people, discourages industrialization, makes administration of justice more costly and difficult, encourages bribery and corruption, increases the rate of unemployment, makes persons in the government see only their own selfish interests, and gives antinational elements the opportunity to take undue advantage. The responsibility to see that these things do not happen, along with the responsibility to protect their freedom, has also devolved on the Nepali people. Every Nepali citizen should work with the full realization of this responsibility so that I may not adopt another measure to fulfill my responsibility. Here I would also like to say that I, too, have some duties—these are to safeguard the sovereignty and independence of the country and to look after such works as are conducive to national welfare. If hindrances really come in the way, I am prepared to do whatever is the need of the hour. What I want is that I should always get the coöperation of the people, as ever.[4]

Although King Mahendra did not refer to the Nepali Congress government specifically, it was obvious that his comments constituted an appraisal of its record to date. What led to this outburst on the part of a monarch who had a reputation for deliberateness and caution is a matter for conjecture. Most of his hypothetically stated accusations had a strong contemporary ring to them, for these were precisely what critics of the government were saying. By repeating their complaints King Mahendra lent the prestige of his high office to their views and a degree of substantiation to the opposition's case. It can hardly have been strictly coincidental that opposition elements grew more demonstrative, vociferous, and obstreperous subsequently.

The royal message issued on the occasion of "National Day," February 18, also contained a veiled criticism of the Nepali Congress government. In what was in effect an exhortation to the government, King Mahendra remarked:

If, discarding anarchism and narrow-mindedness, the government gives priority to the welfare of the country—only then can the people understand the policies of the government.[5]

King Mahendra returned to the theme of need for better rapport between the government and the people during a speech at Rajbiraj on March 12 to mark the unveiling of a statue of the late King Tribhuwan:

All must have realized that those who are actively engaged in nation-building tasks must understand the situation in the country. If we work without understanding this, all our labor will be fruitless and both the people and the government will be blamed. Therefore it has become essential that responsible persons should think twice before starting any work. Without resources no work can be started. It is the duty of the government to start a planned economy and it is also the duty of the people to take part in the national development program.[6]

One feature of the King's critical remarks should be noticed, although perhaps its political import is not completely obvious. On both occassions when the King delivered highly political speeches at Nepalganj and Rajbiraj, the Prime Minister was out of the country, on the former occasion in India and on the latter in China.

When Parliament reconvened on April 1, King Mahendra delivered from the throne an address prepared by the Cabinet in which he cataloged exhaustively—perhaps monotonously—all the principal accomplishments of the government in the past year. About one week later, he left on state visits to Japan, the United States and Canada which kept him away from Nepal for more than three months. A Regency Council under the chairmanship of his brother, Prince Himalaya, was appointed to act on his behalf in his absence. In a message issued on the eve of his departure, he defined the spheres of responsibility of the Cabinet, the Regency Council, and the people:

The Cabinet is there to establish peace and order, expedite reconstruction works, and carry out the day to day administration of the country. We have formed a Regency Council under the leadership of my brother, His Royal Highness Prince Himalaya Vir Vikram Shah Deva, to discharge functions on our behalf during our absence. There is no doubt that, if all the people of the country identify their interests and welfare with that of the whole nation and maintain a liberal and broad outlook, we shall always be accorded an honored seat in the comity of nations, and we shall achieve much progress in every walk of life.[7]

But on the day before the King was to leave the country on his extensive world tour, he was intercepted by refugees from West No. 1 while returning from inaugurating a water filtration plant at Balaju. The demonstrators asked the King to intervene directly to improve law and order in their district, and the King was reported to have assured them that necessary measures would soon be adopted to that effect. This incident, even if deliberately timed by the refugees to coincide with the King's departure, presaged an ominous domestic situation during his prolonged absence.

King Mahendra left Kathmandu on April 10, accompanied by a large personal and official retinue, including Deputy Prime Minister Suvarna Shamsher. At the conclusion of his state visit to Japan (April 18–25), the King and his entourage flew to the

United States at the invitation of the government. During this trip, he had an opportunity to express his opinions upon the political system in Nepal in particular and world affairs in general. In his address to the United States Congress on April 28 he observed:

You are all familiar with the strains and difficulties under which all newly established democracies have to work. . . . Provision for fully representative institutions of government and legislatures, respect for fundamental rights and due process of law, respect for freedom and dignity of the individual are some of the basic principles that underlie our constitution. As is apparent to you, the constitution of Nepal is based on the concepts of law, liberty, and rights prevalent for a long time in your own country.

. . . We believe in an independent foreign policy of judging every international issue on its merits without consideration of anybody's fear or favor and in a policy of non-entanglement. . . . This may sound a little idealistic and a little too impractical but as a small nation we feel that this is the best way in which we can contribute to the discussions and deliberations in the United Nations and to the interests of world peace and friendly relations among them.[8]

Addressing the National Press Club in Washington on April 29, he remarked:

Nepal's is a test case as to whether a small country situated between two big countries [India and China] can, in the realities of power relations in the mid-twentieth century world, preserve its independence, freedom and sovereignty in its own way and manner. On the answer to this question will depend the life and future of the principles of international justice and the ideas of co-existence of big and small nations.[9]

In a speech at a dinner given by the Far East American Council of Commerce and Industry in New York on May 2, King Mahendra invited American businessmen to invest in Nepal and promised them the fullest possible scope for private enterprise. Then he went on to observe that the standard of living in Nepal was one of the lowest in the world, and that if democracy was to survive in that country, it must be able to deliver the goods as quickly as possible.[10] Speaking at a dinner in Los Angeles on May 10, King Mahendra pointed out that the practice of peaceful coexistence had preserved the independence of Nepal for more than three thousand years. The Nepali Ambassador to the United States, Rishikesh Shah, elaborated King Mahendra's point and offered the "unblemished integrity of Nepal as a model for the practice of peaceful coexistence by nations of different ideologies." [11]

King Mahendra began his state visit to Canada on May 25. On the following day he held a press conference in Montreal and observed that Nepal's relations with Communist China were strictly formal and cordial. Referring to the political situation in Nepal, he said that Nepali Communists had been thwarted by the eighteen-month-old democratic Constitution: "Wherever the communists are not banned but are allowed to work openly, they have made slow progress"—an interesting comment in view of his later banning of the Communist party (and all other parties) in December, 1960.[12]

After completing his official visits, King Mahendra left for Nepal on June 16, with visits to Lisbon, Paris, Frankfurt, Vienna, Tehran, Kabul, Srinagar, and New Delhi on the way, and arrived in Kathmandu on July 28. Once again the West No. 1 refugees intercepted the King's procession on the road, demanding the formation of a Royal Commission to investigate their grievances. King Mahendra replied at a public reception:

Upon reaching India, I learnt that disturbances were still continuing in West No. 1 near the capital. If true, this is highly distressing, but I hope that with one year of experience in running the administration, the government must have paid proper attention to it.

Turning to the Chinese incursion into Nepali territory in June, he commented:

The highly unfortunate incident that took place last month on our northern borders had naturally wounded the feelings of the people of Nepal. I am however fully confident that such a mistake will never be repeated by our friendly neighbor. Mere talk is never effective in achieving the progress of the country. In the modern world the wise course is to move patiently according to the time.[13]

Soon after King Mahendra's return, opposition elements—no doubt, taking comfort from the implied criticisms of the government in the royal statements—intensified their agitational activities. Refugees from West No. 1 continued to demonstrate stubbornly for restitution of their lost property and maintenance of law and order in their district. The King, in order to apprise himself fully of the situation in the country, began a series of interviews with members of the Cabinet and with opposition leaders. He met with the entire Cabinet on August 6 and, reportedly, demanded information on the progress of the government's activities.[14] Consequently, the month of August was filled with rumors that the King planned to dismiss the Nepali Congress government because of its shortcomings. B. P. Koirala's allegedly critical remarks about the Constitution at the Nepali Congress party conference in May were widely publicized, and the so-called lack of harmony between the King and the Cabinet was soon described as a personal struggle between King Mahendra, who upheld the Constitution as it was, and B. P. Koirala, who wanted to amend it. Indeed, one of the local weeklies reported that the King had succumbed to Cabinet pressure and had advised the Prime Minister to amend the Constitution if it had any undemocratic features.[15]

While all these ominous rumors were circulating in August, Tulsi Giri resigned from the Cabinet. The reported tension between the King and the Cabinet did not express itself in any conspicuous form, but King Mahendra continued to play an assertive and political role in dealing with opposition groups and individuals. In his reply to the organizers of the Jana Hit Sangha, who had petitioned the King to repeal the government's taxation and land reform measures, he observed:

It is not proper for His Majesty to intervene in any way from time to time. If you think that the government whom you chose has acted in a way detrimental to the interests of the country or any of its citizens, every Nepali citizen has the right to express his opposition according to rules. If, therefore, with the welfare of the people and the country in mind, you initiate any good step in a democratic manner, His Majesty the King will definitely act for the equal protection and welfare of nationalism, the country, and the people.[16]

In the circumstances, this statement was a virtual incitement to the Jana Hit Sangha to continue its agitation, which was aimed specifically at the dismissal of the Nepali Congress Cabinet and the reinstitution of a direct-rule system.

On October 17, the King and the Queen, accompanied by a retinue including Deputy Prime Minister Suvarna Shamsher, arrived in London to begin a three-day state visit, the first ever made there by a Nepali monarch. Having completed the state visit, King Mahendra stayed on for an additional two weeks, inspecting educational establishments and industrial plants throughout the United Kingdom. He returned to Kathmandu on November 9. During his absence the police firing in Gorkha had occurred, resulting in the reported loss of seven lives. In his reply to the civic reception held for him at the Kathmandu airport, King Mahendra commented:

Like other patriots, we have been exceedingly grieved to hear that during our absence, unfortunately, disturbances occurred in some parts of the country and some people were killed. But I have nothing to say further on this matter without understanding the facts properly. We are fully confident that by the grace of God and with the efforts of patriots, law and order will be maintained all over the country and our country will go on marching along the path of progress.[17]

November 11 was the tenth anniversary of the 1950 revolution. The Nepali Congress government decided to commemorate the occasion by inaugurating development projects all over Nepal, estimated to cost more than 100 million rupees, as part of the government's effort to spend the largely unused allocation of the first Five-Year Plan by the end of the fiscal year. King Mahendra took part in some of the inauguration ceremonies, but members of the Cabinet, including Prime Minister Koirala, were far more active and enthusiastic. The King did take this opportunity to issue a message to the people:

The world is always changing, and we feel therefore that revolution is always continuous among men. With this truth in mind, responsible persons should renounce their selfish interests and work honestly for the welfare of all or else they will be regarded as having fulfilled their selfish interests with the blood of brave persons. We therefore pray to Lord Pashupatinath that he should kindle the true revolution in the minds of all the people of Nepal to enable them to remain honest, renounce selfish interests and mutual quarrels, and devote themselves to service.[18]

Viewed after the event, this message may well seem to have been intended to prepare the ground for the royal *coup d'état* that came five weeks later.

THE DECEMBER, 1960, COUP

The Indian Commander in Chief, General Thimayya, arrived in Kathmandu on December 8, 1960, for a one-week official visit. Deputy Prime Minister Suvarna Shamsher left for Calcutta on December 12—for personal reasons. The much-publicized Nepali Youth Conference, attended by a number of delegates from foreign countries, began its session on the morning of December 15. By evening of that fateful day, all the members of the Nepali Congress Cabinet that were in Kathmandu had been arrested, and King Mahendra had sounded the death knell of parliamentary democracy in a broadcast to the country over Radio Nepal.

The Royal Proclamation leveled several specific charges against the Nepali Congress government, alleging that the elected government had (*a*) set aside the interests of the country and the people and wielded authority in a manner designed solely to advance party interests; (*b*) attempted to dislocate and paralyze the administrative machinery in contravention of the laws of the realm; (*c*) encouraged corrupt practices; (*d*) proved incapable of maintaining law and order; (*e*) produced a disturbed and vitiated atmosphere by pursuing impractical measures; (*f*) encouraged antinational elements.[19] With some slight verbal modifications, these vague allegations have been endlessly repeated in government pronouncements and the local press, but have never been substantiated by documentation or appropriate proceedings in any court of law.

Before commencing a discussion of the new political system which King Mahendra has introduced, it would be useful to analyze his apparent motives in discarding parliamentary democracy and also the situation in Nepal which permitted him to take such drastic action with impunity. Only briefly noted in the world press other than in India, these dramatic events were widely interpreted abroad as falling within the same general pattern as similar developments in Pakistan, Indonesia, Burma, Turkey, Iraq and Korea in which Western-style parliamentary institutions had been abolished because of their alleged unsuitability or failure. King Mahendra has himself advanced such an interpretation of the December, 1960, *coup* as, in a sense, justifying and legitimatizing his action.

How valid is this interpretation of these events in Nepal? There is, undoubtedly, a superficial similarity between the December *coup* in Nepal and developments in other Asian countries. On closer observation, however, it is also clear that there were crucial and basic differences which distinguished the Nepal situation. Probably the most important was the relatively minor part played by the military in the royal *coup*—a striking contrast to the situation in Pakistan, Burma, Korea, and Turkey, where military men dominated what were essentially revolutionary movements. There was no "Young Turk" faction in the Nepal state army with pronounced political views and ambitions, demanding and forcing changes in the country's political structure. Indeed, the military establishment has been remarkably quiescent in Nepal in recent years. To the extent that it did play a role in the December *coup*, it functioned as an instrument of the King.

A second feature that distinguished the December *coup* in Nepal from superficially similar developments elsewhere in Asia and Africa was its essentially conservative character. What the *coup* really signified, at least initially, was the restoration of the essential characteristics of the political system as these existed up to the inauguration of parliamentary democracy in 1959. The *coup* had none of the momentum or *esprit de corps* which marked similar developments elsewhere in Asia, nor did it consolidate the position of a new ruling elite. On the contrary, the dominant political and social forces in the new structure were and are the same traditional social and economic groups that the King had depended on before the 1959 general elections.

Never openly discussed, but certainly one of the most vital considerations leading to the abrogation of parliamentary institutions, was King Mahendra's dissatisfaction with the relegation of the Crown to a comparatively minor role in the governmental structure after the installation of the Nepali Congress government. Another factor may have been King Mahendra's suspicion that the "socialist-oriented" Nepali Congress leaders were plotting the eventual abolition of the monarchy. Certain indiscreet remarks by Nepali Congress leaders alluding to the allegedly obstructionist role played by the King and the 1959 Constitution seemed to add substance to the King's apprehensions. Leaders of other political parties and a few disaffected Nepali Congress leaders were only too ready to caution the King about the Nepali Congress's ultimate intentions. In any case, such warnings could count on a receptive audience.

Whether there was any substance to King Mahendra's suspicion that the Nepali Congress government was plotting the overthrow of the monarchy is questionable. The Nepali Congress was predominately a young intellectuals' party and, like most young Nepali intellectuals, was prone to view monarchical institutions as unmodern and, hence, dispensable. But B. P. Koirala and the top echelons of the party seem to have been concerned more with minimizing possible sources of conflict with the King than with plotting his downfall. That the Cabinet would have deliberately instigated a constitutional crisis under the prevailing conditions is unlikely; rather, it would have preferred to leave the question of the ultimate fate of the monarchy to the distant future when a more objective evaluation of its role in the parliamentary system would be feasible.

This does not mean, of course, that a constitutional crisis over the monarchy was not intrinsic to the trend of political developments. There was, indeed, a fundamental difference between the King and the Nepali Congress over the proper role of the monarchy in contemporary Nepal. Since ascending the throne in 1955, King Mahendra has consistently stressed the theory that the monarchy is essential to orderly progress and to the very existence of Nepal as a nation. In this view, the Crown is the only institution capable of providing strong national leadership. It is, therefore, the responsibility of the King to function in the political sphere, directly and decisively when necessary, and as the ultimate source of authority in less critical situations.

While the Nepali Congress has always publicly conceded the central role played by the monarchy, it has also insisted that the Crown can serve in this capacity only as long as it functions constitutionally—i.e., the King should reign but not rule—and that the Crown's role as the symbol of national unity is contingent upon the King's acting as a unifying and nationalizing influence. In contrast, the Nepali Congress has charged King Mahendra with frequently playing upon factionalism within the parties to disrupt them and divide them in order to further his own narrow political goals. Whether he actively instigated the schisms and factional division in the parties, as is alleged, or merely took advantage of their existence is incidental to the question. The effect would have been equally injurious in either case for it, by encouraging instability in the party system and, indirectly, in the administration as well. The Crown, according to the Nepali Congress leaders, should remain above politics, not indulge in them.

Another factor that might have precipitated the King's intervention was his reading of the changing line-up of political forces in the country in 1960. Political observers had sensed the need for a strong opposition party to act as a countervailing force to the Nepali Congress government ever since its formation. There was wide expectation at the time that the Gorkha Parishad leadership would attempt to rally all the anti–Nepali Congress political elements and present a strong opposition to the government. This, however, failed to materialize; instead, the Gorkha Parishad under the leadership of Bharat Shamsher was moving closer to a coalition with the Nepali Congress. It was obvious that a working coalition between these two parties would result in the establishment of a monolithic party government, the extinction of all democratic opposition, and the emergence of the Communist party as the only political alternative to the Nepali Congress's democratic-socialist program. And, more importantly, if the situation had developed along these lines, King Mahendra would have found it extremely difficult to turn down a proposal for a national Cabinet. He would have been caught in the awkward situation of wanting a faster pace of economic development but not at the risk of perpetuating a Nepali Congress–Gorkha Parishad political monopoly in the country.

But it is doubtful that King Mahendra's deep-seated aversion to political parties and party politics would long permit him to play a purely constitutional role, as designated in the 1959 constitutional system. Several of the King's statements, some dating as early as 1951, were caustic in their appraisal of party leaders and frankly skeptical of the capacity of the parties to provide the kind of vigorous, honest political leadership Nepal has needed and has seldom had. In banning the parties after the December *coup,* the King was not only ridding himself of irritating critics and potentially dangerous rivals for power, but was also, in his view, eliminating a pernicious influence upon the body politic in Nepal. A broader, more tolerant and comprehensive perspective of the role played by parties in any democratic political system has never impressed itself upon the King.

SOURCES OF SUPPORT FOR THE ROYAL COUP

Any analysis of King Mahendra's motivations in dismissing the Nepali Congress must necessarily be confined to the realm of mere speculation, for the King has not chosen to speak frankly on this subject as yet. It is possible, however, to explain how it was possible for him, with such little difficulty, to carry out a *coup* against a government that had won a decisive electoral victory twenty months earlier. The answer is that important and articulate groups upon which the King could depend for support were organized and capable of action, while the elements in Nepali society which supported the Nepali Congress were not nearly so well organized or influential.

A large majority of the landowning and commercial interests in Nepal, for instance, were unalterably opposed to the Nepali Congress government's land and taxation policy. The moderate character of the economic legislation enacted by the Koirala Cabinet did not diminish their apprehensions, since these measures were considered to be merely the first in a series of gradually more drastic changes in the land and taxation system. These vested interest groups, with their close ties to various cliques in the palace, had long since concluded that the King was the last effective barrier to the imposition of fundamental economic reforms, and this attitude was crucial in determining their response to the December *coup.*

A small but influential conglomeration of tradition-oriented groups provided the core for another center of resistance to the Nepali Congress regime. Fiercely monarchist in outlook and deeply disturbed by the progressive diminution of the role and powers of the King, they were appalled by the secular, "socialist" aspects of the Koirala government. Orthodox Hindus for the most part, they viewed the refusal of post-1951 governments to apply the dharmashastric clauses (i.e., caste provisions) that the Rana regime had made an integral part of the Nepali legal code as subversive to the principles upon which Nepal's society was based. The monarchy was considered to be the last important obstacle to invidious influences from the outside world, particularly India. Anything that bolstered the throne was assured of their support. This attitude was strengthened by King Mahendra's own traditional Hindu predilections which were reflected in the clauses in both the 1959 and the 1962 Constitutions that barred ascent to the throne to anyone but an "adherent of Aryan culture and Hindu religion."

The allegedly "pro-India" tendencies of the Nepali Congress's foreign policy aroused the opposition of several other groups that differed basically from those so far discussed. These were, in essence, "anti-India and pro-China" in orientation, though for widely varied reasons. Included within this category were the Communists, some students and young intellectuals incensed over what they interpreted as Indian interference in Nepal's internal politics, renascent Buddhist groups resentful of the infliction of "Brahmanic" social regulations on non-Hindu elements of Nepal's society, and even some reformist, modernist groups that strongly opposed the anti-egalitarian features of the caste system, whose presence in Nepal they attributed to age-old influences from India.

Many members of these groups are not pro-Communist in any real sense, and even their ostensibly pro-China attitudes seem to be a thin veneer assumed for the occasion. They are, however, suspicious and resentful of India and are susceptible to anti-Indian slogans, even when used to disguise attacks on policies and institutions they would otherwise be inclined to support. It is on this single issue, moreover, that much of the educated youth of Nepal and King Mahendra can find common ground, for in most other respects their views are widely divergent.

King Mahendra has also drawn considerable support from some elements in the bureaucracy, in particular the royal palace secretariat and some old-line, Rana-trained officials in the government secretariat who lost much of their power and influence through the installation of parliamentary institutions. Both these groups strongly supported the reëstablishment of the pre-1959 governmental system under which they had flourished and, moreover, were well situated to influence King Mahendra in this direction.

Probably the most important mainstay of the King, however,

is the support he has received from the army. This support was particularly crucial in the immediate post-*coup* period. Not only did it provide the King with the physical capactiy to suppress disturbances, but it gave him another source from which reliable appointments could be made to the Central Secretariat and other government posts. A number of army officers were appointed to high positions in the civil administration immediately after the *coup,* replacing public servants suspected of too close ties with the Nepali Congress regime.

That the military has been so docile and easily managed is rather astonishing in Nepal, where the army leadership has had a long tradition of direct and open intervention in politics, going back at least to the days when the country was first unified under the Shah dynasty in the latter part of the eighteenth century. An apolitical military leadership has been the exception rather than the rule in Nepal's history, and the existing situation is largely a tribute to King Mahendra's perceptive and careful planning. Fully cognizant of the role played by the army in mid-nineteenth-century developments which deprived the ruling dynasty of all but nominal sovereign powers, King Mahendra has taken care to emasculate the military as a potent political force—and with considerable success.

To accomplish this end, King Mahendra has utilized various tactics. He has been extremely careful, for instance, to retain complete and direct authority over the military in his capacity as Supreme Commander in Chief. The Defence Ministry at the Central Secretariat has had little influence in military affairs except insofar as it functioned as an instrument of the royal palace. Up to May, 1959, King Mahendra always selected as Defence Minister someone closely connected with the royal family, even when a party Cabinet was in office.

The Nepali Congress Cabinet was the first in which a party member held the Defence portfolio. Nevertheless, the King was careful to retain ultimate and direct authority over the army. Prime Minister Koirala, who also held the Defence portfolio, was probably less involved in Defence Ministry affairs than his predecessors had been. In any case, the King faced no difficulty with the Defence Ministry when he utilized the state army in the course of the December *coup.*

King Mahendra has also paid close attention to the composition of the officer corps since coming to the throne. It has been reported that he has sometimes barred promotion to ambitious young officers suspected of political motivations or interests in favor of men who were more dependable politically. Whether intentionally or not, the officer corps has been remarkably apolitical since 1956, when the King nipped a potentially dangerous plot in which several lower-level officers were involved.

A somewhat less obvious source of support for the December *coup* was provided by opposition party leaders. With relatively few exceptions, most of the opposition leaders welcomed the King's action and promised their coöperation in the establishment of a new political structure. In view of the ban placed on all political parties shortly afterward, and the King's announced intention to dispense with parliamentary government based upon the party system, this attitude would seem to have had masochistic overtones. On closer examination, however, it can be seen that only a few of the opposition party leaders had really benefited from the inauguration of the parliamentary system or held expectations of doing so in the future: the overwhelming victory of the Nepali Congress in the 1959 elections had deprived most of them and their parties of any real influence in Nepali politics.

In these circumstances many opposition politicians had become increasingly unhappy with the parliamentary system, which had proved so ill-suited for the proper appreciation of their talents. Few of them were prepared to undertake the hard task of building a mass-support party from the bottom up, and their only hope for regaining political influence was through royal rather than popular support. These politicians were not particularly distressed with King Mahendra's decision to replace parliamentary institutions with another variation of a direct-rule system under which political advancement would depend primarily on the patronage of the King. Under this system anybody could become a Minister, without reference to the extent of popular support he might enjoy.

CONCLUDING REMARKS

The royal *coup* of December, 1960, will undoubtedly go down in the history of Nepal as an important landmark in the evolution of the political relationship between the Shah rulers and their Prime Ministers. During the pre-Rana period this relationship had been marked by considerable violence and tension. Indeed, until the emergence of Jang Bahadur Rana the careers of Nepali Prime Ministers had ended usually in political disgrace and frequently in violent death. After the establishment of the Rana regime, the Shah monarchy was reduced to a status of political nonentity for a century. The political restoration of the

Shah monarchy was one of the direct outcomes of the 1950 revolution, which, however, also produced a somewhat antithetical and historically unprecedented preoccupation with the establishment of a constitutional democracy in Nepal.

Fundamentally, the December *coup* represented an authoritarian resolution of the basic conflict between these two antithetical by-products of the 1950 revolution. Historically, the nearest parallel to King Mahendra's action was the arrest of Prime Minister Bhimsen Thapa in 1836 by King Rajendra on specious charges, later recanted by the King himself, of disloyalty to the royal family. Those were the days of conspiratorial politics, and vicissitudes in political fortunes were sometimes expressed through poisonings, hired assassins, bloody massacres, and dark dungeons. In 1960 the participants were different, and the political methods and vocabulary were modern, but the basic spirit and idiom of Nepali Court politics remained unchanged.

Panchayat Raj

(1961–64)

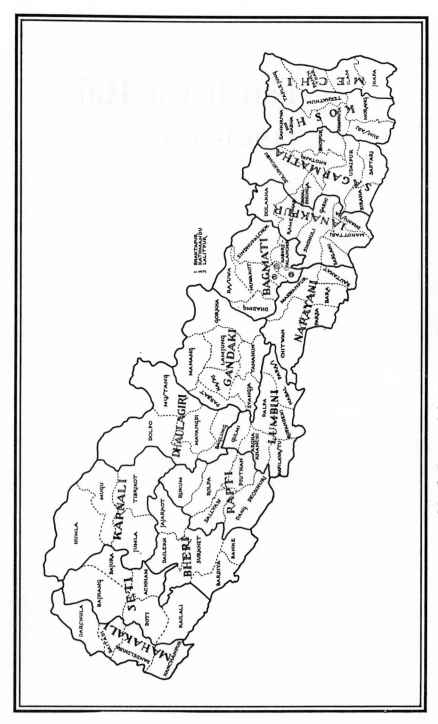

Map 2. Zones and development districts of Nepal, 1963.

19

The 1962 Constitution: Experiments with "Guided" Democracy

THE DECEMBER, 1960, *coup* marked the reinstitution of what was in essence a period of direct rule by King Mahendra. Much of the political pattern characteristic of previous direct-rule periods (1955 and 1957–58) once again became evident. There was, however, one significant distinction. Before the promulgation of the 1959 Constitution, the direct-rule system had been viewed as a stop-gap measure. The ultimate objective, as specified in several of the King's statements, was parliamentary democracy under a constitutional monarchy. All this changed, of course, after the dismissal of the B. P. Koirala Cabinet, and the consequences were even more fundamental than first seemed probable. In justifying his action the King not only criticized the Nepali Congress government, but attacked the parliamentary system itself, which he characterized as a clumsy Western imposition incompatible with Nepal's traditions, history, and objective conditions. What was required, he announced, was a new "Nepali" political system that conformed to the spirit of Nepal's traditions and culture— "Nepalism," in the term used by one of his new Ministers.

Thus, by the end of 1960 it was evident that King Mahendra had more than a change in government in mind in dismissing the B. P. Koirala cabinet. Far more important was the decision to embark once again on new experiments in the structure, functioning, and theoretical basis of the entire political system. That the

395

form this new structure would take was not very clearly defined—
even in King Mahendra's mind, it would seem—was strongly
indicated by the seemingly haphazard manner in which new
institutions of government were created and old institutions that
had been virtually discarded after the 1950 revolution were
resurrected. The approach was so casual as to lead some observers
to question the ultimate intentions of the King. But while
circumstances surrounding the establishment of the new political
system may have appeared chaotic and unplanned, probably this
was owing to uncertainty in the King's mind as to the form the
changes should take rather than to indecision as to the necessity
for change itself.

An unofficial *ad hoc* committee, consisting of four high
officials of the Central Secretariat, was appointed shortly after the
coup to consider institutional innovations. The committee was
instructed to survey political institutions in Yugoslavia, Egypt,
Pakistan, and Indonesia to determine whether recent experiences
in these countries might be instructive in the establishment of a
"Nepali" political system. Approximately a year later, another
committee was appointed to draft a new Constitution. The results
of these and other inquiries, as formalized in the Constitution
King Mahendra bestowed on the country on December 16, 1962,
was a rather odd but ingenious combination of certain features of
the "National Guidance" system in Egypt and Indonesia, the
"Basic Democracy" system in Pakistan, the "Class Organization"
system in Egypt and Yugoslavia, and the panchayat system in
operation in several Indian states. Added onto this basic structure
were the Raj Sabha ("Council of State") and the Daudahas
("Tour Commissions") , more perceptibly "Nepali" in origin and
inspiration.

Not long before the promulgation of the 1962 Constitution
three separate but interdependent institutions had been created
to provide the framework of the new political system: the four-tier
panchayat and class organization systems, supervised by a National Guidance Ministry. There was no necessary and compelling
logic in the decision to establish these three institutions, and their
interconnection was initially more contrived than real. Nevertheless, they were welded into a coherent and integrated mechanism
—in theory, at least—in which each was intended to complement
and supplement the other two. At this stage of developments, all
three institutions seemed to be viewed as integral parts of the new
political structure. Indeed, the lack of detail in many sections of
the 1962 Constitution is probably attributable to the fact that
several of the basic institutions of government provided for in the

organic law had already been established by legislation and had been functioning for several months. In order to comprehend the new political structure in its entirety, therefore, it is necessary to extend the scope of analysis beyond the 1962 Constitution to the relevant supplementary legislation and to the manner of its implementation.

PANCHAYAT RAJ

In a ceremony held in Kathmandu on April 13, 1962, to swear in the elected heads of the Kathmandu Valley panchayats, King Mahendra dwelt at some length on the character and function of the panchayat (literally, a council of five persons, called *panchas*) system.

We have confidently moved toward panchayat democracy by beginning the New Year [Nepali calendar] with the initiation of the panchayat system. This Nepali plant . . . is suited to the climate of our country. There is no Nepali who does not know what a pancha and a panchayat is. The development of culture and civilization in our country . . . has taken place under the panchayat system. Parliamentary democracy has proved unsuitable because it lacks the Nepali qualities which are found in the panchayat system. The nationalistic feelings associated with the awakening are not as possible under any other system as they are under the panchayat system.[1]

Scholars might be inclined to quibble with King Mahendra's emphasis on the role panchayats have played in Nepal's historical development. Institutions given that appellation have functioned in Nepal, but have done so primarily as instruments of caste administration or as judicial bodies in the implementation of Brahmanic social regulations. Whether panchayats had ever served as units of government is open to question, but there is no doubt that they had ceased to function in this capacity during the Rana regime (1846–1951), as was indicated by the difficulties encountered in the efforts to revitalize panchayats before 1962. The Rana regime itself, in its last stages, attempted to contrive a modified parliamentary system based upon panchayats. The post-1950 governments also demonstrated an interest in this institution. A comprehensive Panchayat Act was enacted in 1956, but was never implemented with any vigor, and only a small number of panchayats were actually set up. The Nepali Congress government, however, had projected legislation to expand the powers and functions of the panchayats, and had seemed determined to press for their establishment throughout the whole of Nepal.

Indeed, King Mahendra's policy toward panchayats can be distinguished from that of the Nepali Congress government only in terms of the role assigned these bodies in the total political structure. Previously, they were viewed merely as local government institutions. Under the 1962 Constitution, on the other hand, panchayats constitute the theoretical foundation upon which the entire political superstructure is based.

It is interesting to note, incidentally, that King Mahendra's panchayat system marks a revival in some respects of the principles underlying the panchayat system projected in the 1948 Constitution bestowed on the country by the Rana Prime Minister, Padma Shamsher. Indeed, we can assume that the 1948 Constitution has had a considerable influence upon the King, for the similarities between this document and the 1962 Constitution are too striking to be coincidental. Even the words Padma Shamsher used in announcing the 1948 Constitution have a familiar ring to students of contemporary Nepali politics:

We have tried to mould the elective system of the west to the panchayat system, which is an essential part of our heritage and culture. . . . It is the government's desire that all good, able and energetic elected representatives of the people should come to the centre, and co-operate with the government, but it would be very unfortunate if the introduction of political elections should lead to quarrels or disorder in the country. . . . It is not the intention of the government that the country should be thrown into the vortex of the party system, and the government will never lend its encouragement to the habit of bringing about the election of any candidate by the strength of party machinery rather than by his own ability and eligibility.[2]

These could just as well be the words of King Mahendra in his Royal Proclamation on the establishment of "partyless panchayat democracy" in 1962.

As outlined in the 1962 Constitution, the panchayats have been organized on a four-tier structure, modeled to some extent after the "Basic Democracy" system in Pakistan and the "Panchayati Raj" system in India.* The lowest and primary units are the village *(Gaon)* and town *(Nagar)* panchayats, approximately 3,700 in number. Superimposed on these are district *(Zilla)* panchayats, one for each of the seventy-five Development Districts, and zonal *(Anchal)* panchayats in each of the 14 regional units established under the new administrative reorganization pro-

---

* The description of the panchayat system is based, in part, on interviews with officials of the Panchayat Department and the National Guidance Ministry, October–December, 1961, and October–November, 1963.

gram.* Finally, at the highest level, is the national (*Rashtriya*) panchayat—the "Parliament" under the 1962 Constitution.

By December, 1962—before the promulgation of the new Constitution—legislation defining the powers and functions of the village, town, and district panchayats had been enacted.[3] The Village Panchayat Act provided for the establishment of a village assembly (*Gaon Sabha*) in each panchayat area, consisting of all Nepali citizens twenty-one years of age or older. The assemblies were assigned two principal duties: to elect the members of the panchayat (nine members, elected for six-year terms),† and to hold two annual meetings—a winter meeting to discuss and approve the village budget as formulated by the panchayat, and a summer meeting to discuss development programs.

The village panchayats have been granted limited taxing, administrative, and judicial powers.‡ They can levy a land-tax surcharge amounting to 10 per cent of the central government's land tax, as well as taxes on trades, occupations, and vehicles and fees on specified subjects. Their administrative functions mainly involve assisting development programs in the area, supervising village-owned or village-controlled property, and maintaining certain types of records—census, vital statistics, and so forth. The panchayats eventually will also serve as courts of original jurisdiction in some civil cases and in minor criminal cases. The central government's ultimate authority over the village panchayats is assured, however, by the provisions granting the Panchayat Ministry discretionary power to suspend or dissolve a panchayat and to appoint a provisional panchayat entitled to exercise full powers.

The Town Panchayat Act replaced the Municipality Act (1953), although here again there were only insignificant changes in the powers and functions of the local government units. Under the 1962 Act, any town with a population exceeding 10,000

---

* For a detailed description of this administrative reorganization program see His Majesty's Government, *Anchal Ebam Vikas Zilla Vibhajan Samiti ko Report* [Report of the Zones and Development District Demarcation Committee] (Kathmandu, 1962). The "Development Districts" should not be confused with the old administrative districts, which were eliminated as units of regional government in 1965.

† The procedures for elections under the Village Panchayat (Election) Rules, which permitted balloting by show of hands, were strongly criticized. An amendment to the Panchayat Act, dated April 16, 1962, provided for secret elections, although elections by open vote were permitted for the first panchayat elections then under way. Panchayat Act (Amendment), *Nepal Gazette*, Vol. XI, Extraordinary Issue No. 47, Chaitra 29, 2019 (April 16, 1962).

‡ It was only in 1963, however, that the village panchayats were permitted to use their taxation powers, and then only under strict supervision. By the end of 1965, the village panchayats' judicial powers were still held in abeyance by the government.

(fourteen towns according to the 1961 census), can establish a town panchayat whose members, at least nine in number, are popularly elected. The town panchayat exercizes broad administrative powers, with emphasis placed upon development programs, and has been granted limited taxation powers; in contrast to the village panchayats, it is not vested with any judicial functions. The 1962 Act assures the central government more direct forms of control over municipalities than was the case in the 1953 Act, despite the claims that the new panchayat system represents a deconcentration of political power and functions. Up to one fourth of the membership of the town panchayats is nominated by the government, which also has the power to appoint a "local officer" to exercize broad supervisory powers over the activities of the panchayat. Moreover, the budget prepared by the town panchayat requires the approval of the central authorities.

Quite obviously, the new panchayat system at the primary level did not initially represent any significant deconcentration of political power. Indeed, there were few noteworthy innovations to distinguish recent legislation from earlier laws concerning village and town government. The new panchayat system would seem, at this stage, to constitute an attempt to rationalize the administrative process by creating viable institutions in areas where a serious lacuna had previously existed, thus providing the basis both for a modernized administrative system and for agencies through which economic development programs could be implemented. This first step in the long process of "building democracy from the roots up" can only be characterized as the very soul of caution. But it should also be noted that the royal regime moved with unprecedented vigor and speed to establish panchayats throughout Nepal, a task previous governments had never been prepared or willing to undertake. In this respect the new panchayat system, moderate though its power may be, did represent a significant new development in Nepal's political and administrative structure.

Nationwide elections for the village panchayats were held in the late winter and spring of 1962, and for the town panchayats six months later. Once these elections had been completed, the stage was set for the establishment of the next tier of the panchayat system. Accordingly, the District Panchayat Act was promulgated on November 29, 1962. In the seventy-five new Development Districts, district assemblies were established, consisting of one member from each village panchayat and one third of the membership of each town panchayat within the district area. The district assembly has two primary functions: to hold at least two meetings each year, and to elect the District Panchayat Committee. Meetings are held after the monsoon, to scrutinize and approve the previous year's accounts and to discuss and make final the budget for the coming year, and after the winter harvest, to discuss reform measures and development schemes undertaken by the district panchayat.

The district assemblies elect eleven-member Panchayat Committees, which serve as the executive body in each district. The panchayat, which must meet at least once a month, functions primarily as the expediter of development projects undertaken within the district, but it also supervises the activities and budgets of the village and town panchayats under its jurisdiction, giving directives to them if necessary. It has limited taxing and fee-collecting powers and is entitled to a maximum of 10 per cent of the income of the primary panchayat units.

The government has also expressed its intention to grant broad administrative powers to the district panchayats and, indeed, to substitute them for the Bada Hakims as the principle administrative agency in the districts. Under the scheme proposed in the report of the Administrative Deconcentration Commission in 1963, all of the functions exercised by the Bada Hakims will be gradually transferred to the district panchayats, with the president of the district panchayat serving as the chief executive officer. It seems clear, however, that the central government intends to move slowly and cautiously in devolving powers upon the district panchayats, despite the frequently voiced demands by these bodies for the immediate abolition of the Bada Hakims. The district panchayats argue that they are unable to implement economic development programs under the present system so long as administrative functions on the regional level are retained in the hands of the Bada Hakims. But there are many problems involved in the abolition of the Bada Hakims and the old administrative districts, and supplementary lines of communication and authority will probably have to be developed before the government would be inclined to implement such a drastic program.

As is the case with all other subunits of government in Nepal, the central authorities have retained broad supervisory and control powers over the district panchayats. The Panchayat Ministry may, for instance, issue a cease-and-desist order to any district panchayat undertaking which, in the Ministry's view, is likely to harm the general public, endanger the life of any person, or result in riot. It may also order the district panchayat to perform a prescribed function within a "reasonable time limit." If the district panchayat should fail to discharge its duties or should misuse its powers, it can either be suspended temporarily or be dissolved by order of the central government. All the powers of the district panchayat can then be delegated to "any person or committee" specified by the Ministry, which person or committee can continue to function until the suspension of the panchayat has been lifted or a new panchayat has been elected.

By the end of 1962, legislation pertaining to the zonal panchayats and the National Panchayat had not been promulgated, though the general outlines for the election and functioning of the latter institution had been provided in the 1962 Constitution. Despite this apparent legislative lacuna, King Mahendra announced that the National Panchayat would be established by April 1, 1963, New Year's Day in the Nepali calendar. Frantic preparations were necessary for the elections to the National Panchayat, and seldom has the Nepali administrative system responded so commendably to a challenging situation.

The electoral system provided for the National Panchayat in the 1962 Constitution and supplementary legislation attempts to formulate a representative system within the confines of the newly established "popular" political institutions. The fourteen zonal assemblies elect ninety members to the National Panchayat. The central committees of five of the seven class organizations elect another fifteen.* In addition, Graduate Constituencies, composed of Nepali citizens who have obtained a Shastri or a bachelor's degree, elect four representatives. Finally, the King has the power to nominate a certain number of members, not to exceed 15 per cent of the elected membership.

As a first step in the preparations for the National Panchayat elections, district panchayats were elected throughout Nepal in January and early February of 1963. At the same time, executive ordinances were promulgated in rapid order, specifying procedures under which the zonal assemblies, class organizations, and graduate constituencies would elect representatives to the National Panchayat. Before this could be accomplished, however, these various bodies themselves had to be brought into existence. On January 26, the National Guidance Ministry issued a set of rules regulating the formation of central committees for each of the class organizations. Two days later, the National Panchayat

---

* Five class organizations included are those representing peasants, laborers, women, young persons, and former servicemen. Children's and students' class organizations are excluded from taking part in the National Panchayat elections, presumably because their members are not yet twenty-one years old.

(Graduates' Representation) Act was promulgated, defining procedures under which the four "graduate" representatives to the National Panchayat would be elected. Finally, on February 1, the Zonal Panchayat Act was gazetted, providing for the election of zonal assemblies and zonal panchayats, with powers and functions broadly similar to those exercized by the district-level bodies.

Having provided for the establishment of the electoral institutions themselves, it was then necessary to regulate election procedures. On February 1, the National Panchayat (Formation) Rules were promulgated, specifying certain general principles regarding elections to the National Panchayat. A few days later the National Panchayat (Zonal Assembly Representation) Act and the National Panchayat (Class and Professional Organization) Act were gazetted, regulating elections to the National Panchayat from the zonal assemblies and the central committees of the class organizations.

This spate of legislation was implemented with uncharacteristic speed, and by the end of March most of the representatives to the National Panchayat had been elected by the zonal assemblies, class-organization central committees, and graduate constituencies, all of which had themselves been established in the preceding two or three weeks. Naturally, there has been some degree of skepticism expressed over the democratic character of the elections, owing to the extreme haste with which they were conducted. Charges of ministerial oppression and manipulation were voiced repeatedly during the "campaign" by sections of the Nepali press and probably were not wholly unjustified. Particular exception was taken to the way in which Assistant Ministers were appointed to head Tour Commissions with broad powers in the various zones while the election "campaign" was under way. Even with the advantages heavily weighted in their favor, however, three Assistant Ministers were defeated in their bids for election, though in at least one instance this may have been owing to the opposition of an influential colleague on the Council of Ministers. However questionable some of the circumstances surrounding the elections may have been, they did serve their main purpose, i.e., to bring into existence a national body broadly representative of the different areas and ethnic groups of Nepal. Under prevailing conditions, it is doubtful whether the composition or character of the National Panchayat would have been altered significantly if the elections had been held at a more leisurely pace and under less direct supervision by the central authorities.

Another question that aroused wide discussion among Nepali politicians and intellectuals before the promulgation of the 1962

Constitution concerned the functional character of the National Panchayat. Would it be an advisory body, with recommendatory powers similar to those granted the Legislature under the 1948 Constitution and the 1952 Advisory Assembly Act, or would it be a legislative body with substantial legislative powers comparable to those exercized by the Parliament under the 1959 Constitution?

As defined in the 1962 Constitution, the prerogatives of the National Panchayat fall somewhere in between those granted the advisory assemblies and the Parliament. The National Panchayat can discuss any subject except the conduct of the King, Queen, and Crown Prince and the actions taken by judges in the discharge of their duties. This represents a considerable liberalization over the advisory assembly system. Bills passed by the National Panchayat become law after receiving royal assent. Procedurally, this is similar to the provisions of the 1959 Constitution, but in fact the two situations are quite distinct. Under the 1959 Constitution, royal assent to legislation passed by the Parliament was expected to be automatic unless the King considered the bill unconstitutional. Under the new system, the King functions as the real head of the executive branch of the government and takes a more direct role in the legislative process. The King has been granted broad and essentially unchallengable veto powers which cannot, in the final analysis, be overridden by the National Panchayat. In addition, the King can force the legislature to "submit its opinion" on any bill which it has discussed but not passed. The King "may consider such opinion" and then assent to the bill either "in the form in which it was presented to the National Panchayat" or as amended. The legislative scope of the National Panchayat is further reduced by the provision in the 1962 Constitution barring the introduction of money bills or legislation pertaining to the army without the approval of the King. Thus, while the new "parliamentary" system is somewhat more powerful than the old advisory assemblies, it is definitely in an inferior position vis-à-vis the King, who still retains sufficient powers, both residual and direct, to guarantee him the ultimate decision-making power, even in legislative matters.

The question of the relationship between the National Panchayat and the Council of Ministers had also come in for considerable discussion before the promulgation of the 1962 Constitution. The new political system is a model of equivocation on this issue; it appears to give the National Panchayat substantial powers of control over the Ministers, but at the same time carefully limits and, indeed, nullifies, the applicability of this provision. Members of the Council of Ministers must be selected from the National Panchayat, or must be elected to that body within six months of their appointment. It is the King who appoints the Ministers, however, and nothing in the Constituion obligates him to select persons who have the confidence of the Legislature or to consult with it in making appointments. Nor is the King's choice effectively circumscribed by the provision that Ministers must be members of the National Panchayat, in view of his power to appoint a certain percentage of the membership of that institution. Obviously, if the King should want someone on the Council of Ministers it would be relatively easy to arrange membership in the National Panchayat for him within the prescribed six-month period.

The National Panchayat can also exercise only limited forms of control over a Minister once he has been appointed. Noconfidence votes supported by two thirds of the membership of the National Panchayat present and voting may affect the tenure of a Minister, but would not necessarily lead to his dismissal. The final decision in such a situation is vested in the King, who can retain any Minister if he should so desire. Thus, the system incorporated in the 1962 Constitution represents a significant modification of the principle of ministerial responsibility, for a Minister can be dismissed or retained by the King without reference to the support he may enjoy in the National Panchayat.

In a legalistic sense, therefore, the 1962 Constitution reflects a considerable expansion of royal prerogatives over the 1959 Constitution, and a concomitant reduction in the powers of the Cabinet and the Legislature. Nor are there as yet any indications that the King will abjure his broad constitutional powers, permitting the National Panchayat and Council of Ministers to function with some degree of flexibility, though under his general supervision. The King has continued to serve as his own Prime Minister, even after appointing a chairman of the Council of Ministers in April, 1963. In revamping the Cabinet after the 1963 National Panchayat elections, several Ministers were drawn from the ranks of the nominated members of the new "Parliament," including at least one who had been defeated in the election contest in a zonal assembly. This was widely interpreted as an expression of the King's determination to downgrade the National Panchayat and to clarify beyond all doubt its subordinate position in the new political structure.

But perhaps the government's policy toward political parties and organizations is of more significance on this issue than the Constitutional provisions themselves. A legislature composed of "independents" or "nonpolitical men of integrity" may be attractive in theory—but can it function as anything more than a "rubber stamp" in practice? If no form of political alignment is permitted, as is the case under present laws, the National Panchayat loses much of its significance as a representative institution and is probably impotent as a legislative body. The prospects for lifting the ban on political organizations do not seem very bright, as of the end of 1965. King Mahendra has not altered his attitude toward parties perceptibly, and his public statements still bristle with derogatory comments on parties and party leaders. The 1962 Constitution neither provides for nor bars political parties; theoretically, parties could function within the panchayat system. In the royal address to the opening session of the National Panchayat, however, King Mahendra declared that the objective in establishing a panchayat system was to "create a partyless healthy, clean, and advanced society"—an indication that political parties will not be permitted to function for some time to come.[4] It is primarily for this reason that many of the King's critics charge that the entire panchayat system is merely a subterfuge behind which the King continues to exercise an unchallengeable authority while giving the illusion of a deconcentration of power.

CLASS ORGANIZATIONS

In the course of a long statement to the government newspaper on March 7, 1961, the newly appointed Minister for National Guidance, Vishwabandhu Thapa, criticized the relationship that, since the 1950 revolution, had developed between the parties and what he termed class organizations:

During the past several years, political parties used the class organizations to advance their own interests. The political leaders used the different class organizations only to maintain their own leadership, with the result that leaders of the class organizations also soon began exploiting others. . . . The present regime, under the leadership of the King, wants to strengthen the various class organizations by arousing public consciousness and by overthrowing the political party burden imposed from above. . . . A peasant should be engaged in agricultural pursuits aided by modern scientific equipment, remaining aloof from party politics. The same should be the case with students and other classes as well. Can anything be more important?[5]

To redirect such organizations along the classically conservative lines suggested by the Nation Guidance Minister, the government announced shortly thereafter its intention to establish six class organizations, for peasants, laborers, women, students, young persons, and children. Later, associations of former servicemen were also added to the list.

The class organizations have a four-tier structure, directly paralleling the panchayat system. Where appropriate, primary (i.e., local) class committees have been formed in each village or town panchayat area, elected directly by all the members of each class within the jurisdiction of the panchayat. In addition, district, zonal, and central committees have been set up for each of the class organizations. Every primary unit delegates one member to a district council which elects a five-man District Executive Committee from among its membership, and in turn this committee elects a zonal committee. The president and fourteen of the eighteen members of the Central Committee are elected by a national congress composed of the members of the district and zonal committees of the class organizations. The secretary and treasurer of the Central Committee are appointed by the central government, and the president nominates two other members. The members of the zonal committees elect the fifteen representatives of the class organizations in the National Panchayat.

The class organizations have been guaranteed a monopoly in their respective spheres, as government regulations ban the formation of parallel unofficial organizations. A number of independent students' associations have been ordered dissolved, and the attempted formation of a Nepal Women's Association outside the confines of the women's class organization was declared illegal.[6] All labor unions have been banned unless associated with the government-controlled laborers' organization. Government control has even been extended over some private organizations that do not directly parallel any of the class organizations. The formation of commercial organizations was prohibited, for instance, except when permission had been granted by the National Guidance Ministry.[7] According to one National Guidance official, the Ministry permits the formation of autonomous organizations in related fields, but only under the general supervision of one of the class organizations. Merchants, businessmen, civil servants, and teachers have been classified as falling within the "laborer" category as far as class organizations are concerned. Each of these professional or commercial groups has been allowed to form its own autonomous organization under the general supervision of the Panchayat Ministry.

Government pronouncements on the purposes and functions of the class organizations have been prolific, but seldom specific. An obvious, if unstated motive behind the formation of these bodies is the intention to use them as substitutes for the banned political parties. An attempt has been made to channel political activists into the class organizations, presumably to deter their participation in other forms of politics. Special emphasis was placed on attracting former political party workers. With the exception of one faction of the Nepal Communist party and a few former Nepali Congress workers, however, the response was not enthusiastic until the higher-level class committees were established and the tangible benefits of participation—e.g., a plausible route for election to the National Panchayat—became more evident. The allocation of fifteen seats in the National Panchayat to representatives of the class organizations has certainly enhanced the value of membership among ambitious politicians, and has done more to enliven the proceedings of the class organizations than all the government's exhortations combined.

Numerous pronouncements by government officials have touched on the various functions the class organizations will be expected to undertake. Primary emphasis in these statements has been placed on the necessity for the development of "class consciousness" and on the role of these organizations in protecting "class interests." In the words of one official in the National Guidance Ministry:

. . . the principle of National Guidance presupposes that every citizen belongs to some particular class. On the basis of this theory it aims at making the people understand their class character. Proper protection and preservation of the achievements and legacy of these classes are considered to be of primary importance.*

The Minister for National Guidance has warned, however, that in developing "class consciousness" and advancing the interest of the class, the class organization must avoid assuming a political character:

The government will open wide the door for the classes to give vent to their feelings in the direction of preserving and promoting their interests. But the tendency to move away from the class interest and indulge in politics will be curbed. . . . Every class must confine its activity to its own interests. The history of the past ten years has made amply clear how undisciplined party politics spoils class interests.[8]

---

* Ananta Poudyal, "Rashtriya Nirdeshan Janata ko Sathi" [National Guidance: Friend of the People], *Nirdeshan*, Vol. I, No. 2 (May–June, 1961). This emphasis on "class consciousness" and "class membership" may seem to have Marxist overtones, but it might also be interpreted as a modern adaptation of traditional Hindu attitudes toward caste *dharma* (duties) and, implicitly, *varna shankar* (caste mixture).

Implicit in this statement are two debatable propositions: first, that "class interests" do not necessarily have a political facet, and, second, that the encouragement of "class consciousness" through class organizations is somehow compatible with the discouragement of interclass rivalry and struggle.

It is difficult to perceive how the class organizations can become vital, effective bodies and protect the interest of their memberships without indulging in politics. Is it realistic, for instance, to expect a peasants' organization to abstain from participating in panchayat elections which directly involve the interest of the peasants? Class organizations, as such, have been informed by the Guidance officials that they cannot participate in panchayat elections—except, of course, at the National Panchayat level—but that members of the class organizations can do so as individuals. This is an inadequate arrangement from the viewpoint of the leaders of the class organizations, who are demanding that the policy of compartmentalizing the class organizations and panchayats be abandoned and that representatives of the former be granted *ex-officio* membership throughout all levels of the Panchayat system.

Furthermore, the government is not being wholly realistic, one would suspect, in attempting to effect class harmony through the class organizations system. Quite the contrary, if these should ever become effective, viable organizations, they are far more likely to serve as instruments through which class conflicts are intensified. A prescriptive emphasis upon the common interest of all classes in national development cannot disguise the fact that there are also many spheres in which the interests of the classes clash. Moreover, the class organizations, if granted real autonomy, could become centers of opposition to the government, strongly critical of policies that fail to satisfy class demands. An illustrative incident occurred almost immediately after the formation of the Bhaktapur (a city in Kathmandu Valley) *ad hoc* Peasants' Organization Committee. The committee submitted to the government the apparently reasonable demand that existing land tenure and rent regulations be fully enforced. One National Guidance Ministry official called this "patently impossible" (rightly so under prevailing conditions), and the committee was instructed to "refrain from politics." But if this demand is interpreted as "political," the question arises as to what isn't politics and what is the proper function of the class organizations.

The organizing and coördinating of the activities of the various "classes" in the development programs undertaken by the different levels of government is another duty assigned the class organizations. Indeed, this function would seem to have assumed primary importance in the eyes of the government in view of the need for massive public participation in the Three-Year Plan announced in 1962. The class organizations are also intended to serve as instruments for orienting the public on political, economic, and social questions and thus channelling popular forces and movements into activities the government wishes to further. The Peasants' Organization, for instance, has undertaken to explain the land reform program to the peasants, and the Students' Organization has dispatched teams to various parts of the country to publicize the new legal and social code.

But all these functions are still plans for the future rather than realities. None of the class organizations is effective at levels below the central committee as yet, and there is, at best, minimal public participation in their programs. Most of the attention of the leadership has been directed toward internal struggles for power between presidents and central committees or with resistance to the efforts of the government to furnish supervision and guidance. This state of affairs has largely been the result of two concomitantly operative factors. First, the government has maintained a studied vagueness about the form, functions, and relationships of the new organizations. This results in a constant preoccupation on the part of their members with procedural and organizational squabbles. Second, the leaders acquired their political habits in the days of party politics. Thus they are themselves preoccupied with petty-minded organizational politics, as a safety-valve device, rather than with fundamental analysis of the panchayat system itself. Paradoxically, King Mahendra has helped to bring about the same kind of "politicking" under partyless Panchayat Raj which he had previously accused political parties of promoting on a national scale.

GUIDANCE SYSTEM

In an address to the people of Nepal on "National Day," February 18, 1961, King Mahendra announced the establishment of a new Ministry of National Guidance:

The principal duty of this new Ministry will be to work in the broader interests of the country and to achieve a greater measure of progress and development in all sections of society and among its various classes, to coördinate the rights and interests of the various areas and their people, and to prevent regional interests from conflicting with national interests or with similar interests of other areas.[9]

The new Ministry was given an awesome array of duties and responsibilities under the new political structure. It was, indeed, the focus around which all the other institutions gravitated during the first two years of the royal regime. Its first assignment was the establishment of the panchayats and class organization committees, a task which was carried out with notable vigor and determination, if not always with an evident concern for the principles that were supposed to underlie these institutions.*

A corollary function of the National Guidance Ministry, as projected in legislation promulgated in 1961, was the coördination of the activities of the various levels of the panchayats and the class organizations so as to prevent them from impinging upon each other's spheres or exceeding their proper functions and powers. During 1961, District Guidance Officers were appointed to each of the seventy-five Development Districts to carry out the duties of the Ministry on this level. In December of that year, a National Guidance Act provided for several new institutions that would supplement and assist the Guidance Ministry and the district officials.[10] Under the provisions of this law, joint district and zonal Guidance Committees were to be set up in every district and zone, and a National Guidance Council, appointed by the National Guidance Ministry, was to be formed at the Central Secretariat to "represent different class or professional organizations." [11]

The function of these committees and the Council was to "decide on the general policy in connection with the programs of class or professional organizations at their respective levels and submit their respective suggestions to His Majesty's Government." [12] The purpose was to achieve the maximum coördination of the activities of the various class organizations and to minimize class conflicts. The relationship between the committees and the District Guidance Officers was not specified. The law did, however, grant the National Guidance Ministry the right to "give frequent guidance" to the committees. Presumably, the Ministry was to act through its district officers, when appropriate, in guiding and supervising the proceedings of the committees.

---

* The Panchayat Department, nominally responsible for the establishment of the panchayat system, was initially subordinate to the Ministry of Development rather than the Ministry of National Guidance. Vishwabandhu Thapa held both portfolios at the time of the local panchayat elections, however, and all reports of the elections stressed the role of the National Guidance Ministry. After the elections were over, the Panchayat Department was promoted to a Ministry, but Thapa continued to hold both portfolios until his dismissal in April, 1963.

Before most of the joint Guidance Committees could be set up, some basic changes occurred in the guidance system on the national level which later affected the system at the lower level as well. Upon the completion of the National Panchayat elections in April, 1963, King Mahendra suddenly and unexpectedly abolished the National Guidance Ministry. That guidance *per se* was not being dispensed with was indicated by the fact that all the powers and functions of the National Guidance Ministry were transferred intact to the newly-formed Panchayat Ministry and by the subsequent establishment of a National Guidance Council. But in the process, the guidance system underwent a structural reorganization and, indeed, some confusion of function and jurisdiction. The District Guidance Officer posts were abolished, and the entire burden of guidance on the regional level was placed upon Zonal Guidance Officers and Zonal Guidance Committees, which were under the supervision of the Panchayat Ministry.

The role of the National Guidance Council has never been precisely defined. Quite significantly, the Council functions outside of the Central Secretariat and has no direct relationship— either as a superior or as a subordinate—to the Panchayat Ministry. The King, himself, is the chairman of the Council, which, thus, reports directly to the palace rather than to the Secretariat or the Ministry. In inaugurating the first session of the Council, on August 25, 1963, King Mahendra outlined its duties: to guide and coördinate class organizations; to guide panchayats of all levels and consider problems emanating from the Panchayat system; to prepare a program to activate the people in support of the panchayat system; and to provide "general guidance even to His Majesty's Government" if necessary.[13] As such, the Council assumed most of the functions of the old National Guidance Ministry which legally had been transferred to the Panchayat Ministry. This did not conform with the views of the Panchayat Ministry, which has made it clear that the Council is intended to give "advice" rather than "guidance" to the government, and to serve as a forum for eliciting public opinion. What role the Council eventually will play is still uncertain, for it has so far provided neither advice nor guidance. Indeed, there has been a temporary disarray and confusion in the guidance system during this transitional period, permitting the panchayats and class organizations greater freedom of action than the government may think proper. It may well prove difficult to reimpose the degree of guidance exerted previously by the National Guidance Ministry. Few panchayat and class organization officials will miss the guidance, but its absence could easily lead to a complex struggle between the numerous new institutions whose jurisdictions have only rarely been carefully defined.

There has been no clear indication as yet as to why King Mahendra considered these changes in the guidance system necessary. The National Guidance Ministry was unpopular in some quarters, but there was certainly no irresistible demand for its abolition. But perhaps this was merely another gamit in King Mahendra's efforts to maintain a delicate balance of power between official institutions in order to prevent any dangerous concentration of power anywhere other than the palace. Perhaps the National Guidance Ministry was carving out too central a role for itself in the new political system. It is significant that the guidance function was divided between the Panchayat Ministry and National Guidance Council—the latter not under ministerial control—and that the old National Guidance Minister, Vishwabandhu Thapa, was not included in the new Ministry appointed at the same time.

THE RAJ SABHA AND TOUR COMMISSIONS

While King Mahendra has frequently asserted that the panchayats, class organizations, and guidance system are in conformity with Nepal's traditional political and cultural values, there can be little doubt that in every way but nominally they constituted institutional innovations. There are, however, several other features of the new political structure that are related more directly to earlier Nepali institutions and, indeed, seem to have been inspired by governmental procedures having their origin in the period before the 1950 revolution. Of these, the most important are the Raj Sabha, or Council of State, and the Tour Commissions, both of which fill a vaguely defined but important role in King Mahendra's political structure.

The legal basis for the Raj Sabha is provided by the 1962 Constitution, which stipulates that a Council of State should be appointed by the King to serve in an essentially advisory capacity. The powers and functions of the Raj Sabha are broadly equivalent to those exercized by the Rashtriya Parishad (literally, "National Council," but also usually translated as "Council of State") under the 1959 Constitution. If one is permitted a degree of free association, both these institutions can be traced back, rather indirectly and sporadically, to the Bharadari, the traditional Council of the Nobility, that advised and aided the Shah monarchs before their relegation to a position of nominal sovereignty during the Rana regime.

As outlined in the 1962 Constitution, the Raj Sabha has two primary functions: to supervise succession to the throne or the establishment of a regency in the event of the King's death or incapacity, and to serve as a consultative body when the King and the National Panchayat are not in agreement on proposed legislation. In addition, a Permanent Committee consisting of seven to fifteen members of the Raj Sabha is appointed by the King to act in conjunction with the Steering Committee of the National Panchayat on specified occasions—in particular during periods of national emergency and in the constitutional amendment process.

The size and composition of the Raj Sabha is only partly determined by the Constitution. A number of judicial, governmental, administrative, and religious officials serve as ex-officio members, but the King has the prerogative to appoint as many other members as he thinks fit. If the Raj Sabha appointed by King Mahendra subsequent to the 1963 National Panchayat elections is any indication of the future character of this institution, it is probably fortunate that the Council has only limited consultative powers, since a less homogeneous body could scarcely be conceived. In addition to the ex-officio members, it included, by appointment: three former Prime Ministers (K. I. Singh, M. P. Koirala, and Tanka Prasad Acharya) of diverse political inclinations; the former Home Minister in the Nepali Congress government (Surya Prasad Upadhyaya); the Secretary General of the Nepal Communist party (Keshar Jang Rayamajhi); two Ministers from the previous Council of Ministers (Rishikesh Shah and Lalit Chand); a staunchly pro-Chinese member of the recently dissolved National Planning Council (Poorna Bahadur); and an assorted collection of Ranas and members of the royal family.* This body may cover the Nepali political spectrum fairly adequately, but it is hard to imagine any decision emanating from this group without strong leadership from the palace.

Nothing very definite has been forthcoming as yet to indicate what the general role of the Raj Sabha is expected to be in the new political structure. It is interesting to note that King Mahendra was usually careful to establish high-prestige councils with

---

* Both K. I. Singh, who had been offered the chairmanship of the Raj Sabha's Permanent Committee, and Rishekesh Shah rejected their appointments, Singh because the chairman of the Raj Sabha was placed on a lower official level than the chairman of the Council of Ministers, and Shah because of his stated disapproval of the composition of the Council of Ministers. In late 1963, just before Tulsi Giri's dismissal from the Council, Shah accepted the chairmanship of the Raj Sabha's Permanent Committee.

few apparent responsibilities but important residual powers during periods when he was ruling through a Cabinet. Possibly these are intended to serve as counterbalances to the Ministry and as centers of support in case of any crisis in Palace-Ministry relations, or in any situation where succession to the throne is the issue. The Council of State may also serve another useful purpose —as a sinecure for those political leaders that cannot be safely ignored but are to be kept out of responsible governmental posts.

The Tour Commissions that King Mahendra has appointed on several occasions since the December, 1960, *coup* can also be interpreted as marking the revival of an institutional arrangement with deep roots in Nepal's history. Tour Commissions formed a regular part of the administrative system during the Rana regime, but were abandoned by the postrevolutionary governments—at least, on any formal basis. King Mahendra made one effort to revive the Tour Commission system on ascending the throne in 1955, but the resultant volume of criticism from the political parties led him to put it aside for the time being. The motives behind the reinstitution of Tour Commissions in 1955 and 1961 seem to be related to the King's concern over the lack of direct contacts between the palace and the broad masses of the public as well as to his dissatisfaction with the sources available to him upon which realistic appraisals could be made of trends in public opinion or of political, economic, and social conditions. They seem to serve as substitutes for his own personal tours of the countryside and, indeed, to function in a similar fashion to the royal tours in some respects.

King Mahendra appointed fourteen Tour Commissions, consisting of a chairman, representatives of the military and judiciary, and a secretary, in February, 1961, each of which toured a section of the country and then submitted a report to the palace. The stated objectives of the Commissions were:

. . . to make the administration and judicial administration of the Kingdom of Nepal less expensive, impartial, expedient and efficient, to further promote development works, to organize panchayats in every district, to remove the grievance of the innocent, the old, the poor and women by taking action against and punishing oppressors, cheats, liars, exploiters and other persons of bad conduct and to establish a close relationship between the public and His Majesty's Government.[14]

Unlike the Daudahas under the Rana regime, which were primarily judicial commissions, the Tour Commissions were given broad discretionary powers. (1) The supervision of all government offices within their region, including the power to dismiss nongazetted officers and to suspend gazetted officers on their own initiative, was entrusted to them. They also were instructed to report on the functioning of government offices in their area and to recommend changes. (2) They were to inspect the social and economic conditions of the people and to recommend improvements. The Commissions were granted the power to investigate the operation of development programs in the area and to initiate new development projects, for which limited sums from the Development Fund or Reserved Fund could be expended. Larger projects requiring more substantial expenditures could be recommended by the Commissions, but had to be approved by the relevant Ministry. (3) The Commissions also were granted special judicial powers, equal in substance to those of the Zilla Adalats ("district courts").

In carrying out their duties, some of the Commissions acted with notable vigor and enthusiasm. Several officials were dismissed or suspended, usually on corruption charges, though it was widely suspected that political motivations were more important in some cases. Accomplishments in the judicial sphere were even more impressive, if the statements of several Tour Commission chairmen are reliable. Complaints about the laxity and slowness of the court system are endemic in Nepal, and the backlog of cases in most courts is truly staggering. The Commissions were instructed to set aside the normal judicial procedure and to dispose of as many of these cases as possible. One chairman estimated that his Commission had acted in some two thousand cases, though he admitted that most of the cases had merely been referred back to the regular courts.

The most important task of the Tour Commissions, however, was to note the attitude of the people toward the present regime and to explain to the people the reasons behind the dismissal of the Nepali Congress government. All the Tour Commissions held numerous public meetings in which the King's motivations in the December *coup* were discussed. To a considerable extent, then, the Commissions served as public-relations agencies for the regime and gave an impression of being interested more in discussing King Mahendra's grievances against the Nepali Congress than in noting popular grievances with any and all governments.

After touring their respective areas for approximately three months, the Tour Commissions returned to Kathmandu. Joint conferences were held with several Ministers, reports were prepared incorporating the Commissions' recommendations and observations, and, finally, each Commission was granted an interview with the King. Since none of the Tour Commission reports have been made public, it is impossible to determine the extent to which they have affected subsequent government policy. On basic administrative matters their influence would seem to have been slight, though they may have been of some importance in decisions concerning government personnel in regional and district offices. Nevertheless, the Tour Commissions obviously accomplished some objectives that proved their value to King Mahendra, for in January, 1962, and February, 1963, new Tour Commissions were appointed. In the first instance, the Zonal Commissioners in each of the fourteen zones were appointed as chairmen of the Tour Commissions (and in the process were transferred from the jurisdiction of the Home Ministry to that of the National Guidance Ministry). The powers and functions of the 1963 Tour Commissions approximated those of their predecessors.[15] Headed by several Assistant Ministers, they were used to supervise preparations for the National Panchayat elections held in March of that year.

Will the Tour Commissions become a regular feature of Nepal's new institutional structure? No legislation has yet been enacted to this effect and none is reported to be under consideration. It has been suggested that the Zonal Commissioners can carry out this function, and that new royally-appointed Tour Commissions may not be necessary. But this ignores one of the most useful features of the Tour Commissions from King Mahendra's viewpoint, their affording the Palace direct communication with and control over regional and local officials without the intermediation of the Central Secretariat. Moreover, since the King may view these Commissions as an important part of the process of developing closer ties between the monarchy and the people, useful both for what he learns of popular sentiment and for communicating to the public his views on various questions, new Tour Commissions may occasionally be appointed on an *ad hoc* basis.

CONCLUSIONS

It is much too early, obviously, to attempt an appraisal of the new political structure in Nepal, or to speculate on the ultimate character of the new system, for it is still unclear whether the essential spirit of an absolute monarchy will be retained, thinly disguised, or whether there will be a real deconcentration of power at various levels. Barring a revolutionary change in the governmental system, the political values and concepts of King

Mahendra are likely to be the single most important determinant in the molding of the new institutions.

Speculation on the future of the panchayat system is impossible, therefore, without due consideration of probable future trends in King Mahendra's political ideology. Up to late 1960, the King was careful to consult with a wide range of political leaders even though most of his political education had come by way of persons opposed to the Nepali Congress party. During the first four years of his reign, the King had access not only to criticisms of personalities but also to debates over ideological alternatives to various political programs. The 1960 *coup,* however, narrowed the scope of political dissent to such an extent that the King now hears only personal criticisms of this or that Minister. The panchayat system, as King Mahendra's personal creation, is now treated as sacrosanct and not to be questioned by articulate political elements within Nepal. In this frantic search for political unanimity, there has been a steady deterioration in both the scope and quality of the King's political education, and he is increasingly surrounded by sycophants who are reluctant to raise basic political issues with him.

Nevertheless, direct and immediate challenges to the royal regime do exist and enjoy some degree of popular support. It is still to be seen whether the King's political and economic program will mitigate popular unrest. The reaction to Panchayat Raj has not been overwhelmingly favorable by any means, and what support the new system has engendered has mostly had an obvious political motivation (e.g., Communist participation in class organizations). Even the attitude of some top officials in the Secretariat toward the new institution is equivocal, for they tend to reflect the predominant ethos of the younger Nepali intellectuals who are distinctly "modernist" in orientation and openly disdainful of tradition-oriented institutions. The combination of internal discontent, external pressures, and King Mahendra's demonstrated predilection for political experimentation point to the probability that Panchayat Raj will prove to be an interim arrangement in Nepal's haphazard search for stable, viable political institutions.

In any event, there are certain inherent contradictions within the panchayat system that are likely to prove troublesome in the future. A verbal adherence to the principles of political decentralization under conditions, both internal and external, which would seem to make increasing centralization an essential prerequisite to political unity and economic progress can only have adverse effects. Decentralization may be a necessity in the vastly complex society of India, but the situation in Nepal is quite different. Concessions to local, regional, ethnic, and caste sentiments may be unavoidable, but it is questionable whether they should be incorporated as an essential part of the constitutional system.

And yet the panchayat system does meet some of the most strongly felt needs among articulate political groups in Nepal—in particular, a preference for a political system that is more than a pale reflection of Nepal's two giant neighbors. Indeed, this is sometimes considered a precondition of Nepal's nonalignment policy. As the "philosopher" of the panchayat system, Vishwabandhu Thapa, has expressed it:

I hardly need explain the merits and demerits of parliamentary democracy and communism. Nepal is not only sandwiched between two giant neighbors, but is also confronted by these two great ideologies. The question is: to which of these two political systems should Nepal be attracted. After experimenting with the ideology practised in the south for ten years, Nepal cannot be prepared now to look favorably to the system prevailing in the north . . . The Nepalese desire to stand on their own feet.[16]

Moreover, there is a strong belief that Nepal must evolve its own, unique political personality or else eventually find itself submerged by one or the other of its neighbors. While there may be little that is intrinsically or traditionally Nepali in the panchayat system, it is without question distinct in important respects from both India and China. This in itself is extremely important to the Nepalese, whose primary political objective must be the preservation of Nepal's independence and sovereignty under extremely difficult conditions.

20

The Politics of "Guided" Democracy

In the Royal Proclamation of December 15, 1960, dismissing the Nepali Congress government, King Mahendra announced that until new arrangements could be made he had himself taken up the reins of administration.[1] The next ten days were marked by confusion in Nepali political circles. There was, of course, speculation about the King's intentions. Some observers assumed that a long direct-rule period was inevitable; others predicted that the King would shortly reëstablish the parliamentary system, but with a Cabinet more to his taste. Rumors of extended talks between the King and some of the imprisoned Nepali Congress leaders seemed to add substance to the latter speculation, for such talks might signify that the King was attempting to wean enough Nepali Congress M.P.'s from their allegiance to the party leaders to permit the appointment of a new Cabinet enjoying majority support within Parliament. Perhaps the King had not definitely decided to dispense with the parliamentary system itself on December 15. The subsequent course of events, however, must have convinced him that dramatic new political experiments were both feasible and necessary.

The question of the King's ultimate intentions was not settled by the Royal Proclamation of December 26, in which he rather unexpectedly announced the formation of a new Council of Ministers with himself as chairman. He merely stated: "As we have to make arrangements to save the country from the mischief from which it has suffered, while having at the same time to ensure the establishment of a democratic system in the future, for

420

the present we have formed a Council of Ministers." ² This was obscure enough to encourage speculation that the new Council was an interim arrangement, and that parliamentary democracy would be reëstablished eventually.* The new Ministers and their portfolios are shown in table 12.

TABLE 12

THE COUNCIL OF MINISTERS, 1960

Name	Portfolio
Dr. Tulsi Giri	Foreign Affairs; Defence; Transport and Communications; Electricity and Irrigation; Palace Affairs
Vishwabandhu Thapa	Home and Local Self-Government
Rishikesh Saha	Planning; Economic Affairs; Finance
Surya Bahadur Thapa	Agriculture; Forests; Industry and Commerce
Aniruddha Prasad Singh	Education; Health; Law and Justice; Parliamentary Affairs

Four Assistant Ministers—Nageshwar Prasad Singh, Khagendra Jang Gurung, Kazi Man Limbu, and Bhuwan Lal Pradhan—were also appointed.

There are several aspects of the new ministerial setup deserving of notice. The composition of the Council was particularly significant, for it included only Nepali Congress members or "independents." None of the opposition parties that had loudly denounced the B. P. Koirala government and eagerly demanded royal intervention received any representation. Two Ministers, Tulsi Giri and Vishwabandhu Thapa, and one Assistant Minister, Nageshwar Prasad Singh, were members of the Nepali Congress, and another Minister, Rishikesh Shah, had held prominent posts in the party before his resignation in 1956. These three Ministers held the important portfolios and played the most prominent roles in Council proceedings. Indeed, their position differed from that of their colleagues in that they thought of themselves as advisers to the King and were treated as such by him, while the other members of the Ministry functioned essentially as royal servants who expected to obey instructions, not give advice. This

---

* The comment of the official newspaper, *Gorkhapatra*, pointing out that the majority of the new Ministers were members of the Nepali Congress, which had been victorious in the elections, and expressing the hope that the Council would "lay the foundations of true democracy in Nepal under the direct guidance of the King," lent credence to the view that the King was, at least, open-minded on the question of the reintroduction of the parliamentary system. It was also considered very significant that the Ministry of Parliamentary Affairs was not abolished.

distinction in role consciousness coincided with political background: the first group had been associated primarily with party politics; the latter had conceived of themselves as "independents."

The similarity in the careers of Tulsi Giri, Vishwabandhu Thapa, and, to a somewhat lesser extent, Rishikesh Shah, is striking. All were in their mid-thirties and had first entered politics in the 1947–50 period as members of the anti-Rana group of exiles in India which eventually formed the Nepali Congress. Both Tulsi Giri and Vishwabandhu Thapa had been considered favorite protégés of B. P. Koirala, and their post-*coup* behavior was widely viewed as a betrayal of their erstwhile political "guru." This was not so much the case with Rishikesh Shah, however, as he had been much less closely associated with the Nepali Congress and B. P. Koirala than his two colleagues.

It was generally assumed by the local press that Tulsi Giri was the key figure in the new Council of Ministers. His name came first in the warrant of precedence, and he held the most prestigious portfolios—Foreign Affairs and Defence. Perhaps an even more important indication of the confidence reposed in Dr. Giri by the King was his appointment as head of the newly created Palace Affairs Ministry. It was apparent that the royal palace planned to maintain direct and close supervision over the new Ministry and that Tulsi Giri, as Palace Affairs Minister, would serve as the liaison between the King and his Ministry.

The extreme youth of the Ministry, none of whose members was over forty, presented a distinct contrast to King Mahendra's previous practice of selecting Ministries or Advisory Councils from older, established, tradition-oriented groups. The King gained one very obvious advantage from this procedure. None of these young men had established sources of strength and support, and thus all of them were totally dependent upon the King for their sudden and unexpected rise to exalted rank. Even the Nepali Congress members of the Council had lost contact with most of their former party colleagues and retained only a small coterie of followers, whose attachment in some cases owed more to familial and caste connections than to party membership.

Doubts about the King's ultimate political intentions were finally dispelled on January 5, 1961, by the issuance of yet another Royal Proclamation. In this document, King Mahendra outlined his program for the economic revitalization of the country and then announced:

As political parties may prove obstacles to the task of creating a favorable climate for this new movement of national reconstruction, we have by this proclamation declared illegal and banned for the present all the existing political parties and class organizations affiliated with such parties.*

The first vague outlines of Panchayat Raj were also perceptible in this proclamation when the King declared:

We have to open up a new spring of power which will remove the centuries-old poverty, ignorance, and backwardness of the country and which will nourish to maturity and fruitfulness the tree of democracy rooted in our soil and suited to our conditions. Since panchayats are the basis of democracy, and a democratic system imposed from above has proved unsuitable . . . we have now to build democracy gradually layer by layer, from the bottom upward. It is our aim to associate the people in the administration at all levels and to develop village, district, and municipal panchayats.[3]

Within a few hours all political party offices in the capital were closed and political party activities suspended—though only nominally in the case of the Nepali Congress and the Communist party, as later developments demonstrated.

To provide a legal basis—if somewhat belatedly—for his new Council of Ministers system, the King promulgated an Emergency Arrangements Act on January 12.† Under this Act, the King was given full power to deal with the Ministry as he willed and to accept or reject their advice. Laws and ordinances could be enacted "at the discretion of His Majesty the King or on the advice of the members of the Council of Ministers." The essentially subordinate status of the Ministry was indicated in the "duties of the Ministers" specified in the Act. Each Minister was to report to the King all important matters relating to his Department, to inform the King of departmental affairs as requested by him, and to carry out, or cause to be carried out, those administrative functions that were desired by the King.[4] These terms were even more restrictive than those incorporated in previous "emergency" legislation during direct-rule periods.

The inauguration of a new political system made "guidance" from above essential, and on National Day (February 18), 1961, a new Ministry of National Guidance was created. In the process, a

---

* It was not until July 16, 1961, however, that an executive Order banning parties and political organizations was promulgated by the Home Ministry. *Nepal Gazette*, Vol. II, No. 14, Shravan 2, 2018 (July 16, 1961).

† In dismissing the Nepali Congress government, King Mahendra acted under Article 55 of the 1959 Constitution, which permitted him in cases of "grave emergency" to exercise all of his functions at his own discretion and to assume all powers vested in the Parliament and other governmental institutions. The constitutional provision did not provide for the exercise of these functions through a Cabinet—hence the need for the Emergency Arrangements Act.

reshuffling of portfolios within the Council of Ministers occurred. Dr. Giri was divested of the portfolios of Defence, which was taken over directly by the King, and of Electricity and Irrigation, which was transferred to Aniruddha Prasad Singh. Dr. Giri was compensated with the Home Ministry. Vishwabandhu Thapa, who had held the Home portfolio, became the new Minister of National Guidance. The political implications of the reorganization were not particularly significant except for the King's direct assumption of the Defence portfolio. Under this new arrangement, the Defence Secretary, a high military officer, reported directly to the palace and the Ministry was denied even a nominal role in army affairs. This occurred shortly after some Nepali Congress leaders in India had threatened to launch a movement in Nepal against the royal regime. Perhaps it seemed essential to King Mahendra to bypass the Council, with its Nepali Congress ties, in using the army to deal with any troubles that might arise.

But, all things considered, the first ten months after the royal *coup* were remarkably calm. The extraordinary precautions that had been exercised in the immediate post-*coup* period proved to be, in general, unnecessary. Some new legislation was introduced to provide broader governmental authority, including the State of Emergency Control Act (February 28, 1961) which gave the government the power to restrict the movements of Nepali citizens and to order their return to Nepal from abroad on pain of confiscation of their property, and a special decree issued under the Security Act on March 6 which made it incumbent upon officials, landlords, and retired military and civilian officials to inform against persons engaged in "anti-government" activities. But the lack of any organized resistance led the regime to adopt a more conciliatory policy subsequently. In July all warrants for arrest issued on political grounds since the December *coup* were canceled and one of the leading Nepali Congress Ministers, Surya Prasad Upadhyaya, was released from prison. This was generally considered, though incorrectly, to presage the release of all political prisoners except possibly those against whom civil or criminal cases could be lodged.

Just when it seemed that the royal regime was prepared to make some minor concessions to its critics, the internal and external situation took a sudden turn for the worse. It was obvious that the honeymoon period was over and that major challenges to the regime could be expected shortly. There was widespread dissatisfaction within the country over recent political and economic trends, and even some factions that had previously been staunch in their support of the monarchy were grumbling, quietly but perceptibly. The Nepali Congress and recently ac- quired allies were preparing to launch a terrorist campaign, the scope and consequences of which could not be readily foreseen in Kathmandu. It was also at this time that Nepal's relations with India deteriorated rapidly, and the possibility of New Delhi's supporting and encouraging groups hostile to the regime became the subject of serious consideration in high official quarters in Kathmandu.

Probably no less significant was the increasingly open dissen- sion on policy questions within the Cabinet. Tulsi Giri and Rishikesh Shah represented opposite poles within the limited context of Council of Ministers politics, and most of the contro- versy flared around these two dynamic, flamboyant personalities. As early as March, 1961, there were indications of differences of opinion between these two Ministers on the political prisoners question. It was now apparent that the government did not intend to try any of the Nepali Congress leaders on the charges of treason and other crimes placed against them in the immediate post-*coup* period, and this raised the question of their eventual disposition. In a statement to journalists in New Delhi on March 8, Rishikesh Shah implied that the prisoners would be released if they agreed to coöperate with the new regime.[5] In what amounted to a contradiction of Shah's statement, Tulsi Giri commented that the Council of Ministers had not yet reached any decision about the detained party leaders.[6] According to all available evidence, both Ministers maintained divergent positions on this issue subse- quently. Tulsi Giri worked assiduously to complicate and frus- trate the release of political prisoners, though, of course, without publicly expressing his opposition, while Rishikesh Shah at- tempted to evolve a compromise formula that would be accepta- ble to both the royal palace and the Nepali Congress leaders.

The differences between Tulsi Giri and Rishikesh Shah on foreign policy questions were possibly more crucial and certainly much more open. Toward the end of 1961 and throughout most of 1962, Dr. Giri assumed an increasingly critical public posture toward India, repeatedly questioning New Delhi's motivations and policies toward Nepal. He was also the most vocal advocate of closer ties with Communist China and of a policy of using Peking as a counterfoil to the threat of Indian intervention in domestic Nepali politics. Rishikesh Shah, on the other hand, expressed a marked preference for "quiet diplomacy" in Nepal's relations with India, arguing that there were limits to New Delhi's patience with the kind of statements that were emanating from the Foreign

Ministry in Kathmandu and certain dangers inherent in such practices. While favoring friendly ties with the Peking regime, he also reportedly felt that great caution was necessary in the implementation of Nepal's delicate "balancing of power" policy. Throughout the period from October, 1961, to October, 1962, it was usual whenever any question concerning Indo-Nepali relations arose for Tulsi Giri to allege various kinds of perfidy to Indian leaders and for Rishikesh Shah to issue a moderate statement which, in effect, absolved New Delhi from the charges made by his colleague in the Cabinet.

But perhaps it would be inappropriate to attach very much significance to these strikingly different postures within the Council of Ministers. In the first place, the argument between the positions personified by Tulsi Giri and Rishikesh Shah was primarily tactical rather than policy-oriented. It would seem that the Foreign Minister assumed that the Indian government could best be neutralized as a factor in Nepal's internal politics by what might be termed "bluff and bluster" tactics, while the Finance Minister maintained that an accommodation with India was feasible through a process of quiet negotiation. But Rishikesh Shah was no less intent on achieving the primary objective of the government in all these proceedings—namely, a tacit guarantee from New Delhi that Nepali Congress leaders in India would not be supported or encouraged in launching a movement against the royal regime.

There was, moreover, something of the aura of a puppet show in the scarcely disguised disagreements between the two Ministers, with King Mahendra adroitly manipulating the strings. Both Tulsi Giri and Rishikesh Shah played important roles in the King's foreign and domestic policies, with Dr. Giri assuming essentially the same role in the King's policy toward Peking as V. K. Krishna Menon had once played in Nehru's policy toward Moscow. Dr. Giri was also useful in soliciting popular support for the regime upon the one topic on which there was something approaching a consensus among articulate Nepali groups—that is, real independence and sovereignty for Nepal, which, in the context of Nepali politics, meant major revisions in the traditional structure of Indo-Nepali relations. But Rishikesh Shah was no less necessary to the King, as he was the best guarantee that Nepal's crucial relations with India would not deteriorate beyond the point of no return. The subtle variations in emphasis and direction in Nepal's foreign policy up to October, 1962, were closely reflected in the careers of these two Ministers, but it should be kept clearly in mind that the objectives and basic principles of policy did not fluctuate with these changes in tactics.

POLITICS TAKES A SERIOUS TURN

Under the provisions of the 1959 Constitution, which were still operative, the emergency powers of the King would terminate as of December 15, 1961, one year after their promulgation. This date was eagerly awaited in Kathmandu, where there were still some doubts as to which of the alternatives available King Mahendra would choose. An insight into the probable course of developments was provided by a Royal Proclamation and an Executive Order, both issued on December 10, 1961. The Royal Proclamation extended the emergency indefinitely, but restored the "fundamental rights" clauses of the 1959 Constitution except the clause dealing with contempt of Parliament. The Executive Order largely nullified the significance of the Royal Proclamation by retaining the ban on political parties and political activity.

These maneuvers, widely lauded in the Kathmandu press, did little to assuage the political discontent in the country. This was beginning to assume serious proportions. The hit-and-run tactics of the Nepali Congress and affiliated rebels placed a considerable strain both psychological and physical, upon the government's limited counterinsurgency forces; reports that police and military units had been derelict in their duty circulated in the capital.

The most dramatic incident occurred in January, 1962, during King Mahendra's tour of the Nepal Terai, the scene of the most intense rebel activity, where he was the object of what was officially described as an assassination attempt. An explosive object, described as a bomb by the government and as a firecracker by the Nepali Congress, was tossed at the King's automobile on January 22 as he was touring Tulsi Giri's home town of Janakpur. The King was not injured, and he continued with his tour as if nothing had happened. But the reaction in other quarters was far less restrained, if still within the general pattern of Nepali politics. Within a few hours of the incident, and before any suspects had been apprehended, Tulsi Giri charged that the "assassins" had come from India and that "no local person had a hand in the attempt." [7] He later placed responsibility for the attack on New Delhi because of what was described as

"Indian inaction" in checking the raids "from Indian bases." [8] In a statement in New Delhi on the same day as the assassination attempt, however, Rishikesh Shah asserted that although some Nepalese living in India were responsible for creating disturbances in Nepali territory, neither the government nor the people of India had a hand in these incidents.[9]

With the steady deterioration in the internal situation, King Mahendra moved on several fronts to counter rebel activity and to mobilize popular support behind his regime. Two new ordinances, the Special Circumstances Control Act (February 14, 1962) and the Prevention of Destructive Activities Elements Act (February 27, 1962) were promulgated. The first ordinance granted the government even wider powers over the movements, activities, and associations of Nepali citizens.[10] The second extended the power to exercise such restrictive legislation to the district Bada Hakim, magistrate, or any other officer appointed by the government.[11] The latter ordinance, in particular, was criticized in subsequent months on the charge that these regional-level officials had frequently misused their broad new powers for personal purposes that had nothing to do with the anti-regime activities of Nepali Congress insurgents and their allies.

Two other developments on the political front also attracted wide attention. In April, 1962, King Mahendra announced the formation of a Constitution Drafting Committee. The selection of Rishikesh Shah to head this Committee was widely applauded, since it was generally assumed that the Finance Minister would impart to the new organic law the broadest possible democratic content consistent with the fundamental character of the royal regime. The King also announced in April that an Intellectual's Conference would be held in June. Most of Nepal's most prominent and articulate leaders who had not definitely come out in support of the Nepali Congress movement were invited, along with a large number of intellectuals who had never before been graced with so prestigious a title. The Conference provided a public forum for those leaders who, if they had complaints and grievances against the royal regime, were prepared to play politics within the confines of the existing political structure.

The Conference, held June 6–13, was widely publicized in Nepal. King Mahendra inaugurated the sessions with an admonition to the delegates to deliberate on the various problems confronting the country impartially and with a national perspective. To make his own position on the proper nature of politics perfectly clear, he strongly criticized systems based on political

parties and made a sweeping claim for the effects thus far of
panchayat democracy: ". . . instead of being divided into various
political parties for narrow ends, we have all become one indivisible whole"—a conclusion which subsequent proceedings in the
Conference did little to substantiate. He did, however, hold out
the hope that some form of political organization might be
possible in the future:

I have entrusted with positions of responsibility members of divergent
political parties who have offered their cooperation to me in this
system from a national perspective. . . . It is high time for us to set
aside all obstacles blocking the smooth and speedy progress of our
nation. If we do this, we shall automatically have a basis for a
National Organization.[12]

The 139 delegates to the Conference, in their official statements, generally followed the directions pointed out to them in
the King's inaugural address, but the critical tone of many of the
speeches, cautiously worded though they were, may have exceeded
the limits expected by the government. Even more significant,
perhaps, was the fact that the most critical comments came from
the more prominent delegates, while the faithfully loyalist speakers, though probably in a majority, were frequently from obscure
corners of the country and were unknown to the Kathmandu
audience to whom these proceedings were primarily addressed.
Many delegates expressed their discontent with the way in which
panchayats were being introduced; a significant number expressed doubts about Panchayat Raj itself and wondered whether
this system was really more appropriate to Nepal than parliamentary democracy. One sturdy delegate even demanded negotiations with the Nepali Congress "in order to prevent Nepal from
becoming another Laos or Korea." [13] Several pleaded that the
government permit some form of political organization. The
Conference ended by adopting eight resolutions generally supporting the government's policies, but these were to a certain extent
out of step with the general tone of the Conference and were
probably devised as a face-saving device necessary both to the
royal regime and to the participants.

The political implications of the Intellectual's Conference
became evident almost immediately and were widely interpreted
as strengthening the position of the more moderate wing of the
Council of Ministers. Rishikesh Shah lauded the delegates and
said the administration would now be able to reform itself in the
light of criticisms made at the Conference.[14] He was almost
immediately contradicted by Tulsi Giri, who commented that the

recommendations made by the various speakers had not been discussed by the Cabinet, and that personal views expressed by Ministers should not be considered authoritative as far as the government was concerned.[15]

Approximately three weeks after the conclusion of the Intellectual's Conference, King Mahendra once again reorganized the Council of Ministers, making drastic changes in portfolios and considerably expanding the size of the Ministry (see table 13).

TABLE 13

THE COUNCIL OF MINISTERS, 1962

Name	Title	Portfolio
Tulsi Giri	Vice-Chairman	—
Rishikesh Shah	Minister	Foreign Affairs
Vishwabandhu Thapa	"	Home; Panchayats and National Guidance
Surya Bahadur Thapa	"	Finance; Economic Affairs
Aniruddha Prasad Singh	"	Law and Justice; Parliamentary Affairs
Lalit Chand	"	Public Works, Transport, and Communications
Nageshwar Prasad Singh	"	Health; Electricity and Irrigation
Bhuwan Lal Pradhan	"	Agriculture and Forests
Kirtinidhi Bishta	"	Education
Vedananda Jha	"	Industry and Commerce
Giri Prasad Budathoki	Assistant Minister	Home
Khadga Bahadur Singh	" "	Panchayats and National Guidance
Kaji Man Kandangawa	" "	Finance
Shailendra Kumar Upadhyaya	" "	Agriculture and Forests
Prem Bahadur Shakya	" "	Education

Under the new allocation, Tulsi Giri was given the more prestigious title of Vice-Chairman of the Council, but was divested of the important Foreign and Home Ministries. Rishikesh Shah became Foreign Minister, but lost the Finance and Economic Planning portfolio. Vishwabandhu Thapa was given back the Home Ministry, and Surya Bahadur Thapa now inherited the Finance and Economic Affairs portfolio. Several new Ministers and Assistant Ministers were added. One former Assistant Minister, Kazi Man Limbu, was not included in the new list, while another, Khagendra Jang Gurung, resigned, reportedly because he had not been promoted to full ministerial rank.*

There was no question that this was a far more important ministerial reorganization than that of February, 1961, in both its political and its administrative ramifications. The substantial increase in the size of the Council was justified on the reasonable ground that Ministers had held too many portfolios previously and were unable to devote sufficient energies to any one of them. But the backgrounds and affiliations of several of the new Ministers and Assistant Ministers were particularly interesting in view of the steadily intensifying Nepali Congress campaign. Lalit Chand and Vedananda Jha, for instance, were both from areas of the Terai in which the Nepali Congress was very active. Lalit Chand had been a prominent Nepali Congress leader in the far western Terai districts of Kailali-Kanchanpur, and Vedanand Jha had been president of a regional political party, the Nepal Terai Congress, which had once exercised a limited influence in the area around Birganj. Both men had small coteries of political workers attached to them personally.

Another appointment that caused considerable surprise was that of Shailendra Kumar Upadhyaya, who had once been a prominent member of the Communist party. While after his appointment he claimed that he had resigned from the party in 1958 because he had found it dogmatic and intolerant, his resignation had not been a matter of public record. Upadhyaya admitted that he still believed in Marxism, but expressed himself as being against a bigoted adherence to any ideology.[16] His connections in the party had been with the moderate, pro-regime faction headed by Keshar Jang Rayamajhi, and there was speculation that the King had made the appointment in order to encourage this group to confine its activities within the framework of the existing political system. A pro-Rayamajhi weekly, however, claimed that this showed that the age of sycophancy had died in Nepal and that the King was free from political prejudice.[17]

The two aspects of the reorganization that aroused the most interest were Tulsi Giri's appointment as Vice-Chairman of the Council and Rishikesh Shah's assumption of the Foreign Affairs portfolio. There was some confusion in Kathmandu as to the

---

* K. J. Gurung merely commented: "My resignation was prompted by the fact that there were several circumstances which stood in the way of my working in the interest of my country as well as my community [i.e., the Gurungs of western Nepal] by reason of which I had attained the post." *Samaj*, July 12, 1962. This remark is interesting in view of the King's oft-repeated assertion that his regime was based upon national rather than narrow regional or parochial considerations.

significance of Dr. Giri's ostensible promotion. It was assumed that the King would continue to function as his own Prime Minister, and that the Vice-Chairmanship was more a matter of prestige for Giri than of expanded influence and power—perhaps even a demotion upwards when his divestment of the Foreign and Home portfolios was taken into consideration.

There was no such confusion concerning Rishikesh Shah's transfer from the Finance to the Foreign Ministry, which was correctly interpreted as an indication that the King was prepared to shift tactics in his policy toward India. Tulsi Giri's fulminations had made no perceptible impact upon New Delhi, and now Rishikesh Shah was to be given an opportunity to prove that his "quiet diplomacy" might have better results. But the objective remained the same: New Delhi's agreement to keep Nepali Congress leaders in India under strict supervision and, if feasible, to arrange their repatriation to Nepal.

According to reports current in Kathmandu, the new Foreign Minister was given a limited amount of time to succeed in his mission. On September 4, Rishikesh Shah flew to New Delhi for a series of talks with Indian leaders, including Nehru, Finance Minister Morarji Desai, Defence Minister Krishna Menon, and Home Minister Lal Bahadur Shastri. Abandoning his original plan to proceed from New Delhi to New York to attend the United Nations session, Shah returned to Kathmandu on September 15 with a letter from Nehru to King Mahendra. But it was already apparent that he had not achieved his objective. On September 9, while Shah was still in New Delhi, Prime Minister Nehru told journalists in London that India could not prohibit Nepali refugees from expressing their views in India peacefully— i.e., that the Indian government would not impose further restrictions of their activities and movements—and that he had advised King Mahendra to improve the situation by conducting friendly negotiations with the rebels.[18] This statement raised a furor in the Nepali press, which accused Nehru of interfering in internal Nepali politics.

A series of protracted Cabinet meetings presided over by the King followed Rishikesh Shah's return to Kathmandu, and it was finally decided that the "quiet diplomacy" approach to relations with India should be dropped. Another Cabinet reshuffle occurred on September 22 in which Rishikesh Shah and Aniruddha Prasad Singh were "relieved of their functions," though they retained a status equivalent to ministerial rank. Tulsi Giri once again took over the Foreign Ministry, while Vishwabandhu Thapa, who had usually supported Tulsi Giri in his disagreements with Rishikesh Shah, inherited the Law and Justice and Parliamentary Affairs portfolios. In the communiqué announcing the changes, King Mahendra was more specific than usual in explaining his motivations. Referring to armed raids into Nepal which allegedly originated in India, he declared:

Nepal has, time and again, given friendly notice of all such happenings to the Government of our great neighbour and friendly country, India, through the medium of official correspondence, and also explained the gravity of the situation through personal get-togethers. Notwithstanding all this, however, such happenings have registered an increase and the anti-national elements have been receiving all sorts of help, facilities and cooperation in the friendly country, India.

He then asserted that the two Ministers had been dropped "with a view to bring still more uniformity and solidarity in the Council of Ministers." [19] The "tough line" toward India was renewed, and within the next three weeks relations between the two governments deteriorated to a degree that seemed to threaten a rupture in relations. Before anything so critical could occur, however, dramatic new developments on the Sino-Indian border intervened.

REPERCUSSIONS OF THE SINO-INDIAN CONFLICT IN NEPAL

The scope and intensity of the Chinese attack on the northern border of India commencing on October 20, 1962, came as a traumatic shock to government circles in Kathmandu. While it was assumed that a full-scale war was unlikely, there could be no confidence that the border fighting might not eventually explode into a major conflict involving the entire Himalayan area—inevitably including Nepal. Major changes in the policies and tactics of both the Nepal government and its internal and external opposition were necessary to meet the newly developing situation and were almost immediately forthcoming. There was a sudden, virtually total suspension of mutually recriminatory notes and public statements between Kathmandu and New Delhi, and both governments took steps to remove the more obvious sources of antagonism that had increasingly embittered their relations since December, 1960. Kathmandu may well have received from New Delhi the kind of tacit guarantees it had been seeking. In any case, the Nepali Congress resistance movement was suspended in November and then terminated in December by Suvarna Shamsher, reportedly on the advice of the Indian government.

The sudden, favorable change in the situation permitted King Mahendra to move quickly and decisively to complete the construction of his new political structure without making any major concessions to his opponents and critics. The King's personal prestige was at an unparalleled height and all significant opposition to his regime had been effectively muted. On December 17, the King promulgated the new Constitution which had been prepared by the committee headed by Rishikesh Shah six months earlier. The Constitution went into effect three days later, superseding the 1959 Constitution and the 1961 Special Arrangements Act. Under the provisions of the new Constitution and supplementary legislation, elections were held throughout Nepal in the first quarter of 1963 for district and zonal panchayats and, finally, the National Panchayat.

Once it was apparent that the road to high office lay through the panchayat and class organization systems—which many political activists had doubted previously—there was a hectic scurrying for advantageous positions within these political institutions. The Council of Ministers led the way in this scramble, with Ministers and Assistant Ministers devoting most of their time and energies to "tours" of the zones in which they were seeking election, first to the lower-level panchayats and then to the National Panchayat. There was a constant barrage of complaints in the Nepali press about the activities of the Cabinet members, and allegations that they had misused their official positions to pressure the panchayats in their favor. There seems little doubt that this occurred on a wide scale, and that it was successful in most instances. Tulsi Giri, Vishwabandhu Thapa, and Lalit Chand, for instance, were all elected unopposed by their respective zonal assemblies. Indeed, what is surprising is that several members of the government found these tactics unavailing. One Assistant Minister, Nageshwar Prasad Singh, was defeated in the district panchayat elections at Saptari,[20] while three other Assistant Ministers were defeated in the zonal assembly elections—Shailendra Kumar Upadhyaya and Kaji Man Kandangawa in the Kosi zone[21] and Prem Bahadur Shakya in the Bagmati zone.[22] Surya Bahadur Thapa was also reported to have been defeated in the Dhankuta district panchayat election,[23] but he later denied that he had even entered the contest.[24]

Defeat in the panchayat elections was not necessarily conclusive, however, as there were alternative channels to membership in the National Panchayat. Surya Bahadur Thapa and Bhuwan Lal Pradhan were nominated to this body by the King; Nageshwar Prasad Singh was elected from the Graduates' Constituency;

and Shailendra Kumar Upadhyaya was selected by the Youth Organization as one of their representatives. On the other hand, two Assistant Ministers, Kaji Man Kandangawa and Prem Bahadur Shakya, failed to win seats and therefore were not included in the new government formed in April, 1963.

Most of the prominent political party leaders outside of the government had not participated in the formation of the lower-level panchayats in 1962 and hence were ineligible for election to the higher tiers of the panchayat system in 1963. Lacking the advantages that accrued from membership in the Council of Ministers, the party leaders found it impossible to insinuate themselves into the panchayats and class organizations at the last moment, and none of them managed to win election to the National Panchayat or to be nominated to this body by the King. Nevertheless, a majority of the membership of the National Panchayat had a political party background, although as second-rank leaders at the local and regional level. Estimates of their previous affiliations vary somewhat, but the following approximations were probably nearly correct: Nepali Congress, 20–25 per cent; Communists, 15 per cent; other parties, 20 per cent. By definition, of course, these men were no longer officially affiliated with their parties, but probably their background as party workers was not without significance even under a partyless panchayat system. Moreover, their success in winning election may be attributable in most instances to the reputation and prestige they had acquired as local party leaders before December, 1960.*

Once the panchayat elections had been completed, but before the inauguration of the National Panchayat, King Mahendra announced another reorganization of the Council of Ministers (see table 14). All of the members of the new government were also members of the National Panchayat, providing something of the aura of a parliamentary system to the new setup. The significance of the gesture was somewhat diminished, however, by the fact that the newly elected legislators did not participate in the selection of the Council of Ministers and that four members of the Council were King Mahendra's nominees to the National Panchayat.

Tulsi Giri's promotion to chairman of the Council of Ministers led some observers to conclude that the system under which

---

* It is interesting to note in this respect that the Ministers and Assistant Ministers who were unable to win election to the National Panchayat by way of the lower-level panchayats were mostly "independents," while former party men such as Tulsi Giri, Vishwabandhu Thapa, and Lalit Chand managed to do so without difficulty.

TABLE 14

The Council of Ministers, 1963

Name	National Panchayat membership	Portfolio
Ministers:		
Tulsi Giri (*Chairman*)	Janakpur zone	Foreign; Royal Palace Affairs; General Administration
Surya Bahadur Thapa (*Vice-chairman*)	Nominated	Finance; Economic Planning; Law
Bhuwan Lal Pradhan	Nominated	Food and Agriculture; Forests
Nageshwar Prasad Singh	Graduate's Constituency	Health; Electricity and Irrigation
Kirtinidhi Bishta	Bagmati zone	Public Works, Transportation and Communications; Education
Vedananda Jha	Sagarmatha zone	Industry and Commerce
Khadga Bahadur Singh	Seti zone	Home; Panchayat
Assistant Ministers:		
Shailendra K. Upadhyaya	Youth Organization	Health; Electricity and Irrigation
Giri Prasad Budathoki	Former Servicemen's Organization	Home; Panchayat
Pushkar Nath Upraity	Peasant's Organization	Industry and Commerce
Nagendra Prasad Rijal	Kosi zone	Finance; Economic Planning; Law
Kedar Man "Vyathit"	Nominated	Public Works, Transportation, and Communications
Rajeshwar Devkota	Gandaki zone	Education
Shamsher Bahadur Tumbahamfe	Nominated	Food and Agriculture; Forests

the King served as his own Prime Minister had been abolished and something resembling the old King-in-Council system under the 1951 organic law reinstituted. There is, however, some question as to whether this is what really occurred. Tulsi Giri may have become *primus inter pares* in the Council, but he was not a

Prime Minister in the accepted sense of that term. According to reports, the King still met with the Cabinet frequently, and presided on such occasions. The King also continued to function as head of the Defence Ministry, which was not even mentioned in the allocation of portfolios on April 3—an indication of the equivocal position of the Council of Ministers, not to mention its chairman. Nor was Tulsi Giri referred to as Prime Minister, a title that King Mahendra reportedly finds offensive, either in official documents or, more or less informally, in the press. It could hardly have been an oversight that congratulations to the new chairman came from the Foreign Ministers rather than the Prime Ministers of various countries.

Nevertheless, his promotion did symbolize Tulsi Giri's unchallenged position within the Ministry. Because of the elimination of Vishwabandhu Thapa and Rishikesh Shah, Dr. Giri was now the only Minister with anything resembling a national reputation. Indeed, none of the other members of the Council had played a prominent role in Nepali government and politics before their ascension to ministerial rank, or were likely to be challengers to Tulsi Giri's preëminent position unless, of course, they should be raised to this status by the King. The only other figure of any significance in the Council was the Finance Minister, Surya Bahadur Thapa, who was the Minister in whom the King seemed to repose the most confidence and through whom he acted on occasion, the role played by Purendra Vikram Shah in pre-1959 Cabinets.

Surya Bahadur Thapa has a background very different from that of Tulsi Giri, Vishwabandhu Thapa, and Rishikesh Shah, and is perhaps closer to being the kind of politician that King Mahendra considers ideal for Panchayat Raj. His "independent" politics and royalist proclivities were duly recognized in the post-*coup* period with an appointment to the Council of Ministers while still in his early thirties. His reputation is that of a careful, hard-working administrator, lacking the brilliance and flare of a Tulsi Giri, no doubt, but conforming better perhaps to the King's political pattern.

A new Raj Sabha, or Council of State, was appointed by King Mahendra on April 2, headed by his brother, Prince Himalaya, and with a total membership of sixty-nine. Nominees included six members of the ruling family, six Ranas, three former Prime Ministers, about twenty former Ministers, several members of the Palace Secretariat and the Central Secretariat, an assortment of political leaders ranging from the Communist Keshar Jang Rayamajhi to representatives of orthodox Hindu organizations, and finally the chairmen of five class organizations —as heterogeneous a body as is possible in Nepal. A fourteen-member Standing Committee of the Raj Sabha was also appointed, with K. I. Singh as the chairman and including Tulsi Giri, Vishwabandhu Thapa, Rishikesh Shah, Aniruddha Prasad Singh, and Commander in Chief Nir Shamsher.

Troubles beset the new Council of State almost immediately. K. I. Singh resigned, complaining that the chairman of the Standing Committee of the Council of State should occupy a higher position than the chairman of the Council of Ministers, whereas in the warrant of precedence just issued the opposite was the case. One week later, Rishikesh Shah also submitted his resignation, on the grounds that he had "ideological and fundamental differences of opinion" with Tulsi Giri that might lead to "unnecessary tension" between the Council of State and the Council of Ministers.[25] Surya Prasad Upadhyaya and Tanka Prasad Acharya refused to take the oath of office, reportedly because of their unhappiness at not having been included on the Standing Committee. With four very prominent politicians resigning or declining appointment, the Raj Sabha was off to an inauspicious beginning.

The National Panchayat was inaugurated on April 14. After a message from the King, the first order of business was the election of a Speaker. As expected, Vishwabandhu Thapa was the choice—by a vote of 90 to 29—and the recommendation of him by the National Panchayat was accepted by King Mahendra, who appointed him Speaker. The election of a Deputy Speaker, on April 21, produced something of a surprise. Basudeva Dhungana, a member from Kathmandu with past Communist affiliations, was elected in spite of what was reported to be official pressure in favor of another candidate. Again the National Panchayat's recommendation was accepted by the King.

But this was the only show of independence and spirit from the National Panchayat during its first year, as it proved to be a careful and docile body. The circumstances under which the National Panchayat was inaugurated did little to enhance its prestige or sense of confidence. A large number of important laws, including new land reform legislation and a new social code, were promulgated just before the opening session of the new legislature, which was thus deprived of any opportunity to express itself on these vital issues. Only two unimportant bills were passed by the National Panchayat in this first session, and the budget session that followed was an equally tame affair with the general tendency being to accept bills essentially as presented by the Ministry.

Indeed, the most interesting politics in 1963 were to be found at the lower levels of the panchayat system. The abolition of the National Guidance Ministry, in April, resulted in a temporary aberration in the guidance structure and in a loosening of supervision over panchayats and class organizations. Reports that village panchayats were abusing their taxing powers appeared frequently in the press in the fall of 1963. The district panchayats also commenced a concerted campaign in support of their demands for broader powers at the expense of Bada Hakims and other centrally appointed officials. Even more spectacular was the public meeting held by the Peasant's Organization in Kathmandu in September—the first public "political" meeting permitted since the December *coup*. The meeting was thrown into an uproar when one member of the Peasants' Central Committee criticized the Council of Ministers in the strongest terms heard in Nepal for several years, and even threatened to commence a movement against the Cabinet. The speaker was arrested the next day by the Kathmandu magistrate, but the repercussions of the speech were felt for some time, resulting finally in a serious split within the Peasants' Organization.

But all these were minor problems in comparison to those that had confronted the government in 1962, and were not serious enough to deter King Mahendra and Tulsi Giri from undertaking extended tours abroad. The King visited India, Israel, and Kenya between August 27 and October 11; Tulsi Giri accompanied the King to India and Israel and then set out on a tour of his own to the United States, France, West Germany, the United Kingdom, Switzerland, Denmark, Sweden and the Soviet Union. His tour was a tremendous personal success as far as Nepal was concerned, as he met President Kennedy in Washington, Prime Minister Pompidou in Paris, President Luebke in Bonn, and Premier Khrushchev in the Soviet Union—tangible evidence that Nepal had achieved a respectable position in the international community. He also obtained promises of additional economic assistance from the United States and the Soviet Union and expressions of interest in investment from the West Germans. He returned to Kathmandu on October 30 to the acclaim of the Kathmandu press.

One of the paradoxes of contemporary Nepali politics is that too obvious successes are as dangerous to the careers of Ministers as too obvious failures, as was indicated by Vishwabandhu Thapa's being excluded from the Cabinet just when the system he had nourished as Minister of National Guidance reached fruition. On returning to Kathmandu, Dr. Giri found his position less secure than it had been before his departure. The first public evidence of this was King Mahendra's unexpected appointment of Rishikesh Shah as chairman of the Standing Committee of the Council of State on December 9. The King's choice was believed to have added significance in view of Rishikesh Shah's frequent public statements favoring the release of all political prisoners and, by implication, a settlement with the Nepali Congress. Then, on December 27, King Mahendra announced that he had accepted Tulsi Giri's resignation, for what were described as reasons of health. Dr. Giri had undergone a minor operation two weeks earlier, but no one in Kathmandu accepted this explanation for his resignation. It was common knowledge that he had resigned at the King's request and not on his own initiative. The Foreign Affairs portfolio was given to Kirtinidhi Bishta, and Surya Bahadur Thapa took over the Palace Affairs and General Administration portfolios.

Speculation on these new developments in Kathmandu was rampant, of course, but there was no official clarification. The King did not issue a proclamation explaining his motivation as he had always done in similar circumstances previously. The most plausible, if still unverified, explanation is that King Mahendra had finally decided to seek an accommodation with the Nepali Congress, including the release of all political prisoners, and that Tulsi Giri's dismissal was a necessary prerequisite in view of the Nepali Congress' antipathy to him.* Reportedly, Surya Prasad Upadhyaya, the Home Minister in the B. P. Koirala Cabinet, was sent to India to meet his former party colleagues, and these talks collapsed over the question of the legalization of political parties, as the Nepali Congress was unwilling to accept a partyless panchayat system. This move having failed, King Mahendra restored Tulsi Giri as chairman of the Council of Ministers on February 27, 1964. In a reallocation of portfolios on April 9, Tulsi Giri assumed charge of Home, Panchayats, Royal Palace Affairs, and General Administration, and Khadga Bahadur Singh was given Forests, Food and Agriculture, and Land Reform. Kirtinidhi Bishta retained the Foreign and Education portfolios, but surrendered Public Works and Transport and Communications to Nageshwar Prasad Singh.

Another minor readjustment of portfolios occurred on July 3, when Vishwabandhu Thapa resigned as chairman of the National Panchayat and was reinstated in the Council of Minist-

---

* According to one authoritative Nepali Congress source in India, the King was also quietly releasing numerous Nepali Congress workers at the district level, some of whom had been imprisoned since December, 1960.

ers as vice-chairman of the Council and as Minister of Home and Panchayat Affairs. This left Tulsi Giri with only the Palace Affairs Ministry, but the other vice-chairman of the Council, Surya Bahadur Thapa, retained Finance, Economic Planning, and Law and Justice. After only forty-seven days in office, however, Vishwabandhu Thapa suddenly resigned—"to look after my home and farm as a common citizen and serve my village and district." [26] The Home and Panchayat Affairs portfolios were restored to Dr. Tulsi Giri, but he resigned from the Council on January 26, 1965, for what he described as differences of opinion. The Finance Minister, Surya Bahadur Thapa, was immediately appointed chairman of the Council of Ministers and was given the Palace Affairs and General Administration portfolios in addition to those he already held. Land Reform was assigned to Khadga Bahadur Singh, Panchayat Affairs to Shailendra Kumar Upadhyaya in the redistribution of portfolios, and all the Assistant Ministers were raised to ministerial rank.

As is now the common practice in Nepal, there have been no official explanations of these developments except for the cryptic and cautious comments made by the Ministers at the time of their resignations. Various reports, however, ascribe Vishwabandhu Thapa and Tulsi Giri's resignations to their strong disapproval of the manner in which the power, prestige, and influence of the Council of Ministers have been steadily eroded since December, 1960. This trend was reflected in the editorial reaction of several newspapers which commented that these changes were of no significance since the Council was responsible to the Crown and acted under the direct supervision of the palace. Surya Bahadur Thapa's appointment as chairman of the Council was generally viewed as appropriate because he was the Minister in whom the King reposed the fullest confidence and to whom the King had entrusted the running of the entire administration even during Dr. Giri's tenure as chairman. In any case, one thing was clear. Ministers with significant political backgrounds had been removed from the Council, which now consisted almost entirely of "independents" with a long record of pro-royalist, antiparty activity.

In spite of the increasing homogenity of the Council of Ministers in recent developments, it is nevertheless apparent that partisan politics in Nepal has not been diminished in scope and intensity by the banning of parties and the introduction of Panchayat Raj, even though the patterns and channels of political activity have undergone a significant transformation. King Mahendra has frequently cited the discouragement of "divisive" and "fissiparous" tendencies—usually attributed to political parties—

as a primary objective of his regime. But there are no indications as yet that panchayats and class organizations are less susceptible to regional, parochial, and other narrow interests or are more "national" in perspective than political parties. Indeed, they lack one essential criterion of the party system that was important in this respect: namely, the necessity for parties to make some form of appeal on the national level to have any hope of success in elections. The dynamics of panchayat politics seems to have created a situation in which personality, rather than program, is the decisive factor and at the same time to have blocked most of the channels through which political leaders gained satisfaction in the past. This has certainly been the case with regard to the Council of Ministers since December, 1960, and few would argue that the results have been encouraging. Whether in the end these conditions foster national unity or national frustration is debatable.

21

Political Organizations and Panchayat Raj

THE SPEED AND EFFICIENCY with which the December *coup* was carried out prevented the organization of effective opposition from any quarter. Having come to expect more subtlety and indirection from King Mahendra, the party leaders were stunned by the King's action and it was several weeks before they were able to recover their composure. Their reaction to the total ban imposed on political activity ranged from sullen compliance to a rather smug and expectant acquiescence. Many party leaders issued statements publicly supporting the King, although in some cases only as the price for release from prison or to avoid imprisonment. It was obvious from the enthusiasm with which most of the opposition party leaders greeted the overthrow of the Nepali Congress government and the termination of the parliamentary system that they viewed the *coup* as an unprecedented opportunity to improve their own and, as a secondary consideration, their party's position.

The immediate consequences of the December *coup* were, of course, particularly disastrous for the Nepali Congress, which lost most of its top leadership through imprisonment, exile, or desertion. With only a few exceptions, all the Congress leaders in Nepal either suffered imprisonment or pledged their loyalty to the royal regime. Among this latter group were several who were actively participating in the government; a larger group promised to abstain from political activity in exchange for their freedom. The purge of Nepali Congress workers was carried out with considerable thoroughness, even on the district level. Local party organizations were disbanded and the party workers either imprisoned or dispersed if they exhibited any disinclination to coöperate with the new regime. At all levels, government officials appointed by the Koirala Cabinet or suspected of too close ties with the Nepali Congress were arbitrarily dismissed, often in direct contravention of Nepal's public service regulations.

A few influential Nepali Congress leaders were either in India at the time of the *coup* or else made their way across the border subsequently. Indeed, the first public expression of opposition to the *coup* came during a convention held by approximately 150 political workers from the central Terai district of Birganj, who met in Raxaul (Bihar) in mid-January, 1961. Shortly thereafter, several hundred Nepali Congress leaders and workers held an emergency secret convention in Patna (Bihar), which was also attended by several leaders from other Nepali political parties. The resolutions publicly adopted by the convention were comparatively mild in tone, merely petitioning the King to reconvene Parliament and release political prisoners. According to the party's general secretary, however, this convention secretly "laid down the line of action, and decided to protest against the King's autocratic regime and build a resistance movement." [1]

It was fairly obvious, however, that the Nepali Congress was in no position at this time to launch a major movement against the King, nor was the mood of the country such as to provide much encouragement about the results if one should be attempted. The Congress had virtually disappeared as an effective political organization, and it was only gradually that an underground organization was built, concentrated in the Terai and the far western and far eastern hill areas where Kathmandu's writ has traditionally been tenuous.

There seem to have been some differences of opinion within the Nepali Congress on the objectives of a resistance movement. A moderate faction, led by Suvarna Shamsher, had limited political goals in view, at least as far as the immediate situation was concerned. While the restoration of parliamentary democracy was the ultimate objective, the moderates were obviously prepared to accomplish this in gradual stages if the King could be persuaded to make a few concessions in this direction—e.g., the release of political prisoners and the legalization of political parties. There was a more radical wing in the Nepali Congress-in-exile, however, which grew increasingly influential once it became evident that a compromise settlement with the King would not be easily achieved. This faction insisted that the party should concentrate on preparations for a full-scale armed revolt aimed at the deposition of King Mahendra and, if necessary, the abolition of the monarchical system itself. A revolutionary situation was developing in Nepal, it was argued, and the Nepali Congress must provide leadership for this movement or else see it pass under the control of the Communists.

The relative strength of the more radical wing in the Nepali Congress increased as the ranks of the party were swelled by refugees from Nepal and leaders from other political parties. As the moderates grew increasingly frustrated with their lack of success in opening negotiations with the King, the trend toward extreme solutions became more pronounced. One of the consequences was a series of armed attacks on government installations in the hill areas and the Terai in the late fall of 1961. These tactics presumably represented a compromise between the policies advocated by the moderate and radical factions of the Congress. From their very nature, the attacks had limited objectives and were not intended as the prelude to full-scale revolution. The Congress leaders may have hoped that a demonstration of the party's capacity to stage armed uprisings would intimidate the King and win concessions from him. In this way, the demands for action from the more radical wing of the party could be satisfied, while at the same time the moderate leadership could disown responsibility for the incidents—which were attributed to spontaneous outbursts on the part of the people—thus leaving themselves free to open negotiations with the palace if circumstances should permit.

The King demonstrated no tendency to panic or even to retreat before these tactics, which he correctly appraised as indicative of weakness rather than strength. The royal regime was frankly skeptical of the Congress party's capacity to mount any movement —nonviolent or revolutionary—that could seriously threaten the stability of the government. The policy of the government at the time of the outbreak of the Nepali Congress-inspired uprisings in the fall of 1961 was an intriguing display of politics at its pragmatic best. The government first denied that the incidents had any political significance, attributing them to the maraudings of "dacoit" (bandit) gangs. When the attacks continued and became more obviously political in character, the government completely reversed its position. Suddenly, it was admitted that the uprisings were politically motivated, allegedly the work of "antinational" elements based in India. An anti-Indian propaganda campaign was launched, obviously officially inspired, in which the Indian government was accused of interfering in Nepal's internal affairs by permitting Nepali political refugees to organize and, in some cases, launch attacks on Nepal from Indian soil.

Aside from the question of their authenticity, there can be little doubt that the allegations of Indian interference in Nepal served both the external and the domestic political objectives of the King. The anti-Indian campaign was useful, for instance, in solidifying some degree of popular support behind the regime and in stigmatizing the opposition as puppets of New Delhi intent on reimposing India's dominant influence in Nepal. The King's eager overtures to Peking, which were reaching a crucial stage in the late fall of 1961, were also justified in part on the grounds that the Indian "threat" necessitated closer relations with China. Kathmandu may also have hoped that New Delhi, alarmed by developments along its entire northern frontier, might be moved to grant concessions to Nepal with regard both to political affairs and to the Indian economic aid program.

In spite of or perhaps because of all this maneuvering and posturing by the Nepal government, the scope and intensity of the Nepali Congress campaign increased gradually in the first half of 1962 until by summer there were few areas of the country, except within the immediate periphery of Kathmandu Valley or the more isolated sections of the northern border, that had not witnessed some manifestation of resistance to the royal regime. Most of these were localized affairs of brief duration that never seriously threatened the government's authority yet did place a tremendous strain on both the administration and the military. The steady deterioration in Nepal-India relations during this period, largely owing to the Kathmandu government's suspicion that India was secretly instigating and supporting the rebels, added to the situation a facet with far more dangerous potentialities. The royal regime rather frantically sought a way to get out of the dilemma without compromising its assiduously cultivated "nationalist" posture.

Developments outside Nepal finally permitted the royal regime to emerge from this critical situation intact and, indeed, with its prestige and authority enhanced. The Chinese incursions along the western and eastern extremities of the Sino-Indian border in October, 1962, had an immediate and dramatic impact upon the internal political situation in Nepal. On November 8, Suvarna Shamsher "suspended" the movement, reportedly on the advice of the Indian government, and one month later the campaign was formally terminated.

With these dramatic new developments came some speculation that the King and the Nepali Congress would seek an accommodation under which Suvarna Shamsher and his colleagues would accept Panchayat Raj in its essentials and would, in exchange, be permitted to return to Nepal without endangering their personal freedom. King Mahendra's "private visit" to Calcutta in January, 1963, was rumored to have been motivated by his decision to meet Suvarna Shamsher without the publicity that would have accompanied talks in Kathmandu. But, if reports are correct, the King did not meet Suvarna in Calcutta on that occasion or elsewhere during his tour of India one month later.

Indeed, the subsequent course of events would seem to indicate that the King either lacked interest in or was not inclined toward a settlement with the then much-truncated Nepali Congress. In the April, 1963, reorganization of the government every Minister or Assistant Minister who had been advocating a moderate domestic and foreign policy was excluded. The King's position was demonstrated even more graphically in the decision of the Kathmandu special court that same month, which sentenced Suvarna Shamsher and several colleagues *in absentia* to life imprisonment on the charge of having instigated the transportation of explosive materials to Nepal for subversive purposes. It was assumed that the King would not have permitted this trial to continue or such a rigorous sentence to be imposed if he had been at all interested in a compromise settlement with the Congress. And, indeed, such an accommodation may have seemed unnecessary. The failure of direct action to achieve any positive political gains seriously undermined the Nepali Congress within Nepal and, presumably, among some of its partisans in India. There was, moreover, a broad reconciliation between New Delhi and Kathmandu in 1963 which went far to relieve the King's apprehensions that India might support or encourage forces opposed to the regime.

Nevertheless, most political observers in Nepal would admit that a *rapprochement* between the King and the Nepali Congress is the *sine qua non* for long-term political stability. There have been several attempts to bring the two antagonists together, but these have all proved abortive. The terms of settlement and, perhaps of even greater importance, the manner of the negotiating, have proven to be serious obstacles. The rather clumsy attempts by the Nepali Congress to intimidate the King into basic concessions through the incitement of sporadic violence backfired disastrously; they seem to have strengthened the King's determination to seek a solution on his own terms. Mahendra's view of his own role in Nepali history as the protector and expander of Nepal's national integrity may be of particular significance in this respect. Speculation in the sphere of personality assessment must be tenuous at best, but it is hardly probable that overt intimidation tactics would prove successful against the King—unless, of course, these were supported by an irresistible display of force. The obvious inadequacies of the Congress's revolutionary capacity, combined with its tendency to depend upon Indian influence at Kathmandu for support of its cause, were not well-conceived tactics if the object was to induce the King to agree to a compromise.

The policy pursued by the Congress has had unfortunate consequences, since it would seem that otherwise the points at issue between the King and the party were not incapable of compromise. The debate between the relative merits of parliamentary democracy and Panchayat Raj has an academic air about it, particularly in prevailing conditions. Or perhaps it would be more accurate to say that the King could define Panchayat Raj in such a way as to make it acceptable to most adherents of parliamentary democracy without seriously subverting his own political objectives. The ban on political parties and the stringent restrictions on "fundamental rights" have proved more difficult to negotiate, but the King has usually maintained that these policies would be modified if and when circumstances permitted. How the parties might be fitted into a panchayat system based on indirect elections has never been discussed, but perhaps experiences in India's Panchayat Raj and Pakistan's "Basic Democracy" system, in which elections to the lowest-level bodies are nonpartisan and the higher-level elections are fought on party and partisan lines, may prove instructive. There is, moreover, a general tendency among most Nepali political leaders to accept the fact that the King will continue to play a central role in the governmental system. Indeed, a satisfactory redefinition of "constitutional monarchy" would not seem a major problem if both sides were intent upon reaching an agreement.

Perhaps the question that has most obstructed a settlement has concerned the position of the Nepali Congress political prisoners—in particular, B. P. Koirala. The stature of the former Prime Minister has been enhanced, if anything, by his imprisonment, and the failure of the King to bring him to trial has raised doubts about the allegations of corruption and treason made against him. His refusal to renounce politics in exchange for freedom has also given him something of the aura of a political martyr. But here, again, recent developments indicate that this question may not be so nearly unsolvable as it once seemed.

There were unverified but seemingly authoritative reports in early 1964 that the King was prepared to make concessions on this question if the Nepali Congress accepted the ban on party and political activity for the time being. A number of Nepali Congress workers on the regional level, some of whom had been imprisoned since December, 1960, were quietly released toward the end of 1963. According to these reports, the talks between the King's representative and the Nepali Congress failed over the political party ban issue; but the terms upon which these negotiations were based represented a considerable modification of those rigorously adhered to by both sides previously and a portent of some significance for the future.

THE NEPAL COMMUNIST PARTY

The other political parties in Nepal have not fared much better than the Nepali Congress since the December *coup* and have, indeed, lacked even the limited recuperative powers the Congress, owing to its nationwide organizational basis, has displayed. One possible exception is the Communist Party of Nepal. It is probable that the 1960 ban on political organizations and activity was felt to a lesser degree by the Communists than by the others. The Communists had functioned in an illegal capacity from 1952 to 1956, and thus had more experience with underground operations. Moreover, since the *coup,* the royal regime has taken much less stringent action against the Communists than against the Nepali Congress. Many Communist leaders and workers were able to continue their political activity virtually undisturbed, in striking contrast to the thoroughgoing efforts made to suppress the Nepali Congress at all levels. Thus the Communists have been provided with a considerable operational advantage over the Nepali Congress that may well prove to have significant long-range implications.

Despite these initial advantages, however, the Communists have not been able to seize full benefit from the situation, primarily because of the chronic struggle for power within the party Politburo. The first signs of a fundamental disagreement within the party leadership on the question of the December *coup* became evident in early 1961. The Communists, although as surprised by the King's action as were the other parties, seem to have recovered their poise more quickly. Few of the Communist leaders were apprehended in the general roundup of politicians that followed the *coup*.* Before long, the party was operating underground in much the same fashion as it had done before 1956. At the time of the *coup*, the "moderate" leader, Keshar Jang Rayamajhi, was in Moscow. Thus, the first public reaction of the party to the King's move reflected the views of the "extremist" Kathmandu faction led by a Politburo member, Pushpa Lal Shrestha. On December 24, 1960, a cyclostyled press note was distributed, ostensibly in the name of the party, demanding the cessation of "military terror" and the reconvening of Parliament. By mid-January, 1961, however, Rayamajhi and other moderate Communists had returned to Nepal from Russia, and the struggle for control of the party machinery began in earnest. The moderate faction was in a majority on the Central Committee and was able to gain approval for a more cautious policy toward the new royal regime. In the latter part of January the party issued another press note, this time reflecting the views of the moderate faction. While cautiously critical of the *coup* and demanding the release of political prisoners, the lifting of the ban on political activity, and restoration of fundamental rights, the note did not insist on the reconvening of the Parliament, thus implying acceptance of the new regime.[2]

The intraparty dispute reached a crisis stage at the "secret" plenum session of the Central Committee held at Darbhanga, India, in March. The plenum was attended also by fifty-four delegates representing twenty-four district organizations of the party.† In these stormy meetings, the Rayamajhi faction argued that the party's immediate objectives should be limited to the restoration of fundamental rights, the release of political prisoners, the withdrawal of the ban on political parties, and the election of a new Parliament in the near future. The Pushpa Lal faction, supported by the Kathmandu, Gorkha, and Bandipur party organizations, demanded the reconvening of the dissolved Parliament (i.e., the restoration of the Nepali Congress government) and, if necessary, the launching of a Communist-led movement to achieve this objective. A third, minor faction led by

---

* None of the five members of the Politburo and only three of the seventeen members of the Communist party's Central Committee were arrested in the three months immediately following the *coup*. Others have been arrested from time to time subsequently, but usually only for brief periods.

† Published source materials on the Darbhanga session are both meager and unreliable. The most detailed account of the proceedings was published in the pro-Communist weekly *Samiksha*, March 23, 1961. The reliability of this source is somewhat lessened by the fact that it reflects the views of the Rayamajhi faction. Interesting comments on the session can be found in *Halkhabar*, March 21 and 22; *Dainik Nepal*, March 27; and *Nepal Samachar*, March 22.

the Piuthan party unit demanded the election of a Constituent Assembly to draw up a new Constitution and the eventual establishment of a republican form of government. For all practical purposes, the two latter factions were aligned against the moderates.

The plenum session ended in a virtual stalemate, although the Rayamajhi faction was able to retain control of the Central Committee. Eleven of the seventeen members of the Central Committee were reported to be Rayamajhi supporters, while six followed Pushpa Lal's leadership. The pro-Rayamajhi majority at the Darbhanga session was reduced to one, however, since three members of the Rayamajhi faction were in prison in Nepal and unable to attend, and a fourth resigned from the Central Committee during the session.

To negotiate the differences between the two factions, the plenum session appointed a joint committee to draw up a compromise party program. This thankless task proved to be impossible, however, and the two factions continued their bitter debate over the question of the party's attitude toward the royal regime.[3] There are some reasons for suspecting that the struggle in the party was not conducted solely on the verbal level. Persistent reports circulated in Kathmandu in July, alleging that a colleague had attempted to assassinate Rayamajhi.[4] It was also at this time that the leader of the moderate faction was apprehended by the Kathmandu police under very curious circumstances. What exactly happened in this instance has never been clarified, but one Nepali journal with close ties to the Communists implied strongly that opposition elements in the party had betrayed Rayamajhi to the police.[*] Equally intriguing was the government's sudden arrest of the leader of the "pro-monarchy" faction of the Nepal Communist party while the leader of the "extremist" faction was allowed to wander around Kathmandu, only indifferently disguised. Whatever the reasons may have been, the government reversed itself quickly, for scarcely one month later Rayamajhi was released from prison—and without having signed the usual declaration of loyalty to the King required of political prisoners.

Rumors of collaboration between Rayamajhi and certain members of the government circulated wildly in the Kathmandu bazaar in September when the Communist leader was given a passport and allowed to visit Moscow, ostensibly (and, possibly,

---

* *Pravartak* (Kathmandu), July 12, 1961. It is interesting to note that the day after Rayamajhi's arrest, a leader of the extremist faction, Tulsi Lal Amatya, told reporters in Darjeeling that the Communists had divided Nepal into five zones and that he had been given the task of organizing the revolution in the eastern districts.

actually) for medical treatment. His departure did nothing to reduce the tension in the party, however, and may have been partly responsible for bringing matters to a head. The moderates, bolstered by the return of the three members of the party's Central Committee who had been released from prison at approximately the same time as Rayamajhi, decided to issue a strong warning to the extremists. Pushpa Lal and his associates were threatened with expulsion from the party if they did not mend their ways, accept the decision to support the royal regime, and work within the existing institutional framework.

A serious clash occurred between the two factions at a party Central Committee meeting in Kathmandu, held either in late November or early December. Pushpa Lal insisted that the King's rule was "feudalistic" and had to be overthrown by any means, even revolution. The "bourgeois and reactionary" Indian government was only a slight improvement over the royal regime, Pushpa Lal admitted, but in the circumstances New Delhi could be expected to favor and support "democratic forces" in their struggle to free Nepal from the King's "dictatorship." He also favored an alliance with the Nepali Congress as the necessary prerequisite to a successful revolution. These views were unacceptable to the moderates, and Pushpa Lal and his supporters were threatened with expulsion from the party if they did not cease their "antiparty activities." Shortly thereafter, Pushpa Lal and several colleagues fled to India in order, according to reports, to avoid detention by the authorities.

On arriving in India, Pushpa Lal made two conditional offers of coöperation to the Nepali Congress. These were welcomed by Suvarna Shamsher and his colleagues, though no outright acceptance of the proposal seems to have been made at that time.[5] Indeed, the hard-pressed Congress leaders must have found the offer tempting, for the support of the Pushpa Lal faction would have augmented and supplemented the Nepali Congress's revolutionary potential. Insignificant though they might be numerically, the supporters of the extremist faction of the Communist party were concentrated in some of the most vital areas of Nepal: Kathmandu Valley, Gorkha in the western hills, and Dharan in the lower eastern hills. These were areas in which strong Communist party organizations had existed before the December *coup* and where some residue of this structure must have survived. Even more crucial perhaps were the connections Pushpa Lal had with the Communist-dominated Peasants' Organization through one of his adherents, Tulsi Lal Amatya. Moreover, Pushpa Lal was probably in a position to solicit assistance from sections of the

Communist Party of India that otherwise might have been antagonistic toward the Nepali Congress.

For nearly three months Pushpa Lal toured areas of India in which there were substantial settlements of Nepali migrants—followed very closely, it should be noted, by D. P. Adhikari, then affiliated with the moderate faction of the party. Finally, Pushpa Lal announced in early April, 1962, that a "Congress of the Communist Party of Nepal" would be held the next month. The ostensible purpose of the congress was to formulate policy; actually it was to set up what amounted to a "parallel" Communist party. The announcement brought forth an immediate denunciation from the Rayamajhi faction. Speaking on behalf of the Central Committee of the party, Kamar Sah issued a statement in Kathmandu accusing the Pushpa Lal group of "actively conspiring against the central leadership, violating the Leninist standard of party life, and indulging in factional activities to undermine the very unity of the party." Despite these "antiparty" activities, the announcement continued, the Central Committee was "confident that the rank and file of the party, educated in Leninist principles," would defeat the "nefarious designs of the Pushpa Lal group to split party unity" and that the party would "advance further in its goal to serve the people and the country in its glorious past tradition." [6]

Kamar Sah's warnings were ignored, and a meeting, termed an *Adhibeshan* ("general congress") of the party, was held in Banaras in mid-May, reportedly drawing representatives from eight of the thirty-five districts of Nepal.[7] Seven resolutions were passed, the most important of which called for a revolution against the royal regime, though no date was set for the commencement of the movement. A second resolution expelled ten moderate members of the Central Committee—including Rayamajhi, Sambhu Ram Shrestha, Kamar Sah, D. P. Adhikari, and P. B. Malla—for varying periods, on charges of betraying the party by supporting the King's "antidemocratic" moves. To replace them, a new Central Committee was appointed, of whose nineteen members only four had been members of the old committee. In addition, a new National Council was formed, most of whose fifty-one members were also newcomers.

The Banaras meetings failed to result in an open alliance between the Pushpa Lal faction and the Nepali Congress, but they were effective in completing the split within the Communist Party of Nepal. In late May, the Central Committee of the party (Rayamajhi faction) issued a statement condemning the violent activities of the "antinational elements" in India:

No democratic movement succeeds through violence and terroristic activities. It can succeed only through a mass movement launched inside the country. Violent actions weaken the mass movement. The Communist party therefore condemns such activities.[8]

This statement, astonishing in view of its source, would seem to be directed more at Pushpa Lal and his supporters in the party than at the Nepali Congress. By summer, all efforts to prevent the formalization of the split within the Communist party leadership had come to naught. Finally in September, the Central Committee (Rayamajhi faction) expelled Pushpa Lal, Tulsi Lal Amatya, and Hikmat Singh from the party. Other members of the party who supported these three "deviationists," it was stated, would be dealt with by the appropriate committees of the level on which they worked.

With the revolutionary path to communism discarded (only temporarily, presumably), the Rayamajhi faction adopted another familiar Communist tactic—a "united front of all democratic forces" in Nepal. One of the first indications of the new direction of Communist policy was an article in a pro-Communist weekly complaining that "no united and organized front" had yet been established to meet the challenge of the "Indian-American puppet forces led by Suvarna and Bharat." [9] As the government's ban on party activity was a serious, possibly insurmountable obstacle to the formation of a united front, much of the Communists' persuasive talents was employed in a campaign to convince the King that the dynamics of such a movement were basically in conformity with his own political objectives.

To emphasize even further the "royalist" character of the proposed united front, the Central Committee of the Communist party suggested that the King should call a conference on this subject at the royal palace. "All nationalistic and democratic forces standing for different ideologies and policies and having a program for the solution of national problems" should be invited, the party executive suggested.[10] The use of the adjective "nationalistic" was particularly significant, since in current Nepali political parlance the Nepali Congress and allied "antinational" elements would automatically be excluded from the front. The term "democratic," on the other hand, is interpreted so broadly in Nepal that hardly any organization could reasonably be excluded for being undemocratic; thus any of the parties or groups representing traditional and vested interests could join at their own discretion.

The relationship between the front and the government was also a delicate question upon which the Communists attempted to reassure the King. The front would not be a political party, the Communists said, nor would it be entrusted with the task of running the government:

Of course, it would be indispensable to maintain close contact and hold consultations between such a front and the government. Each will have to respect the other, as otherwise there will be no national unity. In case such a front is formed, it will not be able to assume the form of a "party," though its members following different ideologies and principles may work for nationalism, for the country's development, and for democracy. Instead, such a front would put an end to mutual rivalry and opposition for the sake of opposition and pave the way for a healthy competition for constructive work and service to the country.[11]

As described so enthusiastically by the Communists, the front would be another instrument through which the government could implement its political and economic programs.

Needless to say, there was some doubt in official and intellectual circles in Kathmandu that the Communists intended to allow the front to function in this fashion. There were, it was pointed out, several aspects of such a front that might well prove advantageous to the Communists. First, it would provide the party with an organization within which Communist cadres could operate on a legal level even while the party itself was still banned. Furthermore, the Communists would be assured easier access to such administrative institutions as the panchayats and class organizations, which they had been assiduously attempting to infiltrate. Finally, the party could use its participation in the front to seize a central and possibly dominant position among the remnants of the political party movement in Nepal, in preparation for the time when it might once again have to compete with the Nepali Congress.

The termination of the Nepali Congress-led movement in December, 1962, in the wake of Chinese aggression against India, placed the Pushpa Lal faction in a quandary. Pushpa Lal's policy had been based on the proposition that the overthrow of King Mahendra should be the primary goal of the Communist Party of Nepal, even if the immediate result was a regime dominated by the Nepali Congress. It was now obvious that this policy was unrealistic and that terroristic tactics had been unavailing. Reportedly, a number of Communist party workers in exile in India became disillusioned, returned to Nepal in 1963, and presumably made their peace with the Rayamajhi faction. Further, a serious rift had developed within the extremist faction between the followers of Pushpa Lal and Tulsi Lal Amatya, who succeeded Pushpa Lal as general secretary of the party-in-exile in 1962.[12]

How reliable these reports may be is open to question, but it was apparent, nevertheless, that the challenge to Rayamajhi's leadership was receding. The proroyalist policy of the moderate faction brought tangible political rewards, including Rayamajhi's appointment to the Raj Sabha, the appointment of a former member of the party's Central Committee as an Assistant Minister, and the election of a pro-Communist as Deputy Speaker of the National Panchayat. There are some indications, however, that Rayamajhi's "gradualist" approach has not been popular with party workers who are emotionally anti-monarchical and action-oriented. The party also seems to have lost some of the appeal it formerly had for young intellectuals, who are no longer so prone to view the Communists—at least, the domestic variety— as the wave of the future.

Besides internal factors in the divisions that have rent the Communist party, international developments such as the Sino-Indian border conflict and the Sino-Russian ideological and tactical disputes have had an important impact. There is, as yet, no coherent division of the party into pro-Soviet or pro-Chinese wings—at least, on the public level. Like most others in Asia, the Nepali Communists find it extremely embarrassing to have to make a choice between the two Communist giants. The position of the party is doubly complex because of the Sino-Indian struggle for influence throughout the Himalayan area, which has now become inextricably enmeshed in the Sino-Soviet dispute and in the division of the Indian party into nominally "pro-Soviet" and "pro-China" factions.

No top Nepali Communist leaders have openly declared themselves in the quarrels dividing the Communist world. Tulsi Lal Amatya has been accused of harboring "pro-China" sentiment, but his position as an exile in India makes it imprudent for him to align openly with the Chinese camp.* Rayamajhi's contacts have largely been with the Russians. Presumably his faction would line up with the Soviet Union if it ever became necessary to choose sides; at present it carefully maintains a neutral position and refrains from commenting publicly on any of the issues in

---

* It is significant that Tulsi Lal Amatya has consistently been a supporter of what in Nepal are considered Maoist views on tactics and ideology. As president of a peasants' organization he took the position that, given Nepal's peculiar conditions, the peasantry alone could provide a revolutionary potential. On this point he usually found himself in disagreement with other Nepali Communist leaders, who accepted the more orthodox Marxian position that the working class, supported by the peasantry, must be the instrument of revolutionary change.

dispute. Such discretion is by all odds the better part of valor, for there are indications that both major factions of the party would be even further divided if they had to declare themselves publicly on the Sino-Soviet rift.

OTHER POLITICAL PARTIES

The reactions of the various political parties to the December *coup* was indicative of the basic malaise endemic to the political party movement in Nepal. The abject failure of most party organizations to protest—much less, challenge—the King's action constituted an eloquent commentary on the narrow, self-centered approach of many party leaders and on the lack of a strong popular base for the party movement as a whole. King Mahendra could concentrate his attention on the destruction of the one party with some national support, confident that most of the other party leaders, oblivious of the long-range implications of this policy for their own organizations, would loudly applaud. The King once again proved a shrewd appraiser of the men and organizations competing for political influence, playing upon their recurrent hopes and fears with the skill of a virtuoso.

The objects of the government's repressive actions at the time of the *coup* were not, however, limited to the Nepali Congress leaders. Most of the opposition party leaders, including Tanka Prasad Acharya and Bhadrakali Mishra of the Praja Parishad, Bharat Shamsher and Mrigendra Shamsher of the Gorkha Parishad, K. I. Singh of the United Democratic party, D. R. Regmi of the Nepali National Congress, and Ranga Nath Sharma of the Nepal Prajatantrik Mahasabha, were arrested along with many of their party workers. These leaders were released almost immediately, with one or two exceptions, and they shortly thereafter issued statements lauding the King's action. Enthusiasm among the party leaders diminished perceptibly after the appointment of the new Cabinet, dominated by former Nepali Congress leaders and independents, and turned to frustration when it became apparent that the King had no intention of lifting the ban on political parties.

Subsequent events seem to indicate that some of the opposition party leaders were not nearly so enthusiastic about the December *coup* as the statements issued at the time of their release from detention would suggest. Several leaders, including Bhadrakali Mishra of the Praja Parishad and Kashi Prasad Shrivastav of the United Democratic party, fled to India in early

1961 and joined the Nepali Congress.* For the most part, none of these represented a significant accretion of strength to the Nepali Congress, since they lacked anything more than local centers of support in Nepal. Nor could they even be considered as unofficial spokesmen for their former party comrades in Nepal, who almost without exception vehemently denounced them as traitors to party principles.

Quite a different matter, however, was the flight to India of Bharat Shamsher, the dominant personality in the Gorkha Parishad. Bharat Shamsher was arrested on December 15, 1960, and was not released for nearly three months, long after the other opposition party leaders had been set free. On obtaining his release from detention, the Gorkha Parishad leader issued a statement supporting the King's action, but later claimed that it had been extracted from him under duress. Like most of the other party leaders, he was restricted to Kathmandu Valley for some months. Eventually he received permission to pay short visits to India and Europe. He made two trips abroad, returning each time as scheduled. In the fall of 1961, however, he started off once again, this time not to return. The first indication that this trip differed from his previous excursions was Bharat Shamsher's unexpected attendance at the Rome session of the Second (Socialist) International. On returning to India in November, he held a press conference in New Delhi in which he denounced the royal regime in the strongest possible language and declared his intention to coöperate with the Nepali Congress in a joint effort to overthrow it. Slightly more than a month later, he announced the merger of the Gorkha Parishad with the Nepali Congress, which he described as "a cause, a conviction, and a platform for all democrats," and said that his party's action was guided by the belief that "differences in details of program have to be sacrificed for a bigger cause." [13]

The alliance between the Nepali Congress and the Bharat Shamsher wing of the Gorkha Parishad constituted a potentially serious threat to the King, since it brought a number of trained party workers in various parts of the hill areas of Nepal within the opposition camp. Although Gorkha Parishad leaders in Kathmandu hastened to denounce their erstwhile leader, there are reasons for assuming that Bharat Shamsher, with his well-lined

---

* On May 12, 1961, the Shrivastav faction of the United Democratic party—mostly party workers from the western Terai area—held a secret meeting in Gorakhpur, India, and announced their decision to merge with the Nepali Congress. *Asian Recorder*, VII, No. 24 (June 11–17, 1961), 3996.

pocketbook, retained the loyalty of several party units outside the capital.

Within the Nepali Congress, according to reports, Bharat Shamsher has been a consistent advocate of revolutionary tactics, and several of the armed attacks on government posts in the hill areas in 1962 were allegedly undertaken by his supporters.* Indeed, a decided change in character in Nepali Congress tactics seems to have followed the merger with the Gorkha Parishad. The earlier armed outbreaks in Nepal were hastily and cursorily executed and seemed to be incited for their nuisance value. By February, 1962, the raids were better planned, were carried out on a larger and more ambitious scale, and at times seemed to be genuinely revolutionary in character. Whether this reflected Bharat Shamsher's influence or a change in objective conditions in Nepal, the results were the same—a decided worsening of relations between the Nepali Congress leaders in exile and the King.†

"LOYAL" FORMER PARTY LEADERS

Many of the political party leaders in Nepal have successfully avoided both imprisonment and exile since the December *coup* and have remained around Kathmandu awaiting the magic touch from the palace. Some, like Dilli Raman Regmi, have dropped quietly out of the public eye. Others, such as Tanka Prasad Acharya and Ranga Nath Sharma, have been consistent and vocal supporters of the King and vociferous critics of the Nepali Congress. Rather disappointingly, the tangible benefits accruing to them for their forthright stand have been few and far between. Appointments to minor, usually semiofficial posts have been forthcoming for some of them, but the highly coveted ministerial appointments have gone to former Nepali Congress members and to "independents." Yet there is always the possibility that the King's favor might turn their way, and they stand ready and eager to serve when the call is heard. In a somewhat special category is K. I. Singh, who has kept carefully out of politics but has threatened on a number of occasions to lead a mass movement against the present regime if the political atmosphere did not improve.

All of the anti-Nepali Congress political leaders have chafed

---

* He was reported, for instance, to have opposed Suvarna Shamsher's decision to terminate the resistance campaign in December, 1962. *Samiksha,* February 3, 1963.
† See *The Statesman,* February 4, 1962, for an interesting analysis of these developments by its Darjeeling correspondent.

under the regulations banning party activity and have sought to circumvent these restrictions in various ways, with Tanka Prasad Acharya usually taking the lead in these maneuvers. The former Prime Minister first attempted to obtain the King's approval for the formation of a "country-wide nonpolitical organization on a democratic basis" to assist the government in the struggle against "antinational elements both inside and outside the country." Six leaders from the Praja Parishad, Nepal Prajatantrik Mahasabha, and the United Democratic party (though K. I. Singh kept strictly away from these maneuvers) submitted to the King a petition which stressed the usefulness of such an organization for inculcating nationalist sentiment among the people and resisting "antinational" elements. Also the organization would, it was claimed, "resist and expose the design of any foreign country which might attempt to exercise pressure on Nepal, bring before the government and the people any defects in the policy and work of the Nepal Government," and coöperate in "democratic and constructive tasks." [14]

In replying to the petition, the government expressed its appreciation of the patriotism of the political leaders who had come to realize the need to resist "antinational" forces, and said that it was "always prepared to encourage and extend coöperation to any organized popular force honestly resisting traitorous activities." The reply went on to say, however: ". . . a ban has been imposed on political organizations at present, [and] the government is unable to permit any organization to assume a political color." [15] Tanka Prasad and the other politicians were uncertain as to whether this reply was to be interpreted as a rejection or an approval of their request to form a "nonpolitical" organization and a clarification was sought. [16] The government's reply to this second communication was unequivocal. The objectives mentioned in the petition, the Secretary of the National Guidance Ministry stated, demonstrated beyond doubt that the proposed organization would be "political in character." The political leaders were then reminded of the Home Ministry's notification of December 10, 1961, banning all organized political activity. It was the decision of His Majesty's Government that no permission could be granted to form such an organization. [17]

Thwarted in this endeavor, Tanka Prasad moved to achieve his objective through other tactics. At the Intellectual's Conference held in Kathmandu in June, 1962, the Praja Parishad leader launched a bitter attack on the Council of Ministers and the policy under which "innocent political parties" which supported the King and were "prepared to work for the interest of the country" were penalized for the "misdeeds of a particular party." He suggested that these parties should be allowed to function, while the ban should be retained on "offending" parties such as the Nepali Congress. He waxed particularly indignant over what he alleged was the tendency of some of the present Ministers to argue that if the King should have to replace them, the only "deserving" alternative was the Nepali Congress.[18]

Tanka Prasad has also been the only political leader of note to respond favorably, even enthusiastically, to the Communist party's proposal for a united front, which he apparently views as a vehicle for his reëntry into active politics. But the government has not responded any more favorably to this proposal than it did to Tanka Prasad's earlier bid to form a "nonpolitical" national organization. Frustration continues to be the lot of most of the leaders of the minor political parties, who see little future for themselves in the present administrative structure and even fewer opportunities in any political system in which the Nepali Congress would play an important role. Their only chance for proper recognition seems to be in the hope that developments inside and outside Nepal might force the King to turn to them for support and coöperation.

NONPARTY POLITICAL ELITES

Since December, 1960, King Mahendra has moved, and with some success, to provide as broad a base for his regime as circumstances permitted. One aspect of the current situation that distinguishes the present system from earlier direct-rule periods is the great emphasis the King has placed upon youth in the governmental reorganization. Three of the dominating personalities in the first post-*coup* Cabinet were in their thirties and a number of other men as young or younger were given high posts in the Secretariat. In most instances these were well-educated young Nepalese who had pursued advanced studies in Western or Indian universities and whose ideas and ideals contrasted in many ways with those held by the older, tradition-oriented groups upon whom the King had depended in the past. This emphasis upon youth serves a dual purpose for the King. In the first place, it provides him with a base, and a comparatively competent one technically, upon which he can depend for support in pressing economic and other reforms. At the same time, it associates with the royal regime some of the potential leaders of Nepali society and satisfies their ambitions, at least temporarily, by giving them a status they would not normally attain for another decade.

Presumably King Mahendra hoped and expected that this policy would gain for him wide support among members of the young educated class in Nepal, who would appreciate the new opportunities for advancement opened to them. The response from the young intellectuals has not been altogether positive, as many in this group seem to feel that their view of the world and that of the palace are incompatible. This is not to imply that there is a revolutionary spirit among the young intellectuals, even potentially. On the contrary, cynicism rather than radicalism seems to be the prevailing mood, and there is little to indicate that they are prepared to serve as the core of an opposition movement to the regime, even though few of them may be ideologically in step with the King's political program. The future trends, however, are much less clear and will probably depend upon how this group fares under the present system. Of some significance in this respect is the rapid increase in educated unemployment, previously a minor problem. Many talented young Nepalese are now obtaining higher education, either in Nepal or abroad, without any concomitant expansion of employment opportunities.

While making an appeal to the young educated Nepalese, the King has not neglected the groups which have traditionally held a dominant position in the various institutions of government and which have generally supported the crown vis-à-vis the political parties. In contrast to the policy initiated by the Nepali Congress government, in which such considerations received little attention, the King has reinstituted in its essentials the old system under which certain categories of posts were the virtual preserve of caste or ethnic groups. Most of the King's appointments to the judiciary, for instance, have been Brahmans, the caste that has traditionally filled such posts. Economic vested-interest groups were also guaranteed an important voice in such bodies as the Royal Land Reform Commission and the Royal Taxation Commission, set up to advise the government on economic policies in these crucial spheres. The National Planning Council, which was given the delicate task of preparing a detailed development plan for the country, represented an intricate balancing of economic and political groups having a vested interest in these proceedings if not, unfortunately, much expertise in the task of planning. The far-ranging reforms projected for the land tenure and revenue systems have also been carefully devised not to infringe upon the ancient privileges enjoyed by the landowning classes of the important Kirati and Limbu communities of eastern Nepal. All things considered, the King has been remarkably successful in retaining the support of these normally conservative groups even while advocating economic and political reforms which may prove potentially detrimental to their interests.

The King's handling of the political parties has been no less skillful, if not always so successful. Since his ascent to the throne in 1955, King Mahendra has developed several techniques designed to frustrate the functioning of the political party system. One that was employed with considerable success on at least two occasions before 1959 involved the holding of all-inclusive conferences to which the King invited representatives of innumerable (and sometimes fictitious) political, social, regional, and ethnic organizations. Called theoretically to ascertain public opinion on national issues, the conferences were also used to exacerbate differences between the various political party factions; at the same time they served as platforms for the expression of antiparty views by otherwise anonymous nonpolitical personalities. Their ultimate effect in the past had been to sabotage efforts currently under way to rationalize the party system through a process of amalgamation into three or four basic groups. The way in which minor local parties and "parallel" parties were granted equal status at the conference with the few broader-based parties served to encourage the former to maintain their separate existence. The inclusion of nonpolitical organizations in the conferences was also a useful device for dramatizing one of the King's main criticisms of the party system, namely, that the parties represented special and personal interests rather than the national interest.

The Intellectual's Conference at Kathmandu in June, 1962, exhibited a slight variation on this technique. The ban on political parties obviated the necessity of aiming the conference directly at the subversion of the party system, but it did serve to emphasize the differences in the approaches of the various political party leaders and to obstruct any tendency toward the formation of working agreements among them. It also provided the party leaders—or, rather, those acceptable to the regime—with an opportunity to vent their criticisms of the administration in public without in any way obligating the government to heed their views. The Conference thus served as a substitute of sorts for a Parliament and at the same time suffered from none of the defects, from the King's point of view, of a parliamentary system.

But probably the greatest advantage the King has enjoyed in his relations with the political party movement is the community of interest on certain basic questions between the palace and most of the political party leadership outside of the Nepali Congress. Even after the introduction of parliamentary democracy, the opposition parties displayed a marked preference for traditional political tactics—intrigue, conspiracy, and Court politics. The one unforgivable transgression of the Nepali Congress in the eyes of both the palace and the opposition parties was its refusal to confine itself to these traditional tactics and its increasing emphasis upon alternative approaches to political office and power. The threat was all the more real because the Nepali Congress won an overwhelming victory in the 1959 elections and seemed then to be on the verge of establishing a monolithic party system which would have relegated both the palace and the opposition parties to a permanent position of inferiority.

The opposition parties, therefore, deemed a political system dominated by the Nepali Congress to be more detrimental to their interests than one in which the palace was the source of authority and the dispenser of political rewards. It was with their general approbation that King Mahendra reintroduced the traditional political pattern after the December *coup* and retained it subsequently as an essential characteristic of his new political system. These are the politics with which most party leaders are familiar and within which they can function comfortably and with some degree of sophistication. It is, indeed, paradoxical that political parties, which in view of their public stances and proclaimed ideologies should have been political innovators and apostles of modernization, have served as powerful supports to the traditional political pattern. In the process, moreover, the parties have also been instrumental in solidifying the preëminent position of the monarchy through their readiness to accept the palace as the source of ultimate political authority. In the final analysis, however, it has been the King who has been enabled to use the party leaders for his own purposes, rather than the reverse.

22

Policy and Program
of the Royal Regime

To the surprise of most observers, the radical political changes introduced in Nepal since December 15, 1960, have not been accompanied by substantive changes in policies and programs in most other spheres. Trends in economic, social, administrative, and foreign policy that had been evident at least since 1955, and, in some instances, even in the latter stages of the Rana period, have continued. The royal regime has not represented a significant break with the past and, indeed, the differences that can be perceived are essentially those involving modes of operations and tactics rather than basic objectives.

There was initially considerable confusion about objectives after the *coup,* as some of King Mahendra's earliest pronouncements seemed to imply that major changes in the government's economic, administrative, and foreign policy were imminent. The tone of the Royal Proclamation of December 15 on land reform, taxation, and administrative reorganization, for instance, was such as to encourage the assumption that the new regime would abandon or seriously modify these programs. In retrospect, however, these statements would seem to have been contrived carefully to elicit the maximum political support from those political and economic vested-interest groups that had been hostile to the Nepali Congress without in fact obligating the new government to any definite action.

LAND REFORM

Land legislation enacted between 1951 and 1960 had been restricted to reform of the tenure system, rent control, and protection of tenancy rights. Policy on these issues had been defined most comprehensively in the 1957 Lands Act and the 1959 Birta Abolition Act, although neither program had been implemented with conspicuous vigor or with any notable improvement in the status and position of tenants. Even the Nepali Congress government had moved cautiously on land reform, despite its self-proclaimed adherance to a democratic-socialist ideology.

In the Royal Proclamation of January 5, 1961, King Mahendra stated that the government would "profit by past experience [and] achieve this objective [*Birta* abolition] by means of a clear and scientific policy." [1] This had been generally construed to mean that the 1959 Birta Abolition Act would be implemented in a milder form, if at all.[2] The appointment of a Royal Commission on Taxation and Birta Abolition on February 6, "to submit recommendations with regard to *Birta* abolition" reinforced this impression.[3] Holders of *Birta* land were particularly encouraged by the broad representation they obtained on the Commission, which assured them an important voice in its proceedings. As expected, the Commission's report, submitted to the government on March 27, suggested major revisions in the program, recommending that it be restricted to the imposition of taxes on *Birta* lands at 50 per cent of the rate on adjoining non-*Birta* lands and that the system itself should not be abolished except for *Birta* lands acquired by Ranas after 1847.[4] This report naturally aroused expectations that the abolition program would be drastically amended, and it was an unpleasant shock to *Birta* holders when Finance Minister Rishikesh Shah announced in his budget speech in August that the program would be implemented with only slight modifications. That the report had made little impact on the government was further demonstrated in the Amendment of the 1959 Birta Abolition Act, promulgated on February 6, 1962, which virtually ignored the Commission's recommendations.[5]

In line with its announced intention to reappraise land legislation, the royal regime appointed a second advisory body, the Royal Commission on Land Reform, in June, 1961, headed by Tanka Prasad Acharya, but including conservative landowning interests. The report it eventually submitted seems to have been no more successful in influencing government policy than that of its predecessor.* In any case, the Agricultural (New Arrangements) Act promulgated on April 12, 1963, not only retained

---

* The Commission prepared a series of complex and detailed questionnaires that would have required a large corps of trained social scientists for their proper utilization.

intact most of the controversial provisions of the 1957 Lands Act, but also introduced a radical innovation in land policy by imposing ceilings on the size of landholdings.[6] Surplus lands acquired by the government under this program were to be redistributed, with tenants and landless labor having first priority on their purchase.

The procedures adopted in implementing the land redistribution program, however, seemed to guarantee that the immediate impact would be negligible. The government decided, and announced at the time of the Act's promulgation, that this measure would initially be implemented only on an experimental basis in a few villages in three districts. Nor were the requisite supplementary ordinances enacted to bar the transfer of ownership of land within the family or to traditional familial retainers. In private, the government frankly admitted that the program was unlikely to result in the redistribution of much land, except possibly in a few areas in the Terai.

The Act was defended on the grounds that it would lead to the breakup of large landholdings by forcing redistribution *within* landowning families. This sophisticated, if somewhat obtuse argument presumed that such redistribution would serve the dual purpose of encouraging the disintegration of the joint family system and improving agricultural production methods. Smaller holdings, it was argued, would force landowners to cultivate the land themselves and utilize improved methods of production. Obviously, this would do little to improve the condition of tenants and landless laborers.

The "redistribution" principle in the 1963 Act, thus, may have had more of the character of a radical slogan than of a fundamental land-reform program, but the long-term effects of the acceptance of land redistribution as official policy should not be underestimated. Nor should it be assumed that the timidity displayed by the government in the early stages of implementing this program necessarily implies that it will not be applied with more determination in the future. In 1964 a slightly more stringent version of the 1963 Act was promulgated, to plug a few of the many loopholes of the earlier legislation. The most important and controversial innovation was the clause which set ceilings on landholdings by family (defined to include parents, minor sons, and unmarried daughters) rather than individuals, thus complicating the subdivision of holdings within a family. The government has also shortened the target period during which the land-reform program is to be implemented throughout Nepal to three years (i.e., 1964–67).[7]

TRADE AND COMMERCE

Fundamental dissatisfaction with the system under which Nepal traded abroad has been a constant feature of Nepali politics since 1951. Because more than 95 per cent of Nepal's trade is with India, Indo-Nepali relations have been vitally affected by the gradual crystallization of opinion. The terms of trade with and through India, as prescribed in the 1950 trade treaty, have received the most concentrated criticism, but there has also been widespread resentment at the virtually total dependence upon India for Nepal's general economic well-being. To the educated elite, Nepal's independence and national sovereignty will never be complete without extensive modifications in the trade structure and a reduction of Nepal's exposure to Indian economic domination.

The uncompromisingly aggressive nationalistic posture of the royal regime has placed it directly within the mainstream of articulate Nepali opinion on this subject. Shortly after assuming control in December, 1960, the new government announced its intention to continue the efforts undertaken by previous regimes to diversify Nepal's trade structure. The steady deterioration in Indo-Nepali relations throughout 1961 and 1962 enhanced the importance of this program as Kathmandu grew increasingly concerned with the possiblity that Indian economic pressure might be employed to force political changes in Nepal. Presumably it was to counter this potentiality that King Mahendra first approached China and Pakistan in 1961 in search of alternative channels for Nepal's trade and commerce. While the terms of these proposals were markedly different from those advanced by previous governments, they represented the logical extension of Nepal's efforts since 1947 to expand political and economic relations with countries other than India.

The agreement signed with Communist China in October, 1961, while King Mahendra was on a state visit to that country, provided for a potentially significant contribution to greater flexibility in Nepal's trading system. Peking agreed to finance and supervise the construction of a road connecting Kathmandu with Kodari, a village on the Nepal-Tibet border. It is widely assumed in Nepal that this road, by facilitating trade with Tibet and China, will open another market for Nepal's products and a new source for manufactured goods. Even more important is the expectation that Kathmandu will reëmerge as the principle entrepôt for trade between India and Tibet, a status that contributed to Nepal's affluence for several centuries before the opening of the shorter and easier route through Sikkim around the turn of the century, lately closed by the Sino-Indian border dispute. To regulate the terms of trade between Nepal and Tibet, a new trade agreement was signed by Kathmandu and Peking on May 19, 1964. This agreement, however, was not nearly so comprehensive as had been predicted in certain quarters in Nepal, for it ignored many of the complaints about the treatment of Nepali traders in Tibet that has hampered commercial relations in recent years.

Another aspect of China's economic aid program in Nepal that has affected established trade patterns is the system under which China has provided consumers' goods free of cost to the Nepal government, the goods later being sold on the local market. The funds thus acquired are used to meet Nepali currency requirements for local Chinese aid projects. Because these goods are priced artificially to compete with similar goods imported from or through India, they find a ready market in Kathmandu. Presumably this practice will continue only so long as Chinese aid projects require local currency and less clumsy and expensive means for its acquisition are not available. But in the process China has gained some tangential political benefits and, at the same time, has won a foothold in the Kathmandu market for Chinese-produced commodities that on strictly economic terms of trade could not compete with Indian imports.*

Pakistan probably plays an even more important part in Nepal's trade diversification plans than China. In September, 1961, King Mahendra paid a state visit to West Pakistan, in the course of which he suggested expanded commercial relations between the two countries.[8] In response, a Pakistani trade delegation came to Kathmandu in April, 1962, for preliminary talks on a trade agreement. A Nepali delegation returned the visit a few months later, and on October 19 a trade treaty was signed, providing mutual most-favored-nation treatment. A series of talks in Karachi in January, 1963, culminated in the signing of a trade and transit treaty providing for the free movement of goods between the two countries without custom or transit duties. Air service inaugurated between East Pakistan and Kathmandu in

---

* Not all the so-called Chinese commodities available in Kathmandu are actually manufactured in China. According to reliable reports, the only part of the "Chinese blankets" exported to Nepal in 1963 that was actually produced in China was the label reading "Made in China." The blankets themselves were Japanese products which sold in Japan for a higher price than that asked in Kathmandu.

1963, gave Nepali importers an alternative to Calcutta as a transit port for goods purchased abroad.

In conjunction with these efforts to diversify Nepal's traditional trade pattern, the royal regime has also sought to improve the terms of trade with India or in transit through India. From the economic point of view, the successes achieved here have been of the utmost significance, since the preponderance of Nepal's trade is still with India and is steadily expanding. An Indo-Nepali agreement signed on May 14, 1961, relaxed certain of the procedures under which imports and passenger baggage were transported through India. Irksome features of the 1950 trade treaty system were further reduced by the abolition of the bonding system for Nepali imports in transit through India in October, 1963, and the simplification of the central excise duty refund procedures in January, 1964.

These concessions from New Delhi have gone a long way toward satisfying Nepal's basic objective—recognition of the right of unrestricted transit of goods through India. In furthering its campaign on this question, Kathmandu has actively aligned itself with other landlocked countries at a number of international conferences in pressing for the recognition of the "right of free transit" as an integral part of international law.

The progress made toward trade diversification has had important political implications in Nepal, where it is interpreted as symbolizing fuller recognition of the country's sovereign status, but the immediate economic impact has been slight. Trade with Pakistan and China in 1963 was less than 3 per cent of the total recorded transactions and still less if the widespread and largely unrecorded local trade in agricultural products between the Nepal Terai and the adjoining Indian districts is taken into consideration. The volume of trade with Pakistan and China is likely to grow substantially in absolute terms in the next decade, but its proportion in Nepal's total trade structure may not increase proportionately, as trade with India is also growing rapidly. Moreover, some of the political considerations that made it incumbent upon Nepal to seek alternative trade channels in 1961 and 1962 are no longer as persuasive, while most of the features of the trade system with India that were found objectionable have now been abolished or modified. Diversification is still a stated objective of Nepal's trade policy, but probably is not assigned so high a priority as it was in 1961. There has been an increasing recognition in Kathmandu that Nepal's "natural" trade lines are with India, and somewhat less reluctance to accept certain economic consequences inherent in this situation.[9]

INDUSTRIAL POLICY

In Nepal, as in most "developing" nations, there is a tendency to view industrialization as the remedy for all of the country's economic ills. But industrial expansion since 1951 has been insignificant and directly attributable to foreign aid or Indian investment. A comprehensive industrial policy was not even evolved until the Nepali Congress took office in 1959. The royal regime has retained the essential features of this industrial policy, liberalizing even further the conditions under which both local and foreign capital can invest in industry. The 1950 Company Act was amended in 1961 and an Industrial Enterprises Act was promulgated in 1962. Under the provisions of these laws, new industries, whether foreign or indigenous, have been granted a ten-year exemption from income tax and are permitted to spend up to 70 per cent of their hard-currency earnings on the import of machinery and spare parts. Foreign investors are allowed to repatriate as profits 10 per cent of their capital investment in hard currency annually. A government-sponsored organization, Sajha, has been established to extend financial and other assistance to co-operative industrial and commercial ventures.

Official projections of industrial expansion in Nepal place little stress on private domestic investment. Most new industries scheduled for completion within the next few years are dependent upon foreign aid, either public or private. Several small factories are being constructed under the Russian and Chinese aid programs. The Indian and American aid programs have so far abjured direct involvement in the construction of factories, but have each financed industrial estates near Kathmandu in which a number of private small-scale industries are located. The government has also been negotiating with several Indian industrial firms and with a number of European and Asian governments and private firms in its search for sources of capital investment in industry.

Foreign aid in industrialization has led to some curious misconceptions in Nepal. It is frequently asserted, for instance, that China and Russia support Nepal's industrialization, because they are building a few small factories, while the United States and India are secretly opposed to it—reputedly for capitalist-imperialist motives. What is usually ignored in these allegations is the role played by the United States and India in the development of communications and the expansion of power resources, obvious prerequisites for any serious industrialization program. Indeed, even the Russian and Chinese factories would have been impossible without the roads and power provided by American and Indian aid projects.

THE ROLE OF FOREIGN AID

Among Asian states there is perhaps none whose economic development program is so dependent upon foreign assistance as is that of Nepal. In the 1963/64 budget estimates, for instance, more than 70 per cent of Nepali development expenditure allocations represented foreign assistance.[10] Even these figures were probably misleading, for the estimated revenue resources of the government covered less than 40 per cent of its share of the development budget.[11] When the various other types of indirect assistance are also taken into consideration, it is probable that the proportion of foreign aid in Nepal's development program is close to 85 or 90 per cent. And even then, only around 50 per cent of the funds allocated for development purposes has usually been expended in any single year.

This situation has never been a very happy one from the Nepali viewpoint. The Nepali Congress government, on assuming office in 1959, spoke of the necessity of reducing dependence on foreign aid; but by the time the 1960/61 budget was introduced there was a frank admittance that this goal was unrealistic and would be for some time. Nepal's problem, it was admitted, was to attract more foreign aid and to rationalize the system under which this aid was utilized.

A similar pattern has been evident under the royal regime. In his first budget speech (1961/62), Finance Minister Rishikesh Shah emphasized the need to increase Nepal's proportionate contribution to the development budget; but by the time of his second budget speech (1962/63), this objective received scant attention. The 1963/64 budget speech by the new Finance Minister, Surya Bahadur Thapa, raised the subject once again, but in such terms as to make it apparent that any major reduction in the foreign aid proportion of the development budget was unlikely because of the lack of substantial new sources of indigenous revenue.

The reliance upon foreign aid, unavoidable though it may be in the circumstances, complicates the government's task in formulating a well-conceived and comprehensive program of economic development. The source of aid is undependable and is susceptible to wide fluctuations—at times, for reasons having nothing to do with Nepal. The cement factory promised by Peking in 1956 and again in 1960, for instance, was suddenly canceled in 1964 after surveys conducted by Chinese technicians had approved the project site. The official explanation given was the unsuitability of the site selected, presumably because of the unavailability of adequate supplies of raw materials. But according to other reports, China had to back down at the last moment because the equipment for the factory, which was to have been purchased in Czechoslavakia, was no longer available, owing to the deterioration in Sino-Soviet relations. It can be presumed that these reports are reliable, for Peking did not merely ask to shift the site of the factory, but dropped the project altogether, placing the Nepal government in an awkward situation. Cement is badly required for Nepal's housing and development programs. In 1964, therefore, Kathmandu had to start searching for alternative sources of foreign aid for the construction of a cement factory, at least five years later than would have been the case if reliance had not been placed upon the Chinese commitment.

Under such circumstances, it is difficult for Nepal to evolve a coördinated program of economic development. The four primary sources of foreign aid—the United States, India, the Soviet Union, and China—have different motivations in offering aid and radically different approaches. The Russians and Chinese prefer short-term projects that will make an immediate impact upon the Nepali public, while the United States and India have concentrated upon more basic, long-term programs in such areas as education, agriculture, communications, and power. Nepali views on priorities in economic development have to be fitted into this complex structure, and it is little wonder that the government has never really attempted to conceptualize a pattern of economic development that is anything more than a collection of unrelated and sometimes inconsistent development projects. The Nepal government is in no position to extend much practical guidance to the foreign aid agencies in formulating their programs, much less to insist that they conform to an established pattern. As a result, the foreign sources of aid often decide what is to be offered, and the Nepal government has no alternative but to accept, even when the programs do not conform to its own priority schedule.

This situation is in part a consequence of the Nepal government's decision to seek the maximum diversification of sources of foreign aid, as it does in trade and commerce. Too great a reliance on a single source of aid is considered prejudicial to Nepal's independence and nonalignment policy since there is the assumption—doubtless, correct—that all foreign economic aid programs have a political motivation. Nepali nationalism, which is intensely sensitive to any threat of manipulation from without, prefers a disorganized approach to economic development in which coördination between the various aid programs is kept to a minimum. Indeed, the most telling charges levied against the American program in Nepal is that it works too closely with the Indian program in formulating and proposing development projects. This indicates plainly that in Nepal, as in most other "newly emerging" nations, political considerations have precedence over economic progress.

SOCIAL REFORM

One of the most widely publicized programs of the royal regime is the new Legal Code promulgated in April, 1963. Certain sections of the old Muluki Ain were radically amended to remove provisions based on essentially nonegalitarian, traditional Hindu social concepts. Discrimination on the basis of caste was forbidden, intercaste marriages were legalized, polygamy was prohibited, and women were guaranteed certain rights with regard to divorce and inheritance previously denied them.* August 17, 1963, the date of the enforcement of the new Legal Code, was celebrated in Kathmandu, with untouchables assuming a prominent role in the festivities.

Subsequently, however, the government has moved with caution in interpreting and implementing some of the new legal provisions. In a clarification issued four months later by the Special Complaints Department of the Palace Secretariat it was announced that the caste system itself had not been abolished. The new code, it was explained, "seeks only to introduce equality before the law." The position was made quite clear in the next sentence: "Those who indulge in actions prejudicial to the social customs and traditions of others will be punished." [12] Attempts by untouchables to force an entry into Pashupatinath, the holiest of Hindu temples in Nepal, were forestalled by the police, reportedly on the grounds that the social customs and traditions of high caste Hindus were infringed upon by these actions.

King Mahendra himself issued a cautionary warning in March, 1964, when he stated at a civic reception in western Nepal

---

* Surya Bahadur Thapa, the Law Minister, introduced a bill in the National Panchayat on August 11, 1963, under which persons convicted of offences no longer recognized in the new Legal Code would be released from prison.

that "social reform cannot be achieved all of a sudden . . . least of all by strict legislation." He explained that the new code had been devised so that people could easily observe its provisions, and that society was not to be disrupted in the name of reform.[13] That same month, a five-member Law Commission to study defects in the new Legal Code, "which was hastily drafted by the former Law Commission," was appointed by the government.[14]

Despite the government's apparent responsiveness to the objections raised by some traditionalist elements, the social reforms introduced are likely to be retained. It is an interesting commentary on Nepali politics that the present regime, which draws its most important support from conservative groups with a vested interest in the *status quo,* was able to introduce a social reform program more radical than anything projected by the democratic-socialist Nepali Congress. Here, again, the need for the regime to assume a progressive façade that appeals to younger educated groups, but to implement its program in such a way as not to alienate conservative supporters, is in evidence.

ADMINISTRATIVE REORGANIZATION

Every major political upheaval in Nepal since 1951 had been accompanied by substantial changes in top administrative positions, and the December, 1960, *coup* was no exception. Indeed, the most thorough overhaul of the Secretariat yet attempted in postrevolutionary Nepal occurred in the first year after the *coup.* Civil servants suspected of too close ties to the Nepali Congress were dismissed at all levels of administration and in all branches of government, including the judiciary. The exact number dismissed is difficult to determine from published sources, as district and local level dismissals were never summarized or even reported. The Nepali Congress has placed the number at five thousand, which may be somewhat exaggerated; but if dismissals at all levels of government service are included, it is probable that three thousand is a reliable figure. New appointments to higher administrative posts were openly based upon political considerations, and merit or qualifications were, at best, incidental factors. The Public Service Commission was ignored, its powers being suspended in whole or in part during most of this crucial transitional period.

The procedures adopted by the royal regime in this wholesale purge of administrative personnel nullified and even reversed the efforts made since 1954 to provide some degree of tenure security through the basing of appointments and promotions on merit and seniority. Once the purge was completed, however, the royal regime effected a partial return to the trend toward the standardization of civil service procedures, giving added emphasis to nonpolitical criteria for all but the higher category of posts. But the psychological impact of the massive administrative reorganization in 1961 is still evident. On three occasions since 1955 King Mahendra has suspended established administrative procedures to initiate large-scale changes in personnel, and there is no assurance that this will not occur again. Government servants have been criticized by the press and political groups for allegedly being more concerned with strengthening their contacts with the palace or Ministry than in the competent performance of their duties. But is it reasonable to expect anything else when security of tenure is based upon arbitrary rather than formalized procedures?

The royal regime has not restricted itself to changes in personnel. It has projected reforms in the administrative structure. Probably the most significant, potentially, is the proposed decentralization of the administration to parallel the decentralized political system under Panchayat Raj. In 1962, a new regional structure was superimposed upon the old district administrative system, dividing Nepal into fourteen zones and seventy-five Development Districts which coincide with the territorial jurisdiction of the zonal and district panchayats.

The pattern of administrative decentralization is still unclear in several important respects, and some of the basic policies announced earlier are under periodic reconsideration. A Deconcentration Committee, headed by Vishwabandhu Thapa, was appointed in 1963, but its report merely approved the general policy of decentralization and made little positive contribution to the resolution of the problems this policy has raised.

Doubtless, the most crucial question facing the government at present is the conflict in jurisdiction which has arisen between the various regional units of administration and led to serious confusion as to their respective spheres of authority. The government announced that the old administrative districts were to be abolished eventually, and that the administrative functions of the Bada Hakims would be transferred to the district panchayats. But when this finally occurred in 1965, the Bada Hakim's powers and functions were transferred to centrally appointed zonal commissioners rather than district panchayats.

Confusion is further compounded by the existence of Zonal Commissioners and Zonal Guidance Officers, appointed by the

Central Secretariat, and zonal panchayats elected by the district panchayats, all with vaguely defined and often conflicting spheres of authority within the same territorial jurisdiction as the district panchayats and Bada Hakims. Furthermore, several Ministries and Departments of the central government have their own personnel in the field, and the lines of authority for these officials have not been clearly defined as yet. A Conference of Zonal Commissioners was held in Kathmandu in May, 1964, to study this situation, but no substantive recommendations were forthcoming, except for the usual warning that the government must move cautiously in implementing the decentralization policy.[15]

And there is no doubt that this is the approach adopted by the government, which has moved slowly on the more complex aspects of decentralization and fairly rapidly only when the changes involved a minimal disruption of the existing administrative process. Nor is there any doubt that the Central Secretariat retains final discretionary authority in all administrative matters. The lower tiers of the panchayat system would seem to have been created for two purposes: to fill a serious lacuna in the old administrative system that limited the efficacy of the Central Secretariat's authority in the less accessible areas of the country, and to assist the program of economic development. The decentralization of administrative power so far projected concerns primarily activities essential to the successful exercise of these functions. As such, they involve more the decentralization of duties than of decision-making powers, which are still retained by the Central Secretariat on most important subjects. Thus, the policy of the royal regime on the role of panchayats does not differ markedly from that adopted by previous governments which also projected a limited devolution of functions to local and regional political and administrative units.

INTERNATIONAL RELATIONS

In dismissing the Nepali Congress government, King Mahendra implied that disagreements over foreign policy had been a major factor in his decision. B. P. Koirala and his colleagues were accused of planning to merge Nepal with a neighboring country —never specified, but presumably India—and with having encouraged "antinational" elements, again presumably pro-India groups in Nepal. But there was little in the King's subsequent actions to indicate that there had really been any serious disagreement over the basic principles of Nepal's foreign policy, including such controversial issues as the Gandak treaty and other agreements with India, all of which have been retained.

The differences between the royal regime and the Nepali Congress on foreign policy would seem to have been primarily over the interpretation of certain of these basic principles and, even more important, over the tactics used to achieve policy objectives. "Equal friendship with India and China" was the policy of both but the term apparently had different meanings for King Mahendra and B. P. Koirala. For political consideraions that were essentially domestic, the royal regime permitted and up to October, 1962, even seemed to encourage developments that were likely to disrupt relations with India. The Nepali press, fairly strictly controlled in most other respects, was allowed to indulge in bitter anti-Indian campaigns, often drawing upon the reported remarks of Ministers for support and verification. A similar license was not extended to the anti-Communist or anti-Chinese journals, which occasionally had to suspend publication temporarily because of remarks about Nepal's northern neighbor that were no more critical than those permitted about its southern neighbor.

The royal regime also pushed even more vigorously the policy of expanding Nepal's international relations, with particular emphasis placed upon association with African and Asian powers that followed a policy of nonalignment. Nepal's position on nonalignment and East-West "cold war" issues coincides closely to that followed by India, the objective being maximum contacts with both sides and the avoidance of any direct formal obligations to either. But nonalignment also has a special connotation for Nepal in view of the country's strategic location in an area in which the Sino-Indian border dispute is the most pervasive fact of life. "Nonalignment" plus "equal friendship" equals "neutrality" as far as Nepal is concerned, even though this is neutrality in a dispute between a member of the nonaligned bloc of nations and a Communist state.

Kathmandu has tried to extract recognition of its neutral status from both of its giant neighbors. But there are serious complications in implementing a neutralist policy which is contradictory to some aspects of Nepal's international obligations and internal policy. Nepal cannot simply ignore, for instance, the 1950 treaty of peace and friendship with India which places Nepal in an unofficial alliance with India, the sizable "Gurkha" recruitment for the Indian military forces, the Indian military posts at most key pass areas on the Nepal-Tibet border, and the important role played by Indian military advisers in the reorganization and rearmament of the Nepal state army. When these tangible factors are combined with the intimate social, cultural, economic, and historical ties that have existed between India and Nepal for at least two milleniums, and the incompatibility of Chinese communism and Nepal's social structure and polity, neutrality is possible only as long as the Sino-Indian dispute does not explode into full-scale war.

The delicacy of Nepal's position in the Himalayan border area was dramatically revealed in October, 1962, when Chinese forces launched limited attacks on the extremities of the Sino-Indian frontier—Ladakh and North East Frontier Agency. Kathmandu's response to this critical situation, which at times threatened to expand into a larger conflict, presumably was indicative of its fundamental position in inter-Himalayan politics. Alarmed by the unexpected upsetting of the balance of power in the border area, so vital to Nepal's continuation as an independent entity, Kathmandu moved quickly to improve relations with India. As an earnest of the change in attitude, there was a virtually total cessation of the bitter charges and countercharges that had been exchanged almost daily between the two governments. Kathmandu also refused to heed the suggestion, reportedly from Peking, that "Gurkhas" in Indian military service be recalled or at least barred from service on the disputed border as a token of Nepal's neutrality in the dispute.

Indo-Nepali relations were placed upon a new basis in 1963 by the visit of several Indian leaders, including Home Minister Lal Bahadur Shastri, the Chief of Staff of the Indian Army, and President Radhakrishnan to Kathmandu and several visits by King Mahendra and his Ministers to New Delhi. In the course of the talks held on these occasions, a *rapprochement* was achieved that settled most of the political and economic issues that had previously disrupted relations between the two states. There are still several important issues upon which agreement has not been possible because the interests of the two countries, as perceived by each, diverge; but these are now kept carefully in the background by both governments in contrast to the situation up to October, 1962, when they were often exploited and emphasized.

Kathmandu has been careful to guarantee, however, that the reconciliation with India was not achieved at the expense of friendly ties with Peking. There is, perhaps, a somewhat more cautious attitude toward China, but no evident diminution in either the scope or character of their relationship. China occupies too powerful a position in the Himalayas for Nepal to risk a deterioration in relations, particularly since the defeats inflicted upon India in the 1962 border clashes with China has undermined confidence in its ability to defend Nepal's exposed and probably indefensible northern border.

Nepal's relations with both the Soviet Union and the United States have assumed added importance in view of the critical situation in which it has been placed by the Sino-Indian dispute. That Kathmandu is now attempting to use these two powers as counterbalances to China, as once they were used as counterbalances to India, would seem to be suggested by the role assumed by the Soviet Union in Nepal's economic development and the officially confirmed reports that Nepal had approached the United States and the United Kingdom for military assistance. Nepal's abandonment of an isolationist policy in 1947 has brought many tangible benefits as well as psychological satisfaction for Nepali nationalist sentiment, but it has also exposed the country to numerous and conflicting pressures which threaten its very existence. The skill and tenacity with which succeeding Nepali governments have maneuvered under difficult international conditions deserves commendation. Nevertheless, it is still uncertain as to whether the short-term advantages attained will prove to have equally beneficial long-term results.

CONCLUSIONS

Viewed broadly and with a disregard of meaningless political sloganism, there has been a rather remarkable continuity in the policies and programs adopted by the various Nepali governments since 1951. The present regime has continued for the most part the general trends established earlier, adopting a program of cautious change directed toward the gradual modernization of the Nepali economy, social structure, and administrative system. In spite of his dependence upon the political support of conservative or reactionary elements, King Mahendra has not established an ultraconservative regime dedicated to the preservation of the *status quo*. As may be inevitable in such circumstances, however, there have been certain inconsistencies between policies as adopted and as implemented.

But the contradiction between modernization on the administrative and economic level and certain antimodernist aspects of the new political structure may eventually prove to have more serious consequences. Institutional innovations under Panchayat Raj have resulted in some changes in the channels for political activity, but have made relatively little impact upon the political process, which is still essentially traditional in character. The deficiencies of the political party system in Nepal have received ample consideration in this study. These were, nevertheless, the institutions through which the political process was being modernized—gradually and ineptly, perhaps, but with some success. The prohibition of political party activity has, thus, hampered the modernization process. King Mahendra seems to be aware of this in designing a program to transform Nepal into a twentieth-century society, but the institutions created to replace the political parties—the lower-level panchayats and the class organizations —are of doubtful utility in carrying out this task.

This raises a critical question: Is it possible to modernize the economic, social, and administrative structures without a concomitant modernization of the political process and modes of political behavior? This is not meant to imply that a parliamentary, democratic, or Communist system is a prerequisite to modernization; Japan proved the contrary in the nineteenth century. What would seem to be involved is the utilization of new sources of political initiative, new techniques of political organization, and new patterns in decision making, at both the administrative and the political level. It is still to be seen whether panchayats and related institutions have a positive contribution to make in this respect or whether they will obstruct, delay, and confuse the modernization process upon which Nepal's continued existence as an independent political entity may well depend.

Conclusion

23

Patterns and Trends in Nepal's Political Modernization

AFTER THE EMERGENCE of Nepal as a nation-state in the last quarter of the eighteenth century, the primary goal of the Nepali political system became the maintenance of the *status quo,* which meant the continuation of the delicate balance of power among the various elite families composing the Court. The transfer of the capital from Gorkha to Kathmandu in 1769 gave added emphasis to the nationwide scope of the new political system, but did not result in any significant changes in the political process itself. The political system, like the social system at large, continued to be a highly segmented, pyramidal structure dominated by a handful of families belonging primarily to two castes—the Brahmans and the Kshatriyas. Members of these families supervised the functioning of the political system as part of the inherent rights emanating from their high-caste origins and reinforced by their traditions of familial service at the royal Court.

The traditional political system continued more or less intact until 1951. Whatever political changes occurred in the interim were largely systemic changes brought about by the redistribution of power among the elite families at the top of the political pyramid: the allocation of power among families and individuals changed, but the political system itself remained unchanged. Between 1770 and 1951, there were at least four momentous upheavals at the top level. In 1806, the Thapa family attained a virtual monopoly on political power; in 1846, the Rana family reached a similar position; in 1885, power shifted into the

485

hands of the Shamsher branch of the Rana family; and in 1934, the A Rana group of the Shamsher Ranas came to the top. But none of these developments seriously affected the patterns, goals, or methods of the political system, since these families operated the administration during their tenure in office in more or less the same way, their overriding concern being invariably the enhancement of their material and political fortunes.

The familial basis of the traditional Nepali political system had a pervasive influence on all other organs of government, including the religious establishment, whose primary function was to provide a scriptural legitimation to the person or family in power. The machinery of administration was staffed along familial lines, and positions of power invariably corresponded to status earned by ascription rather than achievement. Similarly, the army was divided among various families or various branches of the same family, and the number of regiments assigned to a family became the most reliable index of its political power.

The Shah family occupied a pivotal position in the process of political change by virtue of its position as the sovereign power in Nepal. The elite families and the army swore ultimate allegiance to the head of the Shah family as the King of Nepal, and the common people, not directly involved in the process, accepted him as a reincarnation of Vishnu, the god of preservation in Hindu mythology. Indeed, the Shah King provided the only enduring basis of continuity and stability through all the complicated maneuvers and countermaneuvers of the elite families. The ruling family was, however, not itself immune to political ambitions, and its political activities were animated by the same spirit of familial gain as was typical of other elite families. Through all the vicissitudes of political change up to 1951, the Shah ruling family served as the ultimate custodian of authority and tradition and also as the ultimate source of all legitimizing powers required by the successive governments formed during this period.

THE NATURE AND CONTEXT OF CONTEMPO-RARY POLITICAL CHANGES

The political change resulting from the 1950 revolution was, on the other hand, a change *sui generis* which should not be equated with the earlier systemic changes. It was, rather, an extrasystemic change brought about by a fortuitous combination of external environmental conditions—mainly, diplomatic pressure from India and the new spirit of political egalitarianism in

Asia—and the activities of a newly emerging "modernizing" Nepali elite which had been educated in Western-style colleges and was alien to the traditional political system. King Tribhuwan was the only systemic agent involved in the change. But the role of the Shah monarch had been so effectively neutralized by the Rana regime that he could just as well be considered as standing outside the periphery of the operational political system and was in certain fundamental respects himself as extrasystemic as the new, modernizing elites. Moreover, his role in the 1950 revolution was more that of a catalyst rather than an active participant. His flight to the Indian Embassy in Kathmandu on November 6, 1950, and later his presence in New Delhi provided a diplomatic leverage to the Indian government in its negotiations with the Rana rulers of Nepal as well as a legitimizing basis for the anti-Rana activities of the Nepali agents of change—i.e., the Nepali Congress party.

The protracted negotiations in New Delhi, which preceded the 1951 political change, demonstrated the determining role of the Indian government and the diplomatic ineffectiveness of the family-centered Rana government. The Indian government was, presumably, representing the viewpoints of both King Tribhuwan and the Nepali Congress in the negotiations with the Rana government, but in reality both the King and the Nepali Congress were only minimally involved in these crucial discussions. Indeed, the Nepali Congress leaders were brought into the picture merely to ratify the agreement—later celebrated as the Delhi compromise—which had been reached between the Indian and the Rana governments.

Thus, the political change which occurred in Nepal under the diplomatic midwifery of the Indian government was a total political change. It was neither an evolution from nor a modification of the traditional political system, but a brand-new innovation whose basic systemic linkages were with the emerging political structure in independent, democratic India. The Delhi compromise not only sounded the death knell of the Rana regime, but also, presumably, ruled out the viability of the traditional political process based on the dominance of a few elite families. Traditional political forms of action were to be superseded by political parties operating on a mass scale; representative democracy was solemnly affirmed as the goal of the new system; the election of a Constituent Assembly, to convene within two years, was envisaged; and the Crown was to function in a constitutional capacity as the symbol of national unity and solidarity far above the reaches of party politics. These new political concepts, which had previously existed only as vaguely defined theories in the minds of a few Nepalese educated in Western-style institutions, formed the basis of the 1951 Interim Government of Nepal Act— a hastily prepared adaptation of the 1950 Indian Constitution which was promulgated in Nepal with no evident concern for the lack of the prerequisites and concomitants which gave meaning to the Indian document.

The 1950 revolution was primarily an intellectuals' revolt against an archaic political system and involved the common people to only a limited degree, but its political aftermath was truly revolutionary and comparable to the effects of more comprehensive revolutions elsewhere. The political innovations introduced by the revolution were so sweeping, unfamiliar, and unprecedented that they were almost paralyzing in their immediate repercussions. None of the usual political infrastructure of a democratic system existed in Nepal; and the agents of the political change soon discovered the magnitude of the task involved in modernizing a basically medieval, feudal, caste-bound society. The entire administrative structure had to be innovated, and once again, since time was of the essence, the Indian model of bureaucracy was sought to be duplicated—in form, at least, if not in operation. The machinery of law and order had to be revamped, and the Indian government undertook the responsibility of reorganizing the police and the military along more modern lines. The bureaucracy, which had traditionally functioned as the custodian of law and order and as a managing agency for the ruling family, now had to add welfare and developmental activities to its functions, necessitating government expenditures on a broad variety of programs. This led to a search for technical skills and economic aid from abroad, and again the Indian government was the first to respond with funds, plans, and programs. Subsequently, other foreign governments responded and a new international image of Nepal came into being.

The introduction of democratic experimentation in 1951 brought in its wake an array of new social and political roles for which there were few if any institutional or traditional supports in Nepal's society. Most of these were direct importations from India, where they had been nurtured under the long-sustained modernizing impact of British colonialism and had been strengthened by decades of anticolonial nationalist politics. Both these factors were conspicuously absent in Nepal; but the new political and administrative roles were tagged on, nonetheless, as an appendage of the incipient political system. Some examples of the new roles thus created were those of the political party leader, the public agitator, the opinion leader, the opposition leader, and the government official.

The newness of these roles stemmed directly from a modernist redefinition of the image of government in the body politic of the country. Traditionally, government in Nepal has been viewed by the people as an omnipotent agency of coercion led by men of inherently superior worth, who knew what was best for the country and whose actions were beyond the comprehension of the common man. The government functioned as an autochthonous institution at a respectable distance from the life-space of the people and made its presence felt only for such purposes as collecting taxes, settling litigations in the courts, suppressing internal dissension, and resisting external aggression. Any public welfare activities, which were always infrequent, were widely publicized as symbolic of the regime's concern for the people, the objective being the enhancement of a benign, if authoritarian, "image" of the government.

When the new, modernizing educated elites assumed leading positions in the 1951 interim government, a revolutionary transformation of the image of government occurred. Political propagandists—including opposition leaders, newspaper editors, and pamphleteers—assiduously created the image of a new government that was no longer the master of the people, as it had been under the Ranas, but a conscientious servant of the people which had to be watched carefully for its acts of omission and commission. The public was cast in the unfamiliar role of critics and masters of the government; the high officials, who had traditionally been considered as objects of awe and reverence, were now described as public servants who could be dismissed outright if they acted against the interests of the people.

This new image of the government contradicted sharply with the *noblesse oblige* concept underlying the Shah or Rana systems of government. The traditional Nepali politician was an inveterate conspirator, one who operated in the deep, dark world of motives rather than overt actions, behind the scenes rather than in a public forum, and one whose public and private political lives were miles apart. Usually he was a "Court influential" who maintained his political preëminence by monopolizing all available channels of information for himself, thus depriving potential rivals of any knowledge other than routine information—often deliberately made misleading—of the crucial decisions under consideration. The Court influential endeared himself to the ruler and his family through a careful manipulation of information access and transmission, and his political fate was usually sealed when his opponents succeeded in establishing a more effective communication network in the Court.

After the 1951 political change, the inveterate conspirator was replaced by the public agitator, who took to street processions and public agitations rather than to palace cliques to advance his political goals. His policies and programs had to be authenticated by opinion leaders, party followers, and the public before he could attain a position of prominence. In theory, the new political influential had to be a person who could mobilize maximum public support in his favor; in practice, however, the recognition of political popularity still had to be validated by a seal of approval from the royal palace. The newspaper editors and the pamphleteers replaced the informers and the rumor mongers of the traditional political system. But their mode of operation—scandalous gossip and character assassination against carefully selected targets—remained the same and provided the context for subsequent political changes. Youthful, inexperienced graduates of Western-style colleges replaced the old civil servants of the Rana regime in the key administrative positions in the new government, and a phenomenal expansion of the administrative staff filled up the scores of new positions in the civil service hierarchy.

The agents of political change, however, had failed to develop a consensus on the contours of the new political landscape that was to emerge in Nepal. The Nepali Congress leaders had acquired only a few years of political experience, and most of this time had been spent in trying to reconcile their individualistic orientation with the needs for corporate activity. As a result, a mature consensus on future political goals and programs was not forthcoming among either the party leaders or the party rank-and-file. The situation was further complicated by the sudden and unexpected collapse of the Rana regime, which found the party leaders unprepared and inadequately trained. Perhaps even more shattering were their experiences once they had taken the reins of administration, for they soon discovered that the governmental machinery that had seemed omnipotent from the outside was, when viewed from the inside and in its reality, quite weak and fragile.

The absence of a well-articulated ideology of political change not only hampered the activities of the government and the political parties, but also acted as a damper on the psychological atmosphere in Nepal. The fall of the Rana regime produced initially a sense of popular exhilaration inspired by buoyant hopes of a political regeneration in the country and an impatient desire to "catch up" with the modern nations of the world. After a few months' experience with the new administration, the popular mood of exuberance underwent a perceptible change. A new political temper manifested itself, expecially in Kathmandu, in the form of cynical, satirical, and often hostile evaluations of the political change and its multifaceted implications. Some Rana revivalists and their old allies sought to exploit this negative political mood in organizing opposition to the new political system. But even more dysfunctional than this Rana-inspired agitation was the conspicuous lack of ideologues, both among the public and in the political parties, who could serve as anchor men for the constantly-shifting, usually unrealistic expectations and moods of the people.

The inevitable outcome of this situation was the emergence of demagogues whose sole objective was the advancement of their personal political fortunes—even, if necessary, at the expense of the new system. This rise in political demagoguery and opportunism was also attributable to the new ethics of public action, regarded at that time as the proper ideological accompaniment of parliamentary democracy, which underscored individualism as the fount of all political actions and ruled out familism as a basis for any corporate social or political activity.

Confusion concerning the nature and consequences of the 1951 political change was by no means limited to the general public. Indeed, there was a woeful lack of consensus among the political parties and their leaders as to what the change entailed in the social, economic, cultural, and educational processes of the country. The one common political denominator was a general awareness that the Rana regime in its historical form had ended; of interpretations and prognostications of the future political process there were as many as there were parties and leaders. The Rana revivalists and their followers foresaw the establishment of a Nepali Congress tyranny bolstered by massive support from India. The non-Rana, non-Communist political opposition also raised the specter of a dictatorial Nepal Congress regime. The handful of Communists interpreted the 1951 political change as a bourgeois revolution, characterized the Nepali Congress leadership as a "national-capitalist bourgeosie," and laid out their own plans for the maturing of a "democratic" proletarian revolution in the future. A few obstreperous politicians who functioned in the guise of "independents" and loudly proclaimed their moral superiority to the party leaders viewed the change as the exclusive handiwork of Indian agents, Rana stooges, or a conspiracy between the Koirala brothers. Even the top-ranking Nepali Congress leaders did not share a common point of view on the nature of transitional politics and, in particular, on the role of the party in the ensuing interim period. This lack of ideological solidarity later proved to be the major cause of the repeated splintering of the party until finally in 1956 the Nepali Congress strengthened its ideological stance by adopting democratic socialism as its goal.

The lack of a well-articulated consensus about the 1951 political change revealed an ideological wasteland, in which the new, embryonic political system had to strike roots. It would have been a near miracle if the period of trial and error that ensued had produced a consensus which was lacking at the beginning of the new political era. This ideological deficit foretold the emergence of a modal political behavior which would be guided more by pragmatic considerations of personal gain and convenience than by any fundamental commitment to political values.

POLITICAL ELITES

The traditional political elites of Nepal consisted primarily of a few Kshatriya and Brahman families having ancestral ties of kinship or service with the early Gorkha kingdom of the Shah rulers. The Brahmans functioned as a sacred elite and also had a monopoly of the legislative and judicial functions of the government, subject to the Shah ruler's veto. The Kshatriyas monopolized the executive branches of the government and filled key positions in the civil and military establishments. After power was seized in 1846 by a Kshatriya family later known as the Ranas, members of the Rana family monopolized all important positions in the government and the army, and a new sacred-elite Brahman family, subservient to the Rana regime, was created. Non-Rana political-elite families were largely liquidated; the few survivors among them were incorporated into the lower echelons of the Rana political system. Some of these families prospered under the Ranas and eventually regained an elite status. Most of them opposed the 1951 political change on pragmatic economic grounds rather than from any ideological attachment to the Rana system. Included within this category were non-Rana Kshatriyas, who abounded in the army, and Brahman and Newar families, who filled the second-level positions in the civil administration. Leading members of these families had acquired considerable property and wealth through their association with the Ranas and were, of course, opposed to the new spirit of economic egalitarianism. Subsequently, they became deeply involved in oppositional politics as "independents," as financial backers of opposition newspapers, and as self-appointed arbiters of interparty conflicts.

The new political elites which achieved prominence in the post-1951 period had mostly served an earlier political apprenticeship in India. They were drawn from a wide variety of Nepali ethnic groups, but their proportional representation in the new "modernizing" oligarchy was largely a reflection of the educational advancement of their respective communities. The ever resourceful Brahmans, who traditionally performed the intellectual functions in the Hindu social system, lost no time in becoming the avid patrons of the secular, liberal, Western-style educational system, in both Nepal and India. It is not surprising, therefore, that Brahmans constituted the largest single caste group in the new oligarchy and provided the core leadership for most political organizations and activities. Ethnic communities such as the Newars, Limbus, and Gurungs, which the Ranas had classified as Mongoloids and treated as second-class citizens, also were important among the new political elites. Their participation followed from their Western-style education or their exposure to modernizing influences in the British or Indian armies. Another important group, the inhabitants of the Terai, became active agents of political change because of their accessibility to educational facilities in India and their contacts with the Indian nationalist movement. They nursed a grievance of long standing for the discrimination practiced against the Terai plains dwellers as persons outside and even alien to the hill-dominated political structure.

The one underrepresented group in the new "modernizing" oligarchy was the Kshatriyas, who had usually been the principal agents of political change before 1951. Their situation is probably attributable to the extreme caution with which the Ranas had treated the non-Rana Kshatriyas, whom they regarded as their most dangerous political rivals, deliberately keeping them at a low educational level by providing places for them at the lower levels of the Rana system, particularly in the army. The only Kshatriyas directly involved in the 1951 political change were a few malcontent Ranas, Shahs, or Kshatriyas whom the Rana regime had failed, wittingly or unwittingly, to accommodate.

In addition to their almost exclusively Indian political apprenticeship, the "modernizing" elite leaders shared other distinguishing characteristics. The great majority were educated in Western-style Indian schools and universities and to that extent shared some core values emphasizing the importance and dignity of the individual. Almost all of them believed that Nepal's salvation lay in modernization and industrialization rather than in some form of tradition-oriented political obscurantism. Even the few traditionalists among them—M. P. Koirala, for example— had a basically modern definition of what was meant by tradition, favored political secularism, and advocated such measures as separation of the religious establishment from the political process and modernization of the Nepali legal code. Another distinguishing characteristic was their comparative youthfulness, the great majority being in their twenties and thirties. In a country long dominated by old age, extended experience, and seniority of birth in its social and political systems, the youthfulness of the modernizers was symptomatic of the drastic challenge to authority and tradition embodied in the 1951 political change. There was an obvious generational conflict between the proponents of the new political order and the supporters of the Rana political system.

A characteristic of the new elites which had far-reaching political consequences was their extreme economic insecurity. Except for a few who were independently wealthy, the new leaders were usually persons of no economic substance or even fixed means of livelihood. In contrast to the British in India, the Rana regime had pursued so ruthless a policy of economic exploitation and political suppression that no middle class worthy of the name had emerged in Nepal. There were no professional groups, such as lawyers, doctors, or teachers, and no organized interest groups such as chambers of commerce, trade-unions, or landlord associations. In India, the leadership of the nationalist movement had been recruited mainly from the professional middle-class. In Nepal, leadership of the anti-Rana movement was mostly provided by members of émigré Nepali families who had been deprived of their traditional means of livelihood by the Ranas and who lived in India on a marginal subsistence basis. Thus, for most of the new elites, the pursuit of politics was not merely a means to an end, but an end in itself. For many, it became an exclusive profession, and economic affluence was directly dependent upon political survival. This situation helps explain the high incidence of opportunism in Nepali transitional politics. Leaders were often forced by sheer economic necessity to compromise their political idealism and pursue a politics of deception and short-term gains rather than of achievement and long-range goals.

The importance of the new political elites in the post-1951 reconstruction of the country was further accentuated because there were no technical elites to supplement and abet their modernizing functions. Of the a handful of engineers, doctors, and educators in the entire country, most were concentrated in the capital. The Rana regime had discouraged the training of all technical elites except those connected with the army; and the few technicians tolerated by the regime to maintain the few appurtenances of the twentieth century in Nepal were required to play strictly subservient roles to the political masters of the Rana military establishment. Legend has it that the regime put to death a Rana engineer of high caliber for fear that his technical innovations would eventually prove to be a political menace to the regime.

In the face of the shortage of technicians and the inexperience of the new administrative class, the political elites frequently had to assume the roles of technicians and administrators when, in fact, the role they were most eligible to fill by virtue of their training and background was that of a literary elite. It is for this reason, presumably, that government policies and programs were frequently imbued with metaphorical grandioseness and literary bombast rather than economic realism and technical precision.

All of the new political elites, whether or not they were systemic components of the traditional political system, could trace back their family history to some event in the past which had caused their dissatisfaction with the old system. These events, usually, were incidents of status withdrawal precipitated by political change; less frequently, they were associated with ideological revolt against the existing sociopolitical system. Two families which exerted important seminal influences on the maturing of the 1951 political change were the Koirala family of Biratnagar under the leadership of Krishna Prasad Koirala (the father of M. P. Koirala and B. P. Koirala) and the Joshi family of Kathmandu under the leadership of Madhava Raj Joshi (the father of Sukra Raj Shastri).* These were both innovational families and the first generation of each paid a heavy price for its political or social nonconformity in the form of exile in India, economic hardships, and precarious existence. The Koirala family did the spadework for the political change of 1951, and the Joshi family laid the background for a new social consciousness and ferment in Nepal through its advocacy of Hindu reform movements.

Of course, other Nepali families in the past had found themselves in conflict with the dominant political faction and sought

---

* Shastri is an academic title indicative of Sanskrit scholarship. He used Shastri rather than his family surname, Joshi.

asylum in India. But these had never been truly innovational families that contemplated major modification of the existing system. Their objective had usually been to introduce systemic changes in the political situation that would rebound to their advantage; they sought to replace the dominant political faction and retain the traditional system. These émigré families had gravitated, for the most part, to a few urban centers in India. The out-group Rana families usually made Calcutta their home-in-exile, while the Brahmanic ones tended to favor Banaras, the holy city of the Hindus. In course of time these two Indian cities became centers of anti-Rana activity. The Banaras group eventually produced the Nepali National Congress and the Calcutta group the Nepal Democratic Congress. The fusion of these two groups into the Nepali Congress signified the emergence of a multifactional and, in a limited but meaningful sense, a national opposition to the Rana regime.

Although the émigré Nepali families maintained links with the larger Nepali society based in Kathmandu, the exigencies of foreign domicile, their marginal means of livelihood, and their aversion to the rulers in Nepal endowed them in the course of time with cosmopolitan and sophisticated sociopolitical attitudes and beliefs. Continued exposure to the varied political ideologies that were flourishing in India, particularly in Calcutta, and participation in the Indian nationalist struggles gave them a political perspective broader than that of the elites in Kathmandu, who had usually a very restricted political socialization. The non-Rana political elites in Kathmandu were largely by-products of the last Rana rulers' reluctant concessions to modernization—a few schools and hospitals intended as a veneer for obsolete political and administrative practices. Thus, the Kathmandu elites had grown up within the framework of the traditional familial and social systems. They were, therefore, far more exposed to the authoritarianism typical of the Nepali familial system than their cosmopolite counterparts in Banaras or Calcutta, and were also obligated to display greater conformity in their social and political behavior. Their oppositional politics had to be conducted with extreme caution and deliberateness since the risks they were courting were infinitely greater.

This significant difference in political socialization between the Nepali political elites in Banaras and Calcutta and those in Kathmandu produced a fundamental split in the post-1951 political process that had an enduring effect. The cosmopolites attained positions of political power in 1951 on the basis of their role in the overthrow of the Ranas and because of their claim to greater expertise stemming from their broad experiences in Indian movements. The Kathmandu elites reacted by accusing the Banaras and Calcutta groups of worming their way into positions of power with the support and blessings of the Indian government. They claimed that they alone were eligible to guide the processes of government during the transitional period since they, in contrast to most of their cosmopolite rivals, possessed the most significant political credential—that is, status as "political sufferers" owing to several years' incarceration in Rana jails. In Nepal, as in India after independence, the primary criteria for political leadership were not training or competence but personal suffering and self-abnegation in the service of a cause. There would seem to be here a reflection of that ideal of Hindu society which glorified the *sadhu,* who had renounced worldly possessions and personal desires and taken to a life of other-worldly contemplation, as the ideal person. In some respects, the ideal political leader was expected to pattern himself after the sadhu in his personal conduct and political behavior.

POLITICAL PARTIES: IDEOLOGY AND COMPOSITION

The political parties were in most cases combinations of elite groups on such bases as friendship ties, kinship ties, and, less frequently, ideological commitments. The elitist nature of political organizations increased the likelihood of leadership conflicts and realignments and complicated the establishing of a mass basis for party activities. This feature highlighted the importance of a few persons who were prominent in other public activities as well as politics. Several of the social and cultural organizations that cropped up in such profusion after 1951 were the creations of political leaders. This interlocking pattern of leadership in public affairs accounts for the overwhelming importance of the *homo politicus* in contemporary Nepal.

Since most of the new political elites professed more or less identical philosophies of modernization and development, their political slogans and nostrums were broadly similar. The single exception was the Communist Party of Nepal, which had a prefabricated ideology and was, therefore, excluded from the typical ideological groupings. The rest of the parties concocted virtually identical manifestoes specifying their objectives and programs. This was particularly noticeable during the 1959 general elections, when the choice available to the voter was essentially between the personal reputations of the candidates rather than their party ideologies or affiliations. The differences between the contending parties were usually those of points of emphasis or the idiosyncratic predilections of a few individual politicians.

Inasmuch as the behavior of the political elites was governed in part by a new ethics of individualism acquired in the process of education at Western-style institutions, their party conflicts and tussles were also imbued with the same spirit. Political opponents, both within a party or in other parties, were designated as traitors to the cause. In support of such charges, insinuations of connections with a foreign government or reactionary elements were usually circulated. When such charges were implausible or unconvincing, the object of the abuse was instead excoriated for violations of party rules and procedures and was sometimes excommunicated from the organization. The activities of the careerists among the political elites often seemed to alternate between impugning the motives of their rivals and denouncing their allegedly unconstitutional acts. In any case, this proclivity for verbal abuse made a substantial contribution to the unstable, yet dynamic nature of the politics of the transitional period.

The rank and file of the political parties was largely recruited from such groups as students, the literati, merchants, former servicemen of the British and Indian armies, and urbanized peasants. In the few urban areas of Nepal, and notably Kathmandu, the introduction of the party system had an unexpected socializing effect in that it helped transform erstwhile unruly, antisocial elements into respectable political leaders. Some of these men even had criminal records and were best known earlier for their propensity for street fighting and other antisocial activities during the celebration of folk festivals. But after 1951, they became party faithfuls and their gangs attained an important status as pressure groups in the various parties. This easy induction of marginal groups into the new political process further underscores the innovational aspect of the 1951 political change in Nepal.

Regionally, most of the rank and file of the political parties was either from the Terai or from Kathmandu Valley. These were politically the most advanced areas in Nepal, and the immediate impact of the 1951 political change was most acutely felt there. With the exception of the Communists, the parties recruited members in a relatively free and open manner. No severe tests of party loyalty or ideological firmness were imposed; and often the rank and file crossed party lines in conjunction with the political maneuvers of their selected leaders. Owing to the undeveloped state of transportation and communication facilities, most party headquarters—usually set in Kathmandu—were unable to exercise adequate control over their branch organizations in the districts. Consequently the branches' activities were typically characterized by a degree of autonomy which was seldom conducive to party strength or unity.

Given the elitist background of party leadership and the composition of the rank and file, it was comparatively easy in the new political context for any sufficiently motivated person to establish a party of his own. The one crucial element was the creation of an effective communication system through such measures as frequent public meetings and processions and, most important, by launching a vigorous and sensational party propaganda campaign. In the years following 1951 the printing presses and public-address systems in the capital were constantly in demand. Scores of party publicity bulletins, newspapers, monthlies, and annuals were launched. None of these publications attained mass circulation proportions, even in the Nepali context. The most widely read probably did not have a circulation exceeding two thousand. Nevertheless, the sum total of this massive scale of publications was a revolution in the Kathmandu communication pattern. This continues to be a special characteristic of the capital even today, although with the emergence of Radio Nepal and the improvement in transportation facilities, communication on a national scale is developing gradually.

The inflation of the communication process in the new political system was also a reflection of the fact that the representative status of the political parties was not tested for nearly seven years by the one universally applicable standard—free elections. In this interim period, any party which could whip up noisy political support in Kathmandu had a good chance of gaining political influence at the royal palace and, thereby, ministerial posts in the government. This explains why a few relatively unrepresentative parties and political leaders, with a communication system that gained attention in places where it mattered the most, were able to continue in power for extended periods.

One characteristic of the new political communication system was the tendency for the contents not to conform to facts and events. Typically, the newspapers and other publicity media placed more emphasis on opinions, judgments, interpretations, and rumors than on straightforward and factual reporting of events. Excessive attention to what was factual did not fit into the prevailing political ethos—and also often hurt rather than helped the already precarious financial condition of a newspaper. It can be argued that the development of a modern communication system in Kathmandu using the printed word rather than the word of mouth did little to improve the factual basis for political acitivity, and only accelerated the tempo of political life with the aid of modern technology.

In this context, one institution which attained an elite political status despite its not having the form of a political party was the Palace Secretariat. Because of its strategic location in the new political process, it became the procurer, purveyor, and censor of all communications channeled to the King for his information in making a decision. The criteria used by the palace staff in screening public information for presentation to the King and the biases in their selections presumably have influenced both the immediate and the long-range future of the country. That King Mahendra has, however, used various techniques to validate reports received through the vested interests–inspired communication network of the Palace Secretariat is evidenced by his establishing direct links with the people on his walking tours and public appearances throughout the country and by his care in soliciting the views of most important political factions on issues under consideration.

It is still unclear what role the Palace Secretariat staff played in bringing about the political crisis of December, 1960, which as an event was primarily a spectacular breakdown in communication between King Mahendra and the Nepali Congress government, especially its Prime Minister. As the authority of the elected government constituted both an ideological and political challenge to the extraparliamentary jurisdiction of the Palace Secretariat, there are grounds for assuming that the latter was responsible for the breakdown in communication.*

The insistent current demand of the "partyless" members of the present Council of Ministers in Nepal that only those who support their political actions are patriots and that those who are critical or even vaguely indifferent to them are necessarily traitors and "antinationals" is yet another index of a one-sided political communication system. A country in which economic development is the prime target can ill afford to lose national consensus

---

* It is also probable that the collapse of the last Rana regime (that of Mohan Shamsher) was hastened by several years because of the distorted, sycophantic communication network in the palace, which misreported and misinterpreted developments both within and outside Nepal to emphasize the durability of the Rana political system when, in fact, it was already beginning to crumble.

and unity—the most valuable "capital" of a poor country—in order to insure the continuation of a few politicians in power. A national unity of purpose and a national consensus of ideology are not born out of political legerdemain or slogan making, but out of a spirit of national participation freely volunteered and constructively used. Any attempt to fabricate an artificial national consensus by such means as coercion, political blackmail, and a manipulated press may be temporarily expedient, but in the long run it is likely to prove self-defeating and destructive of national interests. In the final analysis, the creation of a democratic, modern political system—the stated objective of Panchayat Raj—is nothing more than the creation of a participant society in which each individual or class takes part freely and productively in the affairs of that society. King Mahendra's formulation of the goals of panchayat democracy seems to be based on a similar vision. The translation of these goals into accomplishments is the continuing political preoccupation in Nepal.*

POLITICAL PARTIES: TYPOLOGY AND DESCRIPTION

As noted earlier, the political parties in Nepal have had only superficial differences in their policies and programs. A meaningful typology of the parties, therefore, would have to be based on certain nonideological characteristics of their core leadership rather than on trivial and idiosyncratic differences. The core leadership in any party is that particular collection of persons which has been instrumental in the founding of the group and in sustaining and continuing it through changing political alignments and subsequent fragmentations. The essential novelty of the 1951 political change was that it provided for a new mode of interpersonal relationship in a society which traditionally had sanctioned corporate activity, whether political or social, only along familial or caste lines and related lines of friendship or dependency. The commitment to political change can, therefore, be judged by the nature and stability of the interpersonal relations which characterized the original core leadership of the political parties. In addition, a typology accounting for the organization and disorganization of the parties can be formulated on this basis.

---

* Whether or how far it will succeed is still in the womb of the future. Social scientists can only specify the conditions and processes that may retard or accelerate the transition process so that men of action can take proper heed.

The core leadership of the political parties basically committed to the 1951 political change was multi-ethnic and multifamilial—in short, national—in contrast to that of parties only peripherally or opportunistically committed to political innovations. The leadership of this latter group of parties was based either on the traditional or conventional patterns of interpersonal relationships or on common allegiance to an authoritarian personality.

The qualitative difference in commitment to the 1951 political change also provides a nonideological definition of modernists as opposed to traditionalists. A modernist's political behavior would depart sharply from tradition since it would be governed largely by an enduring multi-ethnic, multifamilial consensus within the

TABLE 15

A Typology of Political Parties Participating in the
1959 General Elections in Nepal

Modern	*Traditional*
Nepali Congress *Core leadership:* B. P. Koirala, Suvarna Shamsher, Ganesh Man Singh, S. P. Upadhyaya *Composition:* Two Brahmans, one Kshatriya, one Newar *Classification:* National	Nepal Praja Parishad (Tanka Prasad Acharya faction) *Core leadership:* Tanka Prasad Acharya, Rama Hari Sharma, Chuda Prasad Sharma *Composition:* Three Brahmans *Classification:* One caste friendship clique
Nepal Gorkha Parishad *Core leadership:* Mrigendra Shamsher, Bharat Shamsher, Ranadhir Subba, Deva Bir Pande Composition: Two Kshatriyas, one Brahman, one Limbu *Classification:* Originally familial, later national	Nepal Praja Parishad (B. Mishra faction) *Core leadership:* B. Mishra Composition: One Terai Brahman *Classification:* One-personality party
Communist Party of Nepal *Core leadership:* Pushpa Lal, Manmohan Adhikari, Tulsi Lal, Keshar Jang Rayamajhi Composition: Two Newars, one Brahman, one Kshatriya *Classification:* Originally ethnic, later national	United Democratic party *Core leadership:* K. I. Singh Composition: One hill Kshatriya *Classification:* One-personality party
	Nepal Terai Congress *Core leadership:* V. Jha Composition: One Terai Brahman *Classification:* One-personality party
	Nepali National Congress *Core leadership:* D. R. Regmi Composition: One Kathmandu Brahman *Classification:* One-personality party
	Nepal Prajatantrik Mahasabha *Core leadership:* Ranga Nath Sharma Composition: One Brahman *Classification:* One-personality party

top echelons of party leadership; a traditionalist's political behavior, on the other hand, would fall within the traditional sanctions for corporate activity such as familial ties, caste, and friendship or dependent relationships. Most political splinter groups that arose in Nepal after the 1950 revolution were essentially authoritarian groups led by a factional leader with the support of small cliques, and were also the most active participants in political alliances and schisms.

The accompanying tabulation presents a typology of political parties in Nepal based on the characteristics of their core leadership.

INTEREST GROUPS AND PRESSURE GROUPS

The traditional Nepali political system developed out of a long-term (if not always peaceful) balancing of the interests of four prominent groups—the royal family, the sacred elite, the military, and the landowning aristocracy. These interest groups usually effected political changes through their participation in or association with the Court—whether Shah or Rana. The 1951 political change did not alter this basic pattern of traditional politics, but only pushed it into the background—temporarily, it turned out—as new interest groups and pressure groups intruded on the political scene, bearing contemporary labels and using a modern political vocabulary.

The new interest groups were the Crown, in its modernized form; the "modernizing" oligarchy; merchants and businessmen; and the political party leaders. The pressure groups through which they sought to exercise influence were the press, student organizations, administrative positions, the party system, and various social and cultural bodies. Among the traditional interest groups, the sacred elite and the military played a fairly dormant role until December, 1960, but the landowning aristocracy continued to play an important and active role in the guise of nonparty "independent" politicians. The crushing defeat suffered by the independents in the 1959 general elections forced them to change their tactics and resort to organized opposition to the Nepali Congress. With the assistance of some commercial interests, they formed the Jana Hita Sangh to oppose the land reform and taxation policies of the Nepali Congress government.

The 1951 political change also provided the conditions under which a multitude of occupational organizations, ranging from a tailors' union to a schoolteachers' association, were established. In most instances, these vocational groups were ill prepared to defend and promote their specialized interest; some, like the drivers' union exerted most of their energy in political activities that often seemed far removed from the nominal objectives of the organization. In general, the occupational groups failed to make a significant impression on the politics of the transitional period, with the possible exception of the Kisan Sangh, a Communist-controlled peasant organization. Since 1961 some of the occupational groups have been combined into a few government-sponsored class organizations, but this has not as yet noticeably increased their effectiveness as pressure groups.

THE CROWN'S ROLE IN TRANSITIONAL POLITICS

After the overthrow of the Rana regime, the Crown became the symbol of national awakening and unity. King Tribhuwan was acclaimed as a liberator for his support of the anti-Rana revolution and as the "father of the nation" and "architect of democracy" after his restoration. During his reign the nonpolitical character of the Crown was widely publicized, although at the same time the failures of the successive political experiments rendered the Crown the most powerful political institution in the country.

King Mahendra's accession to the throne in March, 1955, marked a further stage in the evolution of the Crown's political role. The new King took a direct interest in politics and the government of the country and created a dynamic image of the Crown as an active agent in the political realm by undertaking extensive travels throughout the country, engaging in protracted negotiations with political parties, and experimenting with new administrative and political institutions. Thus the Crown not only superseded the traditional role of the Rana Prime Minister, but acquired new roles befitting the exigencies of the transitional politics. In the process the Crown also became the focus around which traditional interest groups such as the sacred elite, the military, and the landowning aristocracy pivoted. These groups found access to the royal palace through their supporters and representatives on the staff of the Palace Secretariat.

Since December, 1960, the Crown has been directly involved in the establishment and functioning of the new political system, Panchayat Raj, which is often described by official sources as an "absolute" system for which there is no replacement. This equation of the Crown with the panchayat system exposes the former to unnecessary political risks and may well prejudice the long-range interest of both the Crown and the country by seeming to imply that each is dependent upon the other for its own survival. The political system of any backward, underdeveloped country is, by definition, tentative. It is both unrealistic and dangerous, therefore, to think in terms of "ideal" political systems at this stage when changes in Nepal's economic, social, and educational systems will inevitably lead to correlated changes and adjustments in the political structure.

THE "MODERNIZING" OLIGARCHY

The "modernizing" oligarchy which provided the initiative for the 1951 political change and the transitional politics thereafter was the most inchoate and disorganized of the articulate political groups in Nepal. Members of the group were active in forming political parties, starting newspapers, staffing educational institutions, and providing administrators for the new government. But owing to their essentially individualistic outlook and highly personalized interpretations of modernization and change, they were fragmented into numerous small groups and coteries, including political parties, and were never in a position to influence developments as a collective entity.

In addition to political parties, three pressure groups emerged from the "modernizing" oligarchy—the student organizations, the journalists, and the civil service. The students were the best organized and, hence, the group whose support was most eagerly solicited. The agitational activities of political parties, for instance, were largely dependent upon student participation. The journalists—in particular, the "independents"—were usually strong critics of any government in power as the voice of a highly emotional Nepali nationalism and as supporters of the landowning aristocracy, members of which were in most cases their behind-the-scenes financiers.

The new class of administrators emerged as a pressure group in the 1951–59 period primarily as a reaction to the insecurity of tenure at the Central Secretariat and their uneasy relationship with their political bosses—the Ministers. In their search for stability and security they tended to look toward the palace for support and to favor royal intervention in the processes of government. Upon the installation of an elected government in 1959, the administrative machinery was revamped to suit the purposes and procedures of a parliamentary form of government. The comparative stability and expected longevity of the Nepali Congress regime encouraged important elements of the administrative elite to shift their attention from the royal palace to the Ministry, and the role of the administrators as a pressure group encouraging royal participation in politics was temporarily suspended. It was for this reason, presumably, that a wholesale purge was conducted at both the central and the district administrative level after December, 1960, so as to reinsert into the upper-level positions administrators whose personal careers were closely interlinked with the fortunes of the royal palace.

CREATION OF NEW INTEREST GROUPS UNDER THE
PANCHAYAT SYSTEM

The panchayat political experiment in Nepal has involved setting up several new political institutions to replace the banned political parties. Significant among them are the several government-sponsored "class" organizations, which in effect are designed to be nationwide interest groups. The activities of these new groups are still largely programmatic, and it remains to be seen how effectively they can serve their intended purposes in the new political context. One important factor which reduces their effectiveness is the fact that many former political party members, indoctrinated and ingrained in a decade of active party politics, have joined these "nonparty" institutions at both the leadership and the rank-and-file levels. The presence of these people has brought in the spirit of party politics, thus compromising the official message of partyless democracy. Additionally, these various interest groups cannot avoid competing against each other to promote their respective interests. This situation is tantamount to a revival of factional politics and could become more disruptive and antinational than the political party system at its most opportunistic level of operation.

THE NATURE OF TRANSITIONAL POLITICS

In the preceding section a distinction was made between traditional and modern political parties, using a particularistic-universalistic dichotomy to analyze the relationship underlying the composition of their core leadership. The distinction was found to be both conceptually and empirically meaningful in explaining the differences in their activities. It is now to be seen how transitional politics unfolded through the years within the context of tradition-based attitudinal and behavioral constraints and under the impact of an imported ideology of modernization.

The underlying conflict between tradition and modernity gave an indigenous motive force to transitional politics. The absence of clear-cut alien traditions which needed uprooting or, at least, absorption into a new political system brought to the surface the affective or expressive part of the conflict rather than its problem-solving aspects.

In contrast to India, there were no vestiges of foreign rule to erase and no alien cultural legacies to liquidate or assimilate. Despite their tyrannical record, the Ranas were still Nepalese, and their regime was so quickly dismantled that anti-Rana slogans had become superfluous by the end of 1951. Even the handful of non-Rana supporters of the Rana political system were quickly rehabilitated politically. The lack of a foreign scapegoat imparted an inwardness to political conflicts from the very outset. Motives or the interpretations of motives of the political participants were considered more important than their actions as the crucial variables in the political process.

Traditionally, Nepali society granted status to its members strictly on the basis of such ascriptive considerations as caste, ancestry, and connections of kinship or familial service with the elite families. The striving for and maintenance of status was the fundamental motivation of all public activities. A man of status was eligible for almost all positions of power in the society, whether or not he had any specialized skills. Most of the new political elites that emerged after 1951 were profoundly affected by the same traditional concern for status, as was reflected in their readiness to pay any political price to achieve ministerial rank. The search for status among the politicians was only hypothetically based on "modern" concepts of achievement considerations; for the most part, high government offices were sought and distributed as royal favors on the basis of political influence rather than achievement, as the political elites fully understood. In theory, however, the political elites had accepted the concept of an egalitarian society which would break down artificial barriers of status, caste, and other social inequalities and would emphasize personal achievements rather than connections as the basis for advancement. This divorce of practice from theory was most perceptible in the recruitment of the administrative cadres, which was usually effected on the basis of personal or party connections, but was usually rationalized in terms of achievement. The record of the Public Service Commission, which served more as an agency for administrative ritualism than as a proper invigilatory body, is an eloquent tribute to this state of affairs during the transitional period.

There was—and is—a high degree of ritualization in Nepali social life, and the transitional politics also easily acquired similar ritualistic aspects. The Nepali view of the world traditionally had been marked by an absence of causality, rationality, and predictability, especially as it referred to the political and the physical world. As corollaries to such a belief system, elaborate rituals had been created as a protection against unforeseen events, and the role of astrologers as the most important technicians in the country had been institutionalized. Each of the elite families, including the royal family, had its own consulting astrologer, who recommended propitiatory rites when his clients were in distress or danger and auspicious moments for every ritual or new undertaking.

The introduction in 1951 of a political system with implicit biases of rationality in the allocation and legitimation of power ran directly counter to the pervasive astrological frame of reference of Nepali society. It was perhaps inevitable under such circumstances that the new political system would operate in an irrational and unpredictable manner, producing many surprises and uncertainties in the process—of which, the establishment of K. I. Singh's government in July, 1957, and its abrupt dissolution three months later was the most striking example.

The period of transitional politics was thus a period of profound anxiety, uncertainty, and tension in Nepal's public life, revealed in stresses of various kinds in the body politic of the country. At the cognitive level, there was widespread confusion among the political parties and the public; as to the meaning of political democracy; at the emotional level, there was mounting frustration caused by the increasing awareness that the new political system was not the panacea that it had been claimed to be; at the behavioral level, there was a bedlam of confusion and conflict resulting from the free-wheeling enactment of roles imported from abroad and imprecisely defined for the Nepali environment.

The result of this ideological, attitudinal, and behavioral confusion was that Nepali political elites became preoccupied with self-expression rather than with problem solving. The leaders fluctuated uneasily between feelings of omnipotence and impotence; they refused to bow to the discipline of facts, and were more concerned with striking the appropriate political pose than with carrying out a particular course of action. The political process, in turn, became marked by vacillations between extended periods of inaction and short periods of frantic action. Every time there was a Cabinet crisis, all political parties responded to the opportunities inherent in the situation by frantic and noisy demonstrations of their political "high caste," as it were; at other times they engaged in subterranean, tortuous political maneuvers and countermaneuvers to bring about the fall of existing governments. These unstable, demoralizing transitional politics would have been terminated much sooner if the political parties had coöperated and made a concerted effort to hold the general elections as quickly as possible. But the zigzag nature of transitional politics had been so rewarding and promising to the inbred and self-centered political elites that the majority of them sought instead to prolong this period as long as possible.

The course of transitional politics in Nepal from 1951 to 1959 is essentially the career of a political innovation from its initiation through various stages of modification to its culmination. The period of transition was crammed with political activities relating to the adaptation and modification of the innovation. From February, 1951, to March, 1955, King Tribhuwan and the political elites experimented with various governments in the hope that the new political system would somehow be acculturated to Nepali conditions. But the fragmentation of the political elites into many opposing camps, the King's deteriorating health, the lack of institutional supports for new political roles, and the rise of an organized group that rejected the 1951 political change helped to dislocate political innovation patterned after that of neighboring India. Governments formed between 1951 and 1955 were so preoccupied with problems relating to their political survival that they ignored their task orientation almost completely and failed, in the words of King Mahendra, to produce even "four tangible examples of achievement." Popular expectations of rapid progress and development in the country after the overthrow of the Rana regime were thwarted, and the initial fund of public good-will for the political innovation had all but disappeared by March, 1955.

It was on the ground that so-called democratic party governments had failed to deliver the goods to the people that King Mahendra launched another political innovation—amounting almost to a counter-innovation to the 1951 political change—when he ascended the throne in March, 1955. His new political approach was heavily task-oriented, and the new political experiments he introduced were based on a dynamic political role for the Crown, limited participation by the political parties (in the belief that party politics was more conflict-oriented than task-oriented), and a hypothetical commitment to democratic values.

King Mahendra's extensive tours outside Nepal undoubtedly impressed on him the medieval backwardness of his country as well as the need for an accelerated development program. They also perhaps reinforced his conviction that party politics in Nepal was too divisive, personality-centered, and conflict-ridden to be suitable as a means of rapid modernization.

The rise of an indigenous innovation in the form of King Mahendra's dynamic political role received wide support from all those elements which had found the 1951 political change not to their taste. They would have preferred to abandon the so-called democratic experiment completely and immediately, and would have supported revival of the traditional, if benevolent despotism of the Shah rulers. But King Tribhuwan's memory was still fresh in the people's minds, and the early abandonment of parliamentary democracy, which was still acclaimed as his creation, would have been construed as a betrayal of his legacy and an insult to his memory.

Thus, the period from 1955 to 1959 was marked by several compromises with the aims of the 1951 political change and a continuous modification of the interim constitutional system so as to accommodate the new political role of the Crown.

This period was also marked by the emergence of a new class of politicians—the court influentials—who acted as political brokers for King Mahendra's counter-innovations. These elements prepared the ideological and emotional background for the eventual abolition of parliamentary democracy. More concretely, they injected a new public controversy by propounding the thesis that the long overdue general elections should be held for a Parliament and not a Constituent Assembly and that King Mahendra should bestow a Constitution on the people. These proposals directly contradicted King Tribhuwan's Royal Proclamation of February 18, 1951, and were based on two assumptions concerning the political process in the country, namely, that sovereignty in the country resided not in the popular will but in the King, and that the people of Nepal at the present stage of the country's development were incapable of governing themselves and required guidance and supervision from higher authorities.

The debate between the proponents of Constituent Assembly or Parliament raged for nearly two years and divided the political parties and elites neatly into two categories—those who operated on the Indian model and were committed to the aims of the 1950 revolution, and those who opposed the Indian model, criticized Indian influence in Nepal, and were committed to the espousal of King Mahendra's innovations. King Mahendra finally decided the controversy on February 1, 1958, in favor of a Parliament. Subsequently, on February 12, 1959, he approved and bestowed a Constitution on the country. The first general elections commenced a week later, and the period of transitional politics was officially terminated on June 30, the day the new Constitution went into effect and the first elected constitutional government formed by the Nepali Congress was established.

POLITICAL MODERNIZATION: PARLIAMENTARY DEMOCRACY VERSUS PANCHAYAT DEMOCRACY

The establishment of a parliamentary type of government in 1959 and the introduction of a panchayat form of government in 1962 must both be viewed as attempts to bring about the rapid modernization of the country by institutional measures rather than by the long-drawn-out process of developing the correlates of modernization. None of the usual indicators of modernization were present in Nepal when the country broke from its centuries-old geographical and political insulation in 1951. The national rate of literacy was below 5 per cent; industrialization amounted to no more than a handful of factories in the Terai under the entrepreneurship of Indian businessmen; communications and transport facilities were at a primitive stage of development; religion had not been separated from the functions of government; there had been no broadening of the so-called middle-class groups; there was no increasing mobility in social, vocational, and geographical spheres; contractually organized limited-interest associations were nonexistent; scientific and engineering achievements were conspicuous by their absence. In brief, the task of modernizing Nepal was of truly Herculean proportions, involving the revamping of a medieval, disease-ridden, illiterate, poor, and backward country into a modern, national society. Political modernization in such a context meant a revolutionary change in the form and functions of the government, directed toward the creation of a participant society; administratively, it meant an ever growing expansion in the scope of governmental activity; economically, it meant the mobilization of all available internal resources and all procurable foreign assistance to meet the enormous costs of modernization.

During the years of transitional politics (1951–59) only four significant modernization measures materialized. The most important was a phenomenal expansion in educational facilities all over the country, mostly on the initiative of the local communities.

Many schools and colleges were established, and the number of students enrolled in various educational institutions increased tremendously. Second, there was a modernization of the army, under the supervision of the Indian Military Mission. The reorganization of the army took some six years to complete, and its costs told heavily on the slender resources of the successive governments, each of which allocated to it a substantial proportion—at times more than 50 per cent—of the total budget. Third, there was the completion of the first modern highway linking Kathmandu with India and the construction of a modern airport at the capital. It is noteworthy that both the modernization of the army and the construction of the Nepal-India road were possible during the transitional years only because the Indian government took the sole responsibility for these projects as both financier and contractor for the Nepal government. Finally, the Nepal government succeeded in projecting a new image on the world scene and was able to secure technical and economic assistance from several foreign countries, including India, the United States, the Soviet Union, Communist China, and the United Nations. In fact, the volume of foreign aid reached proportions that the unstable administrative apparatus of the country could not absorb and utilize, and economic development was seriously impeded by a faltering administrative machinery, which reflected the weak, unstable political structure in the country.

The establishment of a strong, elected parliamentary form of government in May, 1959, marked the end of the inchoate transitional politics and the introduction of a confident, vigorous political structure for the first time since 1951. It was widely expected that the missing ingredient of political stability, which had hampered reforms in the economic and administrative systems in the preceding years, was finally restored. A long overdue sense of popular optimism was reborn. The new government, embarking upon its modernization program with zeal and vigor, sought to introduce all the textbook features of a modern polity— such as a highly differentiated and functionally specific system of governmental organization, integration within the governmental structure, rational and secular procedures for making political decisions, popular interest and involvement in the political system, and judicial processes based on a secular and impersonal system of law. The administrative services were codified and regularized; the legal system was expanded and modernized; the feudal land system was modified; government revenues were replenished by the imposition of income taxes and property taxes;

and the implementation of development projects was accelerated.

But the activities of the elected Nepali Congress government placed it directly in opposition to all those elements which had dominated transitional politics from 1955 to 1959 and which had been routed nearly out of political existence in the general elections of 1959. All these elements magnified the threat of the new political system to King Mahendra's innovation of a dynamic role for the Crown. The Nepali Congress leaders of the elected government, misjudging the situation, overlooked the important fact that the 1959 Constitution did not in fact provide for the democratic political system under which they presumed they were operating. Most of them had been politically socialized in India, and they conducted themselves in their political roles as if they were operating under the 1950 Indian Constitution. Thus discrepancies between their performance and their role definitions as provided under the 1959 Nepal Constitution were inevitable, and the accumulation exploded finally into the political crisis of December 15, 1960, when King Mahendra swiftly, abruptly, and unceremoniously scuttled the experiment in parliamentary government and resumed his own political innovations, which had been suspended during the parliamentary interlude.

All through 1961 King Mahendra searched for an ideology that would serve not merely as a replacement for parliamentary government but also as a culmination of the innovational process he had introduced in 1955 in the form of a dynamic, authoritarian, politically oriented monarchy. This was finally accomplished through the promulgation of the 1962 Constitution and the inauguration of the National Panchayat in 1963. It is interesting to note that the democratic label is still in wide use in Nepal. Often the present political system is alluded to as panchayat democracy. The use of the term "panchayat" is intended, presumably, to attribute an indigenous and traditional character to the new political system. Except for the attribution, however, all the various bodies that are being established as part of the panchayat system are as ahistorical in Nepal as was the Parliament under the 1959 Constitution. The real rationale of the panchayat system is political rather than ideological or traditional. It is based on a teleological concept of democracy which assumes that the Nepali people are unprepared for autonomous political action except at the lowest levels of task complexity and that the constituted authority—that is, the King—holds ultimate responsibility for the determination of the country's political system.

At the highest level of the political process, the King and his advisers have wide discretionary powers for political decision, and they alone are responsible for articulating the goals of national politics. The so-called decentralization of powers within the panchayat system has provided zonal, district, and local institutions with some degree of autonomy in local administration—but at the price of a complete segregation from national politics. Indeed, one potential danger inherent within the panchayat system is the possibility that concern with local and parochial issues may usurp the importance of national consensus and solidarity in a country which is already saddled with dangerous tradition-based social, ethnic, linguistic, and regional divisions.

The panchayat regime can conceivably be a more effective agent of modernization than parliamentary democracy in some areas of national life. By eliminating the element of competitive politics from Nepali public life, it has made room for speedy implementation of decisions handed down from above. It may have "toned up" the administrative machinery to some extent through the use of such negative incentives as fear of outright dismissals, for even the highest officials cannot be immune from the feeling that they are under the constant scrutiny of the palace. This technique of administrative control was used with considerable success by the Rana regime and may still be effective for directing some categories of present-day administrative personnel. But it is still uncertain what role the administration would play if a serious challenge to the regime should emerge.

The panchayat regime has continued the economic and land-reform measures of its predecessor with only a few minor changes. It is only in the areas of social legislation and foreign affairs that it has some significant achievements to its credit. King Mahendra's promulgation of a new legal code in 1963, banning many discriminatory social practices, marks an important milestone in the social development of the country; it also underscores the point that it is much easier to change some aspects of a traditional society through the application of force than by persuasion. In the realm of foreign affairs, King Mahendra has scored some personal triumphs, though it remains to be seen whether his current diplomatic successes will have enduring value both for his political career and the future of the country. By pursuing a policy of equal friendship with both China and India, and a policy of neutrality in the Himalayan border disputes and armed conflicts between its two neighbors, Nepal has, at least, temporarily received concessions from both sides. On the international scene, King Mahendra projected a new, magnified image of Nepal by personally participating in the Belgrade conference of neutral countries in 1961 and by undertaking extensive tours of several foreign countries.

It is yet too early to forecast how well the new panchayat institutions and class organizations are going to function in Nepal and how effective they are going to be in the process of rapid modernization. The National Panchayat has not achieved a significant role for itself as yet, and the government is still experimenting with the delegation of administrative authority to the local panchayats. Both parliamentary government and panchayat government can be viewed as more or less tentative political instruments of stimulated change. The first sought to promote change by seeking the consent and the participation of the people in the change process, and the latter seeks to promote change by means of directives issued from above on the assumption that the linking of authority with change will accelerate the change process in a traditional society such as that of Nepal. It is possible that the panchayat system, with all its inadequacies as an agent of change, is nevertheless the most viable political structure for contemporary Nepal precisely because it does remove the likelihood of a struggle between the Crown and the Ministry which could otherwise absorb all the attention and energies of the participants in the political process. The King's will reigns supreme and unchallenged under the panchayat system. If a Minister happens to be out of step with the royal will, he is dropped into political oblivion with little fuss or bother since he no longer has a political party which serves as an independent source of political support able to take his case to the people. Indeed, the procedure of appealing to the people on a political issue is contrary to the basic premise of the 1962 constitutional system, which assumes that the interests of the King, the government, and the people are indivisible and identical.

POLITICAL DEVELOPMENT AND NATION BUILDING

The process of nation building is one of the most crucial questions facing most of the newly emerging Asian states, as it is also for those of Africa. At this stage, interest is necessarily centered on the development of political institutions capable of achieving this basic goal. There would seem to be at least three basic prerequisites in any country, no matter how developed or underdeveloped, for the effective implementation of nation-building programs. These are: (*a*) rationalization of the political process in conformity with the circumstances, needs, and history of the country; (*b*) rationalization of the problem-solving administrative machinery; and (*c*) a sense of national unity and solidarity. The success or failure of political development in any country can be judged by its capacity to establish these prerequisites on an enduring basis.

From 1951 to 1960 the political process in Nepal sought various forms of rationalization, the most important being the 1959 Constitution. But this was marked by such a resurgence of political irrationality and emotionalism that the 1959 rationalization of the political process was abruptly aborted in December, 1960. The new rationalization of the political process under the 1962 Constitution may be politically viable, but it has yet to demonstrate the capacity to achieve a rational, task-oriented, and predictable political process. Political tensions and dissidence resulting from the December, 1960, *coup* continue unresolved and perhaps are unresolvable within the confines of the panchayat form of limited democracy. Aware of this undercurrent of hostility, the new government has assumed a posture of rigidity, denying both the need and the possibility of a compromise with its political critics. Since the opposition includes a significant proportion of the new political elites whose support is essential for the successful introduction of innovations in all spheres—political, economic, and social—the present regime finds itself in a basic dilemma. King Mahendra's ability to manipulate and use the traditional elites for his own purposes provides some degree of immediate political stability, but it is probably an obstruction to political development and the rationalization of the political process upon which long-term stability must be based.

The tentative nature of the political experiments carried out since 1951 had highly adverse effects, by thwarting the establishment of a rational, problem-solving administrative machinery. In addition to the unavoidable lack of technical skills and competence, the most serious obstacle to genuine administrative reorganization has been the low morale and insecurity of tenure of the new administrative elite. Almost every government since 1951 has gone through the ritual of "administrative reorganization" at least once during its period in office, but this was usually nothing more than a euphemism for the process of removing the political appointees of the previous regime and appointing its own candidates to these positions. This unhealthy administrative tradition has continued as a normal practice even after December, 1960, obstructing the rationalization of the administrative machinery. The lack of a sound, continuous, merit-based administrative system is probably the greatest single hindrance to the modernization and development of Nepal.

Perhaps the most frustrated and demoralized of the new administrative elites in Nepal are the technicians—engineers, doctors, scientists, and other specialists—who have often spent years in India and the West obtaining the requisite training for their vocations. In a country with a population of nearly ten million, there are only about a hundred and fifty engineers, two hundred doctors, a dozen scientists, and another dozen specialists in other fields. Instead of being valued for their specialized skills, they are often treated with contumely by the politically appointed administrators and even more so by the administrators' transient political bosses. In such a situation, the technical elites often find it necessary to devote attention primarily to the complicated and fascinating game of intra-Secretariat politics, to the detriment of contributions in their fields of specialization. Without the proper recognition and utilization of the technical elites, however, it is inconceivable that any of the programs for the modernization and industrialization of Nepal can achieve any substantial success except for the few essentially symbolic industrial projects established by the various foreign aid programs.

It is, thus, only in the sphere of the third prerequisite for the modernization of Nepal—the development of a sense of nationhood—that there has been some remarkable progress since 1951. Nepali politics has pursued a self-consciously nationalistic policy since the overthrow of the Rana regime. This sense of Nepali nationalism is still largely confined to the people of central Nepal, but there are indications that it is spreading to the remoter hill areas to the east and west of Kathmandu and even to the Terai under the avowedly nationalistic goals of the present regime. The development of transportation and communication facilities, the continuing expansion of educational facilities, and the dominant political role assumed by the Crown may help to unify the country in the psychological as well as the political sense. The crucial question that remains to be answered is whether this still incipient sense of Nepali nationalism can be mobilized for nation-building tasks, and if so under what conditions and at what political price. The early Shah rulers used it for territorial expansion and founded modern Nepal. The present ruler seems to view himself as the consolidator of the task started by his predecessors, but much of what he has attempted since ascending the throne is still programmatic. The panchayat innovation required more than five years of political incubation, and it will obviously require a longer time-span for testing in the world of realities.

Notes

Chapter I: The Setting

(PAGES 1–19)

[1] Quoted in Narahari Nath Yogi and Baburam Acharya, *Rashtrapita Shri 5 Bada Maharaja Prithvi Narayan Shah Divyopadesh* [Divine Counsel of Shri 5 Maharaja Prithvi Narayan Shah the Great] (2d ed.; Kathmandu, 1953); hereafter cited as Yogi and Acharya, *Rashtrapita*.

[2] Giuseppe Tucci, *Nepal: The Discovery of the Malla* (London, 1962), pp. 60–61.

[3] Balchandra Sharma, *Nepal ko Aitihasik Ruprekha* [Historical Outline of Nepal] (Banaras, 1951), p. 197; hereafter cited as Sharma, *Aitihasik Ruprekha*.

[4] Bhui Dal Rai, "Sahi Vansha Ra Kirati" [The Shah Dynasty and the Kiratis], *Gorkhapatra*, June 25, 1962, p. 2.

[5] Mahesh Chandra Regmi, *The State as Landlord: Raikar Tenure* (*Land Tenure and Taxation in Nepal*, Vol. I [Berkeley, 1963]), p. 6.

[6] *Ibid.*, p. 7.

[7] Iijima Shigeru, "Ecology, Economy, and Social System in the Nepal Himalayas," *Developing Economies*, II, No. 1 (March, 1964), 92–105.

[8] See Gerald Berreman, *Hindus of the Himalayas* (Berkeley and Los Angeles, 1963), for a study of an Indian hill community.

[9] Gerald Berreman, "Peoples and Cultures of the Himalayas," *Asian Survey*, III, No. 6 (June, 1963), 289–304.

[10] Regmi, *op. cit.*, pp. 18–21.

[11] Y. P. Pant, "Nepal's Recent Trade Policy," *Asian Survey*, IV, No. 7 (July, 1964), pp. 947–957.

[12] John T. Hitchcock, "A Nepalese Hill Village and Indian Employment," *Asian Survey*, I, No. 9 (November, 1961), 15–20.

Chapter II: The Shah and Rana Political Systems

(PAGES 23–29)

[1] Buddhi Man Singh, "Bhasa Vansavali," [Nepali Genealogy] (MS in collection of Leo E. Rose), leaf 200a; hereafter cited as Singh, "Bhasa Vansavali."

[2] H. A. Oldfield, *Sketches from Nepal* (London, 1880), I, 272–273.

[3] *Ibid.*, pp. 288–292.

[4] Yogi and Acharya, *Rashtrapita*, pp. 5–9.

[5] W. Kirkpatrick, *An Account of the Kingdom of Nepaul* (London, 1811), pp. 197–203.

[6] For his biography see Padma Jung Rana, *Life of Maharaja Sir Jung Bahadur* (Allahabad, 1909).

[7] Oldfield, *op. cit.*, p. 355.

[8] Figures for fatalities and other consequences of the Kot Massacre derived from Singh, *op. cit.*

[9] Oldfield, *op. cit.*, p. 372 n.

[10] Singh, *op. cit.*, leaf 199a.

[11] Sharma, *Aitihasik Ruprekha*, p. 329.

Chapter III: Oppositional Politics Under Rana Rule

(PAGES 40–56)

[1] Padma Jung Rana, *Life of Maharaja Sir Jung Bahadur* (Allahabad, 1909), p. 28.

[2] Singh, "Bhasa Vansavali," leaves 239a–241a.

[3] H. A. Oldfield, *Sketches from Nepal* (London, 1880), II, 20.

[4] Padma Jung Rana, *op. cit.*, p. 302.

[5] Singh, "Bhasa Vansavali," leaves 232a–232b.

[6] Padma Jung Rana, *op. cit.*, p. 303.

[7] *Ibid.*, pp. 155–162.

[8] Oldfield, *op. cit.*, I, 392.

[9] Sharma, *Aitihasik Ruprekha*, p. 336.

[10] P. Landon, *Nepal* (London, 1928), II, 249–250.

[11] Baburam Acharya, "Rana Shahi ra Shadyantra" [Rana Rule and Conspiracy], *Sharada*, XXI, No. 5 (February–March, 1957), 1–8.

[12] Sharma, *Aitihasik Ruprekha*, p. 388.

[13] *Ibid.*, p. 355.

[14] *Ibid.*

[15] *Ibid.*, p. 358.

[16] *Ibid.*, p. 392.

[17] Francis Tuker, *Gorkha* (London, 1957), p. 209.

[18] Raghu Nath Singh, *Jagrit Nepal* [Awakened Nepal], (Banaras, 1950).

Chapter IV: The 1950 Revolution

(PAGES 57–80)

[1] See the report of his conversation with the British Minister and Envoy at Kathmandu, 1940, in Francis Tuker, *Gorkha* (London, 1957), pp. 212–213.

[2] *Free English Rendering of the Government of Nepal Act, 2004 Sambat (1948 A.D.)*, Kathmandu: Government Press, 1948, p. 13.

[3] *The Hindu* (Madras), February 16, 1950.

[4] *Gorkhapatra* (Kathmandu), September 27, 1950.

[5] Politicus, *Inside Story of Nepal* (New Delhi: Hindu Outlook, 1951), pp. 1–20.

[6] Government of Nepal, Department of Publicity, *News Bulletin No. 28*, n.d.

[7] Sharma, *Aitihasik Ruprekha*, p. 413.

[8] K. P. Karunakaran, *India in World Affairs 1950–53* (Calcutta, 1958), p. 194.

[9] G. B. Devkota, *Nepal ko Rajnaitik Darpan* [Political Mirror of Nepal] (Kathmandu, 1959), p. 39; hereafter cited as Devkota, *Rajnaitik Darpan*.

[10] *Ibid.*, p. 44.

[11] *The Hindu*, January 17, 1951.

Chapter V: The "Revolutionary" Governments

(PAGES 83–102)

[1] Devkota, *Rajnaitik Darpan* pp. 49–52.

[2] Jawaharlal Nehru, *India's Foreign Policy, Selected Speeches, September 1946–April 1961* (New Delhi: Government of India, Publication Division, 1961), p. 176.

[3] *The Hindu* (Madras), May 17, 1951.
[4] Devkota, *Rajnaitik Darpan*, pp. 105–106.
[5] *Ibid.*, pp. 113–114.
[6] *Nepal Gazette*, Vol. I, No. 15, Part I Marga 4, 2008 V.S., (November 19, 1951).
[7] *Times of India* (Bombay), February 22, 1952.
[8] *The Statesman* (Calcutta), August 6, 1952.
[9] Devkota, *Rajnaitik Darpan*, pp. 178–179.
[10] *Hindustan Times* (New Delhi), July 8, 1952.
[11] *Ibid.,* July 21, 1952.
[12] *Ibid.,* August 11, 1952.

Chapter VI: King Tribhuwan's Political Experiments

(PAGES 103–123)

[1] King Tribhuwan's Royal Proclamation of August 14, 1952, in Devkota, *Rajnaitik Darpan*, p. 195.
[2] *Ibid.*, p. 198.
[3] *Nepal Gazette*, Vol. II, No. 5, Bhadra 24, 2009 V.S. (September 9, 1952). The abbreviation "V.S." refers to the Vikram Samvat ("era"), prevalent in Nepal as the official calendar and associated with the reign of King Vikramaditya, a monarch of ambiguous antiquity and noted for his legendary qualities of fair-mindedness and benevolence. The Vikram year is based on a lunar calendar and usually begins in March or April.
[4] *Ibid.*, Vol. II, No. 8, Part 1, Aswin 21, 2009 (October 7, 1952).
[5] Devkota, *Rajnaitik Darpan*, pp. 184–185.
[6] News release of the Nepali Congress Central Office, Kathmandu, on the resolution passed at the Working Committee meeting of the Nepali Congress, March 10–13, 1953. See also *The Statesman*, March 15, 1953.
[7] *Ibid.*, March 21, 1953.
[8] *Gorkhapatra*, June 17, 1953.
[9] *The Statesman*, July 4, 1953.
[10] *Ibid.*, July 20, 1953.
[11] *Ibid.*, July 22, 1953.
[12] *The Statesman*, August 4, 1953.
[13] *Nepal Trade Directory* (New Delhi: Nepal Trading Corp., 1959), p. 30.
[14] *Nepal Gazette*, Aswin 4, 2010 (October 19, 1953); also Devkota, *Rajnaitik Darpan*, pp. 224–228.
[15] *Nepal Gazette*, Vol. III, Extraordinary Issue, Falgun 10, 2010 (February 20, 1954).
[16] *The Statesman*, January 10, 1954.
[17] *Ibid.*, August 5, 1954.
[18] *Nepal Gazette*, Vol. III, No. 35, Baisakh 7, 2011 (April 19, 1954).
[19] *The Statesman*, April 14, 1954. See also D. Raj, *Parliament ra Sallahakar Sabha* [Parliament and the Advisory Assembly] (Kathmandu: Nepal Academy, 1959), pp. 315–320.
[20] *The Statesman*, October 5, 1954.
[21] *Ibid.*, October 10, 1954.
[22] *Ibid.*, December 31, 1954.
[23] *Ibid.*
[24] *Ibid.*, January 10, 1955.
[25] *Times of India*, January 18, 1954.
[26] *The Statesman*, January 25, 1955.

Chapter VII: Party Politics in Postrevolutionary Nepal

(PAGES 124–147)

1 *Jatiya Andolanma Nepal Communist Party* [Involvement of the Nepal Communist Party in the National Struggle], Report of the General Secretary at the First Conference of the Nepal Communist Party (Kathmandu, September, 1951) .

2 *Jatiya Janatantrik Samyukta Morcha ko Ghosana Patra* [Manifesto of the National Democratic United Front] (Kathmandu: Pragatishil Adhyayan Mandal, 1951) , p. 3.

3 Devkota, *Rajnaitik Darpan*, pp. 123–124.

4 B. P. Koirala, *Nepali Congress ra Sarkar* [Nepali Congress and the Government] (Biratnagar, 1952) .

5 *Hindustan Times,* September 1, 1952.

6 *Ibid.*

7 *Free Press Journal* (Bombay) , March 25, 1953.

8 *Amrita Bazar Patrika* (Calcutta) , March 8, 1953.

9 *Hindustan Times,* May 2, 1953; *The Statesman,* May 4, 1953.

10 *Ibid.,* June 22, 1953.

11 Devkota, *Rajnaitik Darpan,* p. 218.

12 *Ibid.,* pp. 218–219.

13 *Ibid.,* pp. 220–221.

14 *Ibid.,* pp. 221–222.

15 *The Statesman,* September 22, 1953.

16 *Ibid.,* September 25, 1953.

17 *Ibid.,* October 18, 1953.

18 *Ibid.,* November 2, 1953.

19 *Ibid.,* January 10, 1954.

20 *Ibid.,* March 4, 1954.

21 D. K. Shahi: *Satsal Pachhi Satsal* [Seven Years after 1951] (Kathmandu: Nepali Congress, 1957) , p. 9.

22 *The Statesman,* June 2, 1954.

23 *Ibid.*

24 Devkota, *Rajnaitik Darpan,* pp. 250–251.

25 *The Statesman,* June 6, 1954.

26 *Ibid.,* July 13, 1954.

27 Devkota, *Rajnaitik Darpan,* pp. 273–274.

Chapter VIII: Policies and Programs: 1951–55

(PAGES 148–166)

1 *Nepal Gazette,* Vol. II, No. 17, Poush 1, 2009 (December 15, 1952) .

2 *Ibid.,* Vol. II, No. 18, Poush 8, 2009 (December 22, 1952) .

3 *Ibid.*

4 *The Statesman,* September 22, 1953.

5 D. K. Shahi, *Satsal Pacchi Satsal* [Seven Years after 1951] (Kathmandu: Nepali Congress, 1957, p. 9.

6 "Kathmandu Newsletter", *Hindustan Times,* March 4, 1955.

7 *2010 Sal Magha 7 Gateko Shahi Goshana* [The Royal Proclamation of January 10, 1954] (Kathmandu: Gorkhapatra Press, 1954) .

8 *The Statesman,* February 14, 1954.

9 *Interim Government of Nepal Act (Third Amendment)* (Kathmandu: Gorkhapatra Press, 1954) .

10 *Nepal Gazette,* Vol. I, No. 1, Sravan 22, 2008 (August 6, 1951).

11 *Ibid.,* Vol. II, No. 3, Bhadra 10, 2009 (August 26, 1952).

12 *The Statesman,* May 5, 1954.

13 *Ibid.,* November 6, 1954.

14 *Nepal Gazette,* Vol. I, No. 9, Aswin 15, 2008 (October 1, 1951); see also Vol. I, No. 21, Poush 16, 2008 (December 30, 1951).

15 *Ibid.,* Vol. I, No. 22, Poush 23, 2008 (January 6, 1952).

16 *Ibid.,* Vol. I, No. 26, Part 2, Marga 21, 2008 (February 3, 1952).

17 *Ibid.,* Vol. II, No. 34, Baisakh 1, 2010 (April 13, 1953).

18 *The Statesman,* January 17, 1952.

Chapter X: King Mahendra's Political Innovations

(PAGES 179–204)

1 Devkota, *Rajnaitik Darpan,* p. 97.

2 *Ibid.,* pp. 153–157.

3 *Ibid.,* pp. 278–279.

4 *The Statesman,* April 5, 1955.

5 Devkota, *Rajnaitik Darpan,* pp. 295–299.

6 *Ibid.*

7 *The Statesman,* May 1, 1955.

8 Devkota, *Rajnaitik Darpan,* pp. 295–299.

9 *Ibid.,* p. 309.

10 *The Statesman,* July 6, 1956.

11 *The Commoner* (Kathmandu), July 1, 1957.

12 *Ibid.,* June 30, 1957.

13 *Ibid.,* July 16, 1957.

14 *Ibid.,* July 15, 1957.

15 *Lokvarta* (Kathmandu), July 16, 1957.

16 *Halkhabar* (Kathmandu), July 19, 1957.

17 *Nepal Gazette,* Vol. VII, No. 17, Part 1, Asadh 32, 2014 (July 15, 1957).

18 *Nepal Pukar* (Kathmandu), July 21, 1957.

19 *Diyalo* (Kathmandu), July 17, 1957.

20 *The Commoner,* July 24, 1957.

21 *Diyalo,* July 20, 1957.

22 *Nepal Gazette,* Vol. VII, No. 3, Part 1, Extraordinary Issue, Sravan 11, 2014 (July 26, 1957).

23 *The Commoner,* September 30, 1957.

24 *Karmavir* (Kathmandu), October 10, 1957.

25 *Naya Samaj* (Kathmandu), October 8, 1957.

26 *Samyukta Prayas* (Kathmandu), October 20, 1957.

27 *Rashtravani* (Kathmandu), October 21, 1957.

28 Devkota, *Rajnaitik Darpan,* p. 559.

29 *The Commoner,* September 11, 1957.

Chapter XI: The Prelude to the 1959 General Elections

(PAGES 205–224)

1 *The Commoner,* November 15, 1957.

2 *Naya Samaj,* December 7, 1957.

3 *Ibid.*

[4] Devkota, *Rajnaitik Darpan,* p. 570.
[5] *Naya Samaj,* December 16, 1957.
[6] *Swatantra Samachar* (Kathmandu) , January 31, 1958.
[7] *Halkhabar,* May 7, 1958.
[8] Devkota, *Rajnaitik Darpan,* pp. 586–588.
[9] *Halkhabar,* May 19, 1958.
[10] *Kalpana* (Kathmandu) , May 20, 1958.
[11] *Halkhabar,* May 16, 1958.
[12] Devkota, *Rajnaitik Darpan,* p. 614.
[13] *Halkhabar,* May 19, 1958.
[14] *Nepal Samachar* (Kathmandu) , May 22, 1958.
[15] *Halkhabar,* June 13, 1958.
[16] *Kalpana,* May 29, 1958.
[17] Devkota, *Rajnaitik Darpan,* pp. 675–676.
[18] *Ibid.,* pp. 676–685.
[19] *Kalpana,* June 3, 1958; *Nepal Times,* June 3, 1958.
[20] Dhundiraj Sharma, *Parliament ra Sallahakar Sabha* [Parliament and the Advisory Assembly] (Kathmandu: Nepal Academy, 1959) , p. 67–68.
[21] *Ibid.,* p. 69.
[22] For text see Devkota, *Rajnaitik Darpan,* pp. 673–674.
[23] *Halkhabar,* January 6, 1959.

Chapter XII: King Mahendra's First Four Years: The Record

(PAGES 225–256)

[1] Text in Devkota, *Rajnaitik Darpan,* pp. 406–407.
[2] *Nepal Gazette,* Vol. V, No. 17, Poush 11, 2012 (December 25, 1955) .
[3] Devkota, *Rajnaitik Darpan,* pp. 316–317.
[4] *Ibid.,* p. 319.
[5] *Ibid.,* pp. 356–357.
[6] *The Statesman,* August 15, 1956.
[7] *Ibid.,* September 22, 1956.
[8] *Gorkhapatra,* December 4, 1957.
[9] *Kalpana,* May 25, 1958.
[10] Ministry of Industry and Commerce, *Industrial Policy of Nepal* (Kathmandu, 1958) , pp. 1–4.
[11] *Samaj* (Kathmandu) , June 11, 1958.
[12] *The Motherland* (Kathmandu) , June 9, 1958.
[13] *Kalpana,* August 17, 1958; *Nepal Times* (Kathmandu) , August 18, 1958; *Filingo* (Kathmandu) , August 20, 1958.
[14] *Samaj,* September 3, 1958.
[15] *Naya Samaj* (Kathmandu) , September 7, 1958.
[16] *Halkhabar,* September 13, 1958.
[17] *Kalpana,* July 13, 1958.
[18] *Samyukta Prayas,* August 31, 1958.
[19] *Gorkhapatra,* January 30, 1956.
[20] *The Statesman,* August 21, 1956.
[21] Devkota, *Rajnaitik Darpan,* pp. 437–439.
[22] *Desh Sewa* (Kathmandu) , July 14, 1958.
[23] *Gorkhapatra,* July 19, 1958.
[24] Devkota, *Rajnaitik Darpan,* pp. 651–653.
[25] *Samaj,* November 10, 1956.

Chapter XIII: The Parties Prepare for the Elections

(PAGES 257–279)

[1] *The Statesman,* October 10, 1955.
[2] Devkota, *Rajnaitik Darpan,* p. 24.
[3] *The Statesman,* December 18, 1956.
[4] *Ibid.,* April 16, 1956.
[5] *The Commoner,* June 3, 1957, 1:1.
[6] *Samanantar Nepali Congress Kina* [Why the Parallel Nepali Congress?] (Kathmandu, 1957), p. 12.
[7] *The Commoner,* July 19, 1957.
[8] *Ibid.,* August 18, 1957.
[9] *Naya Samaj,* August 14, 1957.
[10] *The Commoner,* August 29, 1957.
[11] *Halkhabar,* November 15, 1957.
[12] *Kalpana,* February 9, 1958.
[13] *The Commoner,* February 4, 1958.
[14] Devkota, *Rajnaitik Darpan,* pp. 594–595.
[15] *Nepal Pukar,* February 28, 1958.
[16] *Samaya* (Kathmandu), February 5, 1958.
[17] *Swatantra Samachar,* February 15, 1958.
[18] *Filingo,* August 23, 1958.
[19] *Samaj,* July 24, 1958; *Nepal Samachar,* July 23, 1958.
[20] *Ibid.,* July 29, 1958.

Chapter XIV: The 1959 Constitution and the General Elections

(PAGES 280–299)

[1] *Nirvachan Sandesh,* June 30, 1958.
[2] *Ibid.,* July 16, 1958.
[3] *Ibid.,* January 28, 1959.
[4] *Ibid.,* October 1, 1958.
[5] *Ibid.,* January 28, 1959.
[6] Narendra Goyal, *The King and His Constitution: Observation and Commentary on the Constitution of the Kingdom of Nepal* (New Delhi: Nepal Trading Corporation, 1959), p. 1.
[7] *Ibid.,* Article 10 (1), p. 36.
[8] *Ibid.,* Preamble, p. 1.
[9] *Halkhabar,* January 15, 1959.
[10] Devkota, *Rajnaitik Darpan,* p. 698.
[11] *Ibid.,* p. 690.
[12] *Ibid.,* p. 698.
[13] *Swatantra Samachar,* April 4, 1959.
[14] *Samyukta Prayas,* November 10, 1959.
[15] *Naya Samaj,* July 13, 1959.

Chapter XV: The Elected Nepali Congress Government

(PAGES 303–316)

[1] *Halkhabar*, November 24, 1960; *Naya Samaj*, November 27, 1960.
[2] *Nepal Pukar*, November 11, 1959.
[3] *Ibid.*
[4] *Kalpana*, December 7, 1959.
[5] *Swatantra Samachar*, September 12, 1960.
[6] *Kalpana*, November 15, 1960.
[7] *Sahibato* (Kathmandu) , December 9, 1960.

Chapter XVI: Party Politics Under the Nepali Congress Government

(PAGES 317–345)

[1] *Swatantra Samachar*, June 1, 1959.
[2] *Halkhabar*, June 6, 1959.
[3] *Asian Recorder* (New Delhi) , V, No. 22, May 30–June 5, 1959, 2690.
[4] *Ibid.*, No. 24, June 13–19, 1959, 2715.
[5] *Halkhabar*, June 22, 1959; see also issue of June 28.
[6] *Naya Samaj*, July 2, 1959.
[7] *Halkhabar*, July 12, 1959.
[8] *Ibid.*, December 8, 1959.
[9] *Kalpana*, December 20, 1959.
[10] *Halkhabar*, February 9, 1960.
[11] *Dainik Nepal* (Kathmandu) , April 1, 1960.
[12] *Asian Recorder*, VI, No. 37, September 10–16, 1960, 3536.
[13] *Halkhabar*, November 22, 1960.
[14] *Asian Recorder*, VI, No. 6, February 6–12, 1960, 3146–47.
[15] *Halkhabar*, February 29, 1960; see also *Asian Recorder*, VI, No. 12, March 19–25, 1960, 3219.
[16] *Ibid.*, VI, No. 30, July 23–29, 1960. 3449–51.
[17] *Samiksha* (Kathmandu) , August 3, 1960.
[18] *Sahibato*, November 6, 1960.
[19] *Naya Samaj*, December 13, 1960.
[20] *Asian Recorder*, V, No. 23, June 6–12, 1959, 2704.
[21] *Kalpana*, July 6, 1959.
[22] *Navayuga* (Kathmandu) , August 23, 1959.
[23] *Halkhabar*, January 21, 1960.
[24] *Ibid.*, February 14, 1960.
[25] *Ibid.*, January 21, 1960.
[26] *Samaj*, April 16, 1960.
[27] *Ibid.*, April 29, 1960.
[28] *Asian Recorder*, VI, No. 30, July 23–29, 1960, 3449–51.
[29] *Naya Samaj*, September 8, 1960.
[30] *Navayuga*, September 27, 1960.
[31] *Samiksha*, September 26, 1960.
[32] *Halkhabar*, September 2, 1960.
[33] *Dainik Nepal*, May 17, 1960.
[34] *Naya Samaj*, May 28, 1960.
[35] *Halkhabar*, April 24, 1960.
[36] *Kalpana*, May 9, 1960.

[37] *Asian Recorder,* VI, No. 23, June 4–10, 1960, 3557–58.
[38] *Kalpana,* May 14, 1960.
[39] *Naya Samaj,* September 13, 1960.
[40] *Nepal Times,* September 1, 1960.
[41] *Swatantra Samachar,* September 3, 1960.
[42] *Sahibato,* December 9, 1960; *Naya Samaj,* November 27, 1960.
[43] *Samaj,* June 7, 1959.
[44] *Halkhabar,* June 21, 1959.
[45] *Naya Samaj,* April 12, 1960.
[46] *Samiksha,* August 17, 1960.
[47] *Dainik Nepal,* November 26, 1960.

Chapter XVII: Policies and Programs of the Nepali Congress Government

(PAGES 346–373)

[1] Nepali Congress, *Chunao Goshanapatra* [Election Manifesto] (Kathmandu, 1958), pp. 6–7.
[2] His Majesty's Government, Publicity and Information Department, *Budget Speech, 1959–60* (Kathmandu, n.d.), p. 4.
[3] *Ibid., Budget Speech, 1960–61* (Kathmandu, n.d.), p. 26.
[4] *Asian Recorder,* VI, No. 28 (July 9–15, 1960), 3431.
[5] *Kalpana,* December 11, 1960.
[6] *Halkhabar,* April 12, 1960.
[7] *Dainik Nepal,* October 28, 1960.
[8] *Kalpana,* November 8, 1960.
[9] *Dainik Nepal,* December 3, 1960.
[10] *Kalpana,* November 17, 1960.
[11] *Sahibato,* October 24, 1960.
[12] *Asian Recorder,* V, No. 27 (July 4–10, 1959), 2747–48.
[13] *Halkhabar,* June 21, 1959.
[14] *Asian Recorder,* V, No. 51 (December 19–25, 1959), 3060–61.
[15] *Ibid.,* VI, No. 7 (February 13–19, 1960), 3157.
[16] *Ibid.*
[17] *Ibid.*
[18] *Halkhabar,* February 18, 1960.
[19] *Gorkhapatra,* March 16, 1960.
[20] *Asian Recorder,* VI, No. 18 (April 30–May 6, 1960), 3294.
[21] *Ibid.,* VI, No. 19 (May 7–13, 1960), p. 3302.
[22] *Ibid.,* VI, No. 30 (July 23–29, 1960), 3449–51.
[23] *Ibid.,* VI, No. 32 (August 6–12, 1960), 3480–81.
[24] *Ibid.,* VI, No. 37 (September 10–16, 1960), 3536.

Chapter XVIII: King Mahendra and Parliamentary Democracy

(PAGES 374–392)

[1] *Kalpana,* November 6, 1959.
[2] *Halkhabar,* December 3, 1959.
[3] *Dainik Nepal,* January 3, 1960.
[4] *Ibid.,* February 6, 1960.
[5] *Gorkhapatra,* February 19, 1960.

6 *Naya Samaj,* March 12, 1960.

7 *Halkhabar,* April 10, 1960.

8 *U.S. Congressional Record,* April, 1960, pp. 8906–07.

9 *Asian Recorder,* VI, No. 35 (August 27–September 2, 1960) , 3507.

10 *Ibid.*

11 Los Angeles *Times,* May 10, 1960.

12 *Asian Recorder,* VI, No. 35 (August 27–September 2, 1960) , 3508.

13 *Everest News Agency* (Kathmandu) , July 29, 1960.

14 *Samaj,* August 6, 1960.

15 *Samiksha,* August 17, 1960.

16 *Sahibato,* September 21, 1960.

17 *Everest News Agency,* November 9, 1960.

18 *Kalpana,* November 11, 1960.

19 His Majesty's Government, National Guidance Ministry, *On to a New Era: Some Historic Addresses by King Mahendra* (Kathmandu, n.d.) , p. 6.

Chapter XIX: The 1962 Constitution Experiments with "Guided" Democracy

(PAGES 395–419)

1 *Rashtriya Sambad Samiti* (Kathmandu) , April 14, 1962.

2 Government of Nepal, *Free English Rendering of the Government of Nepal Act, 2004 Sambat (1948 A.D.)* (Kathmandu, 1948) , p. 7.

3 Gaon Panchayat Act, *Nepal Gazette,* Vol. XI, No. 39, Magh 11, 2018 (January 24, 1962) ; Nagar Panchayat Act, *Nepal Gazette,* Vol. XII, Extraordinary Issue No. 14, Bhadra 5, 2019 (August 20, 1962) ; Zilla Panchayat Act, *Nepal Gazette,* Vol. XII, Extraordinary Issue No. 24, Marga 14, 2019 (November 29, 1962) .

4 His Majesty's Government, *Unofficial Translation of the Royal Address, April 19, 1963* (Kathmandu: Department of Publicity and Broadcasting, 1963) .

5 *Gorkhapatra,* March 7, 1961.

6 *Ibid.,* March 2, 1962.

7 *Ibid.,* February 28, 1962.

8 *Ibid.,* March 7, 1961.

9 *Sagarmatha Sambad Samiti* (Kathmandu) , February 19, 1961.

10 *Nepal Gazette,* Vol. XI, Extraordinary Issue No. 32, Poush 13, 2018 (December 27, 1961) .

11 *Ibid.*

12 *Ibid.*

13 *Gorkhapatra,* August 26, 1963.

14 "Notification of the Home and Local Self-Government Ministry," *Nepal Gazette,* Vol. X, Extraordinary Issue No. 25, Falgun 8, 2017 (February 9, 1961) .

15 *Nepal Gazette,* Vol. XI, Extraordinary Issue No. 39, Magh 17, 2018 (January 30, 1962) .

16 *Naya Sandesh,* April 27, 1962.

Chapter XX: The Politics of "Guided" Democracy

(PAGES 420–442)

1 *Nepal Gazette,* Vol. X, Extraordinary Issue No. 17, Poush 1, 2017 (December 15, 1960) .

2 *Ibid.,* Vol. X, No. 35, Poush 12, 2017 (December 26, 1960) .

3 *Ibid.,* Vol. X, Extraordinary Issue No. 20, Poush 22, 2017 (January 5, 1961) .

4 *Ibid.*, Vol. X, Extraordinary Issue No. 22, Poush 29, 2017 (January 12, 1961).

5 *Gorkhapatra,* March 9, 1961.

6 *Nepali* (Kathmandu), March 14, 1961.

7 *Nepal Samachar,* January 24, 1962.

8 *Naya Samaj,* January 30, 1962.

9 *Dainik Nepal,* January 23, 1962.

10 *Nepal Gazette,* Vol. XI, Extraordinary Issue No. 42, Falgun 3, 2018 (February 14, 1962).

11 *Ibid.,* Vol. XI, Extraordinary Issue No. 42b, Falgun 16, 2018 (February 27, 1962).

12 Unofficial Translation of King Mahendra's Inaugural Address, Royal Press Secretariat, June 6, 1962.

13 *Gorkhapatra,* June 14, 1962.

14 *Samaj,* June 22, 1962.

15 *Matribhumi* (Kathmandu), July 9, 1962.

16 *Ibid.*

17 *Samiksha,* July 13, 1962.

18 *Naya Samaj,* September 10, 1962.

19 *Asian Recorder,* VIII, No. 42 (October 15–21, 1962), 4841–42.

20 *Halkhabar,* February 1, 1963.

21 *Ibid.,* February 19, 1963.

22 *Nepal News Agency,* February 27, 1963.

23 *Halkhabar,* February 1, 1963.

24 *Nepal Samachar,* February 3, 1963.

25 Swatantra Samachar, April 19, 1963.

26 *Matribhumi,* August 22, 1964.

Chapter XXI: Political Organizations and Panchayat Raj

(PAGES 443–464)

1 P. N. Chowdhury, "From Non-Violence to Violence," *Nepal Today,* I, No. 11 (May 1, 1962), 109.

2 *Kalpana,* January 25, 1961.

3 *Nepal Sandesh,* June 28, 1961.

4 *Motherland,* July 9, 1961.

5 Press statement by Suvarna Shamsher, January 31, 1962, published in the official Nepali Congress organ, *Nepal Today,* I, No. 5 (February 1, 1962), 45.

6 *Himalayan Sentinel,* April 16, 1962.

7 For a detailed report see C. Kesari Prasai, "Nepali Communists in Wilderness," *Janata* (journal of the Praja Socialist Party of India), XVII, No. 23, (July 1, 1962), 4.

8 *Nepal Samachar,* June 1, 1962.

9 Madan Mani Dikshit, "Rashtriya Prajatantric Yekta" [National Democratic Unity], *Samiksha,* August 23, 1962.

10 *Samiksha,* October 14, 1962.

11 *Ibid.*

12 "Communist Volte Face," *Nepal Today,* II, No. 19, (September 1, 1963), 178.

13 *Nepal Today,* I, No. 3 (January 2, 1962), 23.

14 *Naya Samaj,* March 3, 1962.

15 *Gorkhapatra,* March 4, 1962.

16 *Naya Samaj,* March 25, 1962.

17 *Ibid.*

18 *Samaj,* June 10, 1962.

Chapter XXII: Policy and Program of the Royal Regime

(PAGES 465–481)

[1] *Nepal Gazette,* Vol. X, Extraordinary Issue No. 20, Poush 22, 2017 (January 5, 1961).

[2] Mahesh C. Regmi, *Land Tenure and Taxation in Nepal* (Berkeley: Institute of International Studies, University of California, 1963–65), II, 107.

[3] His Majesty's Government, *Shahi Kara Ayog ko Report, 2017* [Report of the Royal Taxation Commission, 1961], (Kathmandu: Department of Publicity and Broadcasting, 1961), p. 2.

[4] *Ibid.,* p. 21–22.

[5] *Nepal Gazette,* Vol. XI, Extraordinary Issue No. 40, Magh 24, 2018 (February 6, 1962).

[6] *Ibid.,* Vol. XII, Extraordinary Issue No. 44a, Chaitra 30, 2019 (April 12, 1963).

[7] *Naya Samaj,* October 23, 1964.

[8] Everest News Agency, September 12, 1961.

[9] Y. P. Pant, "Nepal's Recent Trade Policy," *Asian Survey,* IV, No. 7 (July, 1964), 947–957.

[10] Surya Bahadur Thapa, "Budget Bhashan: 2020–21" [Budget Speech, 1963/64], *Gorkhapatra,* Budget Supplement, Ashadh 26, 2020 (July 10, 1963).

[11] *Ibid.*

[12] *Gorkhapatra,* December 6, 1963.

[13] *Ibid.,* March 13, 1964.

[14] *Nepal Gazette,* Vol. XIII, No. 49, Chaitra 10, 2020 (March 23, 1964).

[15] *Motherland,* May 7, 1964.

Bibliography

PUBLICATIONS IN NEPALI AND HINDI

(Nepali unless otherwise indicated)

Acharya, Baburam. "Rana Shahi ra Shadyantra" [Rana Rule and Conspiracies] *Sharada,* XXI, No. 5 (1957), 1–8.

——. *Chin ra Tibet Sang Nepal ko Sambandh* [Nepal's Relations with China and Tibet]. Kathmandu: Chou En-lai Reception Committee, 1956. 32 pp.

Acharya, Badrinath. *Nepal Jana Kranti* [Nepal's People's Revolution]. Kathmandu: Saraswati Press, n.d. 46 pp.

Adhikari, D. P. "Nepal ko Nayan Samajvadi Sanga" [To the New Socialists of Nepal], *Mashal,* April 27, 1957, p. 8.

Aryal, Vishnu Prasad. *Shahi Kadam Kina* [Why the Royal Move]. Kathmandu, 1961. 27 pp.

Bahadur, Bir (ed). *Nepal ko Pukar* [The Call of Nepal (for K. I. Singh's Return from China)]. Lucknow, 1954. 108 pp.

Bahadur, Poorna. *Nepal ma Antar-rashtriya Drishti* [International Eyes on Nepal]. Kathmandu, 1959. 34 pp.

Bahadur, Ram. *Nepal ko Samvidhan* [Constitution of Nepal]. Kathmandu: Chhatra Mitra Prakashan, 1962. 92 pp.

Baral, Ishwar. *Nepal Aur Bharat ka Sanskritik Sambandha* [Cultural Relations between Nepal and India]. Kathmandu: Jorganesh Press, n.d. 7 pp. (Hindi)

Baral, Lok Raj. "Zilla Prashasan ma Bada Hakim ko Sthan" [The Position of the Bada Hakim in District Administration], *Gorkhapatra,* December 8, 1962, p. 10.

Bhandari, Dhundiraj. *Nepal ko Aitihasik Vivechana* [Historical Analysis of Nepal]. Banaras: Krishna Kumari, 1958. 368 pp.

Basnyat, Surendra Bahadur. *Swatantra Mahasammelan ko Ruprekha* [An Outline of the Independents' Conference]. Kathmandu: Ad Hoc Committee, 1957.

Chemjong, Iman Singh. *Kirat Itihas* [History of Kirat]. Gangtok (Sikkim), 1952. 64 pp.

Devkota, Grishma Bahadur. *Nepal ko Rajnaitik Darpan.* [Political Mirror of Nepal]. Kathmandu: K. C. Gautam, 1959. 766 pp.

Giri, Hari Prasad. *Panchyati Vyabastha ko Ruprekha* [Outline of the Panchayat System]. Kathmandu: Department of Publicity and Broadcasting, 1962. 16 pp.

Giri, Surya Prakash. *Naya Nepal ko Digdarshan* [A Broad Outline of New Nepal]. Kathmandu, 1956. 64 pp.

Giri, Tulsi. *Panchayati Vyabastha ko Saiddhantik Prishthabhumi* [Ideological Foundation of the Panchayat System], *Matribhumi,* September 19 and 25, 1962.

Giri, Tulsi, Bishta, Kirtinidhi, and Jha, Vedananda. *Panchayat*. Kathmandu: Department of Publicity and Broadcasting, 1963. 74 pp.

Gorkha Parishad. *Chunao Ghoshanapatra* [Election Manifesto]. Kathmandu, 1958. 24 pp.

———. *Ghoshanapatra* [Manifesto]. Kathmandu, 1955. 15 pp.

———. *Kosi Samjhauta ko Vibhinna Bichardhara* [Different Lines of Thought on the Kosi Project]. Kathmandu: Pashupati Press, 1954. 28 pp.

———. *Nepali Congress ko Aitihasik Pristhabhumi* [Historical Background of the Nepali Congress]. Kathmandu, n.d. 16 pp.

———. *Nepal Rashtravadi Gorkha Parishad ko Vidhan, 2012* [Constitution of the Nepal Nationalist Gorkha Parishad, 1955]. Kathmandu, 1955. 11 pp.

———. *Nepal Rashtravadi Gorkha Parishad ko Mahasammelan ma Pass Bhayeka Prastab Haru* [Resolutions Passed during the Conference of the Gorkha Parishad]. Kathmandu: Pashupati Press, n.d.

———. *Mahamantri ko Report* [Report of the General Secretary]. Bhojpur, 1956. 12 pp.

Gorkha Vanshavali [Genealogy of the Gorkha Dynasty]. Banaras: Yoga Pracharini Association, n.d. 144 pp.

Jnawali, Surya Vikram. *Amar Singh Thapa*. Darjeeling: Himachal Hindi Bhavan, 1951. 230 pp. (Hindi edition)

———. *Nepal Vijeta Shri Panch Prithvi Narayan Shah ko Jivani* [Life of His Majesty Prithvi Narayan Shah, Conqueror of Nepal]. Darjeeling: Nepali Sahitya Sammelan, 1935. 205 pp.

Hamal, Laxman Bahadur. *Nepal ko Samvidhan* [The Constitution of Nepal]. Biratnagar: Purvanchal Prakash, 1960. 78 pp.

His Majesty's Government. *Gandak Samjhauta ra Janamat* [Public Opinion and the Gandak Agreement]. Kathmandu: Publicity Department, 1960. 34 pp.

———. *Nepal Adhirajya ko Rashtriya Janaganana, 2018 ko Prarambhik Natija* [Preliminary Results of the National Population Census of the Kingdom of Nepal, 1961]. Kathmandu: Central Statistics Department, 1962. 16 pp.

———. *Nepal ko Samvidhan* [The Constitution of Nepal]. Kathmandu, 1959. 20 pp.

———. "Nepal ko Samvidhan" [The Constitution (1962) of Nepal], *Nepal Gazette,* Vol. XII, No. 29, December 16, 1962.

———. *Pancha Barshiya Yojana ko Masauda* [Draft of the Five-Year Plan]. Kathmandu, 1956. 91 pp.

———. *Pradhan Mantri Koirala ko Jeevani ra Sandesh* [Life and Message of Prime Minister Koirala]. Kathmandu: Department of Publicity, 1959.

———. *Press Commission ko Report* [Report of the Press Commission]. Kathmandu, 1958.

———. *Puratatwa Patra Sangraha* [Collection of Archaeological Letters]. Kathmandu: Department of Archaeology and Culture, 1959. 51 pp.

———. *Rajnaitik Sammelan* [Political Conference]. Kathmandu: Department of Publicity, 1959. 80 pp.

———. *Shahi Kadambare Vibhinna Mantavya* [Different Opinions about the Royal Move]. Kathmandu: Department of Broadcasting and Publicity, 1961. 26 pp.

———. *Shahi Kara Ayog ko Report, 2017* [Report of the Royal Taxation Commission], 1961. Kathmandu, Department of Publicity and Broadcasting, 1961. 8 pp.

———. *Shri Panch Maharajadhiraj Bata Bakseka Ghoshana, Bhashan ra*

Sandesh Haru [Proclamations, Messages and Speeches Delivered by His Majesty the King]. Part I. Kathmandu: Department of Publicity and Broadcasting, 1962. 107 pp.

———. *Shri Panch Maharajadhiraj Bata Bakseka Ghoshana, Bhashan ra Sandesh Haru* [Speeches, Messages and Proclamations of His Majesty the King]. Vol. VIII. Kathmandu: Department of Publicity and Broadcasting, 1963. 77 pp.

———. *Anchal Ebam Vikas Zilla Vibhajan Samiti ko Report* [Report of the Development District and Zonal Demarcation Committee]. Kathmandu, 1962. 47 pp.

———, National Guidance Ministry. *Nepal Majdoor Sangathan ko Vidhan* [Constitution of the Nepal Workers' Organization]. Kathmandu: 1961. 16 pp.

———, ———. *Nepal Kisan Sangathan ko Vidhan* [Constitution of the Nepal Peasants' Organization]. Kathmandu, 1961. 16 pp.

———, ———. *Nepal Vidyarthi Sangathan ko Vidhan* [Constitution of the Nepal Students' Organization]. Kathmandu, 1961.

———, ———. *Nepal Bal Sangathan ko Vidhan* [Constitution of the Nepal Children's Organization]. Kathmandu: Ministry of National Guidance, 1961. 16 pp.

———, ———. *Nepal Mahila Sangathan ko Vidhan* [Constitution of the Nepal Women's Organization]. Kathmandu, 1961. 15 pp.

———, ———. *Nepal Yuvak Sangathan ko Vidhan* [Constitution of the Nepal Youth Organization]. Kathmandu, 1961. 15 pp.

Itihas Prakash Mandal. *Itihas Prakash* [Lights on History]. 3 vols. Kathmandu: Nepal Press, 1955–56.

Jatiya Janatantrik Samyukta Morcha ko Ghoshanapatra [Manifesto of the National Democratic United Front]. Kathmandu: Jorganesh Press, 1952. 16 pp.

Joshi, Gokul Prasad. *Dr. K. I. Singh lai Swadesh Aunadewu* [Let Dr. K. I. Singh Return to His Own Country]. Birganj: Durga Press, 1955. 8 pp.

Joshi, Harihar Raj. *Nepal Adhirajya ko Samvidhan ka Kehi Vishesh* [Some Features of the Constitution of Nepal]. Kathmandu: Ratna Pustak Bhandar, 1958. 39 pp.

Joshi, Satya Mohan. "Chini Nepal Sanskritik Sambandha" [Sino-Nepali Cultural Relations], *Gorkhapatra*, September 23, 1960.

Joshi, Ram Hari. *Nepalko Novembar Kranti: Sansmaran* [Nepal's November Revolution: Memoirs]. Patna, 1952.

Karmavir Mahamandal. *Karmavir Mahamandal ko Vidhan* [Constitution of Karmavir Mahamandal]. 1958. 14 pp.

———. *Karmavir ko Parichaya* [An Introduction to Karmavir]. Kathmandu: Karmavir Mahamandal, 1957. 18 pp.

———. *Karmavir Sutra ra Surakshya* [The Karmavir Manual]. Kathmandu, 1958. 8 pp.

Kharidar, Tejraj. *Nepal Rastra Sangthan Janamat* [The Nepali Nation and Public Opinion]. Kathmandu, 1956. 118 pp.

Koirala, Bishweshwar Prasad. *Hamro Antar-rashtriya Niti* [Our International Policy]. Kathmandu: Department of Publicity and Broadcasting, 1960. 14 pp.

———. "Hijo Aj ra Bholi" [Yesterday, Today, and Tomorrow], *Nepal Pukar,* February 28, 1958.

———. *Nepali Congress ra Sarkar* [Nepali Congress and the Government]. Biratnagar: Nepali Congress, 1952.

Nepal Communist Party. *Chunao Ghoshanapatra* [Election Manifesto]. Kathmandu, 1958. 27 pp.

————. *Chunao Sinhabalokan* [An Overview of the Election] Kathmandu, 1959. 15 pp.

————. *Jatiya Andolanma Nepal Communist Party* [Involvement of the Nepal Communist Party in the National Struggle]. Report of the General Secretary at the First Conference of the Nepal Communist Party. Kathmandu, 1951.

————. *Nepal Communist Party ko Vidhan* [Constitution of the Nepal Communist Party]. Kathmandu, n.d. 21 pp.

————. *Nepal Communist Party ko Rajnaitik Prastab Dwitiya Conference ma Swikrit* [Political Resolution Adopted at the Second Conference of the Nepal Communist Party]. Kathmandu: Sharada Press, 1955. 28 pp.

————. *Party Karyakram ma Parivartan Kina* [Why Changes in the Party Program?]. Kathmandu: Azad Press, 1956. 17 pp.

————. *Samvidhan* [Constitution]. Adopted by the First All-Nepal Communist Party Conference, January 26–30, 1954. Kathmandu, 1954.

Nepal Kisan Party. *Nepal Kisan Party ko Ghoshanapatra* [Manifesto of the Nepal Peasant's Party]. Kathmandu, n.d. 12 pp.

Nepal Praja Parishad. *Nepal Praja Parishad ko Ghoshanapatra* [Manifesto of the Nepal Praja Parishad]. Kathmandu, 1956.

————. *Sangharsha Kina?* [Why the Struggle?]. Kathmandu, 1957. 21 pp.

Nepal Prajatantrik Mahasabha. *Nepal Prajatantrik Mahasabha ko Abashyakata ra Uddeshya* [Necessity and Objectives of the Nepal Prajatantrik Mahasabha]. Kathmandu, 1958. 8 pp.

————. *Sabhapati ko Bhashan* [Speech of the President]. Kathmandu, 1957.

————. *Swikrit Prastabharu* [Approved Resolutions]. Kathmandu, 1957. 17 pp.

Nepal Terai Congress. *Nepal Terai Congress ko Goshanapatra* [Manifesto of the Nepal Terai Congress]. Kathmandu, 1957. 13 pp.

Nepali Congress. *Chunao Ghoshanapatra* [Election Manifesto]. Kathmandu: Kalpana Press, 1958. 15 pp.

————. *Kisan Haru ko Nimti Nepali Congressle ke Garyo?* [What did the Nepali Congress do for the Peasants?]. Kathmandu, n.d. 26 pp.

————. *Nepali Congress ko Chhaintho Adhibeshan* [Sixth General Meeting of the Nepali Congress] Patna: Free Press Ltd., 1955. 9 pp.

————. *Nepali Congress ra Nepal ka Pradhan Mantri* [The Nepali Congress and Nepal's Prime Minister]. Kathmandu, 1952. 10 pp.

————. *Shastha Rashtriya Adhibeshan Birganj ko Abasar ma Swikrit Ghoshana Patra* [Manifesto Adopted on the Occasion of the 6th National Conference at Birganj]. Patna: Free Press Ltd., 1956. 20 pp.

————. *Sravan 15 Gate* [(An Account of the Nepal Congress Meeting of) July 30, 1952], Kathmandu: Pashupati Press, n.d. 16 pp.

Nepali, Chitta Ranjan. *Rana Bahadur Shah.* Kathmandu: Shrimati Mary Rajbhandari, 1964. 154 pp.

————. *Janaral Bhimsen Thapa ra Tatkalin Nepal* [General Bhimsen Thapa and the Nepal of His Day]. Kathmandu: Jorganesh Press, 1957. 334 pp.

————. "Nepal ra Tibet ko Sambandha" [Nepal-Tibet Relations], *Pragati*, II, Issue IV, No. 10 (1957) , 103–115.

————. "Nepal-Chin Yuddha" [Nepal-China War], *Sharada*, XXI, No. 2 (April–May, 1956) , 202–216.

————. "Nepal ra British Samrajya" [Nepal and the British Empire], *Sharada*, XXI, No. 3 (May–June 1956) , 11–22.

Nepali National Congress. *Uddeshya, Sangathan, ra Karyakram* [Objectives, Organization, and Program]. Kathmandu, n.d. 116 pp.
———. *Udghatan Samaroha ko Vibaran* [Account of the Inauguration Ceremony]. Calcutta: Aryabhushan Press, 1947. 14 pp.
Nepali, Ramraj. *Kranti ke Purba Nepal* [Nepal before the Revolution]. Banaras: Balwant Printing Works, 1951. 28 pp. (Hindi)
Ojha, Sushilnath. *Communist ke Chahanchha?* [What does the Communist Want?]. Kathmandu, 1956. 31 pp.
Pant, Dibyadeb. *Shah Vansa Charitam* [An Account of the Shah Dynasty]. Banaras: Sangaved Vidyalaya Press, 1935. 49 pp.
Pant, Nayaraj. "Sthiti Malla Tatha Jatpat" [Sthiti Malla and the Caste System], *Purnima*, I, No. 2 (July, 1964), pp. 1–10.
Parallel Nepali Congress. *Samanantar Nepali Congress Kina?* [Why the Parallel Nepali Congress?]. Kathmandu, 1957. 12 pp.
Pith, Gorakhnath. *Shri Tribhuwan Vanshavali* [Family History of King Tribhuwan]. Kathmandu: Saraswati Press, 1953. 8 pp.
Poudyal, Ananta. *Samanya Nagarikvadi Panchayat Darshan* [Panchayat Philosophy for the Common Citizen]. Kathmandu, 1963. 237 pp.
Praja Parishad (B. Mishra faction). *Chunao Ghoshanapatra* [Election Manifesto]. Kathmandu, 1958. 7 pp.
"Prashasan Shakti Vikendrikaran Ayog ko Prativedan" [Report of the Commission on Decentralization of Administrative Authority], *Gorkhapatra*, July 18, 1964.
Rai, Bhui Dal. "Sahi Vansha ra Kirati" [The Shah Dynasty and the Kiratis], *Gorkhapatra*, June 25, 1962.
Ram, Bahadur. *Nepal ko Samvidhan* [The Constitution of Nepal]. Kathmandu: Chhatramitra Prakashan, 1960. 75 pp.
Rashtriya Jana Rajya Parishad. *Party ko Adesh* [Directives of the Party]. Kathmandu, 1957. 14 pp.
Shahi, D. K. *Satsal Pachhi Satsal* [Seven Years after 1951]. Kathmandu: Nepali Congress, 1957. 60 pp.
Sharma, Balchandra. *Nepal ko Aitihasik Ruprekha* [An Historical Outline of Nepal]. Banaras: Madhav Prasad Sharma 1951. 440 pp.
Sharma, Balchandra, Vyathit, Kedar Man, and Sharma, Bharat Mani. *Nepali Loktantrik Samajvadi Ghoshanapatra* [Manifesto of the Nepali Democratic Socialists]. Banaras: Narendra Yantralaya, 1951. 39 pp.
Sharma, Dhundiraj. *Parliament ra Sallahakar Sahba* [Parliament and the Advisory Assembly]. Kathmandu: National Academy, 1959. 439 pp.
Sharma, Lilaraj. *Shri 5 Maharajadiraj ra Sallahakar Raj* [The King and the Advisory Regime]. Kathmandu: Annapurna Press, n.d. 24 pp.
[Shrestha], Pushpa Lal. *Nepali Congress ra Nepal Communist Party ka Ghoshanapatra haru ko Tulanatmak Adhyayan* [A Comparative Study of the Nepali Congress and Nepal Communist Party Election Manifestoes]. Kathmandu, 1958. 16 pp.
Shrivastav, Kashi Prasad. *Nepal ki Kahani* [The Story of Nepal] Delhi: Atmaram & Sons, 1955. 293 pp. (Hindi)
Sijapati, Ganga Vikram. "Nepali Prashasan Vyavastha Vikash ko Ruprekha" [Outline of the Evolution of the Administrative System in Nepal], *Nepali*, No. 13 (November, 1962–January, 1963), pp. 25–56.
Sijapati, Lalit Jang. *Nepal ra Nepal ka Raja* [Nepal and the King of Nepal]. Banaras: Gorkha Bastu Bhandar, 1960. 29 pp.
Singh, Bhim Bhaktaman. *Nepal*. Calcutta, 1948. 73 pp.
Singh, Buddhi Man. "Bhasa Vansavali" [Nepali Genealogy]. MS in collection of Leo E. Rose.

Singh, Jagat Bahadur. *Nepal Praja Parishad ko Adhibeshan ma Swikrit Lakhshya* [Objectives Adopted during the Conference of the Nepal Praja Parishad Party]. Lucknow: Star Press, 1956. 12 pp.

————. *Nepal Praja Parishad ko Sankshipta Itihas* [A Short History of the Nepal Praja Parishad]. Kathmandu, n.d. 10 pp.

Singh, Raghu Nath. *Jagrit Nepal* [Awakened Nepal]. Banaras, 1950, (Hindi)

Thapa, Surya Bahadur. "Budget Bhashan, 2020–21" [Budget Speech, 1963/64], *Gorkhapatra* (Budget Supplement), July 10, 1963.

Thapa, Vishwabandhu. "Nepal Prajatantra Tira" [Nepal Heading toward Democracy], *Gorkhapatra*, July 4, 1963.

————. "Netritwa ko Sankat" A Crisis of Leadership], *Nirdeshan*, II No. 1 (n.d.), 1–4.

————. "Panchayat ra Vibhinna Taha" [Panchayats and the Different Tiers], *Gorkhapatra*, July 9, 1963.

United Democratic Party. *Chunao Ghoshanapatra* [Election Manifesto]. Kathmandu, 1958. 5 pp.

————. *Nepal ko Singh Sarkar ko 110 Din ko Kunai Kam* [Some Achievements of the 110-Day Regime of the Singh Government]. Kathmandu, n.d. 7 pp.

Upadhyaya, Nepal Nath. *Antar-rashtriya Jagatma Shri Panch Mahendra* [King Mahendra in the International Field]. Banaras, n.d. 49 pp.

Upadhyaya, Ramji. *Nepal Digdarshan* [A Survey of Nepali History]. Banaras: Gopal Press, 1950. 486 pp.

————. *Nepal ko Itihas* [History of Nepal]. Banaras: Subba Homnath Kedarnath, 1950.

Upadhyaya, Surya Prasad. *Nepali Congress ko Mahadhibeshan ma Manjur Bhayaka Mukhya Prastab Haruko Adhyayan* [A Study of the Main Resolutions passed during the Sixth Conference of the Nepali Congress]. Patna: Free Press Ltd., n.d. 16 pp.

————. "Vikendrikaran ko Vishleshan" [An Analysis of Decentralization], *Samaj*, September 16, 1964.

Vasistha, M. P. *Nepal ma Antarim Sasan ko Ek Jhalak* [A Glimpse of the Interim Government in Nepal]. Kathmandu, 1956. 17 pp.

"Yami," Dharma Ratna. *Nepal ko Kura* [Facts About Nepal]. Kathmandu, 1956.

Yogi, Narahari Nath. *Gorkhaliharu ko Sainik Itihas* [Military History of the Gorkhas]. Kathmandu: Annapurna Press, 1954. 24 pp.

Yogi, Narahari Nath, and Acharya, Baburam. *Rashtrapita Shri 5 Bada Maharaja Prithvi Narayan Shah ko Divyopadesh* [Divine Counsel of Shri 5 Bada Maharaja Prithvi Narayan Shah the Great]. Prithvi Jayanti Samaroha Samiti [Prithvi Birthday Celebration Committee]. 2d. ed., rev. Kathmandu: Bagishwar Press, 1953. 38 pp.

WORKS IN WESTERN LANGUAGES

Acharya, Tanka Prasad. "Nepal's Fight for Freedom," *India Today*, I, No. 12 (June, 1952), 19–27.

Appadorai, A., and Baral, L. S. "The New Constitution of Nepal," *International Studies*, I (1959–60), 217–247.

Bahadur, Poorna. *Nepal behind the Screen*. Kathmandu: Nepal Youth League Central Committee, 1957. 55 pp.

Bahadur, Prakash. *Hostile Expeditions and International Law*. Kathmandu: Department of Publicity and Broadcasting, 1962. 62 pp.

Bamuniya *(pseud.)* . "The Constitutional 'Crisis' in Nepal," *Eastern World*, V. (January, 1951) , 14–15.

Berreman, Gerald. *Hindus of the Himalayas*. Berkeley and Los Angeles: University of California Press, 1963. 430 pp.

———— "Peoples and Cultures of the Himalaya," *Asian Survey*, III, No. 6 (June, 1963) , 289–304.

Chaudhuri, K. C. *Anglo-Nepalese Relations*. Calcutta: Modern Book Agency Private, Ltd., 1960. 181 pp.

The Citizen King: Biography of Mahendra Bir Bikram Shah Deva, the Ruler of Nepal. New Delhi: Nepal Trading Corporation, 1959. 89 pp.

Deva, Maitra. *Our Ideal Monarch—King Mahendra*. Kathmandu, 1957. 78 pp.

Fisher, Margaret W., and Bondurant, Joan V. *Indian Views of Sino-Indian Relations*. Indian Press Digests Monograph Series No. 1. Berkeley: University of California, 1956, XXIX, 163 pp.

Fürer-Haimendorf, Christoph von. "Caste in the Multi-Ethnic Society of Nepal," *Contributions to Indian Sociology*, IV (April, 1960) , 12–32.

————. "Elements of Newar Social Structure," *Journal of the Royal Anthropological Institute*, 86, Part II (1956) , 15–38.

————. *The Sherpas of Nepal: Buddhist Highlanders*. Berkeley and Los Angeles: University of California Press, 1964. 298 pp.

Government of Nepal. *Free English Rendering of the Government of Nepal Act, 2004 Sambat (1948 A.D.)* . Kathmandu, 1948. 43 pp.

————. *The Interim Government of Nepal Act (1951)*. Kathmandu: Government Press, 1951. 22 pp.

Goyal, Narendra. *The King and His Constitution: Observation and Commentary on the Constitution of the Kingdom of Nepal*. New Delhi: Nepal Trading Corporation, 1959. 140 pp.

Gupta, A. *Politics in Nepal: A Study of Post-Rana Political Developments and Party Politics*. Bombay: Allied Publishers, 1964. 332 pp.

Harris, George L., *et. al. U.S. Army Areas Handbook for Nepal (with Sikkim and Bhutan)*. Washington: Government Printing Office, 1964. 448 pp.

His Majesty's Government. *The Panchayat Way to Prosperity: Collection of the Five Speeches Delivered by His Majesty King Mahendra, February 5 to February 18, 1963*. Kathmandu: Department of Publicity and Broadcasting, 1963. 41 pp.

————. *Statement of Principles: Major Foreign Policy Speeches by His Majesty King Mahendra*. Kathmandu: Department of Publicity and Broadcasting, 1962. 40 pp.

————. Ministry of Law and Justice. *The Constitution of Nepal*. Kathmandu: Jorganesh Press, 1963. 64 pp.

His Majesty's Government, National Guidance Ministry. *On to a New Era: Some Historic Addresses by His Majesty King Mahendra*. Kathmandu, n.d. 45 pp.

————, ————. *Pages of History: A. Collection of Proclamations, Messages, and Addresses Delivered by His Majesty King Mahendra*. Kathmandu, 1963. 114 pp.

——, ——. *Policy and Main Objectives of His Majesty's Government.* Kathmandu: Department of Publicity and Broadcasting, n.d. 22 pp.

Hitchcock, John. *The Magars of Banyan Hill.* New York, Holt, Rinehart & Winston, 1965.

——. "A Nepalese Hill Village and Indian Employment," *Asian Survey*, I, No. 9 (November, 1961), 15–20.

——. "Some Effects of Recent Change in Rural Nepal," *Human Organization*, XXII, No. 1 (Spring, 1963), 75–82.

Hodgson, Brian Houghton. *Essays on the Languages, Literature, and Religion of Nepal and Tibet, Together with Further Papers on the Geography, Ethnology, and Commerce of those Countries.* London: Trubner & Co., 1874. 104 pp.

Iijima, Shigeru. "Ecology, Economy, and Social System in the Nepal Himalayas," *Developing Economies,* II, No. 1 (March, 1964), 92–105.

Jain, Girilal. *India Meets China in Nepal.* New York: Asia Publishing House, 1959. 177 pp.

Joshi, Hora Prasad. *The Way to Political Stability: An Analysis.* Kathmandu: Mercantile Corporation of Napal. 1958. 28 pp.

Karan, Pradyumna P. *Nepal: A Physical and Cultural Geography.* Lexington: University of Kentucky Press, 1960. 100 pp.

Karan, Pradyumna P., and Jenkins, William M., Jr. *The Himalayan Kingdoms: Bhutan, Sikkim, and Nepal.* Princeton: D. Van Nostrand, 1963. 144 pp.

Kirkpatrick, William. *An Account of the Kingdom of Nepaul, Being the Substance of Observations Made during a Mission to that Country in the Year 1793.* London, 1811. 386 pp.

Landon, Perceval. *Nepal.* 2 vols. London: Constable, 1928.

Lévi, Sylvain. *Le Népal: Etude Historique d'un Royaume Hindou.* Annales du Musée Giumet, Bibliotheque d'Etudes, vols. XVII-XIX. Paris, 1905–08.

Malhotra, Ram Chand. "Public Administration in Nepal," *Indian Journal of Public Administration*, IV, No. 4 (October–December, 1958), 451–464.

Nehru, Jawaharlal. *India's Foreign Policy: Selected Speeches, September 1945–April 1961.* Delhi: Ministry of information and Broadcasting. 1961. 612 pp.

"A Nepali." "Political Parties in Nepal," *Economic Weekly,* July 19, 1952, pp. 736–639.

Oldfield, H. A. *Sketches from Nepal.* 2 vols. London, 1811.

Pant, Y. P. "Nepal's Recent Trade Policy," *Asian Survey,* IV, No. 7 (July, 1964), 947–957.

Politicus (*pseud.*). Inside Story of Nepal. New Delhi: *Hindu Outlook,* 1951, 1–20.

Rana, Padma Jung Bahadur. ed. A. C. Mukherji. *Life of Maharaja Sir Jung Bahadur of Nepal.* Allahabad: Pioneer Press, 1909. 314 pp.

Rashtriya Panchayat Secretariat. *The Brief Outline of the Composition and Working of the Rashtriya Panchayat.* Kathmandu: Gorakhapatra Chhapakhana, 1963. 28 pp.

Regmi, Dilli Raman *A Century of Family Autocracy in Nepal.* Banaras: Nepali National Congress, 1950. 267 pp.

——. *Modern Nepal.* Calcutta: Firma K. L. Mukhopadhzay, 1961. 333 pp.

——. *Nepal.* Banaras: Nepali National Congress, 1948. 22 pp.

——. *The Nepali Democratic Struggle.* Banaras: Nepali National Congress, 1948. 45 pp.

——. *Whither Nepal.* Lucknow: Prem Printing Press, 1952. 181 pp.

Regmi, Mahesh Chandra. *Land Tenure and Taxation in Nepal,* 3 vols. Berkeley: Institute of International Studies, University of California, 1963–65.

Rose, Leo E. "Communism under High Atmospheric Conditions: The Party in Nepal," in Scalapino, Robert A. (ed.), *Comparative Communism in Asia,* pp. 243–272. New York: Prentice-Hall, 1965.

———. "Nepal Experiments with 'Traditional' Democracy," *Pacific Affairs,* XXXVI, (Spring, 1963), 16–31.

———. *Nepal: Government and Politics.* New Haven: Human Relations Area Files, 1956. 360 pp.

———. "Sino-Indian Rivalry and the Himalayan Border States," *Orbis,* V, No. 2 (July, 1961), 198–215.

Saksena, Shibbanlal. "Dr. K. I. Singh," *National Herald* (Lucknow), November 18, 1955, p. 4.

Shah, Rishikesh. *Nepal and the World.* Kathmandu: Nepali Congress, 1955. 54 pp.

Shamsher, Suvarna. *Budget Speech, 1959–60.* Kathmandu: Department of Publicity and Information, n.d.

———. *Budget Speech, 1960–61.* Kathmandu: Department of Publicity and Information, n.d.

Shrestha, Badri Prasad. *An Introduction to Nepalese Economy.* Kathmandu: Nepal Press, 1962. 264 pp.

Thapa, Vishwabandu. *National Guidance: Its Origin and Function.* Kathmandu: Department of Publicity and Broadcasting, n.d. 17 pp.

Tucci, Giuseppe. *Nepal: The Discovery of the Malla.* London, George Allen & Unwin, 1962. 96 pp.

Tuker, Francis. *While Memory Serves.* London: Cassel, 1950.

Tuladhar, Tirtha R. *Nepal-China: A Story of Friendship.* Kathmandu: Department of Publicity and Broadcasting, n.d. 48 pp.

———. *Partyless Democracy: Its Basis and Background.* Kathmandu: Royal Palace Press Secretariat, 1962. 34 pp.

"A Wayfarer." *Nepal Today.* New Delhi: New India Press, 1950. 61 pp.

Wright, Daniel *History of Nepal.* Cambridge: Cambridge University Press, 1897. 324 pp.

"Yami," Dharma Ratna. *The Study of Critical Situation in Nepal.* Kathmandu: Himalaya Press, 1958. 25 pp.

NEPALI NEWSPAPERS AND JOURNALS

The Commoner (English daily), Kathmandu.
Dainik Nepal (Nepali daily), Kathmandu.
Desh Sewa (Nepali daily), Kathmandu.
Diyalo (Nepali daily), Kathmandu.
Filingo (Nepali daily), Kathmandu.
Gorkahaptra (Nepali daily), Kathmandu.
Halkhabar (Nepali daily), Kathmandu.
Himachuli (Nepali monthly), Kathmandu.
Jan Chetana (Nepali monthly), Kathmandu.
Jhyali (Nepali weekly), Kathmandu.
Kalpana (Nepali daily), Kathmandu.
Karmavir (Nepali weekly), Kathmandu.

Lokvarta (Nepali daily), Kathmandu.
Mashal (Nepali weekly), Kathmandu. (Communist party organ)
Matribhumi (Nepali weekly), Kathmandu.
Motherland (English daily), Kathmandu.
Navayuga (Nepali weekly), Kathmandu. (Communist party organ)
Naya Samaj (Nepali daily), Kathmandu.
Naya Samaj (Hindi weekly), Kathmandu.
Naya Sandesh (Nepali weekly) Kathmandu.
Nepal Pukar (Nepali weekly), Kathmandu. (Nepali Congress journal)
Nepal Times (Hindi daily), Kathmandu.
Karmavir (Nepali weekly), Kathmandu.
Nepal Bhasa Patrika (Newari daily), Kathmandu.
Nepal Samachar, (Nepali daily), Kathmandu.
Nepal Sambad Samiti (Nepal News Agency), Kathmandu.
News From Nepal (English weekly), Kathmandu. (Published by His Majesty's Government, Department of Publicity and Broadcasting)
Nepal Gazette (Nepali biweekly, frequent Extraordinary Issues), Kathmandu. (Official periodical issued by His Majesty's Government, Department of Publicity and Broadcasting)
Nirvachan Sandesh [Election News] (Nepali), Kathmandu. (Journal published by Election Commission before the 1959 Elections)
Pravartak (Nepali weekly), Kathmandu.
Pragati (Nepali bimonthly), Kathmandu.
Rashtravani (Nepali weekly), Kathmandu. (Gorkha Parishad organ)
Rashtriya Sambad Samiti (National News Agency), Kathmandu.
Sagarmatha Sambad Samiti (Everest News Agency), Kathmandu.
Sahibato (Nepali daily), Kathmandu.
Samaj (Nepali daily), Kathmandu.
Samaya (Nepali weekly), Kathmandu.
Samiksha (Nepali weekly), Kathmandu.
Samyukta Prayas (Nepali weekly), Kathmandu. (National Democratic party organ)
Saptahik Samachar (Nepali weekly), Kathmandu.
Sharada (Nepali monthly), Kathmandu.
Swatantra Samachar (Nepali daily), Kathmandu.

INDIAN NEWSPAPERS AND JOURNALS

Asian Recorder (English weekly), New Delhi.
Amrita Bazar Patrika (English daily), Calcutta.
Himalayan Guardian (English weekly), New Delhi.
Himalayan Sentinel (English weekly), Patna.
The Hindu (English daily), Madras.
Hindustan Times (English daily), New Delhi.
Nepal Sandesh (Hindi weekly), Patna.
Nepal Today (English biweekly), Calcutta. (Published by the Nepali Congress-in-Exile)
The Statesman (English daily), Calcutta.
Times of India (English daily), Bombay.
The Tribune (English daily), Ambala, Punjab.

Glossary

Adalat	government office
Adda	government office or station
Adhikar	rights or privileges
Ain	legal code
Amini	pertaining to government revenues
Bada	big or great
Birta	land grants made by the government to individuals, often tax-exempt
Brahman	member of a Hindu priestly class
Begar	unpaid labor
Beth	conscripted labor, generally for agricultural purposes
Bharadars	nobles; members of the court; Derivatives: *Bharadari* (nobility) ; *Bharadari Sabha* (council of nobles)
Chobdar	court attendant; bearer of the King's umbrella
Dal	corps; an organized group
Daudaha	*ad hoc* judicial commission, usually dispatched to districts outside the capital
Dhakre	an ex-official, no longer on the government pay-roll but liable to be reinstated in the future
Dharmadhikar	the highest religious and judicial authority, usually the Brahman priest of the royal family
Diwani	pertaining to civil law-suits
Duniyadars	commoners
Fouzdari	pertaining to criminal suits
Guru	a teacher; a preceptor
Hukum	royal order which overrides laws and conventions of the land
Jana	people
Jangi	pertaining to war
Jetha-Boora	elderly statesman
Kapardar	a person in charge of the King's wardrobe and jewellery
Kausi	government treasury
Kazi	a high ranking government official who interprets the civil laws of the land
Khajanchi	treasurer

541

Kiput communal land tenure system prevalent among the Limbus
Kisan a peasant
Kshatriya a member of the Hindu warrior caste
Kumari chowk department of audits and accounts

Lal Mohur royal seal of Shah kings

Maharaj king
Mahila woman
Mukhtiyar chief executive officer, equivalent to Prime Minister
Muluki national

Nagarik a citizen

Panchayat an elected committee; literally, a committee of five
Parishad a council; an assembly
Patiya a special expiation for caste defilement
Praja people; Derivatives: *Prajatantra* (people's rule); *Prajatantrik* (democratic)

Raikar land subject to government taxes
Raj kingdom; Derivative: *Rajyas* (principalities)
Rakshya protection
Rashtra nation; Derivative: *Rashtriya* (national)

Sabha council; meeting
Sadhu a Hindu holy man
Samiti a committee
Sanad royal dispensation
Sangha organization; a formal association
Satyagraha passive resistance
Sawal conventions, usually as mandatory as written laws
Shanti peace

Taksali master of the mint

Umrao local commanders

Vidyarthi student

Yogi a Hindu holy man
Yubak a youthful person

Zilla a district

Index

Acharya, Tanka Prasad, 54, 100, 106, 109, 115, 117, 119, 120, 122, 123, 124, 140, 141, 147, 159, 183, 191, 193, 194, 208, 210, 214, 218, 229, 230, 234, 240, 241, 242, 250, 251, 257, 263, 265, 266, 270, 275, 276, 281, 282, 292, 295, 298, 318, 325, 414, 438, 457, 459, 460, 461, 466; dispute as Home Minister with M. P. Koirala, 116; appointed Prime Minister, 186, 188; initiates Parliament vs. Constituent Assembly controversy, 190; forms National Democratic Front, 323; on foreign policy, 240–242

Adhikari, D. P., 453

Adhikaris, 43

Administrative decentralization, 347

Administrative Deconcentration Commission (1963), 401

Administrative reorganization, 155–158, 322, 354, 355, 516, 517

Administrative Reorganization Commission, 229

Advisory Assembly, 89; First Assembly, 97, 150–151; Second Assembly, 116, 117, 120; Third Assembly, 212–213, 221, 222, 223

Advisory Assembly Act (1952), 404

Agriculture in Nepal, 13, 14

Agricultural (New arrangements) Act (1963), 466, 467

Alau invasion, 42

Ale, Hobir, 269

Allen, George V., 146

Aide-memoire controversy, 246–247

Amatya, Tulsi Lal, 331, 332, 451, 452, 456

Amini court, 213

Angdembe, Prem Raj, 313, 314

Anglo-Nepali agreement on "Gurkha" recruitment, 245

Anglo-Nepali treaty of commerce and alliance (1801), 26

Anti-government plot in the police, 107

Appellate court, 213

Arya Samaj, 50; in Nepal, 52

Asian Survey, 245

Bada Kausi, 31

Bahadur, Jang, 11, 33, 37, 40, 44–45, 391; early career, 29; appointed Prime Minister, 31; receives Rana title, 34; trip to England, 38; changes role of succession, 48

Baisi States, 4

Bahadur, Poorna, 414

Bajhang episode, 363–364

Basnyat, Bir Dhoj, 32

Basnyat conspiracy, 32

Basnyat family, 23, 41

Basnyat plot (1857), 42

Basnyat, Surendra Bahadur, 105, 275

Basnyat, Yajna Bahadur, 84, 86, 257

Begar, 232

Belgrade Conference (1961), 515

Beth, 232

Bhadgaon kingdom, 5

Bhagavad Gita, 54

Bhakta, Dharam, 55

Bhandarkhal Parva, 32

Bharadari, 321, 413

Bharadari Sabha, 65

Bharadars, 24, 26, 41

Bhattarai, K. P., 91 n.

Bhave, Vinobha, 309

Bhojpuri, 8

Bhotiyas, 6, 8, 11, 14

Bhutan, 3, 134

Bijuli Garath, 49

Binti Patra Niksari, 38

Biratnagar Jute Mill labor strike, 61

Birta, 14, 111, 346, 348, 356; abolition of, 160, 294, 337, 341, 466

Birta Abolition Act (1959), 352, 466

Bishta, Kirti Nidhi, 430, 436, 440

Bishtas, 43

"Black Act" Day, 143

Bowles, Chester, 165

"Brahman," Purna Prasad, 227, 323

Brahmans, 23, 41, 51, 358, 485, 492–493

British influence in Nepal, 26

British Labour party, 58

Buch, N. B., 158

Buch Committee, 158

Budathoki, Giri Prasad, 430, 436

Buddhist clergy, 11

Buddhist Sabha Sangha, 196

Budget Equalization Fund, 162

Caste system, 11

Chand, Dasarath, 55

Chand, Lalit, 314, 414, 430, 431, 434, 435 n.

Chand, Shamsher, 197, 268, 276

Charkha movement, 53

Chaubise States, 4, 5

Chaudhari, Parashu Narayan, 314

Chautariyas, 25, 26, 27, 32

Chautariya, Guru Prasad, 42

543